diGital

multimedia

Second Edition

digital
multimedia

Second Edition

Nigel Chapman and Jenny Chapman

John Wiley & Sons, Ltd

The following figures are © MacAvon Media Productions
Chapter 1 - Figs. 1.1 and 1.6
Chapter 2 - Fig. 2.12
Chapter 3 - Figs. 3.2, 3.5, 3.7, 3.10, 3.11, 3.14, 3.15 and 3.16
Chapter 4 - Figs. 4.21, 4.22 and 4.44
Chapter 5 - Figs. 5.1, 5.4, 5.6, 5.12, 5.14, 5.16 through 5.24 inclusive, 5.29 and 5.30
Chapter 6 - Figs. 6.3, 6.4, 6.11, 6.16, 6.17 and 6.18
Chapter 7 - Figs. 7.1, 7.2, 7.3, 7.4, 7.8, 7.9, 7.13, 7.16 and 7.19 through 7.30 inclusive
Chapter 8 - Figs. 8.1, 8.2, 8.3, 8.8 through 8.13 inclusive, and 8.15
Chapter 11 - Figs. 11.1 and 11.2
Chapter 13 - Figs. 13.2, 13.4, 13.6, 13.15, 13.22, 13.25 and 13.26
Chapter 16 - Figs. 16.10 and 16.11

Other Wiley Editorial Offices
Hoboken, San Francisco, Weinheim, Queensland, Singapore, Ontario

Wiley also publishes its books in a variety of electronic formats. Some content that appears in print may not be available in electronic books.

British Library Cataloguing in Publication Data

A catalogue record for this book is available from the British Library

ISBN 0-470-85890-7

Produced from authors' own PDF files
Printed and bound in Italy by Rotolito Lombarda SpA
This book is printed on acid-free paper responsibly manufactured from sustainable forestry in which at least two trees are planted for each one used for paper production.

Contents

Preface x

Prologue xii

1 Introduction 1

Historical Context 4

Terminology 6

Delivery 8

Non-linearity 10

Interactivity 13

Social and Ethical Considerations 17

Exercises 29

2 Enabling Technologies 31

Digital Representations 32

Hardware and Software Requirements 42

Networks 50

Standards 57

Exercises 61

3 Introduction to Computer Graphics 63

Vector Graphics and Bitmapped Graphics 66

Combining Vectors and Bitmaps 73

Layers 75

File Formats 78

Exercises 83

4 Vector Graphics   **85**

Fundamentals   86

Shapes   91

Transformations and Filters   101

3-D Graphics   103

Exercises   115

5 Bitmapped Images   **117**

Resolution   118

Image Compression   122

Image Manipulation   130

Geometrical Transformations   148

Exercises   151

6 Colour   **155**

Colour and Science   157

RGB Colour   158

Other Colour Models   170

Channels and Colour Correction   179

Consistent Colour   183

Exercises   187

7 Video   **189**

Digitizing Video   191

Streamed Video   197

Video Standards   199

Introduction to Video Compression   206

QuickTime   220

Editing and Post-Production   223

Exercises   238

NOV TEST

8 Animation **241**

Captured Animation and Image Sequences 245

'Digital Cel' and Sprite Animation 249

Key Frame Animation 251

Web Animation and Flash 254

Motion Graphics 261

3-D Animation 266

Virtual Reality 269

Exercises 272

9 Sound **273**

The Nature of Sound 275

Digitizing Sound 281

Processing Sound 286

Compression 295

Formats 302

MIDI 303

Combining Sound and Picture 309

Exercises 311

10 Characters and Fonts **313**

Character Sets 314

Fonts 324

Exercises 341

11 Text and Layout **343**

Text in Graphics 344

Layout 347

Text Layout Using HTML and CSS 356

Exercises 380

NOU TEST →

12	**Hypertext and Hypermedia**	**383**
	A Short History	385
	The Nature of Hypertext	386
	Browsing and Searching	390
	Links in HTML	395
	HTML and Hypermedia	403
	Exercises	410
13	**Design Principles**	**411**
	Structure and Navigation in Hypermedia	413
	Non-linear Time-based Structures	420
	Design Problems of the WWW	425
	Accessibility	433
	Web Design Issues	442
	Conservatism and Progress	457
	Exercises	459
14	**XML and Multimedia**	**461**
	XML	464
	Namespaces	473
	Stylesheets	477
	Linking	484
	Exercises	495
15	**SMIL and SVG**	**497**
	SMIL	498
	SVG	517
	Exercises	532

16 Scripting and Interactivity **535**

Scripting Fundamentals 537

ECMAScript 538

World Wide Web Client-side Scripting 557

Behaviours 570

Scripting in Flash 573

Exercises 587

17 Multimedia and Networks **589**

Protocols 591

Multicasting 597

Application Protocols for Multimedia 599

Quality of Service 609

Server-side Computation 611

Exercises 616

Projects **619**

Bibliography **638**

Glossary **648**

Index **668**

Preface

This book is a text for introductory courses on digital multimedia. There is at present a diversity of approaches to such courses, ranging from the purely technical, with an emphasis on underlying system technologies or multimedia programming, to those aimed primarily at multimedia content production. Increasingly, courses with a strong practical orientation are being offered within computing and IT departments, to students coming from very mixed backgrounds who are aiming at a career in multimedia. The book will be of use to students on all of these types of course. For multimedia producers, we describe the way media are represented and processed digitally and the consequences that follow. For software engineers, we describe what multimedia producers do with the data and why they want to do it. Ultimately, these are two sides of the same coin, and an understanding of both sides will be of value to anyone seeking to work professionally in multimedia.

In order to fully appreciate the problems and potential of multimedia, it is essential to have a good understanding of the characteristics of the media that are being combined. Armed with such an understanding, much of what happens when media are brought together becomes clear. The book is organized accordingly.

Brent MacGregor's prologue sets the scene, and our introduction expands on some of the subjects he introduces, and considers some additional context. The second chapter lays out the technical underpinnings of digital multimedia. This is followed by four chapters dealing with graphics and colour, three chapters dealing with time-based media and three chapters dealing with aspects of text and hypermedia. In our descriptions of graphics, time-based media and text, we do not lose sight of multimedia, and have emphasized the relevant aspects, while eliding some topics that would normally be central to the study of these individual media as subjects in their own right. With the technical background established, we look, in the next chapter, at various design issues that arise when media are combined. The final four chapters of the book are of a more technical nature, describing XML and languages based on it, scripting and networks. Readers of a non-technical inclination may find the chapter on design provides a good point at which to stop reading, and move on to the projects which follow the main chapters.

Where necessary, we make reference to specific software. We have tried to refer only to widely used programs, which students are likely to encounter in their practical work. We do not go into great detail about how to use individual applications; that is the subject of our companion book, *Digital Media Tools*, the second edition of which was published by John Wiley & Sons in 2003.

Our treatment of multimedia is heavily biased towards the World Wide Web. We have featured the Web, rather than more advanced forms of distributed multimedia, because students are likely to have ready access to the Web itself and to tools for producing Web content; because the emphasis on textual representations and markup languages makes it easy to see and explain what is going on; and because of the ready availability of standards and other documentation. Additionally, although we are reluctant to make predictions about the future, it is clear that the Internet is going to become the major distribution medium for multimedia content. Many graduates of multimedia courses will be hoping to pursue careers in Web design.

We make some assumptions about our readers' prior knowledge. They should have experience of using a modern graphical user interface to an operating system such as the MacOS or Windows, and should have used the World Wide Web and seen other forms of multimedia. We do not assume any mathematical or computer science knowledge, but some programming experience will be valuable in understanding Chapter 16.

Some passages are typeset like this one, in a smaller font, accompanied by a marginal decoration. These passages are 'asides' – they contain material that is somewhat tangential to the main presentation, or at a higher technical level than the surrounding text, and may be omitted without great loss.

Readers familiar with the first edition will notice that we have made extensive revisions to the content, illustrations, organization and presentation to bring the book up to date and improve it. Most noticeably, the book is now printed in full colour. We have also added a glossary of nearly 250 terms. The book is accompanied by a Web site with supporting material at www.digitalmultimedia.org.

Prologue

The Creative Challenge
Brent MacGregor
Edinburgh College of Art

We live in interesting times. Digital technology continues to develop at such a rate that hardware can very often be obsolete before it has been taken out of the box. Software is equally volatile, with exciting tools very often being surpassed by new releases or competing products before users have even learned the features of the old, let alone explored their full creative potential. Even the language is unstable. The expression 'CD-ROM' will soon join the 'televisor', the 'wireless', the 'transistor radio', the '8-track tape deck', 'Betamax', the 'typewriter' and the 'mainframe' in the dictionary of technologies left behind by history. In this context no less an authority than Steve Jobs can be quoted as saying over a decade ago that the very term multimedia was "so overused as to be useless." (*The Daily Telegraph*, December 21, 1992, p. 25). This scepticism is shared by a dynamic young Web developer I know who is equally dismissive of any attempt to put the digital butterfly in any linguistic net: "New media – how twentieth century!" he snorts, more concerned with making the new than describing the already-old. The point of quoting these seemingly dismissive remarks by knowledgeable insiders is to assert that the potential for the future is so enormous that language simply cannot describe or contain it in any way. It is clearly exciting to be working in a growing field which is still so new it hasn't yet found itself the right name. The creative point, however, is not to invent the word, but to make the world. The time has come to fulfil the promise, as we seek to understand multimedia by making it. We must move from the drawings in the sand of the digital age to begin to create the cave paintings.

Developments in computer hardware and software now make it possible for creative visions only dreamed of a few short years ago to be realised easily and routinely. Domestic machines can play complex multimedia product, and easy-to-use tools allow the creation of complex imaginative work on the kitchen table. School-age children can shoot digital video, edit these high-quality moving images with the click of a mouse, author complex multimedia artefacts and publish them to millions on the Web. What might have been considered miraculous some years ago is now everyday. Digital technology is now enabling, not inhibiting; it has delivered its promise. What is needed now is for a creative infrastructure to develop alongside the software and hardware. New creative dreams will be dreamt and realized as multimedia matures and develops in the hands of a wide range of imaginative people. This revolution is only beginning.

User base

I remember an old joke from the early days. (Was this the first multimedia joke?). A developer arrives at the pearly gates having received the final error message. "Who are you and what have you done in your life?" asks the heavenly gatekeeper. "I created multimedia," comes the proud and somewhat overstated reply. Saint Peter answers "That's nothing; God created the world in six days." "But the Lord didn't have to worry about an installed user base," comes the frustrated response. I remember a time, not so long ago, when the phrase 'multimedia computer' was used to describe a PC with a double-speed CD-ROM and a sound card. Multimedia developers worked in niche markets where the expensive workstation hardware needed for consumption could be afforded. Today every sub-$1000 PC or Mac is routinely multimedia-capable. Domestic budgets can now be stretched to purchase video editing packages which replicate the features of $25,000 turnkey systems only a few years old. The tools are with us and the once dreamt-of user base has arrived. What is needed is the creative infrastructure to complement this 'kit'.

Creative possibilities

The printed book dates from the fifteenth century. Photography was developed in the 1830s, while film was invented in 1896. Radio programmes developed during the 1920s and by the mid-1930s television programmes were routinely possible. All these forms have been available to domestic consumers using easily affordable equipment for some time. In short, they are everyday commonplaces. The creative content growing from the technologies in question is mature but none has had its full creative potential realized, let alone exhausted. All have been refined and developed as creative forms since technology made them possible.

Will multimedia be the same and develop over years, decades and even centuries, or will it go the way of the telegram, telex or the newsreel and become a technologically enabled form, quickly eclipsed by subsequent developments? Will the CD-ROM and its silver disk successors become the 'new papyrus' (*Multimedia: The Complete Guide*, Dorling Kindersley, 1998, p. 8) or just a footnote in the history of creative forms? Will the development of multimedia forms and the growth of broadband network distribution be a creative revolution, a Gutenberg shift or just more noise? The answer to this question lies in the hands of creative people in design studios, in teenagers' bedrooms, in university computer rooms, in front of screens all over the world.

A common-sense description of multimedia might be: the ability to combine the creative possibilities of radio and television programmes, newspapers, books, magazines, comic books, animated films and music disks into one set of computer files accessed by the same piece of software to provide an integrated seamless experience, where user input to some extent determines the manner in which the material is accessed. It is therefore interactive. The computer's ability to have rapid access to the files which constitute this material makes the linear model of the radio or television programme seem old-fashioned and limited. Interactivity, where the user to some extent determines the text or, more accurately, the order in which the text unfolds, offers great creative potential. It also offers a great creative challenge, with the possibility of an interactive movie very likely to give the traditional script writer something approaching a migraine headache to the power of 5.

Film and television programme makers quickly saw the possibility for interactive narratives with the arrival of the laser disk in the 1980s. Yet, interestingly, there are no great examples of this form to point to as creative landmarks. Graphic designers who began to work with computers to create two-dimensional printed work, saw the ability to animate text, to add sound and video, as revolutionary extensions of what they do, and they found in the World Wide Web a distribution medium undreamt of. Fine artists have enthusiastically embraced the technology for some time now (Laurie Anderson, *Puppet Motel*, 1995 and Zoë Beloff, *Beyond*, 1996) and will continue to act as the leading edge of development in a way we may not understand the significance of for many years. Animators respond to the challenge of multimedia by saying "We've been doing this for years". The only difference arising with the new technology is random access/interactivity. In fact, there is a case to be made that animation is the most helpful paradigm to apply as we seek to understand and create multimedia from the technical possibilities offered. It is the closest analogue analogue.

Interactivity

Traditional media forms, from books through to animation and live action film and television, are fixed linear texts, unfolding in only one narrative order determined by the creator. With the arrival of multimedia new possibilities have come to the fore: first hypertext and now hypermedia. This new paradigm presents the greatest creative challenge since the arrival not of printing but of writing. The move from linear analogue forms to digital non-linear creative structures will be a gradual one, driven by organic imaginative growth over a relatively long period of time. New multimedia forms will grow, as all new media do, from their immediate predecessors. Television drama grew from its radio, cinema and theatre origins over a period of decades, but is now a creative form wholly itself. The technology existed to create the Victorian serial novel centuries before the genius of Dickens and millions of literate consumers made the form real. Even allowing for the accelerated pace of development in the digital age, there will still be a need for organic creative growth once the technology stabilizes.

Old wine in new bottles?

Digital tools are now routinely used to create traditional linear product. The ubiquitous word processor gives the writer increased non-linear manipulative possibilities in construction, but the product that emerges from this process is an orthodox text, consumed, as the author intended, in a defined linear way. A similar process occurs in film, video and animation production, where digital non-linear editors are now used to create traditional linear narratives. High quality contemporary audio-visual product is shot on film for its still-superior image quality and contrast ratio, but this film is digitized and edited non-linearly, because of the creative flexibility and the speed afforded, while exhibition is still on film, because of the quality and reliability. It is a case of the best horse for the course. Sitting in front of a computer screen is clearly not the best way to read *War and Peace,* which is doubtless best enjoyed as a printed book, but teaching children to read using a speaking multimedia book running on a computer which records their progress adds value and creates a new order of experience.

The encyclopaedia, whether printed books or silver disk, has always been interactive. Its contents are accessed as the user wishes, in a different order for each user, with certain devices to help access. The content of such traditional printed reference work consisted of text and images. The digital multimedia version can add sound, it can animate the illustrations and add full-motion video. Its search tools can be incredibly sophisticated and its content can be arranged and presented in a variety of ways. Crucially however, it still needs a huge team to produce the content. This content is fundamental and its creation requires a vast repertoire of traditional production skills, ranging from making phone calls, through organizing and managing teams, to new skills such as information architecture. In this regard, multimedia production is most like movie making: an expensive team endeavour, where technical specialists from best boy through gaffer and re-recordist are orchestrated by production managers and producers to realize the creative vision of scriptwriters and directors. In multimedia, the equivalent roles are still evolving, sometimes borrowing terminology from older media. If a creative infrastructure is to develop to unleash the potential of multimedia, one must develop the equivalent skills of the producers, directors and the scriptwriters who toil in the television and film industry.

Equally, the role of the graphic design profession in multimedia development should not be underestimated. The typographical knowledge and intuitive skills, the sense of page layout applied to screen design and the ability to communicate concisely in visual language are all skills which are essential to the creation of any multimedia product. Multimedia screens and Web pages all need these creative skills if they are to look anything but amateur. Multimedia tools and Web distribution have given graphic designers the ability to animate text and pages and have moved them into the audio-visual domain. The profession has been presented with an enormous challenge and will continue to rise to it.

Research and multimedia

Technological research in university and industry laboratories has made multimedia hardware and software possible. Industry has taken these insights and developed affordable products for mass-market use. This technological infrastructure is now being used to produce and consume new multimedia products. These new creative forms in turn get researched (some might say over-researched) by cultural theorists, many of whom have never attempted to make the phenomenon about which they write. (For a witty and slightly dismissive summary of this kind of work see particularly: www.newmediastudies.com/webbook1.htm.)

Is there a need for applied research into the making of new media, or is the best way forward simply making digitally enabled products? The pioneers of photography did not have a Kodak-funded Centre for Applied Research in the Photographic Image, founded in 1850; they simply used their imagination and skill to invent a technologically creative form. The games industry, which could be said to be the most developed subset of multimedia, was enabled by research in computer graphics, and certainly some early playful products emerged from computer science labs. However, the form really took off when affordable computers came into the hands of imaginative (and some would say, obsessive) young men who worked alone and in small informal groups, ironically creating a successful industry where such inventive small-scale work is now increasingly difficult.

The distribution system offered by the Internet means that new work can be seen by a wide audience instantly, and virtual communities can form quickly, sharing good practice and effectively speeding the natural organic development of creative forms. Digital media will develop more rapidly than photography did, simply because of the increased speed of communication, enabling practitioners to see each other's work virtually instantly. The growth of digital media is facilitated appropriately by the speed of communication afforded by the very technologies themselves. Commercial imperatives and budgets will help, with advertisers often stealing leads from cutting-edge creative work. The funds poured into pop video production by record companies have helped all aspects of the moving image culture. Equally the slick expensive Web sites now compulsory for all large corporations provide a funding stream which feeds indirectly into all aspects of the developing digital domain. Public money, whether distributed through film funding bodies such as the Australian Film Commission, or arts bodies (Lovebytes, New Media Scotland) or as business development initiatives, has helped the new media grow. And grow they will, in a virtually infinite number of ways, in all manner of settings, limited only by the inventiveness of creative individuals all over the world.

Taxonomy of multimedia

The technical problems have been solved for the most part, the creative challenge remains great. What is likely to be created might be hinted at by a brief taxonomy of existing multimedia product. From these drawings in the shifting sands of the multimedia age we may be able to get a fleeting glimpse of the mature forms that will emerge.

As mentioned above, the reference book, be it the dictionary or encyclopaedia, has been an obvious type of product to produce in multimedia format. In these early days, the interactivity offered by multimedia seems to work best if delivered using the book model which has always been both linear and interactive. The multimedia encyclopaedia is already with us. In the reference book you have an ideal multimedia product which allows for interactivity, indeed demands it. However, a multimedia atlas will never replace the printed version if the maps are not very good, and the production of high-quality maps is not a task to be undertaken lightly. A searchable illustrated multimedia pronouncing dictionary adds value but does it add enough to lure the consumer to part with cash? Virtual museums and galleries can give us access to images and objects which are physically distant, and multimedia technology can be used in the same physical museum space to enhance the actual physical exhibition, but will it replace the experience of standing close enough to world-class art to touch and be touched?

Education is an area where the potential for development is enormous, especially as the young are the most likely adopters of new digitally-enabled products. 'Living books' – children's stories which read to their user and help them to learn to read in the process – are already among us. Mathematics and drawing packages already fill Christmas stockings, put there by dutiful parents acting out of the same noble motives that used to keep door-to-door encyclopaedia salesmen in business. Languages can be taught with multimedia methods and huge, entertaining databases can make all the sciences accessible and exciting. These all exist in rudimentary form, but infinite possibilities remain to be realised.

Computer games already generate more income than Hollywood films and have the added benefit of creating a generation of enthusiastic users unafraid of technology. Some of these end users will go on to become sophisticated creators of multimedia product, which will grow from their experience as gamers.

In terms of adult product for the mature, non-games-playing male and female audience, there is still a golden opportunity to produce a mass-market product. Interactive narrative is often mentioned in this context but this promise remains unfulfilled since it was first made possible with the laser disk in the 1980s. Simply stated there has been no 'killer application' in multimedia. One can talk of software products or games which define an era, but there are no multimedia equivalents, no paradigm-creating breakthroughs, as yet. Multimedia is difficult both to create and to consume; it is demanding but has limitless potential. The challenge remains; the opportunity is still there.

Conclusion

We live in interesting times, times when the young and the creative are taking the new digital technologies and appropriating them to their own uses; uses that could never have been imagined by those who developed the technologies. To work today in the creative uses of digital media is akin to what it must have been like to work in the film business with Eisenstein or Griffith, as they defined the working practices and the very grammar of the film form, or what is was like to have been working in television during the 1950s and early 1960s when that form defined itself creatively as a distinct medium, different from both radio and the cinema. The situation is all the more complicated today as technologies very often become obsolete before they can be fully understood and used. Whatever the technology and however great the pace of change and development, however much the unexpected happens, analogue creativity must inform digital technologies. Those who use any communications medium, whether new or old, digital or analogue, must have something interesting and worthwhile to say. A mastery of the medium and its techniques is crucial, but so is vision and creative daring, imagination and flair, and the ability to work hard to make visions real. It is still all to play for.

Introduction

1

- Historical Context
- Terminology
- Delivery
- Non-linearity
- Interactivity
  - User Interfaces
- Social and Ethical Considerations
  - Access to Multimedia: Consumption
  - Access to Multimedia: Production
  - Control of Multimedia
  - The Control of Content

It was a dark and stormy night. A storyteller might use these portentous words to capture your attention and draw you into a tale. A novelist might use the same words to begin the first page of a book. A radio play based on the same story could open with a crash of thunder and the howling of the wind. A film of the book could open on a scene of darkness, suddenly illuminated by a flash of lightning that reveals trees bent over in the gale, while an artist might paint a picture of a different nocturnal storm.

The dark and stormy night can be represented in different *media*, each of which tells the story through different means, appealing to different senses. One of the key insights in computing is that all these media can be represented *digitally*, as a structured collection of bits, and can then be manipulated by programs on a computer, stored on disks and other storage devices, and transmitted over networks. Their shared digital representation means that different media can be combined into what is loosely called *multimedia*.

The combination of different media is not something new. On the contrary, established forms mix media routinely. A TV news bulletin, for example, might include sound and moving pictures – both live and recorded – still images, such as photographs of politicians, graphic illustrations, such as a histogram showing the trend in unemployment, and text, in the form of subtitles, captions, quotations, and credits, which will usually be accompanied by suitable annunciatory music. A contemporary live theatrical performance may incorporate two- or three-dimensional artwork and design (sets, backdrops, costumes), sound, which may be a mixture of speech and live music, perhaps with tape recordings and synthesized sounds, projected still and moving images, and sometimes text in the form of surtitles (written texts displayed above the stage, which are often used for translation, especially in opera).

The integration of media is natural – we perceive the world through all the senses we have at once; the separation of media is artificial, and may often seem unsatisfactory.

Figure 1.1 'It was a dark and stormy night...'

Consider film, for example. From the earliest days of cinema, in the absence of any method of recording and playing sound in synchronization with picture, separate live sounds were produced at the same time as the film was shown: not just the live piano accompaniment that you may find in contemporary art-house cinema showings of silent classics, but dialogue, singing, and sound effects, produced by actors, singers, and noisemakers in the theatre, often hidden behind the screen. So great was the film-going public's desire to hear sound naturally integrated with moving pictures that in 1927 when Al Jolson spoke his phrase, 'Wait a minute, wait a minute. You ain't heard nothing yet,' in *The Jazz Singer*, audiences stood up and cheered. It is hardly surprising, then, that once the technical obstacles to representing media digitally (which we will consider in Chapter 2) were overcome, the next step should be to combine separate media. In fact, the separation of digital media into distinct data types – different 'sorts of things' to which different operations can be applied – can be seen as a temporary exigency demanded by an immature technology.

What is it, then, if not the combination of media, that distinguishes digital multimedia from previous forms of combined media? It is the fact that the bits that represent text, sound, pictures, and so on can be treated as data by computer programs. The full potential of this fact has not yet been fully explored, but one facet of it immediately distinguishes digital multimedia from its predecessors. A program can control the order in which various components are presented and combined, and can do so in response to input from a computer user. In other words, digital multimedia can be *interactive*, in a way that, for example, a TV news bulletin is not, and that goes far beyond the simple control afforded by a VCR or DVD player.

The digital multimedia version of the story we began this book with could open with a picture depicting a dark and stormy night. By clicking on an icon on the screen, the user could cause the scene to play as a video clip, or add sound effects, according to their choice. Perhaps by clicking on different areas of the scene, details could be revealed, or a new scene could be introduced – a different one for each part of the first scene, allowing the tangled tale of betrayal and redemption that began on that dark stormy night to unfold in more than one way, told through the eyes of different characters. Users whose hearing was poor could choose to have a transcription of any dialogue displayed for them, while users with impaired vision could have a description of what was happening 'read' to them by their computer. Different interface options might be offered for users with different tastes and needs. If the story had attracted critical attention, it might be possible to bring up learned commentaries on particular aspects, or a history of its telling in different media. There might be an opportunity for the user to take an active role, change the story, add new elements or recombine the existing ones.

Historical Context

Compared with established forms such as film or the novel, multimedia is still in its earliest days. The CD-ROM specification was published in 1985, with drives appearing on desktop machines from about 1989; the World Wide Web became publicly available outside CERN at the start of 1992, in the form of a line-based browser giving access to a handful of servers; by January 1997, when the HTML 3.2 specification was adopted as a World Wide Web Consortium Recommendation, audio and video were only supported in Web pages through the use of proprietary extensions. We have become so accustomed to the high speed of technological change in computing that multimedia is already seen as an established feature of the computing landscape. But, on the time-scale of cultural change, it has barely arrived.

The history of film and animation, for example, demonstrates that it takes time – much longer than digital multimedia has existed – for conventions about content and consumption to become established. The very first films exhibited to the public, by the Lumière brothers at the Grand Café on the Boulevard des Capucines in Paris in 1895, showed such subjects as workers going home from a factory, and a train arriving at a station. To be able to reproduce movement was enough, without the farrago of plot, character, or message we normally associate with films. The early trick films of Georges Mélies were shown as part of his magic show, in the same way as the magic lantern projections he used to create illusions. In a similar vein, Winsor McCay's *Gertie the Dinosaur*, one of the first short animations made in America (in 1909), was used as an integral part of his vaudeville act. While Gertie did tricks, McCay stood in front of the screen on stage and talked to her,[†] telling her what to do, and scolding her when she got it wrong, in response to which Gertie started to cry; finally McCay appeared to walk into the frame and ride off on the dinosaur's back.

† In some versions of the film currently in circulation, this monologue has been added as a soundtrack, but the disembodied voice does not convey the presence or interactive nature of the vaudeville act.

At the same time, films, including narrative and animation, were already being shown, particularly in Europe, as entertainments in their own right, purely to be watched on a screen. The diversity of early ways of using film shows that there was originally no consensus about a 'right' way to present a film. Later on, anything other than a cinema screening would be seen as eccentric. Even films that attempted to use the medium in original ways would mainly do so within the cinema context, and a film shown in other ways, for example projected onto the floor of a gallery, would be re-defined – for example, as an 'installation'.

Another notable feature of early cinema is the way in which established forms were translated into the new medium. In particular, the newsreels shown around the time of the First World War were based on the same principles as a newspaper, even to the extent of including an animated cartoon corresponding to a comic strip. Characters were transported from the comic strips to film, and the animators who brought them to life were often (but not always) the artists who had drawn the strips. Perhaps more to the point, one of the most succesful studios producing newsreels and animations was the International Film Service, owned by the newspaper proprietor

William Randolph Hearst – who also owned the syndication rights to many popular comic strips of the period.

Remember that the time we are now describing was twenty years after the invention of cinema, yet we still find film looking to earlier media for its forms and content. In a similar way, multimedia still adopts the format of earlier media; the most obvious example is the multimedia encyclopedia, which has the same form – a series of short articles, accessible through one or more indexes – as its paper equivalent, and is often published by the same organization. Other reference works also follow the form of reference books, sometimes, as in the case of some of Dorling-Kindersley's CD-ROMs, following the distinctive house style of their print originals. Electronic software manuals rarely depart far from the organization of hard-copy manuals, merely adding better searching facilities and sometimes some animation.

One of the things that was needed before film could acquire its distinct character as a medium was an appreciation of the way the movie camera and film could be used to create new sorts of images, by framing, movement, editing and special effects. In multimedia, part of what is presently missing is a real understanding of how we can take advantage of the fact that digital multimedia is data, to integrate the presentation of multimedia with computation. For the moment, we are largely confined to controlling the presentation interactively, and to moving the data across networks.

Terminology

A telling symptom of the immaturity of digital multimedia is the absence of satisfactory terminology. What do you call a mixture of media under software control? Where the display and presentation of the media elements is the sole purpose, as in a Web page or an encyclopedia on CD-ROM, we will usually refer to a *multimedia production*. Where the display of the multimedia is more intimately bound up with computation, we will refer to a *multimedia application*. A simple example of a multimedia production might be a Web page containing a chronological listing of forthcoming film festivals, with some attached images and video clips. A multimedia application using the same data could provide an interface (which might still be a Web page) to a database containing the festivals' details and related material, so that a user could search for festivals in a particular geographical area, or those that accepted material on video tape, and so on. The distinction between the two is not a sharp one. A certain amount of computation might be done to control the presentation of a multimedia production, so there is a continuum from productions that simply present material in a fixed way, through increasingly complex interactivity, to applications that generate multimedia dynamically.

There remains another question. We know that we *read* text, *look at* images, *watch* video and *listen to* sound, but what do we do to a multimedia production? All of these, perhaps, as well as interacting with it. There is no satisfactory term either for the act or for the person who performs it. For the latter, we reluctantly fall back on the over-worked and vague term *user*. The usage at least has the virtue that it draws attention to the active role that, potentially anyway, a user adopts with relation to most multimedia productions. Although much influential critical work has focused on the active role of the reader in creating readings of texts, this activity is of a cerebral and largely unconscious type. In contrast, the user of multimedia is active in a literal sense, using input devices such as the mouse and keyboard to control what goes on – within the limits allowed by the multimedia producer.

It can be useful to distinguish between *multimedia* and *multiple media*. The distinction is best understood from the point of view of the user. It is commonplace that we perceive different media in different ways: we just referred to reading text, looking at pictures, listening to sound, and so on. Cognitive scientists call these different sorts of perception *modalities*. A multiple media production requires us to switch between modalities, for example, by reading some text, then looking at a picture, and so on. Many early 'multimedia' CD-ROM presentations were like this. True multimedia requires us to combine modalities (as we do in real life – think of the experience of walking through a shopping mall, for example), or even develop new ones, to cope with the combination of media. A familiar example is the pop video, where the music and moving images are (usually) presented as a composite – arguably often to the detriment of one or the other considered in isolation – with, for example, visual action illustrating lyrics, and scenes being cut in time to the beat of the music.

While modalities provide a useful way of thinking about multimedia from a cognitive point of view, we prefer to adopt a definition more in keeping with the technical emphasis of this book, and consider digital multimedia to be

> any combination of two or more media, represented in a digital form, sufficiently well integrated to be presented via a single interface, or manipulated by a single computer program.

This definition is broader than some that have been proposed. It is quite common to require at least one of the media to be a time-based one, such as sound or video. It is certainly true that, at present, the addition of time introduces significant new technical difficulties, which may be considered sufficiently challenging to make a qualitative difference between such dynamic multimedia and purely static multimedia, involving only text and images. However, we consider these difficulties to be transient effects of the current state of the underlying digital technologies, and prefer to use the more general definition just given.

Delivery

Some means of delivery is required, to get any multimedia production from its producer to its consumers. It is useful to distinguish between *online* and *offline* delivery.

Online delivery uses a network to send information from one computer, often a server machine providing centralized storage of bulky data, to another, usually a personal computer on somebody's desk. The network in question may be a local area network serving a single organization, but more often it will be the Internet. In particular, the World Wide Web has established itself as the means of delivering multimedia online.

The World Wide Web has achieved such supremacy as a means of accessing data over the Internet that in popular perception the Web and the net are sometimes seen as synonymous. This is not the case, as we will explain in Chapter 2, and in more detail in Chapter 17.

Where multimedia is delivered offline, some removable storage medium must be used. The widespread deployment of CD-ROM drives in personal computers in the mid-1990s was, to some extent, responsible for the surge in interest in multimedia at that time. This is because, for the first time, it made available a form of storage with adequate capacity (around 650 Mbytes, compared to the 1.44 Mbytes of floppy disks) to accommodate the large files characteristic of multimedia data, while still being relatively inexpensive to duplicate. The data transfer rate of early CD-ROM drives was too slow to support playback of video and sound, but more recent models have increased the speed, to the point where multimedia can be played directly from a CD-ROM, although smooth playback of full-screen video from CD-ROM is still impossible without additional hardware support.

Despite a great deal of enthusiasm in certain sectors of the industry, the multimedia CD-ROM never really caught the public imagination; the high development costs of elaborate work in this format meant that the price of such CD-ROMs remained relatively high, and few titles ever made any significant amount of money for their developers. Although some multimedia CD-ROMs continue to be produced, online delivery is widely seen as the future for multimedia. Even for those CD-ROMs which continue to be viable, such as multimedia encyclopedias, there is an increasing trend towards a combination of offline and online delivery, with the CD being used to hold a fixed collection of data, augmented with links to Web sites, where updates and supporting information are available (sometimes for a supplementary fee).

In 1995, an industry consortium announced the specification for a successor to CD-ROM, using the same size and shape platters, called DVD. Originally, this stood for Digital Video Disk, since the format was intended as a replacement for VHS cassettes as a distribution medium for video, as analogue methods of storing video began to be replaced by digital methods. It was immediately understood that DVD could be used equally well for any digital data, just as the audio Compact Disc had been adapted as the CD-ROM. Accordingly, the name was changed, somewhat desperately, to Digital Versatile Disk, thus keeping the abbreviation DVD. DVD offers a much higher storage capacity (up to 17 Gbytes on a double-sided disk), with similar transfer rates to modern ($12\times$ and higher) CD-ROM drives. Although they are sometimes used for distributing software, DVDs have not become a substitute for CD-ROM, being mostly used for their original purpose of distributing high-quality video. DVD players are, in effect, simple computers, which has allowed simple interactive features to be added to DVDs. Many DVD titles use animated menus, from which the user selects sub-titling and language options, accesses extra features, such as movie trailers, jumps to a selected point in the main feature, or plays the movie. Some DVDs include galleries of stills, in the style of a slideshow, and even primitive games. Thus, the DVD has become a new menu for interactive multimedia, albeit of a rudimentary nature.

Online delivery, however, offers possibilities which are not available offline. In particular, it enables the delivery of (almost) live multimedia content, which in turn makes possible novel applications such as video conferencing and broadcast multimedia. Generally, when multimedia is delivered online, the delivery need not be passive, in

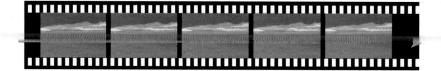

Film: Fixed order of frames defines a single playback sequence.

Book: Physical arrangement of text and pages implies a linear reading order.

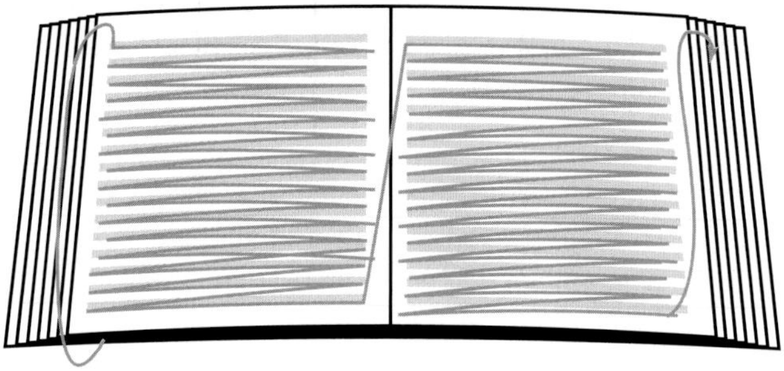

Figure 1.2 Linear structures in conventional media

the way that it is from CD-ROM: things can happen at the delivering end; for example, a database query can be executed.

Non-linearity

Broadly speaking, there are two models currently in use for combining elements of different media types: *page-based* and *time-based*.

In the first, text, images, and video are laid out in a two-dimensional arrangement that resembles the way text and images are laid out in books and magazines. Time-based elements, such as video clips and sound, are embedded in the page as if they were images, occupying a fixed area; controls may be provided to start and stop playback. Individual pages can be combined using *links*, which connect pages, allowing the user to jump from one page to another – not necessarily the next page in any fixed order – by clicking on a representation of the link, such as an underlined word or phrase. Such linked page-based multimedia productions are known as *hypermedia*. The best known example of a hypermedia system is the World Wide Web.

Hypermedia takes its inspiration from paper-based media that are essentially static, and grafts time-based features onto a spatially

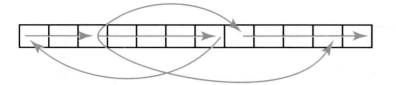

Flash: Jumps between frames controlled by interactivity perr branching and loops.

Hypermedia: Links between pa permit multiple arbitrary readin orders.

Figure 1.3 Non-linear structures

organized framework. In contrast, time-based multimedia makes time the central organizing principle. Elements are arranged in time, often using a timeline, so that they are presented as a sequence. The elements of the sequence may be frames, like those of a film, which are played back at a sufficient speed to provide the illusion of continuous motion in real time, or they may be discrete pages, presented one after another, like slides in a slide show. A multimedia *presentation* (as we will call such a timeline-based production) will often incorporate parallelism: several video clips may be shown at the same time, perhaps overlaid against a static image, or a sound track may play during an animation. Elements may be synchronized, so that, for example, some text may be displayed as long as a video clip is playing, or an image will be displayed ten seconds after the beginning of a video clip. The most widely-used time-based multimedia technology on the Web is Flash; business presentation packages such as PowerPoint usually allow the incorporation of multimedia elements, so PowerPoint slideshows provide the most basic sort of multimedia presentation. (Formerly, Director movies were often used as multimedia presentations on CD-ROM. With the decline of the multimedia CD-ROM, and the increased used of the Internet to distribute multimedia, Director has been superseded by Flash.)

A third model for combining media is exemplified by VRML, which we will describe briefly in Chapter 8, and to some extent, by MPEG-4. Here, the elements are laid out in a three-dimensional scene. The user can move about in the 3-D space and inspect images or objects that they encounter. Links may be incorporated, to provide hypertext functionality, and interactivity can be provided, using the scripting mechanisms that are applied to the other models of multimedia, as we will describe in Chapter 16. Scene-based multimedia of this sort is presently most often found in games, although these are not usually thought of as multimedia productions. The apparent failure of VRML so far to achieve wide acceptance, and the lack of any commercial implementations of the relevant part of the MPEG-4 standard, means that currently there is no standard form for scene-based multimedia.

Multimedia productions based on both of these models are often augmented with interactive features that allow the user to control their progress. As we will describe in Chapter 16, a scripting facility is usually provided that allows multimedia authors to write simple programs that cause actions to occur in response to user input. In this way, a means can be provided for a user to choose to jump forwards or backwards to a specific point in a time-based presentation. This allows for loops and branching structures, which to some extent resemble the linked pages of hypermedia. Scripts can also be written to cause actions to occur after a certain period of time, or in response to events such as a video clip finishing. By using scripts of this sort, temporal organization can be added to page-based multimedia. Since it is also the case that the elements of a time-based multimedia presentation must be arranged spatially, and that Flash movies are often embedded in Web pages and may contain their own links to other pages (which may or may not contain Flash movies) the distinction between our models of media combination is somewhat blurred.

A concept that unifies both models is that of *non-linearity*. In many conventional media, there is an obvious sequence from a well-defined beginning to the end. A play or film is usually watched from its first scene to its last; a novel or magazine article is usually read from beginning to end. We can, if we choose, depart from this linear sequence, by fast-forwarding or rewinding a video tape, jumping to a chapter marker on a DVD, or skipping pages in a book, but the intention of the work's creator is that it should be experienced linearly. In contrast, non-linearity is the essence of hypermedia and of interactive time-based multimedia. Figures 1.2 and 1.3 illustrate the concept. In Chapter 13, we will examine particular non-linear structures commonly used in multimedia.

Non-linearity is not new. Many books are organized for non-linear reading: encyclopedias, dictionaries and other reference books are the most familiar examples of books that are usually accessed in a non-linear fashion. Tables of contents, indexes and cross-references are textual devices that are used in such works to help readers find their way around. You might consider a painting to be non-linear, in as much as the elements are all present at the same time, and you can look at parts of the picture in whatever order or combination you wish. Paintings are usually highly organized visually to make sense when looked at. A performance of a play demonstrates that the distinction between linearity and non-linearity is not entirely clear-cut. Although the play is performed in the linear sequence of scenes, the audience's attention can move around the stage, allowing them to concentrate on different aspects of the action. This is in contrast to a film, where the camera forces you to look at each scene in a particular way.

Interactivity

Interactivity is frequently portrayed as the feature that distinguishes digital multimedia from other forms of combined media, such as television. It is often claimed that it puts the user in control – by implication, in a way that has not previously been possible: "Interactivity empowers the end users of your project by letting them control the content and flow of information."[†] While there is some truth in this, it should be recognized that the amount of control offered is strictly limited within parameters established by the multimedia producer. This must be the case in any situation where interaction takes place with a finite system responding according to a program. Only choices that are coded into the program are allowed. However, providing choices in a computer program is much easier than providing choices via a hardware device – such as through the controls of a VCR – so it is possible in a multimedia production to allow the user to control events at many points. Where a sequence of choices can be made in succes-

† Tay Vaughan, *Multimedia: Making It Work*.

sion, the possibilities expand combinatorially: if, for example, there are four choices at each of five stages of a production, although only twenty branches must be programmed, there is a total of $4^5 = 1024$ possible sequences which can be followed; that is, 1024 possible ways of experiencing the production. Such a range of possible experience might well appear to offer the user endless choice, but ultimate control over "the content and flow of information" remains with the producer, not the user, and even a significantly increased range of choices will not necessarily enhance a production. In certain cases – e.g. the provision of access to information in facilities such as Web site railway timetables – a single, fast, optimized route to the required information is all that is needed. And no amount of interactivity can compensate for poor or dull content, or bad organization of the work – one of the worst cases of this is when, through a series of selections on buttons, etc., one navigates through a site to find that the desired page is an empty space labelled "under construction".

The character of interaction can be appreciated by considering how it operated in the once-popular game *Myst*. The player was presented with a series of images, depicting scenes in an imaginary world. Sometimes, if you clicked on an object, something happened – doors opened, machines operated, and so on. When the cursor was placed near the edge of the screen, it changed shape and a mouse click caused the scene to change, as if you had walked out of the frame into the adjoining space; in this way you could, for example, walk round a building. Apart from that, there were no controls, such as buttons, so the game demanded a process of exploration before you could find out how to make anything happen. Advertising copy and reviews of the game placed great emphasis on the idea that you have a fantastic world to explore. In fact, though, all that your choices and explorations enabled you to do was to complete a few little puzzles, obtaining fragments of a story along the way, until you reached the end. You didn't have any choice over this – if you couldn't work out the combination to open a door, you couldn't attack it with a crowbar instead, for example. All you could do is go off and try a different puzzle, or give up. However, the extraordinary popularity of *Myst* in its heyday demonstrates how interactivity, when embedded in a rich environment with high-quality graphics and evocative sound, can dramatically increase the attractiveness of a production. It is hard to believe that the puzzles presented on their own, or the flimsy piece of fantasy fiction upon which the game is built, would draw the same audience.

'Interactivity' is really a misnomer – although we will continue to use the term in deference to its wide currency. When the computer's role is to present choices and respond to them, it cannot be said to be keeping up its end of an interaction, while at the same time it reduces the user's options for contributing to the intercourse to a few mouse gestures. The application of artificial intelligence can improve the level of discourse, but (with all due respect to Alan Turing) true interaction is only possible where another person is involved. Even then, if the interaction is mediated by a program, the form it can take may be severely limited. In many contemporary networked games, for example, the only way you can interact with your fellow players is apparently by trying to kill them.

Since interactivity is a novel contribution that computers make to multimedia, there is a strong tendency for all multimedia productions to be interactive. It is worth remembering, though, that seemingly endless choice may not only be inappropriate or redundant in the ways described above – it is not necessarily what everybody always wants. In some cases an audience may be quite content to let a story unfold just the way the writer or director intended it to, without the distraction of commentaries, out-takes, or supplementary material. In many of these cases, it would probably be better to read a book or go to the pictures – digital multimedia is not appropriate for everything. There will also be times when producers do not wish to offer interactivity to the user. An increasing number of artists are creating work in the form of digital multimedia, but in many cases they choose to retain control of what is shown, and do not allow their audience to interact with the work. Such productions can be innovative, and even seek to push the boundaries of what can be achieved in the digital domain, without being interactive or departing from an essentially linear form of presentation.

User Interfaces

The means by which choices can be presented to users can vary enormously. At one extreme there is the stylized set of user interface elements – menus, dialogue boxes, outlined buttons, and so on – and conventions used by most operating systems, mainstream applications and Web forms; at the other extreme, interaction with some sorts of game is essentially free-form, with any part of the screen liable to cause a response at some time. Adoption of the conventions has the advantage of predictability: users will generally know what to do when confronted with a form or dialogue box, such as the one

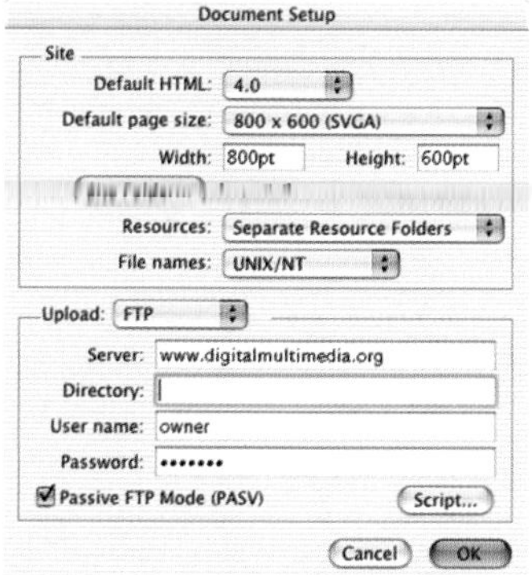

Figure 1.4 A dialogue box with conventional controls

† Because Web pages usually employ a standard collection of interface elements, the Web can be considered a 'platform' in this context.

‡ By default, Bryce's interface takes over the whole screen, obscuring the desktop entirely and hiding the menu bar the way some games do. This is in direct contravention to at least the MacOS user interface guidelines – it's actually quite difficult to do on a Mac – but it doesn't prevent the program from being usable, at least in many users' opinion.

shown in Figure 1.4, containing text entry areas, pop-up menus and buttons: fill in the text, make a selection from the menus, click on the buttons. By following the interface guidelines for the platform your multimedia production is intended for, and designing your dialogues and other interface elements carefully, you can often make it possible for an experienced user of that platform to work with your production without further instruction.† A disadvantage is that users who are not already familiar with the interface conventions might find it harder to use a fully-fledged conventional interface than a specially designed simpler one. Another disadvantage is that everything looks the same; you might have legitimate reasons for wanting to differentiate the appearance of your interface from the operating system. Doing this while at the same time making it clear how your various controls work is a difficult task. The innovative interfaces designed by Kai Krause for products such as KPT and Bryce (see Figure 1.5), for example, have sharply divided users, with some hailing them as a breakthrough while others criticize them for being confusing and affected.‡

The interface elements that have become most familiar to desktop computer users were devised in the context of a static graphical environment. With the incorporation of time-based media – video, animation, sound – new types of operation, such as starting, pausing, rewinding, and adjusting the volume, become possible, so new types of control are required. Menu commands with keyboard shortcuts could be used, but the practice of supplying playback controls in the form of buttons that mimic the operation of those on cassette players and VCRs, and are labelled with the *de facto* standard icons used on such appliances, is more common. Volume controls sometimes have the appearance of sliders or thumb wheels. Since digital video players make it easy to go to a specific point or scrub through a movie, using mouse movements, an additional control is often supplied in the form of a strip, representing the movie, with a marker that can be pulled through it; this marker moves during normal playback to show how much of the movie has been played (see Figure 1.6). The requirements of incorporating time-based media have thus given rise to new interface conventions. As always, these conventions can be ignored, and a free-form or individualistic interface substituted where that is felt to be justified by the nature of a particular production. It should be borne in mind, however, that accepted interface designs are the tried and tested products of expert designers, and the attempt to create a radical or superior interface should not be undertaken too lightly.

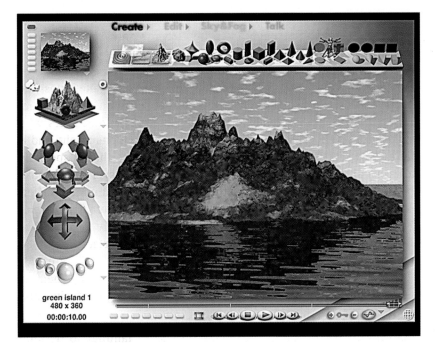

Figure 1.5 An unconventional user interface (Bryce)

Social and Ethical Considerations

It is a commonplace among technologists that technology itself is neutral and without moral value, either good or bad. It is only the uses to which people choose to put technology that need to be subjected to moral scrutiny. While this assertion is literally true – because ethics by definition applies only to the thoughts and actions of sentient beings – it is often the case that, in a specific social, political and economic context, the introduction of new technology presents opportunities for behaviour that were not there before. In such cases, certain ethical problems caused by that behaviour can conveniently be described as arising from particular technological innovations.

Access to Multimedia: Consumption

In the case of multimedia, the issue springing most directly from the nature of the technology itself is that of access. To begin with, access to multimedia depends on access to appropriate hardware and on possession of the necessary skills to use a modern computer system. In developed countries, access to hardware is largely a function of wealth. Although personal computers have become a consumer commodity, they remain among the more expensive of such items: a personal computer equipped to handle multimedia costs substantially

Figure 1.6 Controls for playing video

more than a standard DVD player or a games console, for example. In less developed countries, computers remain rare, and the infrastructure to support modern computer systems – reliable power supplies, ubiquitous telecommunications – is absent. In some countries large numbers of people are still denied the opportunity to acquire basic literacy – this, too, is often a side-effect of poverty. It is sobering for the multimedia developer to remember that substantial numbers of people around the world live without even those basic domestic facilities and appliances which members of the more privileged societies take for granted – in conditions where issues such as access to clean water are of vital importance, and access to computing not even in question. Any talk of the global nature of the Internet, or of multimedia distribution, should be tempered by this knowledge.

The modern world is, however, a complicated and paradoxical place. Although domestic Internet access may be rare in Africa, Internet cafés and other communal forms of access do exist, and often use satellites to provide high-speed access. Even among the wealthiest countries, local conditions can affect the ease with which certain kinds of multimedia can be accessed. 'Broadband' access to the Internet (which we will discuss in more detail in the next chapter) makes it feasible to use the Internet to access certain kinds of multimedia content, particularly video and high-quality audio, which cannot sensibly by accessed using a conventional modem and phone line. However, neither of the most common forms of broadband – ADSL and cable modem – can reach rural areas, the former because customers have to be within a certain, relatively small, distance, of the exchange, the latter because it is not economically viable to lay cables except in densely populated areas. Hence, rural dwellers in countries such as the UK are effectively restricted to a second-class form of access – satellite links, which can be economically viable for the communal facilities in the Third World, are prohibitively expensive for most domestic users in Britain. The Internet is a global phenomenon in principle, but in practice it wears different faces in different places, and in many places it has no face at all.

There are other factors which can prevent access to multimedia. As we stated earlier, the ability to use a computer system is a prerequisite – and this in itself presupposes basic literacy. These skills are by no means universal, even in developed countries. There is conflicting evidence about how computer skills are distributed among age groups. Certainly, young people in most developed countries are now routinely exposed to computers in schools, and often at home, if only through games. But the skills they acquire may be superficial, and the quality of computer education varies as much between schools as any other subject does. The highest levels of computer skills are usually acquired through work, so a failure to master computer technology may be an increasingly significant effect of long-term unemployment. And, of course, not all forms of employment expose people to computers, so disparities of skill are found between occupations, which may, in time, reinforce other social distinctions – e.g. between office and manual workers. People who are too old to have been exposed to computers in schools and who have not used computers as part of their work may find even a user-friendly graphical interface perplexing, so, even if they can afford the hardware to access multimedia, they may not feel able to take advantage of it.

Finally, physical disabilities or learning difficulties may interfere with a person's ability to use computers or experience multimedia content. This is particularly poignant as computers can be of great value in ameliorating some of these difficulties. A range of problems, from arthritis to motor neurone disease, may make it difficult or impossible for someone to operate a conventional keyboard, mouse and other input devices. Blindness and visual impairment raise specific concerns. Voice synthesizers and Braille keyboards and output devices can make it possible for blind people to use computers effectively (again assuming sufficient wealth or social provision makes such devices available), but most multimedia has a marked graphic bias, relying on images not just to convey information, but for navigation and interaction. This is evident on the World Wide Web, where many Web pages use image maps for navigation; the habit of using small images as navigation icons (or merely to provide text labels in a more interesting font than the defaults) means that some Web pages are unusable without images. People who are dyslexic, on the other hand, typically find graphic images and icons more readily intelligible than text, and will be assisted by good design of these elements. Although it is well known that many people have difficulty in distinguishing between certain colours, and most books on design offer advice on how to choose colour combinations to minimize the problems arising from this, few designers appear to apply this advice when it conflicts with their aesthetic intent. The range of difficulties which may be experienced by potential users is very wide, and embraces all media elements, with correspondingly far-reaching implications for the conscientious multimedia designer.

The World Wide Web Consortium has done an exemplary job in addressing the problem of access for the disabled (we will describe the details in Chapter 13), but there is little evidence at present that many Web site designers are taking advantage of the facilities to make their Web pages more accessible to everyone. It is not within the scope of this book, or our own fields of expertise, to do justice to this aspect of access and to provide solutions, but we stress that this is an area which requires the most careful attention.

Provision of computers in public libraries, schools, community centres and Internet cafés, inexpensive set-top boxes and network computers, popular education programmes, and accessibility initiatives can all broaden access to the Internet and other forms of multimedia. But it should be understood that access is not, and probably never will be, universal, especially outside the industrialized nations. As long as the bulk of multimedia is directed to entertainment, this denial of access cannot be considered too serious. Nevertheless, if access to multimedia is portrayed as the norm in a society, to be without that access becomes a marginalizing influence. When advertisements routinely feature URLs, and you have no Internet connection, what message are the advertisements conveying to you? If multimedia does indeed become the primary channel for information dissemination, as some pundits envisage, being denied access to multimedia will mean being denied access to information. On a mundane level, when information about entitlement to social security benefits, refurbishment grants or medical aid is readily available from the home to those with an Internet connection, in the form of a slickly packaged interactive multimedia presentation, but requires a trip to a crowded and depressing government office to pick up a leaflet for those without, it is easy to see how the shift of information provision to new media can deepen existing economic divisions. In extreme cases, simple access to information saves lives, as with health education programmes. Access to information is empowering, and a deliberate denial of access to information has always been one of the most powerful weapons used by governments and the rich and powerful to exercise control and protect their interests. These issues have a social and political reality, and are not simply a matter for peripheral academic debate by multimedia students and producers. The work you make, if it is released to the world at large or to a part of it, will affect other people's lives.

Access to Multimedia: Production

Anybody with access to the Internet can have their own Web site – and anybody without can't. People who cannot use the Internet for any of the reasons given in the preceding section are not only denied access to the information it contains, they are also denied a platform for expression or advertisement. However, in the parts of the world and segments of society where Internet access is readily available, what computing people would call write access is almost as widespread as read access. An Internet Service Provider that did not offer several megabytes of free Web space to its customers is unlikely to survive for long. The availability of inexpensive tools for constructing Web sites (and the possibility of constructing sites by hand in a simple text editor), plus the relatively small effort needed to acquire enough knowledge to use these tools, means that anybody who feels they have something to say to the world can say it on the World Wide Web. Relatively affordable computers, together with very low cost access to the Internet, are bringing about a widespread revolution in access to the means of production and distribution of digital material.

In contrast, access to the means of production and distribution of traditional media is tightly restricted. Probably the most accessible medium is the printed book. It is possible for an author to write, print, and distribute their own books, but the costs involved are considerable, and the likely returns, in the absence of any marketing machinery, are slim. Such personal production is reserved for the independently wealthy. Most books are published through publishers, who are able to take advantage of their size to spread production costs, and to market and distribute their books more effectively. But publishers can only stay in business by making money, so they can only publish books that they think are going to sell. This means that book proposals are submitted to editorial scrutiny and refereeing – with the result that established authors have a better chance of being published than newcomers, and unconventional subject matter or styles of writing that only appeal to a minority of readers are unlikely to appear in print at all. There are small independent publishers – especially in the United States, where there is a tradition of independent and underground presses – who may pick up marginal work, but, like independent authors, their limited resources make it hard for them to achieve wide distribution. Contrast this with the Web, which offers a potentially enormous audience to anybody.

The situation in other traditional media is similar to that for books. Mass distribution of printed images takes place largely through magazines, newspapers and books, and is subject to the same editorial control as the distribution of printed text. Many illustrators and photographers also sell their work to greetings cards, calendar, or postcard manufacturers, or provide images for brochures or corporate publications. Here, the influence of marketing pressures and corporate values will clearly limit the type of work that can be used. Fine artists wishing to exhibit their work are often faced with even higher barriers. Most exhibitions take place in private galleries which survive by taking large commissions on the sale of work, and can therefore not afford to take risks; public galleries, such as the National Gallery or the Museum of Modern Art, if they exhibit work by living artists at all, normally only present the work of established artists. Even if an unknown or unfashionable artist can manage to get their work exhibited, it will only reach the few people who are able to be physically present in the exhibition space. Whereas printed images can be turned into digital form and disseminated through the Internet, the very nature of paintings and other art works means that digital dissemination can only be done at the cost of a substantial degradation of quality, and with a loss of the presence that may well be the essence of the work. However, fine artists, with their trained habits of exploring media, may be in the best position to take advantage of new opportunities that digital media and multimedia offer.

Most recorded music is distributed by a few labels, owned by huge multinational corporations, whose sales dwarf those of the independent labels. Because of the investment that a record label must make to sign, record and promote a band, companies try to ensure that they only make records that will sell, hence the notorious difficulty faced by new musicians trying to break in to the business. Again, contrast this with the ease with which anybody's songs can be placed on the Internet for downloading.

The enormous cost of making even a 'low budget' film means that access to the medium of film is even more tightly restricted than the other forms we have considered. Among the established media, only television can begin to provide any sort of broad access. The relatively low cost of video equipment compared to film, and the absence of any specialized processing requirements, means that video can be produced on a very restricted budget – although not to broadcast quality. Transmission, however, is controlled, as much as in any other medium, if not more, and opportunities for public access to broadcasting are limited to a few derisory slots on a minority channel in the UK, or one cable channel among fifty or so in New York, for example. We will see in Chapters 7 and 17 that emerging network and digital video technologies mean that anyone with a video camera, a contemporary desktop computer and a Web site can broadcast their own video over the Internet.

While the description we have just given is incomplete and simplified, it should convey the fact that access to traditional media is highly exclusive in comparison with access to the World Wide Web – which has the bonus of supporting interactive multimedia. Unfortunately for proponents of democratic access to multimedia, putting up a Web site is not the end of the story. People also have to visit it.

Control of Multimedia

In theory, all Web sites have equal claim on our attention, but, in practice, some exert a stronger appeal than others. Evidence suggests that the metaphor of 'Web surfing' – following links at hazard in the hope of coming across something useful or interesting – is no longer an accurate way of describing people's behaviour (if it ever was). Most people have a limited number of sites that they visit habitually, and only a small number of sites, compared with the vast number that exist, attract more than a few visitors. Many of the most popular sites on the World Wide Web are the home sites of Internet Service Providers, which typically provide a news service, little articles about technology or lifestyles, horoscopes, advertisements, and, increasingly, online shopping. In fact, these Web *portals*, as they are called, are online Sunday supplements, echoing the early development of film, with its impersonation of newspapers. This Sunday supplement model of a Web site is now also provided by sites such as AltaVista and Excite, which originally functioned purely as search engines. The main competition to Web portals is online stores, that is, digital mail-order catalogues. They may be more convenient for home shoppers, but the form of the online catalogues closely mimics their offline originals, and very little extra functionality is offered beyond basic search facilities.

In addition to importing established forms, the World Wide Web is also importing content from established media. In 1999, Apple launched QuickTime TV, providing streamed video over the Internet. Like a conventional cable or satellite service, QuickTime TV is organized as a collection of channels. The current collection of channels includes ABC News, Fox Sports, Warner Brothers, VH-1, Rolling

Stone, WGBH, and the BBC World Service. There is little evidence of public access provision here.

It is hardly surprising that companies should follow established advertising and marketing patterns when confronted with a new medium, or that Web content providers should turn to existing conventional sources for news and entertainment. The notion that the comparative ease with which anybody can put up a Web site provides an opportunity to wrest control of the means of distribution of ideas away from the old establishment does not bear much scrutiny, and is not supported by the evidence. The pattern of domination by identifiable large companies, corporations and institutions has, by and large, been transferred intact to the Internet. However, in addition to this predictable transference to the new media, the Internet has enabled the beginnings of something more interesting: the opportunity to create new kinds of relationship between consumers and producers of multimedia. As well as the one-to-many relationship of conventional broadcasting, publication and marketing, which the Web portals echo, we are seeing a new development of few-to-few relationships, between small groups of individuals with specialized interests, who in reality may be physically very isolated from one another. The structure of the Internet and the low production cost of Web pages provide a support for such relationships which is denied by the politics and economics of the established media.

The Control of Content

> "Then we must speak to our poets and compel them to impress upon their poems only the image of the good, or not to make poetry in our city. [...] He that cannot obey must not be allowed to ply his trade in our city. For we would not have our Guardians reared among images of evil, and [...] gather many impressions from all that surrounds them, taking them all in until at last a great mass of evil gathers in their inmost souls, and they know it not."

> Plato, *The Republic*, Book III

Some issues do not go away or become resolved in a hurry: more than 2300 years have passed since Plato wrote *The Republic*, and yet very similar concerns about the protection of impressionable young people are frequently expressed today. It is precisely the enduring nature of ethical problems – which deal with fundamental issues of how human beings can and should conduct themselves – and the great difficulty in finding satisfactory and practical solutions, that has fuelled the continuation of both academic and real-world debates on these subjects.

Human history to date has shown that any sufficiently complex society has sought to exert some control over what people may read, see, hear, or do, whether this is done by explicit policing or by economic or other, less tangible, means. In the twentieth century this control has usually been justified as a benevolent protective measure, and, in democracies, may well be broadly supported by the electorate. It is interesting that the same type of justification has been used by political systems which were radically opposed to one another – each supposedly protecting their own population from the potentially harmful influences of the other, for example in the ideological combat known as the Cold War.

The rapid growth of the Internet, which offers an unprecedented dissemination of possibly unacceptable or unsuitable material, has given a new impetus to debates about censorship. However, the ethical issues surrounding censorship are complicated, and a very long history of discussion has produced no enduring conclusion or consensus about them. The novelty of the contemporary situation lies in the international reach of the Internet, and its availability within people's homes. Multimedia has not yet managed to raise any new issues of content – and it seems improbable that people will have anything to express in this medium which has not already been expressed many times before in other forms. The new dimension is entirely one of access and distribution. Because the World Wide Web is currently the most effective means of distributing multimedia, anybody who is involved in multimedia production may find themselves drawn into the censorship debate, even though they may be poorly equipped to resolve the difficult ethical problems which have evaded a solution for centuries, and which have only been made more complicated by the very wide reach of the Internet. If you have a serious interest in this debate you will need to do a substantial amount of further reading in ethics generally, and censorship issues in particular, to develop a well-rounded and informed view of the situation. If you prefer to concentrate your efforts elsewhere – as most people working in traditional media have chosen to do – you would be prudent to avoid being drawn in unnecessarily, but you will need to be aware of how the debate is focused, and of the nature of the main issues.

Within a single modern state, mechanisms generally exist for controlling publication, exhibition, performance and so on, which are consistent with the political conditions of that state. The plurality of political and social systems that exist in the world means that it is unrealistic to expect a single model of censorship – whether that means no censorship, rigid centralized control, self-regulation, or any other set of mechanisms – to be acceptable everywhere. And yet, Internet content is available everywhere[†] and the way the network is organized makes it difficult to assign responsibility for the dissemination of content, even in cases where it is desired to do so.

† Subject to the limits we described earlier.

A society's history, its state of development, political system, and religious institutions and beliefs are among the factors that determine precisely what sorts of media or multimedia content are considered objectionable within that society. Some groups of societies may have a broadly similar history and culture, deriving from certain shared roots, which will mean that their basic concerns are concentrated within the same areas. But even in these cases there is often disagreement about the precise limits of acceptability. For example, the level of female semi-nudity that has been commonplace on beaches in the south of France for many years has been, during the same period, considered indecent on the other side of the English Channel (where it is still daring, at least), while at the same time complete nudity of both sexes is acceptable at bathing places in Scandinavia. Where there is greater cultural diversity, there is a corresponding diversity of opinion about decency.

In any society there is often a substantial separation between what is acceptable in a portrayal of life – i.e. in media – and what is acceptable in reality. In some societies, much greater leniency is extended towards representations of behaviour than to the real thing, but in others there is a much closer correspondence between the restrictions which govern media on the one hand and actual human behaviour on the other. In some there are very stringent restraints on specific media, for example on image making. These different sets of standards will be further sub-divided along lines of content: a society may sanction representations of violence while punishing those who actually do violence on others, and at the same time censor images of the sexual activity which in practice that society condones. A quick look at the films of the United States in the 1930s will bear this out. At this period even happily married couples had to be shown as sleeping in separate beds, and never apparently enjoyed any intimacy beyond a kiss and a cuddle, but at the same time gangster films and thrillers portrayed scenes of violence and murder which were illegal and generally condemned in reality. When the complexity of the standards for censorship within a single society is multiplied by the number of societies within the world, and then by the cultural and religious groups within those societies, the result is a set of principles, beliefs and practices which are very diverse indeed.

There is no alternative to accepting this diversity, so how can it be accommodated in the context of the Internet and other modern communication systems? To simply permit everything is not accommodation – restrictions, even when we may not personally approve of them, are part of the diversity. Just as it would be unacceptable to impose one society's set of restrictions on everybody else, so is it unacceptable to impose one society's freedoms on everybody else. (We are not talking here about matters which fall within the scope of 'Human Rights', which is a separate area of ethics in which an international consensus has now more or less been established through, for example, the United Nations Declaration of Human Rights.)

The *Platform for Internet Content Selection (PICS)* is an attempt to provide a mechanism that supports a diversity of attitudes towards content and censorship. The difference between PICS and conventional mechanisms, such as the banning of books or the seizure of video tapes and magazines, is that it restricts reception, not distribution.

An established pattern for the censorship of films, as practised in the United Kingdom and other countries with similar systems, tries to combine restrictions upon reception with some control of distribution. In extreme cases censors can refuse certification, effectively preventing the showing of that film in most venues, or they may require scenes to be edited out before a certificate can be awarded. These measures affect distribution, but by labelling each film which 'passes' with a certificate that defines what age group may legally be admitted to view that film, the censors also attempt to control reception – although in practice in the UK, for instance, this is not put into effect very rigorously. A significant flaw in this system, which has been addressed by certain video tape distributors, is that no indication is given of the nature of the content which was deemed unsuitable. This makes it very difficult for anyone to exercise their own control over what they are exposed to at the movies, unless they have access to information about the film's level of violence, or whatever, from other sources.

Acknowledging the virtual impossibility of preventing material that is unacceptable to somebody somewhere appearing on the World Wide Web, PICS aims to allow the user themselves to prevent unacceptable material reaching them. The underlying idea is simple: labels are associated with each Web page, to provide a rating of its content that can be used to assess its desirability. Undesirable material is rejected by screening software that is either incorporated in a Web browser, or implemented at a lower level to intervene in all network traffic carrying Web pages. All that PICS stipulates is a standard format for content labelling; it says nothing about what the labels should contain, nor how software should deal with them. PICS thus allows for arbitrary criteria to be used for assessing content, and arbitrary strategies for dealing with it.

PICS may sound like a laudably flexible, value-independent, means of blocking the reception of certain sorts of material, but it achieves this by deferring the difficult decisions. Who does determine the criteria for blocking, who ensures that software can apply the criteria, and who attaches the necessary labels to Web pages? In theory, PICS would allow pages to be labelled with, say, a green rating, so that pages that advocated environmentally damaging practices and policies could be filtered out. For this to work, filtering software would have to be made aware of the existence of the green label, so that it could be configured to use it as a filtering criterion. A PICS *service description* is a document that specifies the format of some rating service's labels. Filtering software can download service descriptions so that they can allow users to specify controls based on the labels they describe.

When PICS was first introduced, most filtering was performed by Web browsers which, by default, only understood the labelling system of the Recreational Software Advisory Council (RSAC). This system is restricted to a crude and culturally specific set of measures of violence, sex, nudity, and language. The RSAC has now been succeeded by the Internet Content Rating Association (ICRA). This is an independent international organization which administers the labelling of Web sites. The ICRA does not label sites itself; it provides a questionnaire which Web masters may fill in, detailing items and features within the broad categories of nudity and sexual material, violence, language and other topics, which include promotion of tobacco, alcohol or drug use, incitement to discrimination and 'material that might be perceived as setting a bad example to young children'. As this last sub-category indicates, ICRA perceives its mission as the protection of children; at the same time, it wishes to preserve free speech, so the questionnaire results in a PICS label containing an objective description of the site's features, not a judgement on its suitability for any particular audience. Parents may set up their browsers to permit or deny access to sites on the basis of any combination of features.

The PICS architecture allows labels to be attached either to a page itself, or to its URL at the server, and for enabling the label to be inspected, to determine whether to allow access to the page. The green label could only be applied if concern about green issues was so widespread that Web authors felt an obligation to include green ratings, or if an ecological organization was able to set up a ratings bureau and vet Web pages. However, if there is no third party who shares your concerns, and you do not necessarily trust Web authors to label their pages, you have no means of preventing material you do not want to see from reaching you, except by complete avoidance of anything you think may be unacceptable. Even if a third party service description does embody some criteria you wish to apply to content, you have to trust the labelling service. There is no regulation of such services, so there is room for abuse. There have been allegations that some labelling bureaux have blocked access to pages critical of their own policies, for example.

PICS labels could be used for a number of purposes other than those for which they were intended. For example, it would be trivial to write a Web searching program which sought out Web pages with certain types of content, simply by looking at the PICS labels. Ironically, the mechanism intended to restrict access to certain material is itself the means by which that material may be most easily located.

Exercises

1   Is the idea of making a film of this book an absurd one?

2   The late Kingsley Amis reportedly once asserted that he would never read another book unless it began *A shot rang out!*. How would this opening be realized in

(a) A radio play;
(b) A stage play;
(c) A film;
(d) An animation;
(e) A single created image;
(f) A photograph;
(g) A comic strip;
(h) A song;
(i) A symphony?

If you have access to suitable facilities, produce a rough version of each of your answers.

3   A commonly used means of multimedia delivery is the *information kiosk*, a computer system with limited functionality provided for

the public to learn about, for example, the exhibits in a museum, or tourist facilities in a city. Discuss whether information kiosks are a qualitatively different form of delivery from those described in this chapter.

4   Choose two Web sites and identify at least five (and preferably ten) ways in which you think each of them could be improved. State the criteria you use to judge them by.

5   Look closely at the user interface of any application of your choice, and identify ten features of that interface which you personally do not like. Explain the reasons for your choices, and suggest possible improvements.

6   Choose a straightforward subject, such as a guide to guest accommodation in your neighbourhood. Design a simple one-page layout of graphical material and text, which optimises intelligibility and access to information for potential users of all levels of ability.

7   We stated on page 14 that 'ultimate control over "the content and flow of information" remains with the producer, not the user'. Ignoring feasibility, discuss whether it would be desirable for true control to be transferred to the user.

8   If you are working within a group of people, have each member of the group devise their own set of six filtering labels, which they would choose to apply to a Web site of their making for the guidance of users, and then compare and discuss results. If you are in a position to do so, extend this exercise to include other groups in other countries.

9   A committed vegetarian couple wish to prevent their children from being exposed to images of meat on the World Wide Web. What difficulties would they face in using PICS ratings for this purpose?

Enabling Technologies

- **Digital Representations**
  - Digitization
- **Hardware and Software Requirements**
  - Hardware
  - Software
- **Networks**
  - Clients and Servers
  - MIME Types
- **Standards**

The production and consumption of digital multimedia as we know it depends on the ability of digital computers to perform operations at high speed. In order to benefit from this ability, media data must be in digital form. That is, the rich variety of sensory inputs that make up images, text, moving pictures, and sound must be reduced to patterns of binary digits inside a computer. Once this remarkable transformation has been effected, programs can be used to change, combine, store and display media of all types. Furthermore, the same data can be transmitted over networks, to be distributed anywhere in the world, or conveyed to remote destinations on removable storage such as CD-ROMs or DVDs.

Although a digital representation of data is fundamental, general purpose computers are not the only devices that can manipulate digital data. Digital video can be played by DVD players, digital TV only requires a simple set-top box, and digital audio can be played from CD by any CD player. At present, only a programmable computer can add full interactivity to multimedia, but it seems almost inevitable that, as the technology matures, consumer devices that function as multimedia players will be brought to market. It is to be expected that such devices will be significantly cheaper than personal computers, and that they may bring about the transformation of digital multimedia into a true form of mass communication.

Digital Representations

Computers are built out of devices that can only be in one of two states. Physically, this means that certain points in the devices' circuits are only stable at one of two well-defined voltages. In more abstract terms, we can say that these devices store and operate on *bits*, units of data that can only have one of two values. We might call these values 0V and 3.5V, or **on** and **off**, true and false, yin and yang, but conventionally we denote them by 0 and 1. Bits are usually grouped into larger units such as *bytes*, which consist of an ordered sequence of eight bits, or *words*, whose length depends on the particular model of computer, but is often four bytes, that is, 32 bits. Adopting the convention that a bit is either 0 or 1 suggests an interpretation of these larger groups: they can be read as numbers to base 2, whose digits are the component bits. Thus, the byte containing the eight bits 0, 1, 1, 0, 0, 0, 0, and 1 can be read as the binary number 01100001, which is 97 in decimal. Not only can we interpret bytes and words in this way, we can also build electronic devices that perform the basic arithmetic operations of addition, subtraction, and (with a bit more effort) multiplication and division, and produce an answer in the same format. Hence the once popular notion that computers are just giant high-speed calculating machines.

There is, however, nothing intrinsically numerical about bits and bytes. It is only the way that we choose to interpret them, and the operations that we build into our computers, that make these bits and bytes into numbers. We can choose to interpret patterns of bits in different ways, and this is how the data belonging to different media can be represented digitally. The pattern 01100001 might denote a particular shade of grey occurring in an image, if we wrote software and built display hardware to interpret it in that way.

It is easiest to see what is going on if we describe the interpretation of bit patterns in terms of the interpretation of numbers, since we know how numbers and bit patterns can be associated, and numbers are easier to write down, and have familiar properties. Thus, we represent characters of text by associating a unique number with each letter, digit or other sign we need, in the manner of a code. The widely used ASCII character set, for example, is an association between characters and numbers; it assigns the value 97 (i.e. the bit pattern 01100001) to the lower case letter a, 98 to b, and so on, for 96 different printable characters. For this association to mean anything, we must arrange that hardware – such as keyboards and printers – and software behave in a way that is consistent with it. For example, when you press the key labelled A on your keyboard without holding down the shift key, the number 97 (or rather a sequence of electrical pulses that can be interpreted as the corresponding pattern of bits) is sent to your computer.

As we will see in later chapters, a similar association can be made between numbers and quantities such as the brightness of an image at a point, or the instantaneous amplitude of a sound wave. Although the association is essentially arbitrary, there will normally be some structure to the way numbers are assigned to the quantities they represent: e.g. numbers denoting high brightness have greater values than those denoting low brightness. Such properties tend to fall out naturally from the nature of the quantities represented.

> Ada Augusta, Countess of Lovelace, appears to have understood the nature of digital representations in 1844, when she wrote: "[Babbage's Analytical Engine] can arrange and combine its numerical quantities exactly as if they were letters or any other general symbols; in fact it might bring out its result in algebraical notation were provisions made accordingly."

† Some computers use a different addressable unit, but the principle is the same.

Bits are arranged into bytes, and in the memory of a computer, bytes are arranged in a linear sequence so that each byte can be identified by its position in the sequence, which we usually call its *address*.[†] Addresses behave like numbers, so they can be represented by bit patterns and stored and manipulated like other quantities. This makes it possible to organize collections of bytes into *data structures*. For example, a black and white image is often represented by the values corresponding to the brightness at each point on a fine rectangular grid. We can store these values in a sequence of bytes, and then use the address of the first byte to access the image data; a simple computation allows us to work out the address of the byte corresponding to any grid point, and access the stored value. If we need a sequence of such images, representing successive frames in an animation, say, we can store with each image the address of the next and previous ones, so that we can easily traverse the sequence in either direction.

The most important interpretation of bit patterns in a computer is only incidentally related to multimedia: bit patterns can represent *instructions* that cause the processor to carry out operations on values stored in memory. Again, this interpretation relies on the fact that the hardware is constructed so that the intended effect is achieved when the instruction is presented to the processor. Because instructions are bit patterns, sequences of instructions – *programs* – can be stored in memory and executed. This is the defining characteristic of a computer: it is a *stored program* machine. This is what makes it possible for the same machine to be used for many diverse tasks, from the computation of tax allowances to the precise editing of video footage.

To reiterate a point we made in Chapter 1: the common representation as collections of bits means that data belonging to all media can be manipulated, both individually and in combination, by programs.

At present, there are established ways of representing text, images, sound, video and animation in bits; we can be fully confident that any media developed in the future will also be representable digitally.

Digitization 数字化

Multimedia data sometimes originates in digital form, as it does when images are made using a painting program, but it is frequently necessary to convert from some analogue representation to a digital one, for example, by scanning an image.

A banal illustration of the differences between analogue and digital representations is provided by contemporary time-pieces. Figure 2.1 shows an analogue pendulum clock and a digital alarm clock. The minute hand of the pendulum clock moves steadily, and can point anywhere on the rim of the clock face; it is not constrained to point only at the marks indicating exact minutes. This alarm clock can only display whole numbers of minutes, and its displayed value only changes once every sixty seconds. The digital representation is more convenient than the analogue one for precise computation: for example, if we want to know how long it is until half past twelve, we need only subtract the time displayed on the alarm from 12:30, whereas for the analogue clock we must estimate the difference based on the angular difference between the current position of the hour hand, and a position half way between twelve and one (or else read the clock, and convert the time to its digital form in our heads).

If you are feeling contrary, you will point out that the clock's hands do not really move continuously – there are gears and stepping motors and things inside the case that make it actually move in a series of small jerks. (Nowadays, many new clocks and watches are digital inside, even where the display is analogue, and so the hands can only move in discrete steps, as is evident if you watch the second hand of a clock that has one. Even older, spring-powered, mechanisms such as the one illustrated do not move truly continuously, though, because of the finite size of the moving parts.) There is no such thing as continuous physical movement, if only because of the quantum nature of electrons and photons; the infinitesimally small is a mathematical abstraction. However, as in the case of the pendulum clock, a continuous (analogue) model of behaviour is often more tractable than a digital one, and provides a more accurate description of what is going on than any manageable discrete (digital) model could do.

In multimedia, we encounter values that change continuously in several ways. For example, the amplitude of a sound wave varies

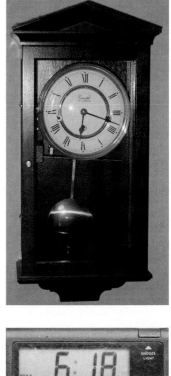

Figure 2.1 Analogue and digital representations

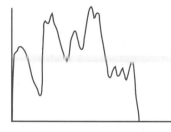

**Figure 2.2 An analogue
signal**

continuously over time, as does the amplitude of an electrical signal
produced by a microphone in response to a sound wave. The brightness of any point on a black and white photograph could in principle
have any value, though in practice this will be restricted by the physical constraints of the process of photography. As you see, we may be
measuring different quantities, and they may be varying either over
time or over space (or perhaps, as in the case of moving pictures,
both). For this general discussion, we will follow tradition, and refer
to the value we are measuring, whatever it may be, as a *signal*, not
usually distinguishing between time-varying and space-varying
signals.

You will observe that, when we have a continuously varying signal,
such as the one shown in Figure 2.2, both the value we measure, and
the intervals at which we can measure it, can vary infinitesimally. In
contrast, if we were to convert it to a digital signal, we would have
to restrict both of these to a set of discrete values. That is, *digitization* – which is what we call the process of converting a signal from
analogue to digital form – consists of two steps: *sampling*, when we
measure the signal's value at discrete intervals, and *quantization*,
when we restrict the value to a fixed set of levels. Sampling and quantization can be carried out in either order; Figure 2.3 shows a signal
being first sampled and then quantized. These processes are normally
carried out by special hardware devices, generically referred to as
analogue to digital converters (ADCs), whose internal workings we
will not examine. We will only consider the (almost invariable) case
where the interval between successive samples is fixed; the number of
samples in a fixed amount of time or space is known as the *sampling
rate*. Similarly, we will generally assume that the levels to which a
signal is quantized – the *quantization levels* – are equally spaced,
although, in this case, other arrangements are sometimes used.

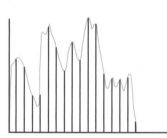

One of the great advantages that digital representations have over
analogue ones stems from the fact that only certain signal values
– those at the quantization levels – are valid. If a signal is transmitted
over a wire or stored on some physical medium such as magnetic
tape, inevitably some random noise is introduced, either because of
interference from stray magnetic fields, or simply because of the unavoidable fluctuations in thermal energy of the transmission medium.
This noise will cause the signal value to be changed. If the signal
is an analogue one, these changes will be more or less undetectable
– *any* analogue value is legitimate, and so a signal polluted by noise
cannot be distinguished from a clean one. If the signal is a digital

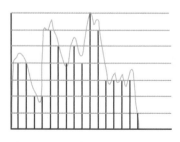

**Figure 2.3 Sampling and
quantization**

one, though, any minor fluctuations caused by noise will usually transform a legal value into an illegal one that lies between quantization levels. It is then a simple matter to restore the original signal by quantizing again. Only if the noise is sufficiently bad to alter the signal to a different level will an error in the transmission occur. Even then, because digital signals can be described numerically, schemes to detect and correct errors on the basis of arithmetic properties of groups of bits can be devised and implemented. Digital signals are therefore much more robust than analogue ones, and do not suffer degradation when they are copied, or transmitted over noisy media.

However, looking at Figure 2.3, it is evident that some information has been lost during the digitization process. How can we claim that the digitized result is in any sense an accurate representation of the original analogue signal? The only meaningful measure of accuracy must be how closely the original can be reconstructed. In order to reconstruct an analogue signal from a set of samples, what we need to do, informally speaking, is decide what to put in the gaps between the samples. We can describe the reconstruction process precisely in mathematical terms, and that description provides an exact specification of the theoretically best way to generate the required signal. In practice, simpler methods that can easily be implemented in fast hardware are used.

One possibility is to 'sample and hold': that is, the value of a sample is used for the entire extent between it and the following sample. As Figure 2.4 shows, this produces a signal with abrupt transitions, which is not really a very good approximation to the original. However, when such a signal is passed to an output device, such as a CRT display or a loudspeaker, for display or playback, the lags and imperfections inherent in the physical device will cause these discontinuities to be smoothed out, and the result actually approximates the theoretical optimum quite well. (However, in the future, improvements in the technology for the playback of sound and picture will demand matching improvements in the signal.)

Clearly, though, if the original samples were too far apart, *any* reconstruction is going to be inadequate, because there may be details in the analogue signal that, as it were, slipped between samples. Figure 2.5 shows an example: the values of the consecutive samples taken at s_i and s_{i+1} are identical, and there cannot possibly be any way of inferring from them the presence of the spike in between those two points – the signal could as easily have dipped down or stayed at the

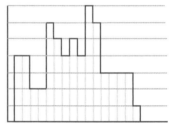

Figure 2.4 Sample and hold reconstruction

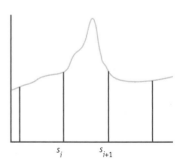

Figure 2.5 Undersampling

same level. The effects of such *undersampling* on the way in which
the reconstructed signal will be perceived depend on what the signal
represents – sound, image, and so on – and whether it is time-varying
or space-varying. We will describe specific instances later. Suffice it
to say, for now, that they are manifested as distortions and artefacts
which are always undesirable.

It is easy enough to see that if the sampling rate is too low some detail
will be lost in the sampling. It is less easy to see whether there is ever
any rate at which we can be sure samples are close enough together
to allow the signal to be accurately reconstructed, and if there is, how
close is close enough. To get a better understanding of these matters,
we need to consider an alternative way of representing a signal. Later,
this will also help us to understand some related aspects of sound and
image processing.

You are probably familiar with the idea that a musical note played on
an instrument consists of waveforms of several different frequencies
added together. There is the fundamental, which is the pitch associated with the note, but depending on the instrument, different numbers
of *harmonics*, or overtones, are also present, and these give the note
its distinctive timbre. The fundamental and each harmonic are pure
tones – sine waves of a single frequency. Any periodic waveform can
be decomposed into a collection of different frequency components,
each a pure sine wave, in a similar way; in fact, with a little mathematical gymnastics, assuming you don't mind infinite frequencies,
any waveform, periodic or not, can be decomposed into its frequency
components. We are using the word 'frequency' in a generalized
sense, to go with our generalized concept of a signal. Normally, we
think of frequency only in the context of time-varying signals, such
as sound, radio, or light waves, when it is the number of times a periodic signal repeats during a unit of time. When we consider signals
that vary periodically in space, such as the one shown in Figure 2.6,
it makes equal sense to consider its frequency as the number of times
it repeats over a unit of distance, and we shall often do so. Hence, in
general discussions, frequencies, like signals, may be either temporal
or spatial. You will probably realize that a spatially varying signal
may vary in two dimensions, not just one. We will consider this complication in Chapter 5, but it can safely be ignored for now.

Figure 2.7 shows one of the classic examples of how pure sine waves
at different frequencies combine to produce more complex waveforms. Starting with a pure sine wave of frequency *f*, we successively

**Figure 2.6 A periodic
fluctuation of brightness**

add components to it with frequencies of *3f, 5f, 7f*, and so on, whose amplitudes are one third, one fifth, one seventh,… the amplitude of the original signal. As you can see, as we add more 'harmonics', the signal begins to look more and more like a square wave; the more frequency components we add, the better the approximation.

Although it may not have the same immediate perspicuity, we could use the frequencies and amplitudes of its components to represent our signal. The collection of frequencies and amplitudes is the signal's representation in the *frequency domain*.[†] It can be computed using a mathematical operation known as the *Fourier Transform*. The result of applying the Fourier Transform to a signal can be displayed, like the original signal itself, in the form of a graph, where the horizontal axis represents frequency and the vertical axis amplitude. A typical signal's *frequency spectrum*, as this representation is called, will consist of a set of spikes at different frequencies, corresponding to the different components. Figure 2.8 shows our square wave in the frequency domain. You will notice that it includes negative frequencies. There is no need to worry about this: negative frequencies are a notational convenience that allow us to deal with phase shifts; where none is present, as here, the representation will be symmetrical, with the negative frequencies matching positive ones. There is also a spike at a frequency of zero, which is called the *DC component*, from the long-standing use of frequency domain representations in electrical engineering. It is equal to the integral of the signal, and provides a measure of its average value.

The square wave example demonstrates a phenomenon that can be shown to be generally true: *higher frequency components are associated with abrupt transitions*. As we add higher frequencies, the leading and falling edges of the waveform become more nearly vertical. Looking at this from the other end, as we omit high frequency components, such abrupt changes get smoothed out. Hence, operations such as sharpening or smoothing an image can be described and implemented in terms of *filters* that remove certain frequencies – this is of fundamental importance in the processing of graphics, as we will see in Chapter 5.

The *Inverse Fourier Transform*, as its name suggests, performs the opposite operation to the Fourier Transform, taking a signal from the frequency domain to the time domain.

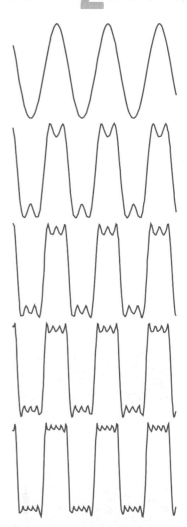

Figure 2.7 Frequency components of a square wave

† Strictly speaking, we also need to know the phase of the components, since it is sometimes necessary to displace them relative to each other, but we will ignore this complication, too.

Returning to the question of whether there is a sampling rate that guarantees accurate reconstruction of a signal, we can now give a precise answer. The *Sampling Theorem* states that, if the highest frequency component of a signal is at f_h, the signal can be properly reconstructed if it has been sampled at a frequency greater than $2f_h$. This limiting value is known as the *Nyquist rate*.

Some authors, especially in the field of audio, use the term 'Nyquist rate' to denote the highest frequency component that can be accurately reproduced. That is, if a signal is sampled at f_s, their Nyquist rate is $f_s/2$. The fact that the term is used with both meanings is unfortunate, but any ambiguity is usually easily resolved by context. We will always use the term in the sense of the lowest sampling rate for proper reconstruction.

The proof of the Sampling Theorem is technical, but the essence of the underlying effect can be illustrated simply. Suppose we have a circular disk, with a single radial line marked on it, which is spinning in a clockwise direction at a rate of n rotations per second, and suppose that we 'sample' this rotation as a movie camera would, by taking snapshots of the disk at equal time intervals. Figure 2.9 shows the snapshots we would obtain by sampling $4n$ times a second. Looking at this sequence (ignoring, for now, the coloured boxes) it is clear that the disk is rotating clockwise, and you can imagine that if these images were successive frames of a film, we would see the disk rotating in its proper direction when the film was projected. Considered as a periodic signal, the rotating disk has a frequency of n and we have sampled at $4n$, comfortably above the Nyquist rate. Consider now what happens if we sample at a rate of $4n/3$; the samples we obtain are the ones identified by red boxes. Looking at the sequence comprising only those samples, it appears from the successive positions of the line more as if the disk is rotating anti-clockwise at a rate of $n/3$. (The phenomenon may be familiar to you from Western movies, in which stagecoach wheels frequently appear to rotate backwards, because the rate at which the film frames were shot is less than the Nyquist rate relative to the actual rotational speed of the wheels.) Note that we must go beyond the Nyquist rate: if we sample our disk at a rate of exactly $2n$, we get samples in which the line alternates between the 12 o'clock and 6 o'clock positions (the blue boxes), so that it is impossible to determine whether the disk is rotating clockwise or anti-clockwise.

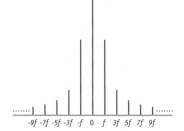

-9f -7f -5f -3f -f 0 f 3f 5f 7f 9f

Figure 2.8 Square wave transformed into the frequency domain

The Sampling Theorem only holds true if the signal is reconstructed from its samples in a particular way – technically, it is necessary to perform the operation in the time domain in such a way that it is equivalent to multiplying the sampled signal by a perfect pulse function in the frequency domain, that is, a function whose value is 1 between a specific pair of frequency values, and 0 everywhere else. By manipulating Fourier Transforms and their inverses, it is possible to arrive at a definition of a function that must be applied to the samples in the time domain to achieve this effect. Unfortunately, this function has non-zero values at points arbitrarily far from the origin. It is therefore impossible to realize the reconstruction operation in this way. In reality, we can only approximate it, with functions that are finitely wide. The practical effect is that it is necessary to sample at a rate still higher than the Nyquist rate to achieve perfect reconstruction.

In general, if we *undersample* a signal – sample it at less than the Nyquist rate – some frequency components in the original will get transformed into other frequencies when the signal is reconstructed, just as our rotating disk's frequency was transformed when we undersampled it. This phenomenon is known as *aliasing*, and is perceived in different ways in different media. With sound, it is heard as distortion; in images, it is usually seen in the form of jagged edges, or, where the image contains fine repeating details, Moiré patterns (see Figure 2.10); in moving pictures, temporal undersampling leads to jerkiness of motion, as well as phenomena similar to the retrograde disk just described.

The effects of an insufficient number of quantization levels are generally easier to grasp intuitively than those of inadequate sampling rates. If we can only represent a limited number of different values, we will be unable to make fine distinctions among those that fall between. In images, it is as if we were forced to make do with only a few different colours, and so had to use, say, crimson for every shade of red we needed. The difference between scarlet and carmine would be lost, and any boundaries between areas of those colours would be elided. The effect on black and white images can be seen clearly in Figure 2.11 which shows a gradient swatch using 256, 128, 64, 32, 16, 8, 4, and 2 different grey levels. The original gradient varies linearly from pure white to pure black, and you can see how, as we reduce the number of different greys, values band together as they are quantized increasingly coarsely. In a less regular image, the effect manifests itself as *posterization*, more formally known as brightness contouring, where coloured areas coalesce, somewhat like a cheaply printed

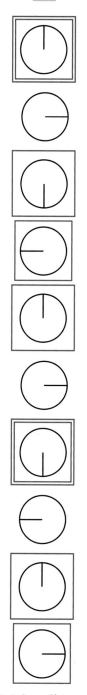

Figure 2.9 Sampling and undersampling

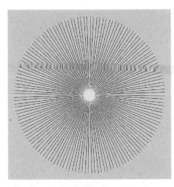

Figure 2.10 Moiré patterns

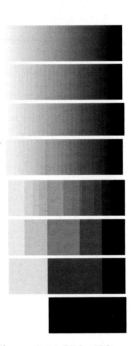

**Figure 2.11 256, 128, ...,
2 grey levels**

poster. Figure 2.12 shows how posterization manifests itself on a colour image: the version on the left is a digital photograph with millions of colours; on the right, we have reduced it to just four colours, and the posterization effect can be seen clearly. (Sometimes you may want to posterize an image deliberately – the result can be quite pleasing.)

The numbers of grey levels in our example were not chosen at random. The most common reason for limiting the number of quantization levels (in any type of signal) is to reduce the amount of memory occupied by the digitized data by restricting the number of bits used to hold each sample value. Here we have used 8, 7, 6, 5, 4, 3, and 2 bits, and finally a single bit. As you can see, although the effect is visible with 128 greys, it only becomes intrusive when the number of levels falls to 32, after which deterioration is rapid.

When sound is quantized to too few amplitude levels, the result is perceived as a form of distortion, sometimes referred to as *quantization noise*, because its worst manifestation is a coarse hiss. It also leads to the loss of quiet passages, and a general fuzziness in sound (rather like a mobile phone in an area of low signal strength). Quantization noise is clearly discernible when sound is sampled to 8 bits (256 levels), but not (except in the opinion of some audiophiles) at the 16 bits (65536 levels) used for audio CDs.

If you have ever used a drum machine or sequencer for making music, you will have met another form of quantization: these devices quantize notes in time, so that they fall on exact beats. A poor drummer can be brought into a tight rhythm by quantizing to sixteenth notes, for example. However, if you quantize to eighth notes, any funky syncopated rhythms will be lost – there are too few quantization levels. (On the other hand, if your drummer is really egregious, and you quantize to sixteenth notes when they are playing in straight eights, you may let in some of their mistakes.)

Hardware and Software Requirements
Hardware

If representing media digitally is conceptually so simple, and if digitization is so well understood mathematically, why is it that digital multimedia is such a relatively new development in computing? What we have so far failed to address is the resource requirements. As subsequent chapters will show, sound, video and most images require large amounts of disk space and memory. Time-based media also have to be captured and played back in real time, so the very large

Figure 2.12 Posterization

quantities of data to be handled imply a requirement for fast processors and data buses capable of high speed transfers. Accessing media data over a network demands high bandwidth. It is only recently that fast enough computers with sufficient memory and large high-speed disks, and broadband network connections have become available. As these developments become routinely available to domestic consumers, a further explosion in the use of multimedia is widely anticipated.

When we look at the hardware requirements of multimedia, there are two distinct cases to consider: requirements for multimedia consumption and requirements for its production. Realistically, in the case of consumption, it is more sensible to consider the capabilities of typical domestic systems, and the limitations which those impose, than some putative set of requirements for ideal playback.

A series of specifications produced by a consortium of PC manufacturers defined the *multimedia PC (MPC)* during the 1990s. The last of these defined the Level 3 MPC as having a 75 MHz Pentium processor, with 8 Mbytes of RAM, running Windows 3.11 (or a binary compatible OS), with at least 500 Mbytes of hard disk, a 4× CD-ROM drive, CD quality audio output, and the capability to play quarter-frame video at full frame rate in 15-bit colour. This probably sounds like a bit of a joke, but you should be aware that at least some

† Because of the fundamentally different nature of the PowerPC and
Pentium processors, clock speeds
cannot meaningfully be compared
between the two popular architectures. A PC rated at 3 GHz will perform at roughly the same speed for
most tasks as a 1.25 GHz Mac.

owners of machines satisfying the MPC specification probably believe
that their hardware is capable of 'doing multimedia'. More realistically, a G4 iMac, running MacOS X on a 1.25 GHz processor, with
512 Mbytes of RAM, 160 Gbytes of hard disk, a DVD-R writer (also
capable of reading and writing CD-ROMs), a built-in 56K modem,
stereo speakers, a powerful graphics accelerator card and a 17-inch
flat-panel display, capable of resolutions up to 1440×900 pixels (or
a Windows MX PC system based on a 3 GHz Pentium IV processor[†]
with the same amount of memory and disk space) represents the sort
of hardware available to digital multimedia consumers in mid-2003.
Even these relatively powerful machines will probably look fairly
feeble by the time you read this. It should be remembered, though,
that domestic users typically upgrade their computers less often than
business users or multimedia professionals, and there are probably
millions of relatively old machines connected to the Internet. It is
also the case that cut-price PCs, which will be attractive to casual
users on price grounds, use older models of processor, and generally
lower specifications than up-to-the-minute luxury models, and that
computers used in business, where they are primarily intended to run
relatively undemanding business applications, like word processors
and spreadsheets, may be based on slower processors and lack powerful graphics and sound cards.

While the best available desktop consumer machines are capable
of flawless video playback from DVD, for example, without special
hardware, at the same time new classes of less powerful devices are
coming into use. Hand-held 'personal digital assistants' (PDAs) are
evolving from simple digital address books into capable computational systems. Their small size makes it difficult to achieve the same
performance as desktop machines, and imposes limitations on the
amount of storage that can be accommodated and the size of the display. The communication facilities of these devices are often based on
the cellular telephone network, which presently provides less bandwidth than the fixed network. A new generation of mobile phones is
also appearing, which can be used for Web browsing and even video
telephony. It seems inevitable that these two classes of device will
converge, giving rise to multimedia phones, which will increasingly
be used for Internet access, including Web browsing. This presents
a challenge to Web designers to produce pages that are accessible
both to powerful desktop machines and to phones and PDAs. At the
system level, it means that multimedia architectures must be scaleable, allowing different versions of a production to be made available

transparently to devices with different capabilities. We will return to this question in Chapter 17.

Although the hardware requirements for high quality multimedia production are more demanding than those for its consumption, a great deal of multimedia is produced on high-end PCs running Windows 2000 and on Macintosh computers. These systems are often augmented with special-purpose graphics acceleration hardware and input devices for video and audio. For example, at the time the iMac described earlier was a typical high-end consumer machine, a G5 Power Macintosh with dual 2 GHz processors, a faster frontside bus and a more powerful graphics card with 64 Mbytes of video memory, would be typical of the better desktop machines used for multimedia production. This would probably be fitted with up to 2 Gbytes of main memory, additional high-speed disks and other specialized peripherals, as described below. More modest equipment can also be used to produce multimedia – many Web pages are produced on ordinary desktop PCs – but the range of material that can be created and manipulated on such machines is limited. At the opposite extreme, high-powered workstations, such as those produced by SGI or Sun, are also used, especially for computationally intensive tasks, such as rendering 3-D animation and video effects, but their use is more common in the film and television industries.

Raw processing power, high-speed data buses, large main memories, and powerful graphics boards are a necessity for producing multimedia content; fast high-capacity secondary storage is equally necessary. We have already noted that sound, video and images require large amounts of storage. During their preparation, they often require substantially more storage than the finished product will need. For example, images may be composed in layers (see Chapter 5), and 'flattened', by combining the separate layers, for delivery. Each layer occupies roughly the same amount of space as the final image, and designers often use up to a hundred layers. High quality audio and, above all, video source material can occupy a very large amount of storage indeed. The degree of compression required for final delivery, especially of video or over a network, usually entails a loss of quality that cannot be tolerated during production, so less compressed, and therefore much larger, files will be in use throughout the production process, with high compression only being applied at the final stage.

Manufacturers are regularly increasing the capacity of hard disks, and several can be used together if necessary. The speed of data transfer to and from large disks is a more serious limiting factor, particularly for digital video, where transfer rates in excess of 3.5 Mbytes per second – sometimes well in excess, up to 30 Mbytes per second are desirable during capture. The ATA buses normally fitted to desktop machines can only cope with data rates for compressed video. However, newer interface standards support higher data rates: FireWire 400 and FireWire 800 offer theoretical speeds of up to 400 and 800 Mbits per second, respectively (50 and 100 Mbytes), USB 2.0 can support 60 Mbytes per second, while new versions of the SCSI standard will transfer data at up to 160 Mbytes per second. FireWire is also used as the standard interface for connecting consumer electronic devices, especially DV cameras (see Chapter 7) and digital stills cameras, to computers.

For video capture it is essential that the data transfer to disk be maintained at a constant rate, or frames may be lost. This is only feasible if the free areas on the disk are contiguous. If a disk becomes fragmented, so that free areas are scattered over its surface in small pieces, the data transfer will be intermittently interrupted, as the disk seeks to a new position. It is important, therefore, that disks to be used for video capture be periodically de-fragmented, using a disk optimizing utility, or simply completely erased before a clip is captured, if this is feasible.

When peripherals are connected via one of the fast SCSI or FireWire buses, the limiting factor becomes the speed at which data can be moved off or onto the disks. With current disk speeds, a single, modestly priced, high-capacity disk connected via FireWire or Fast SCSI 2 to a dedicated computer will provide adequate performance for multimedia production. If, however, it is desired to share data between workstations, using a central server and a local area network, higher performance will be required. Fibre channel or Gigabit Ethernet can provide the transfer speeds. Relatively expensive high-speed disks can be used for storage, but a popular alternative is a *RAID array*. RAID stands for Redundant Array of Inexpensive Disks, and a RAID array is indeed put together out of cheaper, relatively slow, disks: improved performance is achieved by reading from and writing to them in parallel.

More precisely, RAID specifies eight different levels, which offer different degrees of performance and fault-tolerance. The emphasis of most of these levels is on the latter, which explains the 'Redundant' in the expansion of RAID. However, the lowest level, Level 0 RAID, specifies a 'data striping' technique, whereby a data block being written to the array is split into segments which are written to separate disks. The write operations can be overlapped, so that data can be written to the drive buffer faster than it can be physically transferred to any single drive in the array. Read operations can be similarly overlapped. The array looks like a single high-capacity fast drive. RAID 0 offers no protection against disk failure – if one disk fails, the whole array fails. Higher RAID levels are designed to protect against failures, by incorporating redundancy, with more or less sophistication, into the data storage scheme. Level 1 is the least sophisticated: it mirrors disks, which, instead of improving performance, decreases it. Higher levels use more sophisticated schemes, but a popular option is to combine RAID levels 0 and 1, thereby gaining the performance of data striping and the protection of disk mirroring.

In addition to large fast disks, multimedia production requires other, more specialized, peripherals. A graphics tablet with a pressure-sensitive pen is essential for all kinds of graphical work (with the possible exception of some image correction tasks) – you cannot properly draw or paint with a mouse. A large (20 inch or bigger) high-resolution monitor capable of accurately reproducing millions of colours is also desirable (although it should always be remembered that the end user will probably have a smaller, and possibly lower quality, display). It is common practice to attach two monitors to a computer for preparing images, one to display the image, the other, which may be smaller, to hold the plethora of tool bars and palettes that make up the user interface of most graphics programs. High resolution scanners are commonly used for capturing images from photographs and printed media. Digital cameras allow photographs to be downloaded directly to disk, without the expense, time, or specialist laboratories required to process film. Although only the most expensive digital cameras offer anything like the picture quality of conventional 35 mm SLR cameras, the convenience of digital photography makes it a highly popular way of creating images for multimedia. A video camera and sound recording equipment are also needed for recording these media. Nowadays, this equipment is usually itself digital and produces digital output that can be sent directly to the computer, over a FireWire connection, for example. Video and audio capture from conventional analogue equipment requires analogue to digital converters and compression hardware, which will be described in Chapters 7 and 9. The amount and quality of additional studio equipment – microphones, mixers, tripods and heads, lighting, and so on – required will depend on how ambitious and professional a multimedia producer is. Generally, the expectations of domestic consumers are high, so for productions intended for the domestic market, production values must be correspondingly high.

Software

We have emphasized that data of all media types are represented digitally as collections of bits, and can therefore be manipulated by programs on a computer. The things that you might naturally want to do to the bits that represent an image are not the same, though, as the things that you might naturally want to do to the bits that represent a piece of text or an audio clip. Different applications have therefore been developed for the different media types: image editing, painting and drawing programs for graphics; editors and layout programs for text; capture, editing and post-production software for video; special packages for motion graphics and animation; recording, editing, and effects programs for sound, and music synthesizers and sequencers, to name just some.

The essence of multimedia is the combination of the different media elements that can be produced by these programs. One way of carrying out this combination would be by writing a program that reads the different media data and presents it in a combined form, but, while this provides the maximum flexibility, it requires advanced programming skills (which are not always found in conjunction with the necessary skills for effective presentation of multimedia), while being repetitive and error-prone. *Authoring systems*[†] have been devised to carry out the task within an organizational framework that permits the automation of much of the work that would otherwise require programming. Authoring systems may be based on a layout model with a markup language, or on a timeline, as we will describe in detail in Chapters 12 and 13. Some programming, at least in a scripting language, is usually still required, if interactivity is to be provided.

[†] 'Author' isn't a verb, of course, but the usage is too well established to quibble over.

The upshot of all this is that the making of a multimedia production can involve a host of software tools and skills, some of them special to multimedia, others belonging to existing disciplines. A full mastery of any one of the tools required may take years to acquire – Photoshopping can be a career in itself, for example – and each demands a different kind of talent. It is a rare artist who can both write good programs and create high quality images, or direct videos and create striking graphic design work, for example – so professional quality multimedia production will generally require a team. This is not to say that one person working alone cannot produce multimedia, but just that, in most cases, the result is unlikely to be of professional quality. This might be perfectly acceptable in some contexts: personal Web pages probably ought to look amateur, in a sense; scientific visualization is not judged by the same criteria as science fantasy creations; diagrams are judged differently from works of art, and corporate presentations have their own aesthetic. At the low end of the multimedia software market there are packages intended to make multimedia production, especially Web page design, accessible to non-specialists. Such packages hide technical details, such as HTML tags and JavaScript code, and usually provide 'wizards' or 'assistants' that guide the production process. Collections of clip art, basic animations and other prefabricated media elements are available, so simple multimedia productions can be produced quickly with the minimum of effort. They all come out looking much the same, of course.

An essential part of our definition of multimedia is the condition that the combined media be sufficiently well integrated to be presented via a unified interface, and manipulated by a single computer program. This is in complete contrast to the situation we have just described with respect to multimedia production, with its multitude of different software tools and team input. The key to integration is a framework that can accommodate a multiplicity of media and present them to the user. Three distinct approaches can be distinguished (although, as we will see, elements of these approaches can be, and are, combined).

The World Wide Web epitomizes one approach: define a format (in this case, a markup language, HTML or XML) that can accommodate different media, and view it using a dedicated browser. Here, all multimedia productions are collections of Web pages, which are basically text but usually contain embedded graphics and other media elements. Any Web page can be displayed by a sufficiently up-to-date Web browser.

The second approach is to define an architecture, comprising a format that can contain different media types, together with an API (Application Programming Interface) that provides a rich set of functions to manipulate data in that format. The prime example here is QuickTime. A QuickTime movie can contain video, sound, animation, images, virtual reality panoramas, and interactive elements, all synchronized and coordinated. The QuickTime API provides functions for playing and interacting with movies, as well as for editing them. Any program can use the API to provide multimedia functionality;

QuickTime movies can be played by the QuickTime player that is distributed with QuickTime, in the same way that a Web page can be displayed in a browser, but they can also be embedded in word processor documents, or within games, or any special-purpose program that needs to manipulate multimedia as well as performing some other tasks. One can imagine adding code which interprets HTML to any program, of course, but since QuickTime is implemented at the system level and is available to any program, the effort required to add QuickTime support is minimal in comparison.

The third approach is quite the opposite to the previous one: deliver the multimedia production in a 'stand alone' form, that needs no additional software to be used. Flash provides an example of this approach: movies may be saved in the form of a 'projector', which can be delivered on a CD-ROM, for example, and will play on any user's machine (of the right architecture) without their needing Flash itself, or any browser or other movie-playing program. It should be borne in mind that these three approaches are not necessarily separate or incompatible. QuickTime is frequently used purely as a video format with synchronized sound, for example, and so QuickTime movies can often be found embedded in Web pages. Similarly, Flash movies are more often embedded in Web pages to be delivered over the Internet and played inside a browser than delivered as standalone projectors. In order to accommodate these forms of embedded media, Web browsers must be extended with plug-ins, as we will describe in Chapter 12.

Although we have talked about the processes of production and consumption, you should realize that in between these stages a multimedia production may be transmitted over a network, stored in a database, or written to an offline delivery medium.

Networks

Modern computer systems rarely operate in isolation. Local area networks, usually employing some form of Ethernet technology, are used to connect computers within a small organization, or within a single site belonging to a large one. Local area networks are connected together by routers, bridges and switches to form internets. *The* Internet is a global network of networks, communicating via a standard set of protocols loosely referred to collectively as *TCP/IP*. Most of these networks are operated by commercial Internet Service Providers (ISPs) who lease access to other organizations via dedicated lines and routers, and to individuals via the telephone or cable TV networks.

The growth of the Internet since the removal of restrictions on its commercial use in 1991 has been more than adequately described and commented on elsewhere. Although, as we pointed out in Chapter 1, its ubiquity can be exaggerated, in developed countries the Internet is rapidly achieving the status of a public data network, analogous to the public communication network of the telephone system.

Networks, and the Internet in particular, offer valuable opportunities for distributing multimedia, but they also present formidable technical difficulties. In the case of the Internet, an additional factor to be considered is the presence of a largely technologically unsophisticated community of users, who have high expectations of technical quality based on their experience of television, videos, photography and print media. Where multimedia content delivered over the Internet attempts to compete with traditional media, as it is beginning to in news or sports coverage, it must provide some additional value (usually in the form of interactivity) to compensate for inferior picture and sound quality. This situation will, however, change as new high-speed access technologies come into widespread use.

Although the situation is changing rapidly, most domestic Internet access is still provided over a 'dial-up connection', with a modem and the telephone system providing a temporary connection between a user's computer and an ISP's network. The maximum bandwidth available through a modem is 56 kbits per second (kbps).[†]

Many new computers are fitted with modems that conform to the V90 or V92 standard, which should provide this speed for data flowing 'downstream' from the telephone exchange to the modem, with a maximum of 33.6 kbps in the opposite direction, although factors such as noise and the distance between the modem and the telephone exchange make it rare for these figures to be achieved in practice. Speeds between 34 kbps and 48 kbps downstream are more realistic. Many older modems are still in use, providing speeds down to 14.4 kbps. For multimedia delivery it is normal to assume that it is unreasonable to expect to be able to use anything slower than 28 kbps, although it is considerate to provide some alternative to images, sound and video – usually a text substitute – for users with slow connections.

There is good reason to suppose that 56 kbps is the absolute maximum bandwidth achievable using analogue connections between the modem and the exchange. Various new technologies, collectively referred to as *broadband*, avoid this analogue connection to make

† Note that in this section, speeds are quoted, following normal usage in the networking literature, in *bits* per second, although elsewhere, following mainstream computing usage, we quote file sizes and so on in bytes.

direct use of the digital telephone system's potentially higher band-width. Currently, *ADSL* (Asymmetric Digital Subscriber Line) is the leading new method for access over existing copper telephone wires (albeit with different switching equipment). It provides speeds of up to 6.1 Mbps in the downstream direction, and up to 640 kbps upstream (hence 'asymmetric').[†] Telecommunications providers in many countries offer some level of ADSL service to domestic subscribers, although technical restrictions mean that ADSL cannot reach remote homes (more than 5 km from an exchange), and the cost of enabling exchanges for ADSL has meant that in many countries, telecoms companies have considered it financially viable to provide ADSL only in cities and large towns.

[†] Other DSL variants offer lower but symmetrical rates (for example HDSL offers up to 1.5 Mbps in both directions) or even higher asymmetrical rates, up to 50 Mbps downstream).

Another way of avoiding the restriction of the analogue connection between the home and the telephone exchange is to use the cable television network instead of the telephone network, in areas where cable TV is available. Cable modems can transfer data at rates from 500 kbps to 30 Mbps. For remote users, broadband services using satellites are available, but at a cost well in excess of ADSL and cable. Still more broadband technologies are in various stages of development, including delivery of data over the electricity supply network, local wireless networks and the use of high-altitude tethered balloons as an alternative to satellites. All of these broadband services have the additional advantage that the connection to the Internet is permanent, and doesn't tie up the telephone line. (Although ADSL uses the same lines, it allows voice communication at the same time as data transfers.) Many users of broadband find that the convenience of a connection that is always on is more valuable than the increased speed of broadband.

The percentage of households with broadband varies dramatically among countries, even where the infrastructure exists. In June 2001 (the latest date for which detailed figures are available) 14 out of every hundred inhabitants of South Korea had broadband access; in the United States and Japan, the figures were roughly three and one per hundred, respectively; in the UK, less than one household in a hundred had broadband. At the same time, while 92% of the population in South Korea was covered by ADSL services, only 50% of households in the US and UK were. These figures have risen since, but not as dramatically as some commentators had foreseen. It remains the case that in most countries, broadband is still used by only a minority of households.

Commercial Internet users, especially those operating their own Web servers (see below), usually prefer to lease dedicated lines to provide a fixed connection to ISPs. *T1* and *T3* lines provide 1.544 Mbps and 44.736 Mbps, respectively. T1 and T3 lines are also used by small local ISPs to connect to the larger ISPs who are directly connected to the Internet backbone.

The term 'broadband', as it is presently used, is just marketing jargon meaning 'significantly faster than a 56K modem'. An 'official' definition, given in an ITU[†] Recommendation, states that 'broadband' means 'faster than primary rate ISDN', a largely superseded technology giving rates of 1.5 or 2 Mbps. By this definition, broadband would be fast enough to support full frame rate video at a quarter size, but most currently available domestic broadband services come nowhere near this. The FCC suggested a more conservative definition: by their definition, any service with a bandwidth of 200 kbps is 'broadband'. This allows Web pages to be changed as fast as you could flip the pages of a book. This definition comes closer to reality: ADSL and cable services provide at least 256 kbps. You should remember that this is still substantially lower than the speed of CD-ROM drives or LANs.

† See the section on 'Standards' below.

Table 2.1 shows the typical times taken to transfer different media elements over various types of connection, assuming the maximum speed is attained. Although the comparison is striking, it tells only part of the story. The connection between the user and their ISP is not always the factor that limits the speed of data transfer over the Internet. The capacity of the connections between ISPs' networks, and the computing power of the machines from which data is being downloaded may be just as important. It is quite common to find that a file download is not even using all the available speed of a V90 modem. However, anecdotal evidence suggests that both cable modems and

Table 2.1 Data transfer rates over the Internet

	kbps (theoretical)	6 kB text page	100 kB image	4 MB movie
Slow modem	28.8	1.5 secs	28 secs	19 mins
Fast modem	56	1 sec	14 secs	9 mins
T1 line	1544	<1 sec	1 sec	21 secs
Cable modem/ ADSL (typical)	6000	<1 sec	<1 sec	5 secs
T3 line	44736	<1 sec	<1 sec	1 sec

ADSL can provide qualitative improvements in download speeds from powerful servers. However, it is quite easy to see that the advantages of faster access between the user and the ISP can only be maintained if the connections between ISPs are upgraded proportionally as more users acquire faster access, and if data can be delivered by the machines at the far end of the connection at the same rate at which it can be transferred. Since data bus speeds are still considerably higher than network speeds, the latter condition is easily met for a single connection, but as the number of Internet users increases, popular sites will need to service many requests at once.

Local area networks provide much faster data transfer than the Internet. The most common technology for LANs in small organizations is 10 base T Ethernet, which provides 10 Mbps; increasingly, this is being superseded by 100 base T, at 100 Mbps; Gigabit Ethernet is also available. This bandwidth must be shared between all the transfers taking place at any time, so the effective bandwidth between two computers on a LAN will be lower; it is still sufficiently high for multimedia applications that are presently infeasible over the Internet. In particular, video conferencing and other video applications, which can only be implemented on the Internet at very low quality, are possible using a high-speed LAN.

Clients and Servers

Online distribution of multimedia over LANs or the Internet is almost always based on the client/server model of distributed computation. In this model, programs called *servers* 'listen' on a communication channel for *requests* from other programs, called *clients*, which are generally running on a different machine elsewhere on the network. Whenever a server receives a request, it sends a *response*, which provides some service or data to the client. The requests and responses conform to a *protocol*, a set of rules governing their format and the actions to be taken by a server or client when it receives a request or response.

The most popular form of online multimedia delivery is the World Wide Web, whose implementation is an example of the client/server model. Web servers and clients communicate with each other using the *HyperText Transfer Protocol*, usually abbreviated to *HTTP*. HTTP is a very simple protocol, designed for the fast transmission of hypertext information, which is usually in the form of documents marked up using the HyperText Markup Language, HTML, which will be described in Chapters 11 and 12. However, the information in the

World Wide Web is more properly described as hypermedia, and may include graphics, sound, video, MIDI and other sorts of data, and even programs.

HTTP provides communication between Web servers and their clients. A client first contacts a server, and then (usually) sends a request for a Web page. The identity of the server and the location of the file containing the Web page's data are normally extracted from a URL (uniform resource locator), the familiar 'Web address', such as http://www.digitalmultimedia.org/DMM2/index.html, where the initial http:// tells the client to use the HTTP protocol to retrieve the page, www.digitalmultimedia.org is a *domain name* identifying a Web server, and /DMM2/index.html identifies a file in that machine's file system. The server responds by sending the contents of the designated file, if it exists, wrapped up in the form of an HTTP response with some extra information, such as the type of the data (HTML text, GIF graphics, sound, etc.) it is sending. This type information is specified in a format which will be described in the next section.

World Wide Web clients are usually browsers, such as Internet Explorer or Mozilla, which allow us to access Web pages interactively. Despite the foregoing description, Web browsers are usually multi-protocol clients, which can communicate using other protocols, too. (Hence the need for the URL prefix identifying the protocol.) Nearly all browsers allow you to download files using the File Transfer Protocol (FTP), for example, although the interface to that protocol is integrated transparently into the Web browsing interface used for HTTP. Modern browsers also support real-time data streaming for audio and video using several special protocols for this purpose.

Web servers often run on dedicated powerful machines, usually running a special server version of Windows, MacOS X or Unix, to enable them to cope with heavy traffic. A common arrangement is for ISPs to provide Web space on one or more of their machines running a server for the benefit of their customers; small companies and individuals wishing to put up personal Web pages can use the ISP's facilities. Larger companies maintain their own sites and servers. It is perfectly possible to run a Web server on a desktop machine, provided only a reasonable number of hits are expected. The machine running the server must be permanently connected to the Internet, which usually implies that a broadband connection is necessary.

Most servers augment their basic Web page serving function with interfaces to other programs running on the same machine. This allows them to generate Web pages dynamically, incorporating, for example, information retrieved from a database, and to perform computations based on information supplied through a form on a Web page. The Common Gateway Interface (CGI) is a *de facto* standard for such interfaces, but other proprietary mechanisms, such as Microsoft's Active Server Pages, and Apple's WebObjects, and open standards such as PHP and JSP are increasingly preferred, largely because of efficiency and their tighter integration with database management systems.

Many local area networks are based on the same TCP/IP protocols that are used on the Internet, and often they use the same high level protocols, so that, for example, multimedia data can be served over a LAN using HTTP. A LAN organized in this way is often called an *intranet*. It allows familiar Internet clients, in particular Web browsers, to be used with the private network to access information within the organization, but at higher speeds than those that can be attained over the public Internet. Alternatively, proprietary protocols may be used for multimedia applications operating over a LAN. These may provide services that are not available via the Internet, and may be more suitable for private use by a single organization.

MIME Types

The transmission of disparate types of media data across networks connecting heterogeneous computer systems calls for some way of identifying the sort of data contained in a file or data stream. Individual operating systems have their own methods of identifying the type of a file. Most commonly, the extension of a file's name distinguishes the type: a file whose name ends .JPG on a Windows system is assumed to contain a JPEG image, one whose name ends in .MOV a QuickTime movie, and so on. There is nothing standard about the mapping from content type to extension, though – Unix systems may use different extensions from Windows – and not all systems use extensions for this purpose. The MacOS has its own way of storing file type and creator codes with files,[†] and not all media data is stored in a file. Some other means of identifying the content types is required in a networked environment.

† MacOS X uses a combination of filename extensions and the classic MacOS file type and creator codes.

MIME (Multipurpose Internet Mail Extension) is an extension to the Internet mail protocols that supports the inclusion of data other than plain ASCII text in mail messages. Some of its features have been adopted by HTTP, where they provide a simple and convenient way of specifying the type of data included in a server's response to a client's request for a resource. In particular, an HTTP response includes a MIME content type header, which takes the form:

Content-type: *type*/*subtype*

where *type* provides a broad indication of the sort of data, such as text, image, or sound, and *subtype* specifies the precise format, such as HTML, GIF, or AIFF. For example, HTML pages have the MIME content type text/html, while GIF images have type image/gif.

The available types are text, image, audio, and video, which have the obvious meanings; model for 3-D model data, such as VRML; message, which indicates an email message, and application, which means binary data, including executable programs, that must be processed in some way: for example, a GNU Zip (gzip) archive would have the MIME type application/gzip, since it must be passed to an unzipping utility for processing.

The range of subtypes is extensive (none more so than the subtypes of application) and supports most multimedia file formats, although some use 'experimental' subtypes, identified by the prefix x-, which, while not included in the list of supported MIME types maintained by the Internet Assigned Numbers Authority (IANA), are widely supported by Web browsers. For example, the MIME content type video/x-msvideo is recognized by Internet Explorer and Netscape Navigator as identifying AVI movies, although this format is not among the video subtypes registered with IANA. QuickTime movies, on the other hand, have MIME content type video/quicktime: since QuickTime is registered with IANA, the subtype does not have to begin with x-.

We will decribe how MIME types are used by Web servers and browsers in more detail in Chapter 12.

Standards

The International Organization for Standardization (ISO)[†] offers this description of standards:

> "Standards are documented agreements containing technical specifications or other precise criteria to be used consistently as rules, guidelines, or definitions of characteristics, to ensure that materials, products, processes and services are fit for their purpose."

Since standards are agreements, we can assume that things that conform to the same standards are interchangeable. For example, an

† ISO is not a mistyping of IOS, and it does not stand for International Standards Organization. ISO is not an acronym, but a play on words on the prefix iso- meaning 'the same'.

important set of ISO standards is concerned with screw threads. Any manufacturer's standard screws can be fitted in place of any other manufacturer's standard screws, which means that equipment that is assembled using standard screws is not tied to one screw manufacturer. In a market economy, this is supposed to lead to healthy competition. In practical terms, it means that the bankruptcy of one screw manufacturer does not imply that everything built with their screws becomes irreparable. However, only some standards have any legal status, so conforming to a standard is not something that anybody can usually be compelled to do. Nor does conforming to a standard necessarily mean doing something the best way; it just means doing something the standard way.

In multimedia, standards define interfaces, file formats, markup languages, network protocols, and so on, in precise, and usually formal, terms. The role of these standards is broadly analogous to that of the standards for screw threads. If we have a standard file format for image data, for example, then we can incorporate images into a multimedia production without having to worry about which program was used to prepare them originally. Similarly, standards for all the other media types enable multimedia authoring systems to be constructed independently of the applications used to prepare the individual media elements. The alternative would be for each manufacturer of multimedia software to produce a system that could only use its own formats. Whereas this may be attractive to some manufacturers, such closed systems are unacceptable in a world where several different hardware and software platforms are in use, communicating with each other over networks; open[†] systems that can accommodate data from any platform or source are needed.

† We use the word 'open' in a general sense here, without implying the free availability of source code required by adherents to the Open Software credo.

Standards are of particular importance in networking, precisely because a modern network should be capable of connecting different makes of computer running different operating systems. It is only by conforming to standards for protocols and for electrical connections agreed to by all the manufacturers that this can be possible. Because modern networks cross national boundaries, and carry data all over the world, international standards are essential.

Three organizations are involved in making international standards that are relevant to multimedia: ISO, the International Electrotechnical Commission (IEC), and the ITU (International Telecommunication Union). ISO takes responsibility for formulating standards in all technical fields except electrical and electronic engineering, which are the responsibility of the IEC. Information technology defies categorization, and is dealt with by a joint ISO/IEC technical committee. ISO works through the national standards bodies of its member countries – ANSI (the American National Standards Institute) in the United States, BSI (the British Standards Institution) in the United Kingdom, DIN (Deutsches Institut für Normung) in Germany, and so on – who administer the committees that formulate standards, with ISO itself largely operating as a coordinating agency. The IEC operates in a similar way with the relevant national bodies responsible for electrotechnical standards.

Whereas ISO and the IEC are non-governmental agencies – commercial companies, in fact, albeit of a rather special nature – the ITU is an agency of the United Nations.[†] It has a more regulatory function than the other two international standards bodies. For example, it is the ITU that allocates frequencies to radio services; these allocations must be followed to prevent interference, so they have a mandatory status according to international treaty. ITU standards covering video formats and telecommunication are those most relevant to multimedia.

† Although its history goes back much further than the UN's, to 1865.

Although there is broad agreement on the desirability of standards, the process of agreeing standards through these official bodies is a fraught and often a long drawn-out one. Since standards will only be observed if there is a consensus among the concerned parties, a great deal of politics and compromise may be involved in the production of a standard. The major standards bodies require extensive consultative procedures to be followed, designed to ensure that a standard has the broadest possible support, before a draft document can be endorsed as a full standard. These procedures work well for such things as screw threads, where a standard may be expected to remain relevant for very many years after it has been created, but in the rapidly changing environment of computers, networks, and multimedia, standards are often obsolete before they have passed through all the necessary stages and national and international committees. Furthermore, international standards bodies derive some of their income from the sale of standards, and are therefore reluctant to make their documents freely available. This causes some resentment in the computing community, which has become used to free documentation on the World Wide Web – and the high prices charged for some standards put them out of the reach of small software companies. As a result, semi-formal standards and *ad hoc* arrangements play a greater role in these areas than they do in more traditional fields of engineering.

Internet standards are a paradigm of this semi-formal standardization. Since the Internet is, by definition, an open network architecture, it relies on standard protocols to enable different networks to be interconnected. The Internet grew out of Arpanet and NSFNET, which had some degree of central administration; the TCP/IP protocols could be imposed in the early days of internetworking and were inherited as the basis of the Internet. Responsibility for the further development of protocols and for administering information required for the protocols to operate now resides with the Internet Architecture Board (IAB) and its subsidiaries, including the Internet Engineering Task Force (IETF), which deals with technical development, and the Internet Assigned Numbers Authority (IANA), which registers MIME types, language codes, and so on. These bodies have no formal standing outside the Internet community, and no statutory powers – IETF documents, including Internet standards, are almost diffidently called 'Requests for Comments'. Similarly, the organization responsible for defining World Wide Web standards, the World Wide Web Consortium (W3C), has no official status but its Recommendations are treated as standards. As you would expect, these bodies make use of the Internet as a means of disseminating standards, both after they have been adopted, and during the standardization process, thereby providing an opportunity for a wide audience to comment on drafts and proposals.

The advantage of such an *ad hoc* approach to standards is that it accommodates rapid change. The disadvantage is that manufacturers feel less compunction in ignoring, adapting, or extending standards. There is a fine line between such behaviour and legitimate experimentation aimed at advancing a standard. This is illustrated by the history of HTML, where, during the initial period of rapid development of the Web, the two main competing browser companies, Netscape and Microsoft, each implemented their own extensions to HTML 2.0, leading to incompatibilities, but ultimately most of the extensions were incorporated into later versions of the HTML standard.

Sometimes, standards are established without the intervention of standards bodies of any sort. One company's product may come to dominate the market to such an extent that it becomes a standard in all but name. In some cases, a *de facto* standard of this sort may be more widely used than a competing official standard. For example, at the time of writing, the W3C's standard for vector graphics on the Web, SVG, is rarely used in comparison with Macromedia's Flash format, which is implemented by almost all browsers and is in wide use as the 'standard' Web vector format.

Exercises

1 Identify three phenomena in the natural world that exhibit continuous change. What values would you store to represent each one, and how would digitization affect them?

2 Is the sampling rate of 44.1 kHz used for audio CDs adequate to reproduce musical sounds accurately? Justify your answer.

3 Suppose a piece of film depicting a moving stagecoach is shot at 24 frames per second, and that the wheels are rotating at such a speed that when the film is projected at 24 frames per second the wheels appear to move backwards. What would you expect to see if the same film is projected at (a) 12 frames per second; (b) 30 frames per second; (c) 60 frames per second?

4 Digital representations of sounds and images are sometimes accused of being 'limited' (e.g. by the number of quantization levels or the sampling rate), and consequently not to be 'true' representations. Are analogue representations also limited? Explain your answer and give examples.

5 Prove (at least to your own satisfaction) that, if we double the number of bits used to hold a quantized value, then we square the number of quantization levels.

6 Draw up a list of the hardware and software you would recommend for equipping:
(a) A small company specializing in Web page design.
(b) A community college or Further Education college laboratory for introductory courses on multimedia.
(c) A public library's IT facility for community multimedia access.

If possible, talk to people working in the relevant sectors to get an idea of realistic budgets, and try to fit your recommendations within them.

7 Which of the following types of media production are likely to be successful on a Web site, given current technology, and which may cause problems?
(a) A live sports broadcast:
   (i) sound only,
   (ii) sound and video.
(b) The personal home page of a stamp collecting enthusiast.
(c) A video clip from a pop promo.
(d) An art gallery's catalogue of its current exhibition, with text and still images.
(e) An interactive computer game with high quality graphics.

(f) A display of up-to-the-minute share prices for distribution to market traders.

(g) A hi-fi live broadcast of a classical music concert.

Explain each of your answers. For those productions that you do not consider likely to be succesful, what high-end equipment or presently envisaged technological advances would be needed to make them feasible?

8   Explain why upgrading your Internet connection from a 56 kbps modem to a 512 kbps broadband connection would not necessarily cut down the time it takes to download a large image file by a factor of 9.

9   The ISO standard ISO 216 defines a collection of standard paper sizes, including the A sizes, A0, A1, A2, and so on, of which A4 is the most popular for office use. Paper made to this standard is used almost everywhere in the world except in the United States. What problems does this exception cause for hardware and software manufacturers and users? What factors prevent the adoption of ISO standard paper sizes in the United States?

Introduction to Computer Graphics

3

- Vector Graphics and Bitmapped Graphics
- Combining Vectors and Bitmaps
- Layers
- File Formats

We use the term *graphics* in a broad sense to refer to the software and hardware technologies used in a computer system to create, modify and display still images stored in a digital form. Graphics in this sense is of fundamental importance in multimedia, not only because it allows us to generate and display still pictures, but also because it underlies the display of moving pictures and text. Graphics should not, therefore, be considered as just one of the media that make up what we call multimedia, in the sense that sound is, for example. Rather, it is the enabling technology for all the visual elements of multimedia. To understand how it fulfils that role, we need to examine how it works in isolation first. In other words, we need to consider the production and display of still images.

Digital images may originate in a number of different ways. They might already exist in some non-digital medium, and be digitized by a scanner, or they might be captured from the external world in digital form by a digital camera or video frame grabber. Other images might be created on a computer system, by an artist, designer or illustrator using a graphics package, or they might be built up by a programmer using a graphics language. Extensive collections of digital images are available on CD-ROM and on commercial and amateur Web sites. Finally, images might be generated by a computer program operating on some data, mapping it to a simple visual representation such as a pie-chart or a more elaborate visualization, such as a simulated picture of the wave structure of electrons in a solid.

There is a long history of images being made and used as art, entertainment, information, inspiration, devotion, titillation, education, amusement, decoration and communication. In a way, this makes still images the easiest of media: we can draw on centuries of experience when creating images, and, at least within a specific cultural context, we can reasonably expect our audience to understand an extensive range of cultural and visual conventions, such as perspective or caricature. This very familiarity can also make images difficult to deal with in a digital system, because it raises expectations of what can be achieved, which the limitations of the systems available to us often frustrate.

Although some painting programs can simulate the effects of real art materials to a remarkable extent, and high quality scanners can capture much of the detail and subtlety of an original, in the final multimedia production your images will almost certainly be displayed on a low resolution monitor which cannot match even the quality of reproduction provided by photographic methods in glossy magazines. Worse, the available range of colours may be limited, and will be reproduced differently on different systems. It is necessary to understand these limitations, so that you can take appropriate steps to ensure that your artwork looks as good as it can do within them.

Graphic elements of multimedia productions will usually be delivered on CD-ROM, on DVD or over a network, often the Internet. However, digital images are also widely used for print media. It may be necessary to adapt such images for use in multimedia or, contrariwise, to allow for the printing on paper of images originally made for display on a monitor. To do this effectively, it is necessary to take account of the different characteristics of displays and printers, particularly in respect of colour, a topic we will examine in detail in Chapter 6.

There is no doubt that, ultimately, display technology will improve to a point where much higher image quality is achievable. It will always remain the case, though, that an image works – conveys its meaning, evokes its response – differently when it is in a digital form than it does when it is reproduced in print, or framed and hung on a wall. A notable feature of the World Wide Web's shift from a text-based medium to a heavily graphical medium has been the way traditional graphic designers failed to appreciate this difference, and tried to transplant established idioms from print-based design on to the Web. Often the results were cumbersome and unreadable pages that took many minutes to download, looked terrible on most ordinary monitors, and served only to obstruct users trying to find information. Latterly, the Web has begun to develop its own visual vocabulary, which takes account of its limitations and takes advantage of its particular capabilities.

The use of icons as components of graphical user interfaces provides one example of the way in which images can be put to new use in a computer system. Another example is the way in which visual repre-

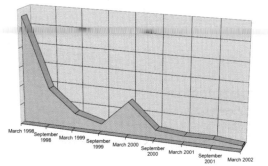

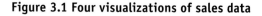

Figure 3.1 Four visualizations of sales data

sentations of data can be generated and displayed to help make large quantities of information more readily comprehensible. Figure 3.1 provides an example of how a set of figures can be mapped to different visual representations that allow trends, which might be hard to see from the raw numbers, to be seen at a glance. As this illustration shows, the same data can be visualized in a variety of styles, whose visual characteristics convey the statistical structure in more or less perspicuous or evocative ways. Such visualizations depend on computers to perform the necessary calculations to generate the image from the data; they are therefore designed with the limitations of display technology in mind.

Vector Graphics and Bitmapped Graphics

The display of images is ultimately controlled by some program: a dedicated picture-displaying application, an image editor, or a Web browser, for example. Monitors display pictures as a rectangular array of *pixels* – small, usually square, dots of colour, which merge optically when viewed at a suitable distance to produce the impression of continuous tones. Figure 3.2 shows an enlarged detail of a digital photograph, with the pixels making up the image visible. To display an image on the monitor, the program must set each pixel to an appropriate colour or shade of grey, in order that the pattern of pixels on the screen produces the desired image. The low level operations required to set pixel values are usually performed by a graphics library, which communicates with the display hardware, and provides a higher level interface to the application program.

A graphics application program must somehow keep an internal model of the image to be displayed. The process of generating a pattern of pixels from a model is called *rendering*. The graphic model

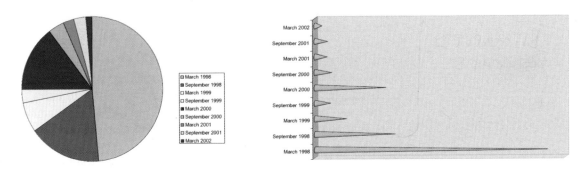

will usually take the form of an explicit data structure that holds a description of the image, but it may be implicit in the sequence of calls to the graphics library which are made as the program executes. Where picture data must be persistent (i.e. must live on after the execution of the program, so that the image can be displayed again at a later time, possibly by a different program), a similar model must be kept in a file. The sequence of events for displaying an image then begins with a program reading an image file, from which it constructs an internal data structure corresponding to the image description in the file; the program then renders the image for display by calling functions from a graphics library, supplying arguments derived from its image model.

It is usual to distinguish between two different approaches to graphical modelling: *bitmapped graphics* and *vector graphics*.

In bitmapped graphics, the image is modelled by an array of pixel values. Where it is necessary to emphasize the distinction between these stored values and the physical dots on a display screen, we will call

Figure 3.2 An image made up of pixels

BITMAPPED
GRAPHICS

✓

them *logical pixels,* and the latter *physical pixels*. In the simplest case, the logical pixels correspond one-to-one to the physical pixels: the model is a map of the displayed image. More generally, the model may be stored at a different resolution from the displayed image, so that some scaling has to be applied to the logical pixels before the image is displayed; the model may also describe a larger image than that to be displayed, so some clipping will have to be applied to extract the desired part for display. Scaling and clipping are the only computations that need to be performed to display a bitmapped image.

VECTOR
GRAPHICS

✓

In vector graphics, the image is stored as a mathematical description of a collection of individual lines, curves and shapes making up the image. Displaying a vector image requires some computation to be performed in order to interpret the model and generate an array of pixels to be displayed. For example, the model will represent a line by storing its endpoints. When the model is rendered for display, the coordinates of all the pixels lying on the straight line between those endpoints must be computed so the pixels can be set to the appropriate colour. For persistent storage in a disk file, such a model is often implemented as a program in a graphics language, for example SVG or PDF.

Neither of the terms 'vector graphics' or 'bitmapped graphics' is entirely accurate. A more accurate term for what we are calling vector graphics would be 'object-oriented graphics', were it not for the potential confusion caused by the meaning of the term 'object-oriented' in the field of programming languages. Bitmapped graphics does not use *bit*maps (except for purely monochrome images), it uses pixel maps, or *pixmaps* for short, but the term 'pixmapped graphics' has never acquired any widespread currency. You will sometimes see the name 'graphics' reserved for vector graphics, and 'images' used to mean bitmapped images, but this usage can cause confusion with the colloquial meaning of these words. Throughout this book, we will stick to the terms introduced in the preceding paragraphs, and hope you will not be misled.

✓

There are profound differences between vector and bitmapped graphics. It should be evident that they will make different demands on your computer system: a bitmapped image must record the value of every pixel, but a vector description can be much more compact. For example, consider the extremely simple picture consisting of a red square with a thick blue outline shown in Figure 3.3. The complete picture is 45 mm square; if it was stored with 72 logical pixels per inch (meaning that it could be displayed on a 72 dpi monitor at its natural size without scaling), then it would be 128 pixels square, so its bitmap would consist of $128^2 = 16384$ pixels. If we assume that the intended destination is a monitor capable of displaying millions of colours at a time, then we need 24 bits to distinguish the possible colours (see Chapter 6), which means that each pixel occupies three bytes, and the entire image occupies 48 kilobytes of memory. The same picture, on the other hand, could be stored in the form of a description of the square's size and the colours of its inside and its outline. One possible format would be a short document in the SVG graphics language, such as the following, which occupies a total of just 284 bytes:

Figure 3.3 A simple picture

```
<?xml version="1.0" encoding="utf-8"?>
<!DOCTYPE svg PUBLIC "-//W3C//DTD SVG 1.0//EN"
  "http://www.w3.org/TR/2001/REC-SVG-20010904/DTD/
svg10.dtd">
<svg  xmlns="http://www.w3.org/2000/svg">
<path fill="#F8130D" stroke="#1E338B" stroke-width="20"
d="M118,118H10V10h108V118z"/>
</svg>
```

Most of this is red tape that identifies the file as SVG and delimits its structure; only the two lines
```
<path fill="#F8130D" stroke="#1E338B" stroke-width="20"
d="M118,118H10V10h108V118z"/>
```
actually define the square, in just 86 bytes. The element, as an entity written between angle brackets is called in SVG and other languages we will meet in later chapters, sets the fill colour to a shade of red, the stroke (outline) colour to blue and the stroke width to twenty pixels; it then defines a path for an imaginary pen to follow in order to draw the square. Whereas displaying the bitmapped image only requires the pixels to be copied onto the monitor, displaying the SVG version requires some software, usually a browser plug-in, to translate it into a displayable form. This not only slows down the display of the picture, it also relies on an SVG plug-in being installed on the computer where the image is to be displayed.

The sizes of bitmaps and vectors are affected by the content of images in different ways. The memory requirement for any 45 mm square, 24-bit colour bitmapped image at a resolution of 72 pixels per inch is 48 kbytes, no matter how complicated the image may be. In a bit-mapped image we always store the value of every logical pixel, so the size of the image and the resolution at which it is stored are the only factors determining the amount of memory occupied (unless we apply

Figure 3.4 A vector poppy

Figure 3.5 A bitmapped iris

compression to it – see Chapter 5). In a vector representation, we store a description of all the objects making up the image; the more complex the picture, the more objects there will be, and the larger the description that will be required, but since we do not actually store the pixels, the size is independent of any resolution.

At least as important as the technical differences between the two different types of graphics are the differences in what you can easily do to your images using each approach. Although many image editing programs now allow you to combine vector and bitmapped graphics, traditionally a distinction has been made between *painting* programs, which operate on bitmaps, and *drawing* programs, which work with vector representations. Even though the distinction is less clear-cut than it used to be, it is still the case that packages such as Illustrator or Freehand are primarily intended for creating and editing vector graphics, and only provide limited facilities for dealing with bitmaps, while packages such as Photoshop and Painter, while providing extensive support for bitmap manipulation, either offer little support for vector graphics, or provide a poorly integrated drawing sub-system.

Figures 3.4 and 3.5 show two flowers; the first is a vector drawing of a poppy, made in Illustrator, the other is a bitmapped image, scanned from a painting of an iris, executed in gouache. The bitmap captures the textures of the original picture and provides a good reproduction of the continuous tones and translucent quality of the paint. The vector drawing has a quite different character, with clearly delineated shapes, made out of a collection of smooth curves, filled in with flat colour.

Figures 3.6 and 3.7 demonstrate the difference between the two formats in another way. With the vector representation, it is easy to select the individual shapes – petals, stem, stamens – and move, rotate or otherwise transform them independently. Each element of the picture retains its identity and can be edited as an object because the position and attributes of each object are stored in the image model. To achieve a similar effect with the bitmapped image would require a painstaking process of masking out the required pixels and then retouching the gap where the petal had been removed, since this image is just an array of pixels, with no underlying model to indicate which belong to the stem, and which to the petals. As a result, editing of parts of the image must be performed by selecting areas, either by painstakingly drawing round them or semi-automatically (and somewhat unreliably) by searching for tonal discontinuities or areas of similar colour. On the other hand, applying a special effect, such as distortion or blurring, to the bitmapped image is simple, whereas producing the same distortion on the vector image could only be done by first transforming it to a bitmapped format, since such effects transform each pixel, possibly using the value of its neighbours, but independently of whether they belong to the same object.

These examples have been deliberately chosen to emphasize the differences between the two types of image. A good illustrator working with a professional drawing package can produce much more subtle effects, but vector images are always based on the same elements of filled shapes.

Figure 3.6 Transforming a vector image

Another major difference between vector and bitmapped graphics is the way they behave when scaled or resized. If a bitmapped image is to be displayed at greater than its natural size, each logical pixel must be mapped to more than one physical pixel on the final output device. This can be achieved either by multiplying up the logical pixels, effectively increasing their size (for example, to double the linear dimensions, each pixel value in the model should be used to set a block of four pixels on the display), or by interpolating new pixels in between the stored ones. In either case, the effect will usually be a readily perceptible loss of quality. Since a vector image consists of a description of the component shapes of the picture, not the values of pixels, scaling can be performed easily as a simple mathematical operation, before the pixel values are calculated. As a result, curves, for example, will remain smooth, no matter how much a vector image is blown up, whereas they will become jagged or blurred if a bitmapped image is scaled up. Figures 3.8 and 3.9 illustrate this effect, being details of the two flower images scaled up by a factor of 8. The outlines of the poppy remain smooth, whereas the iris has become coarse, and the blocks of the original pixels are clearly visible, especially along the edge of the petal.

Figure 3.7 Applying effects to a bitmap

Related problems arise when bitmapped images are displayed on devices with different resolutions, since either they will be the wrong size, or they will exhibit the same loss of quality as occurs when they are scaled. This is more of a problem when images are being prepared for printing than it is with multimedia, since in the latter case we know that our images are going to be displayed on a monitor. Monitor resolutions do vary. As a result, images may appear at a different physical size on different monitors. This is usually considered acceptable, but should be borne in mind by designers.

Figure 3.8 Scaling a vector image

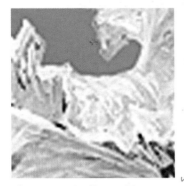

Figure 3.9 Scaling a bitmap

The terms 'drawing program' and 'painting program' introduced earlier express the difference between the visual characteristics of vector and bitmapped graphics. A drawing program lets you build up a vector image out of individual curves, lines and shapes, so the result usually has much of the character of a pen and ink illustration, an air-brushed painting, or a technical diagram: shapes are defined by outlines, and colour is applied to the regions defined by those shapes. A painting program allows you to make a wide range of different marks, and apply colour to arbitrary areas of the image; modern painting programs do a pretty good job at simulating the appearance of natural media such as charcoal, pastel, watercolour or oil paint and the interaction of those media with textured and absorbent supports, such as coarse watercolour paper or canvas.

Drawing and painting programs use different sets of tools to perform the operations that are most appropriate to vector graphics and bitmapped images, respectively. Drawing programs have tools for constructing shapes such as rectangles and ellipses, and for drawing lines and curves, selecting objects, and moving and transforming them by scaling, rotation, reflection and skewing. Painting programs have a quite different set of tools, including brushes for making marks in a variety of styles, colour correction and retouching tools and filters for altering images, and selection tools for picking out areas and groups of pixels.

Painting programs generally offer more expressive possibilities, but at the expense of high memory requirements and scalability problems. For many applications, such as the display of data for scientific or business purposes, technical illustration, and some sorts of graphic design, the expressiveness of painting programs and bitmapped graphics is unnecessary, or even positively undesirable, and vector graphics produced by drawing programs will be preferred.

Memory requirements, the visual characteristics of the image produced, and the possibilities for transformations and effects might influence your decision as to which format to work with. Another important factor is the source of your image. Scanned images, screen shots, photographs from a digital camera, and captured video frames are all inherently bitmaps, because of the way the hardware from which they originate works. Accordingly, for the manipulation and retouching of photographs and for most pre-press work, painting programs are the only possible choice. Charts, diagrams, and other data visualizations generated by a program from data usually, but not invariably, use vector graphics. Artwork made on a computer can be in either form, with the artist's personal preferences, together with the factors mentioned above, and the availability of suitable software, determining the choice.

Combining Vectors and Bitmaps

The different qualities of vector and bitmapped graphics, deriving from the fundamentally different image representations each employs, make them suitable for different tasks. It is not uncommon to find tasks requiring a combination of these qualities that call for images containing elements of both types. For example, a graphic designer might wish to use a scanned image as a background over which drawn (vector) shapes are arranged. There are several ways in which this can be achieved.

The first is to transform vectors into bitmaps, or vice versa. Hence, our designer might prepare their drawn elements in a vector graphics progam, turn the drawing into a bitmap, and composite that with the scanned background in a bitmapped image manipulation program. It is relatively easy to turn a vector graphic into a bitmapped image. The process of interpreting the vector description, known as *rasterizing*, can be accomplished using the same algorithms that are used to display the image on a monitor. The rasterized image loses all its vector properties, though – it ceases to be resolution-independent, so a resolution must be chosen when the rasterization takes place, and the individual shapes can no longer be selected and transformed – they just become areas of pixels. However, as a result they can be treated to the full range of bitmapped effects.

Going in the opposite direction, from pixels to vectors, is more problematical. It requires software to identify the boundaries of shapes within the image, then to approximate those boundaries using the available sorts of curves and lines, and to colour them in appropriately. Generally, this can be done more or less precisely, and parameters can be set to control the accuracy of the vectorization. In Flash, for example, you can set a threshold value, below which two colours will be considered the same, a minimum area to consider when determining the colour of a pixel, and parameters determining the smoothness of the curves in the vectorized version and the extent to which sharp corners are smoothed out. Figure 3.10 shows two vectorized versions of the bitmapped flower image from Figure 3.5, made with different parameter settings. When the original image features subtle tonal graduations, and soft outlines, the vector image

Figure 3.10 Vectorization

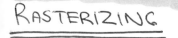

RASTERIZING

turn VECTOR graphic
into BITMAPPED image

produced with the parameters set to give a highly accurate tracing will be made out of many small curves and shapes, which means that it will be neither as compact nor as easy to edit as an image made using vector graphics from the start. (In fact, the file containing the upper vector image is over twice as big as the bitmapped version it was traced from.) Resizing, rotation, and other transformations that can be performed naturally and simply on vectors can be applied to the vectorized image.

Vectorization can be used in other ways than simply as a means of changing the representation of an image. It can be used in a controlled fashion to generate a starting point for a new vector image. Figure 3.11 shows two results of applying Illustrator's autotrace tool to the iris painting. This tool merely traces the outline of a shape, producing the paths shown here. While the simple version at the top is barely recognizable as a version of the original, it could now be worked on inside Illustrator as part of a new composition based on the organic shape of the flower. The autotrace tool will find different shapes depending on where it is applied. The lower half of Figure 3.11 shows the paths produced by deliberately choosing parts of the image to produce a collection of curves that make a better approximation to the iris. Again, these could be used as the basis of a new drawing, retaining the shapes but exploiting the capabilities of the vector tools.

Most drawing programs allow you to import bitmaps without vectorizing them. A bitmap imported in this way is treated as an indivisible object; it can be moved, and some transformations may be applied to it (although they might affect the quality of the image). However, it cannot be broken into its component shapes, the way a vectorized image or any shape drawn in vector form can be, and certain filter effects that rely on being able to change individual strokes cannot be applied to it. Commonly, drawing programs allow pointers to bitmapped images to be imported instead of making a copy of the image itself. This means that the bitmap can be edited in a painting program, after it has been incorporated into a vector image, and the changes will be seen in the vector image.

Sometimes it is not actually necessary to incorporate bitmaps into vector graphics; all that is wanted is for the vectors to have the appearance of bitmapped images. Until recently this could only be achieved by rasterizing and retouching in an image editor. Nowadays, some drawing programs – recent versions of Illustrator and Freehand, for example – allow 'brush strokes' to be applied to the lines and curves making up vector shapes, so that they appear to have been made with natural media, such as watercolour or pencil; calligraphic effects, such as a variation in the thickness of a line depending on its direction, can also be achieved.

This application of a natural media appearance to vector strokes is quite distinct from using a painting tool to draw a smooth curve, for example. In the latter case, the pixels on the path following the brush's movement are coloured to simulate the effect of a painted or drawn line; in the former case, the path is stored in the usual vector form, as the defining parameters of a collection of curves, and the associated appearance is added to it when it is displayed. The path retains all the desirable qualities of vector graphics: it can be transformed, altered, and displayed at any resolution, but it does not have the uniform appearance normally associated with vector graphics. Perhaps most interestingly, the brush stroke applied to a path can be changed, so the appearance of the marks can be altered without re-drawing the path. As far as the appearance of the resulting artwork is concerned, these effects blur the distinction between drawing and painting programs, but internally the strokes are still being applied algorithmically to paths stored in vector form.

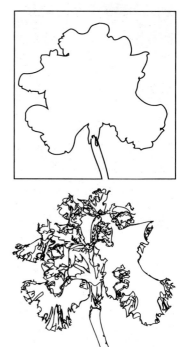

Figure 3.11 Autotraced bitmaps

Layers

The arrangement of artwork in *layers* is an organizational device that is common to both vector and bitmapped images. Since the introduction of the concept of layers in Photoshop 3, it has become one of the most significant ways in which digital technology has affected how artists, designers and illustrators work. As we will see in Chapters 7, 8 and 12, the intuitive appeal of the layer metaphor has led to its adoption in other media, too.

A layer is often likened to a digital version of a sheet of clear acetate material, like an overhead projector transparency. You can draw or paint on parts of the layer, leaving some of it transparent. An image can be constructed by stacking layers on top of each other; where a layer is transparent, the layer below it shows through. This may not sound very exciting – you can always draw things on top of other things – but a layer allows you to collect together part of an image and treat it as a unit.

An immediate consequence of this ability is that it provides a way of distinguishing objects in a bitmapped image. Normally, as we have shown, if you make a picture of a flower as a bitmapped image, there

Photo/Layer 1

Photo 2

Figure 3.12 Compositing layers

is no discrete object corresponding to each petal, just areas of pixels. By placing each petal on a different layer, though, they can be moved or modified individually, much as the individual shapes making up a vector image can be. One specific way in which artists take advantage of the separation that layers allow is by using one layer as a background against which objects on other layers are superimposed. These objects can then be moved about over the background, until a satisfying arrangement is found. If they were not on separate layers, whenever an object was moved it would be necessary to touch in the background where it had been. In a similar way, the use of layers makes it easy to apply effects to parts of an image, since effects can be applied to individual layers. Thus, for example, a background layer might be blurred so that elements on layers placed over it will stand out.

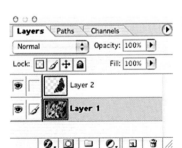

Figure 3.13 Layers for compositing

Figure 3.12 is a simple illustration of combining (or *compositing*) layers. The starting point is the two photographs shown at the left, one a butterfly on a wall, the other a flower. These were scanned into Photoshop, and the butterfly was then extracted from its background (using the magnetic lasso tool, as illustrated in Figure 5.7 in Chapter 5), scaled up and rotated, to produce the third image in Figure 3.12 (the chequerboard pattern indicates transparent areas), which was placed on a layer on top of the flower image. (See Figure 3.13.) The two layers were combined using the Normal blending mode to produce the composite image shown at the extreme right,

Layer 2 extracted from photo 2

Composited layers

where the lower layer shows through the transparent areas of the upper layer, so that the butterfly appears to be perched on the flower.

A different way of using layers is as digital tracing paper. For example, rather than try to vectorize an image like our iris, you might prefer to import it into a drawing program in its bitmapped form, and then create a new layer on top of it, on which you could draw with the vector tools, using the imported image as a guide. (Drawing programs usually allow you to dim layers so that you can more easily see what you are doing on another layer.) Once that task has been achieved, the guide layer can be deleted without affecting any other layer.

Yet another way of using layers is for experimentation. Layers can be reordered without affecting their contents, so that different stacking arrangements can be tried out. Layers can be duplicated, and the duplicates altered separately; any layer can be made invisible, so different versions of a layer can be displayed in turn, to see which is better. When a picture is finished, it is normal to delete any invisible layers, and merge all the remaining ones down to a single layer, since this uses less space.

We have likened layers to transparent sheets of acetate, but, as data structures inside a computer are not subject to the physical limitations of materials, they can behave in ways that acetate cannot. In particular, the degree of transparency can be varied. By using layers that are only partially transparent, backgrounds can be dimmed.

Figure 3.14 Compositing with different blending modes

The precise way in which separate layers are combined may also be modified. The normal behaviour of layers is for the areas that are not transparent to cover any layers beneath. Sometimes, it may be preferable for these areas to be blended with lower layers instead, or dissolved into them. Transparency may be made conditional on the brightness of one or other of the layers, so that blending takes place below a threshold value, but above that value the superposed layer conceals what is below it. More complex blending modes and options may be used by graphic designers to create artificial compositions from layers. Figure 3.14 shows two images produced by compositing the two original photographs from Figure 3.12 using different blending modes.

The layer metaphor has found such favour as a way of organizing images that it has been extended to incorporate effects as well as image elements. Photoshop's *adjustment layers* are described as being a layer through which you can look at the image through a medium that applies some effect, such as a tonal adjustment. In practice, this makes them a tool for applying effects without changing the pixels on image layers. They thus provide a safe means of experimentation.

File Formats

In order to preserve images and exchange them between programs, it must be possible to store image data in a file. There is considerable scope for encoding the data in different ways, compressing it, and adding supplementary information to it. Consequently, a large number of different graphics file formats have been developed. As is the case with programming languages, most of these are only used by a limited circle of enthusiasts, for some specialized applications, or on particular platforms. There remains a significant number of different formats in wide use, with differing characteristics that make them suitable for different types of image.

For bitmapped images, one of the main differences among file formats is the way in which they compress image data. Bitmapped images can contain a large number of pixels, so they require large files, often occupying several megabytes per image at medium to high resolutions. In order to reduce the storage and bandwidth requirements of such images, data compression techniques are often applied to them. We will describe image compression in more detail in Chapter 5, but you need to be aware at this stage of the distinction between *lossless* and *lossy* compression. Lossless compression algorithms have the property that it is always possible to reconstruct the original data exactly from its compressed version; lossy algorithms discard some data – in the case of images, data representing visually insignificant details – in order to achieve greater compression.

We also defer a full description of colour to a later chapter (Chapter 6) but note that one way of reducing the size of a bitmapped image is to restrict the number of different colours that it can contain. If an image uses at most 256 different colours, each pixel only requires a single byte, whereas if it is to be allowed the full range of millions of colours which most monitors are capable of displaying, three bytes per pixel are needed.

The advent of the World Wide Web has had something of a standardizing influence; although it does not specify any particular graphics file formats, the necessity for cross-platform compatibility has led to the adoption of certain formats as *ad hoc* standards.

The first of these is *GIF*, originally developed by CompuServe as a common format for exchanging bitmapped images between different platforms. GIF files use a lossless compression technique, and are restricted to 256 colours. One of this format's most useful features is that one colour can be designated as transparent, so that, if the GIF image is displayed against a coloured background or another image, the background will show through the transparent areas. (See Figures 3.15 and 3.16.) This, in effect, allows you to produce images that are not rectangular. GIFs are most suitable for simple images, such as cartoon-style drawings and synthetic images produced on computers.

Figure 3.15 A GIF with transparency (shown in red)

They are less successful with scanned and photographic images, which may have wide colour ranges and tonal variations.

For these images, *JPEG* is preferred. Strictly speaking, JPEG is a compression technique,[†] and images that have been compressed using it may be stored in any of several file formats – the JPEG standard does not specify any. Colloquially, though, the name 'JPEG file' is used to refer to what are correctly called *JFIF* – JPEG File Interchange Format – files. To complicate matters further, the more recently developed SPIFF format is actually the officially endorsed file format for JPEG images, but as we remarked, JPEG data can be embedded in other files, including TIFF, which we will say more about shortly.

The third, and newest, file format that is widely supported on the Web is *PNG*, which was devised to supersede GIFs. The trouble with GIF is that the compression algorithm it employs is covered by a patent owned by Unisys, who require a licence fee to be paid for any program that implements GIF compression or decompression. PNG, on the other hand, uses a different lossless technique that is not encumbered in this way, and can therefore be implemented freely by anybody. Additionally, PNG is not restricted to 256 colours and it offers a more sophisticated form of transparency than does GIF. The PNG format was developed under the aegis of the W3C, and its specification, published in 1996, has the status of a W3C Recommendation. Support for PNG has been slow to develop, however, and GIF and JPEG remain more popular.

Outside the World Wide Web, other commonly encountered bitmap graphics file formats include *TIFF*, *BMP*, and *TGA* (often called Targa). TIFF (Tag Image File Format) is an elaborate extensible file format that can store full colour bitmaps using several different compression schemes, including JPEG. It is supported by most painting programs on all platforms, although not all programs are equal in the comprehensiveness of their support, so that TIFF files created by one program cannot always be read by another. TIFF is natively supported by Windows, as is BMP. Indeed, BMP is more properly called the

† *Really* strictly speaking, JPEG is the Joint Photographic Experts Group, who developed the compression technique, and after whom it is named.

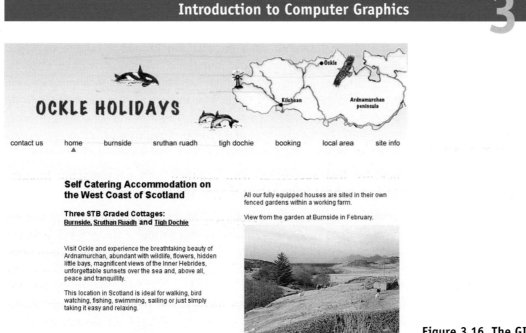

Figure 3.16 The GIF file embedded in a Web page

Microsoft Windows Bitmap format. As such, it is platform-dependent, but the near ubiquity of the Windows platforms means that it is widely understood by programs on other systems. Unlike most other bitmapped formats, BMP only supports a simple form of lossless compression, and BMP files are usually stored uncompressed. TGA files have achieved wide currency, because the format was one of the earliest to support more than 256 colours on PCs. It was designed to accompany a proprietary range of video capture boards, but has become more widely supported by programs on most platforms, although its use is probably declining.

All of the formats mentioned so far store bitmapped images. The situation with respect to vector graphics is slightly different. For a long time, vector graphics was dominated by PostScript. PostScript, developed by Adobe Systems in the mid-1980s, could be described as a programming language with built-in graphics capabilities that allow it to specify the appearance of pages in the form of a program describing how to place graphic elements – paths, shapes, and fills – on the page. Procedures can be defined, so that an application that generates PostScript (it is not the sort of programming language that anyone would want to write by hand) can create a set of operations suited to its own needs and view of page layout.

PostScript is intended as a page layout language, which makes it unsuitable for storing single images in isolation, rather than as components of a page. EPS (Encapsulated PostScript) applies certain conventions to the use of PostScript to ensure that the images in an EPS file are self-contained so that they can be incorporated in other documents. In particular, an EPS file must contain a *bounding box comment*, describing the dimensions of the image. EPS is one of the most widely used vector graphics formats, but a full PostScript interpreter is required to display EPS images.

EPS is thus not an ideal file format for use on the Web. The W3C has defined the Scaleable Vector Graphics format, *SVG* (see Chapter 15). SVG is defined in XML, but in essence, SVG is a derivative of PostScript that uses the same imaging model but a fixed repertoire of operations and is thus easier to implement, and is more compact for transmission over networks. SVG has yet to achieve wide acceptance.

At the same time, the *SWF* format, originally developed for vector animations using Macromedia's Flash (see Chapter 8) but now an open standard, is in wide use for vector images. Although SWF does not have the sanction of the W3C, it has been supported, either via a plug-in or directly, in the major Web browsers for some years, which gives it *ad hoc* status as a standard. SWF is a highly compact format, and can be rendered very quickly. Although, because of its origins, SWF is mostly used for animations, its use for still images is increasing, and may yet pre-empt SVG.

EPS, SWF, and SVG are not just vector formats, although their vector capabilities are their essential feature. It is possible to incorporate bitmaps into these files, too, as self-contained objects. This sort of file format that accommodates both vector and bitmapped graphics, and usually text, too, is sometimes called a *graphics metafile*. Other graphics metafile formats include Macintosh PICT files and Microsoft's Windows Metafiles (WMF). Purely vector-based formats are in fact quite rare and, for the most part, associated with computer-aided design packages: AutoCAD DXF is a complex file format widely used for the exchange of vector data, for example. Vector-based formats are also widely used for three-dimensional models, which we will look at in Chapter 4.

As well as the general purpose formats we have described, certain proprietary formats associated with popular programs are also widely used. In particular, Photoshop and Illustrator files are commonly used as interchange formats for bitmapped and vector graphics, respectively, in the pre-press and publishing industries. One noteworthy feature of these formats is that they preserve any layers that might have been used in making the image. Exporting, say, a Photoshop image to a PICT file will 'flatten' it, combining all the layers into one. This is undesirable if it is intended to make further changes to the image.

Evidently, with so many different file formats in use, conversions between formats are often required. These vary in complexity from a simple reordering of bytes to the sort of vectorization operation described in the previous section. In this context, mention should be made of QuickTime. Although QuickTime is most often considered to be a digital video format (and we will describe it further in Chapter 7) it is better described as a multimedia architecture, which provides a framework and a set of software components for storing and manipulating various digital media formats, of which video is only one – still images are another. QuickTime has its own image format, which generally contains JPEG compressed image data, but more importantly, it provides a collection of import and export components that allow any program that uses QuickTime to work with files in many formats, including JFIF, PNG, GIF, TGA, PICT, TIFF, Photoshop and SWF.

Exercises

1 Describe three significant differences between vector and bitmapped graphics.

2 For each of the following kinds of image, which would be more suitable, bitmapped images or vector graphics?
(a) Circuit diagrams.
(b) Architectural drawings.
(c) Botanical drawings.
(d) Pie charts.
(e) Fingerprints.
(f) A map of the world.
(g) Brain scans.
(h) Illustrations for a children's alphabet book.
(i) A reproduction of the Mona Lisa.
(j) A simple cartoon character, such as Mickey Mouse.

3 Individual objects and groups of objects can be selected in vector graphics, so why do vector drawing programs implement layers?

4   Since GIF files are most suitable for the same sort of images as vector graphics, why would you use them in preference to SWF or some other vector format?

5   What file format would you choose to present the following:
(a) A photograph of yourself
(b) A comic strip cartoon drawing
(c) The floor plan of a museum
for each of the following purposes:
(i) Incorporation in a Web page intended for viewing over a broadband connection.
(ii) Incorporation in a Web page intended for viewing over a dial-up modem.
(iii) Transfer to another platform.
Justify your choice in each case.

Vector Graphics

4

- **Fundamentals**
  - Coordinates and Vectors
  - Anti-aliasing
- **Shapes**
  - Curves
  - Paths
  - Stroke and Fill
- **Transformations and Filters**
- **3-D Graphics**
  - 3-D Models
  - Rendering

Vector graphics provide an elegant way of constructing digital images whose representation is compact, scaleable, resolution-independent, and easy to edit. The compactness of vector graphics makes them particularly attractive for networked multimedia, where the indiscriminate use of bitmapped images can lead to excessive download times, because of the large sizes of the image files. A common complaint amongst domestic Internet users is that the increasing trend towards graphically rich Web sites means that pages take too long to download. Equally, Web designers who are aware of this complaint feel inhibited about using images freely. Vector images can be a fraction of the size of bitmaps, but the absence of any standard format for vector graphics on the Web left little opportunity for using them. As the official SVG and *de facto* SWF standards are increasingly widely adopted, this will change.

Although vector graphics has been eclipsed in recent years by bitmapped representations for two-dimensional images, for three-dimensional work – that is, images that are constructed as projections of a 3-D model – vector techniques are mandatory, since the use of models made out of the three-dimensional equivalent of pixels (*voxels*) is impractical on all but the most powerful equipment.

Fundamentals

In vector graphics, images are built up using shapes that can easily be described mathematically. We expect many readers will be familiar with at least the rudiments of coordinate geometry, the field of mathematics underlying the representation of shapes in vector graphics. For the benefit of those who may not be used to thinking about shapes and outlines in terms of coordinates and equations, we will begin with a very brief review of the basic concepts.

Coordinates and Vectors

Since an image is stored as a rectangular array of pixels, a natural way of identifying any single pixel is by giving its column and row number in that rectangular array. If we number the columns from left to right, and the rows from the bottom of the image to the top, both starting at zero, then any pixel is uniquely identified by the pair (x, y), called its *coordinates*, where x is the column number and y the row. In Figure 4.1, the pixel labelled A is at $(3, 7)$, while B is at $(7, 3)$. The point labelled O is at the *origin* $(0, 0)$.

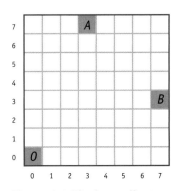

Figure 4.1 Pixel coordinates

The coordinates of pixels in an image must be integer values between zero and the horizontal (for x coordinates) or vertical (for y) dimensions of the image. For the purposes of modelling shapes in a device-independent way, we need to generalize to a coordinate system where coordinates can have any real value. That is, instead of identifying a finite pixel on a grid, coordinates identify infinitely small geometrical points, so that there are infinitely many of them between, for example, $(0, 0)$ and $(1, 0)$. Additionally, the values are not restricted to any finite maximum. We also allow negative coordinates: points with negative x coordinates lie to the left of the origin, while those with negative y coordinates lie below it. The vertical line running through the origin, which consists of all the points with an x coordinate of zero, is called the *y-axis*, while the horizontal line through the origin is the *x-axis*. We can label the x- and y-axes with the x and y coordinates of equally spaced points to produce the familiar graph axes, as shown in Figure 4.2, from which coordinates can easily be read off. Vector drawing programs usually allow you to display axes (usually called *rulers*) along the edges of your drawing.

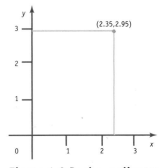

Figure 4.2 Real coordinates and axes

Although mathematical convention employs a coordinate system where y values increase upwards, graphics packages and languages, such as Java Abstract Windowing Toolkit and SVG, often use the opposite convention, with y values increasing downwards. This convention corresponds more closely to the way pixels are drawn onto physical output devices. You generally should not have to concern yourself with the coordinate system used by the output device. Your drawing program will convert from its coordinate system to that of whichever device your drawing is rendered on. This conversion is an example of a *coordinate transformation*, whereby coordinates in one system (the *user space*) are transformed into a different one (the *device space*). Coordinate transformations are inevitable if we are to produce device-independent graphics since, in general, we cannot

rendered = treated

know the coordinate space of the output device. Another example of a coordinate transformation occurs when an image is rendered?? in a window on a display. Since we cannot know when the image is prepared whereabouts on the screen the window will be positioned, there is no possible way of using absolute screen coordinates to specify the objects in the drawing. Instead, the drawing is prepared in the user coordinate space, and transformed to the device space when it is displayed.

Pairs of coordinates can be used not only to define points, but also to define displacements. For example, to get from A to B in Figure 4.1 we must move 4 units to the right, and 4 units down, or, putting it another way, -4 units up. So we can specify the displacement from A to B by the pair $(4, -4)$. In general, for any pair of points $P_1 = (x_1, y_1)$ and $P_2 = (x_2, y_2)$, the displacement from P_1 to P_2 is $(x_2 - x_1, y_2 - y_1)$, which we write as $(P_2 - P_1)$ (see Figure 4.3). When a pair of values is used to specify a displacement in this way, we call it a two-dimensional *vector*. Note that a vector has a direction: $P_2 - P_1$ is not the same as $P_1 - P_2$, since moving from P_1 to P_2 is different from moving in the opposite direction from P_2 to P_1.

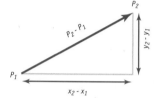

Figure 4.3 A vector

The term *vector graphics* was originally used to refer to the production of images on output devices where the position of the electron beam of a cathode ray tube was controlled directly by setting its (x, y) coordinates, rather than scanning the screen in a raster pattern. By changing the coordinate values, the beam was made to trace out vectors, hence the name. This type of graphics device only lends itself to the drawing of simple shapes, which is why the name is retained for the shape-based graphics systems we are describing here.

A coordinate system lets us identify points in space. The power of coordinate geometry comes from using letters to represent 'unknown' values and using equations in those values to specify relationships between coordinates that characterize geometrical shapes. For example, if (x, y) is *any* point on a straight line that passes through the origin at an angle of 45° from south-west to north-east, then it must be the case that $x = y$, as you can show using simple geometry. We can use the methods of coordinate geometry to derive equations for arbitrary straight lines, circles, ellipses, and so on. Using such equations we can represent shapes simply by storing the appropriate constants that appear in the equations, since it is these which distinguish between different shapes belonging to the same class.

HATE ALGEBRA 😖

finit = limited

Practical considerations might lead us to use a slightly less obvious representation. For example, the equation of a straight line is usually written as $y = mx + c$, where the constants m and c are the slope and intercept, respectively. However, since we can only use finite segments of lines, it is necessary to store the endpoints. The values of m and c can be deduced from these. A bit of simple algebraic manipulation, which many readers will have done at school, demonstrates that, if the line passes through (x_1, y_1) and (x_2, y_2), m is equal to $(y_2 - y_1)/(x_2 - x_1)$ and c is equal to $(x_2 y_1 - x_1 y_2)/(x_2 - x_1)$. Hence, the coordinates of the endpoints are enough on their own to specify both the extent of the line and the constants in its equation.

deduced = derived

In a similar way, the values actually stored for other shapes are not necessarily those that a simple mathematical analysis would suggest.

render = to treat

When it becomes necessary to render a vector drawing, the stored values are used, in conjunction with the general form of the description of each class of object, to set the values of pixels to form an image of the object described. For example, if a line has endpoints (0, 1) and (12, 31), we could compute the y coordinate corresponding to each integer value as x was stepped from 0 to 12. Remember that a pixel's coordinates are always integers (whole numbers), and we cannot set the value of just part of a pixel. The pixel image can, therefore, only ever approximate the ideal mathematical object which the vector model describes. For example, the line just described has equation $y = 5x/2 + 1$, so for any odd integer value of x, y must be rounded up (or down – as long as it is done consistently) to get its corresponding integral value. The coordinates of pixels along the line would be (0, 1), (1, 4), (2, 6), (3, 9).... To get a continuous line, we set blocks of pixels, but the height of the blocks alternates between 2 and 3 pixels, so that the ideal straight line is approximated by an uneven staircase, as shown in Figure 4.4. This is inevitable, since the output devices we are using are based on a grid of discrete pixels. If the resolution of the output device is low (i.e. the pixels are relatively large) the jaggedness of lines, and other effects due to the same cause, can become offensive. This phenomenon is colloquially known as 'staircasing' or, more colourfully, 'the jaggies'.

colloquially = commonly

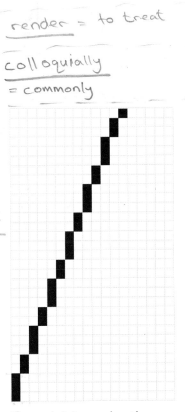

Figure 4.4 Approximating a straight line

Anti-aliasing = making objects look smooth

The process of rendering a vector object to produce an image made up of pixels can usefully be considered as a form of sampling and reconstruction. The abstract line that we would like to draw is a continuous signal – the x and y coordinates can vary infinitesimally – which

infinitesimally = boundless/no limits

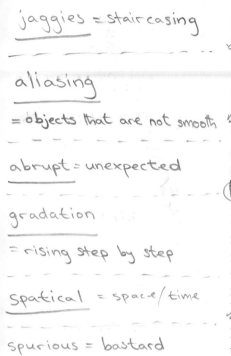

jaggies = staircasing

aliasing

= objects that are not smooth

abrupt = unexpected

gradation

= rising step by step

spatical = space/time

spurious = bastard

has to be approximated by a sequence of pixel values at fixed finite intervals. Seen in this light, jaggies are a form of aliasing caused by undersampling. This is consistent with the common-sense observation that as the resolution of the output device increases – that is, we sample at a higher rate – the individual pixels get smaller, so that the jagged effect becomes less noticeable.

You will recall from Chapter 2 that it is necessary to sample at a rate greater than twice the highest frequency in a signal in order to reconstruct it accurately, and that high frequencies are associated with abrupt changes. If an image contains a sharp hard-edged boundary, its brightness or colour will change directly from one value to another crossing the boundary without any intermediate gradation. The representation in the spatial frequency domain of such a discontinuity in the spatial domain will include infinitely high frequencies. Consequently, no sampling rate will be adequate to ensure perfect reconstruction. In other words, jaggies are always possible, no matter how high the resolution that is used for rendering a vector shape.

In any case, practical and financial considerations impose a limit on the available resolution. In particular, vector graphics that are used in multimedia presentations will usually be rendered on a monitor with a resolution between 72 and 120 dots per inch, and aliasing will be readily visible. To reduce its impact a technique known as *anti-aliasing* is often employed.

Looking back at Figure 4.4, you will see that the staircase effect is a result of the pronounced contrast between black and white pixels. We can soften the effect by using intermediate grey values for some pixels. In terms of the frequency domain representation, we are removing the spurious high frequencies, and replacing them with lower frequencies. We cannot simply tone down the black pixels to produce a grey line instead of a black one; we want to try to use a range of greys to somehow convey to the eye and brain of someone looking at the displayed line the appearance of a smoothness that cannot actually be achieved by the finite pixels.

If we did not have to be concerned about the orientation of the pixel grid, at best we could produce a smooth line one pixel wide, as shown in Figure 4.5. Our original attempt at rendering the line on the basis of its defining equation had the effect of setting to black those pixels whose intersection with this one pixel wide rectangle was at least half the area of the pixel. Anti-aliasing is achieved by colouring each pixel in a shade of grey whose brightness is proportional to the area of the

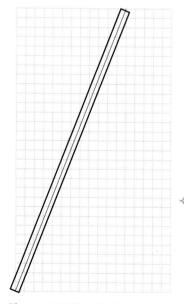

Figure 4.5 The single pixel approximation to a line

intersection, as shown in Figure 4.6. The number of pixels that are no longer white is greater than before, but if we take the grey pixels and multiply the area of each one by the value used to colour it, the total amount of greyness, as it were, is the same as that produced by only using a single black level to colour the original collection of pixels. At this magnification, the result looks fairly incoherent, although it should be apparent that the jaggedness has been subdued somewhat. At normal viewing resolutions, anti-aliasing can significantly reduce aliasing effects, albeit at the expense of a certain fuzziness.

Shapes

When using a drawing program you are restricted to the shapes it provides, which are generally shapes with a simple mathematical representation that can be stored compactly and rendered efficiently. Usually the repertoire of shapes is restricted to rectangles and squares (possibly with rounded corners), ellipses and circles, straight lines, polygons, and a class of smooth curves, called *Bézier curves*, although spirals and stars are sometimes supplied too. Shapes built up out of these elements can be filled with colour, patterns or gradients. Because the program works with a description of the shape, not a map of its pixels, it is easy to move, rotate, scale and skew shapes. It may sound as though vector programs are very limited in their graphic capabilities, but they can be used to achieve complex and subtle effects, especially once you understand how to work with Bézier curves. Vector drawing programs must be approached in a different way from a freehand drawing medium, though.

A good way of appreciating the potential and limitations of vector graphics is by looking at the capabilities offered by a typical drawing program. We will use Illustrator as an example; you will find the same concepts and facilities in any other professional drawing package. Generally, the way in which a drawing package allows you to work with shapes is a reflection of the way in which those shapes are represented in graphics files. For example, you draw a line by selecting a pen tool and clicking the mouse or pressure-sensitive pen at each end of the line: internally, a line is represented by the coordinates of its endpoints. In SVG, a line can be represented by a line element, with the endpoints' coordinates as its attributes.

A sequence of connected lines, such as the one shown in Figure 4.7, is sometimes considered as a single object, called a *polyline*. Closed polylines, whose first and last points coincide, form regular or irregular polygons, and can be used to draw rectangles, for example.

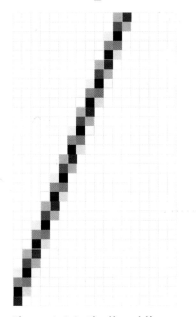

Figure 4.6 Anti-aliased line

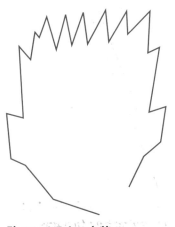

Figure 4.7 A polyline

coincide

= occupy the same place

Alternatively, a rectangle whose sides are parallel to the axes can be drawn by selecting the rectangle tool, holding down the mouse button where you want one corner, and dragging to the opposite corner: a rectangle can obviously be completely described by the coordinates of its opposite corners. In Illustrator, rectangles can also be drawn with the centred rectangle tool. With this, you begin at the point where you want the centre to be, and then drag out one corner. It should be clear that it is possible for the program to compute the coordinates of opposite corners from those of the centre and one corner, and vice versa.

Ellipse = cone shape

Ellipses can be drawn by selecting the appropriate tool and dragging from one point on the perimeter to the opposite point. A pair of points is sufficient to determine the shape and position of the ellipse, and their coordinates can be transformed into one of many convenient representations of the object.

Squares and circles are special cases of rectangles and ellipses, respectively, and so do not need any special representation of their own. It is helpful when drawing to be able to ask the program to restrict rectangles and ellipses to squares and circles. In Illustrator this is done by holding down the shift key while using the rectangle or ellipse tool.

Curves

Lines, polylines, rectangles and ellipses are sufficient for drawing many sorts of technical diagrams (particularly when your lines can be decorated with arrowheads, as they can be in all professional drawing programs). Less constrained drawing and illustration require more versatile shapes, which are supplied by Bézier curves.

Bézier curves are a class of curve that, as we will shortly demonstrate, have several properties that make them especially useful for graphics. A Bézier curve is completely specified by just four points: its two endpoints, and two more points, called *direction points,* which do not usually lie on the curve itself. The endpoints and direction points are collectively referred to as *control points.* The name 'direction points' indicates the purpose of these points: they show the direction in which the curve sets off from each endpoint. This is shown in Figure 4.8: P_1 and P_4 are the endpoints of the curve, P_2 and P_3 are its direction points, and you can see that the curve is accurately described by saying that it begins at P_1, setting off towards P_2, and curving round so that it arrives at P_4 from the direction of P_3.

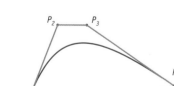

Figure 4.8 A Bézier curve

The lengths of the lines from each endpoint to its direction point determine how wide a sweep the curve makes. You can think of the lengths of these lines as representing the speed with which the curve sets off towards the direction point: the faster it goes, the further out it will curve.

This characterization of the curve is the basis for the way Bézier curves are drawn interactively. After selecting the appropriate tool (usually a pen), you click at the first endpoint, and then drag out towards the first control point, as if you were pulling the curve towards it. You will usually see a *direction line* showing you how far you have pulled. In most applications, for reasons that will be explained in the next section, the direction line usually extends away from the endpoint both in the direction you drag and symmetrically in the opposite direction. Once you have the first one right, you click at the point where you want the curve to end, and drag away from the direction point (see Figure 4.9). You will see the curve being formed as you move the cursor. If you do not like the result when you have finished, you can subsequently select any of the control points and drag it around to change the shape and extent of your curve.

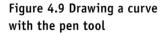

Figure 4.9 Drawing a curve with the pen tool

It is perhaps not immediately obvious that a curve related to four points in the manner just described is unique, or even that it always exists. Since this is not a book about the mathematics of Bézier curves, you will have to take it on trust that it is and does, or consult one of the references at the end of the book. However, it may help to contemplate the following construction for building curves from a pair of endpoints P_1 and P_4 and a pair of direction points P_2 and P_3.

Begin by finding the midpoints of the lines between P_1 and P_2, P_2 and P_3, and P_3 and P_4. Call these P_{12}, P_{23} and P_{34}, respectively, and construct the lines between P_{12} and P_{23} and between P_{23} and P_{34} (see Figure 4.10, top).

Next, find the midpoints P_{123} and P_{234} of these new lines, join *them* together and find the midpoint of this last line. This final midpoint, Q, lies on the curve (Figure 4.10, bottom).

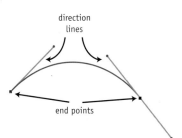

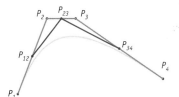

Q lies on the curve, because we assert that this construction is how our curve is to be built. We proceed by taking the two sets of four points P_1, P_{12}, P_{123} and Q, and Q, P_{234}, P_{34} and P_4, and asserting that the curves built using them as control points will be the left and right halves of our complete curve. We therefore apply the same technique of finding midpoints and so on to produce two points on the portions of the curve to the left and right of Q. This in turn leaves us with new sets of control points from which to construct the portions of the curve lying to each side of the new points we have found.

Figure 4.10 Constructing a Bézier curve

tangents

If we were mathematicians, we would go on bisecting our curve forever, until the curve segments became infinitesimally small. If you actually try this construction on paper, or write a program to perform it for you, you will find that the segments very rapidly become indistinguishable from straight lines and your curve becomes as smooth as your drawing medium or display will allow.

However much bisecting we do, the construction lines that pass through the endpoints P_1 and P_4 are part of the lines between P_1 and P_2 and between P_3 and P_4. This remains the case, even if we were to go on bisecting to infinity, so that, in the limit, these lines would be the tangents to the curves at P_1 and P_4. Which is to say that the curve leaves P_1 heading towards P_2, and approaches P_4 from the direction of P_3, as originally described. Furthermore, the further away P_2 is from P_1 the further away will be the midpoint, and, eventually, the curve points we construct, so that the length of the tangents controls how widely the curve sweeps round.

You can construct a Bézier curve using any set of four control points, but the result is not necessarily going to be useful or lovely. Nor is it always obvious, until you have acquired some experience using these curves, exactly what the curve built from any four control points is going to look like. Figures 4.11 to 4.13 show curves produced from the same set of points as were used in Figure 4.8, but in different orders.

Paths

A single Bézier curve on its own is rarely something you want in a drawing. Except in stylized applications for which rectangles, ellipses and straight lines serve adequately, we need to be able to draw a variety of irregular curves and shapes, such as those making up the petals and stamens of the poppy in Figure 3.4. In principle, because the pixels on monitors and printers are finite in size, any shape, no matter how curvaceous, can be approximated as well by a collection of straight lines as by any other method. However, in practice, to produce acceptable approximations to curved shapes, we need to use a lot of very short lines. We thus lose much of the advantage of vector graphics, inasmuch as our descriptions of shapes become large, unwieldy and difficult to work with and edit interactively.

What makes Bézier curves useful is the ease with which they can be combined to make more elaborate curves and irregular shapes. Remember that a Bézier curve with control points P_1, P_2, P_3 and P_4 approaches its endpoint P_4 from the direction of P_3. If we construct a second curve with control points P_4, P_5, P_6 and P_7 (so that it is joined to the original curve at P_4), it will set off from P_4 in the direction of P_5.

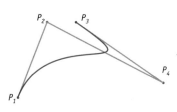

Figure 4.11 P$_1$, P$_2$, P$_4$, P$_3$

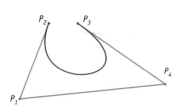

Figure 4.12 P$_2$, P$_1$, P$_4$, P$_3$

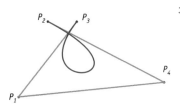

Figure 4.13 P$_3$, P$_1$, P$_4$, P$_2$

Provided we ensure that P_3, P_4 and P_5 are in a straight line, with P_5 on the opposite side of P_4 to P_3, the curve segments will both be travelling in the same direction through P_4, so there will be a smooth join between them, as shown on the left of Figure 4.14. The join on the right is smoother still, because we have made sure that the length of the direction lines is the same on each side of P_4. If you think of the line as a trajectory through space, this ensures that it passes through the shared endpoint at a constant velocity, whereas, if we only make sure the three points are in a straight line, the direction is constant, but the speed changes.

The smoothness of joins when control points line up and direction lines are the same length is the reason behind the display of direction lines in drawing programs. When you drag towards an endpoint, as we saw earlier, direction lines are displayed both to and from it. In other words, you are shown two direction points: one belonging to the curve you are just finishing, the other which could belong to a new curve which joins smoothly on to the end of it. Thus, you can rapidly build up compound curves using a sequence of dragging movements at the points where you want Bézier segments to join.

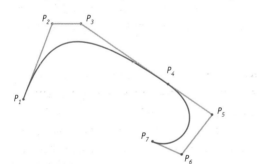

Figure 4.14 Joining two Bézier curves

This property of continuity is not shared by other sorts of curve which might seem to be candidates for the job of curve-drawing primitive. You cannot generally make arcs of circles, parabolas or ellipses join smoothly.

Sometimes you will want your curve to change direction instead of continuing smoothly. To do so, you simply need to arrange that the direction lines of adjacent segments are not lined up (see Figure 4.15). In a drawing program, some expedient is required to break out of the default behaviour of smoothly joining curves. In Illustrator, for exam-

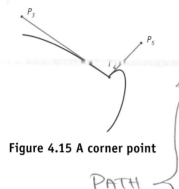

Figure 4.15 A corner point

PATH

ple, you hold down the **option** (or **alt**) key after creating the direction lines at a point; you are then able to drag the direction point for the new curve segment round to where you want it, to make an abrupt corner. By mixing clicking and dragging, it is possible to combine curves and straight lines in arbitrary ways.

Some additional terminology is used to talk about joined curves and lines. A collection of lines and curves is called a *path*. If a path joins up on itself, it is said to be *closed*, otherwise it is *open*. Figure 4.16 shows an open path; Figure 4.17 shows a closed one. Open paths have endpoints, closed paths do not. Each individual line or curve is called a *segment* of the path; the points where segments join (the original endpoints of the segments) are called the path's *anchor points*. Note that any collection of curves and lines may be considered as a path; they do not all have to be connected.

The usual way to construct a path is by constructing the individual segments with the pen tool, which provides great control and permits you to construct very accurate curves. However, if you wish to create artwork with a hand-drawn look, you can use Illustrator's pencil tool. With this tool selected, you can just drag with the mouse or pressure-sensitive pen, as if you were drawing freehand with a pencil or pen. You are not doing so: Bézier curve segments and straight lines are being created to approximate the path your cursor follows. Once the path is complete, you can select it and see anchor points that you can adjust in the usual way. The faithfulness of the approximation can be controlled by a tolerance setting. A higher tolerance leads to a more efficient path, with fewer anchor points, which may, however, smooth out some of the smaller movements you made with the pencil tool.

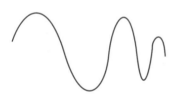

Figure 4.16 An open path

Stroke and Fill

A path, strictly speaking, is an abstract mathematical entity: just as points are infinitesimally small, so a path is infinitesimally thin. Although we have talked about drawing curves, and shown you pictures of paths, you cannot really see a path. You can, however, use it as a specification of something you *can* see. You can do this in two different ways. Either you apply a *stroke* to the path, making it visible as if you had traced it with ink or some other medium, or you treat the path as the outline of a shape, and *fill* it, as if with ink or paint. Or both. Since computer graphics is not bounded by the physical limitations of real art materials, you can stroke or fill paths with more elaborate things than flat colour, such as patterns or gradients.

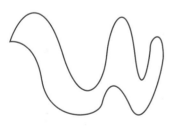

Figure 4.17 A closed path

Practically, you have to be able to see your path while you are drawing it, of course, so drawing programs show you the path as a thin stroke. Once it is complete, each path segment is stroked or filled straight away, so you can see what you are doing.

Consider first applying a stroke to a path. Like physical strokes on paper, the strokes applied by a drawing program have characteristics, such as weight and colour, which determine their appearance. These characteristics can be set and changed by the user of a drawing program. The weight is usually set by specifying the width of strokes numerically, in whatever units are convenient. Specification of colours is more complex, and is described in Chapter 6.

As we noted in Chapter 3, some drawing programs can apply strokes that simulate natural media, such as charcoal or painted brush-strokes.

It is customary for drawing programs to support dashed strokes as well as solid ones. Ideally, the length of dashes and of the gaps between them can be specified. Again, this is usually done by the user entering numerical values in appropriate units.

A more subtle feature of strokes is the shape of their ends – the *line cap.* If a stroke has any appreciable thickness, cutting it off square at the ends with a *butt cap* may produce an undesirable and ugly effect. It may be preferable to use a *round cap*, where the line is finished off with a filled-in semicircle built across its end. A third option is to use a *projecting cap*, with the stroke continued beyond the endpoint of the path by half the width, so that the weight of the stroke relative to the path is the same in all directions. These three line cap options were provided by PostScript, and have been incorporated into PDF and SVG, and are supported by drawing programs like Illustrator. Combining different line caps with dash patterns provides a range of effects, as shown in Figure 4.18.

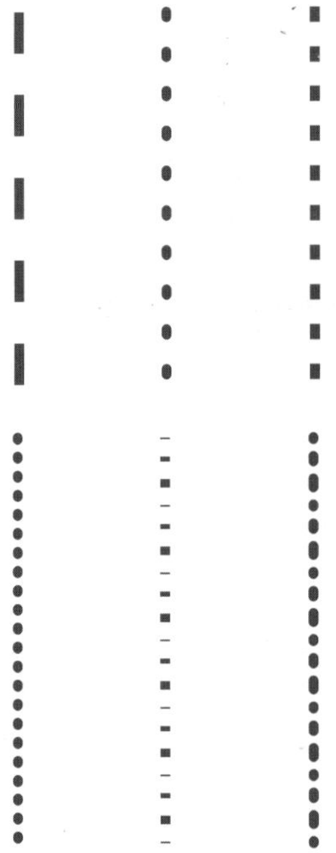

Joins at corner points also need consideration, because wide lines can only meet cleanly if they do so at 90°; when they meet at any other angle an unsightly gap or overlap will result. This can be removed in several ways. The three styles of line join provided by Illustrator are a *mitre* – as in a picture frame, the outside edges of the lines are extended to meet at a point; *round* – a circular arc is used to produce a rounded corner; and *bevel* – the segments are finished off square

Figure 4.18 Dashed effects

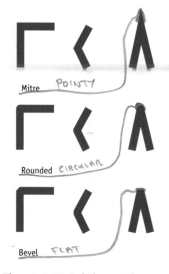

Mitre   POINTY

Rounded   CIRCULAR

Bevel   FLAT

Figure 4.19 Joining styles

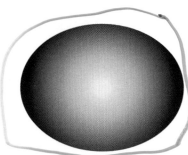

Figure 4.20 Gradient fills

where they join, and the resulting notch is filled in with a triangle to produce a flat ended joint. If mitred joins are used on segments that meet at a very narrow angle, long projecting spikes will result. To avoid this, a limit can be specified, and if the ratio of the spike's length to the stroke width exceeds it, mitres will be replaced by bevels. Figure 4.19 illustrates the different joining styles.

As well as applying a stroke to a path, you can use it as an outline and fill it. Astute readers will observe that you can only fill a closed path, but most drawing programs also allow you to fill an open path – the filling operation implicitly closes the path with a straight line between its endpoints.

The simplest fill is a single colour, and this is often all that is required. When a fill (or, indeed, a stroke) is applied it completely obscures anything underneath it. There is no mixing of overlaid colours, as you would expect if you were using watercolour paints, for example. This means that, among other possibilities, you can use a shape filled with the background colour to knock out areas of objects underneath it.

More interesting and sometimes more attractive effects can be produced by using *gradient fills* and *patterns*.

Figure 4.20 shows two examples of gradient fills. This type of fill is characterized by a gradual transition between colours or tones. In the simplest case – a *linear* gradient – the colours at each end of a region are specified, and a smooth blend of intermediate colours is generated in between. Illustrator provides controls to let you specify intermediate colours, adjust the midpoint of the gradient (where the two colours being blended are of equal intensity) and the line along which the gradient varies. An alternative form of blending, shown at the bottom of Figure 4.20, has the colour varying outwards from a centre point to the outside of the fill. This is called a *radial* gradient. The more sophisticated gradients used in Figure 4.21 were created using Illustrator's gradient mesh tool, which allows the designer or artist to set up a two-dimensional mesh of points (shown on the left of the figure), and specify the colours at each mesh point; the colours are blended in the spaces between the mesh points. The shape of the mesh can be adjusted dynamically until the desired effect is achieved.

Gradient fills are very widely used in artwork created in vector drawing programs, and contribute to the characteristic air-brushed look of much of the graphic design that is produced using these programs.

Figure 4.21 Gradient mesh

Pattern fills, as the name suggests, allow you to use a repeating pattern to fill in an area, as shown in Figure 4.22. Patterns are built out of elements called *tiles*. A tile is just a small piece of artwork, made using the facilities provided by your drawing program (possibly including the facility to import bitmaps as objects). The name embodies the analogy normally employed for describing how an area is filled with a pattern. Imagine that the artwork is rendered onto a rectangular ceramic tile, such as you might use in your bathroom. Copies of the tile are arranged in rows and columns parallel to the *x*- and *y*-axes, butted together as if by a skilled tiler. The resulting pattern is clipped to the area being filled. Constructing tiles that join seamlessly requires a certain amount of skill – in graphics as in bathroom design. Tiles may be used to produce geometrically patterned areas, such as might be appropriate for drawing textiles or wallpaper (or bathrooms), but they can also be designed so that they produce textured effects. Pattern fills are often used as backgrounds.

Some drawing programs allow you to use patterns to stroke paths, producing a textured outline, for example. This is more difficult than using patterns as fills, because one naturally wants the tiles to be arranged perpendicular to the path, not horizontally. This in turn makes it difficult to get tiles to go round corners, so that a pattern intended for tiling a path must include special corner tiles.

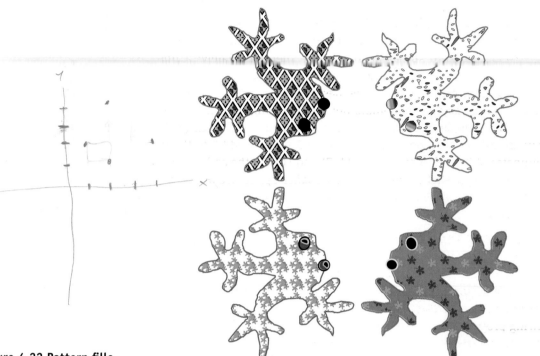

Figure 4.22 Pattern fills

**Figure 4.23 A complex
path...**

If you want to fill a path, you need to know which areas are inside it. For simple shapes, this is a trivial question, but a path may be arbitrarily complex, crossing itself several times. Figure 4.23 shows a single path. Which areas are inside it, and which outside? There is no absolute answer; several different interpretations of the concept of insideness have equal validity. Figure 4.24 shows Illustrator's answer, which is based on the *non-zero winding number rule*, which may be expressed as an algorithm as follows. To determine whether a point is inside a path, draw a (conceptually infinite) line from the point in any direction. Start by setting the winding number to zero. Follow the constructed line, and every time the path crosses it from left to right, add one to the winding number; every time the path crosses from right to left, subtract one from the winding number. After all crossings have been counted, if the winding number is zero, the point is outside the path, otherwise it is inside. Note that this algorithm depends on the path's having a direction, which will depend on the order in which anchor points were added to it.

Transformations and Filters

The objects that make up a vector image are stored in the form of a few values that are sufficient to describe them accurately: a line by its endpoints, a rectangle by its corners, and so on. The actual pixel values that make up the image need not be computed until it is displayed. It is easy to manipulate objects by changing these stored values. For example, if a line runs parallel to the x-axis from (4, 2) to (10, 2), all we need do to move it up by 5 units is add 5 to the y-coordinates of its endpoints, giving (4, 7) and (10, 7), the endpoints of a line running parallel to the x-axis, but higher up. To use a term we introduced earlier in this chapter, we have transformed the image by editing the *model* that is stored in the computer.

Figure 4.24 ...filled

Only certain transformations can be naturally produced in this way. The most important are *translation* (a linear movement of the object), *scaling*, *rotation* about a point, *reflection* about a line, and *shearing* (a distortion of the angles of the axes of an object). These transformations are illustrated in Figures 4.25 to 4.30. Any modern drawing program will allow you to perform these transformations by direct manipulation of objects on the screen. For example, you would translate an object simply by dragging it to its new position.

Briefly, the operations on the model which achieve these transformations are as follows. Any translation can be done by adding a displacement to each of the x and y coordinates stored in the model of the object. That is, to move an object Δ_x to the right and Δ_y upwards, change each stored point (x,y) to $(x + \Delta_x, y + \Delta_y)$. Negative Δs move in the opposite direction. Scaling is performed by multiplying coordinates by appropriate values. Different factors may be used to scale in the x and y directions: to increase lengths in the x direction by a factor of s_x and in the y direction by s_y, (x,y) must be changed to $(s_x x, s_y y)$. (Values of s less than one cause the object to shrink.) Thus, to double the size of an object, its stored coordinates must be multiplied by two. However, this has the effect of simultaneously displacing the object. (For example, if a unit square has its corners at (1,2) and (2,1), multiplying by two moves them to (2,4) and (4,2), which are the corners of a square whose side is of length 2, but it is now in the wrong place.) To scale an object in place, the multiplication must be followed by a suitable, easily computed, displacement to restore it to its original position.

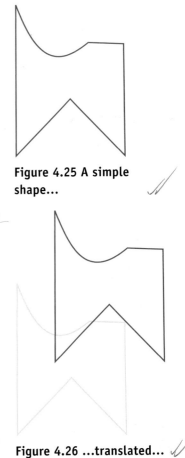

Figure 4.25 A simple shape...

Figure 4.26 ...translated...

Rotation about the origin and reflection about an axis are simple to achieve. To rotate a point (x,y) around the origin in a clockwise direction by an angle

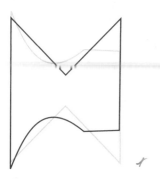

Figure 4.27 ...reflected...

arbitrary

Figure 4.28 ...rotated...

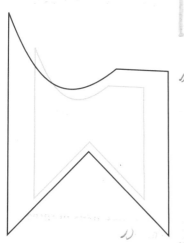

Figure 4.29 ...scaled...

θ, you transform it to the point $(x\cos\theta - y\sin\theta, x\sin\theta + y\cos\theta)$ (which you can prove by simple trigonometry if you wish). To reflect it in the x-axis, simply move it to $(x, -y)$; in the y-axis, to $(-x, y)$. Applying these operations to all the points of an object will transform the entire object. The more general operations of rotation about an arbitrary point and reflection in an arbitrary line require more complex, but conceptually simple, transformations. The details are left as an exercise.

Finally, when an object is sheared, it is as if we took the x-axis and skewed it upwards, through an angle α, say, and skewed the y-axis through an angle β (see Figure 4.31). You can show that the transformation can be achieved by moving (x, y) to $(x + y\tan\beta, y + x\tan\alpha)$.

Other, less structured, transformations can be achieved by moving (i.e. changing the coordinates of) the anchor points and control points of paths. This would normally be done by interactive manipulation in a drawing program. Anchor points and control points may also be added and deleted from paths, so that a designer or artist can fine-tune the shape of objects.

Some commonly required effects which fall between the highly structured transformations and the free manipulation of control points are provided as *filters* in Illustrator and similar programs. (The term 'filter' is taken from photography, where optical filters are used to produce similar effects.) An object is selected, and a filter operation is chosen from a menu of those available. The chosen effect is then applied to the selected object. Filters available in Illustrator include roughening, which produces a rough edge to an object by moving the anchor points of its path in a jagged pattern, scribbling, which moves the anchor points in a random fashion, and rounding corners, which converts corner points into smooth curves. Most filters are parameterized in values such as the maximum distance an anchor point may be moved. The parameters can be set by the user via controls such as sliders.

The important thing to understand about all these transformations is that they are achieved simply by altering the coordinates of the defining points of objects, altering the stored model using nothing but arithmetical operations which can be performed efficiently. Although every pixel of the object must be transformed in the final displayed image, only the relatively few points that are needed to define the object within the model need to be recomputed beforehand. All the pixels will appear in the desired place when the changed model is rendered on the basis of these changed values.

3-D Graphics

Pictures on a screen are always two-dimensional, but that doesn't mean that the models from which they are generated need to be restricted to flat two-dimensional shapes. Models of three-dimensional objects correspond more closely to the way we perceive space. They enable us to generate two-dimensional pictures as perspective projections – or perhaps other sorts of projection – onto a plane, as if we were able to photograph the model. Sometimes, this may be easier than constructing the two-dimensional image from scratch, particularly if we can begin with a numerical description of an object's dimensions, as we might if we were designing some mechanical component, for example, or constructing a visualization on the basis of a simulation. A three-dimensional model allows us to generate many different images of the same objects. For example, if we have a model of a house, we can produce a view of it from the front, from the back, from each side, from close up, far away, overhead, and so on, all using the same model. If we were working in only two dimensions, each of these images would have to be drawn separately.

3-D graphics, as we call vector graphics based on three-dimensional models, is a complicated subject, though, requiring tools that are hard to master, and should be left to specialists most of the time. Here, we can only outline the main features of 3-D technology, in order to provide an appreciation of the difficulties it presents and the opportunities it has to offer.

In abstract mathematical terms, generalizing coordinate geometry from two dimensions to three is straightforward. The x- and y-axes of a two-dimensional coordinate system are perpendicular to each other. If you imagine drawing a set of axes on a flat sheet of paper and pinning it to a vertical wall, you can see that we can place a third axis perpendicular to the other two, coming out of the paper horizontally. Just as we can use x- and y- coordinates to define a point's horizontal and vertical distance along the wall from the origin, we can use a z-coordinate, measured along our third axis, to define its distance from the wall. The three coordinates together define a point in a three-dimensional space (see Figure 4.32).

The primitive geometrical shapes of 2-D graphics are replaced by 3-D objects: instead of a circle, we have a sphere, instead of a square, a cube, and so on. By an obvious extension, a three-dimensional vector defines a displacement in the same way the two-dimensional vectors

Figure 4.30 ...sheared

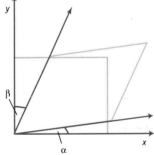

Figure 4.31 Skewed axes

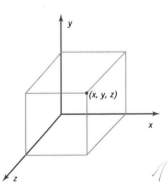

Figure 4.32 Axes in three dimensions

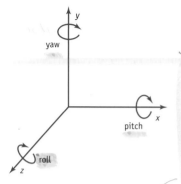

Figure 4.33 Rotations in three dimensions

spatical
= time / space

we used earlier did. This allows us to describe translations of objects in three-dimensional space. We certainly have a basis for 3-D vector graphics.

Even at this stage, it is apparent that three dimensions may be more than one and a half times as complicated as two. Consider rotation. In two dimensions we rotate about a point; in three, we must rotate about a line. Rotations about an arbitrary line can be built out of rotations about the axes, but that still leaves three distinct rotations to consider, as shown in Figure 4.33, which introduces the names used for each of them.

When we introduced a third dimension, we stated that the z-axis points out of the imaginary wall of the x–y plane. Why should it not point into it? There is no reason. The coordinate system we have adopted is no more than a convention. It is known as a *right-handed* coordinate system, a name that Figure 4.34 should explain. A left-handed system is equally valid, and is sometimes used in computer graphics. However, the right-handed system is more widely used, especially by mathematicians, and we will employ it exclusively. We have also adopted the convention that the vertical axis is labelled y, as it was before, but some systems use the x- and y-axes to define a horizontal *ground plane*, with the z-axis adding height to it. In that case, the names of the three rotations are assigned differently to the three variables, although they retain the same spatial meaning – roll is always a movement around the front-to-back axis, and so on.

The added complexity of graphics employing the third dimension goes much further than an extra couple of rotations. Instead of defining shapes by paths, we must define objects by surfaces, which require more complicated mathematics and are much harder for most people to visualize. The fact that we can only work with two-dimensional representations while building models makes visualization generally difficult. This problem is further exacerbated by the fact that only powerful workstations can provide real-time rendering of 3-D models, so it is usually necessary to work with cruder approximations during the design process.

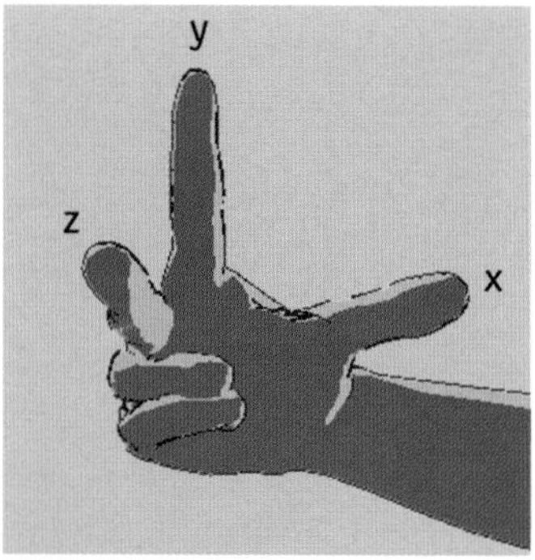

Once a collection of objects has been modelled, they are arranged in space, usually interactively. Often, a complete scene will be constructed from a few objects that are specially modelled and others taken from a library, either developed in earlier projects or brought in as the 3-D equivalent of clip art. (Indeed, some 3-D applications

Figure 4.34 Right-handed coordinate system

intended for consumer or corporate use allow you to do little more than arrange ready-built models in space.)

As well as the spatial relationships between separate objects, we may also wish to consider the relationships between objects that form parts of a larger object. Most complex objects have a hierarchical structure. They can be described as a collection of sub-objects, each of which might be a collection of sub-sub-objects, and so on, until we reach the smallest component objects, which can be modelled in a simple way. For example, a bicycle consists of a frame, two wheels, a saddle, handlebars and front fork. Each wheel is a tyre around a rim, with spokes and a hub. We could model the hub as a cylinder, without decomposing it further. Hierarchical modelling is a well-established way of coping with complexity in many fields. In 3-D it becomes of particular importance when objects are animated, because we can then take advantage of the relationships between components to deduce how the object must move as a whole.

Rendering is no longer a relatively simple matter of generating pixels from a mathematical description. In 3-D, we have a mathematical model of objects in space, but we need a flat picture. Assuming that we want to use conventional Renaissance perspective to project the 3-D model onto a plane surface, we will need to consider the viewpoint, or the position of an imaginary camera, and ensure that the rendered picture corresponds to what the camera sees, while exhibiting the scaling with distance that we expect from perspective.

We also need to consider lighting – the position of light sources, and the intensity and type of illumination they cast, whether it is a diffuse glow or a concentrated beam, for example. The interaction of the light with the surface of objects, and perhaps – in the case of an underwater scene or a smoke-filled room – with the atmosphere must also be modelled and rendered. If we want to achieve any sort of realism, our models must include not just the geometrical features of objects, but also their surface characteristics – not just the colours, but also the texture – so that the surface's appearance can be rendered convincingly in different positions and under different lighting conditions. Although 3-D systems are reasonably good at using lighting models derived from the underlying physics, they are not perfect, and designers sometimes have to resort to physical impossibilities, such as negative spotlights, for absorbing unwanted light.

These added complications mean that the theory of 3-D graphics is a great deal more elaborate than that of 2-D graphics. It also means that

3-D software is more complex and difficult to use. Finally, it means that rendering 3-D models can be an extremely computationally expensive process, that often requires additional hardware (often in the form of 3-D accelerator PCI cards) to achieve acceptable performance on desktop machines.

3-D Models

Broadly speaking, there are three general approaches to modelling 3-D objects, which are often used in conjunction. The simplest approach, which goes by the name of *constructive solid geometry*, uses a few primitive geometric solids, such as the cube, cylinder, sphere and pyramid, as elements from which to construct more complex objects. These elements can be distorted, by squashing or stretching, to produce variations on the simple forms. They can also be combined, using operations usually described in terms of the set theoretical operators union, intersection, and difference.

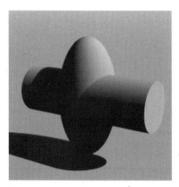

Figure 4.35 Union

† The shadows are just cosmetic additions, which should help make it easier to see the third dimension in these illustrations.

These operations only do anything to two objects that are placed in such a way that they share some of the space that they occupy – normally a physical impossibility, but no problem for a computer model. Their *union* is a new object made out of the space occupied by the two together. Figure 4.35 shows the object formed from the union of a horizontal cylinder and a vertical ellipsoid.† The *intersection* of two objects is the space that the two have in common; Figure 4.36 shows what happens when the same cylinder and ellipsoid are intersected: the shape that is produced is otherwise difficult to describe. Finally, the *difference* of two objects is the space occupied by the first but not the second. This operation is useful for knocking holes out of solid objects, as Figure 4.37 shows.

Constructive solid geometry is especially useful for modelling man-made objects and architectural features, which are often built out of the same elementary solids. It is often found in computer-aided design systems. It can take you a long way with modelling camshafts, triumphal arches and toy steam trains. However, as a glance around your immediate environment will show, many objects in the real world are not made out of geometric solids combined by set operations; these need a different approach.

Figure 4.36 Intersection

Free form modelling uses a representation of an object's boundary surface as the basis of its model. This approach is a 3-D generalization of the use of paths to enclose shapes in two dimensions. Instead of building paths out of lines and curves, we must build surfaces out of flat polygons or curved patches. Surfaces constructed as a *mesh* of polygons can be rendered relatively efficiently, making this a popular representation. (Where fast rendering is required, as in 3-D games, the polygons are often restricted to triangles, which makes rendering more efficient. It also guarantees that the polygons are flat.) However, they suffer from the drawback that, like straight line segments used to approximate a curve, polygons cannot fit together smoothly when they are used to approximate curved surfaces. This is more serious than it may sound, because it affects the way light is reflected off the surface. If reflections are broken up, any irregularities will be readily apparent.

Figure 4.37 Difference

It is possible to generalize Bézier curves to three-dimensional surfaces in order to produce curved patches that can be fitted together smoothly. A cubic Bézier surface patch requires sixteen control points, instead of the corresponding curve's four. Just as we could join curves together smoothly by ensuring that they meet at an anchor point and the connected control points are in a straight line, so we can join patches by ensuring that they meet at a common edge curve and that the connected control points lie in the same plane. This is easy to say, but Bézier patches are hard to work with in interactive 3-D applications, largely because moving a single control point can affect the geometry of the whole patch in a way that may be hard to predict. A more tractable kind of patch is based on surfaces called *non-rational B-splines or NURBs*, which, by using a more complicated construction, ensure that the effect of moving control points is localized. In effect, this makes it possible to sculpt a smooth surface by pulling and pushing it into the desired shape. NURBs are largely confined to high-end systems.

The generality and lack of structure of boundary representations can make it hard to get started with a model. To overcome this problem, most 3-D programs provide a means of generating objects with a certain regular structure or symmetry from 2-D shapes. The resulting objects can then either be used directly, or their surface mesh can be altered to produce a less constrained object.

The basic idea is to treat a two-dimensional shape as a cross section, and to define a volume by sweeping the cross section along a path. The simplest path is a straight line. A shape creates an object with a uniform cross section as it travels along a straight line. For example, a circle creates a cylinder in this way. This process is known as *extrusion*, since the objects it produces resemble those that can be made by industrial processes in which plastic or metal is forced through an opening. Extruded text is an application of this technique that has

Clinche

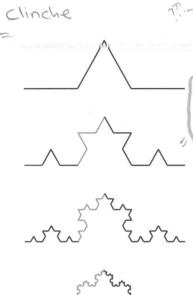

Figure 4.38 Constructing a well-known fractal curve

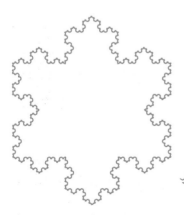

Figure 4.39 A fractal snowflake

been so widely used in producing corporate logos as to have become a cliché. To produce more elaborate objects, a curved path can be used, and the size of the cross section can be altered as it moves along it. If the path is a conventional Bézier path, organic shapes can be generated. If it is a circle, the resulting objects exhibit radial symmetry. If a suitable shape is chosen, circular paths can be used to generate many types of drinking vessel and vase, as well as mechanical components. Because of the resemblance of the resulting objects to traditional turned artefacts, this special case is often called *lathing*.

The third approach to modelling is *procedural modelling*. Here, instead of using models that can be described by equations, and storing only the constants that define a particular instance, we use objects that are described by an algorithm or procedure. Thus, returning to two dimensions for a moment, instead of defining a circle by the equation $x^2+y^2 = r^2$, we could define it by some procedure such as 'draw a curve that maintains a constant distance r from the origin'. In this case, the procedural representation is not very helpful – the equation tells you how to implement the procedure – but for naturally occurring objects with a more complex, less mathematically tractable, structure, algorithms may provide a description where equations cannot.

The best known procedural modelling techniques are based on *fractals*. These are often described as shapes that exhibit the same structure at all levels of detail. Figure 4.38 shows a famous example of such a shape, and its construction. We start with the shape at the top, consisting of four equal line segments, arranged as a straight line with a bump in the middle. We then replace each segment by a scaled-down copy of the entire shape, as shown on the second line. We continue in the same way, replacing each of the segments of each of the scaled-down copies with a copy of the original shape scaled down further, and so on. The bottom two lines show later stages in the procedure. You can imagine that, if we were able to continue in this way to infinity, we would end up with a crinkly curve, with a bulge in the middle and two lesser crinkly bulges to each side. If you were then to magnify any part of the curve and look at it you would see a crinkly curve, with a bulge in the middle and two lesser crinkly bulges to each side, which, if you were to magnify any part of it …

The appearance of certain natural features, such as coastlines, mountains and the edges of clouds, approximates this property: their small-scale structure is the same as their large-scale structure.

Figure 4.39 shows that three of the curves we just constructed can be put together to make a snowflake.

Fractals can be extended to three-dimensional structures that exhibit the same sort of similarity at different scales. Whereas this particular sort of structure cannot be described by equations, it is, as we have just demonstrated, easily described by a recursive algorithm.

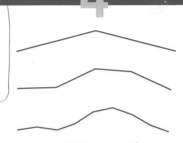

Figure 4.40 Constructing a fractal mountainside

Where fractal algorithms are used to model natural phenomena, an element of randomness is usually introduced. For example, a very simple fractal might be made by splitting a line into two parts, moving the centre point a certain distance, and then applying the construction recursively to the two halves. If the distance moved is not a constant proportion of the length of the segment but a random distance, the resulting shape will still display a recognizable similarity at different scales, without being exactly internally replicated. Figure 4.40 shows a curve being constructed in the manner just described; it could be said to resemble a mountain slope. In three dimensions, a similar construction can be applied to construct terrains out of internally subdivided triangular areas. By joining the midpoints of the three sides of a triangle, it can be divided into four smaller triangles. The midpoints can be randomly displaced perpendicularly to the plane of the original triangle, as indicated in Figure 4.41, and then the construction can be applied to each of the small triangles. This process can be applied to arbitrary polygons, and repeated indefinitely to produce arbitrarily fine detail with the irregular appearance of natural terrain, as exhibited by the landscape in Figure 4.42.

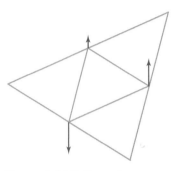

Figure 4.41 3-D random fractal construction

Note that the structures used in this sort of modelling are not, strictly mathematically speaking, fractals. A mathematician's fractal shows the same structure at *all* scales, right on to infinity. Fractals are said to be *self-similar*. In computer graphics, we cannot do this, nor do we want to: we can't show any detail smaller than a single pixel, and in any case, to model natural features we must introduce a random element. The randomized structures commonly used in modelling are a finite approximation to a class of structures known as *random fractals*, which have the property that at any scale the components have the same statistical distribution as the whole structure. This property is a random equivalent of the property of true fractals that at any scale the components are identical to the whole. To ensure such *statistical self-similarity*, constraints must be placed on the random factors introduced at each stage of the construction of these objects.

Figure 4.42 Fractal terrain

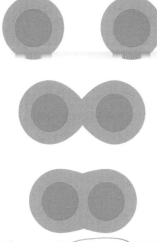

Figure 4.43 Coalescing fields around metaballs

Two other procedural modelling techniques deserve a brief mention. *Metaballs* are sometimes used to model soft objects. Metaballs are just spheres, but their interaction is modelled using the same sort of mathematics as physicists use to model the electric fields around charged spheres. When two metaballs are placed close together, the fields coalesce into a composite field with a smooth boundary (see Figure 4.43). In 3-D graphics, this boundary is used as the surface of a composite shape. Complex objects can be built by sticking metaballs together. The resulting shapes have a soft, organic quality that is difficult to achieve using other methods of modelling. The process of constructing objects from metaballs somewhat resembles modelling using clay, so tools based on this approach can have a more intuitive feel than more traditional, geometry-based, systems. The fields around other shapes besides spheres can be modelled in a similar way, to allow a wider range of soft objects to be constructed easily. These models count as procedural ones because the disposition of the surfaces is computed algorithmically from the positions of the balls; there is no need to shape the actual surface, in the way polygon meshes must be shaped by the designer.

None of the techniques we have described so far is particularly suitable for modelling phenomena such as rain, fountains, fireworks, or grass, consisting of a large number of semi-independent elements, with some shared properties. Often, the elements are moving, and the laws of motion impose certain patterns on them, as in the case of a fountain. To model such things by placing individual drops of water, blades of grass, sparks, and so on, calls for a dedication to detail, and an amount of time, that many 3-D graphic artists lack. *Particle systems* allow features made out of many particles to be specified in terms of a few parameters, from which the positions of the individual particles can be computed algorithmically. Particle systems were first used for film special effects[†] but are now available, at varying levels of sophistication, in desktop 3-D systems.

† Their first reported use was in creating the 'Genesis effect' in *Star Trek II: The Wrath of Khan.*

The modelling technique used in particle systems leads on to the ultimate procedural modelling system: physics. Established modelling techniques are primarily based on the desired appearance of the objects. If, instead, we base our models on the physical characteristics of objects – their mass and its distribution, elasticity, optical properties, and so on – the appearance can be deduced using physical laws. Such physical models could be tremendously powerful, since a single description of an object would suffice to determine its appearance in any position or environment. Combined with the laws of motion, physical models could be used to describe moving objects, and so to generate animation. Unfortunately, although physicists feel able to construct models of the evolution of the entire universe, modelling such things as the way clothing drapes over a figure is beyond current theories. A great deal of research has been carried out in recent years, particularly into modelling textiles, and it is beginning to bear fruit, but it requires intensive computation and its use is still confined to research laboratories and high-budget film production.

Rendering

3-D models only exist inside computers; all we can see is two-dimensional images generated from them. This is the case both when we wish to produce a final image from a model, and when we are working on a model in a 3-D application. In both cases, a rendering operation is needed; in the latter case, this must be done rapidly enough to provide visual feedback. As we will shortly see, rendering high quality images is time consuming, so it is usually necessary to compromise on quality while a model is being built. Because of the complexity of rendering, and its computational demands, it is common for it to be handled by a specialized module, usually referred to as a *rendering engine*. It may be the case that a rendering engine is optimized for multiprocessing, so that rendering can be speeded up by using a collection of processors operating in parallel.

Almost all contemporary 3-D graphics aspires to the sort of realism associated with photographs. That is, it uses Renaissance perspective conventions (distant objects are smaller than near ones) and attempts to represent the effects of light on different surfaces in a way that is consistent with the laws of optics. Figure 4.44 shows an example of the results that can easily be achieved with mid-range software. The mathematics of perspective projection has been understood for a long time, so it is relatively easy for a rendering engine to work out which points on an image plane correspond to each of the nodes of a 3-D model. By joining these points to show the edges of objects and of the polygons making up surfaces, it is possible to produce a *wire frame* image of a model, as shown in Figure 4.45. Wire frames are often used as preview images in modelling programs. They can also be useful in computer-aided design systems, since they contain enough information to provide answers to questions such as 'Does the door provide adequate clearance for the piano when it is fully open?'. For most purposes, though, they are not acceptable.

Figure 4.44 Photo-realism in 3-D graphics

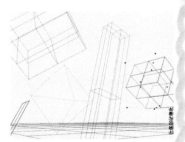

Figure 4.45 A wire frame rendering of 3-D objects

The most noticeable feature of wire frames is the absence of any surfaces. This has the obvious disadvantage that no surface detail can be shown, and the less obvious disadvantage that they do not contain enough information to enable us to determine the orientations of objects unambiguously – in Figure 4.45, can you determine the form and orientation of every object, and which of their vertices is nearest to you? (Look at Figure 4.46 to check your answers.) In order to show the surfaces of objects, it is necessary to determine which of them are visible. The far sides of objects are considered hidden in perspective views, as are surfaces, or parts of surfaces, with other objects in front of them. Determining which surfaces are visible, starting only from a model based on the coordinates of corners of objects, is not a trivial task, but it is one that has received attention almost from the beginning of computer graphics. There are several tried and tested algorithms for performing *hidden surface removal*. Once this has been done, the next task is to determine how to render the visible surfaces.

One answer is to colour them arbitrarily, ensuring that no two adjacent faces are the same colour. This approach makes no pretence at photographic realism, but ensures that the shapes of objects are clearly visible. An alternative is to assign a colour to each object, and render its entire surface in that colour. This is more consistent with our expectations about surfaces, but leaves some visual ambiguity. To resolve this ambiguity, and to begin to produce images that resemble photographs, we must take account of the way light interacts with surfaces. This means that our models must include sufficient information about lights and surface properties. In most 3-D modelling programs, surface characteristics can be associated with an object by setting the values of some parameters, including its colour and reflectivity. (Some systems allow the designer to paint on the surface of models in order to specify their surface characteristics indirectly.) Lights can be created and positioned in the same way as other objects; the designer merely selects a type of light – spotlight or point source (such as the sun), for example – and specifies its position and intensity. It is up to the rendering engine to produce an image that is consistent with the lights and materials that have been used in the model.

Different algorithms – called *shading algorithms* – are employed for this task, each incorporating different models of how light interacts with surfaces,[†] and each using different approximations to allow rendering to be performed with reasonable efficiency. Rendering engines usually allow you to choose the most appropriate shading algorithm for the needs of a particular model. There is usually a trade-off between the final quality of the image – or at least, of its treatment of light – and the amount of computation required.

† The models of illumination are loosely derived from the physics, but also incorporate heuristics aimed at producing an acceptable result and not an optical simulation.

The simplest way of shading an object whose surface is made out of polygons is to calculate a colour value for each polygon, based on the light striking it and its own optical properties, and use that value to colour the whole polygon. Adjacent polygons will often have different colours – they may be at a different angle to the light source, for example – and, as we mentioned earlier, this will make the discontinuities between polygons readily visible. To disguise this effect, and to produce a more convincing rendering of the polygons, more sophisticated algorithms interpolate the colour across each polygon, on the basis of colour values calculated at the vertices. One such interpolation scheme is *Gouraud shading*, named after its inventor. An alternative, which does the interpolation differently, is *Phong shading*. Phong's approach works better when the illumination model being used takes account of *specular reflection* – the light that bounces off the surface of shiny (or partially shiny) objects. The resulting highlights are rendered by Phong shading in a quite convincing way.

The shading algorithms mentioned so far only deal with each object in isolation, but in reality, the appearance of an object may be affected by the presence of others. As an extreme example, the appearance of a glass full of water will depend on what is behind it, while that of a mirror will depend on the objects it reflects. Generally, light may bounce off several objects before reaching the eye, and be influenced by their colour and surface. *Ray tracing* is a shading algorithm that attempts to take account of this. It works by tracing the path of a ray of light back from each pixel in the rendered image to a light source. On the way, the ray may bounce off several surfaces, and the ray tracer will take account of their effect, using a model of illumination and information about the materials of the objects in the scene, to compute the colour and intensity of the starting pixel. Figure 4.46 shows two renderings of Figure 4.45 by a ray tracer, and illustrates the qualities of different surfaces that can be applied to the objects. The ray tracing computation is quite complex, and it must be repeated for every pixel in the rendered image – very possibly millions of pixels. Until recently, therefore, ray tracing was confined to high-performance workstations, but the extraordinary advance in the speed of personal computers has made it feasible to use ray tracing in desktop 3-D systems. It is now the preferred shading algorithm for 'photo-realistic' graphics. It can produce excellent results, particularly in scenes including transparent or semi-transparent objects.

An alternative approach to the interactions between objects is *radiosity*, which attempts to model the complex reflections that occur between surfaces that are close together. This provides a more accurate representation of scattered and ambient light, and is especially useful for interior scenes. Radiosity is more accurately based on the physics of light than other shading algorithms. It also differs from them in computing the lighting on a model independently of any rendered view of it; essentially, it adds the computed light values to the

Figure 4.46 Ray traced rendering with different lighting and surface characteristics

model. This means that the final rendering of an image can be done very efficiently, although the initial computation of lighting values is slow.

These shading algorithms depend on information about the material of which an object is composed. Where the surface contains a great deal of detail, it may not be feasible to specify this information precisely enough for every small feature to be rendered accurately. A popular way of adding surface details to 3-D models is *texture mapping*. An image, typically a pattern representing some particular sort of surface's appearance, such as fur, bark, sand, marble, and so on, is mathematically wrapped over the surface of the object. That is, mathematical transformations are applied to the pixels of the rendered object, based on those of the image, to produce the appearance of an object with the image wrapped around it. To see the effect of this, imagine cutting a picture out of a magazine, wrapping it round a physical object, and sticking it down. This will work quite well for boxes, producing a box whose surface has the appearance of the picture, but it will work much less well for spherical or irregularly shaped objects. If you can further imagine that the picture was printed on a very thin sheet of rubber, you can see that it would be possible to glue it to these shapes, but that it would become distorted in the process. Texture mapping is similar to gluing rubber pictures to objects, and may introduce the same sort of distortion, but it can also provide a convenient means of applying detail to a surface. Related operations include *bump mapping*, where, instead of using the picture to form the surface appearance, we use it to apply bumpiness or roughness, and *transparency mapping* and *reflection mapping*, which modify the corresponding optical characteristics on the basis of a two-dimensional map in the same way.

Rendering algorithms can do a very good job at producing photo-realistic images, but they are not perfect. It is by no means uncommon for a rendered image to be imported into an image manipulation program, such as Photoshop, for further processing of the sort we will describe in Chapter 5.

Exercises

1. Anti-aliasing never affects the appearance of vertical and horizontal lines: true or false? F

2   (For mathematicians.) For many purposes, it is convenient to know the *bounding box* of a vector graphics object, that is, the smallest rectangle that entirely encloses the object.
(a) Show that the bounding box on its own is an adequate representation for an ellipse.
(b) Can a Bézier curve be represented by a bounding box?

3   What happens if two Bézier curves with control points P_1, P_2, P_3 and P_4, and P_4, P_5, P_6 and P_7 are joined at P_4 so that P_3, P_4 and P_5 are in a straight line but P_5 and P_3 are on the same side of P_4?

4   There are 24 possible orders in which the points P_1, P_2, P_3 and P_4 can be used to specify a Bézier curve. Sketch the curves produced by all possible permutations of the points used in the curve shown in Figure 4.8. Their coordinates are $(0,0)$, $(4,10)$, $(8,10)$ and $(20,2)$. Which pairs of curves are identical, and which can be transformed into each other by a geometrical transformation?

5   Gradient fills are not directly provided in some low-level graphics languages. Describe how you would implement linear and radial gradients using the other vector graphics primitives described in this chapter.

6   (a) The algorithm for computing the winding number of a point relative to a path does not tell you what to do if the line you construct coincides with part of the path or touches it tangentially. How would you cope with these possibilities?

(b) An alternative to the non-zero winding number rule that is sometimes used instead is the *odd–even rule*, which is computed in a similar way by constructing a line from a point and counting crossings, only this time you just count the number of times the path crosses the line. If it is even, the point is outside the path; if it is odd, it is inside. Does this rule always give the same result as the non-zero winding number rule? If not, when will they disagree?

7   The difference operation in constructive solid geometry is not commutative, that is, if we subtract shape A from shape B the result is different from what we get by subtracting shape B from shape A. Figure 4.37 shows the effect of subtracting the cylinder from the ellipsoid. Sketch the object that would be obtained by subtracting the ellipsoid from the cylinder.

8   Under what circumstances would you *not* use ray tracing to render a 3-D scene?
– where light is not a factor

Bitmapped Images

- Resolution
- Image Compression
  - Lossless Compression
  - JPEG Compression
- Image Manipulation
  - Selections, Masks and Alpha Channels
  - Pixel Point Processing
  - Pixel Group Processing
- Geometrical Transformations

[handwritten note: maybe read Chp2 - section on SAMPLING]

Conceptually, bitmapped images are much simpler than vector graphics. There is no need for any mathematical modelling of shapes; we merely record the value of every pixel in the image. This means that when the image is created, a value has to be assigned to every pixel, but many images are created from external sources, such as scanners or digital cameras, which operate in a bitmapped fashion anyway. For creating original digital images, programs such as Painter allow visual artists to use familiar techniques (at least metaphorically) to paint images. As we pointed out earlier, the main cost for this simplicity is in the size of image files. There is, though, one area where bitmaps are less simple than vectors, and that is resolution. We touched on this in Chapter 3, but now we shall look at it in more detail.

Resolution

The concept of resolution is a simple one, but the different ways in which the word is used can be confusing. Resolution is a measure of how finely a device approximates continuous images using finite pixels. It is thus closely related to sampling, and some of the ideas about sampling rates introduced in Chapter 2 are relevant to the way resolution affects the appearance of images.

[handwritten margin note: DOTS-PER-INCH]

There are two common ways of specifying resolution. For printers and scanners, the resolution is usually stated as the number of dots per unit length. Usually, in English-speaking countries, it is specified anachronistically in units of dots per inch (dpi). At the time of writing, desktop printers typically have a resolution of 600 dpi, while imagesetters (as used for book production) have a resolution of about 1200 to 2700 dpi; flatbed scanners' resolution ranges from 300 dpi at the most basic level to 3600 dpi; transparency scanners and drum scanners used for high quality work have even higher resolutions.

In video, resolution is normally specified by giving the size of a frame, measured in pixels – its *pixel dimensions*. For example, a PAL frame is 768 by 576 pixels; an NTSC frame is 640 by 480. Obviously, if you know the physical dimensions of your TV set or video monitor, you can translate resolutions specified in this form into dots per inch. For video it makes more sense to specify image resolution in the form of the pixel dimensions, because the same pixel grid is used to display the picture on any monitor (using the same video standard) irrespective of its size. Similar considerations apply to digital cameras, whose resolution is also specified in terms of the pixel dimensions of the image.

PIXEL DIMENSIONS

Knowing the pixel dimensions, you know how much detail is contained in the image; the number of dots per inch on the output device tells you how big that same image will be, and how easy it will be to see the individual pixels.

Computer monitors are based on the same technology as video monitors, so it is common to see their resolution specified as an image size, such as 640 by 480 (for example, VGA), or 1024 by 768. However, monitor resolution is sometimes quoted in dots per inch, because of the tendency in computer systems to keep this value fixed and to increase the pixel dimensions of the displayed image when a larger display is used. Thus, a 14 inch monitor provides a 640 by 480 display at roughly 72 dpi; a 17 inch monitor will provide 832 by 624 pixels at the same number of dots per inch.

There is an extra complication with colour printers. As we will see in Chapter 6, in order to produce a full range of colours using just four or six inks, colour printers arrange dots in groups, using a pattern of different coloured inks within each group to produce the required colour by optical mixing. Hence, the size of the coloured pixel is greater than the size of an individual dot of ink. The resolution of a printer taking account of this way of mixing colours is quoted in *lines per inch* (or other unit of length), following established printing practice. This figure is sometimes called the *screen ruling*, again following established terminology from the traditional printing industry. The number of lines per inch will be as few as one-fifth of the number of dots per inch – the exact ratio depends on how the dots are arranged, which will vary between printers, and may be adjustable by the operator. You should realise that, although a colour printer may have a resolution of 1200 *dots* per inch, this does not mean that you need to use such a high resolution for your images. A line resolution of 137 per inch is commonly used for printing magazines; the illustrations in this book are printed at a resolution of 150 lines per inch.

Now consider bitmapped images. An image is an array of pixel values, so it necessarily has pixel dimensions. Unlike an input or output device, it has no *physical* dimensions. In the absence of any further information, the physical size of an image when it is displayed will depend on the resolution of the device it is to be displayed on. For example, the square in Figure 3.3 on page 69 is 128 pixels wide. When displayed at 72 dpi, as it will be on a Macintosh monitor, for example, it will be 45 mm square. Displayed without scaling on a higher resolution monitor at 115 dpi, it will only be a little over 28 mm square. Printed on a 600 dpi printer, it will be about 5 mm square.[†] In general, we have:

$$physical\ dimension = \frac{pixel\ dimension}{device\ resolution}$$

where the device resolution is measured in pixels per unit length. (If the device resolution is specified in pixels per inch, the physical dimension will be in inches, and so on.)

Images have a natural size, though: the size of an original before it is scanned, or the size of canvas used to create an image in a painting program. We often wish the image to be displayed at its natural size, and not shrink or expand with the resolution of the output device. In order to allow this, most image formats record a resolution with the image data. This resolution is usually quoted in units of *pixels* per inch (ppi), to distinguish it from the resolution of physical devices. The stored resolution will usually be that of the device from which the image originated. For example, if the image is scanned at 600 dpi, the stored *image resolution* will be 600 ppi. Since the pixels in the image were generated at this resolution, the physical dimensions of the image can be calculated from the pixel dimensions and the image resolution. It is then a simple matter for software that displays the image to ensure that it appears at its natural size, by scaling it by a factor of *device resolution/image resolution*. For example, if a photograph measured 6 inches by 4 inches, and it was scanned at 600 dpi, its bitmap would be 3600 by 2400 pixels in size. Displayed in a simple-minded fashion on a 72 dpi monitor, the image would appear to measure 50 inches by 33.3 inches (and, presumably, require scroll bars). To make it appear at the desired size, it must be scaled by 72/600 = 0.12, which, as you can easily verify, reduces it to its original size.

If an image's resolution is lower than that of the device on which it is to be displayed, it must be scaled up, a process which will require the interpolation of pixels. This can never be done without loss of image

[†] Many readers will probably have had the experience of seeing an image appear on screen at a sensible size, only to be printed the size of a postage stamp.

interpolation =

quality, so you should try to ensure that any images you use in your multimedia productions have an image resolution at least as high as that of the monitors on which you expect your work to be viewed.

If, on the other hand, the image's resolution is higher than that of the output device, pixels must be discarded when the image is scaled down for display at its natural size. This process is called *downsampling.* Here we come to an apparent paradox. The subjective quality of a high resolution image that has been downsampled for display at a low resolution will often be better than that of an image whose resolution is equal to the display resolution. For example, when a 600 dpi scan is displayed on screen at 72 dpi, it will often look better than a 72 dpi scan, even though there are no more pixels in the displayed image. This is because the scanner samples discrete points; at lower resolutions these points are more widely spaced than at high resolutions, so some image detail is missed. The high resolution scan contains information that is absent in the low resolution one, and this information can be used when the image is downsampled for display. For example, the colour of a pixel might be determined as the average of the values in a corresponding block, instead of the single point value that is available in the low resolution scan. This can result in smoother colour gradients and less jagged lines for some images. The technique of sampling an image (or any other signal) at a higher resolution than that at which it is ultimately displayed is called *oversampling*.

Figure 5.1 High and low resolution images

Figure 5.1 illustrates the effect of resolution on image quality. The picture on the left has been taken from a high-resolution scan; the picture on the right has been upsampled (to the print resolution of the book) from a screen-resolution version of the same image.

The apparently superior quality of oversampled images will only be obtained if the software performing the downsampling does so in a sufficiently sophisticated way to make use of the extra information available in the high-resolution image. Web browsers are notoriously poor at downsampling, and usually produce a result no better than that which would be obtained by starting from a low-resolution original. For that reason, images intended for the World Wide Web should be downsampled in advance using a program such as Photoshop.

We describe resampling in more detail later in this chapter, when we consider applying geometrical transformations to bitmapped images.

Information once discarded can never be regained. This would seem to imply that one should always keep high resolution bitmapped images, downsampling only when it is necessary for display purposes or to prepare a version of the image for display software that does not downsample well. However, the disadvantage of high resolution images soon becomes clear. They contain more pixels and thus occupy more disk space and take longer to transfer over networks. The size of an image increases as the square of the resolution, so, despite the possible gains in quality that might come from using high resolutions, in practice we more often need to use the *lowest* resolution we can get away with. This must be at least as good as that of an average monitor if the displayed quality is to be acceptable. Even at resolutions as low as 72 or 96 ppi, image files can become unmanageable, especially over networks. To reduce their size without unacceptable loss of quality we must use techniques of data compression.

Image Compression

Consider again Figure 3.3. We stated on page 75 that its bitmap representation required 48 kilobytes. This estimate was based on the assumption that the image was stored as an array, with three bytes per pixel. In order to display the image or manipulate it, it would have to be represented in this form, but when we only wish to record the values of its pixels, for storage or transmission over a network, we can use a much more compact data representation. Instead of storing the value of each pixel explicitly, we could instead store a value, followed by a count to indicate a number of consecutive pixels of that value. For example, the first row consists of 128 pixels, all of the same colour, so instead of using 384 bytes to store that row, we could use just four, three to store the value corresponding to that colour, another to record the number of occurrences. Indeed, if there was no advantage to be gained from preserving the identity of individual rows, we could go further, since the first 2580 pixels of this particular image are all the same colour. These are followed by a run of 88 pixels of another colour, which again can be stored using a count and a colour value in four bytes, instead of as 264 separate bytes all of the same value.

This simple technique of replacing a run of consecutive pixels of the same colour by a single copy of the colour value and a count of the number of pixels in the run is called *run-length encoding (RLE)*. In common with other methods of compression, it requires some computation in order to achieve a saving in space. Another feature it shares with other methods of compression is that its effectiveness depends on the image that is being compressed. In this example, a large saving in storage can be achieved, because the image is extremely simple and consists of large areas of the same colour, which give rise to long runs of identical pixel values. If, instead, the image had consisted of alternating pixels of the two colours, applying RLE in a naive fashion would have led to an increase in the storage requirement, since each 'run' would have had a length of one, which would have to be recorded in addition to the pixel value. More realistically, images with continuously blended tones will not give rise to runs that can be efficiently encoded, whereas images with areas of flat colour will.

It is a general property of any compression scheme that there will be some data for which the 'compressed' version is actually larger than the uncompressed. This must be so: if we had an algorithm that could always achieve some compression, no matter what input data it was given, it would be possible to apply it to its own output to achieve extra compression, and then to the new output, and so on, arbitrarily many times, so that any data could be compressed down to a single byte (assuming we do not deal with smaller units of data). Even though this is clearly absurd, from time to time people claim to have developed such an algorithm, and have even been granted patents for the process.

Run-length encoding has an important property: it is always possible to decompress run-length encoded data and retrieve an exact copy of the original data as it was before compression. If we take the 48 kilobyte array representing Figure 3.3 and apply RLE compression to it, we will be able to apply an obvious decompression algorithm to the result to get back the original array. RLE is an example of a *lossless* compression technique, since no information is lost during

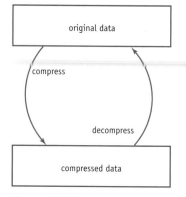

Figure 5.2 Lossless compression

a compression/decompression cycle (see Figure 5.2). In contrast, *lossy* compression techniques work by discarding some information during the compression process. Once discarded, information can never be retrieved, so when data that has been lossily compressed is decompressed, the result is only an approximation to the original data (see Figure 5.3). Lossy compression is well suited to data, such as images and sound, that originates in analogue form, since, as we saw in Chapter 2, its digital representation is an approximation anyway. Clever design of compression algorithms can ensure that only data that is insignificant to perception of the image or sound is discarded, so that substantial savings in storage can be achieved with little or no perceived loss in quality. However, because information is lost during every compression/decompression cycle, if data is repeatedly compressed, decompressed and then compressed again, its quality will progressively deteriorate.

A full description of the mechanics of compression lies beyond the scope of this book; we will just introduce the main algorithms you are likely to encounter.

Lossless Compression

RLE is the simplest lossless compression algorithm to understand, but it is far from the most effective. The more sophisticated lossless algorithms you are likely to encounter fall into two classes. Algorithms of the first class work by re-encoding data so that the most frequent values occupy the fewest bits. For example, if an image uses 256 colours, each pixel would normally occupy eight bits (see Chapter 6). If, however, we could assign codes of different lengths to the colours, so that the code for the most common colour was only a single bit long, two-bit codes were used for the next most frequent colours, and so on, a saving in space would be achieved for most images. This approach to encoding, using *variable-length codes,* dates back to the earliest work on data compression and information theory, carried out in the late 1940s. The best known algorithm belonging to this class is *Huffman coding.*[†]

Although Huffman coding and its derivatives are still used as part of other, more complex, compression techniques, since the late 1970s variable-length coding schemes have been superseded to a large extent by *dictionary-based* compression schemes. Dictionary-based compression works by constructing a table, or dictionary, into which are entered strings of bytes (not necessarily corresponding to characters) that are encountered in the input data; all occurrences of a string

[†] Computer science students will find Huffman coding described in many of their books on data structures, because its implementation provides an interesting example of the use of trees.

are then replaced by a pointer into the dictionary. The process is similar to the tokenization of names carried out by the lexical analyser of a compiler using a symbol table. In contrast to variable-length coding schemes, dictionary-based schemes use fixed-length *codes*, but these point to variable-length *strings* in the dictionary. The effectiveness of this type of compression depends on choosing the strings to enter in the dictionary so that a saving of space is produced by replacing them by their codes. Ideally, the dictionary entries should be long strings that occur frequently.

Two techniques for constructing dictionaries and using them for compression were described in papers published in 1977 and 1978 by two researchers called Abraham Lempel and Jacob Ziv, thus the techniques are usually called LZ77 and LZ78. A variation of LZ78, devised by another researcher, Terry Welch, and therefore known as LZW compression, is one of the most widely used compression methods, being the basis of the Unix **compress** utility and of GIF files. The difference between LZ77 and LZ78 lies in the way in which the dictionary is constructed, while LZW is really just an improved implementation for LZ77. LZW compression has one drawback: as we mentioned in Chapter 3, it is patented by Unisys, who charge a licence fee for its use. As a result of this, the compression method used in PNG files is based on the legally unencumbered LZ77, as are several widely used general-purpose compression programs, such as PKZIP.

JPEG Compression

Lossless compression can be applied to any sort of data; it is the *only* sort of compression that can be applied to certain sorts, such as binary executable programs, spreadsheet data, or text, since corruption of even one bit of such data may invalidate it. Image data, though, can tolerate a certain amount of data loss, so lossy compression can be used effectively for images. The most important lossy image compression technique is *JPEG compression*. JPEG stands for the Joint Photographic Experts Group, which draws attention to a significant feature of JPEG compression: it is best suited to photographs and similar images which are characterized by fine detail and continuous tones – the same characteristics as bitmapped images exhibit in general.

In Chapter 2, we considered the brightness or colour values of an image as a signal, which could be decomposed into its constituent frequencies. One way of envisaging this is to forget that the pixel values stored in an image denote colours, but merely consider them

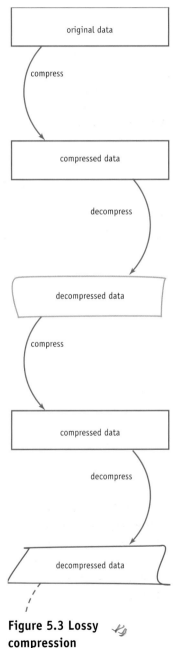

Figure 5.3 Lossy compression

Figure 5.4 Pixel values interpreted as height

as the values of some variable z; each pixel gives a z value at its x and y coordinates, so the image defines a three-dimensional shape. Figure 5.4 shows the iris image from Chapter 3, rendered as a 3-D surface – first as a wire frame, then as a landscape to help you visualize the topography – using its brightness values to control the height. Such a shape can be considered as a complex 3-D waveform. We also explained that any waveform can be transformed into the frequency domain using the Fourier Transform operation. Finally, we pointed out that the high frequency components are associated with abrupt changes in intensity. An additional fact, based on extensive experimental evidence, is that people do not perceive the effect of high frequencies very accurately, especially not in colour images.

Up until now, we have considered the frequency domain representation only as a way of thinking about the properties of a signal. JPEG compression works by actually transforming an image into its frequency components. This is done, not by computing the Fourier Transform, but using a related operation called the *Discrete Cosine Transform (DCT)*. Although the DCT is defined differently from the Fourier Transform, and has some different properties, it too analyses a signal into its frequency components. In computational terms, it takes an array of pixels and produces an array of coefficients, representing the amplitude of the frequency components in the image. Since we start with a two-dimensional image, whose intensity can vary in both the x and y directions, we end up with a two-dimensional array of coefficients, corresponding to spatial frequencies in these two directions. This array will be the same size as the image's array of pixels.

Applying a DCT operation to an image of any size is computationally expensive (the time taken is proportional to the square of the image's size in pixels), so it is only with the widespread availability of powerful processors that it has been practical to perform this sort of compression – and, more importantly, decompression – without the aid of dedicated hardware. Even now, it remains impractical to apply DCT to an entire image at once. Instead, images are divided into 8×8 pixel squares, each of which is transformed separately.

Transforming an image into the frequency domain does not, in itself, perform any compression. It does, however, change the data into a form which can be compressed in a way that minimizes the perceptible effect of discarding information, because the frequency components are now explicitly separated. This allows information about the high frequencies, which do not contribute much to the perceived quality of the image, to be discarded. This is done by distinguishing fewer different possible values for higher frequency components. If, for example, the value produced by the DCT for each frequency could range from 0 to 255, the lowest frequency coefficients might be allowed to have any integer value within this range; slightly higher frequencies might only be allowed to take on values divisible by 4, while the highest frequencies might only be allowed to have the value 0 or 128. Putting this another way, the different frequencies are quantized to different numbers of levels, with fewer levels being used for high frequencies. In JPEG compression, the number of quantization levels to be used for each frequency coefficient can be specified separately in a quantization matrix, containing a value for each coefficient.

This quantization process reduces the space needed to store the image in two ways. First, after quantization, many components will end up with zero coefficients. Second, fewer bits are needed to store the non-zero coefficients. To take advantage of the redundancy which has thus been generated in the data representation, two lossless compression methods are applied to the array of quantized coefficients. Zeroes are run-length encoded; Huffman coding is applied to the remaining values. In order to maximize the length of the runs of zeroes, the coefficients are processed in what is called the *zig-zag sequence*, as shown in Figure 5.5. This is effective because the frequencies increase as we move away from the top left corner of the array in both directions. In other words, the perceptible information in the image is concentrated in the top left part of the array, and the likelihood is that the bottom right part will be full of zeroes. The zig-zag sequence is thus likely to

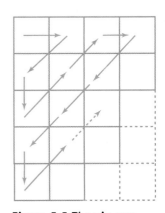

Figure 5.5 The zig-zag sequence

encounter long runs of zeroes, which would be broken up if the array were traversed more conventionally by rows or columns.

Decompressing JPEG data is done by reversing the compression process. The runs are expanded and the Huffman-encoded coefficients are decompressed and then an *Inverse Discrete Cosine Transform* is applied to take the data back from the frequency domain into the spatial domain, where the values can once again be treated as pixels in an image. The inverse DCT is defined very similarly to the DCT itself; the computation of the inverse transform requires the same amount of time as that of the forward transform, so JPEG compression and decompression take roughly the same time (on the same machine). Note that there is no 'inverse quantization' step. The information that was lost during quantization is gone forever, which is why the decompressed image only approximates the original. Generally, though, the approximation is a good one.

The approximation is such a good one that it is not possible to illustrate the effect of JPEG compression here – at the resolution and size of images in this book, even the lowest quality JPEGs of real images were almost indistinguishable from their originals, except at extreme magnification, where the JPEG artefacts are obscured by pixellation. On screen, at screen resolution, however, the effects can sometimes be seen quite clearly.

One highly useful feature of JPEG compression is that it is possible to control the degree of compression, and thus the quality of the compressed image, by altering the values in the quantization matrix. Programs that implement JPEG compression allow you to choose a quality setting, so that you can choose a suitable compromise between image quality and compression. You should be aware that, even at the highest quality settings, JPEG compression is still lossy in the literal sense that the decompressed image will not be an exact bit-for-bit duplicate of the original. It will often, however, be visually indistinguishable, but that is not what we mean by 'lossless'.

The JPEG standard does define a lossless mode, but this uses a completely different algorithm from the DCT-based method used by lossy JPEG. Lossless JPEG compression has never been popular. It has been superseded by a new standard JPEG-LS, but this, too, shows little sign of being widely adopted. Yet another JPEG standard was adopted at the end of 2000: JPEG2000 aims to be the image compression standard for the new century (or at least the first ten years of it). The ISO's call for contributions to the JPEG2000 effort described its aims as follows: "[...] to create a new image coding system for different types of still images (bi-level, gray-level, color) with different characteristics (natural images, scientific, medical, remote sensing imagery, text, rendered graphics, etc.) allowing different imaging models (client/server, real-time transmission, image library archival, limited buffer and bandwidth resources, etc.) preferably within a unified system." JPEG2000 uses a technique called wavelet compression to achieve some of these aims, at the expense of a more complex compression procedure. At the time of writing (late 2003) the new standard shows no signs of replacing JPEG in the immediate future – JPEG2000 is not implemented in any widely available Web browser, for example.

JPEG compression is highly effective when applied to the sort of images for which it is designed: photographic and scanned images with continuous tones. Such images can be compressed to as little as 5% of their original size without apparent loss of quality. Lossless compression techniques are nothing like as effective on such images. Still higher levels of compression can be obtained by using a lower quality setting, i.e. by using coarser quantization that discards more information. When this is done, the boundaries of the 8×8 squares to which the DCT is applied tend to become visible on screen, because the discontinuities between them mean that different frequency components are discarded in each square. At low compression levels (i.e. high quality settings) this does not matter, since enough information is retained for the common features of adjacent squares to produce appropriately similar results, but as more and more information is discarded, the common features become lost and the boundaries show up.

Such unwanted features in a compressed image are called *compression artefacts*. Other artefacts may arise when an image containing sharp edges is compressed by JPEG. Here, the smoothing that is the essence of JPEG compression is to blame; sharp edges come out blurred. This is rarely a problem with the photographically originated material for which JPEG is intended, but can be a problem if images created on a computer are compressed. In particular, if text, especially small text, occurs as part of an image, JPEG is likely to blur the edges, often making the text unreadable. For images with many sharp edges, JPEG should be avoided. Instead, images should be saved in a format such as PNG, which uses lossless LZ77 compression.

Image Manipulation

A bitmapped image explicitly stores a value for every pixel, so we can, if we wish, alter the value of any pixel or group of pixels to change the image. The sheer number of pixels in most images means that editing them individually is both time-consuming and confusing – how is one to judge the effect on the appearance of the whole image of particular changes to certain pixels? Or which pixels must be altered, and how, in order to sharpen the fuzzy edges in an out-of-focus photograph? In order for image editing to be convenient, it is necessary that operations be provided at a higher level than that of altering a single pixel. Many useful operations can be described by analogy with pre-existing techniques for altering photographic images, in particular the use of filters and masks.

Before we describe how images can be manipulated, we ought first to examine why one might wish to manipulate them. There are two broad reasons: one is to correct deficiencies in an image, caused by poor equipment or technique used in its creation or digitization; the other is to create images that are difficult or impossible to make naturally. An example of the former type is the removal of 'red-eye', the red glow apparently emanating from the eyes of a person whose portrait has been taken face-on with a camera using a flash set too close to the lens.† Consumer-oriented image manipulation programs often provide commands that encapsulate a sequence of manipulations to perform common tasks, such as red-eye removal, with a single key stroke. The manipulations performed for the second reason generally fall into the category of special effects, such as creating a glow around an object. Image manipulation programs, such as Photoshop, generally supply a set of built-in filters and effects, and a kit of tools for making selections and low-level adjustments. Photoshop uses an open architecture that allows third parties to produce plug-ins which provide additional effects and tools – the development of Photoshop plug-ins has become an industry in its own right, and many other programs can now use them.

Many of the manipulations commonly performed on bitmapped images are concerned purely with preparing digital images for print, and are therefore not relevant to multimedia. An operation that is typical of multimedia work, on the other hand, is the changing of an image's resolution or size (which, as we saw previously, are essentially equivalent operations). Very often, images which are required for display on a monitor originate at higher resolutions and must be

WHY YOU MIGHT WANT TO MANIPULATE AN IMAGE

† Red-eye is caused by light reflecting off the subject's retinas.

downsampled; an image's size may need adjusting to fit a layout, such as a Web page.

Photoshop is, without doubt, the leading application for image manipulation, being a *de facto* industry standard, and we will use it as our example. There are other programs, though, in particular a powerful package known as *The Gimp*, which has similar capabilities and a similar set of tools to Photoshop's, and is distributed under an open software licence for Unix systems. Both of these programs include many features concerned with preparing images for print, which are not relevant to multimedia. A number of packages, such as Adobe's ImageReady and Macromedia's Fireworks, which are dedicated to preparation of images for the World Wide Web, omit print-oriented features, replacing them with others more appropriate to work on the Web, such as facilities for slicing an image into smaller pieces to accelerate downloading, or adding hotspots to create an 'image map' (see Chapter 12).

Selections, Masks and Alpha Channels

As we have repeatedly stressed, a bitmapped image is not stored as a collection of separate objects; it is just an array of pixels. Even if we can look at the picture and see a square or a circle, say, we cannot select that shape when we are editing the image with a program, the way we could if it were a vector image, because the shape's identity is not part of the information that is explicitly available to the program; it is something our eyes and brain have identified. Some other means must be employed to select parts of an image when it is being manipulated by a mere computer program.

Ironically, perhaps, some of the tools that are used to make selections from bitmapped images are more or less the same tools that are used to draw shapes in vector graphics. Selections may be made by drawing around an area, much as a traditional paste-up artist would cut out a shape from a printed image using a scalpel. The simplest selection tools are the rectangular and elliptical *marquee* tools, which let you select an area by dragging out a rectangle or ellipse, just as you would draw these shapes in a drawing program. It is important to realize that you are not drawing, though; you are defining an area within the image.

More often than not, the area you wish to select will not be a neat rectangle or ellipse. To accommodate irregular shapes, thinly disguised versions of the other standard drawing tools may be used: the lasso tool is a less powerful version of Illustrator's pencil tool, which can be used to draw freehand curves around an area to be selected; the

Figure 5.6 Selection with the magic wand

polygon lasso is like a pen tool used to draw polylines, rather than curves; a fully-fledged Bézier drawing pen is also available. These tools allow selections to be outlined with considerable precision and flexibility, although their use can be laborious. To ease the task of making selections, two tools are available that make use of pixel values to help define the selected area. These are the magic wand and the magnetic lasso.

The magic wand is used to select areas on the basis of their colour. With this tool selected, clicking on the image causes all pixels adjacent to the cursor which are similar in colour to the pixel under the cursor to be selected. Figure 5.6 shows an example of the magic wand selecting a highly irregular shape. The wand was clicked in the dark area of foliage in the top image; the selected area is outlined with a moving marquee, as shown in the detail in the middle image; the selected area can then be removed from its background, as shown at the bottom. The tolerance, that is, the amount by which a colour may differ but still be considered sufficiently similar to include in the selection, may be specified.

The magnetic lasso works on a different principle. Like the other lasso tools, it is dragged around the area to be selected, but instead of simply following the outline drawn by the user, it adjusts itself so that the outline snaps to edges within a specified distance of the cursor. Any sufficiently large change in contrast is considered to be an edge. Both the distance within which edges are detected and the degree of contrast variation that is considered to constitute an edge may be specified. Where an image has well-defined edges, for example, both of these can be set to a high value, so that drawing roughly round an object will cause it to be selected as the outline snaps to the high contrast edges. Where the edges are less well defined, it will be necessary to allow a lower contrast level to indicate an edge, and consequently the outline will have to be drawn with more care, using a narrower detection width. Figure 5.7 shows an example: note how it has been possible to select the butterfly's fine antennae.

Once a selection has been made, using any of the tools just described, any changes you make to the image, such as applying filters, are restricted to the pixels within the selected area. Another way of describing this is to say that the selection defines a *mask* – the area that is *not* selected, which is protected from any changes. Image manipulation programs allow you to store one or more masks with an image, so that a selection can be remembered and used for more than one operation – an ordinary selection is ephemeral, and is lost as soon as a different one is made.

The technique of masking off parts of an image has long been used by artists and photographers, who use physical masks and stencils to keep out light or paint. A cardboard stencil, for example, either completely allows paint through or completely stops it. We could store a digital mask with similar 'all or nothing' behaviour by using a single bit for each pixel in the image, setting it to one for all the masked-out pixels, and to zero for those in the selection. Thus, the mask is itself an array of pixels, and we can think of it as being another image. If just one bit is used for each pixel, this image will be purely monochromatic; by analogy with photographic masks, the white parts of the image are considered transparent, the black ones opaque. Figure 5.8 shows the selection from Figure 5.7 as a one-bit mask.

Digital masks have properties which are difficult to realize with physical media. By using more than one bit, so that the mask becomes a greyscale image, we can specify different degrees of transparency. For reasons which will be elaborated on in Chapter 6, a greyscale mask of this sort is often called an *alpha channel*. Any painting, filtering or other modifications made to pixels covered by semi-transparent areas of the mask will be applied in a degree proportional to the value stored in the alpha channel. It is common to use eight bits for each pixel of a mask, allowing for 256 different transparency values.

Figure 5.7 Selection with the magnetic lasso

To return to the analogy of a stencil, an alpha channel is like a stencil made out of a material that can allow varying amounts of paint to pass through it, depending on the transparency value at each point. One use for such a stencil would be to produce a soft edge around a cut-out shape. In a similar way, the edge of a selection can be 'feathered', which means that the hard transition from black to white in the alpha channel is replaced by a gradient, passing through intermediate grey values, which correspond to partial masking. Any effects that are applied will fade over this transitional zone, instead of stopping abruptly at the boundary. A less drastic way of exploiting alpha channels is to apply anti-aliasing to the edge of a mask, reducing the jagged effect that may otherwise occur. Although anti-aliasing resembles feathering over a very narrow region, the intention is quite different: feathering is supposed to be visible, causing effects to fade out, whereas anti-aliasing is intended to unobtrusively conceal the jagged edges of the selection.

Figure 5.8 Mask formed by the magnetic lasso selection

Normally, a layer in a Photoshop image obscures everything underneath it. However, every layer may have an associated *layer mask*, which is essentially an alpha channel applied to that layer. When two layers are overlaid, if the upper layer has a mask applied, the lower layer will show through the masked-out parts of the upper layer. In the case of a one-bit mask, this means that the lower layer will show through where the mask is black. If the layer mask is a greyscale image, the lower layer will partially show through the grey areas of the mask. The value p of a pixel in the resulting composited image is computed as $p = \alpha p_1 + (1-\alpha)p_2$, where p_1 and p_2 are the values of the corresponding pixels in the two layers, and α is normalized to lie between 0 and 1 – that is, if the α value is stored in 8 bits we divide it by 255.

Layer mask channels can be used to produce a variety of compositing effects. Figure 5.9 illustrates one possibility, using a one-bit layer mask. At the top of the figure are three original images. The tricolour was resized and pasted into a layer on top of the map of Paris. A mask was constructed by painstakingly selecting the Eiffel Tower from the remaining photograph using the magic wand. Photoshop makes it possible to save a selection and then load it into another image, so this cut-out, as shown in the middle of the bottom row of Figure 5.9, was loaded as the layer mask for the tricolour layer, producing the

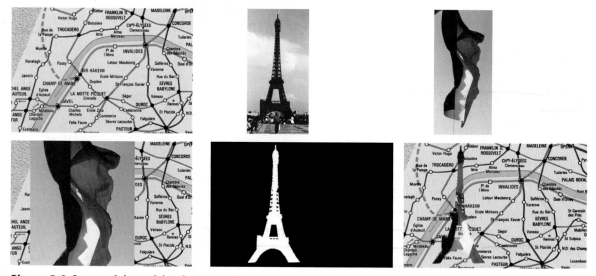

Figure 5.9 Compositing with a layer mask

composite shown in the bottom right corner, where the mask has allowed the map to show through except inside the tower. (This is not the only way to achieve this effect: see Exercise 8.)

A less elaborate example, using a greyscale layer mask, is illustrated in Figure 5.10. Here, a colour and a greyscale version of the same photograph, shown at the top, have been placed on separate layers. A layer mask was constructed by creating a diagonal linear gradient, as shown in the bottom left corner. When this mask is applied, the resulting composite image, at the bottom right, shows colour gradually fading into the picture.

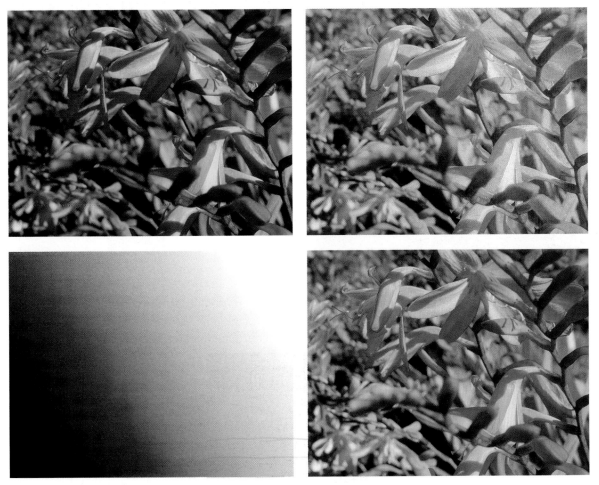

Figure 5.10 Blending with an alpha channel mask

Pixel Point Processing

Image processing is performed by computing a new value for each pixel in an image. The simplest methods compute a pixel's new value solely on the basis of its old value, without regard to any other pixel. So for a pixel with value p, we compute a new value $p' = f(p)$, where f is called the *mapping function*. Such functions perform *pixel point processing*. A simple, if only rarely useful, example of pixel point processing is the construction of a negative from a greyscale image. Here, $f(p) = W - p$, where W is the pixel value representing white.

The most sophisticated pixel point processing is concerned with colour correction and alteration, described fully in Chapter 6. Here, we will only consider the brightness and contrast alterations that are the typical applications of pixel point processing to greyscale images. Colour processing is an extension – although not a trivial one – of these greyscale adjustments. Once again, we will use Photoshop's tools to provide a concrete example, but any image editing software will offer the same functions, with roughly the same interface.

The crudest adjustments are made with the *brightness* and *contrast* sliders, which work like the corresponding controls on a monitor or television set. Brightness adjusts the value of each pixel up or down uniformly, so increasing the brightness makes every pixel lighter and decreasing it makes every pixel darker. Contrast is a little more subtle: it adjusts the range of values, either enhancing or reducing the difference between the lightest and darkest areas of the image. Increasing contrast makes the light areas very light and the dark areas very dark; decreasing it moves all values towards an intermediate grey. In terms of mapping functions, both of these adjustments produce a linear relationship that would be represented as a straight line on a graph: adjusting the brightness changes the intercept between the line and the y-axis; adjusting the contrast alters the gradient of the line.

More control over the shape of the mapping function is provided by the *levels dialogue*, which allows you to move the endpoints of a linear mapping function individually, thereby setting the white and black levels in the image. Graphically, these adjustments stretch or shrink the mapping function horizontally and vertically. To help with choosing suitable levels, a display called the *image histogram* is used. This is a histogram showing the distribution of pixel values: the horizontal axis represents the possible values (from 0 to 255 in an 8-bit greyscale image), the bars show the number of pixels set to each value. The histograms are displayed in the levels dialogue, with two sets of sliders below them, as shown in Figure 5.11. The upper set controls the range of input values. The slider at the left controls the pixel value that will be mapped to black, so, in graphical terms, it moves the intercept of the mapping function's line along the *x*-axis. The slider at the right controls the pixel value that is mapped to white, so it moves the top end of the line along the horizontal line corresponding to the maximum pixel value. The lower slider controls affect the output values in a similar way, i.e. they determine the pixel values that will be used for black and white, so they move the endpoints of the line up and down. In order to spread the range of tonal values evenly across the image, the input sliders are moved so that they line up with the lowest and highest values that have a non-zero number of pixels shown in the histogram. Moving beyond these points will compress or expand the dynamic range artificially.

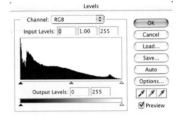

Figure 5.11 Histogram in the Levels dialogue

So far, all the adjustments have maintained a straight-line relationship between old and new pixel values. The third slider that you can see on the upper levels control in Figure 5.11 allows you to produce a more flexible correspondence between original and modified pixel values, by adjusting a third point, corresponding to the mid-tones in the image. If an image's brightness is concentrated in a particular range, you can move the midpoint slider under the corresponding point on the histogram, so that the brightness values are adjusted to put this range in the centre of the available scale of values.

Figure 5.12 shows the effect that level adjustments can achieve in bringing out detail that has been lost in a poorly exposed photograph. The original image, shown at the top left, was shot from inside the room, using the auto-exposure feature of a digital camera. Because of the high contrast between the interior and the view through the windows, the result is disastrous. The histogram of the image is shown next to it, and the uneven light distribution can be clearly seen. This particular problem cannot be solved by adjusting the levels of the whole photograph; different adjustments are needed for the over-exposed exterior and the under-exposed interior, so the first step was to create masks to separate the two problems.

The mask used to isolate the light areas is shown at the top right of Figure 5.12. The second histogram in the margin at the left shows the distribution of pixel values in these areas; you can also see the adjustments that were made to produce the image on the left of the middle row of Figure 5.12. The mask and before and after histograms for the dark areas are shown similarly, with the final adjusted image and its

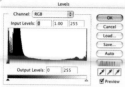

Histogram of original image

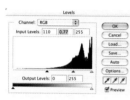

Histogram of light areas

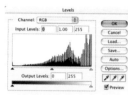

Histogram of light areas after adjustment

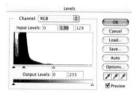

Histogram of dark areas

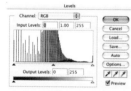

Histogram of dark areas after adjustment

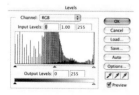

Histogram of complete image after adjustment

Original image

Mask for light areas

Image after adjusting light areas

Mask for dark areas

Image after adjusting light and dark areas

Figure 5.12 Adjusting levels

histogram at the bottom. This final image is somewhat grainy (hence the spikiness of the adjusted histograms), because of the low light levels, but the amount of detail that the adjustments have brought out is remarkable.

All of the brightness and contrast adjustment facilities described so far can be considered as making specialized alterations to the graph of the mapping function f to achieve particular commonly required adjustments to the values of individual pixels. In Photoshop, it is possible to take detailed control of this graph in the *curves dialogue*, where it can be reshaped by dragging control points, or completely redrawn with a pencil tool. The almost complete freedom to map grey levels to new values that this provides permits some strange effects, but it also makes it easy to apply subtle corrections to incorrectly exposed photographs, or to compensate for improperly calibrated scanners.

Before any adjustments are made, the curve is a straight line with slope equal to one: the output and input are identical, f is an identity function. Arbitrary reshaping of the curve will cause artificial highlights and shadows. Figure 5.13 shows a single image with three different curves applied to it. The first adjustment attempts to turn the original sunset scene into a daylit landscape. (For simplicity's sake we applied the adjustment to the entire image. Better results would be obtained by masking and making different adjustments to the light and dark areas, as we did in the earlier levels example.) The second adjustment illustrates what happens if you reflect the original straight line: the colours are inverted. Finally, we show the sort of effects that unsystematic reshaping of the curve will produce. More restrained changes are used to perform tonal adjustments with much more control than the simple contrast and brightness sliders provide. For example, an S-shaped curve such as the one illustrated in Figure 5.14 is often used to increase the contrast of an image: the midpoint is fixed and the shadows are darkened by pulling down the quarter-point, while the highlights are lightened by pulling up the three-quarter-point. The gentle curvature means that, while the overall contrast is increased, the total tonal range is maintained and there are no abrupt changes in brightness.

Pixel Group Processing

A second class of processing transformations works by computing each pixel's new value as a function not just of its old value, but also of the values of neighbouring pixels. Functions of this sort perform *pixel group processing*, which produces qualitatively different effects from the pixel point processing operations we described in the preceding section. In terms of the concepts we introduced in Chapter 2, these operations remove or attenuate certain spatial frequencies in an image. Such *filtering* operations can be implemented as operations that combine the value of a pixel with those of its neighbours, because the relative values of a pixel and its neighbours incorporate some information about the way the brightness or colour is changing in the region of that pixel. A suitably defined operation that combines

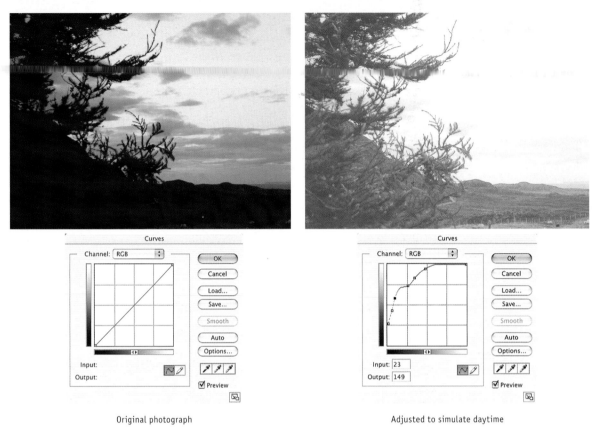

Original photograph   Adjusted to simulate daytime

Figure 5.13 Curves adjustments

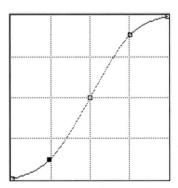

Figure 5.14 The S-curve for enhancing contrast

pixel values alters these relationships, modifying the frequency make-up of the image. The mathematics behind this sort of processing is complicated, but the outcome is a family of operations with a simple structure.

It turns out that, instead of transforming our image to the frequency domain (for example, using a DCT) and performing a filtering operation by selecting a range of frequency components, we can perform the filtering in the spatial domain – that is, on the original image data – by computing a weighted average of the pixels and its neighbours. The weights applied to each pixel value determine the particular filtering operation, and thus the effect that is produced on the image's appearance. A particular filter can be specified in the form of a two-dimensional array of those weights. For example, if we were to apply a filter by taking the value of a pixel and all eight of its immediate neighbours, dividing them each by nine and adding them together

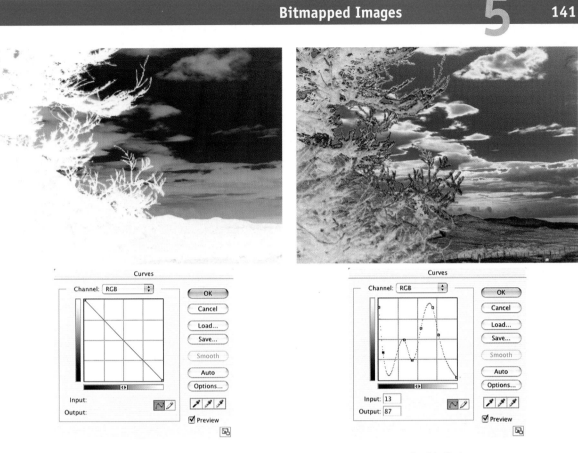

Reversed   Special effects

to obtain the new value for the pixel, we could write the filter in the form:

$$1/9 \quad 1/9 \quad 1/9$$
$$1/9 \quad 1/9 \quad 1/9$$
$$1/9 \quad 1/9 \quad 1/9$$

The array of weights is called a *convolution mask* and the set of pixels used in the computation is called the *convolution kernel* (because the equivalent of the multiplication operation that performs filtering in the frequency domain is an operation in the spatial domain called convolution).

Generally, if a pixel has coordinates (x, y), so that it has neighbours at $(x-1, y+1)$, $(x, y+1) \ldots (x, y-1)$, $(x+1, y-1)$, and we apply a filter with a convolution mask in the form:

$$
\begin{array}{ccc}
a & b & c \\
d & e & f \\
g & h & i
\end{array}
$$

the value p' computed for the new pixel at (x, y) is

$$
\begin{aligned}
p' = \ & ap_{x-1,y+1} + bp_{x,y+1} + cp_{x+1,y+1} \\
& + dp_{x-1,y} + ep_{x,y} + fp_{x+1,y} \\
& + gp_{x-1,y-1} + hp_{x,y-1} + ip_{x+1,y-1}
\end{aligned}
$$

where $p_{x,y}$ is the value of the pixel at (x, y), and so on. You can think of the pixels of the original image passing through the convolution mask nine at a time as a convolution kernel, picking up their weights as they pass through, and then being added together to produce the value for the pixel at the middle of the 3×3 pixel block.

Convolution is a computationally intensive process. As the formula just given shows, with a 3×3 convolution kernel, computing a new value for each pixel requires nine multiplications and eight additions. For a modestly sized image of 480×320 pixels, the total number of operations will therefore be 1382400 multiplications and 1228800 additions, i.e. over two and a half million operations. Convolution masks need not be only three pixels square – although they are usually square, with an odd number of pixels on each side – and the larger the mask, and hence the kernel, the more computation is required.[†]

† Applying certain filters, particularly Gaussian blur (described below), to a large image file is often used to provide 'real world' benchmarking data for new computers.

This is all very well, but what are the visible effects of spatial filtering? Consider again the simple convolution mask comprising nine values equal to 1/9. If all nine pixels being convolved have the same value, let us say 117, then the filter has no effect: $117/9 \times 9 = 117$. That is, over regions of constant colour or brightness, this filter leaves pixels alone. However, suppose it is applied at a region including a sharp vertical edge. The convolution kernel might have the following values:

$$
\begin{array}{ccc}
117 & 117 & 27 \\
117 & 117 & 27 \\
117 & 117 & 27
\end{array}
$$

then the new value computed for the centre pixel will be 105. Moving further into the lighter region, to an area that looks like this:

117 27   27
117 27   27
117 27   27

gives a new pixel value of 57. So the hard edge from 117 to 27 has been replaced by a more gradual transition via the intermediate values 105 and 57. The effect is seen as a *blurring*. One way of thinking about what has happened is to imagine that the edges have been softened by rubbing together the colour values of the pixels, in the same way as you blur edges in a pastel drawing by rubbing them with your finger. An alternative view, based on the concepts of signal processing, is that this operation produces a smoothing effect on the spatial waveform of the image, by filtering out high frequencies. (Engineers would refer to the operation as a *low pass filter*.)

Blurring is often used in retouching scans. It is useful for mitigating the effects of digital artefacts, such as the jagged edges produced by undersampling, Moiré patterns, and the blockiness resulting from excessive JPEG compression.

Although the convolution mask we have just described is a classical blur filter, it produces a noticeably unnatural effect, because of the limited region over which it operates, and the all-or-nothing effect caused by the uniform coefficients. At the same time, the amount of blurring is small and fixed. A more generally useful alternative is *Gaussian blur,* where the coefficients fall off gradually from the centre of the mask, following the Gaussian 'bell curve' shown in Figure 5.15, to produce a blurring that is similar to those found in nature. The extent of the blur – that is, the width of the bell curve, and hence the number of pixels included in the convolution calculation – can be controlled. Photoshop's dialogue allows the user to specify a 'radius' value, in pixels, for the filter. A radius of 0.1 pixels produces a very subtle effect; values between 0.2 and 0.8 pixels are good for removing aliasing artefacts. Higher values are used to produce a deliberate effect. A common application of this sort is the production of drop-shadows: an object is selected, copied onto a new layer, filled with black and displaced slightly to produce the shadow. A Gaussian blur with a radius between 4 and 12 pixels applied to the shadow softens its edges to produce a more realistic effect. A radius of 100 pixels or more blurs the entire image into incoherence; one of 250 pixels (the maximum) just averages all the pixels in the area the filter is applied to. Note that the radius specified is not in fact the limit of the blurring

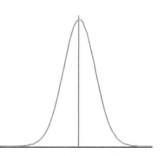

Figure 5.15 The Gaussian bell curve

effect, but a parameter that specifies the shape of the bell curve – the blurring extends well beyond the radius, but its effect is more concentrated within it, with roughly 70% of the contribution to the value of the centre pixel coming from pixels within the radius.

Figure 5.16 shows a typical application of Gaussian blur: a scanned watercolour painting has had a small blur, followed by a slight sharpening (see below), applied to remove scanning artefacts. The result is an image that closely resembles the original, with the filters themselves indiscernible – the blurriness you see is the characteristic spreading of thin watercolour and has nothing to do with the filters. In contrast, the blur in Figure 5.17, with a radius of 29 pixels, transforms the image into something quite different.

Other types of blur are directional, and can be used to indicate motion. Figure 5.18 shows radial blur with the zoom option, which gives an effect that might suggest headlong flight towards the focal point of the zoom.

Blurring is a surprisingly useful effect when applied to digitized images – you might expect blur to be an undesirable feature of an image, but it conceals their characteristic imperfections; in the case of Gaussian blur, it does this in a visually natural way. Sometimes, though, we want to do the opposite, and enhance detail by sharpening the edges in an image. A convolution mask that is often used for this purpose is:

$$
\begin{array}{ccc}
-1 & -1 & -1 \\
-1 & 9 & -1 \\
-1 & -1 & -1
\end{array}
$$

Figure 5.16 A scanned image, corrected by filtering

Figure 5.17 A large amount of Gaussian blur

This mask filters out low frequency components, leaving the higher frequencies that are associated with discontinuities. Like the simple blurring filter that removed high frequencies, this one will have no effect over regions where the pixels all have the same value. In more intuitive terms, by subtracting the values of adjacent pixels, while multiplying the central value by a large coefficient, it eliminates any value that is common to the central pixel and its surroundings, so that it isolates details from their context.

If we apply this mask to a convolution kernel where there is a gradual discontinuity, such as

$$
\begin{array}{ccc}
117 & 51 & 27 \\
117 & 51 & 27 \\
117 & 51 & 27
\end{array}
$$

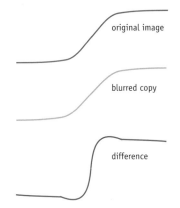

Figure 5.19 Unsharp masking

assuming that this occurs in a context where all the pixels to the left have the value 117 and those to the right 27, the new values computed for the three pixels on the central row will be 317, –75 and –45; since we cannot allow negative pixel values, the last two will be set to 0 (i.e. black). The gradual transition will have been replaced by a hard line, while the regions of constant value to either side will be left alone. A filter such as this will therefore enhance detail.

As you might guess from the example above, sharpening with a convolution mask produces harsh edges; it is more appropriate for analysing an image than for enhancing detail in a realistic way. For this task, it is more usual to use an *unsharp masking* operation. This is easiest to understand in terms of filtering operations: a blurring operation filters out high frequencies, so if we could take a

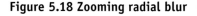

Figure 5.18 Zooming radial blur

Figure 5.20 Enhancing edges by unsharp masking

blurred image away from its original, we would be left with only the frequencies that had been removed by the blurring – the ones that correspond to sharp edges. This isn't quite what we usually want to do. We would prefer to accentuate the edges, but retain the other parts of the image as well. Unsharp masking[†] is therefore performed by constructing a copy of the original image, applying a Gaussian blur to it, and then subtracting the pixel values in this blurred mask from the corresponding values in the original multiplied by a suitable scaling factor. As you can easily verify, using a scale factor of 2 leaves areas of constant value alone. In the region of a discontinuity, though, an enhancement occurs. This is shown graphically in Figure 5.19. The top curve shows the possible change of pixel values across an edge, from a region of low intensity on the left, to one of higher intensity on the right. (We have shown a continuous change, to bring out what is happening, but any real image will be made from discrete pixels, of course.) The middle curve illustrates the effect of applying a Gaussian blur: the transition is softened, with a gentler slope that extends further into the areas of constant value. At the bottom, we show (not to scale) the result of subtracting this curve from twice the original. The slope of the transition is steeper, and overshoots at the limits of the original edge, so visually the contrast is increased. The net result is an enhancement of the edge, as illustrated in Figure 5.20, where an exaggerated amount of unsharp masking has been applied to the original image.

The amount of blur applied to the mask can be controlled, since it is just a Gaussian blur, and this affects the extent of sharpening. It is common also to allow the user to specify a threshold; where the difference between the original pixel and the mask is less than

[†] Originally a darkroom process of combining a photograph with its blurred negative.

Figure 5.21 Unsharp masking applied after extreme Gaussian blur

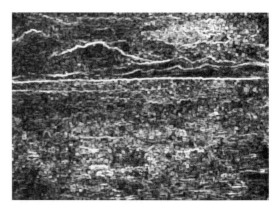

Figure 5.22 Glowing edges

the threshold value, no sharpening is performed. This prevents the operation from enhancing noise by sharpening the visible artefacts it produces. (Notice how in Figure 5.20, the grain of the watercolour paper has been emphasized by the unsharp masking.)

Although sharpening operations enhance features of an image, it should be understood that they add no information to it. On the contrary, information is actually lost, although, if the sharpening is successful, the lost information will be irrelevant or distracting. (It's more intuitively obvious that information is lost by blurring an image.) It should also be understood that although, in a sense, blurring and sharpening are opposites, they are not true inverses. That is, if you take an image, blur it and then sharpen it, or sharpen it and then blur it, you will not end up with the image you started with. The information that is lost when these operations are applied cannot be restored, although it is interesting to see features re-emerging in Figure 5.21 when Figure 5.17 is treated with an unsharp mask. This demonstrates how much information is actually preserved even under intense blurring.

Blurring and sharpening are central to the established scientific and military applications of image processing, but now that image manipulation software is also used for more creative purposes, some rather different effects are called for as well. Photoshop provides a bewildering variety of filters, and third party plug-ins add many more. Many of them are based on the type of pixel group processing we have described, with convolution masks chosen to produce effects that resemble different photographic processes or, with more or less success, the appearance of real art materials. These filters usually

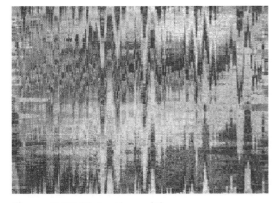

Figure 5.23 Distortion with a square wave

Figure 5.24 Twirled image

work by picking out edges or areas of the same colour, and modifying them; they are not too far removed from the more conventional blur and sharpen operations. Figure 5.22 shows the 'glowing edges' filter's effect on the seascape painting.

If you have access to Photoshop, you should investigate the Custom filter (on the Other sub-menu of the Filter menu). This allows you to construct your own convolution mask, by entering coefficients into a 5×5 matrix. The results are instructive and sometimes surprising.

Another group of filters is based on a different principle, that of moving selected pixels within an image. These produce various sorts of distortion. Figure 5.23 shows the seascape image modified by a square-wave pattern, while Figure 5.24 shows the twirl filter applied to its sharpened version from Figure 5.20, producing an entirely new image. As this example indicates, filters may be combined. It is not untypical for designers with a taste for digital effects to combine many different filters in order to generate imagery that could not easily be made any other way.

Geometrical Transformations

Scaling, translation, reflection, rotation and shearing are collectively referred to as *geometrical transformations*. As we saw in Chapter 4, these transformations can be applied to vector shapes in a very natural way, by simply moving the defining points according to geometry and then rendering the transformed model. Applying geometrical transformations to bitmapped images is less straightforward, since we have to transform every pixel, and this will often require the image to be resampled.

Nevertheless, the basic approach is a valid one: for each pixel in the image, apply the transformation using the same equations as we gave in Chapter 4 to obtain a new position in which to place that pixel in the transformed image. This suggests an algorithm which scans the original image and computes new positions for each of its pixels. An alternative, which will often be more successful, is to compute the transformed image, by finding, for each pixel, a pixel in the original image. So instead of mapping the original's coordinate space to that of the transformed image, we compute the inverse mapping. The advantage of proceeding in this direction is that we compute all the pixel values we need and no more. However, both mappings run into problems because of the finite size of pixels.

For example, suppose we wish to scale up an image by a factor s. (For simplicity, we will assume we want to use the same factor in both the vertical and horizontal directions.) Thinking about the scaling operation on vector shapes, and choosing the inverse mapping, we might suppose that all that is required is to set the pixel at coordinates (x', y') in the enlarged image to the value at $(x, y) = (x'/s, y'/s)$ in the original. In general, though, x'/s and y'/s will not be integers and hence will not identify a pixel. Looking at this operation in the opposite direction, we might instead think about taking the value of the pixel at coordinates (x, y) in our original and mapping it to $(x', y') = (sx, sy)$ in the enlargement. Again, though, unless s is an integer, this new value will sometimes fall between pixels. Even if s is an integer only some of the pixels in the new image will receive values. For example, if $s = 2$, only the even-numbered pixels in even-numbered rows of the image correspond to any pixel in the original under this mapping, leaving three-quarters of the pixels in the enlarged image undefined. This emphasizes that, in constructing a scaled-up image, we must use some interpolation method to compute values for some pixels.

However, it is not just in scaling up that interpolation is required. Whenever we apply a geometrical transformation to an image, it can send values into the gaps between pixels. Consider, for example, something as simple as moving a selected area of an image stored at 72 ppi one-fifth of an inch to the right. Even scaling an image *down* can result in the same phenomenon unless the scale factor is a whole number. It should be clear from our discussion earlier in this chapter that changing the resolution of an image leads to similar problems.

A useful way of thinking about what is going on is to imagine that we are reconstructing a continuous image, so that we can find the required values in between the pixels of our sampled image, and then resampling it. Thus, the general problem is the same as the one we introduced when we discussed digitization in Chapter 2: how to reconstruct a signal from its samples. In practice, of course, we combine the reconstruction and resampling into a single operation, because we can only work with discrete representations.

We know that, for general images which may contain arbitrarily high frequencies because of sharp edges, the reconstruction cannot be done perfectly. We also know from sampling theory that the best possible reconstruction is not feasible. All we can hope to do is approximate the reconstruction to an acceptable degree of accuracy by using some method of *interpolation* to deduce the intervening

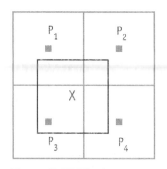

Figure 5.25 Pixel
interpolation

values on the basis of the stored pixels. Several interpolation schemes are commonly employed; Photoshop provides three, for example, which we will describe next. As is usual in computing, the more elaborate and computationally expensive the algorithm used, the better the approximation that results.

Suppose that we are applying some geometrical transformation, and we calculate that the pixel at the point (x', y') in the resulting image should have the same value as some point (x, y) in the original, but x and y are not integers. We wish to sample the original image at (x, y), at the same resolution at which it is stored, so we can imagine drawing a pixel – call it the *target pixel* – centred at (x, y) which will be the sample we need. As Figure 5.25 shows, in general this pixel may overlap four pixels in the original image. In the diagram, X marks the centre of the target pixel, which is shown by a darker red line; P_1, P_2, P_3, and P_4 are the surrounding pixels, whose centres are marked by the small red squares.

The simplest interpolation scheme is to use the *nearest neighbour*, i.e. we use the value of the pixel whose centre is nearest to (x, y), in this case P_3. In general – most obviously in the case of upsampling or enlarging an image – the same pixel will be chosen as the nearest neighbour of several target pixels whose centres, although different, are close enough together to fall within the same pixel. As a result, the transformed image will show all the symptoms of undersampling, with visible blocks of pixels and jagged edges. An image enlarged using nearest neighbour interpolation will, in fact, look as if its original pixels had been blown up with a magnifying glass.

A better result is obtained by using *bilinear interpolation*, which uses the values of all four adjacent pixels. They are combined in proportion to the area of their intersection with the target pixel. Thus, in Figure 5.25, the value of P_1 will be multiplied by the area enclosed by the dark red lines and the lighter intersecting lines in the north-west quadrant, and added to the values of the other three pixels, multiplied by the corresponding areas.

If a and b are the fractional parts of x and y, respectively, then some simple mathematics shows that the value of the pixel at (x', y') in the result, whose target pixel is centred at (x, y), will be equal to

$$(1-a)(1-b)p_1 + a(1-b)p_2 + (1-a)bp_3 + abp_4$$

where p_i is the value of the pixel P_i, for $1 \leq i \leq 4$.

This simple area calculation is implicitly based on the assumption that the values change linearly in both directions (hence '*bi*linearly') across the region of the four pixels. An alternative way of arriving at the same value is to imagine computing the values vertically above and below (x, y) by combining the values of the two pairs of pixels in proportion to their horizontal distances from x, and then combining those values in proportion to their vertical distances from y. In practice, the values are unlikely to vary in such a simple way, so that the bilinearly interpolated values will exhibit discontinuities. To obtain a better result, *bicubic interpolation* can be used instead. Here, the interpolation is based on cubic splines, that is, the intermediate values are assumed to lie along a Bézier curve connecting the stored pixels, instead of a straight line. These are used for the same reason they are used for drawing curves: they join together smoothly. As a result, the resampled image is smooth as well.

Figure 5.26 Nearest neighbour interpolation

Bicubic interpolation does take longer than the other two methods but relatively efficient algorithms have been developed and modern machines are sufficiently fast for this not to be a problem on single images. The only drawback of this interpolation method is that it can cause blurring of sharp edges.

Figures 5.26 to 5.28 show the same image enlarged using nearest neighbour, bilinear, and bicubic interpolation, respectively.

Exercises

1   Explain carefully why the two images in Figure 5.1 appear different, although they are both printed at the same resolution. What sequence of operations do you think was performed on the original scanned image to produce the two illustrations?

Figure 5.27 Bilinear interpolation

2   Suppose you want to change the size of a bitmapped image, and its resolution. Will it make any difference which order you perform these operations in?

3   On page 133 we suggest representing the first 2580 pixels of the image in Figure 3.3 by a single count and value pair. Why is this not, in general, a sensible way to encode images? What would be a better way?

4   Our argument that no algorithm can achieve compression for all inputs rests on common sense. Produce a more formal proof, by considering the number of different inputs that can be stored in a file of N bytes.

Figure 5.28 Bicubic interpolation

Figure 5.29 Iris on its original background

5 We lied to you about Figure 3.5: the original painting was made on black paper (see Figure 5.29). In order to make it easier to reproduce, we replaced that background with the gradient you see in the illustration in Chapter 3. Describe as many ways as you can in which we might have done this.

6 Describe how you would convert a photograph into an imitation Victorian vignette, such as the one shown in Figure 5.30, in the fashion of late nineteenth century portrait photographers. How would you put an ornamental frame around it?

7 Explain why it is necessary to use an alpha channel for anti-aliased masks.

8 Describe how you would produce the composite image in Figure 5.9 if the map was on a layer on top of that containing the flag, instead of the other way round.

9 Describe how the input–output curve of an image should be changed to produce the same effect as moving (a) the brightness, and (b) the contrast sliders. How would these adjustments affect the histogram of an image?

10 Describe the shape of the curve you would use to correct an image with too much contrast. Why would it be better than simply lowering the contrast with the contrast slider?

11 If asked to 'sharpen up' a scanned image, most experts would first apply a slight Gaussian blur before using the sharpen or unsharp mask filter. Why?

Figure 5.30 Creating a vignette (right) from an original photo (left)

12 Motion blur is the smearing effect produced when a moving object is photographed using an insufficiently fast shutter speed. It is sometimes deliberately added to images to convey an impression of speed. Devise a convolution mask for a motion blur filter. How would you allow a user to alter the amount of motion blur? What other properties of the blurring should be alterable?

13 Why are the screen shots published in tutorial articles in computing magazines often hard to read?

14 Explain carefully why pixel interpolation may be required if a rotation is applied to a bitmapped image.

15 An alternative to using bilinear or bicubic pixel interpolation when downsampling an image is to apply a low-pass filter (blur) first, and then use the nearest neighbour. Explain why this works.

6

Colour

- Colour and Science
- RGB Colour
  - Colour Depth
  - Indexed Colour
- Other Colour Models
  - CMYK
  - HSV
  - Colour Spaces Based on Colour Differences
  - Device-independent Colour Spaces
- Channels and Colour Correction
- Consistent Colour

Both vector graphics and bitmapped images can use colour. For most people, colour is such a commonplace experience that it is somehow surprising to discover that it is actually a rather complex phenomenon, in both its objective and subjective aspects. Representing colour in digital images and reproducing it accurately on output devices are consequently not at all straightforward.

Perhaps the most important thing to realize about colour is that you don't always need it. The existence of black and white photography and film demonstrates that people are perfectly well able to recognize and understand an image in the absence of colour – variations in brightness are quite adequate. Indeed, comparing the luminous elegance of a Fred Astaire film from the 1930s with the garish Technicolor of a 1950s MGM musical is enough to demonstrate that the addition of colour is not necessarily an improvement – a fact well understood by advertising agencies and the makers of music videos. Pragmatically, there are advantages to using images without colour. As we will see shortly, black and white bitmapped image files can be much smaller than coloured ones. Furthermore, black and white images are largely immune to the variations in colour reproduction of different monitors. You should not forget that some people do not have colour monitors, or prefer to use them in monochrome mode, and that a few people cannot see in colour at all, while many more cannot always distinguish between certain colours. By working in black and white (or, more accurately, shades of grey) you avoid producing images that may not be seen properly for these reasons.

But people have come to expect colour, and colour can add a great deal to an image, if it is used effectively. Sometimes colour is vital to the purpose for which an image is being used: for example, the colours in a clothing catalogue will influence people's buying decisions, and must be accurate to avoid disappointment and complaints.

The effective use of colour is not something that can be summarized in a few rules. The experience of artists and designers working in traditional media can be put to good use, and in large-scale multimedia production it is wise to ensure that there are artistically trained specialists available, and to leave colour decisions to them. As in most of the other areas we will describe, certain constraints associated with the digital nature of the images we can use in our multimedia productions will modify how we approach colour, so artistic sensibility must be augmented with some technical knowledge.

Colour and Science

Colour is a subjective sensation produced in the brain. In order to reproduce colour electronically, or manipulate it digitally, we need a model of colour which relates that subjective sensation to measurable and reproducible physical phenomena. This turns out to be a surprisingly difficult task to accomplish successfully.

Since light is a form of electromagnetic radiation, we can measure its wavelength – the wavelength of visible light lies roughly between 400 nm and 700 nm – and its intensity. We can combine these measurements into a *spectral power distribution (SPD)*, a description of how the intensity of light from some particular source varies with wavelength. Figure 6.1 shows the SPD of typical daylight. (Notice that it extends beyond the visible spectrum.) In effect, an SPD is constructed by splitting light into its component wavelengths, much as a prism splits a beam of light into a spectrum when we repeat Isaac Newton's optics experiments in school, and measuring the intensity of each component.[†] Subjective experiments show that an SPD corresponds closely to what we mean by 'colour', in the sense that observers can successfully match light with a particular SPD to a specific colour. However, SPDs are too cumbersome to work with when we are specifying colours for use in computer graphics, so we need to adopt a different approach.

† In theory, an SPD ought to be a continuous function, but it is satisfactorily approximated by using samples at wavelengths separated by a suitable interval, for example 10 nm, giving an SPD consisting of 31 components.

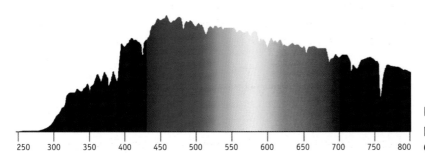

Figure 6.1 The spectral power distribution of daylight

You may have been told at some point in your education that the human eye contains two different sorts of receptor cells: *rods*, which provide night-vision and cannot distinguish colour, and *cones*, which in turn come in three different sorts, which respond to different wavelengths of light. The fact that our perception of colour derives from the eye's response to three different groups of wavelengths leads to the theory – called the *tristimulus* theory – that any colour can be specified by just three values, giving the weights of each of three components.

The tristimulus theory of colour is often summarized (inaccurately) by saying that each type of cone responds to one of red, green or blue light. It follows that the sensation of any colour can be produced by mixing together suitable amounts of red, green and blue light. We call red, green and blue the *additive primary colours*. These are not the artist's primary colours, which will be described later. Putting it another way, we can define a particular colour by giving the proportions of red, green and blue light that it contains. It follows that we can construct television screens and computer monitors using pixels each made up of three dots of different types of phosphor, emitting red, green and blue light, and exciting them using three electron beams, one for each colour. To produce any desired colour we just have to adjust the intensity of each electron beam, and hence the intensity of the light emitted by the corresponding phosphors. Optical mixing of the light emitted by the three component dots of any pixel will make it look like a single pixel of the desired colour.

Since we *can* construct monitors like that, the simplified tristimulus theory is evidently more or less right, and much of the time we can proceed on the basis of it. However, it *is* a simplified theory, and some subtle problems can arise if we ignore the more complex nature of colour. Fortunately, the worst of these are connected with printing, and do not often occur in multimedia work. Reproducing colour on a computer monitor, as we more often need to do, is more straightforward.

RGB Colour

The idea that colours can be constructed out of red, green and blue light leads to the *RGB colour model*, in which a colour is represented by three values, giving the proportions of red (R), green (G) and blue (B) light which must be combined to make up light of the desired colour. The first question that arises is 'What do we mean by red, green and blue?'. The answer ought to be that these are the names of three colours corresponding to three standard primary SPDs, and in the television and video industries several such standards do exist. (In general, the primary blue is actually better described as 'blue-violet', and the red is an orangey shade.) In computing, however, there is no universally accepted standard, although monitors are increasingly being built to use the primaries specified for High Definition TV (HDTV) by the ITU in its Recommendation ITU-R BT.709, and a standard version of RGB colour derived from this recommendation has been proposed. However, there is no real standard for red, green and blue on computer displays, and the colours produced in response to the any particular RGB value can vary wildly between monitors.

It is also important to be aware that it is *not* possible to represent any visible colour as a combination of red, green and blue components, however defined. Figure 6.2 shows a pictorial representation of the relationship between the colours that can be represented in that way – the so-called RGB *colour gamut* – and all the visible colours. The fin-shaped area is a spatial representation of all the possible colours. (For an explanation of exactly what is being plotted see the detailed comments below.) Shades of green lie towards the tip, with reds at the bottom right and blues at the bottom left. The triangular area of the RGB colour gamut is entirely enclosed within the fin, showing that there are some colours that cannot be produced by adding red, green and blue. It should be noted, though, that red, green and blue primaries do produce the largest gamut possible from simple addition of three primaries. Putting that another way, if you were to draw the largest triangle you could fit inside the area of all possible colours, its vertices would correspond to colours you would call red, blue and green.

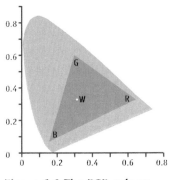

Figure 6.2 The RGB colour gamut

Exactly what is being plotted in Figure 6.2? For a full explanation, you will have to consult the references given in the bibliography, but a rough outline is as follows. The diagram derives from work done under the auspices of the *Commission Internationale de l'Eclairage (CIE)* in 1931. In experiments in which people were asked to mix quantities of red, green and blue lights to produce a colour that matched a displayed sample, it was found that it was necessary to add negative amounts of primaries (by adding them to the displayed sample instead of the attempted match) in order to match some colours. This is now understood to be because the responses of the three type of cone cell are not simply used as colour stimuli, the way the voltages on the three electron guns of a monitor are, but are combined in a more complex way. The CIE defined a set of three primaries, known simply as X, Y and Z, whose spectral distributions matched the inferred spectral response of the eye of their 'standard observer', and could thus be used to produce any visible colour purely by addition. The Y component is essentially the brightness (more properly called *luminance* in this context). If we put $x = X/(X + Y + Z)$, $y = Y/(X + Y + Z)$ and $z = Z/(X + Y + Z)$, you should be able to see that any colour can be fully specified by its x, y and Y values, since X and Z can be recovered from the equations. (Note that z is redundant.) Since Y is the luminance, x and y together specify the colour, independently of its brightness. It is x and y that label the axes in Figure 6.2. (This diagram is called the *CIE chromaticity diagram*, because it plots colour information, independent of brightness.) The curved area is obtained by plotting the value of an SPD comprising a single wavelength as its value varies from 400 nm to 700 nm. The area is closed by a straight line joining the extreme low and high frequencies – the 'line of purples', which corresponds to those colours which do not have a single identifiable wavelength as their dominant spectral component. The RGB gamut is contained inside a triangle with red, green and blue (as defined by the CIE) at its vertices.

Unfortunately, the primaries X, Y and Z cannot be realized by physical light sources.

In practice, the majority of colours perceived in the world do fall within the RGB gamut, so the RGB model provides a useful, simple and efficient way of representing colours. A colour can be represented by three values. We can write this representation in the form (r, g, b), where r, g and b are the amounts of red, green and blue light making up the colour. By 'amount', we mean the proportion of pure ('*saturated*') light of that primary. For example, if we express the proportions as percentages, (100%, 0%, 0%) represents pure saturated primary red, and (50%, 0%, 0%) a darker red, while (100%, 50%, 100%) represents a rather violent shade of mauve. Since black is an absence of light, its RGB colour value is (0%, 0%, 0%). White light is produced by mixing equal proportions of saturated light of all three primaries, so white's RGB colour value is (100%, 100%, 100%). We emphasize that the three values represent the amounts of *light* of the three primary colours which must be mixed to produce light of the specified colour. Do not confuse this *additive mixing* of colours with paint mixing, which is a *subtractive mixing* process, since paint absorbs light. Computer monitors emit light, so any consideration of how colours are produced must be based on an additive model. Scanners work by detecting light reflected from the scanned document, so they too work with additive colours.

The three numbers r, g and b are not absolute values in any sense; it is only their relative values that matter, so we can choose any convenient range, provided it allows us to distinguish enough different values. Like many important questions about colour, 'How many is enough?' can only be answered subjectively. Different cultures have different ideas about when two colours are different, and people differ in their ability to distinguish between different colours, but few, if any, can distinguish more than the nearly 16.8 million distinct combinations provided by using 256 different values for each of the red, green and blue component values.

Colour Depth

Of course, 256 is a very convenient number to use in a digital representation, since a single 8-bit byte can hold exactly that many different values, usually considered as numbers in the range 0 to 255. Thus, an RGB colour can be represented in three bytes, or 24 bits. The number of bits used to hold a colour value is often referred to as the *colour depth*: when three bytes are used, the colour depth is 24. We often also refer to *24 bit colour*, as a shorthand for colour with a 24 bit colour depth. In 24 bits, our mauve shade would be stored as (255, 127, 255), black is (0, 0, 0), as always, and white is (255, 255, 255). (Remember that the values start at zero.)

You may well suppose that 24 is not the only possible colour depth, and this is indeed the case. One other possibility, less common than it used to be, is 1-bit (*bi-level*) colour. A single bit allows us to distinguish two different colours. Usually these will be considered black and white, although the actual colours displayed will depend on the output device – orange and black monitors enjoyed a vogue for a while on ergonomic grounds, for example. A colour depth of 4 bits allows 16 different colours, which is clearly inadequate for displaying anything but the most simple of colour images; 16 different grey levels, on the other hand, can produce respectable greyscale images. Since greys are represented by RGB colour values (r, g, b), with $r = g = b$, a single value is sufficient to specify a grey level, the other two RGB components being redundant. Figure 6.3 shows four versions of the same photograph at different colour depths; note the posterization effect as the number of colours decreases.

The 8 bit colour depth illustrated in the second photograph in Figure 6.3 where a single byte is used to hold a colour value, providing 256 colours, is in widespread use, both in monitors for domestic personal computers and on the World Wide Web. It affords several points of particular interest, and we will return to it shortly. Some computer systems use 16 bits to hold colour values. 16 is not divisible by 3,

Figure 6.3 A photograph in (from left to right) 24, 8, 4 and 1 bit colour

so when RGB values are stored in a 16 bit format, either one bit is left unused, or different numbers of bits are assigned to the three components. Typically, red and blue each use 5 bits, and green is allocated 6 bits, allowing twice as many different green values to be distinguished. This allocation of bits is based on the observation that the human eye is more sensitive to green light than to the other two primaries. (The cone cells in the eye are especially insensitive to blue, to compensate for the high levels of blue in daylight. The high sensitivity to green is presumably an evolutionary response to the preponderance of green in the environment in which human beings evolved.)

Although 24 bits are sufficient to represent more colours than the eye can distinguish, higher colour depths, such as 30, 36 or even 48 bits, are increasingly being used, especially by scanners. Support for 48 bit colour is included in the specification of the PNG file format. These very large colour depths serve two purposes. Firstly, the additional information held in the extra bits makes it possible to use more accurate approximations when the image is reduced to a lower colour depth for display (just as images stored at high resolution will look better when displayed on a low resolution monitor than images stored at the monitor resolution). Secondly, it is possible to make extremely fine distinctions between colours, so that effects such as chroma-key (see Chapter 7) can be applied very accurately.

The common colour depths are sometimes distinguished by the terms *millions of colours* (24 bit), *thousands of colours* (16 bit) and *256 colours* (8 bit), for obvious reasons (although 16 bits allows 65,536 values, so tens of thousands of colours would be a more accurate description).

The names *true colour* and *hi colour* are sometimes used for 24 and 16 bit colour, respectively, but they are often used more loosely by marketing people. We will avoid these terms.

Colour depth is a crucial factor in determining the size of a bitmapped image: each logical pixel requires 24 bits for 24 bit colour, but only 8 for 8 bit, and just a single bit for 1 bit colour. Hence, if it is possible to reduce the colour depth of an image from 24 bits to 8, the image file size will decrease by a factor of three (ignoring any fixed-size housekeeping information that is held in addition to the image data). Returning to an earlier point, an image made up of 256 different shades of grey – more than most people can distinguish – will be one third the size of the same image in millions of colours. Using an arbitrarily chosen set of 256 colours, on the other hand, is unlikely to produce an acceptable result. If the colour depth must be reduced, and greyscale is not desired, then an alternative strategy must be employed.

Indexed Colour

So far, we have implicitly assumed that the stored R, G and B values are used directly to control the intensity of the monitor's three electron beams, thus determining the colour that is displayed.[†] Often this is just what is done, especially in the case of 24 bit colour. This arrangement is called *direct colour*. There is, however, an alternative, which is very widely used on low-end computer systems and the World Wide Web, known as *indexed colour*.

The screen of any colour monitor is capable of displaying the millions of colours that can be represented by 24-bit colour values, but it may

† The relationship between the voltage applied to an electron beam and the intensity of the light emitted by a phosphor when it strikes it is non-linear, as is the response of the eye to the intensity of light which enters it, so the value is not simply used as a voltage, but the hardware is built to compensate somewhat for these non-linearities.

Table 6.1 Colour depth and VRAM

VRAM (Mbytes)	Screen resolution	Max. colour depth
1	640×480	16
	832×624	16
	1024×768	8
	1152×870	8
2	640×480	24
	832×624	24
	1024×768	16
	1152×870	16
4	640×480	24
	832×624	24
	1024×768	24
	1152×870	24
	1280×1024	16
8	640×480	24
	832×624	24
	1024×768	24
	1152×870	24
	1280×1024	24

well be the case that the video RAM (VRAM) provided in the monitor is not sufficient to hold a full-screen image at 3 bytes per pixel. (Table 6.1 shows the amount of VRAM needed to support each colour depth at a selection of common screen sizes.) Another constraint on colour depth is that an image file in 24-bit colour may be considered too large for the available disk space, or it may be felt to take too long to transmit over a network. If, for any of these reasons, we are constrained to use only one byte for each pixel, we can use at most 256 different colours in any one image. Using a standard set of 256 colours for all the images we might need, i.e. attempting to use 8-bit direct colour, is unacceptably restrictive. Indexed colour provides a means of associating a *palette* of 256 specific colours with each image. For example, if we wished to produce a pastiche of Picasso's 'blue period' paintings, we could use a palette holding shades of blue and obtain a reasonable result. If we had had to use only the blues from a set of 256 colours spread evenly over the spectrum, all of the subtlety and possibly much of the content would be lost.

One way of thinking about indexed colour is as a digital equivalent of painting by numbers. In a painting by numbers kit, areas on the painting are labelled with small numbers, which identify pots of paint of a particular colour. When we use indexed colour, pixels store a

Figure 6.4 Images and their colour palettes

small number that identifies a 24-bit colour from the palette associated with the image. Just as each painting by numbers outfit includes only those paints that are needed to colour in one picture, so the palette includes only the 24-bit RGB values for the colours used in the image. When the image is displayed, the graphics system looks up the colour from the palette corresponding to each single-byte value stored at each pixel, and uses the value it finds as the colour of that pixel. Figure 6.4 shows two images with different colour characteristics, together with the palettes used when they are stored using indexed colour.

Experienced programmers will immediately recognize the strategy: it is an example of the folk axiom that all problems can be solved by adding a level of indirection. Hence, instead of trying to use eight bits to hold an RGB value, we use it to hold an index into a table, with 256 entries, each of which holds a full 24-bit RGB colour value. For example, if a particular pixel was to be displayed as the colour whose

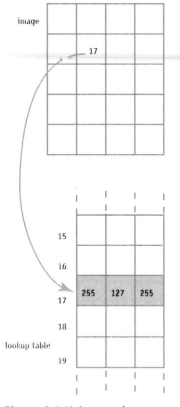

image

17

15

16

255 127 255

17

18

lookup table

19

Figure 6.5 Using a colour lookup table

24-bit RGB value was $(255, 127, 255)$, instead of storing that value in the image, we could store an index identifying the table location in which it was stored. Supposing $(255, 127, 255)$ was held in the 18th entry of the table, the pixel would hold the offset 17 (see Figure 6.5) Such an indexed table of colour values is called a *Colour Lookup Table (CLUT)* or, more simply, a *palette*. You may find it helpful to consider the CLUT as carrying out a mapping from *logical colours*, stored for logical pixels, to *physical colours*, displayed by physical pixels. The looking up operation that performs this mapping is usually carried out by the monitor's video hardware; all the displaying program needs to do is load the correct palette. (Even if the display hardware supports 24-bit direct colour, indexed colour may sometimes be used to reduce the size of image files; in that case, the CLUT lookup may be done by software.) If no palette is supplied, a default system palette will be used (the system palettes on the major platforms are different).

It may help you to understand what is going on when indexed colour is being used if you consider what would happen if, on a computer that only had enough VRAM for 8-bit colour, a program were to display two images in different windows at the same time, and those images used different palettes. Unless the program has been designed to operate in a cleverer way, the colour palette associated with the active window will be loaded. Say this palette is mostly made up of shades of blue, and the 5th entry is a pale sky-blue. Then every pixel with a value of 4 (palette offsets start at 0) will be coloured that pale sky-blue – including pixels in the other image, if its window is still visible. This other image may be made up of shades of brown, with the 5th element of its palette a reddish-brown; nevertheless, while the blue image's window is active, the pixels that should be reddish-brown will be pale sky-blue, since, although the palette is associated with the image, it is applied to the entire screen. Hence, if the brown image became active, the pale sky-blues in the first window would turn reddish-brown. A logical colour value does not identify a colour absolutely, only relative to a palette. You will appreciate that there is a problem if two images are to be displayed in the same window, as they must be if they both occur on the same Web page. It will be necessary to use a single palette to display both. This may require the number of colours in each individual image to be restricted to an even smaller number, unless the colour make-up of both images is the same. Note, though, that if the hardware supports 24 bit colour, all that is necessary is for software (for example, Web browsers) to interpret the palette for each image that uses indexed colour correctly.

If indexed colour is to be used an image file needs to store the palette along with the actual image data, but the image data itself can be smaller by a factor of three, since it only needs eight bits per pixel. For any reasonably sized image, there will be a net saving of space. This saving may be increased if the file format allows palettes with fewer than 256 entries to be stored with images that have fewer colours, and uses the minimum number of bits required to index the palette for each colour value.

Of the file formats mentioned in Chapter 3, PNG, BMP, TGA and TIFF allow the use of a colour palette; GIF requires it as it only supports 8-bit indexed colour images; an SGI image file may have a palette associated with it in a separate file. JFIF and SPIFF files do not support indexed colour: JPEG images stored in 24-bit colour must be reduced to 8-bit if necessary at the time they are displayed. PostScript and its derivatives, such as EPS and PDF, provide sophisticated support for indexed colour, although its use is usually confined to bitmapped images embedded in the PostScript, since its use with vector shapes, where the colour specification is a small part of the image model, is less compelling.

For created images, a palette of 256 colours will often be tolerable and, since you have control over the colours you use, you can work within the restriction, though subtle variations will be lost. However, with photographic or scanned material, or images that already exist in 24-bit colour, it will be necessary to cut down the number of colours when you prepare a version that uses 8-bit indexed colours. What can be done with the areas of the image that should be displayed in some colour which is not in the reduced palette?

Obviously, the missing colour must be replaced by one of those that is in the palette. There are two popular ways of doing this. The first is to replace the colour value of each individual pixel with the CLUT index of the nearest colour. This can have undesirable effects: not only may the colours be distorted, but detail may be lost when two similar colours are replaced by the same one, and banding and other visible artefacts may appear where gradations of colour are replaced by sharp boundaries. As we noted in Chapter 3, these effects are collectively known as *posterization*.

When posterization is unacceptable, the replacement of colours missing from the palette can be done another way. Areas of a single colour are replaced by a pattern of dots of several different colours, in such a way that optical mixing in the eye produces the effect of a colour

Figure 6.6 Dithering patterns

Figure 6.7 Grey produced by dithering

which is not really present. For example, say our image includes an area of pale pink, but the palette that we must use does not include that colour. We can attempt to simulate it by colouring some of the pixels within that area red and some white. This process is called *dithering*. It is done by grouping together pixels in the area to be coloured, and applying colour to individual pixels within each group in a suitable pattern. The process is an extension of the use of *half-toning*, used to print greyscale images on presses that can only produce dots of pure black or white. At low resolutions, dithering may produce poor results, so it is better suited to high resolution work.

Figure 6.6 shows five distinct ways of distributing black and white among a 2×2 block of pixels. If the pixels were small enough and the image was viewed from a sufficient distance, these patterns would be interpreted as five different shades of grey (including black and white) – see Figure 6.7, where we have exaggerated the size of the pixels to show how the half-tones are built up. In general, a block of $n \times n$ pixels can simulate $n^2 + 1$ different grey levels, so you can see that as the size of the block over which we dither is increased, so is the number of grey levels, but at the expense of resolution.

If each pixel can be one of 256 different colours, instead of just black or white, then the corresponding patterns can simulate millions of colours. However, these simulated colours are, in effect, being applied to pixels four times the area of those actually on the screen, hence the effective resolution of the image is being halved, resulting in a loss of detail. While this is usually acceptable for printing, where resolutions in excess of 600 dpi are common, it is often intrusive when images are being displayed on 72 dpi monitors. Other artefacts may also be generated when the patterns are superimposed; these can be minimized by clever choice of dot patterns for the generated colours, although this has the effect of cutting down the number of different colours that can be simulated.

This leaves the question of which colours should be used in a palette. Ideally, you will fill the palette with the most important colours in your image. Often, these will be the most common, in which case it is easy for a program like Photoshop to construct the palette automatically by examining the original 24-bit version when it converts it to indexed colour. Sometimes, though, the use of colour will be more complex, and it may be necessary to construct the palette by hand (or, more likely, edit an automatically constructed palette) to ensure that all the vital colours are present.

You cannot guarantee that every program that displays your image will necessarily use your palette – some may just fall back on the default system palette, with dismaying results. If you have reason to believe that that is a possibility, it is usually better to convert to a system palette yourself when preparing the image, and make any adjustments you can to retrieve some quality instead of letting the system do its own colour conversion. Unfortunately, the system palettes for the major platforms are different. A restricted set of 216 colours, usually referred to as the *Web-safe palette*, is the only palette you can rely on to be reproduced by Web browsers on any system using 8-bit colour, and if you must know which colours are going to be displayed on any platform the Web-safe palette is your best option.

Figure 6.8 illustrates the effect of dithering and the choice of palette on an image. (It is a screenshot of Photoshop's Save For Web dia-

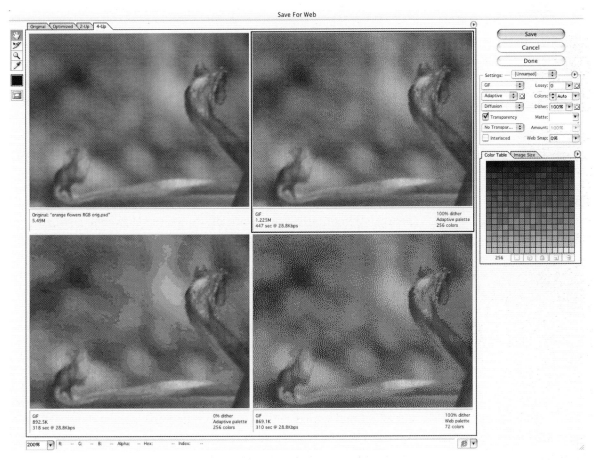

Figure 6.8 Effect of different dithering patterns

logue, with the image being saved as a GIF zoomed in to show the effects clearly.) The original image is at the top left; to its right is a version using an 'adaptive' palette, chosen automatically from the colours in the image, with dithering. At the bottom left, the same palette is used, but without dithering, and posterization can clearly be seen. The final version uses the Web-safe palette with dithering, which in this case produces its own visible artefacts. You will notice that only 72 colours are present in the palette for this final version. This is because the remaining Web-safe colours are not used in this image; they are therefore removed from the palette, which reduces its size without any effect on the image.

Other Colour Models

The RGB colour model is the most important means of representing colours used in images for multimedia, because it corresponds to the way in which colour is produced on computer monitors, and it is also how colour is detected by scanners. Several other colour models are in use, and you should know something about them because you may be required to work with images that have already been prepared for some other medium, especially print, or to use software which is based on a different view of colour from RGB.

CMYK

You have probably seen at some time the experiment, originally devised by Thomas Young in 1801, illustrated in Figure 6.9. Beams of the three additive primaries red, green and blue are shone onto a white surface, which reflects all of the light falling on it, so that they overlap. Where only one colour lands, we see that colour; where all three overlap, we see white, as we would expect from the previous section. Where two colours overlap, we see a new colour formed by the mixing of the two additive primaries. These new colours are a pale shade of blue, usually called *cyan*, a slightly bluish red, called *magenta*, and a shade of *yellow*. Each of these three is formed by adding two of the additive primaries. Since all three additive primaries combine to form white light, we could equally say that cyan, for example, which is the mixture of blue and green, is produced by subtracting the remaining primary, red, from white light.

We can express this effect pseudo-algebraically. Writing R, G and B for red, green and blue, C, M and Y for cyan, magenta and yellow,[†] and W for white, and using $+$ to mean additive mixing of light, and $-$ to mean subtraction of light, we have

Figure 6.9 Complementary colours

[†] The Y that stands for yellow is not to be confused with the Y that stands for luminance elsewhere in this chapter.

$$C = G+B = W-R$$
$$M = R+B = W-G$$
$$Y = R+G = W-B$$

In each equation, the colour on the left is called the *complementary colour* of the one at the extreme right; for example, magenta is the complementary colour of green.

The relevance of this experiment is two-fold. Firstly, it is the basis for a theory of colour aesthetics which has had a great influence on the use of colour in art and design. Secondly, the idea of forming colours by subtraction of light instead of addition provides a colour model appropriate to ink and paint, since these are substances which owe their coloured appearance to the way they absorb light.

An important point to grasp is that the light that is reflected from a coloured surface is not changed in colour by the process of reflection. For example, when you hold a glossy photograph under a bright white light, the light that bounces off it will produce white reflections that interfere with the colour of the photograph itself. The dyes on a surface such as paper do not supply colour to light reflected off the surface, but to light that penetrates through them and gets reflected or scattered back from beneath it. During the light's journey through the particles of dye, ink or paint, the pigments absorb light at some frequencies. The light that emerges thus appears to be coloured. When paints are mixed or dyes are overlaid, the combination absorbs all the frequencies absorbed by the individual components. When, for example, we talk of 'cyan ink', we mean ink that, when it is applied to white paper and illuminated by white light will absorb the red component, allowing the green and blue, which combine to produce the cyan colour, to be reflected back (see Figure 6.10). If we apply a layer of such an ink to white paper, and then add a layer of magenta, the magenta ink will absorb incident green light, so the combination of the cyan and magenta inks produces a blue colour (the additive primary blue, that is), as shown at the bottom of Figure 6.10. Similarly, combining cyan and yellow inks produces green, while magenta combined with yellow gives red. A combination of all three colours will absorb all incident light, producing black. Mixtures containing different proportions of cyan, magenta and yellow ink will absorb red, green and blue light in corresponding proportions, thus (in theory) producing the same range of colours as the addition of red, green and blue primary lights. Cyan, magenta and yellow are called

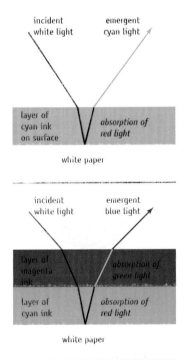

Figure 6.10 Effect of coloured ink

Figure 6.11 Subtractive colour mixing

the *subtractive primaries* for this reason. These subtractive primaries are the primary colours which the artist working in conventional media must use. Figure 6.11 shows (within the limits of the printing process used for this book) the range of colours that can be produced by mixing of primary coloured paint (the three swatches show the only pigments used).

In practice, it is not possible to manufacture inks which absorb only light of precisely the complementary colour. Inevitably, some unwanted colours are absorbed at the same time. As a result, the gamut of colours that can be printed using cyan, magenta and yellow is not the same as the RGB gamut. Furthermore, combining actual inks of all three colours does not produce a very good black. On top of this, applying three different inks is not very good for your paper and leads to longer drying times. For these reasons, in magazine and book printing, the three subtractive primaries are augmented with black. The four colours cyan, magenta, yellow and black, when used in printing, are called *process colours*, and identified by their initials CMYK. Figure 6.12 shows the CMYK colour gamut and compares it with the RGB gamut displayed earlier. You will see that the CMYK gamut is smaller than RGB, but is not a strict subset – there are CMYK colours that fall outside the RGB gamut, and vice versa. You will also see that, because of the different colour mixing method and the presence of the black, the gamut is not triangular.

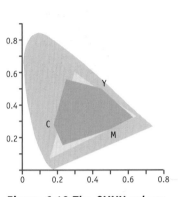

Figure 6.12 The CMYK colour gamut

For printing, an understanding of the subtractive CMYK model of colour, and also of the properties of inks and papers, is vital to high quality colour reproduction. For multimedia, CMYK is of less direct relevance. If it should happen that you wish users of your multimedia production to be able to print copies of the images it contains, in colour, then you should ensure that they only contain colours within the CMYK gamut, otherwise there will be colour shifts on the printed version. If you are incorporating images that have previously been used in some print medium, you may find they are stored in a format in which colours are specified as C, M, Y and K values, instead of R, G and B. When the images are converted to a suitable file format for multimedia, it may be necessary also to convert the CMYK colour values into RGB. (Programs such as Photoshop can do this.) Having done so, you may be able to apply some colour transformations to improve the appearance by taking advantage of the larger RGB gamut.

HSV

Breaking a colour down into its component primaries makes sense from a theoretical point of view, and reflects the way monitors, scanners and colour printers work, but as a way of describing colour, it does not correspond to the way in which we experience colours in the world. Looking at a pale (cyan) blue, you probably don't relate it to a mixture of green and blue-violet light, but rather to other blues, according to how nearly pure blue it is, or how much of a greenish or purplish blue it appears, and to how light or dark it is.

In more formal terms, we can consider a colour's *hue*, its *saturation*, and its *brightness*. In physicists' terms, hue is the particular wavelength at which most of the energy of the light is concentrated (the *dominant wavelength*); if you like, hue is the pure colour of light. In less scientific terms, we usually identify hues by names. Famously, Isaac Newton identified seven hues in the spectrum, the familiar red, orange, yellow, green, blue, indigo and violet of the rainbow. Newton had his own mystical reasons for wanting seven colours in the rainbow and it is more normal to distinguish just four: red, yellow, green and blue, and define hue informally as the extent to which a colour resembles one, or a mixture of two, of these.

A pure hue can be more or less 'diluted' by mixing it with white: the dominant hue (wavelength) remains the same, but the presence of other hues makes the colour paler. A colour's saturation is a measure of its purity. Saturated colours are pure hues; as white is mixed in, the saturation decreases. A colour's appearance will be modified by the intensity of the light: less light makes it appear darker. The brightness of a colour is a measure of how light or dark it is.

The equation of hue with the measurable quantity dominant wavelength is appealing, but not quite as simple as one would hope. Some hues cannot be identified with a single wavelength. Most people would consider purple to be a hue, but the SPD for purple has peaks at both short and long wavelengths (red and blue). We know, though, from the discussion of subtractive mixing, that we could consider purple to be made by subtracting light at the dominant wavelength of a shade of green from white light. In other words, the hue purple is associated with a dominant wavelength, but the dominance takes the form of a negative peak. This notion is, perhaps, no more incongruous than the physicists' idea that a hole is where an electron isn't.

In terms of paint, a hue is a pure colour. Adding white decreases its saturation, producing a *tint*. Adding black decreases its brightness, producing a *tone*.

Since the early nineteenth century, painters and other visual artists who like to systematize their thinking about colours have organized them into a 'colour wheel': the different hues are organized in a circle, with the subtractive primaries equally spaced around the perimeter, and the additive primaries in between them so that each primary is opposite its complement (see Figure 6.13). In art terms, it is the subtractive primaries which are usually referred to as primary colours. Their complements are called secondary colours, and the colours produced by mixing primaries and secondaries are tertiary colours. (The tertiary colours are sometimes added to the colour wheel in between the primaries and secondaries.)

This colour wheel can be extended to produce an alternative colour model. First, the distinct primary, secondary and tertiary hues can be augmented to produce a continuum extending all the way round

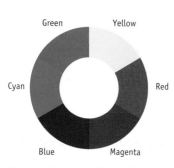

Figure 6.13 A colour wheel

a circle. Any hue can be specified as an angle around the circle, usually measured counter-clockwise, relative to red at 0°. Saturation can be added to the model by putting white at the centre of the circle, and then showing a gradation of tints from the saturated hues on the perimeter to the pure white at the centre. To add brightness to this model, we need a third dimension. Imagine the colour disk just described as being on top of a cylinder, made up of similar slices whose brightness decreases as we move downwards, so that, instead of white at the centre we have increasingly dark greys, until at the bottom, there is black. On each slice, the colours will be correspondingly toned down. A particular colour can be identified by its hue (H) (how far round the circle from red it is), its saturation (S) (how near the central axis) and its brightness value (V) (how far up the cylinder it is), hence this form of colour description is called the HSV model. Its structure is illustrated in Figure 6.14, together with two sample slices through the cylinder.

As we move towards the ends of the HSV cylinder, the variability in saturation will be smaller. At the bottom, there is less light, so less scope for adding white, while at the top, there is more light, and less scope for adding black. Accordingly, a better model is actually provided by a double cone, rather than a cylinder, which narrows towards a single black point at the bottom, and a single white point at the top. The colour model based on this geometry is called *HLS*, which stands for hue, saturation, and lightness.

You may sometimes see references to the *HSB* model. This is identical to the HSV model just described, using the B to stand for brightness instead of the less obvious V for value.

Industrial designers use a different approach to colour specification, based on swatches of standard colours that can be reproduced accurately. The Pantone system is widely used for this purpose, and has been adapted for incorporation into computer graphics applications.

Although the HSV model superficially resembles one of the ways in which painters think about colour, it should be remembered that the arrangement of hues around the circle is really no more than a visual mnemonic for colour harmony – it is otherwise arbitrary and has no physical basis.

All colour models provide a way of specifying a colour as a set of numbers, and of visualizing their relationships in a three-dimensional space. This way of describing colour is independent of the many subjective factors which normally play a part in our perception of colour.

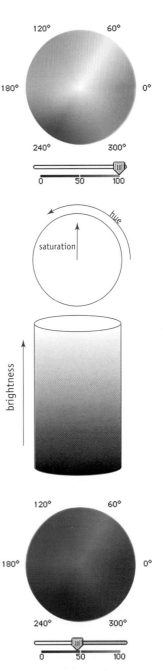

Figure 6.14 The HSV model

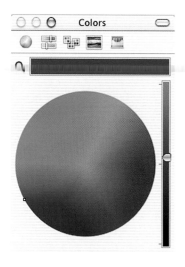

Figure 6.15 Colour pickers

For computer programs, a numerical, objective, colour specification is necessary. For people, it is less so, and most people find the numerical specification of colours non-intuitive. Within graphics programs, though, it is normal to choose colours interactively using a *colour picker* dialogue. These may be based on any of the colour models we have discussed, and allow you to choose colours by manipulating controls that affect the values of the components, while seeing a sample of the resulting colour displayed. Figure 6.15 shows some of the colour pickers provided by the Macintosh system software, as examples of some different styles of picker. In the HSV colour picker at the top, a slider is used to control the *V* value, while the corresponding slices through the cylinder are displayed, and a colour is selected by clicking on a point in the disk. The RGB picker below simply uses sliders to control the three components, while the spectrum picker at the bottom lets you pick your colour directly by clicking.

Colour Spaces Based on Colour Differences

For some purposes it is useful to separate the brightness information of an image from its colour. Historically, an important motivation for doing this was to produce a means of transmitting colour television signals that would be compatible with older black and white receivers. By separating brightness and colour, it is possible to transmit a picture in such a way that the colour information is undetected by a black and white receiver, which can treat the brightness as a monochrome signal. Once a means of separating colour and brightness had been devised, it became possible to process the two signals separately in other ways. In particular, it is common practice in analogue broadcasting to use less bandwidth to transmit the colour than the brightness, since the eye is less sensitive to colour than to brightness. There is evidence to suggest that the human visual apparatus processes brightness and colour separately, too, so this form of representation also holds some physiological interest.

The basis of the RGB representation of colour is that light can always be broken down into three components. What we consider as brightness – the extent to which a pixel appears to be lighter or darker – is clearly related to the values of the red, green and blue components of the colour, since these tell us how much light of each primary is being emitted. It would be tempting to suppose that the brightness could be modelled simply as $(R + G + B)/3$, but this formula is not quite adequate, because it takes no account of the eye's differing sensitivity to the different primaries. Green contributes far more to the perceived brightness of a colour than red, and blue contributes hardly at all. Hence to produce a measure of brightness from an RGB value, we must weight the three components separately. There are several different formulae in use for performing this computation; that recommended for modern cathode ray tubes, as used in most computer monitors and TV sets, is: $Y = 0.2125R + 0.7154G + 0.0721B$. The quantity Y defined here is called *luminance*.

You should be able to see that red, green and blue values can be reconstructed from luminance and any two of the primaries. It is normal, though, for technical reasons, to use some variant of a representation consisting of Y together with two *colour difference* values, usually $B - Y$ and $R - Y$. We say 'some variant' because different applications require that the three components be manipulated in different ways. For analogue television, a non-linearly scaled version of Y, properly denoted Y', is used together with a pair of weighted colour difference values, denoted U and V. Out of carelessness, the term *YUV colour* is often used to refer to any colour space consisting of a brightness component together with two colour difference components. Digital television uses a variant called $Y'C_BC_R$, which is like Y'UV but uses different weights for the colour difference computation.

Device-independent Colour Spaces

RGB and CMYK are the most commonly used colour models, but they are both *device-dependent*: different monitors provide different red, green and blue primaries; different sorts of ink and paper produce different cyan, magenta, yellow and even black. Given an RGB value such as $(255, 127, 255)$, you don't know exactly what colour is going to be produced on any particular monitor, and you have no guarantee that it will be the same on any two monitors, or even on the same monitor at different times.

As we mentioned in the technical note on page 169, the *Commission Internationale de l'Eclairage (CIE)* has carried out work to produce an objective, *device-independent* definition of colours. Its basic model, the *CIE XYZ colour space*, uses three components X, Y and Z to approximate the three stimuli to which the colour-sensitive parts of our eyes respond. This model is device-independent, but as well as being awkward to work with and impossible to realize with physical light sources, it suffers (as do the RGB, CMYK, HSV and most other colour models) from not being *perceptually uniform*. A perceptually uniform model would be one in which the same change in one of the values produced the same change in appearance, no matter what the

Figure 6.16 An RGB colour image and (from left to right) its red, green and blue channels

original value was. If, for example, RGB was a perceptually uniform model then changing the *R* component from 1 to 11 would produce the same increase in perceived redness as changing it from 101 to 111. However, it doesn't. This means that computations of the distance between two colours based on their RGB values do not reflect what we consider the degree of difference between them, which in turn makes finding a closest colour match when reducing an image to a restricted palette difficult.

For many years, the CIE tried to produce a colour model that was perceptually uniform, but never quite succeeded. Two models, refined from the original XYZ model to be much more nearly perceptually uniform, were produced in 1976. These are the L*a*b* and L*u*v* models (often written simply Lab and Luv, or CIELAB and CIELUV).

In both models, the L* component is a uniform luminance and the other two components are colour differences. In L*a*b*, they specify colour in a way that combines subtractively, as in CMYK. 'Lab colour' is widely used in the pre-press industry as a standard specification of colour difference values for printing. L*u*v* is a similar model, but the colour difference values work additively, as in RGB, so L*u*v* provides a device-independent model of colour suitable for monitors and scanners.

These models do not correspond to any easily understandable way of thinking about colour, so you are unlikely to use them directly. However, they do provide a basis for the device-independent treatment of colour, and are used as a reference point for systems that try

to guarantee that the colours we specify in our images will look as nearly as possible the same on whatever output device is being used.

Channels and Colour Correction

Earlier, we implied that in a 24-bit RGB colour image, a single 24-bit value is stored for each pixel. While this is the way colours are stored in some file formats, there is another possibility: for each pixel, three separate 8-bit values, one for each of red, green and blue, are stored. That is, in terms of data structures, instead of storing an image in a single array of 24-bit values, we store it in three arrays, each consisting of single bytes. This representation has some computational advantages, since 3-byte quantities are awkward to manipulate on most machines. It also provides a useful way of organizing colour images conceptually, irrespective of whether the physical storage layout is actually of this form.

Each of the three arrays can itself be considered as an image. When we consider each colour separately, it only makes sense to consider these as greyscale images. Each of the three greyscale images making up the colour image is called a *channel*, so we speak of the red channel, or the green or blue channel. Figure 6.16 shows an RGB colour image and its three channels.

Each channel can be manipulated separately: since it is an image, the manipulations can be done using the usual image editing tools provided by Photoshop and similar programs. In particular, levels and curves can be used to alter the brightness and contrast of each channel independently. When the altered channels are recombined,

Figure 6.17 Correcting and over-correcting a colour cast

the colour balance of the composite image will have changed. Colour correction operations performed in this way are frequently required to compensate for the deficiencies of scanners and other input devices. Figure 6.17 shows an example: the scanned photograph on the left has a marked colour cast; in the middle image, this has been corrected; the image on the right shows how colour adjustment can be taken further to produce an artifically coloured image.

The previous paragraph may make adjusting the levels of each channel sound like a simple operation. In practice, although some colour adjustments are straightforward – maximizing the contrast in all three channels, for example – producing a desired result can be very time-consuming, calling for considerable experience and fine judgement. Some image manipulation programs come equipped with 'wizards' or 'assistants', software modules with some degree of artificial intelligence, to help in some common situations calling for colour correction.

Sometimes, though, a simpler approach is adequate. Just as the brightness and contrast controls encapsulate a class of tonal adjustments, so the *colour balance* and *hue and saturation* adjustments provide a less refined interface to the adjustment of levels in the three colour channels. Colour balance provides three sliders, one for each of the pairs of complements cyan and red, magenta and green, and yellow and blue, which allow you to adjust the relative proportions of each pair. The adjustment can be applied to shadows, midtones, or highlights separately. The hue and saturation adjustment performs a similar operation, by allowing you to vary each of the *H*, *S*, and *V* components of colours within specified ranges: reds, greens, blues, and so on. This provides a more intuitive way of adjusting the colours if you are used to working with HSV specifications. Figure 6.18 shows an example of what can be achieved with these adjustments. The photograph on the left, taken in February (in the northern hemisphere), has been transformed into a spring scene, merely by adjusting the hue and saturation sliders as shown.

A different way of making colour changes which, like the two sets of controls just described, works across all the channels at once, is

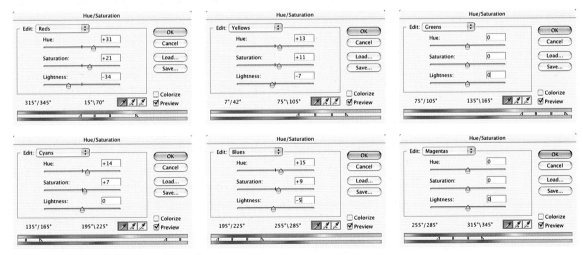

Figure 6.18 Hue and saturation adjustments

to replace a specified colour wherever it appears with a different one. This is like doing a search and replace operation on a text file using an editor, except that the target and replacement are colours, not text strings. Photoshop's version of this operation is somewhat more sophisticated: you can set a tolerance value, which causes pixels within a certain percentage of the target value to be altered, and use H, S, and V sliders to specify a change to those components of pixels that match the target, instead of just specifying an exact replacement colour. In effect, this command creates a mask, in a similar manner to the magic wand described in Chapter 5, and then makes colour adjustments to selected areas of the image.

Although we are only discussing RGB colour, images stored in any colour space can be separated into channels. In particular, the channels of a CMYK image correspond to the colour separations needed by commercial printing processes, while the channels of a $Y'C_BC_R$ image correspond to the components of a video signal. Furthermore, the idea that a greyscale image can be considered to be one channel of a composite image is extended in the concept of alpha channel, which we introduced in Chapter 5. Although alpha channels behave completely differently from the colour channels that make up the displayed image, their common representation has some useful consequences.

One of the most common applications of this duality is in inserting people into a separately photographed scene, often one where it is impossible for them to be in reality. This can be done by photographing the person against a blue background (ensuring that none of their clothing is blue). All of the image data for the person will be in the red and green channels; the blue channel will be an image of the area not occupied by the person. An alpha channel constructed as a copy of the blue channel (an operation built in to any software that manipulates image channels) will therefore mask out the background, isolating the figure. It is then a simple matter to copy the figure, using the mask to define it as the selection, and paste it into, for example, an underwater scene. This *blue screen* technique is commonly used in video and film-making, as well as in constructing fake images.

Other sorts of colour image processing can be implemented by applying some greyscale processing to each of the channels separately. An important example is JPEG compression, which, although it is most commonly applied to colour images, is defined in the standard to operate on 8-bit quantities, so that each channel is compressed individually. One advantage of this is that the compression algorithm is unaffected by the colour space used for the image; it just takes whatever channels are there and compresses them. This offers the freedom to choose a colour space, and apply pre-processing to the channels. It is common for JPEG compressors to transform an image into $Y'C_BC_R$, and then downsample the colour difference components, since the eye is less sensitive to colour variation than to brightness variations. This same 'chroma downsampling' step is routinely applied to video signals, for both compression and transmission, as we will see in Chapter 7.

Consistent Colour

Colour adjustment is messy, and getting it wrong can cause irreparable damage to an image. It would be much better to get things right first time, but the varying colour characteristics of different monitors and scanners make this difficult. Some recent developments in software are aimed at compensating for these differences. They are based on the use of *profiles*, describing how devices detect and reproduce colour.

We don't need much information to give a reasonable description of the colour properties of any particular monitor. We need to know exactly which colours the red, green and blue phosphors emit (the R, G and B *chromaticities*). These can be measured using a suitable scientific instrument, and then expressed in terms of one of the CIE device-independent colour spaces. We also need to know the maximum saturation each component is capable of, i.e. we need to know what happens when each electron beam is full on. We can deduce this if we can characterize the make-up and intensity of white, since this tells us what the (24-bit) RGB value (255, 255, 255) corresponds to. Again, the value of white – the monitor's *white point* – can be specified in a device-independent colour space.

You will sometimes see white point specified as a *colour temperature*, in degrees absolute. This form of specification is based on the observation that the spectral make-up of light emitted by a perfect radiator (a so-called 'black body') depends only on its temperature, so a black body temperature provides a concise description of an SPD. Most colour monitors for computers use a white point designed to correspond to a colour temperature of 9300 K. This is far higher than daylight (around 7500 K), or a conventional television monitor (around 6500 K), in order to generate the high light intensity required for a device that will normally be viewed under office lighting conditions. (Televisions are designed on the assumption that they will be watched in dimly lit rooms.) The 'white' light emitted by a monitor when all its three colours are at full intensity is actually quite blue.

Computer monitors are not actually black bodies, and so their SPDs deviate from the shape of the black body radiation, which means that colour temperature is only an approximation of the characteristic of the white point, which is better specified using CIE colour values.

Finally, the most complex element in the monitor's behaviour is the relationship between the RGB values presented to it by the graphics controller, and the intensity of the light emitted in response. This relationship is not a simple linear one: the intensity of light emitted in response to an input of 100 is not ten times that produced by an input of 10, which in turn is not ten times that produced by an input of 1. Physical devices do not work as conveniently as that. However, the response can be captured to some extent using a single number, referred to as the display's γ (often written out as *gamma*).

Why γ? Because the *transfer characteristic* of a display – the relationship between the light intensity emitted by the screen (I) and the voltage applied to the electron gun (V) is often modelled by the transfer function $I = V^\gamma$, where γ is a constant. Unfortunately, this model is not entirely accurate, and one of the sources of variability between monitors lies in the use of incorrect values for γ which attempt to compensate for errors in the formula. Another is the fact that some display controllers attempt to compensate for the non-linearity by adjusting values according to an inverse transfer function before they are applied to the electron guns, while others do not.

Armed with device-independent values for red, green and blue, the white point and gamma, it is possible to translate any RGB colour value into an absolute, device-independent, colour value in a CIE colour space that exactly describes the colour produced by the monitor in response to that RGB value. This is the principle behind the practice of *colour management*.

In a typical situation calling for colour management an image is prepared using some input device, which might be a monitor used as the display by a graphics editor, or a scanner. In either case, the image will be stored in a file, using RGB values which reflect the way the input device maps colours to colour values – its *colour profile*. We say that the image is stored using the input device's colour space. Later, the same image may be displayed on a different monitor. Now the RGB values stored in the image file are mapped by the output device, which probably has a different profile from the input device. The colours stored in the colour space of the input device are interpreted as if they were in the colour space of the output device. In other words, they come out wrong.

One way of correcting this is to embed information from the input device's profile in the image file. EPS, PDF, TIFF, JFIF, PNG and other types of file are able to accommodate such information, in varying degrees of detail. At the least, the R, G and B chromaticities, white point and gamma can be included in the file. Software on the machine being used to display the image can, in principle, use this information to map the RGB values it finds in the image file to colour values in a device-independent colour space. Then, using the device profile of the output monitor, it can map those values to the colour space of the output device, so that the colours are displayed exactly as they were on the input device. In practice, it is more likely that the two profiles would be combined and used to map from the input device colour space to the output device colour space directly. It is, of course, possible that some of the colours in the input device colour space are not available in the output device colour space, so colour management can only actually guarantee that the colours will be displayed exactly as they were intended within the capabilities of the output device. If software uses colour management consistently, the approximations made to accommodate a restricted colour gamut will be the same, and the output's colour will be predictable. If the display software has not been written to take advantage of device profiles, the display will be no better than it would be without colour management.

An alternative way of using colour management software is to modify the colours displayed on a monitor using the profile of a chosen output device. In this way, colour can be accurately previewed. This mode of working is especially useful in pre-press work, where actually producing printed output may be expensive or time-consuming.

To obtain really accurate colour reproduction across a range of devices, device profiles need to provide more information than simply the RGB chromaticities, white point and a single figure for gamma. In practice, for example, the gammas for the three different colours are not necessarily the same. As already stated, the actual transfer characteristics are not really correctly represented by gamma; a more accurate representation is needed. If, as well as display on a monitor, we also wished to be able to manage colour reproduction on printers, where it is necessary to take account of a host of issues, including the

C, M, Y and K chromaticities of the inks, spreading characteristics of the ink, and absorbency and reflectiveness of the paper, even more information would be required – and different information still for printing to film, or video.

Since the original impetus for colour management software came from the pre-press and printing industries, colour management has already been developed to accommodate these requirements. The *International Colour Consortium (ICC)* has defined a standard device profile, which supports extremely elaborate descriptions of the colour characteristics of a wide range of devices. ICC device profiles are used by colour management software such as Apple's ColorSync, the Adobe colour management system built into Photoshop and other Adobe programs, and the Kodak Precision Color Management System, to provide colour management services. ColorSync provides colour management at a system software level, making it easy for individual Macintosh applications to incorporate extremely sophisticated colour management services. Manufacturers of scanners, monitors and printers routinely produce ICC profiles of their devices. TIFF and EPS files can accommodate complete ICC profiles.

Colour management is not much use unless accurate profiles are available. Unfortunately, no two devices are exactly identical. In the case of monitors, the situation is even worse, since tubes age and their colour characteristics change over time. Although a generic profile produced by the manufacturer for one line of monitors is helpful, to take full advantage of colour management it is necessary to calibrate individual devices, at relatively frequent intervals (once a month is often advised). Some high-end monitors are able to calibrate themselves automatically. For others, it is necessary to use a special measuring device in conjunction with software that displays a sequence of colour values and, on the basis of the measured output of the screen, generates an accurate profile.

You may wonder why the profile data is embedded in the file. Why is it not used at the input end to map the colour values to a device-independent form, such as L*a*b*, which can then be mapped to the output colour space when the image is displayed? The work is split between the two ends and no extra data has to be added to the file. The reason is that most existing software does not work with device-independent colour values, so it could not display the images at all. If it ignores a device profile, things are no worse than they would have been if it was not there.

Clearly, though, it would be desirable to use a device-independent colour space for stored colour values. The sRGB (standard RGB) colour model attempts to provide such a space. As you can guess, it is based on the RGB model, and specifies standard values for the R, G and B chromaticities, white point, and gamma. The standard values have been chosen to be typical of the values found on most monitors.[†] As a result, if the display software is not aware of the sRGB colour space and simply displays the image without any colour transformation, it should still look reasonable. Use of sRGB colour is especially suitable for graphics on the World Wide Web, because there most images are only ever destined to be displayed on a terminal. A standard colour space based on RGB is of no help in maintaining consistency of colours for printing.

Having read this section, you may well ask 'Why bother?'. It may not seem like the end of the world if the colours in your image are a bit off when it is displayed on somebody else's monitor. Consider, for example, the use of Web pages as online shopping catalogues. For many products, the colour is important. (To take an extreme example, think about buying paint over the Internet.) One of the factors driving the development of colour management and its incorporation into Web browsers is the desire to facilitate online shopping. As well as the development of the sRGB colour space, this has led to the development of browser plug-ins providing full colour management facilities. If online shopping seems crassly commercial, consider instead the use of the World Wide Web by art galleries to deliver catalogues. Here again the best possible colour reproduction is vital if the catalogues are to serve their function properly.

[†] Or so its proponents claim. Other experts believe the chosen values are not the best. Photoshop 5.0 used sRGB as its default colour space; in response to users' reactions, this default was almost immediately changed in the 5.01 update.

Exercises

1 Comment on the advisability of using translucent tangerine coloured plastics in the surround of a computer monitor.

2 If you consider the three components of an RGB colour to be cartesian coordinates in a three-dimensional space, and normalize them to lie between 0 and 1, you can visualize the RGB colour space as a unit cube, as shown in Figure 6.19. What colours correspond to the eight corners of this cube? What does the straight line running from the origin to $(1,1,1)$ shown in the figure represent? Comment on the usefulness of this representation as a means of visualizing colour.

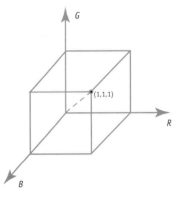

Figure 6.19 The RGB colour space

3   Why do RGB colour values (r, g, b), with $r = g = b$ represent shades of grey?

4   If a CLUT has 256 entries (so pixels only need a single byte), each 3 bytes wide, how large must an image be before using indexed colour provides a net saving of space?

5   For which of the following images would the use of indexed colour be satisfactory?
(a) A reproduction of your national flag.
(b) A photograph of the surface of Mars.
(c) A photograph of yourself on the beach.
(d) A still from a black and white Fred Astaire movie.
In which cases is the system palette likely to be acceptable without dithering?

6   Give an example of an image whose most important colour is not one of its most commonly occurring colours. When might this cause a problem?

7   If you gave a child a paintbox containing red, green and blue paints only, will they be able to mix an adequate range of colours to paint the ceiling of the Sistine chapel?

8   Which colour space should be used for storing images and why?

9   Suppose you had an image with too much red in it, perhaps because of poor lighting. Explain what adjustments you would make to its red channel to compensate. What undesirable side-effect would your adjustment have, and what would you do about it?

10 The most noticeable effect of the adjustments shown in Figure 6.18 is to turn the bracken bright green, but if you look at the screenshots you will see that no changes were made to the greens. How can this be so?

11 Superman's uniform is blue, with a yellow S on the chest, and a red cape. How would you make an image of Superman flying, without recourse to his superpowers?

7 Video

- Digitizing Video
- Streamed Video
- Video Standards
  - Analogue Broadcast Standards
  - Digital Video Standards
  - DV and MPEG
- Introduction to Video Compression
  - Motion JPEG
  - DV
  - MPEG Video
  - Other Codecs for Multimedia
  - Codec Comparison
- QuickTime
- Editing and Post-Production
  - Film and Video Editing
  - Digital Video Editing and Post-Production
  - Preparing Video for Multimedia Delivery

All current methods of displaying moving pictures, whether they are on film or video, broadcast to a television, or stored on a computer system or some digital storage medium, depend on the phenomenon known as persistence of vision – a lag in the eye's response to visual stimuli which results in 'after-images' – for their effect. Because of persistence of vision, if a sequence of still images is presented to our eyes at a sufficiently high rate, above what is called the fusion frequency, we experience a continuous visual sensation rather than perceiving the individual images. If consecutive images only differ by a small amount, any changes from one to the next will be perceived as movement of elements within the images. The fusion frequency depends on the brightness of the image relative to the viewing environment, but is around 40 images per second. Below this frequency, a flickering effect will be perceived, which becomes more pronounced as the rate at which successive images are presented is decreased until, eventually, all illusion of motion is lost and we see the sequence of still images for what it really is.

There are two different ways of generating moving pictures in a digital form for inclusion in a multimedia production. We can use a video camera to capture a sequence of frames recording actual motion as it is occurring in the real world, or we can create each frame individually, either within the computer or by capturing single images one at a time. We use the word *video* for the first option, and *animation* for the second. Since both video and animation are forms of moving pictures they share some features, but there are also technical differences between them. For live-action video it is necessary both to record images fast enough to achieve a convincing representation of real-time motion, and to interface to equipment that conforms to requirements and standards which were defined for broadcast television – even though, when we come to play back the video on a computer, these requirements and standards are largely irrelevant. To make matters worse, there are several different standards in use in different parts of the world.

As we will see, video places considerable strains on the processing, storage and data transmission capabilities of computer systems. Video is also much in demand from consumers, whose expectations are typically based on their experience of broadcast television; it is probably the area of multimedia which is presently most subject to technical change. Typically, video targeted at consumer equipment will be played back at reduced frame rates, possibly even with jittering from dropped frames, in windows much smaller than the smallest domestic television set, and it will often exhibit visible compression artefacts. In order to accommodate the limitations of low-end PCs, considerable compromises over quality must be made. Video should therefore be used judiciously in multimedia productions intended for low-end platforms. Consumers who are used to broadcast digital TV will not be impressed by what has been disparagingly, but not unjustifiably, described as 'dancing postage stamps'. Good video production for general consumption therefore requires both a careful choice of material and a mode of presentation that does not draw attention to its defects.

Contemporary film is shot at a rate of 24 frames per second, but film projectors are equipped with a device that interrupts the projection, effectively displaying each frame twice, so that the projected frame rate is 48. In countries that use the NTSC system for television and video, frames are displayed at a rate of roughly 30 per second, but again the rate at which the picture is refreshed is effectively doubled, because each frame is broken into two interlaced halves, known as fields, which are displayed one after the other (see below). The PAL and SECAM systems work in a similar manner, at a rate of 50 fields (25 frames) per second. When we are displaying images on a computer monitor, we can choose the rate at which they are displayed. The relatively high refresh rate of the monitor avoids flicker, so digital display does not require interlaced fields, but images must still be displayed rapidly enough to produce the illusion of motion. A rate of 12–15 frames per second is just about sufficient, although higher rates are to be preferred.

Digitizing Video

The one thing that you need to keep constantly in mind when considering digital video is the size of the data it generates. A video sequence consists of a number of frames, each of which is a single image produced by digitizing the time-varying signal generated by the sensors in a video camera. We invariably use bitmapped images

Figure 7.1 A video sequence is a set of still frames

for video frames (because that is what video equipment generates). The size of the image produced for each frame of NTSC video, as used in North America and Japan, is 640 pixels wide by 480 pixels high. If we use 24-bit colour, each frame occupies 640×480×3 bytes, which is 900 kilobytes. One second of uncompressed NTSC video comprises almost exactly 30 frames, so each second occupies just over 26 megabytes, each minute about 1.6 gigabytes. The figures for the PAL system used in Western Europe and Australia are slightly higher: 768×576 at 25 frames per second gives 31 megabytes per second or 1.85 gigabytes for each minute. At these rates, you could not get very much video on to a CD-ROM or DVD; nor could you transmit it over any but the fastest network – certainly not the Internet as we know it. By using a good-sized disk array, you would be able to store an entire feature film, and the required data transfer rate is within the reach of the latest SCSI and Firewire standards. Storing video in such a form is therefore a feasible option for film and TV studios, but not (quite) for the domestic consumer.

Notice that the need for very high rates of data transfer arises from the fact that these are *moving* pictures, and we must deliver them one after another, fast enough for them to be perceived as a representation of continuous motion. The high volume of each frame arises from the storage requirements of bitmapped images. As we saw in Chapter 5, we can reduce this requirement by applying some form of compression to our images. It should come as no surprise, therefore, to learn that we also apply compression to video. For transmission over a relatively slow network such as the Internet, or for playback directly from CD-ROM, we must apply severe compression, as well as using other methods, such as limiting the frame size, to reduce the volume of data. For capturing video in real-time, this compression must be carried out so fast that dedicated hardware is needed. In the remainder of this discussion, we will ignore the possibility of working with uncompressed video, since this is only feasible on very high-end equipment at the present time.

Digital video may be captured either directly from a camera, or indirectly from a video tape recorder (VTR) or (leaving aside questions of legality) from a broadcast signal. Current technology offers two sites for performing the digitization and compression: in the camera, or in the computer. If a VTR intervenes, or a signal is broadcast, the nature of the signal is not changed by the recording or broadcasting process – digital VTRs record digital signals, analogue VTRs record analogue signals.

In the case of digitization and compression being performed using circuitry inside a camera, the purely digital signal (now better described as a data stream) is then passed to the computer via a high speed interface. The most widely used combination of hardware for capturing video in this way comprises a digital camcorder or VTR using one of the variants of the *DV* format – mini-DV (often simply called 'DV'), DVCAM or DVCPRO – connected to a computer by a *FireWire* interface. (FireWire was formerly known as IEEE 1394, but the more colourful name has now been officially adopted; equipment made by Sony uses the name iLink for the same interface.) The three DV variants use different tape formats and provide differing degrees of error correction and compatibility with analogue studio equipment, but all send digital video as a data stream to a computer in the same format, so software does not need to distinguish between the three types of equipment. Mini-DV is essentially a consumer format, although it is also used for semi-professional video production. The other two formats are more suited for professional use, being especially widely used for news gathering. All DV equipment supports *device control*,

Figure 7.2 Every fourth frame of a 25 fps video sequence

Figure 7.3 An uncompressed frame (left) and a DV version (right)

the ability for the tape to be stopped, started and moved to a specific position by signals sent from the computer by software.

Although the subjective quality of DV is very good, it is a compressed format, and as we saw in the case of bitmapped still images in Chapter 5, compression causes artefacts and interferes with subsequent processing and recompression. Figure 7.3 shows a frame of uncompressed video and the same frame compressed as DV. It is hard to see any difference at this scale. However, as the blown-up details in Figure 7.4 show, there are compression artefacts in the DV. As the extreme blow-ups in Figure 7.5 demonstrate, the actual pixels have changed considerably in some areas.

'DV' stands for 'digital video', but that expression is also used in a more general sense, to refer to the storage and manipulation of video data in a digital form. We will usually use the term in this general sense, and use 'DV' whenever we mean the specific standard we have just introduced.

If digitization is to be performed in the computer, an analogue video signal, conforming to some broadcast video standard, is fed to the input of a *video capture card* attached to the computer. Within this card, the analogue signal is converted to digital form. Usually, the resulting digital data is compressed in the card, before being passed on for storage on disk or transmission over a network, although sometimes it may be possible to perform the compression using software running on the computer's central processor. A variant on this approach is to feed the analogue signal into an externally connected device which converts it into a DV signal, which can then be sent to the computer via Firewire. This is an attractive option, if the best quality is not required, since it allows software to treat the output from any video source as a DV stream.

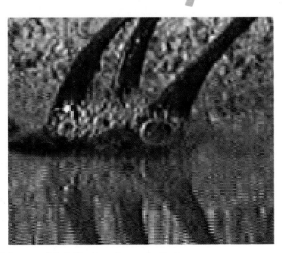

Figure 7.4 Detail of uncompressed frame (left) and DV frame (right) showing artefacts

Digitization in the camera has one great advantage over digitization in the computer. When an analogue signal is transmitted over a cable, even over a short distance, it will inevitably be corrupted, if only to a small extent, by noise. Noise will also creep in when analogue data is stored on magnetic tape. Composite video signals, the type normally used in domestic equipment, are also subject to distortion caused by interference between the colour and brightness information, especially when stored on VHS tape. Until DVD players and digital TV became common, we had all become used to noise and distortion in broadcast television and VHS video, and didn't usually consider it objectionable, but these phenomena can reduce the effectiveness of compression. They typically produce small random fluctuations in colour, so that, for example, areas that should be composed of a single colour, and would compress well, will lose their coherence and compress less well. Some video compression techniques are based on the similarity between adjacent frames. Again, the random nature of any signal degradation will undermine this similarity, making compression less effective, and the resulting picture less satisfactory. If digitization is carried out inside the camera, only digital signals, which, as we pointed out in Chapter 2, are resistant to corruption by noise and interference, are transmitted down cables and stored on tape. Compression is applied to a clean signal at its source and so it will be more effective.

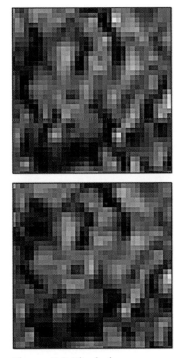

Figure 7.5 Pixels in uncompressed frame (top) and DV frame (bottom) showing shift in colour values

Coincidentally, as consumers have become used to the clean picture quality of DVDs and broadcast digital TV, VHS noise has come to seem less and less acceptable. It is only a matter of time before analogue video disappears.

The disadvantage of digitization performed in the camera is that the user has no control over it. The data stream produced by a digital video camera must conform to an appropriate standard, usually DV, which stipulates the data rate for the data stream, and thus the amount of compression to be applied. Analogue video capture boards and their associated software normally offer the user control over the compression parameters, allowing a trade-off to be made between picture quality and data rate (and hence file size).

DV devices and video capture boards can usually perform not only digitization and compression, but also their inverses, decompression and digital to analogue conversion. Devices which compress and decompress signals are known as compressor/decompressors, invariably contracted to *codecs*. Using a hardware codec, either in a DV camcorder or on a capture card, it is possible to capture video signals, store them on a computer, and then play them back at full motion to an external video monitor (i.e. a TV set) attached to the camcorder's (analogue) line-out socket or the video card's output. When distributing multimedia, we cannot know, however, whether our audience will have any hardware codec available, or if so, which one, and generally we will want the video to play back on their computer's monitor. So, we need a *software codec*: a program that performs the same function as the dedicated hardware codecs we have described, in order to ensure that the audience will be able to play back the video on their computer's ordinary monitor. Generally, software is slower than dedicated hardware, but playing full-screen video at broadcast frame rates using a software codec is possible on the fastest of contemporary desktop computers. Many older or less well specified machines are not capable of smooth playback at full size and speed, though, and as we will see, networks are not generally capable of delivering video fast enough, so video on the Web usually uses smaller frames and lower frame rates, and may have to sacrifice many aspects of quality.

Generally, compression algorithms that are suitable for software codecs are different from those suitable for hardware implementation, so we will often have to recompress captured video material – resulting in a type of generational loss of quality – in order to prepare it for incorporation in a multimedia production.

Streamed Video

It's one thing to play a pre-recorded video clip from a hard disk, DVD or even a CD-ROM; it's quite another to play video over a network. By this we mean delivering a video data stream from a remote server, to be displayed *as it arrives*, as against downloading an entire video clip to disk and playing it from there. Such *streamed video* resembles broadcast television, in that the source video is held on the server, which acts like a TV transmitter sending out the signal, which is played back straight away on a client machine. Downloading the entire clip is as though the TV company sent a courier round with a videotape whenever you wanted to watch a programme. Streamed video opens up the possibility of delivering live video, bringing one of the modes of conventional broadcasting to video on computers. It goes beyond conventional broadcast TV in this area, though, because it is not restricted to a single transmitter broadcasting to many consumers: any suitably equipped computer can act as both receiver and transmitter, so users on several machines can communicate visually, taking part in what is usually called a *video conference.*

The fundamental obstacle to streamed video is bandwidth. As we will show, even heavily compressed and down-sampled video at a quarter of normal frame size requires a bandwidth of 1.86 Mbits per second. For now, therefore, decent quality streamed video is restricted to local area networks, T1 lines and broadband connections (ADSL and cable modems); dial-up Internet connections using V90 modems cannot handle the required data rate. Even where the bandwidth is available, the network has to be capable of delivering data with the minimum of delay, and without undue 'jitter' – a variation in the delay that can cause independently delivered video and audio streams to lose synchronization. We will return to this subject in Chapter 17.

It may help you to understand the nature of what we will sometimes call *true streaming* by contrasting it with alternative methods of video delivery you may meet on the World Wide Web. The simplest method is embedded video, where a movie file is transferred from a server to the user's machine, where it is played back from disk once the entire file has arrived. A refinement of this method is called *progressive download* or *HTTP streaming*. With this mode of delivery, the file is still transferred to the user's disk, but it starts playing as soon as enough of it has arrived. This will be when the time it will take for

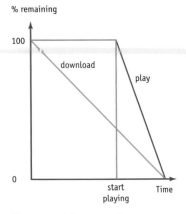

Figure 7.6 Progressive download

the remainder to be downloaded is equal to the duration of the entire movie. This is illustrated in Figure 7.6.

There is usually an appreciable delay before playback starts, since progressively downloaded movies are typically made with a data rate that exceeds the bandwidth of the network connection, in order to maintain quality. The movie file usually remains on the user's hard disk – at least in their Web browser's cache – after playback is completed. Thus, enough disk space to store the whole movie must be available, so progressive download cannot be used for huge files, such as complete feature films. Also, since an entire file is downloaded, this method of delivery cannot be used for live video, nor does it allow you to skip over parts of the file without downloading them.

In contrast, true streaming video is never stored on the user's disk. A small buffer may be used to smooth out jitter, but effectively each frame in the stream is played as soon as it arrives over the network. This means that streams can be open-ended, so true streaming can be used for live video, and the length of a recorded movie that is streamed is limited only by the amount of storage available at the server, not by the viewer's machine. Random access to specific points in a stream is possible, except for live streams. True streaming is thus suitable for 'video on demand' applications.[†] Its drawback is that the network must be able to deliver the data stream fast enough for playback. Looked at from the other side, this means that the movie's data rate, and thus its quality, is restricted to what the network can deliver. Even with the best connections, Internet streamed video will not provide the picture quality of broadcast television.

† The fact that no copy of the entire movie is held on the user's machine makes it even more attractive where copyright material is involved.

Why bother, then? The answer is sometimes summed up in the slogan, 'Every Web site a TV station'. Streaming video server software is available free, or (for a small number of simultaneous streams) at a modest cost. Anyone with a permanent Internet connection can therefore transmit streamed video content; many ISPs provide streaming facilities to their customers who do not run their own servers. Internet streaming is thus much more accessible than conventional TV broadcasting facilities, and so it provides a new communication channel for minority voices and unconventional video (experimental and underground work, as well as the more notorious sort) that is denied access to conventional channels. As we will explain in Chapter 17, though, the broadcasting establishment may not be undermined to the extent that might seem possible... or desirable. Another answer, more often given by conventional broadcasters, is that streamed video can be interactive. It is not entirely clear, though, what sort of interaction, if any, people want to

have with video. Facilities that have been proposed for broadcast digital TV appear to be restricted to allowing viewers to select between different camera angles, and to call up 'instant replays' on demand. Initial provision of such facilities, for example by the satellite TV company BSkyB, is being targeted at sports coverage. It is not clear that this sort of interactivity, when provided over the Internet, would compensate for poor picture quality. The two factors of democratic access and interactivity are combined in video conferencing, which may currently be the most successful application of streamed video, but is somewhat marginal from our viewpoint on multimedia, opening up, as it does, questions better considered in the context of computer-supported collaborative working.

Video Standards

Digital video is captured from devices that are also used to record pictures for playing back on television sets – it isn't currently economically practical to manufacture cameras, except for cheap Webcams, purely for connecting to computers. Therefore, in multimedia production we must deal with signals that correspond to the standards governing television. The newer digital devices must maintain compatability with old analogue equipment in essential features such as the size of frames and the frame rate, so in order to understand digital video we need to start by looking at its analogue heritage.

Analogue Broadcast Standards

There are three sets of standards in use for analogue broadcast colour television. The oldest of these is *NTSC*, named after the (US) National Television Systems Committee, which designed it. It is used in North America, Japan, Taiwan and parts of the Caribbean and of South America. In most of Western Europe a standard known as *PAL*, which stands for Phase Alternating Line, referring to the way the signal is encoded, is used, but in France *SECAM* (*Séquential Couleur avec Mémoire*, a similar reference to the signal encoding) is preferred. PAL is also used in Australia and New Zealand and in China, while SECAM is used extensively in the former Soviet Union and in Eastern Europe. The standards adopted in Africa and Asia for the most part follow the pattern of European colonial history. The situation in South America is somewhat confused, with NTSC and local variations of PAL being used in different countries there.

The NTSC, PAL and SECAM standards are concerned with technical details of the way colour television pictures are encoded as broadcast signals, but their names are used loosely to refer to other characteristics associated with them, in particular the frame rate and the number of lines in each frame. To appreciate what these figures refer to, it is necessary to understand how television pictures are displayed.

Like computer monitors, television sets work on a raster scanning principle. Conceptually, the screen is divided into horizontal lines, like the lines of text on a page. In a CRT (cathode ray tube) set, three electron beams, one for each additive primary colour, are emitted and deflected by a magnetic field so that they sweep across the screen, tracing one line, then moving down to trace the next, and so on. Their intensity is modified according to the incoming signal so that the phosphor dots emit an appropriate amount of light when electrons hit them. The picture you see is thus built up from top to bottom as a sequence of horizontal lines. (You can see the lines if you look closely at a large TV screen.) Once again, persistence of vision comes into play, to make this series of lines appear as a single picture.

As we remarked above, the screen must be refreshed about 40 times a second if flickering is to be avoided. Transmitting an entire picture that many times a second requires an amount of bandwidth that was considered impractical at the time the standards were being developed. Instead, each frame is divided into two *fields*, one consisting of the odd-numbered lines of each frame, the other of the even lines. These are transmitted one after the other, so that each frame (still picture) is built up by *interlacing* the fields (Figure 7.7). The fields are variously known as odd and even, upper and lower, and field 1 and field 2. Originally, the rate at which fields were transmitted was chosen to match the local AC line frequency, so in Western Europe, a field rate of 50 per second, and hence a frame rate of 25 per second, is used for PAL; in North America a field rate of 60 per second was used for black and white transmission, but when a colour signal was added for NTSC, it was found to cause interference with the sound, so the field rate was multiplied by a factor of 1000/1001, giving 59.94 fields per second. Although the NTSC frame rate is often quoted as 30 frames per second, it is actually 29.97.

odd field

even field

Figure 7.7 Interlaced fields

When video is played back on a computer monitor, it is not generally interlaced. Instead, the lines of each frame are written to a frame buffer from top to bottom, in the obvious way. This is known as *progressive scanning*. Since the whole screen is refreshed from the frame buffer at a high rate, flickering does not occur, and in fact much lower frame rates can be used than those necessary for broadcast. Fields may be combined into frames when an analogue video signal is digitized, or

Figure 7.8 Video frame and detail of separated fields

they may be stored separately and only combined when the material is played back. Since fields are actually separated in time, combining them in this way can cause undesirable effects. If an object is moving rapidly, it may change position between the two fields. The detailed blow-ups of the frame in Figure 7.8 show an example: between the fields the actress turns and moves so that the cloak on the left of the frame comes forward, appearing bigger in the second field than in the first. When the fields are combined into a single frame for progressive display (or exported as a still image), the edges of moving objects will have a comb-like appearance where they are displaced between fields, as shown in Figure 7.8, and in detail in Figure 7.9. To prevent this effect, it may be necessary to 'de-interlace' by averaging the two fields when constructing a single frame; this, however, is a relatively poor compromise. Another option is to discard half the fields – say all the even fields – and to interpolate the missing information for the fields that remain, to give full frames. This also gives predictably poor results. On the other hand, the fact that there are 60 or 50 fields per second in analogue video can sometimes usefully be exploited by converting each field into a single frame, thus giving two seconds of slower but fluid video for each second captured. If the resulting video is played either at full speed (30 or 25 fps), or at a small size, the loss

Figure 7.9 'Comb effect' in combined fields (detail)

of image quality resulting from the interpolation necessary to create frames from fields will scarcely be noticeable.

Each broadcast standard defines a pattern of signals to indicate the start of each line, and a way of encoding the picture information itself within the line. In addition to the lines we can see on the picture, some extra lines are transmitted in each frame, containing synchronization and other information. An NTSC frame contains 525 lines, of which 480 are picture; PAL and SECAM use 625 lines, of which 576 are picture. It is common to quote the number of lines and the field rate together to characterize a particular scanning standard; what we usually call NTSC, for example, is 525/59.94.

It is possible that you might need to digitize material that was originally made on film and has been transferred to video tape. This would be the case if you were making a multimedia film guide, for example. Most film footage is projected at 24 frames per second so there is a mismatch with all the video standards. In order to fit 24 film frames into (nearly) 30 NTSC video frames, a stratagem known as *3–2 pulldown* is employed. The first film frame is recorded for the first three video fields, the second for two, the third for three again, and so on. If you are starting with material in this form, it is best to remove the 3–2 pulldown after it has been digitized (a straightforward operation with professional video editing software) and revert to the original frame rate of 24 per second. Using PAL, films are simply shown slightly too fast, so it is sufficient to adjust the frame rate.

Digital Video Standards

The standards situation for digital video is no less complex than that for analogue video. This is inevitable, because of the need for backward compatibility with existing equipment – the use of a digital data stream instead of an analogue signal is orthogonal to scanning formats and field rates, so digital video formats must be capable of representing both 625/50 and 525/59.94. The emerging HDTV (high-definition television) standards should also be accommodated. Some attempt has been made to unify the two current formats, but unfortunately, different digital standards for consumer use and for professional use and transmission have been adopted.

Like any analogue data, video must be sampled to be converted into a digital form. A standard officially entitled *Rec. ITU-R BT.601* but more often referred to as *CCIR 601*[†] defines sampling of digital video. Since a video frame is two-dimensional, it must be sampled in both directions. The scan lines provide an obvious vertical arrangement;

† CCIR was the old name of the organization now known as ITU-R.

CCIR 601 defines a horizontal sampling picture format consisting of 720 luminance samples and two sets of 360 colour difference samples per line, irrespective of the scanning standard. Thus, ignoring chrominance and interlacing for a moment, an NTSC frame sampled according to CCIR 601 will consist of 720×480 pixels, while a PAL frame will consist of 720×576 pixels.

Observant readers will find this perplexing, in view of our earlier statement that the sizes of PAL and NTSC frames are 768×576 and 640×480 pixels, respectively, so it is necessary to clarify the situation. PAL and NTSC are analogue standards. Frames are divided vertically into lines, but each line is generated by a continuous signal, it is not really broken into pixels in the way that a digital image is. The value for the number of pixels in a line is produced by taking the number of image lines (576 or 480) and multiplying it by the *aspect ratio* (the ratio of width to height) of the frame. This aspect ratio is 4:3 in both PAL and NTSC systems, which gives the sizes originally quoted. Video capture cards which digitize analogue signals typically produce frames in the form of bitmaps with these dimensions. The assumption underlying the calculation is that pixels are square. By relaxing this assumption, CCIR 601 is able to specify a sampling rate that is identical for both systems, and has desirable properties such as providing the same number of horizontal samples in every line. CCIR 601 pixels, then, are not square: for 625 line systems, they are slightly wider than high, for 525 line systems they are slightly higher than wide. Equipment displaying video that has been sampled according to CCIR 601 must be set up to use pixels of the appropriate shape.

Video sampled according to CCIR 601 consists of a luminance component and two colour difference components. The colour space is technically $Y'C_BC_R$ (see page 187) – you can consider the three components to be luminance Y, and the differences $B-Y$ and $R-Y$. As a first step in reducing the size of digital video, fewer samples are taken for each of the colour difference values as for luminance, a process known as *chrominance sub-sampling*. It is justified by the empirical observation that human eyes are less sensitive to variations in colour than to variations in brightness. The arrangement of samples used in CCIR 601 is called *4:2:2* sampling; it is illustrated in Figure 7.10. In each line there are twice as many Y samples as there are samples of each of $B-Y$ and $R-Y$. Since, for those pixels whose colour is sampled, all three values are sampled at the same point, the samples are said to be *co-sited*. The resulting data rate for CCIR 601 video, using 8bits for each component, is 166 Mbits (just over 20 Mbytes) per second.

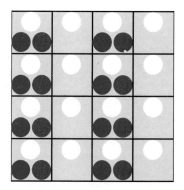

Figure 7.10 4:2:2 chrominance sub-sampling

Why 4:2:2 and not 2:1:1? Because other sampling arrangements are possible. In particular, as we will see when we consider DV, some standards for digital video employ either 4:1:1 sampling, where only every fourth pixel on each line is sampled for colour, or 4:2:0, where the colour values are sub-sampled by a factor of 2 in both the horizontal and vertical directions – a somewhat more complex process than it might at first appear, because of interlacing. (The notation 4:2:0 is inconsistent; it certainly does not mean that only one of the colour difference values is sampled.)

DV and MPEG

Sampling produces a digital representation of a video signal. This must be compressed and then formed into a data stream for transmission. Further standards are needed to specify the compression algorithm and the format of the data stream. Two separate sets of standards are emerging, both based on $Y'C_BC_R$ components, scanned according to CCIR 601, but with further chrominance sub-sampling.

As we remarked earlier, digital video equipment intended for consumer and semi-professional use (such as corporate training video production) and for news-gathering is based on the DV standard; studio equipment, digital broadcast TV and DVD are based on *MPEG-2*, one of several ISO standards produced by the ISO/IEC *Motion Picture Experts Group (MPEG)*. Their earlier MPEG-1 standard, primarily intended for the Video CD format (which never became very popular), has provided a basis for subsequent MPEG video standards. One of these, MPEG-4, has recently emerged as one of the leading formats for streamed video.[†]

† The main rival to MPEG-4 in this area is Microsoft's proprietary Video for Windows format.

DV and its main variations – DVCAM and DVPRO – all use the same compression algorithm and data stream as DV, which always has a data rate of 25 Mbits (just over 3 Mbytes) per second, a compression ratio of 5:1. There are, however, a high quality DVPRO and a professional Digital-S format, which use 4:2:2 sampling, unlike DV which uses 4:1:1, and offer better quality at correspondingly higher bit rates. These are for professional use. Finally, HDDV is a high-definition version of DV, suitable for low-budget film making.

Each of the MPEGs was designed as a family of standards, organized into different *profiles* and *levels*. Each profile defines a subset of features of the data stream; as we will see in the next section, for instance, MPEG-2 allows some scope for different ways of encoding the digital video data. Each level defines certain parameters, notably the maximum frame size and data rate, and chrominance sub-sampling. Each profile may be implemented at one or more of the levels, although not every combination of level and profile is defined. The most common combination in MPEG-2 is *Main Profile at Main Level (MP@ML)*, which uses CCIR 601 scanning with 4:2:0 chrominance sub-sampling; it supports a data rate of 15 Mbits per second and allows for the most elaborate representation of compressed data provided by MPEG-2. MP@ML is the format used for digital television broadcasts and for DVD video.

MPEG-4 is an ambitious standard designed to support a range of multimedia data at bit rates from as low as 10 kbits per second all the way up to 1.8 Mbits per second or higher. This allows MPEG-4 to be used in applications ranging from mobile phones to HDTV. To accommodate these requirements, MPEG-4 defines many profiles, each of which provides tools for one of the types of media data that the standard envisages being encoded as an MPEG-4 data stream. At present, it is the visual profiles concerned with video data that have attracted most attention. In particular, the *Visual Simple Profile (SP)* can be used for low-bandwidth video streaming over the Internet, and its relatively low computing requirements for decompression make it suitable for use on less powerful devices, such as PDAs. The slightly more sophisticated *Visual Advanced Simple Profile (ASP)* is suitable for broadband streaming of video to desktop computers. For each of these profiles, different levels specify the values of parameters such as frame size and bit rate. For example, SP@L1 (level 1 of the Simple Profile) specifies a bit rate of 64 kbps, for a frame size of 176×144 pixels; ASP@L5 specifies 8000 kbps at full PAL CCIR 601 size, 720×576. Hence, even within these two profiles, MPEG-4 provides for a full range of bit rates, frame sizes and image quality. Potentially, MPEG-4 video could supersede MPEG-2 for applications such as DVD video, but the existing investment in DVDs using MPEG-2 makes it likely that the two will coexist for a long time to come.

MPEG-4 compression is supported in QuickTime and RealMedia (see below), and is the basis for the Sorensen Squeeze codec used for adding video to Flash movies. MPEG-4 was also supported by Windows Media in versions lower than 9, but has now been superseded by Microsoft's own proprietary codec in Windows Media 9. MPEG-4 video is also used by the DivX system. DivX video files use the AVI file format, with an MPEG-4 codec that supports SP and ASP. The resulting files are small (for video) and of good quality, so DivX is becoming popular as a format for distributing video over the Internet.

It has been compared to the MP3 audio format in this respect, since it makes it possible to create files that are compact enough to be downloaded over domestic broadband connections, which can be played back using a free codec. An inexpensive version of the DivX codec can also be used encode video, so independent film makers can easily make their work available over the Internet in DivX format. Fears have been expressed about the possibility of unscrupulous persons using DivX to encode commercial movies ripped from DVD and exchanging them, in the same way that MP3 music files have been widely illicitly exchanged.

Introduction to Video Compression

We have seen that video data is usually compressed when it is digitized. Digital video formats are intimately bound up with compression, so before we can consider how video may be represented and manipulated inside a computer we must look at compression techniques that are applied to it.

The form of compression applied by digital video cameras and video capture boards is usually optimized for playback through the same devices. For example, DV video is best played back through a DV deck or camcorder, not directly to a computer monitor. When we want to use a video sequence as part of a multimedia production, we cannot rely on our users having any particular video hardware, so the only safe assumption is that the video is going to be played back using their computer's processor. Additionally, we have to assume that the video data must be delivered from a hard disk, at best, or from a CD-ROM or DVD, or even over a network connection. We will usually prepare video material using a software codec, to apply a form of compression that is more suited to the capabilities of the hardware that is likely to be used by consumers. Typically, therefore, our video data will need to be compressed twice: first during capture and then again when it is prepared for distribution. To appreciate the implications of this, we need to understand the general features of the compression algorithms employed at both of these stages.

All video compression algorithms operate on digitized video consisting of a sequence of bitmapped images. There are two ways in which this sequence can be compressed: each individual image can be compressed in isolation, using the techniques introduced in Chapter 5, or sub-sequences of frames can be compressed by only storing the differences between them. These two techniques are usually called *spatial compression* and *temporal compression*, respectively, although the more accurate terms *intra-frame* and *inter-frame* compression are also used, especially in the context of MPEG. Naturally, spatial and temporal compression can be used together.

Since spatial compression is really just image compression applied to a sequence of images, it makes sense to distinguish between lossless and lossy methods – the distinction, and the trade-offs implied, are the same as they are for still images. Generally, lossless methods do not produce sufficiently high compression ratios to reduce video data to manageable proportions, except on synthetically generated material (such as we will consider in Chapter 8). However, although lossily compressing and recompressing video usually leads to a deterioration in image quality, and should be avoided if possible, recompression is often unavoidable, since the compressors used for capture are not suitable for delivery for multimedia. Furthermore, for post-production work, such as the creation of special effects, or even fairly basic corrections to the footage, it is usually necessary to decompress the video so that changes can be made to the individual pixels of each frame. For this reason, it is wise, if you have sufficient disk space, to work with uncompressed video during the post-production phase. That is, once the footage has been captured and selected, decompress it and use uncompressed data while you edit and apply effects, only recompressing the finished product for delivery.

There is considerable irony in the fact that one of the most loudly voiced advantages of digital video (and audio) is that it suffers no 'generational loss', unlike analogue video, which inevitably degrades every time you copy a tape, as you must whenever you perform any editing, and when you prepare material for distribution. Digital data can be copied as many times as you like, without any loss of quality – provided all you are doing is making an exact copy. As soon as you start decompressing and recompressing between copies, something very much like generational loss, only uglier, happens after all. The irony is compounded by the fact that considerable effort is being expended on devising methods to prevent people making exact copies, for fear of widespread piracy of digital video.

The principle underlying temporal compression algorithms is simple to grasp. Certain frames in a sequence are designated as *key frames*. Often, key frames are specified to occur at regular intervals – every sixth frame, for example – which can be chosen when the compressor is invoked. These key frames are either left uncompressed, or more likely, only spatially compressed. Each of the frames between the key frames is replaced by a *difference frame*, which records only the differences between the frame originally in that position and either the most recent key frame or the preceding frame, depending on the sophistication of the decompressor. For many sequences, the differences will only affect a small part of the frame. Consider, for example, a typical 'talking head' shot, of a person's head and upper body against a background, such as you might see on a news report. Most of the time, only parts of the speaker's face will be moving; the background, and perhaps the speaker's upper body, will remain static, so the pixels corresponding to these elements will keep the same values from frame to frame. Therefore, each difference frame will have much less information in it than a complete frame. This information can be stored in much less space than is required for the complete frame.

You will notice that we have described these compression techniques in terms of frames. This is because we are normally going to be concerned with video intended for progressively scanned playback on a computer. However, the techniques described can be equally well applied to fields of interlaced video; while this is somewhat more complex, it is conceptually no different.

Compression and decompression of a piece of video need not take the same time. If they do, the codec is said to be *symmetrical*, otherwise it is *asymmetrical*. In theory, this asymmetry could be in either direction, but generally it is taken to mean that compression takes longer – sometimes much longer – than decompression. This is acceptable, except during capture, but since playback must take place at a reasonably fast frame rate, codecs which take much longer to decompress video than to compress it are essentially useless.

The quality of lossily compressed video can only be judged subjectively – we can measure how much information has been discarded, but not whether it matters to the viewer. Consequently, any terms used to describe video quality are vague at best. One of the most commonly employed terms is 'broadcast quality', which does not mean the quality you receive on a TV set, it means good enough *to be* broadcast or used in post-production – a much higher quality, usually only achieved in a professional studio, using high-end equipment. 'Near broadcast quality', a favourite term of marketing people, means 'not broadcast quality'. 'VHS quality' is a vague term, as VHS tape is available in a very wide range of grades, from the cheapest commonly used in domestic VCRs to tapes described as 'professional' or 'broadcast'. Generally, though, it is reasonable to take 'VHS quality' to mean 'just about acceptable'.

Motion JPEG

Many video compression schemes are based, like JPEG image compression, on the use of the Discrete Cosine Transform. the most straightforward approach is to apply JPEG compression to each frame, with no temporal compression. JPEG compression is applied to the three components of a colour image separately, and works the same way irrespective of the colour space used to store image data. Video data is usually stored using $Y'C_BC_R$ colour, with chrominance sub-sampling, as we have seen; JPEG compression can be applied directly to this data, taking advantage of the compression already achieved by this sub-sampling.

The technique of compressing video sequences by applying JPEG compression to each frame is referred to as *motion JPEG* or *MJPEG* compression,[†] although you should be aware that, whereas JPEG is a standard, MJPEG is only a loosely defined way of referring to this type of video compression. MJPEG is used by most analogue capture cards, which usually employ special-purpose hardware to allow the complex computations required by the JPEG algorithm to be carried out fast enough to keep up with the incoming video signal. Individual hardware manufacturers have implemented motion JPEG independently, and in the absence of any standard, implementations differ slightly, especially in the way that the compressed data is stored. Recently, a consortium of digital video companies has agreed a standard format known as *MJPEG-A*, which is supported by QuickTime (see below), ensuring that compressed data can be exchanged between systems using different hardware. As DV and other purely digital formats take over from analogue video, the use of MJPEG compression will decline.

† Not to be confused with MPEG.

Like still-image JPEG, motion JPEG codecs allow the user to specify a quality setting, trading off high compression against image quality. Instead of specifying the quality directly, video codecs often allow the specification of a maximum data rate, from which a suitable quality setting is deduced. This is appropriate, for example, if you wish your video to be played back from a DVD, where the maximum data rate is known in advance. Data rates of around 3 Mbytes per second, corresponding to a compression ratio of around 7:1, are commonly achieved by low- to mid-range capture cards. More expensive cards offer higher data rates (lower compression ratios) and therefore better quality. (The more you pay for compression, the less of it you get.) However, for multimedia use, it is invariably necessary to apply a

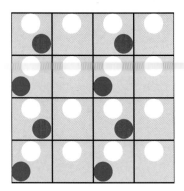

Figure 7.11 4:2:0 chrominance sub-sampling (PAL DV)

† Actually, DVCPRO uses 4:1:1 for PAL as well as NTSC.

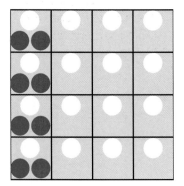

Figure 7.12 4:1:1 chrominance sub-sampling (NTSC DV)

high degree of compression to the video data for delivery, so although the principle of starting with the highest possible quality material is a sound one, it may not be worthwhile working with the best capture boards if the final product is destined for CD-ROM or the Internet.

Provided the device on which the compressed video data is stored is capable of delivering it at the rate required by the card, MJPEG video can be played back at full frame size at standard frame rates.

DV

DV compression also uses the DCT and subsequent quantization to reduce the amount of data in a video stream, but it adds some clever tricks to achieve higher picture quality within a constant data rate of 25 Mbits (3.25 Mbytes) per second than MJPEG would produce at that rate.

DV compression begins with chrominance sub-sampling of a frame with the same dimensions as CCIR 601. Oddly, the sub-sampling regime depends on the video standard, PAL or NTSC, being used. For PAL, 4:2:0 sub-sampling with co-sited sampling is used, but for NTSC 4:1:1 is used instead.† As Figures 7.11 and 7.12 show, the number of samples of each component in each 4×2 block of pixels is the same.

Blocks of 8×8 pixels from each frame are transformed using the DCT, and then quantized and run-length and Huffman encoded along a zig-zag sequence, just as in JPEG compression. There are, however, a couple of additional embellishments to the process.

First, the DCT may be applied to the 64 pixels in each block in one of two ways. If the frame is static, or almost so, with no difference between the picture in each field, the transform is applied to the entire 8×8 block, which comprises alternate lines from the odd and even fields. However, if there is much motion, so that the fields differ, the block is split into two 8×4 blocks, each of which is transformed independently. This leads to more efficient compression of frames with motion. The compressor may determine whether there is motion between the frames by using motion compensation (described below under MPEG), or it may compute both versions of the DCT and choose the one with the smaller result. The DV standard does not stipulate how the choice is to be made.

Second, an elaborate process of rearrangement is applied to the blocks making up a complete frame, in order to make best use of the space available for storing coefficients. A DV stream must use exactly

25 Mbits for each second of video; 14 bytes are available for each 8×8 pixel block. For some blocks, whose transformed representation has many zero coefficients, this may be too much, while for others it may be insufficient, requiring data to be discarded. In order to allow the available bytes to be shared between parts of the frame, the coefficients are allocated to bytes, not on a block-by-block basis, but within a larger 'video segment'. Each video segment is constructed by systematically taking 8×8 blocks from five different areas of the frame, a process known as *shuffling*. The effect of shuffling is to average the amount of detail in each video segment. Without shuffling, parts of the picture with fine detail would have to be compressed more highly than parts with less detail, in order to maintain the uniform bit rate. With shuffling, the detail is, as it were, spread about among the video segments, making efficient compression over the whole picture easier.

As a result of these additional steps in the compression process, DV is able to achieve better picture quality at 25 Mbits per second than MJPEG can achieve at the same data rate.

MPEG Video

MPEG-4 is currently the most important of the MPEG standards for multimedia, but its handling of video is based on the earlier MPEG-1 standard, which is also sometimes used for video on the Web and CD-ROM, so we will begin by describing MPEG-1 compression in some detail, and then indicate how MPEG-4 differs from it.

MPEG-1

The MPEG-1 standard[†] doesn't actually define a compression algorithm: it defines a data stream syntax and a decompressor, allowing manufacturers to develop different compressors, thereby leaving scope for 'competitive advantage in the marketplace'. In practice, the compressor is fairly thoroughly defined implicitly, so we can describe MPEG-1 compression, which combines temporal compression based on motion compensation with spatial compression based, like JPEG and DV, on quantization and coding of frequency coefficients produced by a discrete cosine transformation of the data.

A naive approach to temporal compression consists of subtracting the value of each pixel in a frame from the corresponding pixel in the previous frame, producing a difference frame. In areas of the picture where there is no change between frames, the result of this

[†] ISO/IEC 11172: 'Coding of moving pictures and associated audio for digital storage media at up to about 1.5Mbit/s'.

Figure 7.13 An object moving between frames

Figure 7.14 Area of potential change (in white)

Figure 7.15 Area of potential change allowing for motion of the object

subtraction will be zero. If change is localized, difference frames will contain large numbers of zero pixels, and so they will compress well – much better than a key frame. Often, though, we may be able to do better, because pictures are composed of objects that move as a whole: a person might walk along a street, a football might be kicked, or the camera might pan across a landscape with trees. Figure 7.13 shows a simple example, in which the clapperboard – a distinct and clearly delineated object – moves through two consecutive frames of a movie. As the clapperboard moves across the screen, it obscures different parts of the sea shore behind it, while everything else in the scene stays still. Figure 7.14 shows the area within which pixels may have changed, which would have to be stored in a difference frame. If we could somehow identify the coherent area corresponding to the clapperboard, we would only need to record its displacement together with the changed pixels in the smaller area shown in Figure 7.15. *Motion compensation* is an attempt to do this.

MPEG-1 compressors do not attempt to identify objects in a scene. Instead, they divide each frame into blocks of 16×16 pixels known as *macroblocks* (to distinguish them from the smaller blocks used in the DCT phase of compression), and attempt to predict the whereabouts of the corresponding macroblock in the next frame. No high-powered artificial intelligence is used in this prediction: all possible displacements within a limited range are tried, and the best match is chosen. The difference frame is then constructed by subtracting each macroblock from its predicted counterpart, which should result in fewer non-zero pixels, and a smaller difference frame after spatial compression. The price to be paid is that, in addition to the difference frame, we now have to keep the *motion vectors* describing the predicted displacement of macroblocks between frames. These motion vectors can, however, be themselves compressed: the motion vector for a macroblock is likely to be similar or identical to the motion vector for adjoining macroblocks (since these will often be parts of the same object), so, by storing the differences between motion vectors, additional compression, analogous to inter-frame compression, is achieved.

Temporal compression has to start somewhere. MPEG key frames are called *I-pictures*, where I stands for *intra*. These frames are purely spatially (intra-frame) compressed. Difference frames that use previous frames are called *P-pictures*, or 'predictive pictures'. P-pictures can be based on an earlier I-picture or P-picture. MPEG goes further and allows for frames that are predicted from later frames; these are

B-pictures. Figure 7.16 shows why backward prediction can be useful. In the top frame, from the beginning of the sequence, the figure of the actress is hidden, but as the sequence proceeds, she appears from behind the moving clapperboard. If we wished to use this frame as an I-picture, the following P-pictures would have to record all the pixels of the figure. However, she is present in a later frame, so if the intermediate frames are predicted from both the upper and lower frames shown in Figure 7.16 (i.e. not just a preceding frame, but a later one too), further compression will be achieved. B-pictures can use motion compensation from the next I- or P-pictures, or both, hence their full name 'bi-directionally predictive' pictures.

A video clip can be encoded in compressed form as a sequence of I-, P- and B-pictures. It is not a requirement that this sequence be regular, but encoders typically use a repeating sequence, known as a *Group of Pictures* or *GOP*, which always begins with an I-picture. Figure 7.17 shows a typical example. (You should read it from left to right, like a time line.) The GOP sequence is **IBBPBB**; the picture shows two such groups: frames 01 to 06 and 11 to 16. The arrows indicate the forward and bi-directional prediction. For example, the P-picture 04 depends on the I-picture 01 at the start of its GOP; the B-pictures 05 and 06 depend on the preceding P-picture 04 and the following I-picture 11. All three types of picture are compressed using the MPEG-1 version of JPEG compression. Published measurements indicate that, typically, P-pictures compress three times as much as I-pictures, and B-pictures one and a half times as much as P-pictures. However, reconstructing B-pictures is more complex than reconstructing the other types, so there is a trade-off to be made between compression and computational complexity when choosing the pattern of a GOP. An additional factor is that random access to frames corresponding to B- and P-pictures is difficult, so it is customary to include I-pictures sufficiently often to allow random access to several frames each second. Popular GOP patterns include **IBBPBBPBB** and **IBBPBBPBBPBB**. However, as we remarked, the MPEG-1 specification does not require the sequence of pictures to form a regular pattern, and sophisticated encoders will adjust the frequency of I-pictures in response to the nature of the video stream being compressed.

Figure 7.16 A hidden object revealed in a later frame

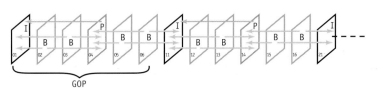

Figure 7.17 An MPEG sequence in display order

For the decoder, there is an obvious problem with B-pictures: some of the information required to reconstruct the corresponding frame is contained in an I- or P-picture that comes later in the sequence. This problem is solved by reordering the sequence. The sequence of pictures corresponding to the actual order of frames is said to be in 'display order'; it must be rearranged into a suitable 'bitstream order' for transmission. Figure 7.18 shows the bitstream order of the sequence shown in display order in Figure 7.17. All the arrows showing prediction now run from right to left, i.e. every predicted frame comes later in the sequence than the pictures it depends on.[†] You will notice that the first GOP is reordered differently from the second; any subsequent groups will extend the pattern established by the second.

† For the B-pictures, we have run the arrows to the relevant P- and I-pictures together, with an intermediate arrowhead, in an attempt to keep the diagram less cluttered.

Figure 7.18 An MPEG sequence in bitstream order

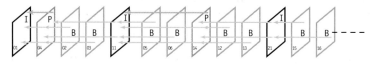

Before any of this compression is done, MPEG-1 video data is chroma sub-sampled to 4:2:0. If, in addition to this, the frame size is restricted to 352×240,[‡] video at a frame rate of 30 fps can be compressed to a data rate of 1.86 Mbits per second – the data rate specified for compact disc video. This is the typical format for MPEG-1 video, although it can be used with larger frame sizes and other frame rates. MPEG-1 cannot, however, handle interlacing or HDTV formats, hence the need for MPEG-2 for broadcasting and studio work.

‡ 4:2:0 video of this size is said to be in *Source Input Format (SIF)*.

If nothing else, the preceding description should have made it clear that MPEG compression and decompression are computationally expensive tasks – and there are further complications which we have glossed over. Initially, MPEG video, like MJPEG, could only be played back using dedicated hardware. Indeed, the parameters used for CD video were chosen largely so that MPEG decoders could be accommodated in VLSI chips at the time the standard was drawn up (1993). Advances in processor speed mean that it has since become feasible to play back MPEG-1 video using software only. File sizes are by no means small, however. A 650 Mbyte CD-ROM will only hold just over 40 minutes of video at that rate; an 8.75 Gbyte DVD has room for over nine hours. (You would only use MPEG-1 on DVD if your video was part of a multimedia production, though. DVDs employ MPEG-*2* when they are Digital *Video* Disks.)

MPEG-4

MPEG-4 is an ambitious standard, which defines an encoding for multimedia streams made up of different types of object – video, still images, animation, textures, 3-D models, and more – and provides a way of composing scenes at the receiving end, from separately transmitted representations of objects. The idea is that each type of object will be represented in an optimal fashion, rather than all being composited into a sequence of video frames. Not only should this allow greater compression to be achieved, it also makes interaction with the resulting scene easier, since the objects retain their own identities.

At the time of writing, however, it is the video compression algorithms described in the MPEG-4 standard which have received the most attention, and for which commercial implementations exist.

As we remarked earlier, MPEG-4 defines a collection of profiles for video data. The higher profiles employ a method of dividing a scene into arbitrarily shaped *video objects*, for example a singer and the backdrop against which she is performing, which can be compressed separately. The best method of compressing the background may not be the same as the best method of compressing the figure, so by separating the two, the overall compression efficiency can be increased. However, dividing a scene into objects is a non-trivial exercise, so the lower profiles – *Simple Profile* and *Advanced Simple Profile* – are restricted to rectangular objects, in particular complete frames, and it is these profiles which have been implemented in widely used systems such as QuickTime and DivX. For practical purposes, therefore, MPEG-4 video compression is a conventional, frame-based codec, which is a refinement of the MPEG-1 codec just described. I-pictures are compressed by quantizing and Huffman coding DCT coefficients, but some improvements to the motion compensation phase used to generate P- and B-pictures provide better picture quality at the same bit rates, or the same quality at lower bit rates, as MPEG-1.

The Simple Profile uses only P-pictures (those that depend only on earlier pictures) for inter-frame compression. This means that decompression can be more efficient than with the more elaborate schemes that use B-pictures (which may depend on following pictures), so the Simple Profile is suitable for implementation in devices such as PDAs and portable video players. The Advanced Simple Profile adds B-pictures and a couple of other features. *Global Motion Compensation* is an additional technique that is effective for compressing static scenes with conventional camera movements, such as pans and zooms.

The movement can be modelled as a vector transformation of the original scene, and represented by the values of just a few parameters. *Sub-pixel motion compensation* means that the displacement vectors record movement to an accuracy finer than a single pixel; in the case of Simple Profile, half a pixel, and for the Advanced Simple Profile, a quarter of a pixel. This prevents errors accumulating, resulting in better picture quality, with little additional overhead.

Other Codecs for Multimedia

MPEG-4 is emerging as the preferred codec for video on the Web, but you will often encounter video compressed using older codecs. The three most common of these are called *Cinepak*, *Intel Indeo*, and *Sorenson*.

All three are based on a technique known as *vector quantization*, which works in the following manner: each frame is divided up into small rectangular blocks of pixels, the 'vectors' in vector quantization. The codec uses a collection of constant vectors, known as a *code book*; the code book vectors represent typical patterns that might occur in an image, such as flat areas of colour, sharp or soft edges, or different textures. Quantization is the process of allocating each vector in the image to the vector in the code book which approximates it most closely. (It is a generalization of scalar quantization, familiar from our description of digitization, when a value from some continuous range is approximated by one of a number of fixed levels.) Vector quantization provides compression, because each vector in the image can be replaced by an index into the code book. The image can be reconstructed from these indices and the code book by a simple process of putting together copies of the code book vectors corresponding to the stored indices. Decompression is thus very efficient, and can be carried out without special-purpose hardware. Compression, on the other hand, is a computationally intensive process, so these codecs are highly asymmetrical: compressing a frame using Cinepak, for example, typically takes more than 150 times as long as decompressing it.

Cinepak, Intel Indeo and Sorenson all augment their vector quantization compression with temporal compression using key frames and difference frames. The first two use a straightforward differencing scheme, while Sorenson uses a more sophisticated scheme, including motion compensation, which is closer to that used in MPEG compression.

Even though the decompression process is relatively efficient, full-motion full-screen playback cannot be achieved on mid-range processors with these codecs. Therefore, they are usually applied to small frames to be played back at reduced frame rates. Respectable (VHS quality) images can be achieved at quarter-frame size (320×240 pixels) and 12 frames per second – certainly not good enough for the discerning viewer, but acceptable for many purposes. The Sorenson codec (the most efficient of the three) can compress video with these parameters so that it has a data rate of only 50 kilobytes per second, which is well within the capabilities of a 'multimedia PC' and can even be delivered by a 1× speed CD-ROM drive. (It should be borne in mind, though, that this data rate is still well in excess of that of a modem, so there is no chance of using these codecs to achieve real-time playback over a dial-up Internet connection. They could be used in this way over a 10 base T ethernet, though.)

Of the three, Cinepak has been established the longest. It remains popular, because of the high compression ratios it can achieve, and the efficiency with which it plays back compressed material, which makes it especially suitable for use on older computers. Intel's Indeo is similar in its general characteristics, but is less asymmetrical, being roughly 30% faster than Cinepak at compressing. It was originally intended for hardware implementation, but is now available in an efficient software version. It is generally held that Cinepak is superior for material with a lot of motion, but Indeo is better for more static material, for which it does a better job of preserving colours accurately. However, the quality of neither is particularly good. Sorenson is the most recently produced of these three codecs, and was widely hyped on its appearance as being superior to the other two, both in quality and in the compression ratios it can achieve.

Codec Comparison

Figures 7.19–7.24 provide a simple comparison of the quality of three leading codecs, compared with a DV original. As we showed earlier in the chapter, the DV frame already shows some compression artefacts, but it serves as an appropriate reference point, since it was the format in which the footage was captured, and is thus the best quality attainable.

As you can see, the MPEG-4 and DV frames are virtually indistinguishable, but the two other codecs show degradation of the image, and a noticeable shift in brightness. The Cinepak version, in particular, is extremely poor, as the highly magnified comparisons

Figure 7.19 Sample DV frame

Figure 7.20 DV frame detail

Figure 7.21 MPEG-4 detail

of the girl's face illustrate graphically. All the codecs were used at their medium quality setting. (For MPEG-4, accurate compression was chosen in preference to fast compression.) The average amount of memory per frame was 161 kbytes for the original DV, 95 kbytes for the MPEG-4 version, 114 kbytes for Sorenson video and 68.5 kbytes for Cinepak. Thus, Cinepak does produce the smallest file size, but at a considerably lower quality. MPEG-4 produces a significant amount of compression with no perceptible loss of quality, and would be the best choice of codec, unless the efficiency of decompression was important.

This single comparison does not, of course, provide comprehensive evidence of the relative virtues of the different codecs, which may perform differently on different types of source material, but it does show, in broad terms, the type of result you can expect on live footage with a natural subject.

Figure 7.24 Comparison of DV (top) and Cinepak (bottom) magnified

Figure 7.22 Sorenson detail

Figure 7.23 Cinepak detail

QuickTime

As preceding sections have shown, there exists a plethora of digital video compression schemes and data formats: DV, MPEG-1, MPEG-2 and MPEG-4, several varieties of MJPEG, various software compressors, including the ones described earlier, proprietary schemes devised by particular manufacturers of digital video workstations, not forgetting uncompressed video. Each of these schemes requires the information to be encoded in a different way; within each encoding there is scope for defining incompatible file formats – some standards, such as the MPEGs, only define a data stream, not a file format. Because of the diversity of requirements, there is little hope of being able to design a universal video file format, and the usual political considerations make it unlikely that all the parties involved would agree to it, even if one could be devised. A more profitable approach to standardization is to base it on an architectural *framework*, defined at a sufficiently abstract level to accommodate a multiplicity of concrete video representations. Several such approaches have been proposed, but *QuickTime* has established itself as a *de facto* standard.

QuickTime was introduced by Apple in 1991, and has been extended through new versions ever since. The objects that QuickTime manipulates are *movies*. For the present, you can consider a movie to be an abstraction of a video sequence, although, in fact, QuickTime movies can contain other types of media as well. Although we speak of a movie containing data, the movie itself is really just a framework for organizing, accessing and manipulating the data that represent the actual video frames, which may be stored separately from the movie itself.

Originally, QuickTime's focus was on the temporal aspects of time-based media, including video. Every movie has a *time base*, which records the rate at which it should be played back and its current position; both are specified relative to a time coordinate system which allows the time base to be synchronized to a clock so that movies can be played back at the correct speed on any system. When a movie is played, if the frames cannot be displayed fast enough to maintain the required frame rate, some are dropped so that the overall duration of the movie will be correct and synchronization (for example with an associated sound track) will be maintained. The time coordinate system also makes it possible to identify specific points in a movie, so that individual frames can be accessed; this in turn facilitates non-linear editing of movies – a topic which will be described in the next section.

The success of QuickTime is largely due to its being a component-based architecture. This means that it is possible to plug components (small programs conforming to certain interface conventions) into the QuickTime structure in order to deal with new formats and provide new implementations of operations. A set of standard components is supplied as part of the distribution. These include a number of *compressor components*, implementing MPEG-4, Sorenson, Cinepak, and Intel Indeo codecs, as well as several others developed for specific tasks such as compressing computer-generated animation. *Sequence grabber components* are used to digitize video. They use lower level components to obtain any necessary parameters from the user, and to communicate with digitizing hardware. A standard *movie controller* component is used to provide a user interface for playing movies. There are also components called *transcoders*, which translate data between formats that use the same compression algorithm, without the need for decompression and recompression.

QuickTime can also be used for streaming video. Its streeaming implementation is based on open Internet standard protocols, particularly RTSP, the Real Time Streaming Protocol, which is used to control the playback of video streams, which are carried over the network using the Real Time Protocol, RTP. These protocols are described in Chapter 17. Streaming QuickTime streams can be embedded in Web pages and in any application that incorporates QuickTime. Several different versions of a movie can be provided, compressed to match the requirements of different types of connections – a 28.8 kbps version, a 56 kbps version, a T1 version, and a cable modem version may all be provided so that, to the user, there only appears to be one movie; the server chooses the appropriate one to fit the speed of the user's connection. Tools are available for integrating the QuickTime streaming server with capture facilities, allowing live video to be streamed to the Internet. As well as true streaming, progressive download is supported by QuickTime.

Since Streaming QuickTime is essentially just QuickTime delivered in a special way, all of the QuickTime codecs can be used for streaming. However, to obtain sufficient compression to stream a movie over most network connections, these have to be used on their lowest quality settings, and the movie will generally have to be scaled down to a small frame size. With current technology, best results are obtained using QuickTime's MPEG-4 codec.

QuickTime does have its own file format, which provides a very flexible way of storing video and other media.[†] To avoid imposing this format on everybody, and to enable application software based on QuickTime to access other types of file, components have been added to make it possible to manipulate files in other formats as if they were native QuickTime. Formats supported in this way include MPEG-1, MPEG-4 and DV, OMF (a high-end professional format), and Microsoft's AVI, and its extension OpenDML. As this demonstrates, QuickTime's component architecture makes it easily extensible. For example, DivX Networks have produced a component that allows QuickTime to be used to play DivX movies. Another common example occurs when a new video capture card is developed, with its own features and idiosyncrasies. Provided its manufacturer writes a (relatively simple) *video digitizer component*, any application program based on QuickTime can capture and play back video using the new card, edit that video, and convert it to other formats. Looking at this from the other side, anybody who devises a new video format or codec does not have to implement all the high level editing operations that are necessary to make it useful – QuickTime provides all that, using the interface supplied by the components associated with the type of data in question. This abstraction away from specific formats is passed on to end users of video editing and playback software. For example, when a video editor wishes to save an edited movie, he or she is presented with options for selecting a compression method. If a new codec is added to their system, it will show up as a new alternative within the same interface.

QuickTime is available in a fully compatible form on the 32-bit Windows platforms as well as MacOS, and QuickTime is also supported on SGI workstations for professional use. A version of QuickTime for Java has also been developed. As well as the basic functionality implemented in the QuickTime system software, a plug-in for popular Web browsers is distributed with QuickTime, which means that QuickTime files can be used as a format for distributing video over the World Wide Web.

There are two other major video formats that you might encounter or consider for use in multimedia. Real Networks' RealVideo is a widely used streaming video format, with many resemblances to Streaming QuickTime. It is based on the same protocols and supports MPEG-4,

[†] The QuickTime file format was used as the basis for the MP4 format for MPEG-4 data.

but it also has its own proprietary codec, which is claimed to achieve better compression than MPEG-4. RealVideo was the first commercially available streaming video format, and remains popular on the Web.

The other major video format is AVI. AVI files are the native format for Microsoft's Windows Media, a system with similar objectives to QuickTime. It is less comprehensive in its support for codecs and formats than QuickTime, and uses a proprietary codec. Because of the pervasiveness of Windows operating systems, AVI is very widely used, especially on Microsoft systems, but it has failed to achieve QuickTime's status as a *de facto* cross-platform standard. As we stated earlier, QuickTime can handle AVI files directly.

Editing and Post-Production

Shooting and recording video only provides raw material. Creating a finished piece of video – whether it is a feature film or a small clip for a Web site – requires additional work. *Editing* is the process of making a constructed whole from a collection of parts. It comprises the selection, trimming and organization of the raw footage, and where sound is used, its combination with the picture. *Transitions*, such as dissolves, may be applied between shots, but no changes are made to the footage itself. We contrast this with *post-production*, which is concerned with making changes or adding to the material. Many of the changes made at this stage are generalizations of the image manipulation operations we described in Chapter 5: colour and contrast corrections, blurring or sharpening, and so on. Compositing – the combination or overlaying of elements from different shots into one composite sequence – is often carried out during post-production; for example, figures may be inserted into background scenes that were shot separately. Elements may be animated during post-production, and animation may be combined with live action, in the manner that has become characteristic of film special effects.

People have been making films for over a hundred years, and during that time an elaborate set of conventions about how film – and, by extension, video – is edited have developed. For example, action sequences in Hollywood films are typically cut 'on the action'; that is, cuts are made while something is happening, in order to distract the viewer's attention from the cut itself. In contrast, flashback sequences are often introduced by a long dissolve, typically starting from a shot of a person starting to tell a story about earlier events, with the narration continuing over the first shot of the flashback. Here, the transition is used to signify the change of time frame, and is supposed to be evident to the viewer, or this method of signification will not work. Viewers expect film to be edited in accordance with conventions such as these. If it is not, as in certain types of avant garde work, then that fact in itself makes a statement. Thus, in contrast to Hollywood directors, some of the French *nouvelle vague* directors during the 1960s deliberately used 'jump cuts', occurring apparently gratuitously in the middle of a scene, to draw attention to the constructed nature of their films, and cut straight to flashbacks instead of using dissolves, acknowledging that film is only seen in its own time. This kind of editing requires the audience to be more alert – to work harder – if they are to appreciate what the film-maker is doing (or even follow the narrative, in some cases). Early film makers, such as Dziga Vertov and Sergei Eisenstein, experimented with editing as much as with the process of shooting film, and their work is still referred to by students of film today.

All film and video is constructed. A common example is the way in which a conversation between two people facing each other is conventionally presented: each person occupies the field of view while they speak; when the speaker changes, a cut occurs to a 'reverse shot', with the camera apparently moving instantaneously through nearly 180° to face the new speaker – as if the camera were each person in turn, watching the other speak. You have probably seen this so often that you barely think about it, but, in fact, the two actors in the scene were probably not carrying on a conversation in real time while the dialogue was shot; they may not even have been filmed speaking their lines on the same day. The conversation is created in the editing, on the basis of a convention that does not resemble the way anybody could see that conversation if it really took place. This is a particularly blatant example of the artifice involved in constructing sequences of moving pictures, but some artifice is always involved – even the picture from a live Webcam is framed in a certain way. While most Hollywood film makers seek to make the construction of a film invisible, and concentrate on telling a story, other directors, such as Jean-Luc Godard, prefer to expose the mechanics of film making, and still others, such as Eric Rohmer, prefer to minimize their reliance on convention, and shoot and edit in a more realistic way, using third person viewpoints and extended shots for dialogue scenes, with the sound recorded live, for example. But, however a piece of film or video is to be constructed, it will be necessary both to shoot footage and to edit it.

Even if nobody had ever wanted to display video on a computer, incorporate it into a multimedia production, or broadcast it digitally, video would have been digitized, because the advantages of non-linear editing which digitization brings are too compelling to resist. To appreciate this, and to understand the metaphors used by digital editing systems, you have to consider traditional methods of film and video editing.

Film and Video Editing

Editing film is a physical process. To a film editor, a 'cut' is not merely a figurative reference to an edit that produces a discontinuity in the flow of pictures, it is a real severing of the film itself, which divides a strip of film into two clips which may then be spliced together with others to compose a scene. Clips can be trimmed, cut and spliced, arranged and rearranged, for as long as the fabric of the film holds up. The main problem with this basic editing is keeping track of everything – a good deal of labelling and hanging strips of film from hooks is called for.

Although making straight cuts in film is straightforward, creating other types of transition between clips is much less so, and requires special equipment. Suppose, for example, you wanted a scene of someone falling asleep to dissolve into a dream sequence. Such an effect is conventionally achieved using a device called an *optical printer*, which is a rig that directs the light from a pair of projectors into a camera.[†] Optical filters and masks can be interposed to control the amount of light from each projector reaching the camera. For our dissolve, we would put the end of the falling asleep scene on one projector and the beginning of the dream sequence on the other; initially, filters would be set up so that all the light from the first projector and none from the second reached the camera. Gradually, the filters would be adjusted, so that the two beams were mixed, with the proportion from the second projector increasing as that from the first decreased. The result would be a piece of film with the required dissolve effect; this would then be spliced in place of the corresponding frames of the two original clips.

Despite the apparent simplicity of the set-up, exceptionally sophisticated effects can be achieved using such 'opticals', in conjunction with techniques such as matte painting or with models. One drawback is that opticals are usually done by a specialist laboratory, so the film editor cannot actually see what the transition looks like until the film has been developed. This leaves little room for experimentation.

[†] There are different types of optical printer. Some only use a single projector, but expose the film in the camera more than once, to achieve the same effects as the set-up described here.

It is no coincidence that the straight cut forms the basis of most films' structure.

Traditional video editing, although the same as film editing in principle, is quite different in practice. It is virtually impossible to cut video tape accurately, or splice it together, without destroying it. The only way to rearrange pictures recorded on video tape was to copy them onto a new tape in the desired order. If, for example, we wanted to cut from an outside view of a house to a scene in a room inside it, and had first recorded interior scenes and then added some outside shots to the end of the same tape, we could use two tape machines (call them A and B) to assemble the material in the required order. The output signal from machine A is fed to the input of machine B, so that B records what A plays. The original tape is put on machine A and wound forward to the point at which the desired part of the exterior scene begins, then B is started and records that scene. Recording is stopped while machine A is rewound to the exact beginning of the interior, which is then copied onto the tape in machine B, which now holds the required material in the right order.

A more powerful arrangement is to use three machines, designated A, B and C. The three-machine edit suite is still the paradigm for most desktop video editing software. If you can arrange that your two scenes are on separate tapes, you load one on to each of A and B, and set the *in point* (first frame) and *out point* (last frame) of each. A device known as an *edit controller* can now start machine A at the in point of the first scene, copying it on to machine C until it reaches its out point, when machine B is started at its in point, adding the second scene to the tape on machine C. One virtue of this arrangement is that the cut can be previewed, by running machines A and B without actually recording on C, so it is possible to experiment with adjusting in and out points until a perfect cut is obtained. The signals can be mixed and modified electronically, so this arrangement also provides a video equivalent of the optical printer, for some standard operations. A rich variety of transitions can be produced this way, and, unlike film transitions, they can be reviewed straight away, and parameters such as the speed of a dissolve can be controlled in real time. Three machines also make insert editing straightforward. Suppose, for example, that part of a scene has had to be reshot after a first edit of the scene has been done. The original edit can be played off one machine, until the point where the defective footage occurs, at which point the signal is taken from the other machine, and then switched back after the replacement shot has been inserted.

Note that these operations require that the machines be able to start and stop in precisely the right place. As it is physically impossible to start a tape transport instantaneously, some *pre-roll* is always required, as the machine comes up to speed. This method of editing requires not only extremely accurate control mechanisms, but also some means of identifying positions on tapes. *Timecode* is used for this purpose. There are several standards in use, but the only one of any importance is *SMPTE* timecode. A timecode value consists of four pairs of digits, separated by colons, such as 01:14:35:06, representing hours, minutes, seconds, and frames, so that the complete value identifies a precise frame. A trivially obvious scheme, you may well think – the tricky bit is writing the code onto the tape so that its current frame can be read by a machine. Standards for doing so are in place, and so 'frame-accurate' positioning of tape is possible.

Timecode behaves differently depending on the frame rate: for a PAL system, the final component (which identifies the frame number) ranges from 0 to 24, for NTSC it ranges from 0 to 29, but not in the obvious way, because the NTSC frame rate is 29.97. Since there is not an exact number of NTSC frames in a second, SMPTE timecode, which must use exactly 30, drifts with respect to the elapsed time. The expedient adopted to work round this is called *drop frame timecode*, in which frames 00:00 and 00:01 are omitted at the start of every minute except the tenth. (It's a bit like a leap year.) So your count jumps from, say, 00:00:59:29 to 00:01:00:02, but runs smoothly from 00:09: 59:29 through 00:10:00:00 to 00:10:00:01. Whether or not it handles drop frame timecode correctly is one measure of how professional a digital video editing program is.

Editing video on two or three machines requires tapes to be copied every time a change is made, and it is inevitable that there will be generational loss as noise is introduced by the copying process. Even the best analogue systems used for commercial video always introduce some loss every time a copy is made. With VHS tape, just two copying operations are usually sufficient to produce serious loss of quality. A second drawback is that the final tape has to be constructed linearly, from beginning to end, in contrast to film, which can be spliced together in any order. This imposes a less flexible way of working, which inevitably has implications for the nature and quality of video editing. Now that digital video is being widely used, the analogue three-machine edit suite is falling into disuse and most video editing is being done on computers.

Digital Video Editing and Post-Production

The unique visual qualities of film might make the process of cutting and splicing worthwhile, but analogue video is such a poor medium that it offers little return for the hardships that must be endured in a three-machine edit suite. Digitization has opened the way to a different mode of working, that brings video editing closer in kind to film editing, but without the physical process. An imperfect, but useful, analogy of the difference between linear analogue and non-linear digital video editing is the difference between writing with a typewriter and using a word processor. On a traditional typewriter, words have to be written in their final order, with the potential for corrections limited to what can be achieved with Tipp-Ex, unless an entire sheet is thrown away and retyped – which might upset subsequent pagination. In the latter case, corrections can be made anywhere, text can be composed in any order, without regard to pagination or layout. The ability to access and change data randomly, which is fundamental to the way we build computers, engenders these capabilities in text processing software, and analogous ones in video editing software.

Besides random access, digital video editing's other big advantage is that it is non-destructive. Source clips are never changed. This means that it is possible to cut and recut, potentially forever, as the editor changes his or her mind. Furthermore, in contrast to film, edited digital video can be played back as soon as the hardware on which it is being edited allows. With top-end equipment, this is instantaneously; on desktop machines, there may be some delay, but the delays are measured in minutes or hours at worst, not the days that it may take for film to be processed. Recent advances in hardware and software mean that now even desktop equipment often provides instant playback of edited digital video.

Developments in hardware, including DV camcorders and FireWire and the increased speed of processors and capacity of hard disks, have led to a broadening of interest in digital video editing at all professional levels and among consumers. There is now a range of software, from basic consumer-oriented editors, designed for editing home videos, up to the state-of-the-art editing suites used by film and television studios. Now that DV is widely used, many mid-range editing and post-production applications provide a 'DV-native' editing environment, in which most operations are performed on DV data, which ensures that picture quality is maintained at the highest possible level for material in this format. Recompression is only required where transitions and effects are applied.

Each editor will evolve their own method of working with a particular program, but the facilities provided by different editing applications are basically the same. One simple, idealized procedure for editing with a desktop application would begin with assembling all the clips for a project – capturing them where necessary, and importing them into a library, where they may be arranged for convenient access. Next, each clip is opened within the application, and roughly trimmed. Note that trimming does not actually discard any frames, as it would with film; it merely suppresses those before the in point and after the out point. If necessary, the in and out points can be readjusted later; if the out point is subsequently moved to a later frame in the clip, or the in point is moved to an earlier one, frames between the old and new points will reappear. The initial trimming operation will leave the editor with the material that they believe should appear in the final movie. The next step is to arrange clips in the desired order on the timeline, assembling them into a rough cut, which can be previewed. Still images can also be used; given a duration, they will behave as clips with no motion. For movies with sound, the picture and sound track can be combined. Almost always, adjustments will have to be made, particularly if it is necessary to match up sound and picture. Clips may need to be trimmed again, or more drastic changes may be required, such as the substitution of completely different material when ideas fail to work out.

For some basic projects, editing will be complete at this stage, but for others, the desired transition from one clip to the next cannot be achieved simply by cutting directly. Using other types of transition changes the style, rhythm and mood of a piece. A dissolve, for example, in which one clip fades into another (Figure 7.25), is less emphatic than a cut, and tends to convey a sense of gradual change or smooth flow from one thing to another. A dissolve to black and then into a new scene is often used to indicate that time has passed between the two scenes. More fanciful transitions, such as wipes, spins and page turns, draw attention to themselves, and function almost as decoration. As most transitions can be described relatively easily in terms of mathematical operations on the two clips involved, digital video editing software usually offers a vast range of possibilities – some video editing applications have well over fifty transitions built in (most of them showy gimmicks), plus a means of defining your own – of which the majority will never be used by a good editor.

Figure 7.25 A dissolve

Many transitions are parameterized: for example, the 'clock wipe' transition (Figure 7.26) may play clockwise or anti-clockwise.

There are two important practical differences between cuts and other transitions. Firstly, in a cut, the two clips are butted; in all other transitions, they overlap, and some part of each contributes to the resulting picture. For sequences which are not going to be edited just with basic cuts it is therefore necessary to ensure that when shot and captured to disk, each clip has sufficient extra frames, beyond the period where it is to play alone, to cover the transition. Secondly, because image processing is required to construct the transitional frames, transitions must be rendered, unlike cuts, which can be implemented simply by copying. Hence, there will inevitably be some loss of image quality where dissolves and so on are used instead of straight cuts.

Video editing is primarily concerned with the arrangement of picture through time, and its synchronization with sound. While frame accuracy may be required to set precise in and out points, or to eliminate faulty footage, it is rarely necessary while editing to consider whole sequences of footage as individual frames. In post-production procedures, however, the temporal dimension may assume less importance, and a movie may be dealt with as a sequence of individual still images. Most digital post-production tasks can be seen as applications of the image manipulation operations we described in Chapter 5 to the images in such a sequence, and contemporary applications that include post-production facilities normally describe them in the same terms as are used when dealing with bitmapped still images. Two important classes of post-production operation that can be described in these terms are those concerned with image correction, and with compositing.

A video sequence may suffer from the same defects as a single image: for example, it may be over- or under-exposed or out of focus; it may have a colour cast, or it may display unacceptable digitization artefacts. Each of these defects has its characteristic remedy: adjust the levels, sharpen, or apply a Gaussian blur. Post-production systems therefore provide the same set of adjustments as image manipulation programs – some support the use of Photoshop plug-ins – but allow them to be applied to sequences instead of a single image.

Most adjustments have parameters, such as the slider positions for the levels controls. When adjustments are made to sequences, it may be appropriate to use the same parameter values for each image, or it may be preferable for them to change. If, for example, a whole, mostly static, sequence has been shot under incorrect lighting, the same correction will probably be needed for every frame, so the levels can be set for the first, and the adjustment will be applied to as many frames as the user specifies. If, however, the light fades during a sequence, when it was intended to remain constant, it will be necessary to increase the brightness gradually to compensate. It is possible to apply a suitable correction to each frame individually, and this may occasionally be necessary, but often it is adequate to specify parameters at a few key frames and allow their values at intermediate frames to be interpolated. The panel at the bottom of Figure 7.27 shows a typical interface for defining interpolation. Varying parameter values over time can be used to achieve certain special effects, as Figure 7.28 illustrates.

Just as some of the image manipulation operations we described in Chapter 5 combined separate layers into a composite result, so some post-production operations combine separate video tracks into a composite. As with still images, for superimposition to achieve anything useful, some parts of the superimposed tracks must be transparent. In video, selecting transparent areas is called *keying*. Good video editing and post-production software will offer several different keying methods.

The method of blue screening, which we described for single images in Chapter 6, has long been used in video for inserting isolated elements into shots. Traditional examples of its use include adding models to live footage, or placing actors in impossible or dangerous situations. Digital post-production systems support both traditional blue screening, where the actor or model is shot in front of a screen that is a particular shade of blue and then the blue channel is removed, and a more general form of *chroma keying*, where any colour in a scene can be selected and designated as transparent. Chroma keying is essentially the same as building an alpha channel from a selection made using a magic wand tool. An alternative is *luma keying*, where a brightness threshold is used to determine which areas are transparent.

In some applications, it is possible to select a transparent area explicitly, using selection tools to create a mask. In film and video, a mask used for compositing is called a *matte*. Mattes are frequently used for removing unwanted elements, such as microphone booms, from a scene, in which case the matte is called a *garbage matte*, or

Figure 7.26 A clock wipe

Figure 7.27 A colour offset filter applied to video over time

for allowing live footage to be combined with a still image. A typical example of such a use of mattes occurs when actors are filmed on a set containing just a few foreground elements such as trees and plants. The top of the picture (typically just a plain backdrop on the set) is matted out, and subsequently replaced with a painting of a landscape, so that the foreground scene appears to be taking place in front of a mountain range, a medieval castle, or whatever. Mattes can also be used for split-screen effects.

Another way of creating transparency is to use an alpha channel created in some other application. This is often the most satisfactory method of creating mattes to be used in conjunction with still images, since Photoshop provides much more sophisticated selection tools than most video applications. Alternatively, an imported greyscale image can be used as a matte.

Figures 7.29 and 7.30 illustrate the complexity of layered compositions that can be achieved using a video application. Alpha channel and luma key masking have been used to insert a luminous sparkling dove into the scene, which is itself created by applying effects to multiple layers.

Since a video clip is a sequence of images, a new possibility arises that is not present when single images are being composited: transparency can be made to vary over the course of the sequence (that is,

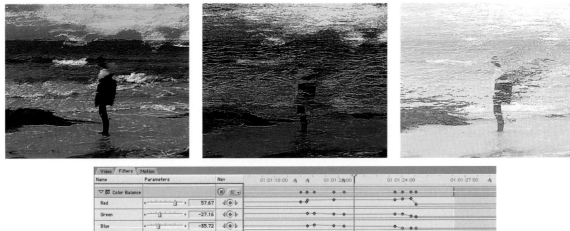

Figure 7.28 A complex set of filters applied to video over time to achieve a special effect

to vary over time when it is played back). This happens automatically with chroma and luma keying, as the colour and brightness distribution changes between frames. In order to produce masking that varies over time, it is necessary to use a sequence of masks as the matte. Such a sequence – often called a *travelling matte* – is naturally stored in a separate video track, when it is called a *track matte*. Although, in principle, the content of any suitable video track could be used as

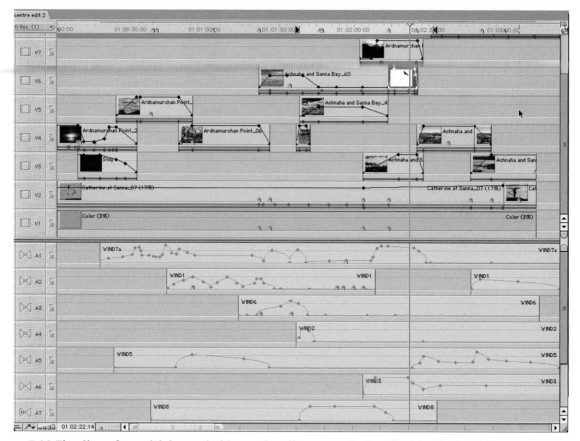

Figure 7.29 Timeline of a multi-layered video and audio composited project in Final Cut Pro

a travelling matte, a specially designed sequence of masks will often be required in practice. Track mattes may be created painstakingly by hand, but are more usually generated from a single still image, by applying simple geometrical transformations over time to create a varying sequence of mattes, in a way that we will describe in Chapter 8. Travelling mattes are often used in title sequences, where they are especially favoured for news bulletins.

The quality of picture achieved after applying effects and filters will depend on which video application is being used Where an editing program such as Premiere may allow you to apply a filter to a clip, and vary it over time, a more sophisticated program will provide a wide range of controls for the filter's parameters, and for the more sophisticated interpolation between key frames that it offers. For example, in Premiere, the parameter values are interpolated linearly between key frames, whereas in AfterEffects, the interpolation can

Figure 7.30 A five-layer video composition using luma key and masking to produce a richly textured result (left) at the edit point shown in the timeline of Figure 7.29

also use Bézier curves, which can be specified using handles and control points, as they can in Illustrator. Increasingly, such high-end post-production facilities are also being seen in the more powerful editors, such as Final Cut Pro.

Preparing Video for Multimedia Delivery

Editing and post-production are performed in roughly the same way whether the final video is intended for multimedia delivery – off-line or on-line – or for conventional transmission or recording on video tape. For multimedia, an additional step of preparing the material for delivery is usually required. The reason for this step is the need to cope with limitations of the final delivery medium and playback platforms that are not usually relevant on the platform used for editing and post-production. (Recall from Chapter 2 that multimedia production usually takes place on specially equipped top-of-the-range desktop machines or workstations, whose performance far exceeds that of consumer machines.) Compromises must be made at this stage, which will involve choosing what is to be sacrificed in order to bring the resource requirements of video within the capabilities of delivery media and low-end machines. Different material will permit and suggest different choices.

What might be sacrificed in this way? The possibilities include frame size, frame rate, colour depth, and image quality. Reducing the size of video frames is usually a relatively painless way of reducing the size and bandwidth of video files. People usually sit close to their monitors, so a large picture is not necessary, and monitor resolution is usually better than that of television sets, so a down-sampled image on a computer screen can appear smoother than the images we are familiar with on television (assuming the down-sampling is done intelligently). Similarly, reducing the frame rate is often acceptable: the illusion of continuous motion can often be satisfactorily maintained with frame rates around 12 fps. Higher frame rates are needed to eliminate flicker only if the display is refreshed at the frame rate. This is not the case with computer monitors, which are refreshed at a much higher rate from VRAM. By using quarter frames and reducing the frame rate from 30 fps to 15, the volume of data is reduced by a factor of eight.

A further factor of three can be obtained by reducing the colour depth from the 24 bits usually used for video to eight bits. As we explained in Chapter 6, this can be done by limiting the colours to those in a standard palette (usually the Web-safe palette), using indexed colour with a custom palette, or by reducing to 256 shades of grey. We argued in Chapter 6 that the last option may be preferable to using a limited range of colours. Unfortunately, not all video codecs support the use of greyscale images.

If these compromises are unacceptable, or – as may easily be the case – they do not sufficiently reduce the resource requirements of your video, it will be necessary to squeeze bytes out with compression, at the cost of a loss of image quality. We have already described suitable codecs, and their characteristics. It should be emphasized that, despite all the clever algorithms they use and despite the claims that are sometimes made, all codecs introduce visible artefacts when very high compression ratios are needed. It may be necessary to apply filters in order to minimize their effects, but this will also result in a further loss of picture information.

As well as taking steps to minimize the size of video, it is also necessary to ensure that it is fit to play on any platform. QuickTime movies prepared on a Macintosh computer must be flattened, for example, so that they do not store any data in the resource fork that is unique to MacOS files. Where necessary, movies must be made self-contained. That is, where the file format allows pointers to other files to be used as part of a movie, these pointers must be replaced by the data they refer to. It may be necessary to produce different versions of a movie for different platforms, to compensate for the different gamma of PC and Mac monitors, for example. For video that is to be delivered over a network it is common practice to produce a range of different versions matched to the speed of users' network connections. QuickTime allows different versions to be combined into a single movie.

Video editing programs provide facilities for performing the necessary preparation for delivery, but as with post-production tasks, their facilities are relatively crude, and it is better to use a dedicated application, such as Discreet Cleaner. This provides improved control over settings for codecs, and integrates compression with the other tasks we have described for preparation. Suitable filters can be applied to mitigate the effects of aggressive compression, and multiple versions can be constructed at the same time, and integrated. Additional facilities that are especially useful at this stage of production include a data rate analyzer, and a split-pane preview window for showing the effects of different settings.

Exercises

1   Under what circumstances will you need a hardware codec when working with video?

2   Specify the ideal video components of a system for the following projects:

(a) A video interview with a celebrity, to be recorded at their home, and incorporated into a Web page for which you will need to extract high quality still images as well as the video footage.

(b) A live video conference to be conducted across the Internet.

(c) A video recording of the close finish of a 100 metre sprint, for a multimedia production on the Olympic games, which will allow the user to determine the winner for themselves.

(d) A surveillance system in a bank which would provide visual evidence for a forensic multimedia presentation in a court of law.

(e) Video footage of a fast flowing mountain stream, which is to be presented as smoothly as possible in slow motion, in a small sized window on a Web page.

(f) Time-lapse footage of the opening of a flower, for use on a Web site devoted to gardening.

3   Specify a practical system, based only on the equipment available to you, for realising the same projects.

4   Suppose you were involved in the design of a multimedia software application for domestic use, intended to allow users to create 'home' multimedia productions such as a record of a child's birthday to send on CD-ROM to a grandparent on the other side of the world. What assumptions will you make about video for this program, and what facilities will you supply?

5   A user starts to download a 905 kilobyte movie of 30 seconds' duration, using progressive download over a connection that provides an average data rate of 2500 bytes per second. How long will it be before the movie starts to play? Why might the user experience jerky playback?

6   How much storage would be occupied by a 90 minute feature film stored in each of the following forms?

(a) CCIR 601

(b) MP@ML MPEG-2

(c) DV

(d) SP@L1 MPEG-4

(e) ASP@L5 MPEG-4

For each format, indicate what applications it is suitable for.

7 What effect will each of the following common video idioms have on a compression scheme that includes temporal compression?

(a) Cuts

(b) Dissolves

(c) Hand-held camera work

(d) Zooms

(e) Pans

In which cases does motion compensation help?

8 Suppose an MPEG encoder uses the nine-frame sequence IBBPBBPBB as a GOP. Draw a diagram showing the dependencies between the first 18 frames of a compressed clip produced by this encoder. Show how the pictures would be reordered into bitstream order. Explain carefully why the pattern of I, P and B pictures in the bitstream order of the first nine frames is different from that of the second nine frames.

9 Capture a short clip[†] from TV or a video tape of each of the following:

(a) A classic black and white *film noir*

(b) A contemporary soap opera

(c) A silent comic piece by Chaplin or Keaton

(d) A serious documentary

(e) A musical comedy in Glorious Technicolor

Observe how each has been edited to give it its particular character. Re-edit each clip to give it the style and feel of one of the others. For example, make a silent comedy clip out of the documentary, or *film noir* clip out of the musical comedy.

(a) Do this simply with basic transitions, i.e. cuts, dissolves, and wipes.

(b) If post-production tools are available to you, take this further, by changing colours, contrast, or the quality of sound. For example, render the contemporary soap opera in grainy black and white with crackly sound, or the re-edited *film noir* in three-colour Technicolor.

10 If you look closely at the frames in Figure 7.26, you will see combing in the area swept out by the clock wipe. Explain what causes this. What can you deduce about the speed with which this particular transition plays?

† Pay attention to copyright and use these clips only for your own work. Do not attempt to publish or broadcast them in any medium, including from a Web site.

Animation 8

- Captured Animation and Image Sequences
- Digital Cel and Sprite Animation
- Key Frame Animation
- Web Animation and Flash
  - The Timeline and Stage
- Motion Graphics
- 3-D Animation
- Virtual Reality
  - VRML
  - QuickTime VR

Animation may be defined as the creation of moving pictures one frame at a time; the word is also used to mean the sequences produced in this way, as in 'a Disney animation' or 'Web animation'. Throughout the twentieth century, animation was used for entertainment, advertising, instruction, art and propaganda on film, and latterly on video; it is now also widely employed on the World Wide Web and in multimedia presentations.

To see how animation works, consider making a sequence of drawings or paintings on paper, in which those elements or characters intended to change or move during the sequence are altered or repositioned in each drawing. The changes between one drawing and the next may be very subtle, or much more noticeable. Once the drawings are complete, the sequence of drawings is photographed in the correct order, a single frame at a time. When the film is played back, this sequence of still images is perceived in just the same way as the sequence of frames exposed when live action has been filmed in real time: persistence of vision causes the succession of still images to be perceived as a continuous moving image. If you wish to convey the illusion of fast movement or change, the differences between successive images in the sequence must be much greater than if the change is to be gradual, or the movement slow.

'Animate' literally means 'to bring to life', which captures the essence of the process: when played back at normal film or video speeds, the still characters, objects, abstract shapes, or whatever, that have been photographed in sequence, appear to come to life.

As film is projected at 24 frames per second, drawn animation in traditional media, as we have just described it, technically requires 24 drawings for each second of film, that is, 1440 drawings for every minute – and even more for animation made on video. In practice, animation that does not require seamlessly smooth movement can be shot 'on 2s', which means that two frames of each drawing, or whatever, are captured rather than just one. This gives an effective frame rate of 12 frames per second for film, or 15 for NTSC video. Digital animation can actually be played back at these lower frame rates, with the same saving in labour.

If an animation is made solely from drawings or paintings on paper, every aspect of the image has to be repeated for every single frame that is shot. In an effort to reduce the enormous amount of labour this process involves, as well as in a continuing search for new expressive possibilities, many other techniques of animation have been devised. The best known and most widely used – at least until very recently – has been *cel animation*. In this method of working, those elements in a scene that might move – Homer Simpson, for example – are drawn on sheets of transparent material known as 'cel', and laid over a background – the Simpsons' living room, perhaps – drawn separately. In producing a sequence, only the moving elements on the cel need to be redrawn for each frame; the fixed parts of the scene need only be made once. Many cels might be overlaid together, with changes being made to different ones between different frames to achieve a greater complexity in the scene. To take the approach further, the background can be drawn on a long sheet, extending well beyond the bounds of a single frame, and moved between shots behind the cels, to produce an effect of travelling through a scene. The concepts and techniques of traditional cel animation have proved particularly suitable for transfer to the digital realm, and many popular cel-like cartoons on TV are now produced digitally.

Largely because of the huge influence of the Walt Disney studios, where cel animation was refined to a high degree, with the use of multi-plane set-ups that added a sense of three-dimensionality to the work, cel has dominated the popular perception of animation. It was used in nearly all the major cartoon series, from *Popeye* to *The Simpsons* and beyond, as well as in many full-length feature films, starting with *Snow White and the Seven Dwarfs* in 1937. However, from the very beginnings of moving pictures in the 1890s, animation has been successfully created by employing a variety of other means. Many artists do indeed work by drawing each frame separately on paper, while others, even more painstaking, have painted directly on to film, or scratched the emulsion of blackened film stock; others have worked with sand or oil paint on glass, or chalks on paper or card, making changes to the created image between every shot; still others have manipulated front or back lit cut-outs under the camera

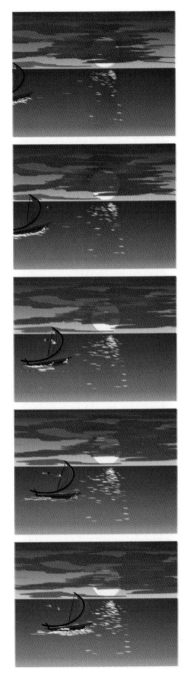

– Terry Gilliam's distinctive work for the *Monty Python* TV series is a well-known example of cut-out animation. Sometimes animators have invented a completely new way of working for themselves, such as Alexeïeff and Parker's pin screen, in which closely spaced pins are selectively pushed through a board and lit so that the shadows they cast form an image, which is changed between each shot.

A distinct alternative to all of these essentially two-dimensional forms is three-dimensional, or *stop-motion,* animation. This encompasses several techniques, but all use miniature three-dimensional sets, like stage sets, on which objects are moved carefully between shots. The objects may include articulated figures, whose limbs can be repositioned, or solid figures whose parts are replaced, or substituted, between shots, to produce an effect of gestures, walking, and so on. Figures and other objects made out of a malleable modelling material, such as Plasticine, may be used instead; these can be manipulated between shots, to produce both natural movement and otherwise impossible changes and transformations. This latter form of animation – often called *clay animation* – has achieved recent prominence with the work of the Aardman studios whose output includes the *Wallace and Gromit* films.

Although it may be convenient to consider the various techniques of animation separately, hybrid forms of animation are often produced – mixing cel and 3-D, for example. There is also a long tradition of combining animation with live footage. The most celebrated example of this is perhaps *Who Framed Roger Rabbit?* (1988), but a mixture of live action and animation was employed in some of the earliest films ever made, including Georges Méliès' well known 'trick films', and Max Fleischer's *Out of the Inkwell* series of the 1920s, which did much to popularize animation as a form of entertainment. Recently, the eager adoption of digital technology by the film industry has led to a substantially increased use of animation in conjunction with live action, particularly in special effects movies. It is perhaps not always realised by an audience that much of what they perceive as 'special effects' has been achieved by basic animation techniques, whether traditional, as in the 1933 classic *King Kong* and many other monster movies, or digital, as in *The Matrix* and its sequels, for example.

All of the traditional forms of animation have their counterparts in the digital realm. Moreover, digital technology affords new opportunities for using animation and techniques derived from it in new contexts.

Captured Animation and Image Sequences

As we will see, digital technology has brought new ways of creating animation, but computers can also be used effectively in conjunction with the older methods discussed above, to produce animation in a digital form, suitable for incorporation in multimedia productions. Currently, preparing animation in this way – using digital technology together with a video camera and traditional animation methods – offers much richer expressive possibilities to the animator working in digital media than the purely computer-generated methods we will describe later in this chapter.

Instead of recording your animation on film or videotape, a video camera is connected directly to a computer, to capture each frame of animation to disk – whether it is drawn on paper or cel, constructed on a 3-D set, or made using any other technique that does not depend on actually marking the film. Instead of storing the entire data stream arriving from the camera, as you would if you were capturing live video, you only store the digital version of a single frame each time you have set up a shot correctly. Many small utilities are available for performing *frame grabbing* of this sort, and some video editing applications provide the facility – Premiere, for example, offers a Stop Frame command on its Capture menu. Frame grabbers all work in roughly the same way: a recording window is displayed, showing the current view through the camera. You can use this to check the shot, then press a key to capture one frame, either to a still image file, or to be appended to an AVI or QuickTime movie sequence. You then change your drawing, alter the position of your models, or whatever, and take another shot. Frames that are unsatisfactory can be deleted; usually, an option allows you to see a ghost image of the previously captured frame, to help with alignment and making the appropriate changes. When you have captured a set of frames that forms a sequence, you can save it as a QuickTime movie or a set of sequentially numbered image files (see below). The latter option is useful if you want to manipulate individual images in Photoshop or import them into Flash, for example.

Capturing animation to disk in the manner just outlined not only opens up the possibilities of non-linear editing and post-production that we described in Chapter 7, it also allows animation in traditional media to be combined with purely digital animation and motion graphics; Figure 8.2 shows an example from a work produced in this hybrid fashion.

Figure 8.1 A cel-like digital animation sequence

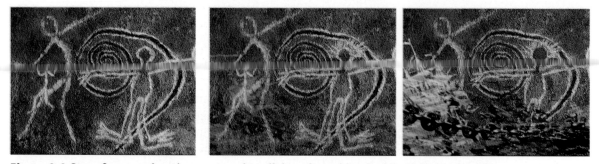

Figure 8.2 Stop-frame animation captured to disk and combined with digital animation

For certain types of traditional animation, it is not even necessary to use a camera. If you have made a series of drawings or paintings on paper, you can use a scanner to produce a set of image files from them. You can also manipulate cut-outs on the bed of a scanner, almost as easily as under a camera. A film scanner will even allow you to digitize animation made directly onto film stock. You can to use a digital stills camera instead of a video camera, provided it allows you to download images directly to disk. In all of these cases you are able to work at higher resolution, and with a larger colour gamut, than is possible with a video camera.

For drawn or painted animation you can dispense with the external form and the digitization process entirely by using a graphics program to make your artwork, and save your work as a movie or as a sequence of image files. You can use the natural media brushes of Painter or recent versions of Photoshop to produce animation that looks (somewhat) as if it was produced with traditional materials, or you can take advantage of the pixel manipulating facilities of these programs to produce work with a characteristic digital look. Even when you are producing your animation a frame at a time, a program can sometimes save you work, by letting you record macros or scripts for drawing repeated elements or applying filters to many frames.

Sequences of image files provide a very flexible representation of an animation. Individual files can be opened in a graphics program to be altered; single files can be removed from the sequence, replaced or added. The sequence can then be imported into a video editing application and converted into an AVI or QuickTime movie. However, managing a collection of image files can become complicated, especially if you eventually want to import them into a video editing program. In order for this to be possible without tying you to a particular combination of programs, the files' names must conform to some convention. For example, on the Macintosh, Premiere can only import a

sequence of PICT files if they are all in the same folder, and all the files have a suffix consisting of a period followed by the same number of digits, for example Animation.001, Animation.002, … **Animation.449**. (Failure to provide the necessary leading zeroes will have consequences that you can probably guess at.) If you make any changes to the set of images, you must take care not to disturb the numbering, or to adjust it if necessary.

Several computer programs, including Painter and Flash (which we will describe in more detail later) let you open a movie and modify its individual frames. (Photoshop can open files in a special filmstrip format, which Premiere can export and re-import, for similar purposes.) This offers new possibilities. You can, for example, paint onto or otherwise alter original video material, which is one way of adding animation to live action.[†] Another option is to trace, frame by frame on a layer, selected elements from a live action video clip, which is subsequently deleted. This process, whether achieved digitally or by older means, is what is properly referred to as *rotoscoping*, and has long been used to create animation that accurately reproduces the forms and natural movements of people and animals.

[†] In computer graphics circles, this process of painting onto existing video frames is sometimes called 'rotoscoping', but the use of the term is inaccurate, as explained below.

Rotoscoping is named after the *rotoscope*, a device patented by Max Fleischer (of *Betty Boop* and original animated *Popeye* fame) in 1915. Fleischer's device projected movie footage, one frame at a time, onto a light table, giving a back-projected still image over which the animator could place a sheet of animation paper. When the tracing of one frame was complete, the film was advanced to the next by means of a hand crank.

Instead of using a set of still image files to hold an animation sequence, you can sometimes use a single 'image' file to hold several images. While a surprising number of file formats – including, but not exclusively, formats intended for use with animation software – offer this facility, by far the most common is GIF.

GIF files' ability to store a sequence of images has been used to provide a cheap and cheerful form of animation for Web pages. Most Web browsers will display each image contained in a GIF file in turn when they load the file. If the displaying happens fast enough, the images will be seen as an animation. The GIF89a version of the format provides for some optional data items that control the behaviour of an *animated GIF*, as these files are called. In particular, a flag can be set to cause the animation to loop, either for a stipulated number of times or indefinitely, and a minimum delay between frames, and hence a frame rate, can be specified. However, animated GIFs do not provide a very reliable way of adding animated features to Web pages. As with most aspects of a browser's behaviour, the way in which animated GIFs are displayed can be changed by users – looping can be turned off, animation can be prevented, and if image loading is disabled, animated GIFs will not appear at all – and not all browsers offer a proper implementation. The main advantage of animated GIFs is that they do not rely on any plug-in, or the use of scripting (see Chapter 16), so they will be viewable using a wider range of browsers.

Several free or inexpensive utilities are available on the major platforms for combining a set of images into a single animated GIF; Premiere and Flash allow you to save a movie in this form, too, and dedicated Web graphics programs, such as ImageReady and Fireworks, can be used to create animated GIFs from scratch or by altering existing images. Potentially, therefore, GIF files can be used to store any form of animation. However, even when GIF animation is properly implemented and enabled, it has many shortcomings. You cannot add sound; you are restricted to a 256 colour palette; your images are losslessly compressed, which may conserve their quality, but does not provide much compression, a serious consideration that effectively prevents the use of this format for any extended animation sequences. Usually, each frame of an animated GIF is displayed by the browser as it arrives. Network speeds mean that there may be excessive, and probably irregular, delays between frames, making any frame rate that may be specified in the file irrelevant. However, if an animation is set to loop, once it has played through the first time it will have been copied into the browser's local cache (unless it is too big), and subsequent loops will play at a speed only limited by the user's processor and disk (which are completely unknown to the animator). In general, there is little chance of an animated GIF consistently playing back at a sufficiently high frame rate to give smooth animation, unless it is small. Usually, therefore, animated GIFs are not used for realistic animation, but for more stylized changing images, often resembling neon advertising signs. Possibly for this reason, by association of ideas, Web page advertising is what animated GIFs are most often used for. It is probably fair to say that, because of the ease with which animated advertisements can be incorporated into a Web page by almost anybody, they have been used for some of the worst animation ever produced. (Possibly as a result, the use of animated GIFs has declined in recent years.)

For captured animation of any duration, especially if it is accompanied by sound, the best results will be achieved using a video format. Once you have captured or painted an animation sequence and saved it as, or converted it to, QuickTime, for example, what you have is just an ordinary QuickTime movie, so it can be edited, combined with other clips, have effects applied, and be embedded in a Web page, just like any other video clip. However, animation clips may have some distinctive features which affect the way you deal with them. In particular, certain styles of drawn animation tend to feature simplified shapes and areas of flat colour. (This is *not* invariably the case; the characteristics of the images depend on the individual animator's style.) Material of this type may be more amenable to lossless compression than other types of video. QuickTime's *Animation* codec is designed to take advantage of the characteristics of simple cartoon-style drawn animation, which, as we will see later in this chapter, are often shared by computer-generated 3-D animation. Compression is based on run-length encoding (RLE), and, when the codec is used at its highest quality setting, is lossless. There is also a lossy mode that can be used to achieve higher compression ratios. Because it is based on RLE, this codec can compress areas of flat colour well, which is what makes it suitable for animation in the particular styles just mentioned.

'Digital Cel' and Sprite Animation

Our earlier description of cel animation may have put you in mind of layers, as described in Chapter 3. Layers allow you to create separate parts of a still image – for example, a person and the background of a scene they are walking through – so that each can be altered or moved independently. The frames of an animated sequence can be made by combining a background layer, which remains static, with one or more animation layers, in which any changes that take place between frames are made. Thus, to create an animation, you would begin by creating the background layer in the image for the first frame. Next,

on separate layers, you create the elements that will move; you may want to use additional static layers in between these moving layers if you need to create an illusion of depth. After saving the first frame, you begin the next by pasting the background layer from the first; then, you add the other layers, incorporating the changes that are needed for your animation. In this way, you do not need to recreate the static elements of each frame, not even using a script.

Where the motion in an animation is simple, it may only be necessary to reposition or transform the images on some of the layers. To take a simple example, suppose we wish to animate the movement of a planet across a background of stars. The first frame could consist of a background layer containing the star field, and a foreground layer with an image of our planet. To create the next frame, we would copy these two layers, and then, using the move tool, displace the planet's image a small amount. By continuing in this way, we could produce a sequence in which the planet moved across the background. (If we did not want the planet to move in a straight line, it would be necessary to rotate the image as well as displace it, to keep it tangential to the motion path.)

Using layers as the digital equivalent of cel saves the animator time, but, as we have described it, does not affect the way in which the completed animation is stored: each frame is saved as an image file, and the sequence will later be transformed into a QuickTime movie, an animated GIF, or any other conventional representation. Yet there is clearly a great deal of redundancy in a sequence whose frames are all built out of the same set of elements. Possibly, when the sequence comes to be compressed, the redundant information will be squeezed out, but compressing after the event is unlikely to be as successful as storing the sequence in a form that exploits its redundancy in the first place. In general terms, this would mean storing a single copy of all the static layers and all the objects (that is, the non-transparent parts) on the other layers, together with a description of how the moving elements are transformed between frames.

This form of animation, based on moving objects, is called *sprite animation*, with the objects being referred to as *sprites*. Slightly more sophisticated motion can be achieved by associating a set of images, sometimes called *faces*, with each sprite. This would be suitable to create a 'walk cycle' for a humanoid character, for example (see Figure 8.3). By advancing the position of the sprite and cycling through the faces, the character can be made to walk.

QuickTime supports sprite tracks, which store an animation in the form of a 'key frame sample' followed by some 'override samples'. The key frame sample contains the images for all the faces of all the sprites used in this animation, and values for the spatial properties (position, orientation, visibility, and so on) of each sprite, as well as an indication of which face is to be displayed. The override samples contain no image data, only new values for the properties of any sprites that have changed in any way. They can therefore be very small. QuickTime sprite tracks can be combined with ordinary video and sound tracks in a movie.

We have described sprite animation as a way of storing an animated sequence, but it is often used in a different way. Instead of storing the changes to the properties of the sprites, the changed values can be generated dynamically by a program. Simple motion sequences that can be described algorithmically can be held in an even more compact form, therefore, but, more interestingly, the computation of sprite properties can be made to depend upon external events, such as mouse movements and other user input. In other words, the move-ment and appearance of animated objects can be controlled by the user. This way of using sprites has been extensively used in computer games, but it can also be used to provide a dynamic form of interac-tion in other contexts, for example, simulations.

Key Frame Animation

During the 1930s and 1940s, the large American cartoon produc-ers, led by Walt Disney, developed a mass production approach to animation. Central to this development was division of labour. Just as Henry Ford's assembly line approach to manufacturing motor cars relied on breaking down complex tasks into small repetitive sub-tasks that could be carried out by relatively unskilled workers, so Disney's approach to manufacturing dwarfs relied on breaking down the production of a sequence of drawings into sub-tasks, some of which, at least, could be performed by relatively unskilled staff. Disney was less successful at de-skilling animation than Ford was at de-skilling manufacture – character design, concept art, storyboards, tests, and some of the animation, always had to be done by experienced and talented artists. But when it came to the production of the final cels for a film, the role of trained animators was largely confined to the creation of *key frames*.

We have met this expression already, in the context of video compres-sion and also in connection with QuickTime sprite tracks. There,

Figure 8.3 Sprite faces for a walk cycle

key frames were those which were stored in their entirety, while the frames in between them were stored as differences only. In traditional animation, the meaning has a slightly different twist: key frames are typically drawn by a 'chief animator' to provide the pose and detailed characteristics of characters[†] at important points in the animation. Usually, key frames occur at the extremes of a movement – the beginning and end of a walk, the top and bottom of a fall, and so on – which determine more or less entirely what happens in between, but they may be used for any point which marks a significant change. The intermediate frames can then be drawn almost mechanically by 'in-betweeners'. Each chief animator could have several in-between-ers working with him[‡] to multiply his productivity. (In addition, the tedious task of transferring drawings to cel and colouring them in was also delegated to subordinates.)

In-betweening (which is what in-betweeners do) resembles what mathematicians call *interpolation*: the calculation of values of a function lying in between known points. Interpolation is something that computer programs are very good at, provided the values to be computed and the relationship between them can be expressed numerically. Generally, the relationship between two key frames of a hand-drawn animation is too complex to be reduced to numbers in a way that is amenable to computer processing. But this does not prevent people trying – because of the potential labour savings.

All digital images are represented numerically, in a sense, but the numerical representation of vector images is much simpler than that of bitmapped images, making them more amenable to numerical interpolation. To be more precise, the transformations that can be applied to vector shapes – translation, rotation, scaling, reflection and shearing – are arithmetical operations that can be interpolated. Thus, movement that consists of a combination of these operations can be generated by a process of numerical in-betweening starting from a pair of key frames. This means that cartoon-like animation can be created digitally in programs like Flash with considerable savings of effort compared with traditional methods.

If we just consider motion in a straight line, the simplest form of inter-polation is *linear*. This means that an object moves an equal distance between each frame, the distance moved per frame being the total distance between the object's positions in the starting and ending key frames, divided by the number of frames in the sequence. Putting it

[†] The mass production approach to animation is almost invariably associated with cartoons featuring characters.

[‡] This 'him' is not a casual slip: the big cartoon studios of those days did not have what we would consider an enlightened attitude to women as animators.

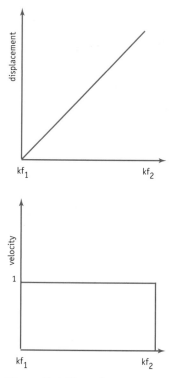

Figure 8.4 Linearly interpolated motion

more simply, the symbol moves at a constant velocity, which causes two problems.

First, motion begins and ends instantaneously, with objects attaining their full velocity as soon as they start to move, and maintaining it until they stop. Nothing really moves like that. To produce a more natural movement, programs that implement interpolated motion (including Flash) borrow a technique from hand-made animation: the transition from stasis to movement is made more gradual by using smaller, slowly increasing, increments between the first few frames (i.e. the object accelerates from a standstill to its final velocity), a process referred to as *easing in*. The converse process of deceleration is called *easing out*. Figure 8.4 shows the way the horizontal displacement and velocity of an object changes with time when it is moved from an initial position in key frame 1 (kf_1) of (0, 0) to a final position in key frame 2 (kf_2) of (50, 50), using linear interpolation over 50 frames. Figures 8.5 and 8.6 show how the change might be modified when the motion is eased in or out – we have shown a style of easing that uses *quadratic* interpolation, that is, the acceleration is constant. More complicated styles are possible and might be preferred. When applying easing in Flash, the animator can set the degree of easing using a slider that moves from maximum easing in, through a constant velocity, to maximum easing out. In effect, this moves the displacement curve from one like Figure 8.5, via similar curves with less pronounced bulge, through Figure 8.4 and beyond to Figure 8.6. (That is, the acceleration goes from some maximum positive value, through zero, to a maximum negative value.)

The second problem with linear interpolation can be seen in Figure 8.7, which shows how displacement and velocity change if we now append to our original sequence a second one of 50 frames, during which our object moves from its position in kf_2 of (50, 50) to a new position at (75, 75) in kf_3. Because each sequence is interpolated separately as a straight line, there is a sharp discontinuity at kf_2; as the velocity graph clearly shows, this will appear as a sudden deceleration at that point in the animation. Again, this is an unnatural sort of movement, that will rarely be what is desired. By clever manipulation of the easing slider, it would be possible to smooth out this abruptness, but a more general solution to the problem is available. In Chapter 4, we stressed that Bézier curves' most attractive property is that they can be joined together smoothly by aligning their tangent vectors. By using Bézier curves instead of straight lines to interpolate between key frames, smooth motion can be achieved. Note that we do

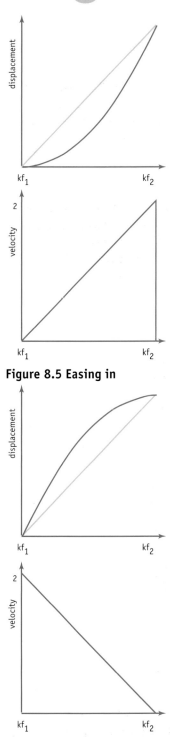

Figure 8.5 Easing in

Figure 8.6 Easing out

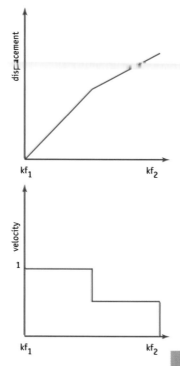

Figure 8.7 Abrupt change of velocity

not mean that objects should follow Bézier shaped paths, but that the *rate* at which their properties change should be interpolated using a Bézier curve. Flash does not offer the option of any form of non-linear interpolation but other, more elaborate, key frame animation systems do. Although we have only considered displacement in one direction, you should be able to see that similar considerations apply to any transformations that might be interpolated.

Web Animation and Flash

Animation can be added to Web pages in the form of animated GIFs or embedded video, but the most popular Web animation format is *Shockwave Flash (SWF)*, which is usually generated using Macromedia Flash. SWF is a vector animation format, which makes it particularly suitable for Web animation, since graphic objects can be compactly represented in vector form, and, as we outlined in the previous section, motion can be represented as numerical operations on the vector data. Thus, SWF animations can have lower bandwidth requirements than video or any bitmapped format. The price paid for this lower bandwidth is that vector animations do not offer the full range of visual possibilities available in bitmaps.

Although SWF files *may* be small, only needing low bandwidth, they are not necessarily so. Flash does allow bitmapped images to be imported into animations, and certain styles of drawing and animation lead to vector animations that are of considerable size. In fact, many Flash animations found on the Web take an unacceptable time to load over a dial-up connection. If bandwidth considerations are important to you, you need to make a conscious effort to avoid using bitmaps, draw simple vector shapes and use interpolated motion as much as possible in your animations.

Flash is more than an animation program. It supports a powerful scripting language, called ActionScript, which makes it possible to add interactivity to animations and to build Web applications with user interfaces created in Flash. We will return to these aspects of Flash in Chapter 16. Scripting can also be used to create animations in Flash, by using algorithms to set the position of movie clip symbols. Instead of creating motion by hand, objects can be made to move according to the laws of physics, or some mathematical description of behaviour, such as the way flocks of birds move as a group.

The Timeline and Stage

An animation being created in Flash is organized using a *timeline*, a graphical representation of a sequence of frames, similar to the timeline in video editing applications. Animations can be built up a single frame at a time, by inserting key frames into the timeline sequentially.

Flash's *stage* is a sub-window in which frames are created by drawing objects. Objects can be created on the stage using some built-in drawing tools, similar to but less comprehensive than those of Illustrator or Freehand, or they can be imported from those applications. Bitmap images, in formats including JPEG and PNG, may also be imported and auto-traced to make vector objects; images can be used in bitmap form within a Flash frame, but cannot then be rotated or scaled without potentially degrading the image. Comprehensive support is provided for text; characters in outline fonts can be decomposed into their component outline paths, which can be edited or animated separately. Layers can be used to organize the elements of a frame; they also play a key role in interpolating motion. Figure 8.8 shows the stage and timeline as they appear in Flash. The Flash interface also contains a toolbox, containing the vector drawing tools, and a host of palettes, for colour mixing, alignment, applying transformations, setting typographic options, and so on.

Figure 8.8 The timeline (top) and stage (below) in a simple Flash movie

When a movie is first created, it contains a single empty key frame. When a key frame is added to the timeline immediately after an existing key frame, it starts out with a copy of the contents of the preceding key frame. Since most animation sequences exhibit only small changes between frames, an efficient way of working on animations created a frame at a time is by adding key frames incrementally at the end of the current sequence and making changes to their contents. To assist with this sort of animation, Flash provides an *onion-skinning* facility; when this is turned on, up to five preceding frames are displayed semi-transparently under the current frame. This makes it easier to see the changes between frames, and to align objects correctly.

As well as key frames, the timeline can also hold simple frames. These contain no objects of their own; when the movie is played back, they continue to display the contents of the most recent key frame. That is, they hold on the key frame. You can add frames and key frames independently to different layers, so one layer may hold a static background image with moving elements on layers above it. The background layer will have just one key frame at the beginning, while the moving layers will have key frames at every point where an object moves. This may be every single frame.

Symbols and Tweening

Graphical objects can be stored in a library in a special form, called a *symbol*, that allows them to be reused. Multiple *instances* of a symbol may be placed on the stage. They will all be fundamentally identical, but transformations can be applied, to change the size and orientation of each instance. Instances remain linked to the symbol; if the symbol is altered, every instance is automatically altered too.

Since interpolated animations, almost by definition, reuse objects, interpolating (or *tweening*, as Flash puts it) the motion of an object turns it into a symbol. You can create tweened motion in several ways. In the simplest, a key frame is selected in the timeline, and an object is drawn on the stage. The command **Create Motion Tween** is selected from the **Insert** menu; this sets up the tweening and, as a side-effect, stores the object in the library as a symbol. Another key frame is created at the end of the tweened sequence, and the symbol is moved to a new position in this new frame. The tweening is shown on the timeline as an arrow between the two key frames, as you can see in Figure 8.8, where the two character layers have been tweened to move the creature across the screen in a straight line, as shown in Figure 8.9. (The figure only shows every fourth frame of the animation.) An animation may be built up as a sequence of automatically tweened segments, between key frames that have been arranged by hand, by repeating this process.

Moving a single symbol about the stage in a straight line offers little in the way of artistic gratification. Tweening can be applied to different layers, with key frames in different places, though, allowing the independent animation of many symbols, each of which may be part of a single character. To further ease the work of animating motion, an object can be moved along a path drawn on a hidden layer; this *motion path* need not be a straight line, so movements that would have to be constructed using many key frames if only rectilinear movements were possible can be achieved in a single tweened sequence with just two key frames. Finally, although the process we have described is referred to as 'motion tweening', an object's size, orientation, opacity and colour may also be interpolated in the same way.

As well as motion tweening, Flash supports *shape tweening*, or *morphing*, as it is commonly known. This is a form of interpolation where the shapes of graphical objects are transformed between key frames, for example, a square can be turned into a circle. In the animation shown at the beginning of this chapter and in Figures 8.10 to 8.12, the motion of the spray and ripples on the sea was created by shape tweening.

There are, in fact, three different sorts of symbol in Flash. *Graphic* symbols are simply reusable vector objects; the symbols created for motion tweening are graphic symbols by default. *Button* symbols are a specialized type of symbol, used for adding interactivity to Flash movies; we will describe them in Chapter 16. *Movie clip* symbols are self-contained animations with their own timelines, that play within the main movie. For example, the dolphins leaping picturesquely out of the water in the animation of the sailing ship were added to the basic animation of the ship, sea and clouds by creating a movie clip symbol of a single dolphin jumping, as in Figure 8.10; instances of this single dolphin symbol were added to the main movie, to make a school of dolphins to accompany the ship on its voyage.

Since movie clip symbol instances have their own timelines, they will continue to play, even when the main movie has been stopped. Figure 8.12 shows that the schools of dolphins carry on leaping, even when the ship has been frozen (by stopping the movie in the player). Compare these frames with the ones at the beginning of the chapter, to see how the compound animation has been built out of the independent movement of its elements. Figure 8.13 shows how the

Figure 8.9 A simple animation created by motion tweening

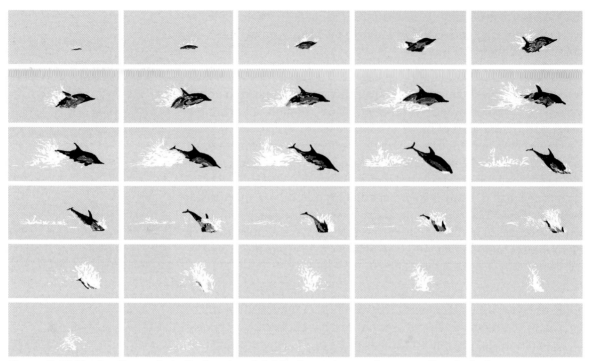

Figure 8.10 Movie clip symbol of a leaping dolphin (superimposed on grey for clarity)

Figure 8.11 Movie clip symbols playing in sync with other action in the main movie

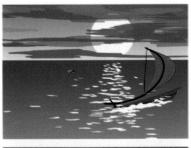 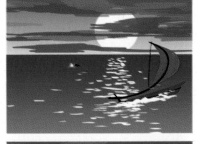 

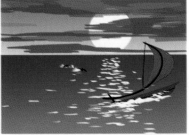 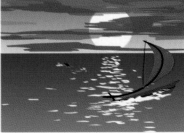 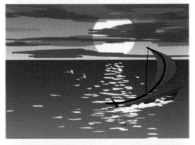

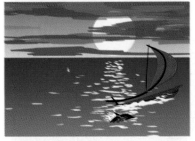  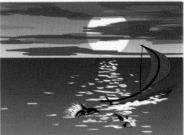

  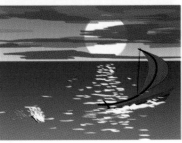

Figure 8.12 Movie clip symbols playing independently of the main movie

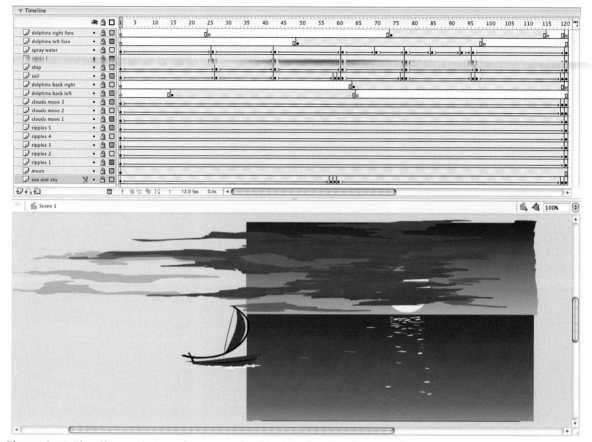

Figure 8.13 Timeline and stage for a complex Flash animation

composition was created out of many layers, with shape and motion tweening, as well as movie clips. Note how the images on the stage extend beyond the frame; tweening causes them to move into shot in the completed animation.

The nature of vector drawing and tweening leads to a compact representation of animations created in this way. An SWF file consists of *items*, which are divided into two broad classes: *definitions* and *control items*. The former are used to store definitions of the symbols used in an animation into a dictionary; the latter are instructions to place, remove, or move a symbol (identified by its name in the dictionary). Placement and movement are specified using transformation matrices, so that the position and any scaling or rotation are specified at the same time. An SWF file is thus rather like a program, comprising as it does definitions of some objects and instructions that manipulate them. SWF data is encoded in a binary form and compressed, resulting in very small files.

Motion Graphics

Interpolation between key frames can be applied to bitmapped images. Since bitmaps do not contain identifiable objects, the use of layers to isolate different elements of an animation is essential. The analogy with cel animations is more or less complete – each layer is like a transparent sheet of acetate with something painted on it. Layers can be moved independently, so an animation can be constructed by placing different elements on different layers, and moving or altering the layers between frames. Where the movement or alteration is easily described algorithmically, it can be interpolated between key frames, just as in-betweeners interpolate between a chief animator's key frames. Typically, between key frames, a layer may be moved to a different position, rotated or scaled. These geometrical transformations are easily interpolated, but since we are now concerned with bitmapped images, they may require resampling, and consequently cause a loss of image quality, as we explained in Chapter 5.

AfterEffects is the leading desktop application for animation of this kind. Because of their shared provenance, AfterEffects works well in conjunction with Photoshop and Illustrator. A Photoshop image can be imported into AfterEffects, with all its layers – including adjustment layers – and alpha channels intact; an Illustrator drawing can be imported and rasterized, again with its layers intact. A common mode of working, therefore, is to use the tools and facilities of Photoshop or Illustrator to prepare the elements of an animation on separate layers, and import the result into AfterEffects where the layers are animated. Photoshop images should be prepared at an appropriate resolution and size for your intended delivery medium. If they are to be scaled down, they must be large enough to accommodate the maximum reduction that will be applied. Illustrator files can be either rasterized when they are imported and then treated as bitmaps, or continuously rasterized for each frame in the animation. This means that if they are scaled, for example, no detail will be lost.

The simplest animations are made by repositioning layers, either by dragging them or by entering coordinates, and interpolating motion between key frames. By combining layers and adding effects and filters that also vary over time, moving graphic designs are obtained. The countdown sequence shown in Figure 8.14 was made by importing a set of still images into AfterEffects and animating them in this way. Apart from the interpolated motion of the complete bitmaps, no moving elements were used. The effects that can be achieved using

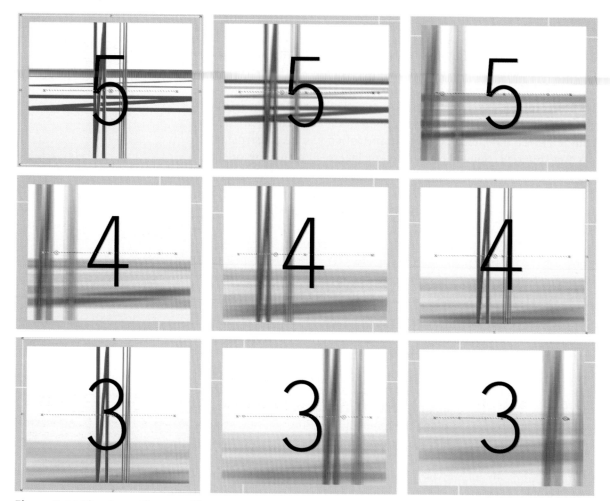

Figure 8.14 Simple motion graphics

motion and time-varying filters on bitmapped images have more in common with graphic design than with mainstream cartoons or art animations. They are often known by the more suggestive name of *motion graphics*. Many of the techniques first appeared in title sequences for feature films, and credit sequences remain a typical application.

Interpolation can be applied to other properties of a layer. In particular, its angle can be varied, so that it appears to rotate. Angles may be set by hand in key frames and interpolated, or the rotation may be determined automatically in conjunction with movement, to maintain the orientation of a layer with respect to its motion path. Scaling, which may be used as a perspective effect to convey the impression of

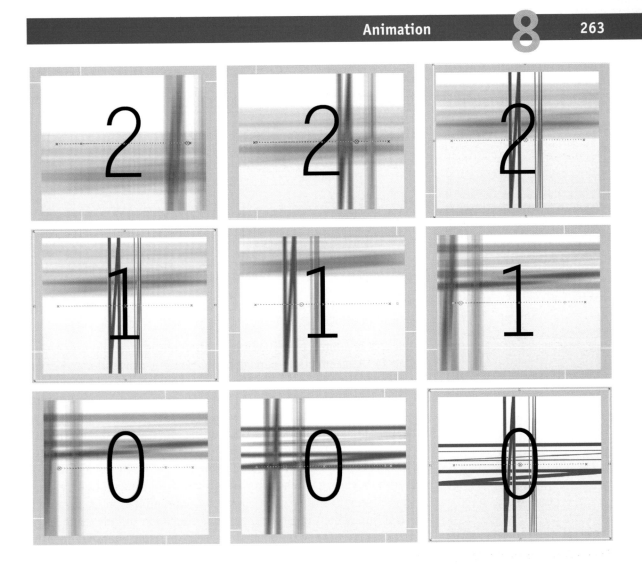

approaching or receding movement, or as a zoom in or out, can also be set in key frames and interpolated.

AfterEffects supports both linear and Bézier interpolation, in both space and time. Linear interpolation leads to abrupt changes in direction; with Bézier interpolation the changes in direction are smooth. These are different forms of spatial interpolation, which are set by moving the layer in the window that shows the image. Temporal interpolation affects the rate of change of position with respect to time. Again, this may be linear, with a constant velocity and instantaneous starting and stopping, as discussed earlier in connection with Flash, or Bézier, where the acceleration is smooth. The temporal and

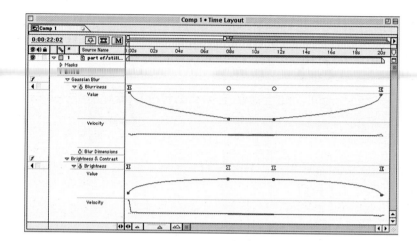

Figure 8.15 Interpolating filters

spatial interpolation methods are independent: you can use linear temporal interpolation with Bézier motion paths, and vice versa.

The degree of control over the interpolation of these spatial properties offered by AfterEffects is considerable. Using a conventional Bézier pen tool, the graphs showing how a value varies with time may be redrawn. Key frames are inserted automatically when control points are added to the graph. Absolute values may be entered numerically, allowing complete control over positioning and the rate of movement. Nevertheless, the type of motion that can be produced by interpolating the position, angle, and size of a single layer is restricted. Objects appear to move as a whole, with an unrealistic gliding motion, resembling that seen in simple, low-budget, cut-out animation, as favoured for some pre-school entertainment and education on television. Key frame animation of bitmapped images is therefore more frequently used for stylized motion. As we mentioned in Chapter 7, travelling mattes are often made by animating a still image in AfterEffects. Another popular application is the animation of text. Individual characters or words can be placed on layers and animated, just like any other layer, or text may be placed on a path, as in Illustrator, and then moved along that path over time.

As our countdown example demonstrates, bitmapped representation allows other properties of the image besides its position, angle and size to be altered over time. So, in addition to geometrical transformations, more radical time-based alterations of the layers can be achieved. As we described in Chapter 5, bitmapped images can be treated with many different effects and filters. Most of these filters have parameters, such as the radius of a Gaussian blur, or the brightness of glowing edges. Such parameters can be made to change over time, using the same mechanism of interpolation between key frames as is used for interpolating motion. Doing so allows some unique effects to be generated.

For example, Figure 8.15 shows a sequence of frames extracted from the title sequence of a short film. The title, 'part of', emerges from darkness as a vague blur, becomes sharper and brighter until it reaches maximum clarity, where it is held for a few seconds before receding back into the darkness. This was achieved by applying a time-varying Gaussian blur to the text, in conjunction with varying the brightness. The actual text was a single still image, made in Photoshop, that was otherwise unaltered. Figure 8.15 also shows the graphs of the Gaussian blur and brightness values that were used. The blur starts with a very high value, which renders the text illegible; in the same key frame, the brightness is substantially reduced. The values are interpolated to a point where the blur is removed and the brightness brought right up. Bézier interpolation is used to ensure a smooth fade up. The values are held constant between the middle two key frames, as shown by the flat portions of the graphs, and then, to make the title fade back into nothing, a symmetrical interpolation is used to a final key frame where the values are identical to those at the beginning.

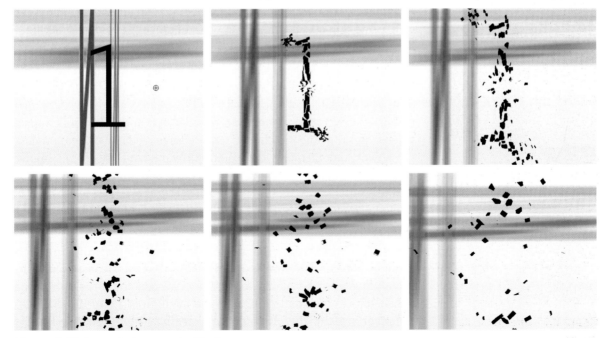

Figure 8.16 A purely temporal effect

As well as varying the parameters of still image filters and effects over time, you can also apply new effects which become possible when a temporal dimension is added to images. Figure 8.16 shows part of an alternative version of the countdown animation, with a chatter effect applied to the numerals.

3-D Animation

3-D animation is easy to describe, but much harder to do. No new concepts beyond those already introduced in this chapter and in Chapter 4 are needed to understand the essence of the process. The properties of 3-D models are defined by numerical quantities. Changing the numbers changes properties such as an object's position in space, its rotation, its surface characteristics, and even its shape. The intensity and direction of light sources and the position and orientation of a camera are also numerically defined. In order to animate a three-dimensional scene, therefore, all that is necessary is to set up an initial scene and render it as the first frame of the animation, make some changes to parameters, render the next frame, and so on. Because the values that are being changed are numerical, some kinds of change can be interpolated between key frames; a timeline can be used as a convenient way of organizing the animation, and motion paths in three dimensions (often 3-D Bézier splines) can be used to describe movement. Because 3-D models must be rendered as 2-D images, which implies the presence of a viewpoint or camera, as well as moving objects in a scene, we can move the camera, making it fly through a landscape or round some objects, as in Figure 8.17.

Whereas simple 3-D animations, such as tumbling logos and rotating globes, really can be made very easily – and there are dedicated packages available for such tasks – high-quality photo-realistic animations, such as those employed in television advertisements, music videos, and film special effects, require huge resources: time, processor power and memory, dedicated software, and above all, highly skilled specialized personnel. Multimedia production can rarely afford these resources. For this reason our description of 3-D animation is limited – readers interested in a fuller treatment of the subject should consult the relevant references given in the bibliography.

There are several factors that make 3-D animation more difficult than it might appear. The first is the difficulty that most people have in visualizing in three dimensions. When we add time, there are four dimensions to be handled through the medium of a two-dimensional computer screen. This difficulty is exacerbated by the second problem, which is the amount of processing power needed to render a 3-D animation. Advanced shading algorithms, such as ray tracing, take a long time to process a single image. In animation, we need at least 12, and up to 30, images to be processed for every second of completed animation. This makes generating fully rendered previews impossible on anything but the most powerful workstations or networks of distributed processors.

Large budgets, patience and practice can overcome these problems, but what remains is the necessity to change a large number of parameters in such a way as to produce convincing movements. At the very highest level of 3-D computer-generated animation, the solution that is adopted is to provide a rich interface giving the animator complete control over movement. For animating figures, this resembles the type of control used by a puppeteer to control a mannequin – body suits equipped with motion sensors, like those used to control animatronic puppets, are even used sometimes. This is in marked contrast to the approach taken to animation by computer programmers, whose well-trained instinct is to try to automate everything. In an attempt to overcome the limitations of simple interpolation schemes, considerable research efforts have been expended on ways of producing convincing motion in three dimensions automatically.

One of the key approaches is to provide certain kinds of behaviour that can be applied to objects and the way they interact. A simple type of behaviour consists of making one object point at another. This is most useful when the pointing object is a camera or light. If a camera is pointed at an object, it will maintain that object in its field of view, no matter where it moves; a spotlight pointed at an object will automatically follow it, as a real spotlight follows a dancer on a stage, for example. Actual objects in the scene can also be made to point at each other: a sunflower can be made to point always at the sun, for example. A variation on this behaviour is to have one object track another, i.e. follow its motion at a distance. This can be used crudely to animate chase scenes. Like pointing, it can be applied to a camera, allowing it to follow an object or character through a scene, even in places where it would be physically impossible for a real camera to go.

Some 3-D animation systems incorporate behaviour based on the physical laws of motion. For example, they allow the user to specify that an object should accelerate from zero under the influence of an external force whose magnitude is specified as a parameter. Taking

Figure 8.17 Moving the camera around a 3-D scene

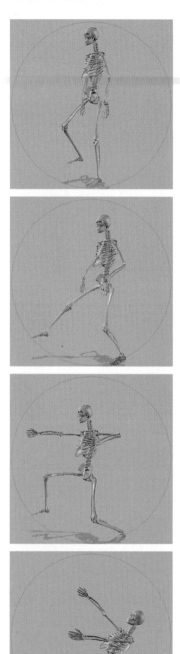

this further, moving objects can be made to collide realistically, or bounce off solid surfaces. These behaviours are based on simple laws of physics that encapsulate the possible motion in a few equations. Unfortunately, many realistic types of movement cannot be so easily described, and other methods must be used.

Kinematics is the study of the motion of bodies without reference to mass or force. That is, it is only concerned with how things can move, rather than what makes them do so. In animation, it is most useful in connection with jointed structures, such as the limbs of human or animal figures. Because they are joined together, the various parts of your arm, for example, can only move in certain ways. To produce realistic movement, a 3-D model of an arm must obey the same *kinematic constraints* as a real arm: if the upper arm is raised, the lower arm and hand must come with it, for example. Whereas, in reality, it is the motion of the upper arm that propels the rest of the arm, in an animation system, modelling movement in this way – from the beginning of a chain of connected elements to the end – is not very helpful to the animator. It is more useful to be able to position the object which is at the end of the chain – a hand, say – and then make the other elements – the rest of the arm – move to accommodate it. It is usually the extremities that impose limitations on movement; when walking, a foot must stay above the ground, resting on it at each step, for example. It takes considerable understanding of the way limbs move to ensure that this will happen correctly by moving the thigh, so it is preferable for the software to work out the movements of the leg from the animator's placement of the foot, and so on. This type of modelling is called *inverse kinematics*, since it works backwards from effect to cause. Inverse kinematics can be applied to any structure that is modelled as a linked chain of objects. It is routinely provided by 3-D animation programs that support such structures. Poser, for example, can be set to automatically apply inverse kinematics to the arms and legs of figures.

A little experimentation will show you that computation of movement using inverse kinematics is not entirely straightforward. In particular, the kinematic constraints on arms and legs do not uniquely determine the possible movements that the limbs can make to accommodate movements of the extremities. Try lifting your right hand to touch the tip of your nose with your first finger. How many different ways can your right elbow move while you do so? In order to fix a particular type of movement, extra constraints, such as minimizing the potential energy of the whole structure, must be added. To produce movements that defy these constraints, while still being physically possible, inverse kinematics must be abandoned, and the parts must be positioned by hand.

Virtual Reality

Originally, the phrase 'virtual reality' was used to describe an immersive sensory experience of a synthetic world. Head-mounted displays, which are sensitive to head movements, are used to project images on the user's eyes, modifying them as the head is moved, so that the user appears to be inside a 3-D world, looking around. Data gloves track hand movements, allowing the display to incorporate an image of the user's arm; haptic interfaces provide tactile feedback, so that users can touch and feel objects in the virtual world. Taken to the extreme, virtual reality of this sort would be the ultimate in multimedia, stimulating all the senses at once.

The high cost of the interface hardware required by immersive virtual reality (together with the understandable reluctance on the part of most of the adult population to immerse their body in strange electronic devices) has confined it to flight and industrial simulations, and specialist games arcades. A more modest vision of virtual reality (VR), as 3-D graphics that can be explored, has evolved. Even this version of VR has not yet achieved widespread acceptance, largely because the heavy demands it makes on processor power lead to disappointing results on desktop computers. Two VR technologies deserve a brief mention, since they can be incorporated in Web pages with some success, and promise to become more important as computer power catches up with the vision of VR enthusiasts.

VRML

The *Virtual Reality Modeling Language (VRML)* was created on a wave of enthusiasm for VR and the World Wide Web in 1994. The intention was to provide a mechanism for distributing virtual worlds over the Internet, using Web browsers as the interface. To this end, VRML was a text-based language, that allowed 3-D objects and scenes to be described in a programming language-like notation. VRML 1.0 did little more; the main additional feature was the capability of embedding hyperlinks in scenes, using URLs. Subsequently VRML 2.0 added support for interactivity, via scripting of the sort to be described in Chapter 16, and allowed for video and audio to be embedded in VRML worlds (so, for example, a television set could be made to show a movie). VRML became an ISO standard in December 1997.

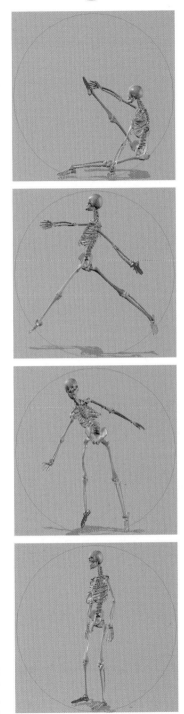

Figure 8.18 'Knee bone's connected to the thigh bone...'

VRML allows the specification of objects, in terms of their geometry (whether they are a cube, cylinder, sphere, and so on) and the material of which they are composed. Textures can be mapped onto the surfaces of objects, which can be placed in 3-D space using transformations. Scenes can be lit in a variety of ways, by specifying the type and position of light objects. The basic language thus provides a way of describing the sorts of scenes that can be constructed with conventional 3-D modelling programs, although it lacks some of the more elaborate features, such as NURBS and metaballs. The description is explicit: for example, a terrain might be modelled as an elevation grid, a type of VRML object that specifies a set of points, forming a grid, each at a different height. In VRML, the dimensions of the grid and the height of each grid point must be explicitly specified. Constructing VRML scenes by hand is thus a painstaking and error-prone business. Most 3-D modellers will generate VRML as output from their normal interactive modelling tools, however, which provides an easier way of constructing scenes.

It might appear that VRML is no more than an alternative representation of the output of a modeller, and, as far as the language goes, this is more or less the case. It does, as we noted earlier, provide additional features for interactivity and embedding multimedia, but the main distinctive feature lies not so much in the language as in the way it is displayed. Once a VRML file has been downloaded into a suitable browser – either a Web browser with an appropriate plug-in, or a dedicated VRML browser – the user can explore the 3-D world it describes. That is, they can move the viewpoint through the space of the model, as if they were moving about in it. To that extent, VRML deserves to be considered a form of virtual reality.

To create the illusion of moving through a 3-D space, VRML must be rendered in real-time. As we have stated several times, realistic rendering of 3-D models is a computationally intensive task, which is usually only feasible with special hardware, such as 3-D accelerator cards. This is one of the main obstacles to the widespread use of VRML, although a lack of commitment to the format by major software vendors may be more significant. At the time of writing, a host of competing – mostly proprietary – formats for delivering 3-D models over the World Wide Web is available, with none, as yet, achieving any widespread use.

QuickTime VR

QuickTime VR (or *QTVR*, for short), part of QuickTime, offers a very basic VR experience. There are two types of QuickTime VR movies: panoramic movies and object movies. The former presents a 360° view of a scene – the interior of a room, or a valley surrounded by mountains, for example. Using their mouse, a user can drag the scene, as if looking around. It is also possible to zoom in or out, in order to view the scene in more or less detail. Object movies, in contrast, allow the user to examine an object from different angles, as if by walking round it, again by dragging with the mouse. QTVR movies of either sort may contain *hot spots*, which are active areas that contain links to other movies. Clicking on a hot spot causes the linked movie to replace the current one. A typical use of hot spots is to allow a user to go through a door from one room into another.

QTVR movies can be generated from some 3-D programs, such as Bryce. They can also be made from photographs, allowing them to represent real scenes and objects. To achieve the best results, a special rotating rig is used to hold the camera (for panoramas) or an object. A sequence of pictures is taken, with the rig being rotated a fixed amount between each picture. These are then scanned (or read in to the computer if a digital camera is being used) and special software 'stitches' them together and renders the result as QTVR. The purpose of the rig is to ensure that the individual pictures fit together perfectly. If an ordinary tripod is used for panoramas, or a record turntable or similar device for object movies, there may be discontinuities; stitching software will attempt to compensate for these, but the result may be distortion of the images.

Since QTVR is part of QuickTime, panoramas and object movies can be combined with audio and video. Most usefully, they can be viewed by any software that uses QuickTime; in particular, the QuickTime plug-in for Web browsers allows QTVR to be embedded in Web pages, in the same way as video clips can be (see Chapter 12).

QuickTime VR and VRML might be considered travesties of the original vision of immersive virtual reality, but they have the advantage of being implementable without special interface devices or powerful workstations. They offer the possibility of new approaches to interfaces to multimedia, based on the organization of media in three-dimensional spaces.

Exercises

1 What are the advantages and disadvantages of using a scanner or a digital stills camera to capture traditional art work as animation sequences? For what types of animation, if any, would you have to use a video camera connected to a computer?

2 How could you incorporate drawn animation into a live-action video sequence without using a special effects program?

3 If an animation sequence is to be saved as QuickTime, what factors will influence your choice of codec? Under what circumstances would it be appropriate to treat the animated sequence exactly like a live-action video sequence?

4 When would it be appropriate to use an animated GIF for an animation sequence? What problems are associated with animated GIFs?

5 In what ways is a sprite animation track radically different from a video track containing animation?

6 For what type of work would sprite animation be particularly suitable and why?

7 What problems are associated with using basic linear interpolation to do 'in-betweening' between key frames?

8 How would you use Flash's easing facility to set up a movement that eases in *and* out?

9 Describe the motion of an object whose position is animated in AfterEffects using Bézier interpolation for the motion path, and linear interpolation for the velocity.

10 Create a very simple title for a video clip as a single image in a bit-mapped graphics application such as Photoshop or Painter, and save it as a still image file. Using whatever tools are available (Premiere, AfterEffects, etc.), create a pleasing 10-second title sequence by simply applying time-varying effects and filters to this single image. (If you want to go for a more sophisticated result, and have the necessary tools, you might create your original image on several layers and animate them separately.)

11 Do the models generated by 3-D applications contain enough information to be used in conjunction with a haptic interface to provide tactile feedback to a user? If not, what extra information is needed?

9

Sound

- The Nature of Sound
- Digitizing Sound
  - Sampling
  - Quantization
- Processing Sound
  - Recording and Importing Sound
  - Sound Editing and Effects
- Compression
  - Speech Compression
  - Perceptually Based Compression
- Formats
  - MP3
  - Streaming Audio Formats
- MIDI
  - MIDI Messages
  - General MIDI
  - MIDI Software
- Combining Sound and Picture

S ound is different in kind from any of the other digital media types we have considered. All other media are primarily visual, being perceived through our eyes, while sound is perceived through the different sense of hearing.[†] Our ears detect vibrations in the air in a completely different way from that in which our eyes detect light, and our brains respond differently to the resulting nerve impulses. Sound does have much in common with one other topic we have considered, though. Although sound is, for most of us, a familiar everyday phenomenon, like colour, it is a complex mixture of physical and psychological factors, which is difficult to model accurately.

Another feature that sound has in common with colour is that you may not always need it. Whereas a multimedia encyclopedia of musical instruments will be vastly enriched by the addition of recordings of each instrument, few, if any, Web pages need to play a fanfare every time they are visited. Sounds can be peculiarly irritating; even one's favourite pieces of music can become a jarring and unwelcome intrusion on the ears when inflicted repeatedly by a neighbour's sound system. Almost everyone has at some time been infuriated by the electronic noises of a portable games console, the cuter varieties of ringing tone of a mobile phone, or the rhythmic hiss that leaks out of the headphones of a personal stereo. The thoughtless use of such devices has become a fact of modern life; a similar thoughtlessness in the use of sound in multimedia productions should be avoided. At the very least, it should always be possible for users to turn the sound off.

Some users, though, don't need to be able to turn sounds off, because they can't hear them anyway. Not only are some people unable to hear, many others use computers that are not equipped to reproduce sound. Although new PCs intended for domestic use (and all Macs) have sound cards, older PCs, and those used in the business environment, are rarely fitted with them. It is always considerate to provide

[†] Text may exceptionally be rendered in other ways, but the graphic representation is the norm.

some alternative to sound, such as captions or transcripts of speech, for the benefit of those who cannot hear. If you know that your multimedia production is destined to be used in an environment where sound hardware is not typically available, then it may be advisable to avoid the use of sound altogether.

There are two types of sound that are special: music and speech. These are also the most commonly used types of sound in multimedia productions. The cultural status of music and the linguistic content of speech mean that these two varieties of sound function in a different way from other sounds and noises, and play special roles in multimedia. Representations specific to music and speech have been developed, to take advantage of their unique characteristics. In particular, compression algorithms tailored to speech are often employed, while music is sometimes represented not as sound, but as instructions for playing virtual instruments.

The Nature of Sound

If a tuning fork is struck sharply on a hard surface, the tines will vibrate at a precise frequency. As they move backwards and forwards, the air is compressed and rarefied in time with the vibrations. Interactions between adjacent air molecules cause this periodic pressure fluctuation to be propagated as a wave. When the sound wave reaches the ear, it causes the eardrum to vibrate at the same frequency. The vibration is then transmitted through the mechanism of the inner ear, and converted into nerve impulses, which we interpret as the sound of the pure tone produced by the tuning fork.

All sounds are produced by the conversion of energy into vibrations in the air or some other elastic medium. Generally, the entire process may involve several steps, in which the energy may be converted into different forms. For example, if one of the strings of an acoustic guitar is picked with a plectrum, the kinetic energy of the musician's hand is converted to a vibration in the string, which is then transmitted via the bridge of the instrument to the resonant cavity of its body, where it is amplified and enriched by the distinctive resonances of the guitar, and then transmitted through the sound hole. If one of the strings of an electric guitar is picked instead, the vibration of the string as it passes through the magnetic fields of the pickups induces fluctuations in the current which is sent through the guitar lead to an amplifier, where it is amplified and used to drive a loudspeaker. Variations in the signal sent to the speaker coil cause magnetic variations, which are used to drive the speaker cone, which then behaves as a sound source, compressing and rarefying the adjacent air.

While the tines of a good tuning fork vibrate cleanly at a single frequency, most other sound sources vibrate in more complicated ways, giving rise to the rich variety of sounds and noises we are familiar with. As we mentioned in Chapter 2, a single note, such as that produced by a guitar string, is composed of several components, at frequencies that are multiples of the fundamental pitch of the note. Some percussive sounds and most natural sounds do not even have a single identifiable fundamental frequency, but can still be decomposed into a collection – often a very complex one – of frequency components. As in the general case of representing a signal in the frequency domain, which we described in Chapter 2, we refer to a sound's description in terms of the relative amplitudes of its frequency components as its *frequency spectrum*.

The human ear is generally considered to be able to detect frequencies in the range between 20 Hz and 20 kHz, although individuals' frequency responses vary greatly. In particular, the upper limit decreases fairly rapidly with increasing age: few adults can hear sounds as high as 20 kHz, although children can. Frequencies at the top end of the range generally only occur as components of the transient attack of sounds. (The general rule that high frequencies are associated with abrupt transitions applies here.) The highest note on an ordinary piano – which more or less defines the limit of most Western music – has a fundamental frequency of only 4186 Hz when in concert pitch.[†] However, it is the transient behaviour of notes that contributes most to the distinctive timbre of instruments: if the attack portion is removed from recordings of an oboe, violin, and soprano playing or singing the same note, the steady portions are indistinguishable.

† That is, using even temperament, with the A above middle C equal to 440 Hz.

Interesting sounds change over time. As we just observed, a single musical note has a distinctive attack, and subsequently it will decay, changing its frequency spectrum first as it grows, and then as it dies away. Sounds that extend over longer periods of time, such as speech or music, exhibit a constantly changing frequency spectrum. We can display the *waveform* of any sound by plotting its amplitude against time. Examination of waveforms can help us characterize certain types of sound.

The idea of a sound's frequency spectrum changing might be slightly confusing, if you accept that any complex waveform is built out of a collection of frequency components. Strictly, Fourier analysis (as introduced in Chapter 2) can only be applied to *periodic* signals (i.e. ones that repeat indefinitely). When analyzing signals with a finite duration, various expedients must be adopted to fit into the analytic framework. One approach is to treat the entirety of a signal as one cycle of a periodic waveform; this is roughly what is done when images are broken down into their frequency components. An alternative is to use a brief section of the signal as if it were a cycle, thus obtaining a snapshot of the frequency make-up at one point. For audio signals, this provides more useful information. A spectrum analysis is typically obtained by sliding a window through the waveform to obtain a sequence of spectra, showing how the signal's frequency components change over time.

Figures 9.1 to 9.7 show waveforms for a range of types of sound. Figure 9.1 is a short example of speech: the main speaker repeats the phrase 'Feisty teenager' twice, then a more distant voice responds. You can clearly identify the syllables, and recognize that the same phrase is repeated, the second time faster and with more emphasis. In between the phrases there is almost silence – the sound was recorded in the open air and there is background noise, which is visible as the thin band running along the axis. You can see that it could be possible to extract individual syllables and recombine them to synthesize new words, and that, if it were necessary to compress speech, a lot could be achieved by removing the silences between phrases. The clearly demarcated syllables also provide a good basis for synchronizing sound with video, as we will see later.

The next four figures show the waveforms of some different types of music. The first three are purely instrumental, and do not exhibit the same character as speech. The first, Figure 9.2, is taken from an Australian aboriginal didgeridoo piece. This is characterized by a continuous drone, which requires the musician to employ a 'circular breathing' technique to maintain it. The waveform shows this drone, as the thick continuous black region, with its rhythmic modulation. Figure 9.3 shows the waveform of a piece of boogie-woogie, played

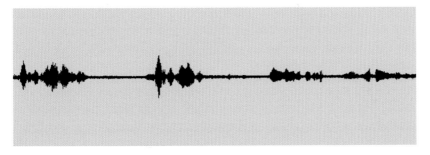

Figure 9.1 'Feisty teenager'

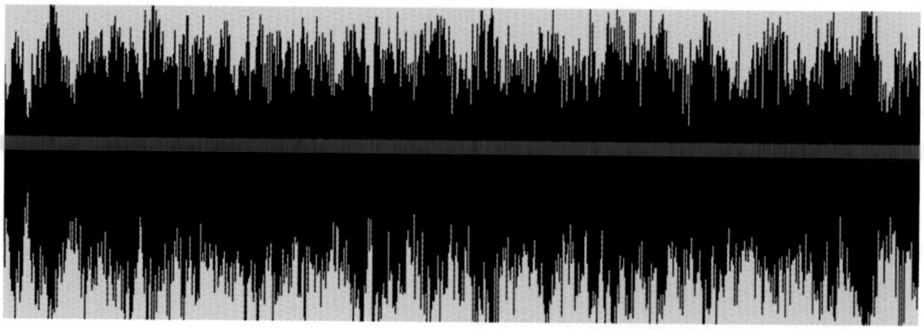

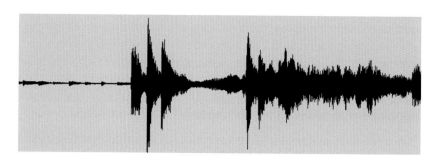

Figure 9.2 Didgeridoo

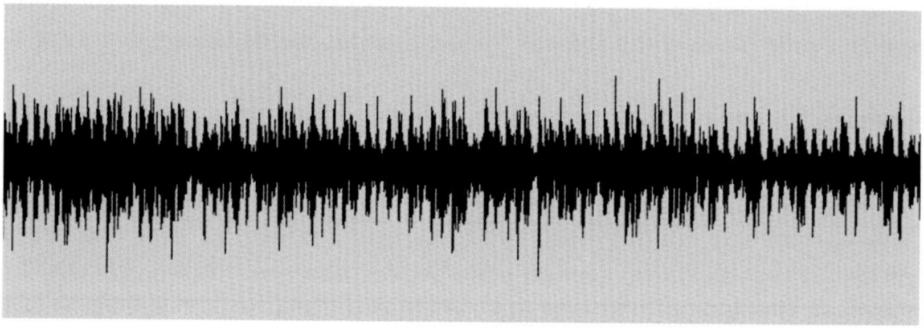

Figure 9.3 Boogie-woogie

Figure 9.4 Violin, cello and piano

by a pianist accompanied by a small group. The rhythm is clearly visible, but it is not possible to distinguish the melody played by the right hand (unless, perhaps, you are a very experienced audio technician). Figure 9.4 is a completely different waveform, corresponding to a very different piece of music: a contemporary work arranged for violin, cello, and piano. It shows a great dynamic range (difference between the loudest and quietest sounds). Although the steep attack of the louder phrases tells you something about the likely sound of this music, there is no obvious rhythm, and it is not possible to pick out the different instruments (although they can be clearly identified when listening to the music).

As you would expect, singing combines characteristics of speech and music. Figure 9.5 is typical: the syllables of each word are easily identifiable, as is the rhythm, but the gaps between sung phrases are filled

Figure 9.5 'Men grow cold...'

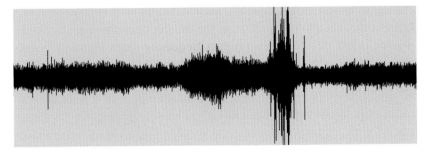

Figure 9.6 A trickling stream

Figure 9.7 The sea

with the musical accompaniment. It is possible to see the singer's phrasing, but quite impossible to deduce the lyrics,[†] and, although voice prints are unique to each individual, we doubt whether any readers could identify the singer from this waveform, despite her distinctive voice. (It's Marilyn Monroe.)

Figures 9.6 and 9.7 are both natural water sounds. The first is a recording of the trickling sound of water in a small stream; it is almost continuous. The random spikes do not correspond to any audible clicks or other abrupt sound; they are just slight variations in the water's flow, and some background noise. The second waveform was recorded on the seashore. There is a constant background of surf and two distinct events. The first is a wave breaking fairly close to the microphone, while the second is the water splashing into a nearby

† Men grow cold, as girls grow old/And we all lose our charms in the end.

rock pool and then receding through a gap in the rocks. This wave-form can almost be read as a story.

As these illustrations show, a waveform display can show a certain amount of the gross character of a sound, but it does not convey the details, and it is not always easy to correlate against the sound as it is heard. The main advantage of these visual displays is their static nature. A piece of sound can be seen in its entirety at one time, with relationships such as the intervals between syllables or musical beats visible. This makes analysis of the sound's temporal structure – which is especially useful for synchronization purposes – relatively simple, compared to performing the same analysis on the dynamically chang-ing sound itself, which is only heard an instant at a time.

Waveforms and the physics of sound are only part of the story. Sound only truly exists as a sensation in the mind, and the perception of sound is not a simple registering of the physical characteristics of the waves reaching the ears. Proofs of this abound, both in the literature and in everyday experience. For example, if a pure 200 Hz tone is played, first softly, then louder, most listeners will believe that the louder tone has a lower pitch than the quieter one, although the same illusion is not perceived with higher frequency tones. Similarly, com-plex tones sometimes seem to have a lower pitch than pure tones of the same frequency. Most people with good hearing can distinguish the sound of their own name spoken on the opposite side of a noisy room, even if the rest of what is said is inaudible, or carry on a suc-cessful conversation with someone speaking at a volume lower than that of the ambient noise.

One of the most useful illusions in sound perception is *stereophony.* The brain identifies the source of a sound on the basis of the differ-ences in intensity and phase between the signals received from the left and right ears. If identical signals are sent to both ears, the brain interprets the sound as coming from a non-existent source that lies straight ahead. By extension, if a sound is recorded using a pair of microphones to produce two monophonic channels, which are then fed to two speakers that are a suitable distance apart, the apparent location of the sound will depend on the relative intensity of the two channels: if they are equal it will appear in the middle, if the left channel is louder (because the original sound source was nearer to the left-hand microphone) it will appear to the left, and so on. In this way, the familiar illusion of a sound stage between the speakers is constructed.

Because of the psychological dimension of sound, it is unwise, when considering its digitization and reproduction, to place too much reliance on mathematics and measurable quantities. Pohlmann's comments[†] about the nature of sound and its reproduction should be borne in mind:

† Ken C Pohlmann, *Principles of Digital Audio*, p. 5.

> "Given the evident complexity of acoustical signals, it would be naive to believe that analog or digital technologies are sufficiently advanced to capture fully and convey the complete listening experience. To complicate matters, the precise limits of human perception are not known. One thing is certain: at best, even with the most sophisticated technology, what we hear being reproduced through an audio system is an approximation of the actual sound."

Digitizing Sound

The digitization of sound is a fairly straightforward example of the processes of quantization and sampling described in Chapter 2. Since these operations are carried out in electronic analogue to digital converters, the sound information must be converted to an electrical signal before it can be digitized. This can be done by a microphone or other transducer, such as a guitar pickup, just as it is for analogue recording or broadcasting.

Sampling

A sampling rate must be chosen that will preserve at least the full range of audible frequencies, if high-fidelity reproduction is desired. If the limit of hearing is taken to be 20 kHz, a minimum rate of 40 kHz is required by the Sampling Theorem. The sampling rate used for audio CDs is 44.1 kHz – the precise figure being chosen by manufacturers to produce a desired playing time[‡] given the size of the medium. (The same rate is used in mini discs.) Because of the ubiquity of the audio CD, the same rate is commonly used by the sound cards fitted to computers, to provide compatibility. Where a lower sound quality is acceptable, or is demanded by limited bandwidth, sub-multiples of 44.1 kHz are used: 22.05 kHz is commonly used for audio destined for delivery over the Internet, while 11.025 kHz is sometimes used for speech. Another important sampling rate is that used by DAT (digital audio tape) recorders, and also supported by the better sound cards. Although these commonly offer a variety of sampling rates, 48 kHz is used when the best quality is desired. DAT is a very suitable medium

‡ According to legend, the time to play von Karajan's recording of Beethoven's 9th symphony.

for live recording and low budget studio work, and is often used for capturing sound for multimedia.

DAT and CD players both have the advantage that they can generate digital output, which can be read in by a suitably equipped computer without the need for extra digitizing hardware. In this respect, they resemble DV cameras. Where a digital signal cannot be produced, or where the computer is not fitted with the appropriate digital audio input, a digitizing sound card must be fitted to the computer, in the same way as a video capture board must be used for analogue video. Digital audio inputs are surprisingly uncommon, so it is often necessary for the (analogue) line output of a DAT or CD player to be redigitized by the sound card. This is clearly unfortunate, since it is preferable to work entirely with digital data and prevent noise and signal degradataion. It does, however, avoid the problem of incompatible sampling rates that can occur if, say, a recording on DAT is to be combined with an extract from a CD. Resampling audio is as undesirable as resampling images.

The necessity to resample data sampled at 48 kHz often occurs if the sound is to be combined with video. Some video applications do not yet support the higher sampling rate, even though DAT is widely used for capturing sound, and sound cards that support 48 kHz are becoming common. For multimedia work it may therefore be preferable to sample sound at 44.1 kHz, which is supported by all the major desktop video editing programs.

Sampling relies on highly accurate clock pulses to determine the intervals between samples. If the clock drifts, so will the intervals. Such timing variations are called *jitter*. The effect of jitter is to introduce noise into the reconstructed signal. At the high sampling frequencies required by sound, there is little tolerance for jitter: it has been estimated that for CD quality sound, the jitter in the ADC must be less than 200 picoseconds (200×10^{-12} seconds).

Even if they are inaudible, frequencies in excess of 20 kHz are present in the spectra of many sounds. If a sampling rate of around 40 kHz is used, these inaudible components will manifest themselves as aliasing when the signal is reconstructed. In order to avoid this, a filter is used to remove any frequencies higher than half the sampling rate before the signal is sampled.

Quantization

We mentioned in Chapter 2 that the number of quantization levels for analogue to digital conversion in any medium is usually chosen to fit into a convenient number of bits. For sound, the most common choice of sample size is 16 bits, as used for CD audio, giving 65,536 quantization levels. This is generally sufficient to eliminate quantization noise, if the signal is *dithered*, as we will describe shortly. As with images, smaller samples sizes (lower bit-depths, as we would say in the context of images) are sometimes needed to maintain small file sizes and bit rates. The minimum acceptable is 8-bit sound, and even this has audible quantization noise, so it can only be used for applications such as voice communication, where the distortion can be tolerated. In the search for higher fidelity reproduction, as many as 24 bits are sometimes used to record audio samples, but this imposes considerable demands on the accuracy of ADC circuitry.

Quantization noise will be worst for signals of small amplitude. In the extreme, when the amplitude is comparable to the difference between quantization levels, an analogue signal will be coarsely approximated

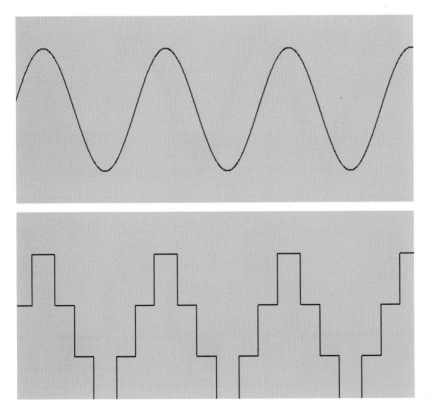

Figure 9.8 Undersampling a pure sine wave

by samples that jump between just a few quantized values. This is shown in Figure 9.8. The upper waveform is a pure sine wave; below it is a digitized version, where only four levels are available to accommodate the amplitude range of the original signal.[†] Evidently the sampled waveform is a poor approximation of the original. The approximation could be improved by increasing the number of bits for each sample, but a more economical technique, resembling the anti-aliasing applied when rendering vector graphics, is usually employed. Its operation is somewhat counter-intuitive.

Before sampling, a small amount of random noise is added to the analogue signal. The word 'dithering' (which we used with a somewhat different meaning in Chapter 6) is used in the audio field to refer to this injection of noise. The effect on sampling is illustrated in Figure 9.9. The upper waveform is the original sine wave with added dither;[‡] the lower waveform is a sampled version of this dithered signal. What has happened is that the presence of the noise has caused the samples to alternate rapidly between quantization levels, instead of jumping cleanly and abruptly from one to the next, as they

‡ We have used rather more noise than is normal, in order to show the effect more clearly.

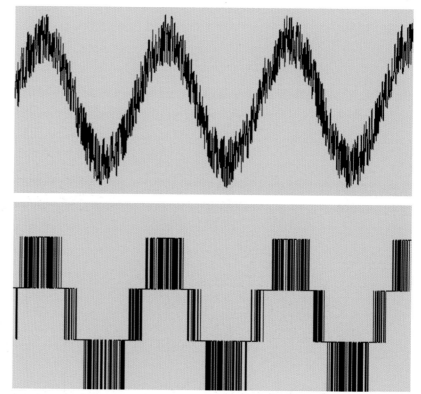

Figure 9.9 Dithering

do in Figure 9.8. The sharp transitions have been softened. Putting it another way, the quantization error has been randomized. The price to be paid for the resulting improvement in sound quality is the additional random noise that has been introduced. This is, however, less intrusive than the quantization noise it has eliminated.

Figure 9.10 illustrates the effect of sampling and dithering on the signal's frequency spectrum. In these pictures, the horizontal *x*-axis represents frequency, the vertical *y*-axis amplitude, with the colours being used as an extra visual indication of intensity, and the back-to-front *z*-axis represents time. The first spectrum is the pure sine wave; as you would expect, it is a spike at the wave's frequency, which is constant over time. To its right is the spectrum of the sampled signal: spurious frequencies and noise have been introduced. These correspond to the frequency components of the sharp edges. Below the pure sine wave is the spectrum of the dithered version. The extra noise is randomly distributed across frequencies and over time. In the bottom left is the sampled version of this signal. The pure frequency has re-emerged clearly, but random noise is present where before there was none. However, although this noise will be audible, the ear will be able to discern the signal through it, because the noise is random. Where the undithered signal was sampled, the noise was concentrated near to the signal frequency, in a way that is much less easily ignored.

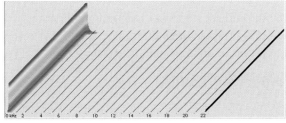

Pure sine wave

Sine wave with dithering noise

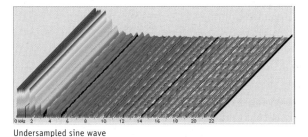

Undersampled sine wave

Undersampled dithered sine wave

Figure 9.10 Audio frequency spectra showing the effect of sampling and dithering

Processing Sound

With the addition of suitable audio input, output and processing hardware and software, a desktop computer can perform the functions of a modern multi-track recording studio. Such professional facilities are expensive and demanding on resources, as you would expect. They are also as complex as a recording studio, with user interfaces that are as intimidating to the novice as the huge mixing consoles of conventional studios. Fortunately, for multimedia, more modest facilities are usually adequate.

There is presently no single sound application that has the *de facto* status of a cross-platform desktop standard, in the way that Photoshop and Dreamweaver, for example, do in their respective fields. Several different packages, some of which require special hardware support, are in use. Most of the well known ones are biased towards music, with integrated support for MIDI sequencing (see page 317) and multi-track recording. Several more modest programs provide simple recording and effects processing facilities; where hardware support is not provided, real-time effects are not usually achievable. Video editing packages usually include some integrated sound editing and processing facilities, and some offer basic sound recording. These facilities may be adequate for multimedia production in the absence of special sound software, and are especially convenient when the audio is intended as a soundtrack to accompany picture.

Given the absence of an industry standard sound application for desktop use, we will describe the facilities offered by sound programs in general terms only, without using any specific example.

Recording and Importing Sound

Many desktop computers are fitted with built-in microphones, and it is tempting to think that these are adequate for recording sounds. It is almost impossible to obtain satisfactory results with these, however – not only because the microphones themselves are usually small and cheap, but because they are inevitably close to the machine's fan and disk drives, which means that they will pick up noises from these components. It is much better to plug an external microphone into a sound card, but if possible, you should do the actual recording onto DAT (or good quality analogue tape) using a professional microphone, and capture it in a separate operation. Where sound quality is important, or for recording music to a high standard, it will be necessary to use a properly equipped studio. Although a computer can form the basis of a studio, it must be augmented with microphones and other equipment in a suitable acoustic environment, so it is not really practical for a multimedia producer to set up a studio for one-off recordings. It may be necessary to hire a professional studio, which offers the advantage that professional personnel will generally be available.

Before recording, it is necessary to select a sampling rate and sample size. Where the sound originates in analogue form, the choice will be determined by considerations of file size and bandwidth, which will depend on the final use to which the sound is to be put, and the facilities available for sound processing. As a general rule, the highest possible sampling rate and sample size should be used, to minimize deterioration of the signal when it is processed. If a compromise must be made, the effect on quality of reducing the sample size is more drastic than that of reducing the sampling rate: the same reduction in size can be produced by halving the sampling rate or halving the sample size; the former is better. If the signal is originally a digital one – the digital output from a DAT recorder, for example – the sample size should be matched to the incoming rate, if possible.

A simple calculation suffices to show the size of digitized audio. The sampling rate is the number of samples generated each second, so if the rate is r Hz and the sample size is s bits, each second of digitized sound will occupy $rs/8$ bytes. Hence, for CD-quality, $r = 44.1 \times 10^3$ and $s = 16$, so each second occupies just over 86 kbytes,[†] each minute roughly 5 Mbytes. These calculations are based on a single channel, but audio is almost always recorded in stereo, so the estimates should be doubled. Conversely, where stereo effects are not required, the space occupied can be halved by recording in mono.

† In kHz, k represents 1000, following normal usage, but in kbytes, the k is 1024, in accordance with the conventions of computing.

Professional sound applications will record directly to disk, so that the possible length of recordings is limited only by the available disk space and any file size limitations built in to the operating system. Many lower-level programs record to RAM, however, and subsequently carry out all their processing in memory. While this is more efficient, it imposes severe restrictions on the length of sound that can be managed.

The most vexatious aspect of recording is getting the levels right. If the level of the incoming signal is too low, the resulting recording will be quiet, and more susceptible to noise; if the level is too high, *clipping* will occur; that is, at some points, the amplitude of the incoming signal will exceed the maximum value that can be recorded. The

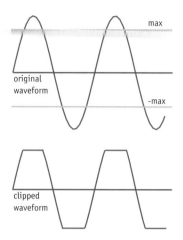

Figure 9.11 Clipping

value of the corresponding sample will be set to the maximum, so the recorded waveform will apparently be clipped off straight at this threshold. (Figure 9.11 shows the effect on a pure sine wave.) The result is heard as a particularly unpleasant sort of distortion. Ideally, a signal should be recorded at the highest possible level that avoids clipping. Sound applications usually provide level meters, so that the level can be monitored, with clipping alerts. Where the sound card supports it, a gain control can be used to alter the level. Some sound cards do not provide this function, so that the only option is to adjust the output level of the equipment from which the signal originates. Setting the level correctly is easier said than done, especially where live recordings are being made: to preserve the dynamic range of the recording, the same gain must be used throughout, but the optimum can only be determined at the loudest point. When the sound is live, this cannot be known in advance, and only experience can be used to choose gain settings. Where the material already exists on tape or CD, it is possible – and usually necessary – to make several passes in order to find the best values.

Some software includes automatic gain controls, which vary the gain dynamically according to the amplitude of the signal, in order to prevent clipping. They must, therefore, reduce the volume of louder passages, so as a side-effect, they reduce the dynamic range of the recording. This is generally undesirable, but may be necessary if suitable levels cannot be maintained throughout the recording.

It may be obvious, but it seems worth emphasizing: once a signal has been clipped, nothing can be done to restore it. Reducing the amplitude subsequently just produces a smaller clipped signal. There is no way to recover the lost waveform. Similarly, although sound programs often provide a facility for 'normalizing' a sound after recording, by amplifying it as much as possible without causing clipping, this stretches the dynamic range of the original without adding any more detail. In practice it may be necessary to use this facility, or to select and amplify particularly quiet passages within a sound editing application after the recording has been made. In principle, though, the gain should always be set correctly, both when recording to tape, and when recording or capturing to disk.

A technically simpler alternative to recording sound is to import it from an audio CD. Although audio CDs use a different format from CD-ROM, they are nevertheless a structured collection of digital data, so they can be read by suitable software. QuickTime includes an audio CD import component that allows any sound application based on

QuickTime to open tracks on a CD just like any other file. This is the simplest way of importing sounds, but most recorded music is copyrighted, so it is necessary to obtain permissions first. Copyright-free collections can be obtained, much like royalty-free image libraries, although they tend to the anodyne. Composers and musicians with access to professional recording facilities may supply their work on CD, avoiding the need for the multimedia producer to deal with the sound recording process. However, even when importing sounds from CDs there can be difficulty in getting the levels right.

The Internet is a rich source of ready-made sounds, but many are made available illegally, and others may not be legally reproduced without payment of a fee. Increasingly, though, record companies are arriving at mechanisms to provide music online, in the form of MP3 or AAC files (see below). While it may be legal to download these files and listen to them, it remains generally illegal to use them in any published form without obtaining clearance from the copyright holders.

Sound Editing and Effects

We can identify several classes of operation that we might want to apply to recorded sounds. Most of them have counterparts in video editing, and are performed for similar reasons.

First, there is editing, in the sense of trimming, combining and rearranging clips. The essentially time-based nature of sound naturally lends itself to an editing interface based on a timeline. A typical sound editing window is divided into tracks, in imitation of the separate tape tracks used on traditional recording equipment, providing a clear graphic representation of the sound through time. The sound in each track may usually be displayed as a waveform; the time and amplitude axes can be scaled, allowing the sound to be examined in varying degrees of detail. Editing is done by cutting and pasting, or dragging and dropping, selected parts of the track. Each stereo recording will occupy two tracks, one for each channel. During the editing process many tracks may be used to combine sounds from separate recordings. Subsequently, these will be mixed down onto one or two tracks, for the final mono or stereo output. When mixing, the relative levels of each of the tracks can be adjusted to produce the desired balance – between different instruments, for example.

A special type of edit has become common in audio: the creation of loops. Very short loops are needed to create voices for the electronic musical instruments known as samplers (whose functions are increasingly performed by software). Here, the idea is to create a section of sound that represents the sustained tone of an instrument, such as a guitar, so that arbitrarily long notes can be produced by interpolating copies of the section between a sample of the instrument's attack and one of its decay. It is vital that the sustained sample loops cleanly; there must not be abrupt discontinuities between its end and start, otherwise audible clicks will occur where the copies fit together. Although some software makes such loops automatically, using built-in heuristics such as choosing zero crossings for each end of the loop, the best results require a detailed examination of the waveform by a person. Longer loops are used in certain styles of dance music – techno and drum'n'bass, for example – which are based on the combination of repeating sections. Again, there is a requirement for clean looping, but this time at the coarser level of rhythmic continuity. Software is also available that puts together even longer loops from a pre-recorded library, pitch- and time-shifting them so they are in the same key and tempo, to allow non-composers to produce music of a sort.

As well as editing, audio has its equivalent of post-production: altering sounds to correct defects, enhance quality, or otherwise modify their character. Just as image correction is described in terms of filters, which are a digital equivalent of traditional optical devices, so sound alteration is described in terms of gates and filters, by analogy with the established technology. Whereas analogue gates and filters are based on circuitry whose response produces a desired effect, digital processing is performed by algorithmic manipulation of the samples making up the signal. The range of effects, and the degree of control over them, that can be achieved in this way is much greater than is possible with analogue circuits. Several standard plug-in formats are in use that allow effects to be shared among programs. Although it is not an audio application, Premiere's effects plug-in format is becoming widely used; at a more professional level, the formats associated with Cubase VST and with DigiDesign ProTools are popular.

The most frequently required correction is the removal of unwanted noise. For example, in Figure 9.1, it might be considered desirable to remove the background noises that were unavoidably picked up by the microphone, since the recording was made in the open. A *noise gate* is a blunt instrument that is used for this purpose. It eliminates all samples whose value falls below a specified threshold; samples above the threshold are left alone. As well as specifying the threshold, it is usual to specify a minimum time that must elapse before a sequence of low amplitude samples counts as a silence, and a similar limit before a sequence whose values exceed the threshold counts as sound. This prevents the gate being turned on or off by transient glitches. By setting the threshold just above the maximum value of the background noise, the gaps between words will become entirely silent. Since the noise gate has no effect on the speaker's words, the accompanying background noise will cut in and out as he speaks, which may well turn out to be more distracting than the original noise. This illustrates a general problem with noise removal: the noise is intimately combined with the signal, and although people can discriminate between the two, computer programs generally cannot.

Noise gates can be effective at removing hiss from music, since, in this case, the noise is hidden except in silent passages, where it will be removed by the noise gate. There are more sophisticated ways of reducing noise than the all-or-nothing filtering of the noise gate, though. Filters that remove certain bands of frequencies can be applied to noise that falls within a specific frequency range. *Low pass* filters, which allow low frequencies to pass through them, removing high frequencies, can be used to take out hiss; *high pass filters*, which pass the high frequencies and block the low, are used to remove 'rumble':

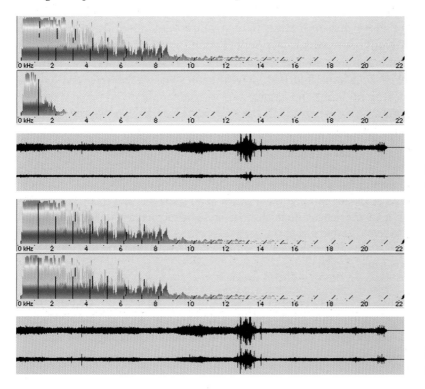

Figure 9.12 Low pass filtering

Figure 9.13 High pass filtering

low frequency noise caused by mechanical vibrations. Figures 9.12 and 9.13 show the effect of low and high pass filters on the spectrum and waveform of the sea sound from Figure 9.7. (The upper spectrum and waveform in each figure are the original sound; the lower after filtering.) A *notch filter* removes a single narrow frequency band. The commonest use of notch filters is to remove hum picked up from the mains: this will have a frequency of exactly 50 or 60 Hz, depending on the part of the world in which the noise was recorded. Some sophisticated programs offer the user the ultimate facility of being able to redraw the waveform, rubbing out the spikes that correspond to clicks, and so on. To do this effectively, however, requires considerable experience and the ability to interpret the visual display of a waveform in acoustic terms, which, as the examples shown earlier demonstrate, is not always easy.

Specialized filters are available for dealing with certain common recording defects. A *de-esser* is a filter that is intended to remove the sibilance that results from speaking or singing into a microphone placed too close to the performer. *Click repairers* are intended to remove clicks from recordings taken from damaged or dirty vinyl records. (There are also effects plug-ins that attempt to add authentic-sounding vinyl noise to digital recordings.) Although these filters are more discriminating than a noise gate, they are not infallible. The only sure way to get perfect sound is to start with a perfect take – microphones should be positioned to avoid sibilance, and kept well away from fans and disk drives, cables should be screened to avoid picking up hum, and so on.

Although the noise reduction facilities available in desktop sound applications are fairly crude and ineffectual, more elaborate – and computationally expensive – approaches have been developed. One approach is based on attempting to analyze the acoustic properties of the original recording apparatus on the basis of the make-up of the noise in quiet passages, and then compensating for it in the music. Sophisticated noise reduction techniques are used to restore old records from the early part of the twentieth century, and also to reconstruct other damaged recordings, such as the tapes from voice recorders of crashed aircraft.

When we consider effects that alter the quality of a sound, there is a continuum from those that perform minor embellishments to compensate for poor performance and recording, to those that radically alter the sound, or create new sounds out of the original.

A single effect may be used in different ways, at different points in this continuum, depending on the values of parameters that affect its operation. For example, a *reverb* effect is produced digitally by adding copies of a signal, delayed in time and attenuated, to the original. These copies model reflections from surrounding surfaces, with the delay corresponding to the size of the enclosing space and the degree of attenuation modelling surfaces with different acoustic reflectivity. By using small delays and low reflectivity, a recording can be made to sound as if it had been made inside a small room. This degree of reverb is often a necessary enhancement when the output from electric instruments has been recorded directly without going through a speaker and microphone. Although cleaner recordings are produced this way, they are often too dry acoustically to sound convincing. Longer reverb times can produce the illusion of a concert hall or a stadium. Still longer times, with the delayed signals being amplified instead of attenuated, can be used creatively to generate sustained rhythm patterns from a single chord or note. Figure 9.14 shows the effect of adding an echo to our sea sound.

Other effects can be put to a variety of uses in a similar way. These include *graphic equalization*, which transforms the spectrum of a sound using a bank of filters, each controlled by its own slider, and each affecting a fairly narrow band of frequencies. (Analogue graphic equalizers are commonly found on mid-range domestic sound

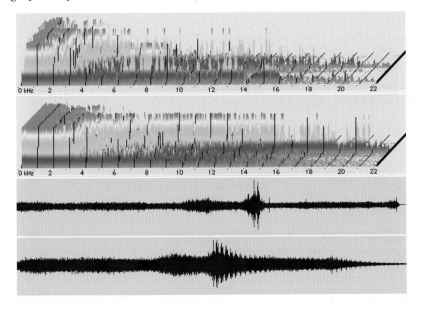

Figure 9.14 Echo

systems.) These can be used to compensate for recording equipment with idiosyncratic frequency response, or to artificially enhance the bass, for example, to produce a desired frequency balance. *Envelope shaping* operations change the outline of a waveform. The most general envelope shapers allow the user to draw a new envelope around the waveform, altering its attack and decay and introducing arbitrary fluctuations of amplitude. Specialized versions of envelope shaping include *faders*, which allow a sound's volume to be gradually increased or decreased, and *tremolo*, which causes the amplitude to oscillate periodically from zero to its maximum value.[†]

Time stretching and *pitch alteration* are two closely related effects that are especially well-suited to digital sound. With analogue recordings, altering the duration of a sound can only be achieved by altering the speed at which it is played back, and this alters the pitch. With digital sound, the duration can be changed without altering the pitch, by inserting or removing samples. Conversely, the pitch can be altered without affecting the duration.

Time stretching is required when sound is being synchronized to video or another sound. If, for example, a voice-over is slightly too long to fit over the scene it describes, the soundtrack can be shrunk in time, without raising the pitch of the speaker's voice, which would happen if the voice track was simply played at a faster speed. Time stretching can also be applied to music, to alter its tempo. This makes

[†] To classical musicians, 'tremolo' means the rapid repetition of a single note – this does produce a periodic oscillation of amplitude. The 'tremolo arm' fitted to Fender Stratocasters and other electric guitars actually produces a periodic change of *pitch*, more accurately referred to as 'vibrato'.

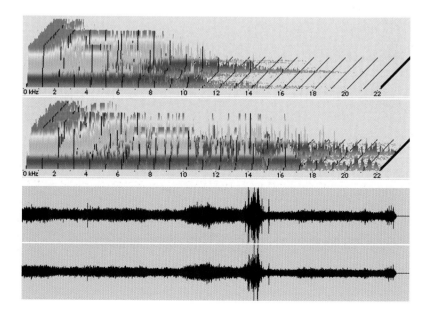

Figure 9.15 Pitch shifting

it possible to combine loops that were sampled from pieces originally played at different tempos.

Pitch alteration can be used in several ways. It can be applied uniformly to alter the pitch of an instrument, compensating for an out-of-tune guitar, for example. It can be applied periodically to add a vibrato (periodic fluctuation of pitch) to a voice or instrument, or it can be applied gradually, to produce a 'bent note', in the same way a blues guitarist changes the tone of a note by bending the string while it sounds. The all-important shape of the bend can be specified by drawing a curve showing how the pitch changes over time. Pitch alteration can also be used to transpose music into a different key; again, this allows samples from disparate sources to be combined harmoniously. Figure 9.15 shows the result of shifting the pitch of the sea up an octave (i.e. doubling the frequencies).

Beyond these effects lie what are euphemistically called 'creative' sound effects. Effects such as flanging, phasing, chorus, ring modulation, reversal, Doppler shift, and wah-wah, which were pioneered in the 1960s on albums such as the Beatles' *Sergeant Pepper's Lonely Hearts Club Band* and Jimi Hendrix's *Electric Ladyland*, have been reproduced digitally, and joined by new extreme effects such as roboticization. These effects, if used judiciously, can enhance a recording, but they are easily over-used, and are generally best enjoyed in private.

Compression

While the data rate for CD-quality audio is nothing like as demanding as that for video, it still exceeds the bandwidth of dial-up Internet connections, and lengthy recordings rapidly consume disk space. A single three-minute song, recorded in stereo, will occupy over 25 Mbytes. Hence, where audio is used in multimedia, and especially when it is delivered over the Internet, there is a need for compression. The complex and unpredictable nature of sound waveforms makes them difficult to compress using lossless methods. Huffman coding can be effective in cases where the amplitude of the sound mainly falls below the maximum level that can be represented in the sample size being used. In that case, the signal could have been represented in a smaller sample size, and the Huffman algorithm, by assigning short codes to the values it does encounter, will effectively do this automatically. This is a special case, though, and, in general, some form of lossy compression will be required.

An obvious compression technique that can be applied to speech is the removal of silence. That is, instead of using 44,100 samples with the value of zero for each second of silence (assuming a 44.1 kHz sampling rate) we record the length of the silence. This technique appears to be a special case of run-length encoding, which, as we said in Chapter 5, is lossless. However, as Figure 9.1 shows, 'silence' is rarely absolute. We would obtain little compression if we simply run-length encoded samples whose value was exactly zero; instead, we must treat samples falling below a threshold as if they were zero. The effect of doing this is equivalent to applying a noise gate, and is not strictly lossless, since the decompressed signal will not be identical to the original.

The principles behind lossy audio compression are different from those used in lossy image compression, because of the differences in the way we perceive the two media. In particular, whereas the high frequencies associated with rapid changes of colour in an image can safely be discarded, the high frequencies associated with rapid changes of sound are highly significant, so some other principle must be used to decide what data can be discarded.

Speech Compression

Telephone companies have been using digital audio since the early 1960s, and have been forced by the limited bandwidth of telephone lines to develop compression techniques that can be effectively applied to speech. An important contribution of this early work is the technique known as *companding*. The idea is to use non-linear quantization levels, with the higher levels spaced further apart than the low ones, so that quiet sounds are represented in greater detail than louder ones. This matches the way in which we perceive differences in volume.

Figure 9.16 shows an example of non-linear quantization. The signal value required to produce an increase of one in the quantized value goes up logarithmically. This produces compression, because fewer bits are needed to represent the full range of possible input values than a linear quantization scheme would require. When the signal is reconstructed an inverse process of expansion is required, hence the name 'companding' – itself a compressed version of 'compressing/ expanding'.

Different non-linear companding functions can be used. The principal important ones are defined by ITU Recommendations for use

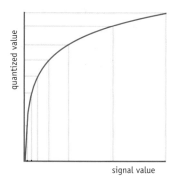

Figure 9.16 Non-linear quantization

in telecommunications. Recommendation G.711 defines a function called the μ-*law*, which is used in North America and Japan. It has been adopted for compressing audio on Sun and NeXT systems, and files compressed in accordance with it are commonly found on the Internet. A different ITU Recommendation is used in the rest of the world, based on a function known as the *A-law*.

Telephone signals are usually sampled at only 8 kHz. At this rate, μ-law compression is able to squeeze a dynamic range of 12 bits into just 8 bits, giving a one-third reduction in data rate.

The μ-law is defined by the equation:

$$y = \log(1 + \mu x)/\log(1 + \mu) \text{ for } x \geq 0$$

where μ is a parameter that determines the amount of companding; μ = 255 is used for telephony.

The A-law is:

$$y = \begin{cases} Ax/(1 + \log A) & \text{for } 0 \leq |x| < 1/A \\ (1 + \log Ax)/(1 + \log A) & \text{for } 1/A \leq |x| < 1 \end{cases}$$

Another important technique that was originally developed for, and is widely used in, the telecommunications industry is *Adaptive Differential Pulse Code Modulation (ADPCM)*.[†] This is related to inter-frame compression of video, in that it is based on storing the difference between consecutive samples, instead of the absolute value of each sample. Because of the different nature of audio and video, and its origins in hardware encoding of transmitted signals, ADPCM works somewhat less straightforwardly than a simple scheme based on the difference between samples.

Storing differences will only produce compression if the differences can be stored in fewer bits than the sample. Audio waveforms can change rapidly, so, unlike consecutive video frames, there is no reason to assume that the difference will necessarily be much less than the value. Basic *Differential Pulse Code Modulation (DPCM)* therefore computes a predicted value for a sample, based on preceding samples, and stores the difference between the prediction and the actual value. If the prediction is good, the difference will be small. *Adaptive DPCM* obtains further compression by dynamically varying the step size used to represent the quantized differences. Large differences are quantized using large steps, small differences using small steps, so the amount of detail that is preserved scales with the size of the

† Pulse Code Modulation is the term used in audio and communications circles for encoding digital data as a sequence of pulses representing ones and zeros. Whereas this is more or less the only sensible representation for computer use, alternatives, such as Pulse Width Modulation, exist where the data is to be represented as a stream for transmission, rather than as stored values.

difference. The details of how this is done are complicated, but as with companding, the effect is to make efficient use of bits to store information, taking account of its rate of change.

ITU Recommendation G.721 specifies a form of ADPCM representation for use in telephony, with data rates of 16 kbps and 32 kbps. Lower rates can be obtained by a much more radical approach to compression. *Linear Predictive Coding* uses a mathematical model of the state of the vocal tract as its representation of speech. Instead of transmitting the speech as audio samples, it sends parameters describing the corresponding state of the model. At the receiving end, these parameters can be used to construct the speech, by applying them to the model. The details of the model and how the parameters are derived from the speech lie beyond the scope of this book. Speech compressed in this way can be transmitted at speeds as low as 2.4 kbps. Because the sound is reconstructed algorithmically, it has a machine-like quality, so it is only suitable for applications where the content of the speech is more important than a faithful rendition of someone's voice.

Perceptually Based Compression

The secret of effective lossy compression is to identify data that doesn't matter – in the sense of not affecting perception of the signal – and to throw it away. If an audio signal is digitized in a straightforward way, data corresponding to sounds that are inaudible may be included in the digitized version. This is because the signal records all the physical variations in air pressure that cause sound, but the perception of sound is a sensation produced in the brain, via the ear, and the ear and brain do not respond to the sound waves in a simple way.

Two phenomena in particular cause some sounds not to be heard, despite being physically present. Both are familiar experiences: a sound may be too quiet to be heard, or it may be obscured by some other sound. Neither phenomenon is quite as straightforward as it might appear.

The *threshold of hearing* is the minimum level at which a sound can be heard. It varies non-linearly with frequency, as shown in Figure 9.17. A very low or very high frequency sound must be much louder than a mid-range tone to be heard. It is surely no coincidence that we are most sensitive to sounds in the frequency range that corresponds to human speech. When compressing sound, there is no point in retaining sounds that fall below the threshold of hearing, so a com-

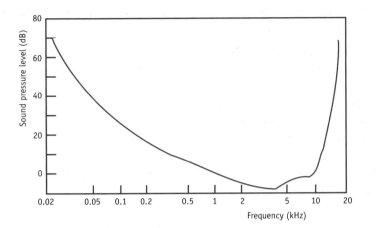

Figure 9.17 The threshold of hearing

pression algorithm can discard the corresponding data. To do this, the algorithm must use a *psycho-acoustical model* – a mathematical description of aspects of the way the ear and brain perceive sounds. In this case, what is needed is a description of the way the threshold of hearing varies with frequency.

Loud tones can obscure softer tones that occur at the same time.[†] This is not simply a case of the loud tone 'drowning out' the softer one; the effect is more complex, and depends on the relative frequencies of the two tones. *Masking*, as this phenomenon is known, can be conveniently described as a modification of the threshold of hearing curve in the region of a loud tone. As Figure 9.18 shows, the threshold is raised in the neighbourhood of the masking tone. The raised portion or *masking curve* is non-linear, and asymmetrical, rising faster than it falls. Any sound that lies within the masking curve will be inaudible, even though it rises above the unmodified threshold of hearing. Thus, there is an additional opportunity to discard data. Masking can be used more cleverly, though. Because masking hides noise as well as some components of the signal, quantization noise can be masked. Where a masking sound is present, the signal can be quantized relatively coarsely, using fewer bits than would otherwise be needed, because the resulting quantization noise can be hidden under the masking curve.

It is evident that the phenomena just described offer the potential for additional compression. It is not obvious how a compression algorithm can be implemented to take advantage of this potential.

† In fact, they can also obscure softer tones that occur a little later or, strange as it may seem, slightly earlier.

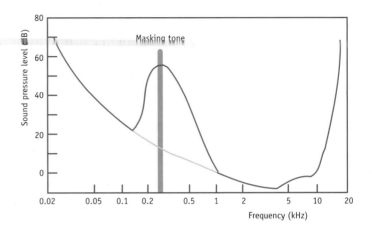

Figure 9.18 Masking

The approach usually adopted is to use a bank of filters to split the signal into bands of frequencies; 32 bands are commonly used. The average signal level in each band is calculated, and using these values and a psycho-acoustical model, a masking level for each band is computed. That is, it is assumed that the masking curve within each band can be approximated by a single value. If the signal in a band falls entirely below its masking level, that band is discarded. Otherwise, the signal is quantized using the least number of bits that causes the quantization noise to be masked.

Turning the preceding sketch into a working algorithm involves many technical details that lie beyond the scope of this book. The best known algorithms that have been developed are those specified for audio compression in the MPEG standards. MPEG-1 and MPEG-2 are primarily video standards, but, since most video has sound associated with it, they also include audio compression. MPEG audio has been so successful that it is often used on its own purely for compressing sound, especially music.

MPEG-1 specifies three *layers* of audio compression. All three layers are based on the principles just outlined. The encoding process increases in complexity from Layer 1 to Layer 3, while as a result, the data rate of the compressed audio decreases: the quality obtained at 192 kbps for each channel at Layer 1 only needs 128 kbps at Layer 2, and 64 kbps at Layer 3. (These data rates will be doubled for stereo.) MPEG-1 Layer 3 audio, or *MP3* as it is usually called,[†] achieves compression ratios of around 10:1, while maintaining high quality.

† MP3 does not, despite what you may sometimes read, stand for MPEG-3. There is no MPEG-3.

A typical track from a CD can be compressed to under 3 Mbytes. The sound quality at this rate is sometimes claimed to be 'CD quality', but this is something of an exaggeration. Higher bit rates can be used at Layer 3, however, giving correspondingly better quality; variable bit rate (VBR) coding is also possible, with the bit rate being changed, so that passages that do not compress easily can be encoded at a higher rate than those which do. MP3 can also encode audio at lower bit rates, for example for streaming. At 64 kbps, stereo quality is claimed to be as good as FM radio.

The audio part of the MPEG-2 standard includes an encoding that is essentially identically with MPEG-1 audio, except for some extensions to cope with surround sound. The MPEG-2 standard also defined a new audio codec, *Advanced Audio Coding (AAC)*. Unlike MP3, AAC is not backwards compatible with earlier MPEG standards, or lower layers. By abandoning backwards compatibility, AAC was able to achieve higher compression ratios at lower bit rates than MP3. Like MP3, AAC is based on perceptual coding, but it uses additional techniques and a more complicated implementation. Subjective listening tests consistently rate AAC quality as superior to MP3 at the same bit rates, and the same subjective quality is attained by AAC at lower rates than MP3. For instance, AAC audio at 96 kbps is considered to be superior to MP3 at 128 kbps. AAC has been incorporated and extended in MPEG-4, where it forms the basis of coding of natural audio (as distinct from speech and synthesized sound).

Lossy compression always sounds like a dubious practice – how can you discard information without affecting the quality? In the case of MPEG audio, the argument is that the information that has been discarded is inaudible. This contention is based on extensive listening tests, and is supported by the rapid acceptance of MP3 as a format for downloading music. (It should also be borne in mind that, although some people care obsessively about the quality of audio reproduction, most people aren't very particular, as witnessed by the enduring popularity of the analogue compact audio cassette.) As with any lossy form of compression, though, MPEG audio will deteriorate progressively if it is decompressed and recompressed a number of times. It is therefore only suitable as a delivery format, and should not be used during production, when uncompressed audio should be used whenever possible.

Formats

Most of the development of digital audio has taken place in the recording and broadcast industries, where the emphasis is on physical data representations on media such as compact disc and digital audio tape, and on data streams for transmission and playback. There are standards in these areas that are widely adhered to. The use of digital sound on computers is a much less thoroughly regulated area, where a wide range of incompatible proprietary formats and *ad hoc* standards can be found. Each of the three major platforms has its own sound file format: AIFF for MacOS, WAV (or WAVE) for Windows, and AU[†] for Unix, but support for all three by applications is common on all platforms. The standardizing influence of the Internet has been less pronounced in audio than it is in graphics. QuickTime, Windows Media and RealAudio are all widely used as container formats for audio compressed with different codecs. The popularity of music swapping services using MP3 has led to its emergence as the leading audio format on the Internet.

† More properly, WAV is the Audio Waveform file format, actually a variety of Microsoft RIFF file, and AU is the NeXT/Sun audio file format.

MP3

MP3 has its own file format, in which the compressed audio stream is split into chunks called 'frames', each of which has a header, giving details of the bit rate, sampling frequency and other parameters. The file may also include metadata tags, oriented towards musical content, giving the title of a track, the artist performing it, the album from which it is taken, and so on. MP3 files have been widely used for downloading and storing music on computers and mobile music players. (The growth of legal music download services, as against informal peer-to-peer swapping services that have caused so much agitation in the music industry, may see MP3 superseded as the format of choice.)

MP3 is, however, primarily an encoding, not a file format, and MP3 data may be stored in other types of file. In particular, QuickTime may include audio tracks encoded with MP3, and Flash's SWF movies use MP3 to compress any sound they may include.

Streaming Audio Formats

In Chapter 7, we explained that streamed video resembles broadcast television. Streamed audio resembles broadcast radio. That is, sound is delivered over a network and played as it arrives, without having to be stored on the user's machine first. As with video, this allows live transmission and the playing of files that are too big to be held on an average-sized hard disk. Because of the lower bandwidth required by audio, streaming is more successful for sound than it is for video.

The first successful streaming audio format was Real Networks' RealAudio, a companion to RealVideo, which has now been incorporated into Real G2. This uses a range of proprietary compressors to maintain reasonable sound quality at data rates suitable for dial-up and broadband Internet connections. RealAudio also uses downsampling to reduce its bandwidth requirements. Streaming QuickTime can also be used for audio, on its own as well as accompanying video. QuickTime includes an AAC codec for high quality audio. Windows Media audio can also be streamed. All three of these formats, as well as MP3, are used for broadcasting live concerts and for the Internet equivalent of radio stations, and also for providing 'play on demand' music – the Internet as the biggest jukebox in the world.

MIDI

If we had written a piece of music, there are two ways we could send it to you. We could play it, record the performance, and send you the recording, or we could write it down using some form of notation, indicating the arrangement, and send you the sheet music, so you could play the piece for yourself. There is a parallel here with bit-mapped and vector graphics. In the first case, we send you the actual sound; in the second, we send you what amounts to a set of instructions telling you how to produce the sound. In either case we are making some assumptions about what you can do. For the recording, we assume you have a machine capable of playing back whichever medium we have recorded our performance on. For the sheet music, we are making the more demanding assumptions that you can read our chosen music notation, have access to the instrument or instruments indicated in the arrangement, and can either play yourself or get musicians to play those instruments. If the music is arranged for a symphony orchestra, this may present some difficulties for you, whereas, if we were to send a recording, all the difficulties would lie at our end.

In the digital realm, there is a similar choice of options for delivering music. So far, we have considered ways of delivering digitized sound, that is, the equivalent of recordings. There also exists an equivalent to delivering the sheet music, i.e. a way of delivering instructions about how to produce the music, which can be interpreted by suitable software or hardware. Similar assumptions must be made: for sound files, you must have software that can read them – as we have seen, this is not a demanding requirement. For instructions, you must have software that can interpret the instructions, and some means of producing sounds that correspond to the appropriate instruments.

MIDI (Musical Instruments Digital Interface) provides a basis for satisfying these requirements. Originally, MIDI was devised as a standard protocol for communicating between electronic instruments, such as synthesizers, samplers, and drum machines. By defining a standard hardware interface, and a set of instructions indicating such things as the start and end of a note, it provided a means of controlling a collection of such instruments from a single keyboard, removing the requirement for the huge banks of keyboards beloved of certain 1970s rock stars, and opening the way for playing traditional keyboard instruments, particularly synthesizers, with other controllers, such as drum pads or wind instruments.

More significantly, perhaps, MIDI allowed instruments to be controlled automatically by devices that could be programmed to send out sequences of MIDI instructions. Originally, *sequencers*, as these devices are known, were dedicated hardware devices, programmed using their own built-in, relatively clumsy, interfaces. It was not long before it was realized that computer programs could offer a more convenient and flexible means of sequencing, provided that a computer could be fitted with a MIDI interface so that it could send the necessary signals to other MIDI devices. Such an interface is a relatively simple and inexpensive device, so computer-based sequencers rapidly became available. A software sequencer provides editing and compositional functions, so it needs to store MIDI sequences in files. This requirement led to the development of a standard file format for MIDI files, that is, a way of storing MIDI on disk. Clearly, such files can be exchanged between computers equipped with MIDI software. They can also be incorporated into multimedia productions.

Playing back MIDI files requires an instrument that understands MIDI, but a computer, equipped with suitable hardware or software, can be such an instrument itself. Sounds can be either synthesized on a sound card, or held on disk in the form of samples, to be played back in response to MIDI instructions. MIDI files are therefore a means of communicating music. Because they do not contain any audio data, they can be much more compact than actual digitized sound files. For the same reason, though, they cannot guarantee the same fidelity: the samples available when the file is produced may be of higher quality than those used to play it back – just as the musician who plays a piece of music from a score may not be sufficiently accomplished to realize the composer's intentions. In both cases, the result is unpredictable.

MIDI Messages

A MIDI *message* is an instruction that controls some aspect of the performance of an instrument. Messages are encoded in much the same way as machine instructions: a *status byte* indicates the type of the message, and is followed by one or two *data bytes* giving the values of parameters. Although wind instruments, drum pads, and guitars are used as MIDI controllers (as devices that transmit MIDI signals are called), MIDI is markedly biased towards keyboard instruments. Thus, for example, the most commonly used message is 'Note On', which takes two parameters: a number between 0 and 127 indicating the note to be sounded, and a key velocity, indicating how fast the key was pressed, and hence the attack of the note. When an actual keyboard is being used to generate MIDI messages, these values will be sensed by the keyboard's hardware as the musician plays the key. When the message is being generated by software, the values are specified by the user.

Other notable MIDI messages include 'Note Off', which ends a note, 'Key Pressure', which indicates the degree of 'aftertouch' to be applied, and 'Pitch Bend', to change note values dynamically, as a guitarist does by bending the string (on MIDI keyboards, a wheel is used for this function).

The status and data bytes in a stream of MIDI instructions are distinguishable by the value of their most significant bit. This makes possible an optimization: where a sequence of messages all have the same status byte, it may be omitted from the second and subsequent messages, for which it will be inferred from the most recent value. This arrangement is called *running status*; it can save an appreciable number of bytes where a sequence of notes is being played with no modifications. Using the convention that the end of a note can be indicated by a 'Note On' message with a velocity of zero, the whole sequence can consist of a single 'Note On' status byte, followed by a series of data bytes giving the notes to be played and the velocities to be applied to them.

When a MIDI message is interpreted, we say that an event occurs. In live performance, the timing of events is determined by the player in real time. In a MIDI file, it is necessary to record the time of each event. Each message is preceded by a *delta time*, that is, a measure of the time since the preceding event. Near the beginning of the file is a specification of the units to be used for times.

General MIDI

The preceding account indicates how notes are produced, but leaves unanswered the question of how they are to be associated with particular sounds. Typically, the sorts of instruments controlled by MIDI – synthesizers and samplers – provide a variety of *voices*. In the case of synthesizers, these are different synthesized sounds, often called *patches* by synthesists; in the case of samplers, they are different instrument samples. A MIDI 'Program Change' message selects a new voice, using a value between 0 and 127. The mapping from these values to voices is not specified in the MIDI standard, and may depend on the particular instrument being controlled. There is thus a possibility that a MIDI file intended to specify a piece for piano and violin might end up being played on trombone and kettle drum. To help overcome this unsatisfactory situation, an addendum to the MIDI standard, known as *General MIDI*, was produced, which specifies 128 standard voices to correspond to the values used by Program Change messages. The assignments are shown in Table 9.1.

For drum machines and percussion samplers, Program Change values are interpreted differently as elements of drum kits – cymbals of various sorts, snares, tom-toms, and so on (see Table 9.2).

General MIDI only associates program numbers with voice *names*. There is no guarantee that identical sounds will be generated for each name by different instruments – a cheap sound card may attempt to synthesize all of them, while a good sampler may use high quality samples of the corresponding real instruments. Adherence to General MIDI offers some guarantee of consistency, though, which is otherwise entirely missing.

QuickTime incorporates MIDI-like functionality. QuickTime Musical Instruments provide a set of instrument samples, and the QuickTime Music Architecture incorporates a superset of the features of MIDI. QuickTime can read standard MIDI files, so any computer with QuickTime installed can play MIDI music using software alone. QuickTime can also control external MIDI devices. MIDI tracks can be combined with audio, video or any of the other media types supported by QuickTime.

Table 9.1 General MIDI voice numbers

1	Acoustic Grand Piano	44	Contrabass	87	Synth Lead~7
2	Bright Acoustic Piano	45	Tremolo Strings	88	Synth Lead~8
3	Electric Grand Piano	46	Pizzicato Strings	89	Synth Pad~1
4	Honky-tonk Piano	47	Orchestral Harp	90	Synth Pad~2
5	Rhodes Piano	48	Timpani	91	Synth Pad~3
6	Chorused Piano	49	Acoustic String Ensemble~1	92	Synth Pad~4
7	Harpsichord	50	Acoustic String Ensemble~2	93	Synth Pad~5
8	Clavinet	51	Synth Strings~1	94	Synth Pad~6
9	Celesta	52	Synth Strings~2	95	Synth Pad~7
10	Glockenspiel	53	Aah Choir	96	Synth Pad~8
11	Music Box	54	Ooh Choir	97	Ice Rain
12	Vibraphone	55	Synvox	98	Soundtracks
13	Marimba	56	Orchestra Hit	99	Crystal
14	Xylophone	57	Trumpet	100	Atmosphere
15	Tubular bells	58	Trombone	101	Bright
16	Dulcimer	59	Tuba	102	Goblin
17	Draw Organ	60	Muted Trumpet	103	Echoes
18	Percussive Organ	61	French Horn	104	Space
19	Rock Organ	62	Brass Section	105	Sitar
20	Church Organ	63	Synth Brass~1	106	Banjo
21	Reed Organ	64	Synth Brass~2	107	Shamisen
22	Accordion	65	Soprano Sax	108	Koto
23	Harmonica	66	Alto Sax	109	Kalimba
24	Tango Accordion	67	Tenor Sax	110	Bagpipe
25	Acoustic Nylon Guitar	68	Baritone Sax	111	Fiddle
26	Acoustic Steel Guitar	69	Oboe	112	Shanai
27	Electric Jazz Guitar	70	English Horn	113	Tinkle bell
28	Electric clean Guitar	71	Bassoon	114	Agogo
29	Electric Guitar muted	72	Clarinet	115	Steel Drums
30	Overdriven Guitar	73	Piccolo	116	Woodblock
31	Distortion Guitar	74	Flute	117	Taiko Drum
32	Guitar Harmonics	75	Recorder	118	Melodic Tom
33	Wood Bass	76	Pan Flute	119	Synth Tom
34	Electric Bass Fingered	77	Bottle blow	120	Reverse Cymbal
35	Electric Bass Picked	78	Shakuhachi	121	Guitar Fret Noise
36	Fretless Bass	79	Whistle	122	Breath Noise
37	Slap Bass~1	80	Ocarina	123	Seashore
38	Slap Bass~2	81	Square Lead	124	Bird Tweet
39	Synth Bass~1	82	Saw Lead	125	Telephone Ring
40	Synth Bass~2	83	Calliope	126	Helicopter
41	Violin	84	Chiffer	127	Applause
42	Viola	85	Synth Lead~5	128	Gunshot
43	Cello	86	Synth Lead~6		

Table 9.2 General MIDI Drum Kit Numbers

35	Acoustic Bass Drum	47	Low -Mid Tom Tom	59	Ride Cymbal~2
36	Bass Drum~1	48	Hi Mid Tom Tom	60	Hi Bongo
37	Side Stick	49	Crash Cymbal~1	61	Low Bongo
38	Acoustic Snare	50	Hi Tom Tom	62	Mute Hi Conga
39	Hand Clap	51	Ride Cymbal~1	63	Open Hi Conga
40	Electric Snare	52	Chinese Cymbal	64	Low Conga
41	Lo Floor Tom	53	Ride Bell	65	Hi Timbale
42	Closed Hi Hat	54	Tambourine	66	Lo Timbale
43	Hi Floor Tom	55	Splash Cymbal		
44	Pedal Hi Hat	56	Cowbell		
45	Lo Tom Tom	57	Crash Cymbal~2		
46	Open Hi Hat	58	Vibraslap		

MIDI Software

MIDI sequencing programs, such as Cakewalk Metro and Cubase, perform capture and editing functions equivalent to those of video editing software. They support multiple tracks, which can be allocated to different voices, thus allowing polytimbral music to be constructed. In addition, such packages support composition.

Music can be captured as it is played from MIDI controllers attached to a computer via a MIDI interface. The sequencer can generate metronome ticks to assist the player to maintain an accurate tempo. Although it is common to use the sequencer simply as if it were a tape recorder, to capture a performance in real time, sometimes MIDI data is entered one note at a time, which allows musicians to 'play' music that would otherwise be beyond their competence. Facilities normally found in conventional audio recording software are also available, in particular the ability to 'punch in': the start and end point of a defective passage are marked, the sequencer starts playing before the beginning, and then switches to record mode, allowing a new version of the passage to be recorded to replace the original.

Sequencers will optionally *quantize* tempo during recording, fitting the length of notes to exact sixteenth notes, or eighth note triplets, or whatever duration is specified. This allows rhythmically loose playing to be brought into strict tempo, which may be felt desirable for certain styles of music, although the result often has a machine-like feel, since live musicians rarely play exactly to the beat. Quantization is usually necessary if it is desired to produce a transcription of the music, since otherwise the program will transcribe exactly what was played, even if that involves dotted sixty-fourth notes and rests.

Most programs allow music to be entered using classical music notation, often by dragging and dropping notes and other symbols onto a stave. Some programs allow printed sheet music to be scanned, and will perform optical character recognition to transform the music into MIDI. The opposite transformation, from MIDI to a printed score, is also often provided, enabling transcriptions of performed music to be made automatically. Those who do not read music usually prefer to use the 'piano-roll' interface, which allows the duration of notes to be specified graphically, essentially using a timeline. For music constructed out of repeating sections, loops can be defined and reused many times.

Once a piece of music has been recorded or entered, it can be edited: individual notes' pitch and duration can be altered, sections can be cut and pasted, or global changes can be made, such as transposing the entire piece into a different key, or changing the time signature. The parameters of individual MIDI events can be changed – the velocity of a note can be altered, for example. Voices can be changed to assign different instruments to the parts of the arrangement.

Because digital audio is very demanding of computer resources, but MIDI is much less so, the two forms of music representation were originally separated, with different software being used for each. Now that computers have become powerful enough to take audio in their stride, the two are commonly integrated in a single application, which allows MIDI tracks to be combined and synchronized with full audio. This arrangement overcomes one of the major limitations of MIDI, namely the impossibility of representing vocals (except for 'Oohs' and 'Aahs'). MIDI can be transformed into audio, much as vector graphics can be rasterized and transformed into pixels. The reverse transformation is sometimes supported, too, although it is more difficult to implement. MIDI captures the musical structure of sound, since MIDI events correspond to notes. Being able to transform audio into MIDI allows music to be recorded from ordinary instruments instead of MIDI controllers – it can even be recorded from somebody's whistling – and then edited or transcribed in terms of musical notes.

Combining Sound and Picture

Sound is frequently used as a part of a video or animation production. When it is, synchronization between sound and picture becomes a matter of considerable importance. This is seen most clearly where the picture shows a person talking, and the soundtrack contains their speech. If synchronization is slightly out, the result will be disconcerting; if it is considerably out, the result will at best be unintentionally funny, but more likely incoherent. Although speech makes the most exacting demands on synchronization, wherever sound and picture are related it is necessary that the temporal relationship between them is maintained. Voice-overs should match the picture they describe, music will often be related to edits, and natural sounds will be associated with events on screen.

In order to establish synchronization, it is necessary to be able to identify specific points in time. Film is divided into frames, which provide a natural means of identifying times. Video tape does not have physical frames, but, as we mentioned in Chapter 7, timecode can be written to a video tape, allowing the frames to be identified. Audio tape can be similarly augmented with timecode, and the codes can be used to synchronize tape recorders, both audio and video. As long as the timecodes on two machines agree, they must be in sync.

Sound is effectively continuous, though, even in the digital domain – the high sampling rates used for digital sound mean that a single sample defines too short a time interval to be useful. For sound, the division into frames imposed by timecode is just a useful fiction. This fictional division continues to be used when synching digital audio and video. It enables sound and picture tracks in a video editing application such as Final Cut Pro to be arranged on the same timeline. Unlike the soundtrack on a piece of film or a video tape, a sound track in a digital video editing program is physically independent of the video it accompanies, so it is easy to move the sound in time relative to the picture, simply by sliding the sound track along the timeline. This is not something you would normally want to do if the sound and picture had originally been recorded together. In that case, you will usually want to maintain their synchronization during editing. For this purpose, tracks can be locked together, so that, for example, cutting out part of the video track will remove the accompanying sound.

Audio tracks may be displayed as waveforms. When a sound track has been made independently of the picture – a voice-over or musical accompaniment, for example – it will be necessary to fit the sound to the picture. By looking at the waveform to identify the start of syllables in speech, or stressed beats in music, an editor can identify meaningful points in the sound track, which can be lined up with appropriate picture frames. Performing this matching by eye is difficult, so a method that is often used is to scrub through the sound to identify the precise cue point by ear, and place a marker that can then be lined up on the timeline with the video frame (which can also be marked for identification). Sometimes, it may be necessary to apply a time-stretching filter to adjust the duration of the sound to fit the picture, as described earlier.

Synchronization can thus be established in a video editing program, but it must then be maintained when the video and its soundtrack are played back – possibly over a network. If the sound and video are physically independent – travelling over separate network connections, for example – synchronization will sometimes be lost. This is a fact of life and cannot be avoided. Audio and video data streams must therefore carry the equivalent of timecode, so that their synchronization can be checked, and they can be resynched, if necessary. Usually, this will require some video frames to be dropped, so that picture can catch up with sound – the greater data rate of the video means that it is the more likely to fall behind.

Where video and audio are played back from a local hard disk, it is easier to maintain synchronization, although it still cannot be guaranteed, owing to the different speeds of the components involved. For very short clips, it is possible to load the entire sound track into memory before playback begins, eliminating any potential delays caused by reading from disk. This is impractical for movies of any significant duration. For these, it is normal to *interleave* the audio and video, that is, the audio is divided into chunks, which are interspersed between video frames. The size of chunk can be varied, and optimized for particular hardware configurations.

QuickTime provides highly flexible support for specifying time within a movie. A movie has a *time base*, specifying the current time and the rate (and direction) at which time passes, relative to a *time coordinate system*, which specifies the units in which time is to be measured. The time coordinate system is chosen to suit the data; for example, sound sampled at 44.1 kHz may use a time coordinate in which each time unit is 1/44.1 ms. A *clock component* is used to obtain real time values, usually from the clock chip built in to the computer on which the movie is being played. By synchronizing the time base to the clock, the required playback rate is maintained. Whenever some data, such as a frame of video, is to be played, the time base is passed to the software component responsible for playing the data. The current movie time can then be used to determine the appropriate portion of the data to play. If sound and picture start to drift, this will ensure that they are brought back into the correct temporal relationship.

Exercises

1   Give an example of a natural sound that has an identifiable pitch.

2   Why are the sampling frequencies normally used for 'lo-fi' digital sound exact sub-multiples of 44.1 kHz?

3   Given that singing has characteristics of both speech and music, which compression algorithms would you expect to be most successful on songs?

4   A problem commonly encountered when recording in the open air is that a microphone will pick up the sounds made by the wind blowing against it. Describe how you would attempt to remove such noise from a digitized recording. How successful would you expect your attempts to be? Suggest an alternative approach to eliminating wind noise.

5   When we described anti-aliasing of vector graphics in Chapter 4, it was as an antidote to insufficiently high sampling rates. In this chapter, we have described dithering as a way of mitigating the effect of insufficient quantization levels. Would this kind of dithering help improve the apparent quality of under-sampled audio? Is there any connection between dithering sound and dithering colour, as described in Chapter 6?

6   Explain how you would apply a 'cross-fade' to a stereo recording of a solo instrument, so that the sound would appear to move gradually from the extreme left to the extreme right of the sound stage.

7   What could you do to correct a sound that was digitized with its levels (a) too high; (b) too low? How would you prepare a sound recording with an extremely wide dynamic range for a multimedia production?

8   Is there a limit on how far you can (a) stretch, (b) contract a digitized sound successfully? What aspects of particular kinds of sound might affect the limits?

9   (a) Describe the alterations that must be made to the digital representation of a sound to raise its pitch by an octave, without changing its duration. (Raising the pitch by an octave is the same as doubling the frequency.)
(b) Describe the alteration that must be made to a MIDI Note-On message to raise the note's pitch by an octave.

10   Under what circumstances might you expect to lose synchronization between sound and picture in a multimedia production? What steps could you take to minimize the chances of this happening?

Characters and Fonts

- Character Sets
  - Standards
  - Unicode and ISO 10646
- Fonts
  - Accessing Fonts
  - Classification and Choice of Fonts
  - Font Terminology
  - Digital Font Technology

10

Text has a dual nature: it is a visual representation of language, and a graphic element in its own right. Text in digital form must also be a representation of language; that is, we need to relate bit patterns stored in a computer's memory or transmitted over a network to the symbols of a written language. When we consider the display of stored text, its visual aspect becomes relevant. We then become concerned with such issues as the precise shape of characters, their spacing and the layout of lines, paragraphs and larger divisions of text on the screen or page. These issues of display are traditionally the concern of the art of *typography*. Much of the accumulated typographical practice of the last several centuries can be adapted to the display of the textual elements of multimedia.

In this chapter, we consider how the fundamental units of written languages – characters – can be represented in a digital form, and how the digital representation of characters can be turned into a visual representation for display. We will show how digital font technology makes it possible to approximate the typographical richness of printed text in the textual components of multimedia.

Character Sets

In keeping with text's dual nature, it is convenient to distinguish between the lexical *content* of a piece of text and its *appearance*. By content we mean the characters that make up the words and other units, such as punctuation or mathematical symbols. (At this stage we are not considering 'content' in the sense of the meaning or message contained in the text.) The appearance of the text comprises its visual attributes, such as the precise shape of the characters, their size, and the way the content is arranged on the page or screen. For example, the content of the following two sentences from the short story *Jeeves and the Impending Doom* by P.G. Wodehouse is identical, but their appearance is not:

```
The Right Hon was a tubby little chap who looked as if he
had been poured into his clothes and had forgotten to say
```
'When!'

THE RIGHT HON was a tubby little chap who looked as if he had been *poured* into his clothes and had forgotten to say 'When!'

We all readily understand that the first symbol in each version of this sentence is a capital T, even though one is several times as large as the other, has some additional strokes, and is darker. To express their fundamental identity, we distinguish between an *abstract character* and its graphic representations, of which there is a potentially infinite number. Here, we have two graphic representations of the same abstract character.

As a slight over-simplification, we could say that the content is the part of a text that carries its meaning or semantics, while the appearance is a surface attribute that may affect how easy the text is to read, or how pleasant it is to look at, but does not substantially alter its meaning. In the example just given, the fixed-width, typewriter-like font of the first version clearly differs from the more formal book font used for most of the second, but this and the gratuitous initial dropped cap and use of different fonts do not alter the joke. Note, however, that the italicization of the word 'poured' in the second version, although we would normally consider it an aspect of the appearance like the use of the small caps for 'Right Hon', implies an emphasis on the word that is missing in the plain version (and also in the original story). Hence, the distinction between appearance and content is not quite as clear-cut as one might think. Nevertheless, it is a useful distinction, because it permits a separation of concerns between these two qualities that text possesses.

Abstract characters are grouped into alphabets. Each particular alphabet forms the basis of the written form of a certain language or group of languages. We consider any set of distinct symbols to be an alphabet.† This includes the set of symbols used in an ideographic writing system, such as those used for Chinese and Japanese, where each character represents a whole word or concept, as well as the phonetic letters of Western-style alphabets, and the intermediate syllabic alphabets, such as Korean Hangul. In contrast to colloquial usage, we include punctuation marks, numerals, and mathematical symbols in an alphabet, and treat upper- and lower-case versions of the same letter as different symbols. Thus, for our purposes, the English alphabet includes the letters A, B, C, … Z, and a, b, c, … z,

† We do not define 'symbol'. In the abstract, an alphabet can be any set at all, but in practical terms, the only symbols of interest will be those used for writing down some language.

but also punctuation marks, such as comma and exclamation mark, the digits 0, 1, ..., 9, and common symbols such as + and =.

To represent text digitally, it is necessary to define a mapping between (abstract) characters in some alphabet and values that can be stored in a computer system. The only values that we can store are bit patterns. As we explained in Chapter 2, these can be interpreted as integers to base 2, so the problem becomes one of mapping characters to integers. As an abstract problem, this is trivial: *any* mapping will do, provided it associates each character of interest with exactly one number. Such an association is called, with little respect for mathematical usage, a *character set*; its domain (the alphabet for which the mapping is defined) is called the *character repertoire*. For each character in the repertoire, the character set defines a *code value* in its range, which is sometimes called the set of *code points*. The character repertoire for a character set intended for written English text would include the 26 letters of the alphabet in both upper- and lower-case forms, as well as the 10 digits and the usual collection of punctuation marks. The character repertoire for a character set intended for Russian would include the letters of the Cyrillic alphabet. Both of these character sets could use the same set of code points; provided it was not necessary to use both character sets simultaneously (for example, in a bilingual document) a character in the English alphabet could have the same code value as one in the Cyrillic alphabet. The character repertoire for a character set intended for the Japanese Kanji alphabet must contain at least the 1945 ideograms for common use and 166 for names sanctioned by the Japanese Ministry of Education, and could contain over 6000 characters; consequently, it requires far more distinct code points than an English or Cyrillic character set.

The mere existence of a character set is adequate to support operations such as editing and searching of text, since it allows us to store characters as their code values, and to compare two characters for equality by comparing the corresponding integers; it only requires some means of input and output. In simple terms, this means that it is necessary to arrange that when a key is pressed on a keyboard, or the equivalent operation is performed on some other input device, a command is transmitted to the computer, causing the bit pattern corresponding to the character for that key to be passed to the program currently receiving input. Conversely, when a value is transmitted to a monitor or other output device, a representation of the corresponding character should appear.

There are advantages to using a character set with some structure to it, instead of a completely arbitrary assignment of numbers to abstract characters. In particular, it is useful to use integers within a comparatively small range that can easily be manipulated by a computer. It can be helpful, too, if the code values for consecutive letters are consecutive numbers, since this simplifies some operations on text, such as sorting.

Standards

The most important consideration concerning character sets is standardization. Transferring text between different makes of computer, interfacing peripheral devices from different manufacturers, and communicating over networks are everyday activities, and continual translation between different manufacturers' character codes would not be acceptable, so a standard character code is required. The following description of character code standards is necessarily somewhat dry, but an understanding of them is necessary if you are to avoid the pitfalls of incompatibility and the resulting corruption of texts.

Unfortunately, standardization is never a straightforward business, and the situation with respect to character codes remains somewhat unsatisfactory.

ASCII (American Standard Code for Information Interchange) has been the dominant character set since the 1970s. It uses 7 bits to store each code value, so there is a total of 128 code points. The character repertoire of ASCII only comprises 95 characters, however. The values 0 to 31 and 127 are assigned to *control characters*, such as form-feed, carriage return and delete, which have traditionally been used to control the operation of output devices. The control characters are a legacy from ASCII's origins in early teletype character sets. Many of them no longer have any useful meaning, and are often appropriated by application programs for their own purposes. Table 10.1 shows the ASCII character set. (The character with code value 32 is a space.)

American English is one of the few languages in the world for which ASCII provides an adequate character repertoire. Attempts by the standardization bodies to provide better support for a wider range of languages began when ASCII was adopted as an ISO standard (ISO 646) in 1972. ISO 646 incorporates several national variants on the version of ASCII used in the United States, to accommodate, for example, some accented letters and national currency symbols.

Table 10.1 The printable ASCII characters

32		33	!
34	"	35	#
36	$	37	%
38	&	39	'
40	(	41	)
42	*	43	+
44	,	45	-
46	.	47	/
48	0	49	1
50	2	51	3
52	4	53	5
54	6	55	7
56	8	57	9
58	:	59	;
60	<	61	=
62	>	63	?
64	@	65	A
66	B	67	C
68	D	69	E
70	F	71	G
72	H	73	I
74	J	75	K
76	L	77	M
78	N	79	O
80	P	81	Q
82	R	83	S
84	T	85	U
86	V	87	W
88	X	89	Y
90	Z	91	[
92	\	93	]
94	^	95	_
96	`	97	a
98	b	99	c
100	d	101	e
102	f	103	g
104	h	105	i
106	j	107	k
108	l	109	m
110	n	111	o
112	p	113	q
114	r	115	s
116	t	117	u
118	v	119	w
120	x	121	y
122	z	123	{
124	|	125	}
126	~		

A standard with variants is no real solution to the problem of accommodating different languages. If a file prepared in one country is sent to another and read on a computer set up to use a different national variant of ISO 646, some of the characters will be displayed incorrectly. For example, a hash character (#) typed in the United States would be displayed as a pound sign (£) in the UK (and vice versa) if the British user's computer used the UK variant of ISO 646. (More likely, the hash would display correctly, but the Briton would be unable to type a pound sign, because it is more convenient to use US ASCII (ISO 646-US) anyway, to prevent such problems.)

A better solution than national variants of the 7-bit ISO 646 character set lies in the provision of a character set with more code points, such that the ASCII character repertoire is mapped to the values 0–127, thus assuring compatibility, and additional symbols required outside the US or for specialized purposes are mapped to other values. Doubling the set of code points was easy: the seven bits of an ASCII character are invariably stored in an 8-bit byte. It was originally envisaged that the remaining bit would be used as a parity bit for error detection. As data transmission became more reliable, and superior error checking was built in to higher level protocols, this parity bit fell into disuse, effectively becoming available as the high order bit of an 8-bit character.

As is customary, the different manufacturers each developed their own incompatible 8-bit extensions to ASCII. These all shared some general features: the lower half (code points 0–127) was identical to ASCII; the upper half (code points 128–255) held accented letters and extra punctuation and mathematical symbols. Since a set of 256 values is insufficient to accommodate all the characters required for every alphabet in use, each 8-bit character code had different variants; for example, one for Western European languages, another for languages written using the Cyrillic script, and so on.[†]

† Under MS-DOS and Windows, these variants are called *code pages*.

Despite these commonalities, the character repertoires and the code values assigned by the different manufacturers' character sets are different. For example, the character é (e with an acute accent) has code value 142 in the Macintosh Standard Roman character set, whereas it has the code value 233 in the corresponding Windows character set, in which 142 is not assigned as the value for any character; 233 in Macintosh Standard Roman, on the other hand, is É. Because the repertoires of the character sets are different, it is not even always possible to perform a translation between them, so transfer of text between platforms is problematical.

Clearly, standardization of 8-bit character sets was required. During the 1980s the multi-part standard ISO 8859 was produced. This defines a collection of 8-bit character sets, each designed to accommodate the needs of a group of languages (usually geographically related). The first part of the standard, ISO 8859-1, is usually referred to as *ISO Latin1*, and covers most Western European languages. Like all the ISO 8859 character sets, the lower half of ISO Latin1 is identical to ASCII (i.e. ISO 646-US); the code points 128–159 are mostly unused, although a few are used for various diacritical marks; Table 10.2 shows the 96 additional code values provided for accented letters and symbols. (The character with code value 160 is a 'non-breaking' space.)

The Windows Roman character set is sometimes claimed to be the same as ISO Latin1, but it uses some of the code points between 128 and 159 for characters which are not present in ISO 8859-1's repertoire.

Other parts of ISO 8859 are designed for use with Eastern European languages, including Czech, Slovak and Croatian (ISO 8859-2 or Latin2), for languages that use the Cyrillic alphabet (ISO 8859-5), for modern Greek (ISO 8859-7), Hebrew (ISO 8859-8), and others – there is a total of 10 parts to ISO 8859, with more projected, notably an ISO Latin0, which includes the Euro currency symbol.

ISO 8859 has several shortcomings. In practical terms, the worst of these is the continued use of manufacturers' proprietary non-standard character sets. These are firmly entrenched in use and entangled with their corresponding operating systems and other software. Experience shows that, in time, standards are adopted if they can be seen to provide benefits, but there are fundamental problems with 8-bit character sets, which make it seem likely that ISO 8859 will not achieve universal adoption, but that newer standards will render it obsolete. The main problem is simply that 256 is not enough code points – not enough to represent ideographically based alphabets, and not enough to enable us to work with several languages at a time (unless they all happen to use the same variant of ISO 8859).

Unicode and ISO 10646

The only possible solution is to use more than one byte for each code value. A 16-bit character set has 65,536 code points; putting it

Table 10.2 The top part of the ISO Latin1 character set

Code	Char	Code	Char
160		161	¡
162	¢	163	£
164	¤	165	¥
166	¦	167	§
168	¨	169	©
170	ª	171	«
172	¬	173	
174	®	175	¯
176	°	177	±
178	²	179	³
180	´	181	µ
182	¶	183	·
184	¸	185	¹
186	º	187	»
188	¼	189	½
190	¾	191	¿
192	À	193	Á
194	Â	195	Ã
196	Ä	197	Å
198	Æ	199	Ç
200	È	201	É
202	Ê	203	Ë
204	Ì	205	Í
206	Î	207	Ï
208	Ð	209	Ñ
210	Ò	211	Ó
212	Ô	213	Õ
214	Ö	215	×
216	Ø	217	Ù
218	Ú	219	Û
220	Ü	221	Ý
222	Þ	223	ß
224	à	225	á
226	â	227	ã
228	ä	229	å
230	æ	231	ç
232	è	233	é
234	ê	235	ë
236	ì	237	í
238	î	239	ï
240	ð	241	ñ
242	ò	243	ó
244	ô	245	õ
246	ö	247	÷
248	ø	249	ù
250	ú	251	û
252	ü	253	ý
254	þ	255	ÿ

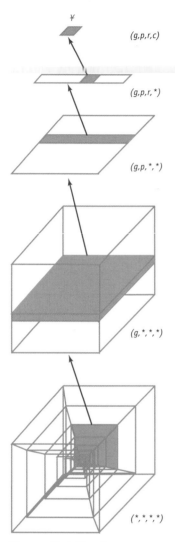

(g,p,r,c)

(g,p,r,*)

(g,p,*,*)

(g,*,*,*)

(*,*,*,*)

Figure 10.1 The four-dimensional structure of ISO 10646

another way, it can accommodate 256 variants of an 8-bit character set simultaneously. Similarly, a 24-bit character set can accommodate 256 16-bit character sets, and a 32-bit character set can accommodate 256 of those. The ISO (in conjunction with the IEC) set out to develop a 32-bit character set, designated ISO 10646, structured along the lines of the previous two sentences: a collection of 2^{32} characters can be arranged as a hypercube (a four-dimensional cube) consisting of 256 groups, each of which consists of 256 planes of 256 rows, each comprising 256 characters (which might be the character repertoire of an 8-bit character set). The intention was to structure the immense character repertoire allowed by a 32-bit character set with alphabets distributed among the planes in a linguistically sensible way, so that the resulting character set would have a clear logical structure. Each character can be identified by specifying its group g, its plane p, and a row r and column c (see Figure 10.1). Each of g, p, r and c is an 8-bit quantity, which can fit in one byte; four bytes thus identify a unique character, so, inverting our viewpoint, the code value for any character is the 32-bit value which specifies its position within the hypercube.

To make the structure of the character set evident, we usually write code points as quadruples (g,p,r,c). By extension, such a quadruple also identifies a subset of the character set using a * to denote all values in the range 0–255. Thus $(0,0,0,*)$ is the subset with all but the lowest-order byte zero. In ISO 10646 this subset is identical to ISO Latin1.

At the same time as the ISO was developing this elegant framework for its character set, an industry consortium was working on a 16-bit character set, known as *Unicode*. As we noted above, a 16-bit character set has 65,536 code points. This is not sufficient to accommodate all the characters required for Chinese, Japanese and Korean scripts in discrete positions. These three languages and their writing systems share a common ancestry, so there are thousands of identical ideographs in their scripts. The Unicode committee adopted a process they called *CJK consolidation*,† whereby characters used in writing Chinese, Japanese and Korean are given the same code value if they look the same, irrespective of which language they belong to, and whether or not they mean the same thing in the different languages. There is clearly a cultural bias involved here, since the same process is not applied to, for example, upper-case A and the Greek capital alpha, which are identical in appearance but have separate Unicode code values. The pragmatic justification is that, with Chinese,

Japanese and Korean, thousands of characters are involved, whereas with the European and Cyrillic languages, there are relatively few. Furthermore, consolidation of those languages would interfere with compatibility with existing standards.

Unicode provides code values for all the characters used to write contemporary 'major' languages, as well as the classical forms of some languages. The alphabets available include Latin, Greek, Cyrillic, Armenian, Hebrew, Arabic, Devanagari, Bengali, Gurmukhi, Gujarati, Oriya, Tamil, Telugu, Kannada, Malayalam, Thai, Lao, Georgian, and Tibetan, as well as the Chinese, Japanese and Korean ideograms and the Japanese and Korean phonetic and syllabic scripts. It also includes punctuation marks, technical and mathematical symbols, arrows, and the miscellaneous symbols usually referred to as dingbats (pointing hands, stars, and so on). In addition to the accented letters included in many of the alphabets, separate diacritical marks, such as accents and tildes, are available and a mechanism is provided for building composite characters by combining these marks with other symbols. (This not only provides an alternative way of making accented letters, it also allows for the habit mathematicians have of making up new symbols by decorating old ones.) Code values for nearly 39,000 symbols are provided, leaving some code points unused. Others are reserved for the UTF-16 expansion method (described briefly later on), while a set of 6400 code points is reserved for private use, allowing organizations and individuals to define codes for their own use. Even though these codes are not part of the Unicode standard, it is guaranteed that they will never be assigned to any character by the standard, so their use will never conflict with any standard character, although it might conflict with those of other individuals.

Unicode is restricted to characters used in text. It specifically does not attempt to provide symbols for music notation or other symbolic writing systems that do not represent language.

Unicode and ISO 10646 were brought into line in 1991 when the ISO agreed that the plane $(0, 0, *, *)$, known as the *Basic Multilingual Plane (BMP)*, should be identical to Unicode. ISO 10646 thus utilizes CJK consolidation, even though its 32-bit code space does not require it. The overwhelming advantage of this arrangement is that the two standards are compatible (and the respective committees have pledged that they will remain so). To understand how it is possible to take advantage of this compatibility, we must introduce the concept of a character set *encoding*.

An encoding is another layer of mapping, which transforms a code value into a sequence of bytes for storage and transmission. When each code value occupies exactly one byte, it might seem that the only sensible encoding is an identity mapping: each code value is stored or sent as itself in a single byte. Even in this case, though, a more complex encoding may be required. Because 7-bit ASCII was the dominant character code for such a long time, there are network protocols that assume that all character data is ASCII, and remove or mangle the top bit of any 8-bit byte. To get round this limitation, it may be necessary to encode 8-bit characters as sequences of 7-bit characters. One encoding used for this purpose is called *Quoted-Printable (QP)*. This works quite simply: any character with a code in the range 128–255 is encoded as a sequence of three bytes: the first is always the ASCII code for =; the remaining two are the codes for the hexadecimal digits of the code value. For example, é has value 233 in ISO Latin1, which is E9 in hexadecimal, so it is encoded in QP as the ASCII string =E9. Most characters with codes less than 128 are left alone. An important exception is = itself, which has to be encoded, otherwise it would appear to be the first byte of the encoded version of some other character. Hence, = appears as =3D.

To interpret a sequence of bytes correctly we need to know which encoding and which character set is being employed. Many systems rely on convention, or stipulate (or quietly assume) that all text is encoded in ISO Latin1. A more flexible approach is to use an additional feature of the MIME content type specifications which we introduced in Chapter 2. Following the type and subtype, a character set specification of the form

> ; charset = *character set*

may appear. A set of 'official' character set names is maintained by IANA. For example, the type of a Web page composed in ISO Latin1 is

> text/html; charset = ISO-8859-1

This information should be included in HTTP response headers and MIME-encoded email messages. It can also be specified using appropriate tags in a mark-up language, as we will explain in Chapter 11.

For ISO 10646 the obvious encoding scheme, known as UCS-4, employs four bytes to hold each code value. Any value on the BMP will have the top two bytes set to zero; since most values that are currently defined *are* on the BMP, and since economic reality suggests that for the foreseeable future most characters used in computer systems and transmitted over networks will be on the BMP, the UCS-4 encoding wastes space. ISO 10646 therefore supports an alternative encoding, UCS-2, which does the obvious thing and drops the top two bytes. UCS-2 is identical to Unicode.

Unicode encodings go further. There are three *UCS Transformation Formats (UTFs)* which can be applied to Unicode code values. UTF-8 takes the reasoning we just applied to 32-bit values a step further. ASCII code values are likely to be more common in most text than any other values. Accordingly, UTF-8 encodes UCS-2 values so that if their high-order byte is zero and the low-order byte is less than 128, the value is encoded as the single low-order byte. That is, ASCII characters are sent as themselves. Otherwise, the two bytes of the UCS-2 value are encoded using up to six bytes, with the highest bit of each byte set to 1 to indicate it is part of an encoded string and not an ASCII character. Text encoded with UTF-8 is thus a string of 8-bit bytes, and is therefore vulnerable to mangling by protocols that can only handle ASCII. UTF-7 is an alternative encoding which uses a technique similar to that described for QP to turn Unicode characters into streams of pure ASCII text, which can be transmitted safely.

The UTF-16 encoding has a different emphasis. This encoding allows pairs of 16-bit values to be combined into a single 32-bit value, thus extending the repertoire of Unicode beyond the BMP. Only values in a limited range can be combined this way, with the result that UTF-16 only provides access to an additional 15 planes of the full ISO 10646 character set. These comprise nearly a million characters under UTF-16, which seems to be sufficient for present purposes.

To summarize: ISO 10646 is a 32-bit character code, arranged in 256 groups, each of which consists of 256 planes accommodating 65,536 characters each. The UCS-4 encoding utilizes four bytes to hold the full 32-bit code value for any character; the UCS-2 encoding utilizes just two bytes, to hold 16-bit values for characters on the $(0,0,*,*)$ plane. UCS-2 is identical to Unicode. ISO Latin1 is the 8-bit code equivalent to the $(0,0,0,*)$ row of ISO 10646, and ASCII is a subset of ISO Latin1. UTF-8 allows any ISO 10646 or Unicode value to be encoded as a sequence of 8-bit bytes, such that ASCII values are left unchanged in a single byte. UTF-16 is an extension mechanism which provides Unicode with access to an extra 15 planes of the full ISO 10646 character set.

The markup languages HTML and XML, described in Chapters 11 and 14, and the Java programming language use Unicode as their character set. Once it also becomes adopted as the native character set of the major operating systems, the task of transferring text that uses characters beyond the US-Anglophone ASCII repertoire should be substantially eased.

Fonts

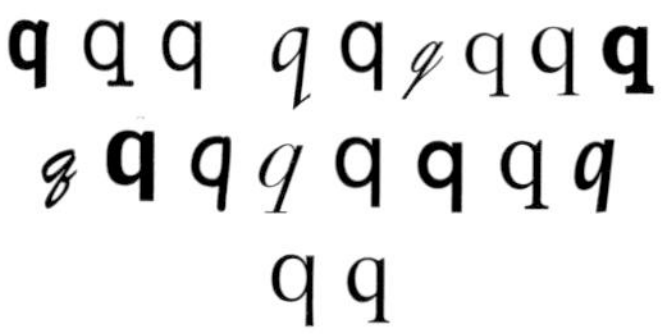

To display a piece of text, each stored character value must be mapped to a visual representation of the character's shape. Such a representation is called a *glyph*. As Figure 10.2 shows, a single character can be represented by a multitude of different glyphs. Many small details can be changed without destroying the fundamental identity of the abstract character being represented. We can recognize all the glyphs in Figure 10.2 as lower-case letter q. In addition to the variations in shape which that figure illustrates, glyphs can vary in size, from tiny subscripts to banner headlines over an inch tall. If we are to be able to use glyphs systematically, it is necessary to impose some organization on them.

Figure 10.2 Glyphs for lower case q

Glyphs are arranged into collections called *fonts*. The name has been taken from traditional printing. In the letterpress (or 'cold metal') technique a page is assembled out of individual pieces of type, each one of which is a metal block, with a mirror image of a letter or other symbol in relief on one end. These blocks are clamped in a frame together with spacers, and pages are printed by inking the faces of the type and pressing the paper against them. In this context, a font is a collection of pieces of type – actual metal objects. Usually, the type-setter works from a cabinet in which the type is arranged in drawers holding multiple instances of each letter shape at each size that is required. All the shapes in a particular font will have been made from masters produced by a type designer so that they share certain visual characteristics, and combine well with each other to make a harmonious and readable page.

Letterpress has been largely superseded, first by mechanical hot metal technologies, such as Monotype and Linotype machines, and now by digital typesetting. The concept of a font has been retained through these technological changes, although its realization has evolved, first into a set of moulds into which hot lead is poured to make letters for typesetting machines, and then into a computer file that holds a description of the graphic forms of the glyphs. The idea that a font combines a set of glyphs that are visually related and designed to work together has not changed. In fact, many of the fonts available for use on computers today are versions of traditional typesetters' fonts, some of them based on original designs from the fifteenth century.

Accessing Fonts

Text originates as a stream of character codes. To turn it into a form that can be displayed, these must be replaced by glyphs chosen from one or more fonts. Once this replacement has been performed, the content of the text (the character codes) becomes lost and can only be retrieved with difficulty. Essentially, the text turns into graphics, which cannot easily be searched or edited. (A person can still read the text, of course – in fact, they can't read it in any other form – but a program cannot manipulate it in any way.) What is more, since a stream of character codes is much more compact than an image representing the same text, replacement of character codes by glyphs also increases the size of the text. The graphical representation of text is inefficient because it takes no advantage of the repetitive nature of text: the same character will typically occur many times, so if glyphs are substituted, many copies of the same glyph will be used, and each will be much larger than the corresponding character code.

There is an exception to our observation that text originates as a stream of character codes. If a page of printed text is scanned the result is a bitmapped image of the page. If you want to get hold of the characters from a scanned text you need to use special *optical character recognition (OCR)* software, which uses pattern recognition techniques to analyze the shapes within the bitmapped image and deduce the characters they represent. OCR is a mature technology, but 100% accurate recognition is rarely achieved.

Because of these considerations, it is normal to keep text in some character-based form, and only to use glyphs when it is actually displayed or incorporated into a graphic image. The simplest case is that of *monostyled* text: text that is displayed in a single font. In that case, a text file need only contain the characters of the text itself: it is the familiar 'plain ASCII' (or perhaps plain ISO 8859) file. When such a file is displayed, the character codes are used to select glyphs from a font, either a default system font, or a single font selected by the user from within the program being used to display the text.

Monostyled text is rarely adequate for multimedia production, where a richer typographic experience is usually required. The principle of selecting glyphs using character codes remains the same, but additional information is needed to control the selection of fonts. We will describe various forms this information may take in Chapter 11. At this point, we must consider the question: Where might fonts be found?

There are only two possibilities. Glyphs must be taken either from fonts stored on the system being used to display the text, or from fonts embedded in the text file. In the latter case, the fonts must originally have been stored on the system used to prepare the text, and therein lies the most important advantage of this approach: multimedia designers can use fonts of their own choosing, confident that they will be available when they are needed, because they are embedded in the same file as the text. If they are not, then only the fonts on the user's system will be available, and there is no reason to suppose that the user's selection will be the same as the designer's, so there is a possibility that some font required by the text will not be available. The probability of this occurring increases if the designer chooses esoteric fonts – as designers sometimes will.

Why then might you prefer not to embed fonts in your text files? One potent reason is that not all text file formats allow you to do so. In particular, HTML has no facility for embedding fonts, although, in conjunction with CSS stylesheets, it does allow you to specify the fonts you wish to be used to display textual elements of Web pages. The other reason for preferring to rely on fonts on the user's system is that fonts are fairly bulky objects: the fonts used for this book, for example, vary in size between about 32 and 50 kilobytes each. It is quite easy to find yourself using half a dozen fonts on a page, so including the fonts with the text can lead to bloated files and consequently to extended download times.

If a font is not available, various more or less undesirable consequences can result. In the extreme, the result might be a system crash. More likely, text in the missing font will not be displayed, or it will be displayed in some other font that has been substituted. The last case is the least serious, and the most common, but it is far from ideal. As we will see in the next section, every font has its own distinctive character, so substituting another in its place can seriously impair a carefully thought out design. Furthermore, the widths of the glyphs in the substituted font will probably be different from those in the intended font, so that the positioning of individual glyphs on the page will be incorrect. Depending on how the layout of text for display is done, this might result in ragged margins where straight ones were intended, uneven gaps between words, or gaps within words. Any of these defects will have a detrimental effect on the appearance of your text, and may make it hard to read.

Classification and Choice of Fonts

There are thousands of fonts available, each with its own special personality. Some broad characteristics are used to help classify them.

A major distinction is that between *monospaced* (or *fixed-width*) and *proportional* fonts. In a monospaced font, every character occupies the same amount of space horizontally, regardless of its shape. This means that some letters have more white space around them than others. For example, the narrow shape of a lower-case l must be surrounded with white to make it the same width as a lower-case m. In contrast, in a proportional font, the space each letter occupies depends on the width of the letter shape. Paradoxically, this produces a more even appearance, which is generally felt to be easier to read in most contexts. In addition, it allows you to fit more words on to a line. Text in a monospaced font looks as if it was produced on a typewriter or a teletype machine. It can sometimes be used effectively for headings, but is especially suitable for typesetting computer program listings. It is also useful for conveying a 'low-tech' appearance, for example in correspondence where you wish to convey a slightly informal impression. Text in a proportional font has the appearance of a traditional book, and is usually preferred for setting lengthy texts. It is generally felt to be more readable, since letters appear to be tightly bound together into words. Figures 10.3 and 10.4 illustrate the difference between monospaced and proportional fonts.

Probably the most widely used monospaced font is Courier, which was originally designed for IBM typewriters, and has achieved wide currency because it is one of the fonts shipped as standard with all PostScript printers. Many proportional fonts are in common use. As you can no doubt discern, the font used for the main text in this book, ITC Slimbach, is proportionally spaced. Most of the classical book fonts, such as Times, Baskerville, Bembo, and Garamond are also proportional, as are many newer fonts, such as Helvetica.

Another very broad distinction is between *serifed* and *sans serif* (sometimes *sanserif*) fonts. *Serifs* are the little strokes added to the ends of character shapes (see Figure 10.5). These strokes are present in serifed fonts, but omitted in sans serif fonts, which consequently have a plainer look. Serifs originate in marks produced by chisels on Roman stone inscriptions, so serifed fonts are sometimes called Roman fonts. Figure 10.6 shows some text in Officina Sans – a bold version of this font is used for figure captions in this book.

`Monospaced Font:`
`Courier`

`Each letter`
`occupies the`
`same amount of`
`horizontal space,`
`so that the text`
`looks as if it`
`was typed on a`
`typewriter.`

Figure 10.3 A monospaced font

Proportional Font: Giovanni

Each letter occupies an amount of horizontal space proportional to the width of the glyph, so that the text looks as if it was printed in a book.

Figure 10.4 A proportional font

Figure 10.5 Serifs

Sans Serif Font: Officina Sans

The letters of a sans serif (or sanserif) font lack the tiny strokes known as serifs, hence the name. They have a plain, perhaps utilitarian, appearance.

Figure 10.6 A sans serif font

Italic Font: Giovanni Italic

The letters of an italic font slope to the right, and are formed as if they were made with an italic pen nib. Italics are conventionally used for emphasis, and for identifying foreign words and expressions.

Figure 10.7 An italic font

Sans serif fonts are a comparatively new development, on a typographical time scale, and have only gradually gained acceptance for general use – in some typographical catalogues they are still identified by the alternative name of grotesques. In the nineteenth century, sans serif fonts were indeed rather grotesque, being crude designs used mostly for advertising and posters. Only in the twentieth century have they become accepted for use in books, with the development of more elegant and refined designs. The best known sans serif font is probably Helvetica, which again is one of the standard PostScript fonts. Other sans serif fonts you may meet include Univers and Arial (the latter popularized by Microsoft). Gill Sans, another very popular sans serif font, was based on the font used for the signs on the London Underground, which had helped to generate interest in sans serif type.

There is contradictory evidence as to whether serifed or sans serif fonts are more readable – spacing probably makes more difference. However, serifs are very small features, and therefore difficult to render accurately at low resolutions, which can mean that text in a serifed font is hard to read on a computer screen, simply because the letters are not being accurately reproduced. Sans serif fonts are widely used for such features as window titles and menu entries on these grounds.

Spacing and serifs are independent properties: sans serif and serifed fonts can equally well be either monospaced or proportional.

A third classification of fonts is based on broad categories of *shape*. In particular, we distinguish between fonts with an *upright* shape, and those with an *italic* shape. Upright fonts, as the name implies, have characters whose vertical strokes (stems) are indeed vertical. Italic fonts imitate a certain style of handwriting, and have letters that are slanted to the right. Additionally, the letter shapes in an italic font are formed differently from those in an upright font, so that they share some of the characteristics of italic handwriting. When digital fonts first appeared, 'italic' fonts were sometimes produced simply by applying a shear transformation to an upright font. The effect is rather different, since the calligraphic features of true italic fonts are missing. Such fonts are now used in their own right, not as substitutes for italics. They are said to have a *slanted* shape. The difference is illustrated in Figures 10.7 and 10.8, which show italic and slanted versions of two upright fonts.

Most italic fonts are variations on or designed as companions to upright fonts. For example, Giovanni Italic is an italic version of Giovanni Book. There are, however, some fonts with an italic shape which are designed on their own; these are usually intended to have the character of handwriting, and to be used where something more human than a conventional typeface is desired. Among the best known calligraphic fonts are several versions of Chancery, including Zapf Chancery. Specialist fonts based on samples of real handwriting are also available. Figures 10.9 and 10.10 are examples of a relatively formal calligraphic font and a handwriting font.

One type of font that doesn't quite fit our classifications is the *small caps* font, in which small versions of the upper-case letters are used as lower-case letters. This variation is sometimes considered to be a shape, although the sense is somewhat different from that in which italic is considered a shape. Small caps fonts are most useful for trademarks and so on, which are normally written entirely in upper-case: full-size upper-case words stand out awkwardly in ordinary text, but small caps are less intrusive.

Digital technology has made it relatively easy to create new fonts, which has led to a great deal of experimentation and whimsy. Fonts which depart radically from convention are sometimes grouped together under the heading of 'fantasy fonts'. Figure 10.11 shows an example – although, by the very nature of fantasy fonts, there can really be no such thing as a 'typical' example. Such fonts should be used judiciously, if at all.

Some fonts appear somewhat squashed horizontally, compared with the normal proportions of most fonts. They are referred to as *condensed* fonts, and are intended for applications, such as marginal notes or narrow newspaper columns, where it is desirable to be able to fit text in as tightly as possible. In contrast, some fonts, described as *extended*, are stretched out horizontally, making them more suitable for headings and other isolated text elements.

Finally, fonts can be classified according to their *weight*, that is, the thickness of the strokes making up the letters. Thicker strokes make text look darker and more solid. Conventionally, we call fonts with a heavy weight (thick strokes) *boldface* or simply *bold*. Like italics, bold fonts are usually versions of other fonts with a lighter weight. As a result, boldness is not an absolute property: a bold version of a font whose normal weight is particularly light may be lighter than the normal version of a heavy font, whose own bold version will be

Slanted Font: Lucida Bright Oblique

The letters of a slanted font share the rightward slope of italic fonts, but lack their calligraphic quality. Slanted fonts are sometimes used when a suitable italic font is not available, but may be preferred to italics when a more modern look is wanted.

Figure 10.8 A slanted font

Calligraphic Font: Apple Chancery

Calligraphic fonts usually resemble 'round hand' or 'copperplate' handwriting, unlike italic fonts.

Figure 10.9 A calligraphic font

Handwriting Font: Kidprint

Handwriting fonts are based on samples of real people's handwriting, so they are often quite idiosyncratic.

Figure 10.10 A handwriting font

even heavier. Some fonts may exist in several versions, exhibiting varying degrees of boldness. Under these circumstances, individual styles are described by terms such as *ultra-bold*, *semi-bold*, *light* and *ultra-light*.

Conventional typesetting wisdom has it that boldface is intrusive, and should be reserved for headings and similar uses. Because of the limitations of computer displays, it is sometimes advisable to use boldface more widely than would be appropriate in text intended for paper. For example, conventionally you *never* use boldface for emphasis, always italics. However, italic text, because of its slant, often renders badly at low resolutions, making it hard to read on a computer monitor. Under these circumstances, the use of bold text for emphasis may be justified. Bold fonts are also used quite widely for window titles and menu items, because they show up well.

Word processors often treat underlining as a styling option similar to italicization and emboldening, so you might think that there would be underlined versions of fonts, too. Underlined fonts are extremely rare, though: underlining is scorned in typographic circles, where it is considered to be a poor substitute for italicization, only suitable for typewriters which lack italics. Like most conventional typographical wisdom, the undesirability of underlining is no longer unquestioned. Since more flexible effects can be produced by combining ordinary fonts with lines of various thicknesses, this questioning has not led to an outbreak of underlined fonts.

Because it makes sense to talk about an italic version or a bold version of an upright font, fonts can be grouped into families. A font family corresponds closely to what is traditionally called a *typeface*. A font is a particular style of some typeface. In pre-digital typography each different size would be considered a separate font, but nowadays we usually consider that the same font can be rendered at different sizes.

Fantasy Font: Jokerman

Fantasy fonts defy characterization, and often break all the rules. They are easily over-used.

Figure 10.11 A fantasy font

Usually, an upright serifed font is considered to be the normal form, which is augmented by versions in different weights, perhaps an italic form or a sans serif form. Variations are often combined to produce additional versions, such as bold italics, or slanted sans serif. The Lucida Bright family is an extreme example, consisting of 20 fonts: Lucida Bright is an upright serifed font; it is also available in bold, italic, and bold italic. Lucida Sans is the sans serif version, which comes in the same four versions, as do Lucida Typewriter, a fixed width Lucida font, and Lucida Fax, a variant form designed to be especially readable at low resolution. Three calligraphic fonts and a slanted font complete the family. All 20 fonts share a similar feel so that they can be combined without any obtrusive visual discontinuities. In contrast, when fonts from different families are combined, their differences can be very noticeable, as Figure 10.12 shows. Traditionally, such discontinuities have been carefully avoided, but in recent years designers have taken advantage of the ease with which desktop publishing software allows them to combine fonts to explore new combinations that defy the established conventions. As a general rule, if you want to combine fonts, they should be either from the same family, or from families with quite different characteristics. Fonts that are similar but not the same look worst of all together.

In the days of letterpress and hot metal typesetting, to produce text at different sizes required different sets of type, which would qualify as separate fonts. Only a limited number of different sizes could easily be made available. With digital fonts, arbitrary scaling can be applied to glyphs, so that fonts can be printed at any size. Purists maintain that simple scaling is not adequate, and that letter shapes should be designed to look their best at one particular size, and should only be used at that size. Contemporary font technology, however, tends to the idea that a font should exist at only one size and should be scaled to produce any other size that is needed. Special information contained in the font is used to help maintain a pleasing appearance at all sizes, as we will describe in a later section.

As well as the objective factors of spacing, serifs, shape, weight and size that can be used to classify type, there is a more subjective classification based on the sort of jobs for which a font is most suitable. The basic distinction is between *text fonts* and *display fonts*. The terminology is slightly silly, since all fonts are used for text. The distinction is between fonts suitable for continuous text, such as the body of a book or article, and those suitable for short pieces of isolated text, such as headings, signs or advertising slogans on posters.

Text in Lucida Bright goes well with *Lucida italic and **demibold italic*** but looks quite wrong with Slimbach.

Figure 10.12 Mixing fonts from different families

Sometimes, a finer distinction is drawn within the class of display fonts. *Decorative* fonts are those for which appearance is the primary design consideration. They often incorporate ornaments and other features that make them quite unsuitable for extended use. *Headline* fonts, as the name implies, are designed for use in headlines and other situations where it is important to attract the reader's attention. This leaves a category to which the name display fonts is often attached, consisting of fonts intended especially for use at large sizes, with other features designed to take advantage of the possibilities offered by large characters; for example the serifs might be especially fine.

Text fonts must be unobtrusive, so that they do not intrude on the reader and interfere with the primary message of the text. They must also be easy to read, so that they do not cause fatigue when they are read for hours at a time. To some extent, whether or not a font is intrusive depends on whether it is familiar; at the same time, the criteria for selecting text fonts have not changed over the years. The combination of these factors means that text fonts tend to be conservative. Invariably they are upright, more often serifed than not, and of a medium weight.

Display fonts are another matter. Here, the intention is to get across a short message. Garish design that would be offensive in a text font becomes eye-catching; innovation attracts attention. Fantasy fonts that would be completely useless for continuous text can often serve very well for display. Nevertheless, the choice of appropriate fonts, and the combination of display fonts with each other and with text fonts, calls for considerable judgement. There is a far greater diversity of design among display fonts than among text fonts, and whereas the same text fonts continue to be used year after year, display fonts are subject to fashion.

Conventional ideas about font usage are based on centuries of experience of making books, pamphlets, posters, packaging, road signs, shop fronts and other familiar forms of printed matter. While much of this experience can be applied to the textual components of multimedia, some aspects of the new media demand a fresh approach. Generally, display fonts can be used on a computer monitor in much the same way as they can on paper, so where text is combined with images, fonts can be used as they would be on a poster; attention-grabbing headings can effectively use the same display fonts as you might find in a book. Continuous text is more problematical: the low resolution of most monitors can lead to distortion of letter shapes, making fonts that work well on paper hard to read, especially at small sizes. The obvious solution is to use fonts at larger sizes than is customary in books, and this is often done: text for electronic display is often set as much as 60% larger than text in ordinary books. An alternative is to look for a font that has been designed to be readable at low resolution; Verdana and Arial are examples of such fonts. Sans serif fonts tend to survive better at low resolutions, which makes them more suitable for this purpose.

The way the text in multimedia productions is arranged gives rise to some less technical questions concerning fonts. Long continuous passages covering many pages are cumbersome and tiring to read on a screen, and do not integrate well with other media. It is common, therefore, to find multimedia text elements constructed as small pieces that fit onto one or two screenfuls. These pieces will often resemble, in form and style, the short explanatory placards attached to museum displays and zoo exhibits. This sort of text partakes of the character of both continuous text for which we would use a text font – it has a non-trivial extent and content – and the shorter texts normally set in a display font – it is succinct and usually has a message to get across. A restrained display font will often work well in this situation, as will some quite unconventional solutions, such as a text font in a large bold version, or coloured text on a contrasting background.

Text for multimedia is often prepared using the same tools as are used in 'desktop publishing' (DTP). It is important to remember that the output from conventional DTP programs is intended for printing on paper. We reiterate that text that will look excellent when printed on paper may well be unreadable when viewed on a computer monitor. It is necessary to adapt the way you use these tools, bearing in mind the actual medium for which your output is destined, or to use tools that have support for output to alternative media.

One final consideration which is unique to digital text is that, in many cases, the multimedia designer has no control over the fonts that will be used when text is finally displayed. As we explained previously, it may be necessary for completely different fonts to be substituted on different computer systems; in some cases, the software used for display may let users override the original fonts with those of their own choosing. Consequently, unless you know that neither of these circumstances will arise, there is no point in carefully exploiting the features of a particular font to achieve some special effect – the effect may never be seen by anyone except you.

Most of the preceding description of fonts has concentrated on letters, implicitly in the Latin alphabet. However, as the discussion of character sets in the previous section indicated, we use far more characters than these letters, and just as we need character sets to provide code values for a large character repertoire, so we need fonts to provide glyphs for them. In fact, you can think of a font as a mapping from abstract characters to glyphs, in much the same way as a character set is a mapping from abstract characters to code points. Like a character set, a font is only defined for a specific character repertoire. Most fonts' repertoires consist of the letters from some alphabet, together with additional symbols, such as punctuation marks. You might be forgiven for hoping that fonts would be structured around one of the character set standards, such as ISO Latin1, but this is not usually the case. It is generally possible to access the individual glyphs in a font using a numerical index, but, although the printable ASCII characters are usually in their expected positions, other symbols may well be in positions quite different from that corresponding to their code values in any ISO character set.

The way in which glyphs are grouped into fonts owes more to printing tradition than to the influence of character code standards, with the alphabet being the focus of design. Even then, some fonts may not include lower-case letters, if the designer intended the font only to be used for headlines, for example. Specialized non-alphabetic symbols, such as mathematical symbols, are usually grouped into their own fonts, known as *symbol fonts* or *pi fonts*. Some fonts consist entirely of graphic images: you may encounter fonts of arrows, or fonts of pointing hands, for example. Some images are considered to be symbols and are included in character sets – fonts containing these symbols are called *dingbat fonts* – but others are put together by font designers for special applications, and do not fit into any character set framework.

As a result of all this, another level of encoding is required in order to map stored character codes in some character set to glyphs. Additionally, some mechanism may be needed to combine separate fonts, for example, an alphabetic font and a symbol font, to provide glyphs for all the characters used in a document – a problem which will become acute as the wider range of characters provided by Unicode comes into wider use. Fortunately, the mechanisms for accessing glyphs are usually handled transparently by text layout software.

Font Terminology

Typography has its own specialized vocabulary, some of which it is necessary to understand if you are to find your way around among fonts and their descriptions.

Much of the description of a font's characteristics consists of measurements. These are usually given in units of *points (pt)*. In digital typography, one point is 1/72 of an inch, which makes 1 pt equal to just under 0.3528 mm. A point is thus a very small unit, suitable for measuring the dimensions of such small objects as typeset characters. For slightly larger quantities, such as the distance between lines of text, we often use a *pica (pc)*, which is equal to 12pt (or 1/6 in or 4.2333 mm).

Unlike other units of measurement, such as the metre or the foot, the point does not have an internationally agreed standard magnitude. The value of exactly 1/72 in is a comparatively recent innovation, pioneered by PostScript. In English-speaking countries, the printer's point is 1/72.27 in, and some software, such as TEX, still uses this value by default. In France, the Didot point, which is about 7% larger than the printer's point, is preferred.

A font's size is quoted in points, as in '12pt Times Roman' or '10pt Lucida Sans'. The value specified is technically the font's *body size*. In the days of letterpress, the body size was the height of the individual pieces of metal type, each of which were the same size so that they could be fitted together. Hence, the body size was the smallest height that could accommodate every symbol in the font. This remains the case: the size is not necessarily equal to the height of any character in the font (although parentheses are often as tall as the body size), but is usually the height between the top of the highest character and the bottom of the lowest. However, the body height is actually an arbitrary distance, chosen to provide a suitable vertical space for the letters to sit in when they are set in lines. A font with a particularly open character might have a body size somewhat larger than is necessary just to accommodate all its characters, so that there is always some extra space around them when text is set in that font on conventional baselines.

In normal text, characters are arranged so that they all sit on the same horizontal line, just as, when we write on lined paper, we ensure that all our letters are on the lines. This line is called the *baseline*; the space between successive baselines is called the *leading*.[†] An important font dimension is the height between the baseline and the top of a lower-case letter x. This value is the font's *x-height*; the bodies of most lower-case letters fit in between the baseline and the x-height. Some letters, such as h, have strokes that rise above the x-height; these are called *ascenders*. Similarly, letters such as y extend below the baseline; the extending strokes are called *descenders*. These terms are illustrated in Figure 10.13. Sometimes, the size of the largest ascender (the distance between the x-height and the top of the body) is called the *ascent*, and the corresponding descending dimension is called the *descent* of the font.

† Named after the thin strips of lead formerly inserted between lines of print in letterpress printing. 'Leading' is pronounced to rhyme with 'heading'.

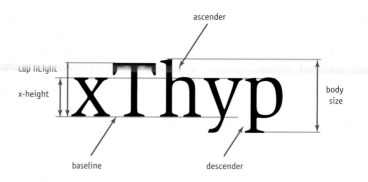

Figure 10.13 Some font terminology

Ascenders are not the only things that extend above the x-height: capital letters do so as well. In many fonts, though, the capitals do not extend to the full height of ascenders, so we need another quantity, the *cap height*, also shown in Figure 10.13, to characterize the vertical extent of capitals. (In English text, the difference between cap height and ascent is most obvious when the combination 'Th' occurs at the beginning of a sentence.)

The ratio of the x-height to the body size is one of the most important visual characteristics of a font. Since the bulk of the text lies between the baseline and the x-height, a font with a relatively high x-height will look bigger than a font with a lower x-height at the same size. If you look back at Figure 10.12, you will be able to see that one of the things that prevents the text in Slimbach merging happily with that in Lucida Bright is that the latter font has a higher x-height. This feature is common to the entire Lucida family, so the Lucida Italic mixes easily with the upright Lucida Bright.

If you look closely at Figure 10.13 you will see that the curved tops of the h and p actually extend through the x-height. This phenomenon is called *overshoot*, and helps make the letters look more uniform in size. The extent of the overshoot is another factor that characterizes the look of a font.

The x-height of a font is used as a unit of measurement, usually written ex. It has the useful property of not being an absolute unit, like a point, but a relative one; it changes with the font's size, and is different for different fonts, but always stands in the same relation to the height of lower-case letters, so it provides a convenient way of expressing vertical measurements that should change in proportion to this quantity. A similar unit of horizontal distance is the em. Traditionally, 1 em is the width of a capital letter M. In many fonts, M is as wide as the body size, so the meaning of 1 em has migrated over the years, and is now often taken as a unit of length equal to the font size;[†] for a 10pt font, 1 em is equal to 10 pt, for a 12pt font it is equal to 12 pt, and so on. Long dashes — like these — which are sometimes used for parenthetic phrases, especially in books published in the United States, are 1 em long, so they are called *em-dashes*. You will sometimes see another relative unit, the *en*, which is the width of a capital N, and usually defined as 0.5 em. An *en-dash* is 1 en long; en-dashes are used for page or date ranges, such as 1998–99, or instead of em-dashes (as in this book).

[†] The em unit is defined like this in CSS (see Chapter 11), for example.

Other features which characterize the look of a font include the size and shape of serifs, and the ratio of the thickness of thick and thin strokes. For example, so-called *modern* fonts (actually based on designs about 200 years old) are characterized by high contrast between the thick and thin strokes, and serifs without brackets (the curves that join the serif to its stem). Fans of these fonts believe these features produce a brilliant, sophisticated appearance on the page, while their detractors find them affected and illegible, compared to the *old-style* fonts with their more uniform solid appearance, or the cleaner lines of twentieth century sans serif fonts. The implications for display at low resolution should by now be clear.

The features of individual letters are not all we need to consider in a font. We also have to look at how letters are combined. As we stated earlier, most text fonts are proportionally spaced, with each letter occupying as much horizontal space as it needs to. As Figure 10.14 shows, each letter has a *bounding box*, which is the smallest box that can enclose it. Normally, a slight gap is left between the bounding boxes of adjacent characters. In other words, when drawing a glyph immediately following another one, it is drawn relative to a *glyph origin*, which lies outside the bounding box, usually to its left, by a distance known as the character's *left side bearing*, as shown in Figure 10.14 (where we have considerably exaggerated the magnitude of the side bearing).

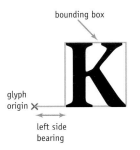

Figure 10.14 Side bearings

Sometimes, when two particular letters are placed next to each other, the total amount of space between them looks too great or too small. Typographers normally adjust the spacing to make it look more uniform. (Once again, you will notice the apparent contradiction that it is necessary to introduce non-uniformity to achieve the subjective appearance of uniformity.) This process of adjustment is called *kerning*, and is illustrated in Figure 10.15. (Look closely, kerning is subtle.) The kerning pairs for a font are defined by its designer.

Figure 10.15 Kerning

Carefully produced fonts may have hundreds of kerning pairs, each with its own spacing. The information about which pairs of characters are to be kerned, and by how much, is stored as part of the font.

The measurements which describe the size of individual characters and the spacing between them are collectively known as *font metrics*. Programs that perform typesetting need access to font metric information, in order to determine where to place each glyph as they build up lines, paragraphs and pages. The organization of this information depends on the font format, computer system and typesetting software being used.

Two operations related to kerning are *letter spacing* and *tracking*. Letter spacing is the process of changing the space between all letters in a font, stretching or squeezing the text. This may be done either to change the appearance of the font, or to fit an awkward line of text on to a page. (The latter operation is severely frowned on in the best typesetting circles.) Tracking is a systematic application of letter spacing depending on the font size: large letters need proportionally less space between them to look right.

Certain character combinations just will not look right, no matter how you space them. Printers traditionally replace occurrences of such troublesome sequences by single composite characters, known as *ligatures*. In English text, commonly used ligatures in traditional printing include ff, fl, fi and ffl. There is no standard set of ligatures, and some fonts provide more of them than others. Monospaced fonts do not usually provide any. The extent of support for ligatures also depends on the font format: most PostScript and TrueType fonts only offer ff and fi ligatures; OpenType fonts may provide a full set. (Font formats are described in the next section.) Figure 10.16 shows why we need ligatures, and the improvement achieved by using them. Ligatures are stored as extra characters in the font.

without fine fluffy soufflés
with   fine fluffy soufflés

Figure 10.16 Ligatures

High quality text layout software will automatically deal with kerning and ligatures, making the appropriate spacing corrections and character substitutions when it encounters the codes for combinations of characters that require such treatment. Word processors and Web browsers cannot generally do this.

Digital Font Technology

Glyphs are just small images, which can be stored in a font using either bitmaps or vector graphics. This leads to two different sorts of fonts, *bitmapped* fonts and *outline* fonts, based on these two graphics technologies. Glyphs in bitmapped fonts exhibit the same characteristics as bitmapped images, while outline glyphs share the characteristics of vector graphics. Since character shapes are usually built out of simple curves and strokes, and lack any subtle texture, there is little advantage in using bitmapped fonts on the grounds of expressiveness. The main advantage of bitmapped fonts is that glyphs can be rendered on-screen simply and rapidly, using a bit copying operation. This advantage is being eroded by the wider availability of efficient graphics hardware and faster processors, but bitmapped fonts remain widely available.

The considerable disadvantage of bitmapped fonts is that, like any other bitmapped image, they cannot be scaled gracefully. The need for scaling arises in two different contexts: when a font is required at a different size from that at which it was prepared, and when it is required at a different resolution. The latter case is unlikely to arise with multimedia productions designed for display on screen, since the bitmapped fonts installed on computer systems are usually designed for use at screen resolution, but it presents serious problems if text must also be printed on a high resolution printer. The first case – scaling bitmapped fonts to produce type at a different size – always presents a problem. The irregularities that result from scaling a bitmap are especially intrusive with character shapes, owing to the amount of fine detail in their design. When bitmapped fonts are used, it is normal to provide versions of each font at several different sizes. Characters will then look as good as is possible at those sizes, but not at any others, so the designer is forced to use only the standard sizes.

Each platform has its own native bitmapped font format, usually optimized in some way to work efficiently with the system software routines responsible for text display. In contrast, outline fonts are usually stored in a cross-platform format. The two most widely used formats are Adobe *Type 1* (often simply referred to as *PostScript fonts*, although there are other types of PostScript fonts) and *TrueType*.

Outline fonts can be scaled arbitrarily, and the same font can be used for display at low resolution and for printing at high resolution, provided that the display software can interpret the outline shapes. The utility Adobe Type Manager (ATM) performs this function at the system level for Type 1 fonts for operating systems that do not have it built in; rendering of TrueType fonts is built into both the Windows and MacOS operating systems, hence outline fonts of both types can be used by any application program. Because of the supremacy of text preparation software directed towards print-based media, outline fonts are more widely used than bitmaps for elaborately formatted text.

Outline fonts in either of the popular formats can contain up to 256 glyphs. The glyphs in a Type 1 font are simply small programs, written in a restricted subset of PostScript. The restrictions are intended to make it possible for the glyphs to be rendered efficiently on screen at sufficient quality to be acceptable at screen resolution. TrueType is an alternative format, based on quadratic curves instead of the cubic Bézier curves used by PostScript. A character outline in a TrueType font is stored as a series of points which define the lines and curves making up its shape. A newly developed format, *OpenType*, unifies Type 1 and TrueType fonts, by providing a file format that allows either sort of outline to be stored, and provides a cross-platform font format. OpenType fonts are superior to the older formats in many ways. Their encoding is based on Unicode, and they can accommodate many more than 256 characters. This allows a single font to include glyphs for more than one alphabet – Latin and Cyrillic, for example – which would otherwise have to be kept in separate fonts. OpenType also has better support for the niceties of fine typography, such as an extended range of ligatures, old-style numerals, small capitals and fractions.

As well as descriptions of the glyph shapes, Type 1 and TrueType fonts both include extra information that can be used by a rendering program to improve the appearance of text at low resolutions. This information concerns rather subtle features, which tend to lose their subtlety when only a few pixels can be used for each stroke. In Type 1 fonts, it takes the form of declarative *hints*, which provide the values of parameters that can be used to direct glyph rendering at low resolutions. For example, some hint information is intended to cause overshoots to be suppressed. As we stated on page 336, overshoots normally help improve the regular appearance of a font. However, at low resolutions, when the amount of overshoot is rounded to the nearest pixel, the effect will be exaggerated and text will appear to be more irregular than it would if all lower-case letters were exactly as high as the x-height. The point at which overshoot suppression is effective depends on the design of the font, so it cannot be applied without information from the font designer. The Type 1 hints allow this information to be supplied. Other hints similarly suppress variations in stem width, which while aesthetically pleasing at high resolutions, merely look uneven at low resolutions. Another example of the use of hints concerns bold fonts. It is quite conceivable that the rounding effect of rendering at low resolution will cause the strokes of a normal font to thicken to such an extent that it becomes indistinguishable from the boldface version of the same font. A hint allows rendering software to add additional width to boldface fonts to ensure that they always appear bold. TrueType fonts achieve the same sort of improvements using a more procedural approach, allowing the font designer to write *instructions* that specify how features of a character should be mapped to points on a pixel grid at any resolution.

Although the use of hints and instructions improves the appearance of fonts at small sizes as well as at low resolutions, it only causes minor changes of shape to compensate for the small number of pixels available. Traditional typographers sometimes produce separate designs of the same font at different sizes, which is said to produce a more pleasing appearance than simply scaling one design to fit. Such niceties have until now rarely been encountered with digital fonts, but the new OpenType format does allow a font to include up to four different optical variations for different ranges of size: caption, regular, sub-head and display.

As with other sorts of vector graphics, the appearance of outline fonts can sometimes be improved by anti-aliasing – softening a hard, and inevitably jagged, edge between those pixels that are on and off by using a pattern of grey pixels over a wider area. The smoothing effect thereby achieved is illustrated in Figure 10.17: the upper letter A is not anti-aliased, the lower one is. As this figure shows, anti-aliasing is very effective with large characters; it also works well at medium resolutions, such as that of a laser printer. At low resolutions, small type (below about 12pt), although noticeably smoother, also begins to look blurred, which may leave it harder to read than it would be if left jagged, so anti-aliasing should be applied to fonts judiciously.

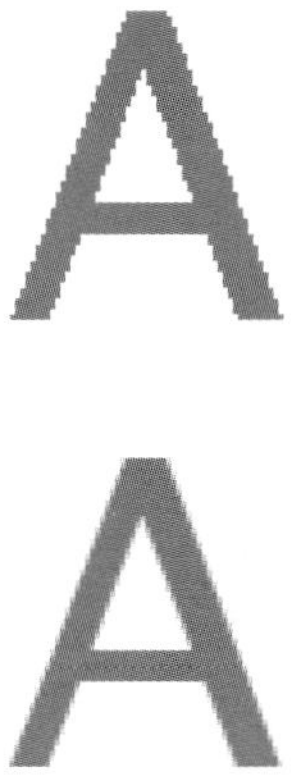

Figure 10.17 Anti-aliased text

Exercises

1   In Chapter 3, we described how a graphics application program keeps track of a model of an image, which it renders to make it visible. Discuss the extent to which a sequence of character codes can be considered a model of text, which has to be rendered as glyphs.

2   Naive commentators sometimes claim that using Unicode or ISO 10646 is wasteful of space, when documents can be adequately represented in ASCII. Explain why this is not so.

3   Although Unicode can represent nearly a million different characters, keyboards cannot have that many keys. Discuss ways in which keyboards can be made to accommodate the full range of characters.

4   Look at a newspaper. Compare and contrast the way fonts are used in news stories and in advertisements.

5   Find out which fonts are available on your computer, and print samples of each. Which would you consider to be suitable for display purposes and which for text?

6   Which of the fonts available on your system would you use for each of the following jobs?
(a) The opening credits of a science fiction movie.
(b) Your *curriculum vitae*.
(c) The body copy of a community newsletter.
(d) A wedding invitation.
(e) The list of ingredients on the back of a jar of jam.
Explain each of your choices.

7   Is there a meaningful distinction to be made between fonts that are *readable* and those that are *legible*? If so, what is it?

8   Fonts designed to be used on low-resolution devices usually have a relatively high x-height. Why?

9   Design a font for Scrabble tiles. You only need the upper-case letters. You will have to ensure that your letter forms fit harmoniously and legibly into the square tile (and don't forget the little number for the letter's value). If you don't have access to font design software, such as Fontographer or Metafont, you should design the character shapes on squared paper in sufficient detail to be mapped to pixels; otherwise, use the software available to you to generate a font in a suitable format and use it to typeset some sample words.

11

Text and Layout

- Text in Graphics
- Layout
  - Inline formatting
  - Block formatting
  - Markup
  - Stylesheets
- Text Layout Using HTML and CSS
  - Elements, Tags, Attributes and Rules
  - HTML Elements and Attributes
  - CSS Properties

In Chapter 10, we considered the storage and display of individual characters. When characters are combined into words, sentences and extended passages of text, we need to think about how they should be arranged on the screen. How are paragraphs to be broken into lines? How are headings, lists and other textual structures to be identified and laid out? How are different fonts to be used?

As well as being a vital component of multimedia, text can play an additional role by specifying the structure of a multimedia production. Layout commands and visual characteristics can all be specified using a text-based *markup language*. In later chapters we will show how links to other documents, the location of images and video clips, interaction with users, and synchronization of time-based media can also be specified textually in a markup language. The best known such languages are HTML, which we will introduce in the next chapter, and the newer and more powerful XML, which is described in Chapters 14 and 15.

Our primary focus is on markup, not on the tools, such as word processors and desktop publishing packages, that present users with an environment for preparing text. Multimedia authoring systems usually include similar facilities for preparing text. It is, however, common practice to use a dedicated system to prepare text, which is then imported into the authoring environment already formatted. In either case, the formatting operations available are equivalent to what can be expressed using the languages described later in this book.

Text in Graphics

The maximum flexibility in the layout of text can be obtained by treating text as graphics and manipulating it with a graphics program. Text can then be placed at will, possibly using layers to overlay it, and treated with effects and transformations. The integration of text and graphics occurs naturally, so this approach to text is ideally suited to graphic design incorporating text, such as posters, packaging, company logos and letterheads, Web pages, book jackets, and CD covers. As always, there is a choice between vector and bit-mapped graphics, which determines how the text can be manipulated.

If text items are created from outline fonts, they can be treated as objects in a vector graphics program: they can be arranged on the page arbitrarily, and all the transformations and effects that can be applied to other graphical objects can be applied to them. Words and letters can be scaled, rotated, reflected and sheared. They can be stroked with colours, gradients, or even patterns. The leading drawing programs provide extra facilities for laying out text, which take account of its sequential nature. Tools allow you to fill areas with text, arranged either horizontally or vertically. (Vertical text is intended for languages that are normally written that way, but can be applied to horizontal languages for a special effect.) The text flows automatically to stay within the area, with line breaks being created automatically as required. Text can also be placed along a path.

Figure 11.1 shows some typical ways of treating text in a vector graphics program. The design down the left was made by setting the name Shakespeare vertically, using a mid-blue to colour the text, taking a copy and reflecting it about the vertical axis. The mirrored copy was then filled with a lighter shade of blue and displaced slightly vertically and horizontally. Glendower's speech is set in red on a Bézier path, while Hotspur's reply is centred within an oval. Again, slightly different shades have been used to distinguish the components. The attribution has been rotated; all the elements were scaled to fit their spaces. The text remains editable: spelling mistakes can be corrected – you can even use a spelling checker – and the fonts and type size can be changed. The shapes into which the text has flowed, and the paths along which it is placed, can be changed using the normal vector editing tools, and the text will move to accommodate the changes.

By treating text as bitmapped graphics, quite different results can be obtained. Once text has been converted into pixels, it becomes susceptible to all the retouching and filtering that painting programs provide. (However, unless the text is set in a large font, many effects either do not show up, or obliterate it entirely.) Text can be warped and distorted, embossed and bevelled, set in burning metal, or weathered and distressed. Figure 11.2 provides some examples, with a host of filters and effects applied to different textual elements. This text has been incorporated into a bitmapped image and can no longer be

Figure 11.1 Vector text

Figure 11.2 Bitmapped text

edited as text, but must be retouched like any other part of the image. Using the terminology from Chapter 10, text in vector graphics form retains its lexical content, whereas in a bitmapped image it is reduced entirely to appearance.

Evidently, both approaches to text in graphics have their uses, and they can be profitably combined. For most purposes, vector-based text is more manageable; it was formerly common practice for designers to prepare text in Illustrator, then import it into Photoshop, where it is rasterized so that bitmapped effects can be applied. With the release of Photoshop 5.0, vector-based text was incorporated directly into Photoshop. Text on its own layer can be edited, as it can in Illustrator, although the full range of vector effects is not available. The text must still be rasterized before bitmapped effects can be used. The distinction between the two approaches to graphics and text remains: programs are increasingly combining the two, but the underlying representations remain distinct.

Graphics programs offer complete control over the appearance and placement of text, but this is not always what is required. Quite the contrary, in fact. If you are preparing some conventional text, such as a letter or an article, you want to be able to just type the words, and have a program do as much of the layout as possible for you. For this, we have to turn to a different class of programs, and consider some new questions, in particular, how do we exercise control over layout without having to place everything explicitly? Before we can do that, though, we need to have a clearer idea of the layout and formatting that are conventionally applied to text.

Layout

Advertisements, posters and CD and DVD covers may use graphic text effects such as the ones illustrated in the preceding section, but most text is laid out according to conventions developed over many years and familiar to us all from books and magazines. The book you are reading now illustrates most of these conventions. The text is arranged on lines, which are combined into paragraphs, and these are placed on the page. Formatting may be applied to characters within a paragraph – the font may be changed, for instance – and to entire paragraphs – space may be added within lines so that all the lines in a paragraph, except the last, are the same length, or the lines may be allowed to be of different lengths. These are fundamentally different types of formatting operation, and it is usual to distinguish between *inline* or *character* formatting, and *block level* or *paragraph* formatting. At a still higher level, there are questions of how blocks should be positioned relative to each other. Usually, paragraphs are placed one after the other vertically, with approximately even space between them, to be read in sequence, but, as you will see if you look at any magazine, blocks of text may be positioned in other ways. Captions are placed under or beside illustrations, for example, and supplementary material is often set off in sidebars, sometimes with distinctive background shading. Blocks are also set in a special style for headings, and they may be arranged to form lists of items.

The sophistication and elegance with which formatting is applied to text varies widely, depending on the program being used. Word processors provide a basic set of facilities suitable for business documents, and produce results that are adequate but lack many of the typographical niceties offered by page layout applications such as InDesign, which can generate output comparable to the best typography achieved by traditional means. Typography for Web pages is limited by the facilities of the markup languages employed, and by the capabilities of Web browsers, which tend to be limited in this respect. We will look at this special case later in this chapter, after describing layout and formatting in more general terms.

Text layout for print has to deal with issues of page make-up. These include how blocks are placed within the fixed area of the page, how text is broken between pages, and the placement of fixed elements, such as running headers and page numbers, on each page. In multimedia work intended for display on screen these issues do not arise, since text is not usually systematically broken into pages, but arranged within a window, using scroll bars to deal with overflowing text. On Web sites, each Web page may have a similar layout, however, and page templates are commonly used to ensure consistency. However, the allocation of text to pages is usually performed manually by the Web author.

Inline formatting

Inline formatting is applied to sequences of characters, often called *spans*, within a block; where blocks are organized sequentially, as consecutive paragraphs for example, it may be possible to apply the same format to spans that extend across blocks. Inline formatting specifies the font properties described in Chapter 10. The font family and variant and size of the characters within each span can be set. Where text is destined for an output medium that supports colour, characters may be set in different colours. For subscripts and superscripts, a baseline offset may be set, so that the characters (which will usually be set at a smaller size) will be moved vertically into an appropriate position. Note that this will increase the height of the span, as will setting characters in a larger size, which may necessitate increasing the leading[†] for affected lines.

† See page 335.

Most modern word processors and page layout applications allow you to define named *character styles*, which collect together a set of properties used for a particular purpose, such as emphasis, and allow you to apply them by name, instead of setting the individual properties separately. This ensures consistency and makes modifying styles easier.

Block formatting

In conventional documents, each block will be treated as a paragraph, even though some blocks, such as headings, will just be single lines. Each paragraph will have default settings for the formatting properties of characters; in the absence of any explicit inline formatting, the text of the paragraph will be set in the default font, using a default value for the leading. The block treated as a whole has additional formatting properties concerned with the way space is added to the lines within

Lorercillan henisisi bla at, velit at autem zzrit praese facidunt aut lore consequipit, sum vullan velesenit aut nismolorer il utet loboreet at. Duiscinci blam eu feuis niam dolor sum quam zzriure con hendre min veliqua corperostrud do odoloreet at wisis at, consequisl eu facillum nis aliquisl ut nonullaore dunt aciduis adignisi.

Lorercillan henisisi bla at, velit at autem zzrit praese facidunt aut lore consequipit, sum vullan velesenit aut nismolorer il utet loboreet at. Duiscinci blam eu feuis niam dolor sum quam zzriure con hendre min veliqua corperostrud do odoloreet at wisis at, consequisl eu facillum nis aliquisl ut nonullaore dunt aciduis adignisi.

Lorercillan henisisi bla at, velit at autem zzrit praese facidunt aut lore consequipit, sum vullan velesenit aut nismolorer il utet loboreet at. Duiscinci blam eu feuis niam dolor sum quam zzriure con hendre min veliqua corperostrud do odoloreet at wisis at, consequisl eu facillum nis aliquisl ut nonullaore dunt aciduis adignisi.

Lorercillan henisisi bla at, velit at autem zzrit praese facidunt aut lore consequipit, sum vullan velesenit aut nismolorer il utet loboreet at. Duiscinci blam eu feuis niam dolor sum quam zzriure con hendre min veliqua corperostrud do odoloreet at wisis at, consequisl eu facillum nis aliquisl ut nonullaore dunt aciduis adignisi.

Figure 11.3 Left aligned, centred, right aligned and justified paragraphs

the block, and the way the block is placed relative to its surroundings and other blocks.

Figure 11.3 demonstrates the four common ways of dealing with spacing of lines.[†] If the inter-word spacing is kept uniform, text may be *left aligned*, so that the left margin is straight, but the right margin is ragged, *right aligned*, with a straight right and ragged left margin, or *centred*, with both margins ragged but equal. Left alignment is the norm (for languages that are read from left to right), with right aligned and centred text normally reserved for headings and other displayed items. For more formal publications, such as most books, text is *justified*. Extra space is added between words, if necessary, to make each line, except the last, the same length. This may be done in different ways. The crudest is to add words to a line until no more will fit, then insert equal amounts of space between every word to fill up the line. This can produce badly stretched-out lines. Usually, words may be broken and hyphenated at the ends of lines, to reduce the need for inter-word space. The rules and conventions governing how words may be hyphenated are complex and somewhat arbitrary, and differ among languages, so automatic hyphenation is not always very

[†] It also illustrates the typographer's habit of using garbled Latin text to demonstrate layout features, so that the text's meaning does not intrude on the layout.

successful. To obtain more even text, and to avoid 'rivers of white' when spaces line up on consecutive lines, more elaborate algorithms, which consider the entire paragraphs, instead of individual lines, may be employed. For justified text, the last line of each paragraph is usually set left aligned, but for some sorts of document, every line is justified. Occasionally, the last line of a justified paragraph is centred, which can look very elegant for isolated blocks of text, but is not very readable for long passages consisting of many paragraphs.

Fully justified text has a neat and orderly appearance, whereas ragged right is less formal, some say more restless. However, even if you wish to present a formal appearance, justification is best avoided for text to be displayed on a monitor. Because of the low resolution of monitors, text is usually set in relatively large sizes, which means that fewer words can be fitted on to a line of reasonable length; this in turn provides fewer gaps between which to distribute the extra space needed for justification, with the result that the text may acquire large or uneven gaps, rivers of white, and other undesirable artefacts that interfere with readability.

Every block of text may be surrounded by space on all four sides. Setting space above and below a block marks it off from its neighbours. The space between the left edge of the block and the edge of the page or window is usually called the *indent*. Sometimes, the first line of a paragraph is indented differently from the other lines. One convention for indicating the start of a paragraph is to indent the first line relative to the others. First lines may also be *exdented*, that is, indented a negative amount relative to the rest of the paragraph. This form of layout is often used for lists. (See, for example, the way exercises are laid out at the end of each chapter of this book.) The items in a list may be numbered, or introduced by bullets or other dingbat characters.

Sometimes frames are put around blocks. This gives rise to extra places to insert space: between the text and the frame, and between the frame and its surroundings. All of these spaces must be controlled when text is laid out. It is also fairly common to allow blocks to have a background colour; frames too may be coloured.

Just as named character styles are used to abstract inline formatting, so a collection of values for a block's formatting – its default font settings, alignment, indentation and spacing – may be given a name as a paragraph style, and used to set paragraphs in a consistent fashion.

Blocks of text are sometimes arranged in rows and columns as tables; generally the cells of a table can contain images as well as text. Although tables are intended for the tabular display of data and other information, the regular grid that a table imposes may be found convenient for other formatting tasks, such as attaching a caption to an image, or setting text in two columns. (As we will explain in Chapter 13, the use of tables for this purpose should be avoided.) The formatting of tables can be complicated: the height of rows and the width of columns must be specified, or determined automatically. The text inside each cell of the table must be formatted, and arranged within the space of the cell; the vertical alignment of cells with respect to each other must be set. Adjacent cells may be merged in some of the rows so that they span more than one column, or in columns to span more than one row. Columns may have headings set in a different style from the contents of the cells. Rules (lines) may be used to separate some or all of the rows and columns.

Finally, at the highest level of organization of text, blocks must be positioned and combined into a printed page or a Web page. Normally, paragraph and heading blocks are arranged one after the other vertically, with the surrounding space as specified for each. Where less conventional layouts are used, each block may need to be placed at a specific point, either relative to the origin of the page, or relative to another block. Some systems allow you to embed a block within another block. Within the enclosing block, the embedded block is treated as if it was a single character, although most inline formatting does not then make sense. Baseline offsets may, however, fruitfully be applied.

Markup

In the days before desktop publishing and word-processors, authors' manuscripts were usually produced on a typewriter. Consequently, they could not be laid out in exactly the same form as the final published book or paper. The author, the publisher's copy editor and possibly a book designer would annotate the manuscript, using a variety of different coloured pens and a vocabulary of special symbols, to indicate how the text should be formatted by the typesetter when it was printed. This process of annotation was called *marking up* and the instructions themselves were often referred to as *markup*. With the transition to computer-based methods of publication, the function of markup has been transferred to the instructions inserted (often by the author) into the text file that now corresponds to the manuscript.

The form of these instructions is determined by the program being used to prepare the manuscript.

A distinction is often drawn between *WYSIWYG* formatting systems, and *tag-based* systems. WYSIWYG stands for 'What you see is what you get', a phrase which succinctly captures the essence of such systems: as you type, text appears on the screen laid out just as it will be when printed or displayed. Font and size changes, indentation, tabulation, and other layout features are controlled by menus, command keys or toolbar icons, and their effect is seen immediately. The markup, although present, is invisible; only its effect can be seen, giving the illusion that the formatting commands do not insert markup, but actually perform the formatting before your very eyes, as it were. In contrast, with a tag-based system, the document is normally prepared using a plain text editor; the text is interspersed with the markup, which takes the form of special layout commands, often known as *tags*. Tags are lexically distinguished from the text proper, by being enclosed in angle brackets or beginning with a backslash character, for example.[†]

† Text editors often have modes for common markup languages, in which the tags can be inserted using a single keystroke or menu selection.

Tags do the same job as the commands in a WYSIWYG system, but their effect is not necessarily immediately visible. A separate processing phase is usually required, during which the formatting described by the tags is applied to the text, which is converted into a form that can be displayed or printed, such as PDF. Word processors such as MS Word are invariably WYSIWYG, as are most commercial page layout tools, such as Quark Express and Adobe InDesign. Tag-based layout has, until recently, been largely confined to the academic and technical sectors, where tools such as troff and LᴬTᴇX were in use since long before the phrase 'desktop publishing' was coined. In recent years, the popularity of HTML has brought tag-based text formatting to a wider audience.

Although the experience of preparing text using these two different types of system is very different, calling for different skills and appealing to different personalities, a moment's reflection will show you that their differences are mostly superficial and concern the interface much more than the way in which layout is actually controlled. Underneath any WYSIWYG system is a tag-based text formatter, although the tags are more often binary control codes than readable text tags, and are inaccessible to the user of the WYSIWYG editor. The rash of WYSIWYG HTML editors and the re-targeting of page layout packages to produce HTML demonstrate that there is no real incompatibility between using tags to control layout and using a WYSIWYG approach to document preparation.

For the most part, we will concentrate on layout using textual tags, partly because it is easier to see what is going on, and partly because, after years in the shade of layout based on hidden control codes, it has acquired a new importance because of the World Wide Web. An advantage of using textual markup, instead of binary codes or some data structure, is that the marked up document is plain text, which can be read on any computer system and can be transmitted unscathed over a network. This is particularly important for the Internet, with its heterogeneous architectures. Here, HTML has brought tagging into wide use. XML, and a clutch of languages developed from it, promise to extend the use of this sort of markup into other areas of multimedia.

The difference between tag-based and WYSIWYG layout is merely a cosmetic difference between interfaces. A more profound distinction is that between *visual* markup and *structural* markup. In visual markup, tags or commands are used to specify aspects of the appearance of the text, such as fonts and type sizes. In structural markup, tags identify logical elements of a document, such as headings, lists or tables, and the visual appearance of each type of element is specified separately.

The distinction exists in a crude form in any word processor that supports the use of paragraph and character styles. For instance, if you were writing a paper divided into sections, you would almost certainly want to distinguish the section headings from the body text, let's say by setting them in a large boldface sans serif font, and inserting some extra space above the heading. A purely visual approach to markup would lead you to select each heading, insert space above it and set the font, its size and shape, using the appropriate menu commands or controls on the formatting palette. You would have to apply the correct settings to each section heading.

However, if you were to adopt a more structural approach, you would define a paragraph style, **sectionheading**, say, which abstracted the correct font and spacing settings for section headings. Whenever you added a new section, you would just apply the **sectionheading** style to its heading. If you were adopting this approach, you would probably also define styles for the body text, sub-headings, paper title, and so on, for all the textual elements in your paper. You could go further and create a document template containing all these style definitions, which you could use to produce papers with a consistent layout.

Structural markup has distinct advantages over visual markup. Perhaps most obviously, it allows us to change the appearance of a document globally by changing the definitions of the styles just once. If, for example, we wanted to use a more imaginative layout for our section headings – right-aligned in uppercase boldface italics, say – we would only have to edit the definition of the sectionheading paragraph style and every section would be reformatted in the new style. Consistency is ensured. In contrast, if we had marked up each section heading individually, we would have had to find and change the markup of each one.

The ease with which structural markup allows layout to be changed offers more than a licence to experiment with different typographical effects at whim. A more substantial advantage is the easy localization of documents which it permits. Centred layouts, for example, which are fairly standard in the United States, are much less popular in Europe. Changing the layout of a document such as a software manual to make it look more agreeable to customers in different parts of the world can be achieved by redefining the heading styles, while leaving the text of the manual alone. Similarly, while an author is working on a manuscript, it might be desirable to preview it using a simple layout, perhaps double-spaced. By using a different set of definitions for the styles, the same markup can be used to produce a final version, laid out in a more professional way.

Even better, a sufficiently powerful system based on structural markup would allow you to redefine the effect of your markup tags for different output media. For example, if you wished to produce a version of your document to be 'read' to blind people by a speech synthesizer, you might redefine a section heading so that the words of the heading were read with increased emphasis. This sort of application is best suited to tag-based structural markup, in which the structural tags themselves need not specify any form of processing but just identify different sorts of textual element. Hence, they can be used as the basis for presentation of the document in any medium, including media not invented when the document was written.

A related advantage of structural markup is that it permits a separation of concerns, and a division of labour, between the appearance of a document and its structure. The writer need only concentrate on identifying the logical divisions within the document while he or she is writing. The question of what typographical features should be used to identify those divisions in a perspicuous and pleasing way can be dealt with separately, ideally by a specialist book designer. If visual markup is used, the processes of writing and layout become intertwined, and control over appearance is left to the whim of the author.

The final advantage of structural markup is that identifying the structural elements by name makes it easy for a computer program to analyze the structure of the document. Although people can identify the structural elements from their appearance, this depends on knowledge and understanding, things which it is notoriously difficult to incorporate into computer programs. Programs are extremely good at searching text for strings with a specific form, such as XML tags, or word processor control codes, however. This makes it relatively easy to write programs to extract tables of contents or other tagged pieces of information. It also makes it easier to translate between different forms of a document. For instance, both Word and InDesign use paragraph and character styles. An import filter allows Word documents to be placed into InDesign, while mapping named styles from the former program to styles with the same name in the latter. Thus, an author can type a manuscript in Word, and apply styles, whose names are specified by a designer, but whose appearance in Word is irrelevant; when the document is placed into InDesign, each of the author's placeholder styles is replaced by the book designer's styles for the same element, so that section headers which were merely bold-faced in Word can be set in a more elaborate, carefully spaced way in InDesign, without any new markup being applied explicitly.

Stylesheets

If you take the idea of structural markup to its logical conclusion, it leads to the complete separation of structure and content from appearance. Markup tags should only indicate structure. However, when documents are displayed or printed, they have some appearance, and it is natural to want to specify this. Where pure structural markup is used, the specification of appearance is left to a separate mechanism.

If the same set of tags is used to mark up a sufficiently large class of documents, it may make sense to construct display software specifically for that class of documents, and to hardwire the layout rules into the software. That way, every document will be laid out consistently by a particular display program. A variation on this approach is to build facilities into the display program allowing its user to control some aspects of the layout. This is the approach adopted by the first generations of Web browsers. Most of the formatting of headers, lists, tables and other elements is controlled by the browser, but some details, specifically fonts, type sizes and colours, may be controlled by preferences set by the user. This is quite a radical departure from traditional publishing, since it gives the reader control over some aspects of the appearance of the document.

The alternative is to provide a separate specification of the layout, complementing the tagged document. Such a layout specification is usually called a *stylesheet*. For each tag being used, a stylesheet provides a rule describing the way in which elements with that tag should be laid out. There may be more than one stylesheet for a particular document or class of documents, providing a different appearance to the same structure, as, for example, one corresponding to typographical styles favoured in the US, and another corresponding to those in Western Europe. Stylesheets are written using a stylesheet language, which is designed for the purpose.

Text Layout Using HTML and CSS

Originally, the World Wide Web was intended as a means of dissemination of scientific research, so the markup language for Web pages, HTML (Hypertext Markup Language), contained tags corresponding to the main elements of a scientific paper: a title, headings that can be nested several levels deep to introduce sections, subsections, subsubsections and so on, and lists of various types such as enumerations and bullet points. Additionally, HTML provides some typographical control, by allowing you to mark text as italicized or bold, although it does not allow you to specify particular fonts;[†] HTML also provides generic styling tags, to mark text as, for example, emphasized or strong, without specifying anything about the typographical rendering of such text – these tags are more in the spirit of structural markup than are the explicit typographical tags. Later revisions of HTML added tables and interactive forms to its repertoire. As well as these layout tags, HTML crucially includes tags for hypertext linkage and for inclusion of images and other media elements, as we will describe in later chapters.

[†] Font selection was introduced in HTML 3.2, having been provided as an extension in popular browsers previously, but is deprecated in HTML 4.0 and XHTML in favour of stylesheets.

Our main interest in describing HTML is to introduce you to the syntax of markup on the Web, and to illustrate structural markup. Similarly, with CSS we intend to show how stylesheets can provide sophisticated layout control to complement the markup. We assume that most readers will have some knowledge of HTML, but will not necessarily be acquainted with CSS. Those readers needing additional detailed information should consult the references given in the bibliography.

HTML is a language that has evolved – not always in an entirely controlled manner – and its design goals have changed over the years. As a result it displays inconsistencies, especially between its current structural markup ethos and left-over visual markup features from an earlier phase of its evolution. Thus, whereas some tags are little more than hooks on which to hang stylesheet-based formatting, others provide direct control over typography. Because of the need for browsers to be able to display old Web pages, HTML must provide backwards compatibility with its older versions, so this mixture of features will persist. Looking at this situation in a positive light, HTML will continue to support a plurality of approaches to markup.

The features of HTML described in this book correspond to the XHTML 1.0 specification, adopted as a W3C Recommendation in January 2000. For the most part, XHTML is compatible with the earlier HTML 4.0 recommendation, in the sense that legal XHTML is also legal HTML 4.0, but the opposite is not true, since XHTML is stricter than HTML in some respects. (In fact, the XHTML Recommendation consists of a few pages describing the differences from HTML 4.0.) Except where the distinction is crucial, we will use the name HTML to refer to either XHTML or HTML 4.0.

Although we have referred to Web pages being displayed by a Web browser, such as Mozilla or Internet Explorer, the structural markup of HTML can also be interpreted by other programs, such as a text-to-speech converter. In the following pages, we will adopt the name *user agent*, used in HTML specifications, to mean any program that interprets HTML markup. A user agent, such as a conventional Web browser, that formats HTML documents and displays them on a monitor, is an example of a *visual user agent*; a text-to-speech converter is an example of a non-visual user agent.

Elements, Tags, Attributes and Rules

HTML markup divides a document into *elements*, corresponding to its logical divisions, such as sections and paragraphs. In general, elements may contain other elements: a section typically contains several paragraphs, for example, and this containment is reflected in the markup. Each element is introduced by a *start tag* and ends with an *end tag*; between these two tags is the element's *content*, which, as we just observed, may include other elements with their own start and end tags. Elements must be properly nested, that is, if an element starts inside another, it must end inside it, too. This means that each element forms part of the content of a unique *parent* element that immediately encloses it.

Every type of element available in HTML has a name. Its start tag consists of the name enclosed in angle brackets, as, for example, <p>, which is the start tag of the p element, used for paragraphs. In XHTML the names of tags consist of lower-case letters and numbers. (In earlier versions of HTML, the case was irrelevant, with <p> and <P> being considered the same; in XHTML they are different.) The end tag is similar, except that the element's name is preceded by a slash: the end tag for paragraphs is </p>. So every paragraph in an HTML document has the form:

```
<p>
```
content of the paragraph element
```
</p>
```
All other elements have the same form – start tag, content, end tag – but with their own identifying tags.

An inevitable problem arises if tags are written in the same character set as the text proper: we must lexically distinguish tags from text, using some special characters (in HTML the angle brackets that sur-round the element name in a tag) so we need some mechanism for representing those special characters when they appear in the text as themselves. In HTML, a symbol can be represented by the *character entity reference* < (the terminating semi-colon is part of the entity reference). This now leaves us with the problem of representing an & so as not to cause confusion. Again, a character entity reference is used; this time it is &. Strictly speaking, there should be no trouble using > symbols in text – there is always sufficient context to determine whether or not it is part of a tag – but some user agents do get confused by them, so it is advisable to use > except at the end of a tag.

As you may have guessed, character entity references provide a general mechanism for inserting characters that are hard to type or are not available in the chosen character encoding. References are available for all the char-acters in the top half of ISO 8859-1, as well as for mathematical symbols and Greek letters, and for layout characters, such as an em-dash. Some examples are given in Figure 11.4; for the full list, consult section 24 of the HTML 4.0 specification. There are many Unicode characters without character entity

references. For these you can use a *numeric character reference*, which specifies a character using its ISO 10646 character code. A character with code *D* is
written as &#*D*;, so, for example, < is an alternative to <. (If you are
more comfortable with base 16 numbers, you can write your numeric entity
references in hexadecimal, putting an x after the # to indicate you are doing
so. Another alternative to < is &#x3c).

Whitespace consists of space, tab and formfeed characters, and line
breaks, which may be of the form used on any of the major platforms:
carriage return, linefeed or both. In text, whitespace separates words
in the usual way. Visual user agents will format the text in accordance
with the conventions of the writing system being used; in English this
will usually mean that runs of spaces are replaced by a single space.
(In pre elements, described later, whitespace is left exactly as it is
typed.) Whitespace immediately following a start tag or preceding
an end tag is ignored, so that the following two examples will be
displayed identically.

```
<p>
Shall I compare thee to a summer's day?
</p>

<p>Shall I compare thee to a summer's day?</p>
```

An HTML document may be annotated with *comments*. These are
introduced by the character sequence <!-- and terminated by -->. For
example,

```
<!-- This section was revised on
      31st October 2003 -->
```

As the example shows, comments may occupy more than one line.
Comments are not displayed with the rest of an HTML document.
They are intended for information about the document, for the benefit
of its author or anyone who needs to read the marked up source.
However, as we will see later, comments have also been appropriated
for the purpose of maintaining compatibility between current and
older versions of HTML, by providing a mechanism for hiding content
that older browsers cannot deal with.

Some elements have no content; they are called *empty elements*. An
example is the hr element, which produces a horizontal rule (line).
There is no sensible content that can be supplied to such an element
– it just *is* a horizontal rule – so there is nothing for an end tag to do.
You can put an end tag anyway, but it is more customary to run the
start and end tags together, into a single tag, where the fact that the
element is empty is indicated by putting a / before the closing >, as

&iexcl;	¡
&pound;	£
&sect;	§
&Aring;	Å
&aring;	å
&piv;	π
&forall;	∀
&exist;	∃
&isin;	∈
&ni;	∌
&mdash;	—
&dagger;	†
&Dagger	‡

**Figure 11.4 A few examples
of character entity
references**

in < hr />. (The space before the / is not required, but putting it in makes it easier for older browsers to treat XHTML as HTML.)

Although it does not have any content, a horizontal rule element has some properties, including its width and colour. In HTML such properties are called *attributes*. The attributes associated with a particular element are specified as part of its definition in the language. Values for each attribute may be assigned within the start tag of an element. For example, to set the length of a rule to one half of the width of the displayed page and its width to 12 pt, we would use the following tag:

<hr size = "12" width = "50%" />

Attribute names must be in lower case. Values are assigned using an = sign. The values assigned to attributes must be enclosed in double or single quotes, even if they are numbers.

Some attributes function as flags or Booleans, turning some property on or off. The noshade attribute of hr is an example: if it is set, the rule is set as a solid block, and not as the pseudo-3D groove which is the default. Such a flag is turned on by assigning its own name to it, as in

<hr size = "12" width = "50%" noshade = "noshade" />

Flags are turned off by omitting them from the tag, as in the first 12pt rule example.

HTML experts might cringe at the preceding examples, because all the attributes to hr that we have used are *deprecated* in HTML 4.0 and XHTML. Actually, most of the attributes of simple text elements are deprecated, because they control some aspect of appearance. This can now be controlled much better using stylesheets. In principle, since stylesheet information is separate from markup, any stylesheet language can be used with HTML. In practice, most Web browsers only support *Cascading Style Sheets (CSS)*, a simple stylesheet language which works well with HTML, and can be easily mastered.

Let's return to paragraphs to demonstrate how a stylesheet can be used to control layout. For now, do not worry about how the stylesheet and HTML document are combined.

A paragraph element is a logical division of the text of a document. In the absence of any stylesheet, a user agent is free to express this division in whatever way it chooses. In English text, several different conventions are employed for laying out paragraphs. The visually simplest relies only on the insertion of additional vertical space between paragraphs; commonly this visual cue is augmented or replaced by applying an indentation to the first line of each paragraph. Most, if not all, visual user agents use the simplest convention by default. Suppose we want to use the more elaborate form, with indentation.

CSS allows us to specify various visual properties of each document element. One of these properties is, luckily for our example, the indentation of the first line. We specify that the first line of each paragraph should be indented by 4 pc (see page 335) with a CSS rule like this:

```
p {
      text-indent: 4pc;
}
```

The rule has two parts: a *selector* (here p) which indicates which elements the rule applies to, and some *declarations* (here there is only one) which provide values for some visual properties. Here the declaration specifies a **text-indent** (the name of the property controlling the amount of indentation applied to the first line) of 4 pc. The declaration part of a rule is enclosed in curly brackets, as you can see.

Whenever the rule just given is in force, every paragraph will be displayed with its first line indented by any user agent that implements CSS stylesheets (and is configured to do so). Suppose now that we did not wish to apply this indentation to every paragraph. Many manuals of style suggest that the first paragraph of a section should not be indented, for example. In order to be more selective about which paragraphs a rule applies to, we need some way of distinguishing between different classes of paragraph, such as those that are indented and those that are not. The HTML attribute **class** can be used for this purpose. This attribute is a property of virtually every HTML element; its value is a distinguishing name that identifies a subset of that element. For example, we might use a class **noindent** for paragraphs we wished to be displayed with no indentation.

In a CSS rule, a selector can consist of an element name followed by a dot and a class name. To specify that paragraphs of class **noindent** should not be indented, we would add the following rule to the previous one:

```
p.noindent {
      text-indent: 0pc;
}
```

As you would probably expect, when there is a general rule for some element, like our first example, and a more specific rule for some

Lore veraessissit ulla alit dolorero od do dolorem nit ulputat accumsan ut praesequam, veniamet doleniatuero er am, quisl et aut prationsecte el eugueros et incidunt nostie magna feu faccumsan hent prat, vullum ilit la feugiamcommy nullaorem dolor am quis acidunt velissenibh exerat. Ut adio erci tetumsan volum veliquat ad te feugait loreet dunt nullaore dolorper sisi.

Lore veraessissit ulla alit dolorero od do dolorem nit ulputat accumsan ut praesequam, veniamet doleniatuero er am, quisl et aut prationsecte el eugueros et incidunt nostie magna feu faccumsan hent prat, vullum ilit la feugiamcommy nullaorem dolor am quis acidunt velissenibh exerat. Ut adio erci tetumsan volum veliquat ad te feugait loreet dunt nullaore dolorper sisi.

Lore veraessissit ulla alit dolorero od do dolorem nit ulputat accumsan ut praesequam, veniamet doleniatuero er am, quisl et aut prationsecte el eugueros et incidunt nostie magna feu faccumsan hent prat, vullum ilit la feugiamcommy nullaorem dolor am quis acidunt velissenibh exerat. Ut adio erci tetumsan volum veliquat ad te feugait loreet dunt nullaore dolorper sisi.

Figure 11.5 Browser display of paragraphs with different indents

class of that element, like our second example, the more specific rule is applied to elements of that class, and the general rule is only applied to elements belonging to no class, or to some class for which no specific rule is available. If, for example, we had some paragraphs of class unindent, they would be displayed with a 4 pc first line indent, since the only rule that applies to them is the general one with selector p.

Rules can be used to control a range of properties; even a simple rule with only a couple of declarations can produce effects that are not usually available in HTML. For example, the following rule causes paragraphs to be displayed with a hanging indent.

```
P.hang {
    text-indent: -4pc;
    margin-left: 4pc;
}
```

The effect of these three rules is shown in Figure 11.5, which shows the display of the following HTML document by a user agent that understands stylesheets.

```
<!DOCTYPE html PUBLIC "-//W3C//DTD XHTML 1.0 Strict//EN"
 "http://www.w3.org/TR/2000/REC-xhtml1-20000126/DTD/xhtml1-
strict.dtd">

<html>
<head>
```

```
<meta http-equiv="content-type" content="text/html;charset=iso-
8859-1" />

<title>Paragraphs</title>

<style type="text/css">
p {
        text-indent: 4pc;
}
p.noindent {
        text-indent: 0pc;
}
p.hang {
        text-indent: -4pc;
        margin-left: 4pc;
}
</style>
</head>

<body>
<p class="noindent">
Lore veraessissit ulla alit dolorero od do dolorem etc.
</p>
<p class="unindent">
Lore veraessissit ulla alit dolorero ...
</p>
<p class="hang">
Lore veraessissit ulla alit dolorero ...
</p>
</body>
</html>
```

This document also illustrates some features of HTML that have not
been described yet. The very first line is a *document type declaration*,
which identifies the version of HTML being used, in this case
XHTML 1.0. The enigmatic form of the specification should just be
treated as red tape until Chapter 14, when it will be explained; the
declaration is not actually needed by most current browsers, but it
can be used by verification programs to check the legitimacy of the
HTML markup. Next comes the start tag for the html element. This
is the root of the entire document structure; all the elements of the
document proper are contained within it. There are only two document elements that can come immediately inside the html element:
head followed by body. The head of the document contains information about the document, which is not displayed within it; the body
contains the real text.

There are three elements contained in the head of this document. The meta element should also be treated as red tape: it specifies that the character set is ISO 8859-1. This is the default usually applied, but it is good practice to specify the character set explicitly in this way. If you do so, the meta element should be the first thing in the head (for reasons that are hopefully obvious). The title element contains a short title, which is usually displayed in the title bar of the browser's window. It is not displayed within the window, because it is not part of the text contained in the body.

The next element in the head is a style, which is where the stylesheet rules governing the layout of this page are to be found. (This is not the only place they can be; we will see an alternative later.) The start tag has an attribute type whose value is the MIME type of the stylesheet. For CSS rules, this is always text/css. The body of the document contains the paragraphs themselves, with their class attributes. The style in the head is applied to them to produce the desired display.

To summarize: text in the body of an HTML document is marked up with tags that delineate the document elements corresponding to the logical divisions of the text. Stylesheet rules, which may be put in a style element in the document's head, control the layout of these elements; the selector of each rule determines which elements it applies to, and the corresponding declarations set properties that control the appearance on screen. The class attribute is used to distinguish between different subsets of an element type, so that finer control can be exerted over their layout.

We are now in a position to describe the HTML tags that can be used to mark up text, and the CSS properties that can be used to control its layout. Although we are describing these particular languages, you should appreciate that the underlying principles of markup and layout apply to any system of text preparation.

Please note that the account we are about to give is not exhaustive. Some additional details will be provided later – in particular, we will look at facilities for incorporating other media besides text in later chapters – but we are not attempting to give a definitive reference guide to or tutorial on HTML and CSS. For that, consult the specifications and books listed in the bibliography.

HTML Elements and Attributes

The HTML 4.0 specification, and thus the XHTML specification, defines 91 elements, of which 10 are 'deprecated', meaning that they may be removed from future revisions of HTML, since there are now preferred ways of achieving the same effect. Only a few of these elements are concerned purely with text layout. Those that are can conveniently be divided into *block-level* and *inline* elements. Block-level elements are those, such as paragraphs, that are normally formatted as discrete blocks; i.e. their start and end are marked by line breaks. Inline elements do not cause such breaks; they are run in to the surrounding text. Thus, the distinction corresponds to the general distinction between block and inline formatting described earlier.

The most frequently used block-level textual element is the paragraph (p) element, which we have looked at already. Other block-level elements concerned purely with text layout include level 1 to level 6 headers, with element names h1, h2, ..., h6; br, which causes a line break; and hr, the horizontal rule element which we saw previously. The blockquote element is used for long quotations, which are normally displayed as indented paragraphs. Note, though, that using blockquote as a way of producing an indented paragraph is an example of the sort of structural markup abuse that should be avoided: markup is not intended to control layout. This being so, you will appreciate that the pre element, which is used for 'pre-formatted' text and causes its content to be displayed exactly as it is laid out, is something of an anomaly, yet it is useful for cases where the other available elements do not serve, and elaborate stylesheet formatting is not worthwhile.

The only elaborate structures that HTML supports as block-level elements are lists and tables. Tables are relatively complex constructions (as they inevitably must be to accommodate the range of layouts commonly used for tabulation); since their use is somewhat specialized we omit any detailed description. Lists, in contrast, are quite simple. HTML provides three types: ordered lists, in the form of ol elements, unordered lists, ul elements, and definition lists, dl elements. ol and ul elements both contain a sequence of list items (li elements), which are laid out appropriately, usually as separate blocks with hanging indentation. The difference is that user agents will automatically number the items in an ordered list; the items in an unordered list are marked by some suitable character, often a bullet. The items of a dl element are somewhat different, in that each consists of two elements: a term (dt) and a definition (dd). The intended use of a dl is, as its name suggests, to set lists of definitions; typically each item consists of a term being defined, which will often be exdented, followed by its definition. Figure 11.6 shows the appearance of lists produced by the following HTML fragment. Note that a list item element can contain a list, giving nested lists.

```
<ul>
   <li>first item, but not numbered 1;
   <li>second item, but not numbered 2;
   <li>the third item contains a list, this time a numbered one:
   <ol>
      <li>first numbered sub-item;
      <li>second numbered sub-item;
      <li>third numbered sub-item;
   </ol>
   <li>fourth item, but not numbered 4;
</ul>
<dl>
   <dt>ONE <dd>the first cardinal number;
   <dt>TWO <dd>the second cardinal number;
   <dt>THREE   <dd>the third cardinal number
</dl>
```

The most abstract block-level element is div, which simply identifies a division within a document that is to be treated as a unit. Usually, a division is to be formatted in some special way. The class attribute is used to identify types of division, and a stylesheet can be used to apply formatting to everything that falls within any division belonging to that class. We will see some examples in the following sections. Even in the absence of a stylesheet, classes of divisions can be used to express the organizational structure of a document.

Although we emphasize the use of the class attribute and stylesheets for formatting, HTML provides most textual elements with (deprecated) attributes that provide some primitive layout control. For example, the p element has an attribute align, which may take the values left, center, right or justify, causing the paragraph to be left-aligned, centred, right-aligned or justified. The align attribute may also be used with hr elements and all levels of heading. When it is used with div, it causes all the block-level elements contained within the division to be aligned according to its argument. Although stylesheets provide superior formatting facilities, it may be necessary to use attributes such as align so that user agents that do not support stylesheets can produce an approximation to the intended layout.

Inline elements are used to specify formatting of phrases within a block-level element. As such, they might be seen as being in conflict

- first item, but not numbered 1;
- second item, but not numbered 2;
- the third item contains a list, this time a numbered one:
    1. first numbered sub-item;
    2. second numbered sub-item;
    3. third numbered sub-item;
- fourth item, but not numbered 4;

ONE
    the first cardinal number;
TWO
    the second cardinal number;
THREE
    the third cardinal number

Figure 11.6 Display of HTML lists in a browser

with the intention of structural markup. It is, however, possible to identify certain phrases as having special significance that should be expressed typographically without compromising the principle of separating structure from appearance. Examples of elements that work in this way are em for emphasis, and strong for strong emphasis. Often the content of these elements will be displayed by a visual user agent as italicized and bold text, respectively, but they need not be. In contrast, the i and b elements explicitly specify italic and bold text. These elements *are* incompatible with structural markup and should be avoided (especially since a stylesheet can be used to change their effect).

There is an inline equivalent to div: a span element identifies a sequence of inline text that should be treated in some special way. In conjunction with the class attribute, span can be used to apply arbitrary formatting to text, as we will see.

In this section we have considered textual elements that can appear in the body element of an HTML document, but there is one element that can *replace* the body, and that is frameset. A frameset divides a page up into a collection of individual *frames*, which can be updated independently, arranged in a rectangular grid. A frameset element can only contain frame elements or other framesets. Each frame is (perhaps unexpectedly) an empty element; it uses an attribute named src ('source') to specify another HTML file, whose contents will be displayed within the frame. The value of the src attribute is a URL.[†]

† See Chapter 12 if you have managed to avoid knowing what a URL is.

When they were first implemented, frames became popular, because they provided a means of laying out text in independent blocks, where previously HTML had only supported a single flow of paragraphs. There is ample anecdotal evidence to suggest that many users find frames confusing, though, because the elements of a page become independent of each other, which undermines the metaphor of a printed page that is generally used to make sense of Web browsing. There are also practical difficulties deriving from the fact that a frameset has a single URL, although the content displayed will change as individual frames are updated. This makes bookmarking frames impossible, and leads to confusion in history lists. Frames have never been an official part of HTML, and CSS positioning now offers better layout facilities, so frames should generally be avoided.

All the elements we have described can possess a class attribute, which permits subsetting. Additionally, each may have an id attribute, which is used to specify a unique identifier for a particular occurrence of the element. For example,

```
<p id="para1">
```

is the start tag of a paragraph identified as para1. This identifier can be used in various ways, one of which is in a CSS selector, where it must be prefixed by a # symbol instead of a dot. For example,

```
p#para1 { text-indent: 6pc; }
```

will cause the paragraph with its id set to para1 to be set with a special indent. The values of id attributes must be unique with in a document, so CSS selectors that include a # can be used to apply custom formatting to single elements.

CSS Properties

It is now time to see how CSS can be used to transform the sparse text markup provided in HTML into an expressive and flexible formatting system. Again, note that the principles of layout – the values that can be changed and the ways they can be combined, for example – apply to many text preparation systems. Master pages in a DTP system such as InDesign, and paragraph and character styles in a word-processor, perform a very similar function to that of stylesheets and are applied to the text of a document via its markup in a similar way. In turn, these formatting operations closely resemble the tasks that have been performed in setting type by hand for hundreds of years.

It should be emphasized that CSS is a language for visual formatting, so it can only be meaningfully interpreted by visual user agents. Non-visual user agents have their own stylesheet languages.

CSS allows you to control the typography of your document, by choosing fonts and setting the type size. Five properties control the font characteristics described in Chapter 10. Several of them display some ingenuity in coping with the inevitable uncertainty about the capabilities of user agents and the availability of fonts. This is most evident in the font-family property: its value may be a list of font names (separated by commas) in decreasing order of preference. For example:

```
p.elegant { font-family: "The Sans",Verdana,Helvetica,sans-serif }
```

says, in effect, that we would ideally like text in paragraphs of class elegant to be set in a rather recherché font called 'The Sans'. (Note that we must surround the name by double quotes in the CSS declaration because it contains a space.) Should that font not be available, we will settle for Verdana, failing which Helvetica will do. If even Helvetica is not possible, any sans serif font should be used. Our fallback choices are based on pragmatic considerations: Verdana is similar to the preferred font, and is distributed with Internet Explorer, so there is a good chance that it will be available. Next we try for a sans serif, which, although not as good a match, is almost certain to be on any user's system. Finally, we have used a generic font family, in the expectation that a user agent will substitute an appropriate font that falls into that family. CSS provides five such generic families: serif, sans-serif, monospace, cursive and fantasy, which correspond to the font styles introduced in Chapter 10. The actual font selected when a generic font must be used will depend on the configuration of the browser. There is no actual guarantee that it will fall into the class identified by the name: the standard set of fonts included on a MacOS system does not include any font that would qualify as a fantasy, for example, so something more down-to-earth would have to be used.

The naming of fonts is not standardized, so you must be careful to include in a list of font family names all the pseudonyms by which your chosen font is known. For example, Times New Roman is often identified simply as Times or Times-Roman. If you wanted to be as sure as possible that this font would be used you would have to include all three names at the beginning of your font family list.

The search for a font is carried out for each character – remember that HTML uses ISO 10646 as its character set. Where a document contains text in several languages, or mixes mathematical symbols with text, the glyphs for different characters will be found in different fonts. The list of fonts in a declaration for the font-family property can be used to group together a set of fonts that should be used to provide glyphs for all the characters that might occur in a document.

The two properties font-style and font-variant are used to select different font shapes. The font-style property can have the values normal, italic, or oblique, normal being upright, and oblique what we have termed 'slanted'. The value of font-variant may be normal or small-caps – CSS considers small-caps a variant form rather than a different style, in theory allowing for small-caps italic fonts, and so on. The effect of declarations for these properties is to select an appropriate member of the font family chosen on the basis of the value of font-family. A slanted font is considered to be an appropriate choice for the font style italic if no real italic font is available.

The font-weight property has to deal with the fact that the terms used for font weights only make sense within a font family; as we remarked in Chapter 10, the bold version of some typeface may well be lighter than the medium version of another. For simple situations, CSS lets you use the values normal and bold for this property, with the expected effect. However, many font families provide more than two different weights, but with no universal naming convention to distinguish between them. Instead of imposing a single naming scheme, CSS uses numbers to identify different weights. You can set font-weight to any of the nine values 100, 200, ..., 900, which represent an ordered sequence of fonts, such that, as the font-weight value increases (numerically), the font's weight will not decrease, and may increase. Thus, if there are nine different weights (TrueType fonts always have nine different weights), each value will select a different one, but if the font has fewer, some values will be mapped to the same weight of font. Finally, you can use the values bolder and lighter. This requires a slight digression on the subject of inheritance.

The formatting described by a CSS rule's declaration is applied to any document element that matches the rule's selector. As you know, each element has a parent element. Any properties that are not explicitly changed by a rule for an element are left with the values they had in the parent – the properties' values are *inherited*. This is almost certainly what you would expect. It introduces the possibility of specifying property values not in absolute terms, but relative to the inherited values. Values for font-weight of bolder and lighter are the first example of this that we have seen. Their effect is to set the font weight to the next larger or smaller numerical value that corresponds to a different font from the inherited one, if such a font exists. (You cannot, for example, make a font any bolder than 900.)

A similar option is available for the **font-size** property. This may take on the values **smaller** or **larger**, which cause a relative size change. Font sizes can also be specified as a percentage of the parent element's font size, or as a multiple of the em or ex of the inherited font. Sizes can also be specified independently of the parent font. Here the range of values can be chosen from **xx-small**, **x-small**, **small**, **medium**, **large**, **x-large** and **xx-large**; it is suggested that these values correspond to sizes forming a geometric progression, with a ratio of 1.5. The absolute values will be determined by the choice of size for **medium**, which will be the 'natural' size of the font, as determined by the user agent. There is no guarantee that all user agents will produce the same set of sizes, even for the same font. Sizes can also be specified as absolute lengths, in any unit, although points will usually be preferred.

Normally, when we select a type size, we also specify the leading. In CSS, the **line-height** property is used for this purpose. The default value, **normal**, allows the user agent to select a 'reasonable' size. This is invariably too small: most user agents (following the advice in the CSS specification) choose a value between 1.0 and 1.2 times the font size. This follows convention for printed matter. This convention is partly dictated by economic considerations: if the lines are closer together, it is possible to fit more words on a page. This consideration is irrelevant for screen display, where the more open appearance lent to text by more widely spaced lines can compensate for the physical strain most people experience when reading from a screen. A line height of about 1.5 times the font size is more suitable. This can be set with any of the following declarations, which illustrate some of the different values available for this property.

```
line-height: 150%;
line-height: 1.5;
line-height: 1.5em;
```

Line heights may be expressed as a percentage, a ratio or in units of ems, all of which are relative to the font in use in the current element. Heights may also be specified as absolute values in any units.

All of the font properties may be combined in a shorthand declaration for the **font** property. Its value is a list comprising the values for the five font properties; the individual property values are separated by spaces, leaving enough context to identify a list of font styles separated by commas.[†] A value for **line-height** can be combined with the **font-size**, separating the two with a slash. This closely follows print-

† It should not matter what order the values appear in, but browsers are sometimes picky: style, variant, weight, size, family is a safe choice.

ers' conventions: 12pt/14pt is the way a printer specifies a 12pt font on 14pt baselines. A typical font declaration would look like:

```
p { font: italic bold 14pt/21pt "The Sans",Verdana,Helvetica
      sans-serif }
```

Where no attribute is supplied for a font property (such as font-variant here) the default is used. This is usually the value inherited from the parent element.

One of the important differences between printing and displaying text is that printing in colour is an expensive process, but displaying in colour is free – although you cannot guarantee that everyone has a colour monitor. Therefore, using coloured text and text on coloured backgrounds is an option which should be considered and is often to be preferred to imitating ink on paper by using black text on a white background. This is because the white areas of a screen are actually emitting light, which is usually quite bright and, as we noted in Chapter 6, has a very high colour temperature; it can therefore be quite a strain to look at for long – it is as if the monitor was shining a bright light in your eyes. Furthermore, the high contrast between black text and a white background can result in an optical illusion, whereby the type appears thinner, as if the background had spread over it. The same effect occurs in reverse if white text is placed on a black background. A combination of pale grey text on a dark grey background is surprisingly effective: the dark background reduces the strain caused by the light, and the lessened contrast reduces or eliminates the apparent distortion.

In some circumstances, the use of coloured type can serve other ends. For example, if you are making a multimedia production for small children or primary school teachers, the use of primary colours for the text may make it appear more cheerful and inviting. Red on black may produce a more sinister effect, suitable for a digital Fanzine for a Goth band, perhaps. Many style guides will tell you to be restrained in your use of colour, especially bright colours and harsh contrasts, and your own experience probably tells you that over-use of coloured text can be initially irritating and ultimately boring. But a timid and conservative approach to colour is boring too.

The two CSS properties background-color and color control the colour of the background and the text, respectively. Their values specify colours in the sRGB colour space (see Chapter 6), although user agents are given considerable latitude in how faithfully they approximate sRGB colours. Several formats are provided for colour specifications.

The most intuitive takes the form rgb(r%,g%,b%), where r, g and b are the percentages of red, green and blue in the desired colour. Instead of percentages, you may use numbers in the range 0–255 if you prefer. The most commonly used form of colour specification is the least readable: the three components are expressed in hexadecimal (base 16), and combined into a single, six-digit number, preceded by a #. The following specifications all describe the same shade of mauve: rgb(80%,40%,80%), rgb(204,102,204) and #CC66CC.

If, as in this example, each of the component values consists of a pair of repeated digits, the specification can be abbreviated to a three-digit form, with each being given just once, as in #C6C. If the digits are taken only from the set 0, 3, 6, 9, C and F, the resulting colour will necessarily belong to the 216 colours of the 'Web-safe' palette. You can also use names for some colours, but the only ones sanctioned by the standard are the 16 belonging to the VGA colour palette, so this option is of limited use.

Applying colour, fonts and line spacing to different document elements, such as the body text, headers, emphasized passages and general divs and spans, goes a long way to producing attractive and expressive text for use in multimedia. CSS – and DTP packages – provide control over several more aspects of a document's appearance. We will briefly describe some of the more useful of these, leaving the details to the references given in the bibliography.

Control over alignment in CSS is provided by the text-align property, which takes values left, right, center or justify. For example, to set the body text of a document ragged right (i.e. left-aligned), except for paragraphs of class display, which should be centred, the following rules could be used.

```
body { text-align: left }
p.display { text-align: center }
```

Text layout for multimedia has more in common with magazine and advertising layout than with mainstream book design. Rather than trying to construct a layout for extended reading of flowing text, the multimedia designer is concerned with arranging text on a screen, so that each screenful stands on its own and communicates its message or makes its impact as effectively as possible. An established approach to such layout is to place individual blocks of text on a grid. Designers have been using HTML tables as grids, positioning each block in a table cell, but CSS provides direct control over the positioning of document elements, a facility comparable to the control offered by page layout programs such as PageMaker. To understand positioning in CSS you need to know about CSS's model of text rendering, which is typical of the models employed by layout programs.

The model is fundamentally simple, although the fine detail (which we will gloss over) gets quite involved in places. You will recall that HTML document elements can be classified as either block-level or inline. The layout algorithm reflects this classification. Each element is notionally placed into a box. Text that is not contained in any inline element is placed into an anonymous box. These anonymous boxes and those containing inline elements are placed next to each other horizontally, and then this line of boxes is, as it were, folded up to fit into the available width. The alignment specified for the parent element is used to control the distribution of space between the boxes. In this folding process, some boxes may be split between adjacent lines; for example, an **em** element may need to be broken across lines. When the inline elements and text contained in a block-level element have been arranged as described, they are placed in a box corresponding to the whole block. The boxes for blocks are placed vertically, one below another. For computer displays, there is no notion of 'available height' – windows scroll – so no further adjustment or selection of page breaks is necessary.

In the absence of any further stylesheet information, this layout algorithm produces the familiar sequence of uniformly spaced blocks of text, all fitted into lines of the same width. CSS lets you exert some control over the disposition of text, to produce more interesting and effective layouts.

Lists are treated slightly differently, since we usually want to display the label or marker for each list element outside the block containing the element itself. The modification to the basic algorithm is simple. A somewhat more complicated algorithm is used to lay out tables, although in all cases, layout is performed by arranging boxes next to each other horizontally and vertically. Full details can be found in the CSS specification.

Each box can be surrounded by a *border*, which is separated from the box's contents by some *padding*; beyond the border, *margins* can be used to separate the box from its neighbours, or from the edges of its enclosing box. Each box's width and height can be specified explicitly, subject to certain constraints. Colour and background can be specified separately for each box. These properties permit such effects as shaded and outlined boxes, narrowed columns and superimposed or overlapping elements (using negative margins). Borders, margins and padding are controlled by a plethora of CSS properties, which provide control over each of them on each of the four sides of the box.

It is also possible to make boxes float to the left or right margin, while text flows around them. This facility is most often used for embedding images into paragraphs of text, but it can also be used, in conjunction with margin settings, to float text past text, as shown in Figure 11.7. The float property can take the values left or right, with the expected effect. A complementary property clear is used to control the placement of text that might be flowing past a floated box. It takes values left, right, both or none, indicating which sides of the box may not be adjacent to a floating box. Putting it another way, a value of left for clear forces a box to go below the bottom of any left-floating element, and so on.

The ultimate in layout control comes from using *absolute positioning* of elements. If an element is formatted according to a rule that sets the property position to absolute, then you can assign lengths to the properties top and left, thus determining the position of the top left hand corner of the box. In conjunction with width and height these properties allow you to place boxes arbitrarily on the screen. This, of course, allows you to place boxes on top of each other, which raises the question of their stacking order. The z-order property can be used to control this: its value is a number; elements with higher z-order values are placed in front of those with lower values. Use of the absolute positioning properties allows you to lay out text with the same degree of control over its positioning as you could achieve using a graphics program, as described in the first section of this chapter, but without having to convert to a graphics format, and without losing the text content or its markup. You cannot, however, apply filters and effects, or place text on a path.

The calculations and measurements needed for absolute positioning can be tedious, so most designers will prefer to use software that enables them to manipulate text boxes interactively on their screens, and generates the markup and stylesheet automatically. Such programs essentially provide the layout capabilities of conventional page layout packages.

Figure 11.8 is a simple demonstration of absolute positioning. Several words of caution are in order. You should never forget that user agents may ignore (or fail to correctly interpret) stylesheets. It can be quite difficult to ensure that a document that is laid out using absolute

```
<html>
<head>
<title>Box effects</title>
<style type="text/css">
p {
    margin-left: 2pc;
    margin-right:2pc;
    color: #19338F;
}
p.leftfloater {
    margin-left: 0;
    float: left;
    width: 30%;
    color: #FB0F0C;
    font: bold;
}
p.rightfloater {
    margin-right: 0;
    float: right;
    width: 30%;
    font: bold x-large sans-serif;
}
p.clear {
    clear: both;
    width: 50%;
}
</style>
</head>
<body>
<p class="leftfloater">
Left floated text will move to the left of the page, while the main
body flows sublimely past it.</p>
<p class="Rightfloater">
Right floated text will move to the right of the page.</p>
<p class=boxed>
The main text flows past the floaters, accommodating itself to the
space in between them, until a paragraph belonging to the class
"clear" is encountered.</p>
<p class="clear">
At which point, the layout resumes below the floated material, like
this.</p>
</body>
</html>
```

Figure 11.7 Floated elements: HTML/CSS source and browser display (opposite)

Left floated text will move to the left of the page, while the main body flows sublimely past it.

The main text flows past the floaters, accommodating itself to the space in between them, until a paragraph belonging to the class "clear" is encountered.

Right floated text will move to the right of the page.

At which point, the layout resumes below the floated material, like this.

positioning remains comprehensible when it is laid out using a user agent's default interpretation of the structural markup alone. The effect of positioning directives interacts with font sizes, which may be overridden by user preferences. You should also remember that your documents may be rendered by a non-visual user agent, perhaps for the benefit of people with impaired vision. Here again you should avoid producing documents whose comprehensibility depends on their layout.

In our examples, we have shown stylesheets embedded in HTML documents. Where a stylesheet is to be applied to more than one document, duplicating it in every one is wasteful and leads to maintenance problems. Under these circumstances, a stylesheet is usually stored in its own file, and incorporated into every HTML document that needs it, by way of a link element, which for this purpose has the form:

<link href="*stylesheet's URL*" rel="stylesheet" type="text/css" />

(We will describe link elements more fully in Chapter 12.)

Our intention in presenting this description of CSS is to illustrate the sort of control over text layout that is available to designers, by examining in some detail one particularly accessible means of achieving it. We have by no means described all its features, and have simplified some of those we have discussed. Two features in particular that are worthy of note in passing are context-sensitive selectors and media types. The first of these allows you to stipulate that a declaration should only be applied to elements that occur within another specified element type. For example, you might wish to apply a special sort of formatting to em elements that occur within other em elements, or within paragraphs belonging to the class special, say. Media types allow you to specify that certain parts of a stylesheet apply only when the document is being rendered to certain media. Thus, you can specify different fonts for printing on paper and for displaying on screen, for example.

Returning to the introduction of CSS on page 360, you may be wondering why *Cascading* Style Sheets. Stylesheets may be provided by

```html
<html>
<head>
<title>Absolutely Positioning</title>
<style type="text/css">
h1 {
   position: absolute;
   top: 0%;
   left: 25%
}
h1.over {
   top: 8%;
   left: 35%;
   z-index: 2;
   color: #000000;
   font: normal bold 36pt palatino, times, serif;
}
h1.under {
   z-index: 1;
   color: #808080;
   font: normal italic 54pt palatino, times, serif;
}
p  {
   border-color: #FB0F0C;
   border-style: solid;
   border-width: thin;
   padding: 2pt;
}
p.q1 {
   position: absolute;
   width: 125pt;
   height: auto;
   left: 10pt;
   top: 90pt
}
p.src1 {
   position: absolute;
   left: 40pt;
   top: 190pt
}
p.q2 {
   position: absolute;
   width: 125pt;
   height: auto;
   left: 200pt;
   top: 90pt;
}
```

Figure 11.8 Absolutely positioned elements: HTML/CSS source and browser display (opposite)

```
p.src2 {
    position: absolute;
    left: 250pt;
    top: 150pt;
}
body {
    color: #19338F;
    background: #B5B5D6;
}
</style>
</head>
<body>
<h1 class="under">Shakespeare</h1>
<h1 class="over">William</h1>
<p class="q1">
Keep thy foot out of brothels, thy hand out of plackets, thy pen
from lenders' books, and defy the foul fiend.</p>
<p class="src1">
King Lear, Act IV</p>
<p class="q2">
He thinks too much; such men are dangerous.</p>
<p class="src2">
Julius Caesar, Act I</p>
</body>
</html>
```

document designers, but they may also be provided by the user; user agents must necessarily provide a default stylesheet. The term 'cascading' refers to the way in which stylesheets from these sources are combined. Basically, designers' stylesheets supplement or override the users', which in turn supplement or override the user agent's. A user's stylesheet may, however, designate certain rules as important, in which case they override any conflicting rules in the designer's stylesheet. A user with poor eyesight might, for example, use an important rule to ensure that text is always set in a large size. However, designers' rules can also be important, and in that case, override any users' rules. This is a facility that should be used with discretion – it is, at the least, impolite to insist on imposing your vision on all users, even though you are a sensitive artist, when you don't know what special needs they might have.

Exercises

1   By default, em elements in HTML documents are usually displayed in italics. As we stated in the previous chapter, for display on screen, it may be preferable to use boldface for emphasis. Write a CSS rule to specify this appearance for em elements.

2   How would you specify that an entire HTML document should be displayed with one and a half times the normal leading?

3   Write a CSS rule to set level 1 headings as 'call outs', that is, the heading text should be typeset in the margin with its top on a level with the top of the first paragraph of the following text. (You will need to specify a wide margin.)

4   For pages that use CSS extensively, it would be polite to display some text that could only be seen by browsers that could not interpret stylesheets, explaining that the layout was being ignored by the browser. There is no simple way of discovering whether a user agent supports stylesheets. Devise a means of embedding such a message in a page, using only HTML and CSS.

5   Construct a CSS stylesheet in which all the block-level and inline HTML elements described in this chapter are distinguished purely by their colour. Choose a colour scheme that is visually appealing, and ensures that people with defective colour vision can still distinguish the different elements.

6   Construct a simple example of a document that has a different meaning depending on whether or not a user agent correctly interprets stylesheets.

7   Find a Web page that uses visual layout tags and attributes. (You will have to view the HTML source to discover this.) Take a copy of the page, remove the visual layout and replace it with a CSS stylesheet that produces an identical layout on a suitably equipped browser.

8   Rewrite your CSS stylesheet from the previous exercise to change every aspect of the page's layout without altering the HTML tags.

9   There are three approaches in use for creating and editing Web pages. They are (a) use a text editor to edit HTML tags by hand; (b) use an 'almost-WYSIWYG' visual editor, such as Dreamweaver, to edit HTML indirectly by changing the layout on screen; (c) use an HTML generator, such as Freeway, to edit a layout, and then create equivalent HTML from it. Discuss the relative advantages and disadvantages of these three approaches.

Hypertext and Hypermedia

12

- A Short History
- The Nature of Hypertext
  - Links
- Browsing and Searching
- Links in HTML
  - URLs
  - Anchors
- HTML and Hypermedia
  - Links and Images

In Chapters 10 and 11, we described the character of digital text, one of the most important components of multimedia. As well as the simple text described up to now, multimedia productions often make heavy use of *hypertext*. Hypertext is text augmented with *links* – pointers to other pieces of text, possibly elsewhere in the same document, or in another document, perhaps stored at a different location. A navigational metaphor is usually employed to describe how these links work: the place a link occurs is called its *source*, the place it points to is its *destination*. A user *follows* a link from its source to its destination: when a representation of the source is selected, usually by clicking with a mouse, the part of the document containing the destination is displayed, as if the user had jumped from the source to the destination, much as one follows a cross-reference in an instruction manual. Hypertext thus allows us to store a collection of related texts and browse among them.

Because the user's interaction with hypertext is more complex than that with text, we must consider more than just appearance when we look at the interface to hypertext. As well as the question of how a link is to be displayed, we must consider whether and how to store a record of links that have been followed, so as to permit backtracking, and we must consider what additional navigational facilities should be provided. For most people, the most familiar example of hypertext is the World Wide Web, and the navigational facilities provided by the popular Web browsers illustrate the sort of facilities that are required if users are to be able to browse a collection of hypertext documents comfortably.

You will almost certainly be aware, though, that the World Wide Web is not just made up of hypertext. Web pages can have images, sounds, video, and animation embedded in them, and scripts associated with them to perform interaction with the user. This network of media elements connected by links is an example of *hypermedia*, of which hypertext is a special case, restricted to the single medium of text. Despite the added technical complexity of dealing with a multitude of media types, the generalization from hypertext to hypermedia is conceptually a simple one, so we can safely begin our technical discussion by considering hypertext. The development of the two is inseparable, though, so, as we wish to begin by reviewing this development, we will start by considering hypertext and hypermedia together.

A Short History

Although popular perceptions of hypermedia focus on the World Wide Web, the concept has a long history. Its origin is generally traced to an article[†] written in 1945 by Vannevar Bush, a scientific advisor to President Roosevelt, in which he described a machine for browsing and annotating a large collection of documents. The *Memex*, as Bush's device was known, included a mechanism for creating links between documents, allowing documents related to the one currently being read to be retrieved, in much the same way as Web pages related to the current one can be accessed by following a link. The Memex was a mechanical device, based on photosensors and microdots, and it is hardly surprising that it was never built – digital computer technology provides a much more suitable mechanism for linked data retrieval.

[†] V. Bush, "As We May Think", *Atlantic Monthly*, July 1945.

Bush's contention was that association of ideas was fundamental to the way people think, and that document storage systems should work in a way that reflects these associations, hence the need for links. This interest in matching retrieval to a hypothesized way of thinking persisted in the earliest work on computer-based hypertext: one of the first working hypertext systems was developed under the aegis of an institution with the grandiose title of the Augmented Human Intellect Research Center.[‡]

[‡] We leave it to the reader to judge whether the majority of contemporary Web sites can be said to augment the human intellect.

Another feature of early writing and research on hypertext is the assumption that links would be added dynamically by different users of the system, so that the linked structure would develop over time on the basis of interactions between a community of users. There remains a considerable overlap between hypermedia systems and computer-supported collaborative working.

Among several experimental systems developed in the late 1960s and early 1970s, Ted Nelson's Xanadu project deserves mention, because it was intended to be a global system, storing the entire world's literature. In this sense, it foreshadowed modern distributed hypermedia systems, unlike the smaller scale, but more practical, systems that were developed in the years that followed. It was in connection with Xanadu that the word 'hypertext' was devised.

A number of experimental systems were developed throughout the 1970s and early 1980s. As experience with hypertext grew, some of these systems began to be used in earnest, particularly in information kiosks and similar applications. At this stage, much attention was paid to human interface issues, and to developing formal models of hypertext systems. Further work on these lines was rendered largely irrelevant by the arrival of *HyperCard* in 1987.

HyperCard, developed by Apple, was for several years distributed free with every Macintosh computer. The consequent sudden mass distribution of a hypertext system allowed HyperCard to establish itself as the paradigm of such a system – for a while, HyperCard 'stacks' become synonymous with hypertext – irrespective of any flaws in its interface and model of hypertext. Most, if not all, of the features to be found in HyperCard were derived from earlier systems, particularly Xerox's NoteCards; its importance lies not in innovation, but in popularization. Among those features were a card-based metaphor for organizing linked material, support for a variety of media, and the provision of a scripting language that allows actions to be associated with events and controls on a card. This language, HyperTalk, is sufficiently powerful to have allowed users to develop sophisticated applications in HyperCard – *Myst* was a HyperCard stack, for example.

HyperCard brought hypermedia out of the laboratories and into the world; the World Wide Web made it into a cultural phenomenon. Unlike earlier systems, which used proprietary formats and were largely closed and self-sufficient, the Web uses publicly available technology – anyone can create a Web page with a text editor – and plug-ins and helper applications allow browsers to handle arbitrary media types. This technology is, in fact, fairly crude, and it took over five years for the World Wide Web to evolve from a simple distributed hypertext system to a full hypermedia system with interactivity. The ubiquity of the World Wide Web means that its continuing evolution is likely to define the nature of hypermedia for some time to come.

The Nature of Hypertext

Text becomes hypertext with the addition of links which connect separate locations within a collection of hypertext documents. Links are active: using some simple gesture, usually a mouse click, a user can follow a link to read the hypertext it points to. To make this happen, a piece of software called a *browser* is required. Usually, when you follow a link, the browser remembers where you came from, so that you can backtrack if you need to. The World Wide Web is an example of a (distributed) hypertext system, and a Web browser is a particular sort of browser.

Browsers tend to encourage people to read hypertext in a non-linear fashion: instead of starting at the beginning and reading steadily, you might break off to follow a link, which in turn might lead you to another link that you can follow, and so on. At some point, you might go back to resume reading where you left off originally, or you may find it more fruitful to go on pursuing links.

It is a common misconception that such non-linear browsing is the distinctive innovation of hypertext. The following quotation is an extreme expression of this view:

> "All traditional text, whether in printed form or in computer files, is sequential. This means that there is a single linear sequence defining the order in which the text is to be read. First, you read page one. Then you read page two. Then you read page three. And you don't have to be much of a mathematician to generalize the formula to determine what page to read next."[†]

† Jakob Nielsen, from 'Usability considerations in introducing hypertext' in *Hypermedia/Hypertext*, ed. Heather Brown, Chapman and Hall (1991).

A glance at any magazine will show just how mistaken is the notion of a single linear sequence for reading printed text. What we find is a collection of articles that can be read in any order, broken up by pages of advertisements, to be skipped over or glanced at between paragraphs; a contents page contains pointers to each article. Many magazines feature 'sidebars', with information tangential to the main text of the article; picture captions interrupt the linear flow of text; and articles may be split ('continued on page 52'), with their continuation many pages further on and parts of several other articles intervening.

Other forms of printed matter also display non-linearity. An encyclopedia is made up of short articles, which are often cross-referenced, so that having read one you may be led on to another. Cross-referencing is also common in manuals for software and in all sorts of technical reference material. The tiresome scholarly apparatus of footnotes and bibliographic references comprises a sort of system of links, and much academic research consists in following those links. Even novels, which usually have a linear structure, are often read non-linearly: a reader might find it necessary to go back to an earlier chapter ('Piotr? Was he Ivan's brother-in-law or his faithful servant?') or even to go to the end to find out who murdered the Colonel; it may be necessary to stop reading the novel and resort to a dictionary to find out what 'tergiversate' means. Some novels explicitly use non-linear structures: Vladimir Nabokov's *Pale Fire*, and Flann O'Brien's *The Third Policeman*, for example, both include extensive notes, arranged in the same way as academic endnotes and footnotes, which must, therefore, be read out of the linear sequence of the text, but nevertheless play a major role in telling the story.[†]

† It might be argued that the notes in *The Third Policeman* actually tell part of the story of the same author's *The Dalkey Archive*, thereby providing an example of inter-document linkage.

It would not be going too far to say that, taken over all the varieties of reading, non-linearity is the norm when it comes to reading text. What is novel and distinctive about computer-based hypertext is the immediacy with which links can be followed, which creates a qualitatively different experience. Contrast waiting six weeks for a copy of a conference paper you have ordered on inter-library loan because you saw a reference to it in a journal with clicking on a link in a Web page and being shown the text of the same paper, as stored on a computer somewhere on the other side of the world, within a few seconds (on a day when Internet traffic is flowing briskly). Although text on paper does not have a unique linear sequence for reading, it does have a unique linear physical sequence, so following cross-references, even within a single text, requires the reader to flip forwards and backwards between pages, using page numbers to identify the destinations of cross-references. Even though computer memory is also arranged linearly and addressed sequentially, layers of abstraction imposed by software on top of this arrangement, together with the speed of operation of modern computers and networks, makes this linearity transparent, so that hypertext systems can provide the illusion that links connect together disparate pieces of text into a network (you might even call it a web) that you can travel on.

Links

Hypertext raises some new issues of storage and display. How are links to be embedded in a document? How are their destinations to be identified? How are they to be distinguished typographically from the surrounding text? To appreciate the answers to those questions, we need a clear understanding of what a link is, and what sort of thing links connect.

The simplest case is exemplified by the World Wide Web. If we confine ourselves for the moment to pages consisting purely of text, these are self-contained passages, which may be of any length, but usually fit on a few screens. Their only connection with other pages is through links (even though a link may be labelled 'next' or 'previous', such sequential connections between pages must be explicit). Within a page, though, the normal sequential structure of text is exhibited: you can sensibly read a page from beginning to end (although you don't have to), and elements such as headings and paragraphs are used to structure the content of the page. The HTML source of a Web page is often held in a file, but some pages are generated dynamically, so you cannot always identify pages with files, or indeed, with any persistent stored representation.

Hypertext systems are generally constructed out of self-contained elements, analogous to Web pages, that hold textual content. In general, these elements are called *nodes*. Some systems impose restrictions on their size and format – many early hypertext systems were built on the analogy of 3 by 5 index cards, for example – whereas others allow arbitrarily large or complex nodes.

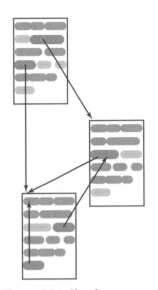

Figure 12.1 Simple unidirectional links

In general, hypertext links are connections between nodes, but since a node has content and structure, links need not simply associate two entire nodes – usually the source of a link is embedded somewhere within the node's content. To return to the World Wide Web, when a page is displayed, the presence of a link is indicated by highlighted text somewhere on the page, and not, for example, by a pop-up menu of links from that page. Furthermore, a link may point either to another page, or to a different point on the same page, or to a specific point on another page. Hence, Web links should be considered as relating specific locations within pages, and, generally, links connect parts of nodes (see Figure 12.1).

In HTML, each link connects a single point in one page with a point (often implicitly the start) in another, and can be followed from its source in the first page to its destination in the other. We call links of this type *simple unidirectional links*. XML and other more elaborate hypertext systems provide a more general notion of linking, allowing the ends of a link to be regions within a page (*regional links*), links that can be followed in either direction (*bidirectional links*), and links that have more than just two ends (*multi-links*). Figure 12.2 illustrates these generalized forms of link, collectively known as *extended* links.

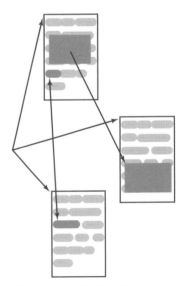

Figure 12.2 Regional, bidirectional and multi-links

Browsing and Searching

The possibility of disorientation – being 'lost in hyperspace' as the cliché happily puts it – has been anticipated since the earliest experiments with hypertext. The division of text into nodes leads to fragmentation and a disruption of the context supplied by conventional linear structures; the multiple branching paths provided by links, while offering ample opportunity to browse endlessly, can resemble a maze to a user searching for one specific piece of information.

Much early thinking about this problem concentrated on the provision of graphical views of the link structure between a collection of nodes. This approach has many problems – for any non-trivial collection of nodes and links the diagram itself becomes a confusing tangle. It is difficult to provide enough information about a node's content for users to determine whether it is interesting, or remind them whether they have visited it before – and, despite various ingenious embellishments, such as the use of 'fish-eye' views, showing nodes close to the current one in more detail than those further away, these graphical navigation aids have been largely abandoned in favour of navigation based on browsing history, indexing and searching.

Often, browsing in hypertext entails following side-tracks from a linear sequence and then returning to pursue it further. Providing a 'go back' command is a natural way of supporting this mode of reading. To do so requires the browser to maintain a stack of recently visited nodes, so it is straightforward to extend the facility by making this stack visible to the user in the form of a *history list*, and allowing users to jump directly to any node on the list, going back an arbitrary number of steps. A simple 'go back' facility provides a form of backtracking whereby a path is followed through the hypertext until it is no longer fruitful, and then the user backs up to a point where there was a different choice of link to follow and tries another path. In an alternative way of working, direct transfers to nodes on the history list allow a collection of recently visited nodes to be treated as a cluster, with arbitrary jumps being made between them. In effect, the history list provides an *ad hoc* set of dynamically constructed links.

History lists are always of limited size. Even if they were not, a complete history of your browsing activity will soon become as confusing to find your way around as the hypertext network itself. It is more useful to summarize this activity over a period of time in the form of a collection of pointers to previously visited interesting nodes. On the World Wide Web, pointers are URLs,[†] and, since these are just text strings, maintaining a collection of *bookmarks* or *favourites*, as URLs of interesting sites are usually called, is simple. Typically, Web browsers allow you to bookmark a page when you visit it, recording its URL together with the page title (this can be replaced by a mnemonic name subsequently, if the title is not sufficiently meaningful); bookmarks can be organized into a hierarchy and sorted. A menu of bookmarks is provided by the browser, which shows their names; selecting a bookmark from this menu causes the browser to retrieve the corresponding page. Instead of following trails of links, users can construct a collection of bookmarks that enables them to go directly to their chosen sites. This way of working is extremely common: you will notice that it entails rejecting the browsing approach to finding information in favour of direct access to a relatively small number of familiar sites.

†See page 395.

Browsing is based on looking for information by its associations. An alternative, and often more natural, procedure is to look for information on the basis of its content. This approach is closer to information retrieval and database querying; it can serve as a way of finding a starting point for browsing as well as being an alternative to it. In a small hypertext network, stored on a single computer, it makes sense to search through the whole network for a keyword or phrase by applying a conventional text-searching algorithm to each of the stored nodes. For larger networks, and especially for distributed networks such as the World Wide Web, this approach is not practical. Instead, we would like to construct an index (which can be kept on a single Web site), consisting of keywords together with URLs of nodes that they describe, and search that. Such an index could also be organized into categories using a suitable classification scheme, so that it can serve as a subject index, rather like a library's classified catalogue.

Many small indexes have been constructed simply by users publishing their bookmarks, sometimes supplying a simple facility to search through them. Where these form a coherent set of pages on a single topic, for example MPEG video, the result can be a useful access point for specialized browsing on that topic. Wider coverage is available from commercial index sites, such as Yahoo! and the Open Directory. Here, huge numbers of URLs have been collected, classified, and provided with a powerful search engine that supports the full range of Boolean query operations normally found in information retrieval systems.

There are two broad approaches to constructing index sites: manual and automatic. Using the manual approach, sites are classified on the basis of people's evaluation of their content. A URL for a Web site is normally added to the index in response to a request from its author, who suggests an initial position in the classification – usually a hierarchy of topics – and supplies a brief description of the contents. The site is then visited, and the classification is refined if necessary. The description is kept along with the URL, so it is possible to find a site either by navigating through the classification hierarchy, or by searching through the descriptions for keywords.

The search facility helps to compensate for the limitations of hierarchical classifications, which are well known to information scientists and will be familiar if you have ever used a hierarchical library catalogue: a site cannot be in more than one place in the hierarchy even though there is often good reason to classify it in more than one way. For example, should a Web site devoted to the use of MPEG-2 video for broadcast television be classified under television, which may be a sub-category of entertainment, or under digital video, a sub-category of multimedia within the computing category? To get round this sort of problem, indexes use aliases to make a sub-category appear to be in more than one category. However, following an alias leads you into the category under which the topic is actually stored, so if you then work back up the hierarchy, you won't get back the way you came down.

Evidently, a great deal depends on the structure of the hierarchy. Most classifications used by Web index sites are heavily slanted towards computing, communications and physical sciences, reflecting the origins of the World Wide Web. For example, Yahoo!'s top-level categories include one devoted entirely to computers and Internet, while another is devoted to everything concerning business and economy. Such imbalances may be alleviated by replacing the simple hierarchical classification by one of the more sophisticated schemes developed by information scientists, or by changing the structure of the classification as the content of the material being indexed changes. Whereas libraries' classification schemes tend to ossify, because of their relationship to the physical books and their shelving, a Web index, which exists and deals with objects that exist only on computers, can be changed much more easily.

While the manual approach to constructing indexes has the considerable advantage that human intelligence is applied to classifying and filtering the entries, it is labour-intensive – to be done properly, it requires somebody to actually go and visit each Web site submitted for indexing – which makes it difficult for the indexes to keep up with the rapid pace of change of the World Wide Web. Automatically constructed indexes avoid this problem. They are built by programs variously known as *robots*, *spiders* or *Web crawlers*, which simply follow links, collecting URLs and keywords from the pages they encounter. A highly efficient search engine running on some very powerful computers is used to process queries against the database of indexed words. When a user submits a query containing any of the words found on a page, the first few lines of that page, together with its URL, are displayed among the query results. The success of this approach depends on the robot's success in extracting meaningful keywords, on the heuristics used to classify sites on the basis of key-words, and on the efficiency and sophistication of the search engine used to query the database of keywords and URLs.

This brute force approach to indexing can produce some idiosyncratic results. A Web crawler cannot in any sense understand natural lan-guage, or differentiate between different uses of a word in different contexts, so, for example, a search for 'the blues' will find Web pages devoted to Birmingham City Football Club and the St. Louis Blues NHL hockey team as well those dealing with blues music. Indexing based on keywords is also vulnerable to attempts by unscrupulous Web masters to attract extra hits by planting inappropriate keywords on pages, although search engines do make an effort to detect such abuses.

As the number of sites on the World Wide Web grows, indexing and searching must become more sophisticated to help users find infor-mation they are looking for. The Google search engine extends the use of keywords by also looking at the number of links pointing at a page, and using this as a weighted measure of its importance. Pages which are referred to by links in many other sites, or in sites that are considered particularly significant, will appear higher in the listing than sites which have no incoming links.

It is possible, though, that the actual text of a page may not include the words one would normally use to describe its subject: that may be implicit in the content, or the author may have used a synonym – for example, in writing about automatic indexing of Web pages, they may have written about 'spiders' without mentioning 'robots', so a search on the latter term would fail to find their page. Furthermore, the opening lines of text from a Web page do not always provide a very helpful indication of its content. The current state of the art in natural language understanding by software does not provide a practical way of improving matters. Instead, the problem has to be approached from the other end by providing a means of adding a description that can be easily processed by a simple program to a Web page.

A description for the benefit of indexing software is just one useful example of *metadata* – data about data; in this case, data about a page, as against data that is part of the content of a page. HTML uses **meta** elements to provide a simple mechanism that allows metadata to be attached to any Web page. In particular, a collection of explicitly specified keywords and a short description can be given, which Web crawlers can use to collect their data for indexing. The **meta** element is empty and can only appear in the head of an HTML document. Two attributes, **name** and **content**, are used to allow it to specify arbitrary metadata as a pair of values, the name serving to identify the type of information, the content providing the corresponding value. This scheme avoids a proliferation of elements and leaves the maximum flexibility for choosing properties to use to describe a document.[†]

† You may recall from Chapter 11 that meta elements are also used to specify the character set of a document. The attribute used is different but the principle of using the element for data about the document is the same.

Two named properties are recognized by most search engines: **description** and **keywords**, whose intent is clear from the chosen names. The description, if present, is used instead of the first lines of the page when the results of a query are displayed. The keywords provide additional index terms, which may not be present in the text itself. Thus, if a Web page was devoted to the life and times of the blues singer Robert Johnson, it could usefully include the following:

```
<meta name="description" content="The life and times of the
blues singer Robert Johnson" />
<meta name="keywords" content="blues, music, King of the Delta
Blues" />
```

While effective, this mechanism is crude, and the absence of any structure in the metadata makes it difficult to use it for any complex processing. The *Resource Description Format (RDF)* incorporates ideas from conventional relational and object-oriented databases to provide a way of organizing metadata more formally, so that it can be processed by computer programs. The extensive use of metadata to allow information to be extracted automatically is likely to be the next step in the evolution of the Web, leading to what is called the *Semantic Web*.

Links in HTML

The links that can be embedded in a Web page composed in HTML are simple and unidirectional. What distinguishes them from links in earlier hypertext systems is the use of *Uniform Resource Locators (URLs)* to identify destinations.

URLs

A URL uniformly locates a resource, but the concept of 'resource' thus located is quite hard to pin down. The specifications are not unambiguously helpful here: "A resource can be anything that has identity [...] The resource is the conceptual mapping to an entity or set of entities, not necessarily the entity which corresponds to that mapping at any particular instance in time." (IETF RFC 2396 *Uniform Resource Identifiers (URI): Generic Syntax*). "[R]esource: A network data object or service that can be identified by a URI, ..." (IETF RFC 2068 *Hypertext Transfer Protocol -- HTTP/1.1*). In practice, a resource is anything that can be accessed by one of the higher level Internet protocols such as HTTP, FTP, or SMTP. Often, but by no means always, a resource is a file, or some data, but the way in which you can access that data is constrained by the protocol you use. For example, a mailto resource identifies a user's mailbox, but only allows you to access the mailbox by sending a message to it. An ftp resource identifies a file, and might even be used to identify a user's mailbox on systems where mailboxes are stored as files, but an ftp resource can be fetched over the network from its remote location. A resource is thus something like an abstract data type, identifying some data and providing a set of operations that can be performed on it.

All recent W3C Recommendations, including XHTML 1.0, stipulate the use of Uniform Resource *Identifiers* (URIs), rather than URLs. URIs are a superset of URLs, which also include *Uniform Resource Names* (URNs). URNs are intended to provide a location-independent way of referring to a network resource, unlike URLs which pin a resource down to a specific location for all time. In practice, Web pages invariably use URLs, so we will stick to the more familiar term and concept.

The URL syntax provides a general mechanism for specifying the information required to access a resource over a network. For Web pages, three pieces of information are required: the *protocol* to use when transferring the data, which is always HTTP, a *domain name* identifying a network host running a server using that protocol, and a *path* describing the whereabouts on the host of the page or a script that can be run to generate it dynamically. The basic syntax will be familiar: every Web page URL begins with the prefix http://, identifying the HTTP protocol. Next comes the domain name, a sequence of sub-names separated by dots,[†] for example www.wiley.co.uk, which usually identifies a machine within an organization, within a sector within a country. In the US, the country is usually implicit, and the top-level domain is the sector – commercial, educational, government, etc.[‡] There may be more intermediate domains in a domain name than we have shown in this example: universities, for example, typically assign sub-domains to departments, as in www.cs.ucl.ac.uk, a Web server in the computer science (CS) department of University College London, an academic institution in the United Kingdom. Domain names are registered with a central agency for a small fee.

After the domain name in a URL comes the path, giving the location of the page on the host identified by the preceding domain name. A path looks very much like a Unix pathname: it consists of a /, followed by an arbitrary number of segments separated by / characters. These segments identify components within some hierarchical naming scheme. In practice, they will usually be the names of directories in a hierarchical directory tree, but this does not mean that the path part of a URL is the same as the pathname of a file on the host – not even after the minor cosmetic transformations necessary for operating systems that use a character other than / to separate pathname components. For security and other reasons, URL paths are usually resolved relative to some directory other than the root of the entire directory tree. However, there is no reason for the path to refer to directories at all; it might be some access path within a document database, for example.

In advertisements and other published material, you will frequently see the URLs of Web pages given with the leading http:// omitted, and most Web browsers allow you to omit the protocol when typing URLs, making intelligent guesses on the basis of the rest. Although such usage in these contexts is sanctioned in the relevant standards, within an HTML document, you must always use a complete URL, or a partial URL of the form, and with the meaning, described below.

The only characters that can be used in a URL belong to the ASCII character set, because it is important that URL data can be transmitted safely over networks, and only ASCII characters can be considered

[†] Occasionally, the numerical IP address is used here (see Chapter 17).

[‡] However, organizations in other countries may also register domain names without a country code. Having a .com address is considered good for a company's image, even if it is based in the UK. Some countries' domain names are available in all parts of the world, allowing companies to register memorable domain names that are not available in their own country.

safe for this purpose – and not even all ASCII characters. Certain characters that may get corrupted, removed or misinterpreted must be represented by escape sequences, consisting of a character's ASCII code. In particular, spaces must be written in a URL as %20.

A URL with the components described so far can identify a Web page in one of three ways. In all cases, the domain name identifies the host running an HTTP server. The path might be a complete specification of the location of a file containing HTML, as in http://digitalmultimedia.org/downloads/index.html or, if it ends in a / character, the specification of the location of a directory. As a special case, if the path consists only of a /, it may be omitted: http://digitalmultimedia.org/ and http://digitalmultimedia.org both identify the root directory of the support site for this book. Where a path identifies a directory, the configuration of the Web server determines what resource the URL specifies, and thus what is retrieved when the URL is used in a request. Often, it is a file within that directory with a standard name, such as index.html.

The third way in which a URL identifies a Web page is via a program that generates the content dynamically. Again, the precise mechanism depends on the server's configuration, but usually such programs must reside in a specific directory, often called cgi-bin, or must have a special extension, such as .acgi. The occurrence of the letters CGI in both of these conventions indicates that a mechanism known as the *Common Gateway Interface* is being invoked. This mechanism provides a means for a server to pass information to and receive it from other programs, known as CGI scripts. CGI scripts are commonly used to provide an interface – or *gateway* – between the Web server and databases or other facilities. Several mechanisms are provided to pass parameters to CGI scripts, including appending a *query string* to the end of the URL used to invoke the script. The query string is separated from the path by a ?, as in http://ink.yahoo.co.uk/bin/query_uk?p=macavon.[†]

† For more information on the Common Gateway Interface and CGI scripting see Chapter 17.

Although the Common Gateway Interface was intended to provide a standard for interaction between a Web server and other resources, many Web server programs and database systems provide their own methods for performing the same function. The widely used Apache server had its own system of modules, while Microsoft servers support the use of Active Server Pages (ASP). Other non-proprietary mechanisms include Java servlets and PHP. These solutions are often more efficient or easier to write than CGI scripts, and have been widely adopted in commercial Web sites.

We have described a hypertext network as consisting of nodes connected by links, but the nodes (i.e. pages) of the World Wide Web are grouped into Web *sites*, each comprising a relatively small number of pages, usually held on the same machine, maintained by the same organization or individual, and dealing with related topics. Within a site, links pointing to other pages on the same site are common. *Partial URLs* provide a convenient shorthand for such local links.

Informally, a partial URL is a URL with some of its leading components (the protocol, domain name, or initial segments of the path) missing. When a partial URL is used to retrieve a resource, the missing components are filled in from the *base URL* of the document in which the partial URL occurs. This base URL is usually the URL that was used to retrieve the document, although sometimes it might be specified explicitly (see below). The way in which base and partial URLs are combined is very similar to the way in which a current directory and a relative path are combined in hierarchical file systems, particularly Unix. For example, if the relative URL videoindex.html occurs within the document retrieved via the URL http://www.digitalmultimedia .org/chapters/index.html it will be equivalent to the full URL http:// www.digitalmultimedia.org/chapters/videoindex.html Within the same document, /catalogue/ would be equivalent to http://www. digitalmultimedia.org/catalogue/. The special segments . and .. are used to denote the current 'directory' (component in the hierarchy described by the URL path) and its immediate parent, so, again within the same document, the relative URL ../links/index.html is the same as http://www.digitalmultimedia .org/links/index.html. Generally, if a relative URL begins with a /, the corresponding complete URL is constructed by removing the pathname from the base URL and replacing it with the relative URL. Otherwise, just the last segment of the pathname is replaced, with . and .. being interpreted as described.

A little thought will show you that, if relative URLs are resolved using the URL of the document in which they occur as the base URL, it is possible to move an entire hierarchy of Web pages to a new location without invalidating any of its internal links. This is usually something you want to be able to do, but occasionally you may need the base URL to be independent of the location of the document containing relative URLs. Suppose, for example, that you have constructed a table of contents for some Web site. You will want to use relative URLs, because all your links point to pages on the same server. If, however, you wish to be able to duplicate the table of contents (but not the site itself) on several sites, you will not want to use each copy's own location as the base URL for these relative URLs; instead, you will always want to use a URL that points to the site you are indexing. To achieve this, you can explicitly set the base URL in a document using the HTML base element. This is an empty element, with one attribute href, whose value is a URL to be used as a base for resolving relative URLs inside the document. The base element can only appear within a document's head. Base URLs specified in this way take precedence over the document's own URL. Hence, if a document included the element <base href="http://digital_multimedia.org" />, then, no matter where the document itself was stored, the relative URL links/index.html would be resolved as http://digital_multimedia.org/links/index.html.

One more refinement of URLs is needed before they can be used to implement simple unidirectional links as we have described them. We emphasized that links connect parts of nodes, but a URL specifies a complete page. To identify a location within a page – a particular heading, or the beginning of a specific paragraph, for example – the URL needs to be extended with a *fragment identifier*, consisting of a # character followed by a sequence of ASCII characters. The fragment identifier functions roughly like a label in assembly language programs: it can be attached to a particular location within a document (we will see how shortly) and then used as the destination for a 'jump'. A fragment identifier is not really part of a URL: it is not used by HTTP requests, but is stripped off by the user agent making the request, which retains it. When the requested document is returned, the user agent will find the location designated by the fragment identifier, and display the document with that part of it in the window.

Anchors

We have glossed over some of the fine detail of HTTP URLs – if you need to know everything about URLs consult the specifications – but the description just given should suffice to show that URLs provide the information required to access a Web page from anywhere on the Internet. The HTTP protocol provides a means of retrieving a Web page, given its URL, and therefore the combination of URLs and HTTP can be used to implement hypertext links in the World Wide Web provided we have a means of embedding URLs as links in HTML documents. This is provided by the a (anchor) element, which can be used as both the source and destination of a link, depending on which of the attributes href, name and id are provided.

The href attribute is used when an anchor is to serve as the source of a link. Its value is a URL, which may be absolute, if the link points to a document elsewhere on the World Wide Web, or relative, if it points to a document within the same hierarchy. The URL may have a fragment identifier appended to designate a specific location within the destination document, or it may consist solely of a fragment identifier, for links within the same document. The anchor element has content, which is displayed by user agents in some special way to indicate that it is serving as the source of a hypertext link. For example, most popular browsers by default show the content of anchor elements in blue and underlined; when a link's destination has been visited, a different colour (often purple) is used to display the visited link whenever the document containing the source is displayed again within a designated period of time.

A CSS stylesheet can provide rules for formatting a elements, just like any other element. To cope with the desire to change the appearance of a link when it is visited, CSS provides special *pseudo-classes* link, visited, hover and active that can be applied to a selectors. They identify subsets of the class of anchor elements, just as a class name does, but whether an anchor belongs to the subset depends on its condition in the browser, not on any attribute values. To distinguish pseudo-classes from ordinary classes, they are separated from the element name in selectors by a colon instead of a dot. The link and visited pseudo-classes are used in selectors to identify hypertext links (which will be a elements in any current version of HTML), and visited links, respectively. Formatting specified for the active pseudo-class is applied to a link when the user has clicked on it, and that for hover is applied when the cursor is over the link. These pseudo-classes can therefore be used to identify links by special formatting, and also to implement simple rollovers that do not depend on scripting.

The following rules stipulate that links should be set in boldface and blue until they have been visited, when they revert to the normal text font in green. When the cursor rolls over a link, it will turn red, and when the user clicks on the link, it will briefly appear extra large.

```
a:link { font-weight: bolder; color: blue; }
a:visited { font-weight: normal; color: green; }
a:hover{ font-weight: normal; color: red; }
a:active { font-size: xx-large; }
```

Despite the elegance of this way of controlling the appearance of links, it should perhaps be used judiciously. Some usability studies have concluded that users rely on their chosen browser's default for the appearance of links in order to recognize them. Interfering with this recognition can detract from the usability of your Web pages. On the other hand, the hover pseudo-class provides a simple and reliable way of implementing rollovers.

An anchor element with a name attribute is presently the most common way of attaching a name to a location within a document. The value of the name can be any string that would be legal HTML, although when the name is used as a fragment identifier any characters other than the subset of ASCII that is legal in a URL must be escaped. Although an anchor attribute that is being used as the destination for hypertext links in this way has content, this is not usually displayed in any special way by user agents. An alternative to anchors with names is provided in HTML 4.0 and XHTML: *any* element may have an id (identifier) attribute with a unique value; this may be used for several purposes, among them the specification of link destinations, by using the identifier as a fragment identifier. The use of identifiers instead of anchor names for this purpose has the advantage that any document element – for example, a header – can be used as the destination of a link, without the necessity of enclosing it in a dummy anchor. The disadvantage is that older browsers do not recognize identifiers.

There is nothing to stop you using the same anchor as both the source of a link, and a potential destination of other links, by providing it with an href attribute and a name or identifier. Within a document, each name or identifier must be unique, for obvious reasons. Although it would appear to be possible to distinguish between identifiers and names with the same value, this is not done, and it is not permitted for a name and an identifier to be the same. The behaviour of a user agent in the face of name clashes is not defined.

The following HTML code shows examples of links within a document, using both named anchors and a header with an identifier; a link to a section of a separate document is also shown.

```
<h1>Links and URLs</h1>
```

```
<h2 id="links">Links</h2>
<p>Hypertext links are implemented in HTML using the &lt;a&gt;
element and <a href="#urls">URLs</a>.</p>
[etc, etc.] </p>
<a name="urls"><h2>URLs</h2></a>
```

```
<p>An introduction to the use of URLs in HTML can be found in
<a href= "http://www.w3.org/TR/REC-html40/intro/intro.html#h-
2.1.1"> the HTML4.0 specification</a>. They are the basis of <a
href="#links"> links </a> in Web pages. </p>
```

Colloquially, we say that when a user clicks on a highlighted anchor element in a Web page, the browser 'goes to' the page that is the destination of the link; by extension, we talk about 'visiting' Web sites and pages. This metaphor of visiting has achieved almost universal currency, despite the fact that, in reality, the opposite takes place: we do not visit Web pages, they come to us. Clicking on a link that references a separate document causes the resource identified by the URL that is the value of the href attribute of the anchor to be retrieved via HTTP. Assuming that the resource is a Web page, the browser interprets the HTML and any associated stylesheet and displays the page. If a fragment identifier is appended to the URL, the browser will find the corresponding anchor (assuming it is there) and scroll the display to it. Usually, the newly retrieved page replaces any page being currently displayed by the browser, hence the idea of 'going to' the new page.

HTML anchors provide a flexible and general linking mechanism, but this very generality may be its weakness. There is nothing to suggest why a link has been established; in other words, simple a elements do not capture any of the semantics of linking. Thus, a user can have no way of knowing what sort of relationship the link expresses, and hence whether it is worth following, and programs cannot provide automatic navigational hints based on, for example, similarities between a link and those previously followed. The rel (relationship) and rev (reverse relationship) attributes are an attempt to capture more of links' semantics. Their value is a *link type*, which is a string designating a type of relationship that may be expressed through linkage. For example, an occurrence of a technical word in a document may be linked to an entry in a glossary; the rel attribute of the source anchor for this link could have the value glossary, as could the rev attribute of the destination anchor at the entry for that word in the glossary:

```
... by means of a <a href="../terms.html#url" rel="glossary">URL
</a> ...
```

and

```
<dt><a name="url" rev="glossary">URL</a></dt> <dd>Uniform
Resource Locator ... </dd>
```

A related issue concerns relationships between entire documents, such as one document being a translation of another into a different language, that are not expressed naturally by hypertext links between anchors within documents. The link element is provided to express such relationships. links can only appear in a document's head; they have an href attribute, whose value is a URL identifying the linked document, and may have rel or rev attributes, serving the same function as they do with anchors. Since they are in the document's head, link elements are not displayed by browsers – in fact, they have no content. It is envisaged that they might be used to construct special purpose menus or toolbars to assist with navigation among a set of related documents.

A collection of standard link types is defined to designate common relationships between documents, such as Next, Prev, and Start, which can be used to connect together a sequence of documents, or Chapter, Section, Subsection, and Contents which can be used to organize a collection of documents in the form of a conventional book. We have previously seen the use of a link element, with a rev value of Stylesheet to connect a document to an external stylesheet definition. In addition to the standard relationships, Web page authors are free to invent their own, although these are of less use in helping programs and users understand the structure of a collection of documents.

HTML and Hypermedia

In HTML, links are implemented as anchors, with an href attribute whose value is a URL pointing to the destination. In previous sections, we assumed that the URL points to a page of HTML. What if it doesn't?

HTTP doesn't care. If you ask a server to return the resource identified by a URL it will do so. As we mentioned in Chapter 2, it will include in its response, as well as the resource's data, an indication of what sort of data it is, in the form of a MIME content type. The presence of MIME content types in HTTP responses answers a question that may have bothered you: how does a Web browser know that what it is receiving is an HTML document? Because the content type is specified as text/html. The question begs another: How does an HTTP server know what MIME type to specify when it sends a response? It would be unrealistic to expect the server to analyze the data and deduce its type; a more prosaic solution is adopted. The server has access to a configuration database, maintained by whoever looks after the server, which provides a mapping from filename extensions, or file type and creator codes, to MIME types.

The upshot of all this is that when a browser receives a document it also receives information about the type of data it contains, in the form of a MIME content type. This brings us back to the original question, which we can now rephrase: What does the browser do if the content type is not text/html? Either the browser will be intelligent enough to deal with it anyway, or it will have to get another program to do so.

Consider the second option first. Web browsers can be configured so that, for each MIME type, a program is nominated to deal with documents of that type. The nominated programs are usually called *helper applications*. When a document arrives that the browser cannot display itself, it starts up the appropriate helper application to do so instead. For example, suppose your browser had been configured so that the Adobe Reader was the helper application for data of type application/pdf (PDF documents). If you click on an anchor whose href attribute's URL points to a PDF file, the data will be retrieved as usual. When it arrives, the browser will use the OS's facilities to start up another process to run Adobe Reader, handing it the retrieved data. The PDF document will be displayed in a new window belonging to Adobe Reader, with that program's interface, independent of the Web browser. Thus, although you read the PDF after retrieving it via a Web page, it is not integrated with any other Web data – we have not really achieved hypermedia, although we can link together different media using hyperlinks.

In order to properly integrate the display of media besides formatted text into a Web browser we must extend the capabilities of the browser so that it can render other media, and we must provide some extra HTML tags to control the layout of pages with embedded graphics, video and sound. It is not realistic to expect a Web browser to be able to cope with absolutely any imaginable type of data; for some obscure types a helper application will always be the best option. On the other hand, some types, especially image types and plain text, are so common that it is reasonable to expect browsers to have code to display them built in. Other types, such as video and audio, fall in between: it would be nice to handle them in the browser, but they are not yet so common that the necessary implementation effort on the part of the browser manufacturer is justified, and not all users will be happy with the resulting increased resource requirements of their browsers. The solution to this dilemma is *plug-ins*: software modules that can be installed independently by users who need them. Plug-ins are loaded by a browser when it starts up and add functionality to it, specifically the ability to deal with additional media types. The major browsers all use the same interface that allows them to incorporate plug-ins, and they can be configured to use a plug-in instead of a helper application for certain media types. An example of a widely used plug-in is Macromedia's Flash Player plug-in, which transparently incorporates all the functionality of the standalone Flash Player into any browser that implements the Netscape plug-in interface (this includes Internet Explorer). It is written by the Flash engineers, who presumably know more about SWF files than anyone else, so it provides a better implementation of SWF displaying than is likely to have been provided if the browsers had been extended by their own developers. Users only need to install the plug-in (usually simply by placing it in an appropriate place) if they want to view SWF movies within their browsers; this way, users with no interest in Flash and Web animation do not incur the associated overhead.

Once a browser becomes capable of rendering non-textual data without the aid of a helper, the possibility exists of integrating the display of such data with the other elements of Web pages. This leads to a mode of multimedia presentation based on a *page layout* model. This model is derived from long-established practice in print-based media for combining text and graphics. It can be fairly naturally extended to incorporate video and animation, by treating them as if they were pictures to be placed on the page, but with the added property that they can be made to move. Sound sits much less comfortably on a page, being purely non-visual. An expedient often employed is to represent a sound by an icon or set of controls, which can be treated as a graphic element, and then activated to play the sound in the same way as a video element is activated. An alternative is simply to associate a sound with a page, and have it play when the page is loaded. This approach has the disadvantage that users have no control over whether the sound is played.

Special markup is required for embedding these new elements in Web pages. In XHTML, the **object** element is provided for embedded media of all types – it is flexible enough to accommodate new media types that have not yet been implemented, as well as embedded executable content, in particular, Java applets. Early versions of HTML only provided support for bitmapped images, in the form of the **img** element. Use of this element has become so well established that, for the most popular image formats – JPEG, GIF, and possibly PNG – it is unlikely to be superseded by object. Before HTML 4.0 there was no officially endorsed method for embedding any other type of media, but Netscape implemented an embed element (subsequently also adoped by Microsoft in Internet Explorer) for including video, sound, and other media types. Although embed never had any official status, it has been widely used, and is routinely generated by HTML authoring programs.

Part of the enduring attraction of img is its simplicity. It is an empty element; in the simplest case, it has a single attribute, src, whose value is a URL pointing to an image file. img is an inline element, so the image is displayed where the tag occurs. This enables you to run images in with text, use them as headings or labels on list items, and so on; alternatively, you can isolate an image by enclosing it in its own paragraph.

To understand the necessity for img, consider the following two fragments of HTML.

Let us show you a <a href="still1.jpg">picture</a>.

and

```
<p>This picture has more presence:</p>
<p>
<img src="still1.jpg" />
</p>
```

In the first case, the word 'picture' would be highlighted as a link, just as if it pointed to another page. When the highlighted text is clicked, the image is displayed alone in the browser window, replacing the current page. In the second case, the image is displayed as part of the page, like a picture in a newspaper or magazine.

Like any other HTML document element, an img can be laid out in imaginative and pleasing ways using CSS rules. Margins and borders can be set around images, which can be aligned and floated, using the properties introduced in Chapter 11. For complete layout control, absolute positioning, including z-index, can be used to put images exactly where you want them – subject always to the proviso that not all user agents interpret stylesheet information. (For the benefit of older browsers, img elements have a set of attributes, including height, width, border and align, to provide some degree of control over their placement.)

The object element is the preferred way of embedding multimedia and executable content in Web pages.[†] We will not consider the latter at this stage, but we note that there are additional attributes for this purpose. For embedding images, video, sound, and so on, the data attribute is used; the value is a URL that points to the data to be rendered as the object's content. It is advisable also to specify the MIME type of the data, as the value of the type attribute. Although the server will supply this information if the data is requested, providing it in the object's start tag means that a user agent that cannot render data of that type need not waste time downloading it – possibly a non-trivial consideration if the object is a large video clip.

The way in which object provides for the possibility of a user agent's being unable to display the specified object is ingenious, but slightly counter-intuitive. Unlike an img element, an object has content, but the content is not the object – that is specified by the data attribute. The content is displayed only if the user agent is unable to display the object. This means that the content can be used to provide a replacement version of the object. The following use is typical:

```
<p>Here's a QuickTime movie</p>
<p>
<object data="movies/clip2.mov" type="video/quicktime">
      <object data="images/still2.jpg" type="image/jpeg">
          A 5 second video clip.
      </object>
</object>
</p>
```

If possible, a movie clip is displayed. If the necessary plug-in is not there, or some other reason prevents playing the movie, a still image is put in its place. If even this cannot be done, some text describing the missing object is used.

It is often necessary or desirable to specify some aspects of the way in which an object is displayed. For example, a video clip might be shown in a standard video controller component, with play, pause and fast-forward controls, or it might be displayed with no controls and play itself automatically. A page designer would want to be able to specify which of these styles is used. However, different options make sense for different media: you cannot sensibly attach a video controller component to a still image, for example. Furthermore, object elements are intended to be able to support arbitrary media, including those not yet invented. Consequently, it is not possible to define a set of attributes for the object element type that will provide

[†] Preferred, that is, by the W3C. At the time of writing, the implementation of object in contemporary browsers is patchy, but embed is almost universally supported.

for all possible eventualities. Instead, parameters required to control the display of objects are set using a special element type: param. This is similar to meta, in that it has attributes name and value, which are used to provide a value for a named parameter. The parameters for an object are set in param elements contained in the object element. The precise set of names that is applicable depends on the type of the object's data (or on the plug-in used to display the object).

For example, the QuickTime plug-in understands several parameters that can have the value "true" or "false", including controller, which determines whether a movie is displayed with a standard movie controller component, autoplay, which causes the movie to start playing as soon as the page is displayed, if it is true, and loop, which makes it play as a continuous loop. Hence, to make a movie play automatically forever without any visible controls, the following HTML markup could be used.

```
<object data="movies/clip2.mov" type="video/quicktime">
<param name = "controller" value = "false" />
<param name = "autoplay" value = "true" />
<param name = "loop" value = "true" />
</object>
```

Links and Images

One of the places you can use images is between the start and end tags of an a element with an href attribute. The effect is to produce a clickable image that serves as the source of a link. This may be indicated by outlining it in a special colour. A common use of this facility is to create clickable icons or buttons; another is to produce image catalogues consisting of small 'thumbnail' pictures: clicking on a thumbnail causes a full-sized version of the picture to be displayed. Alternatively, it may just be considered more appropriate to have an image serve as the linking element, if it somehow captures the semantics of what it links to. For example, an image of a book's cover may be used as the source of a link to a page of an on-line book store from which it can be purchased. (It is, however, more difficult to convey a link's meaning unambiguously using an image than it is using words.)

A slightly more elaborate way of using images as links is extremely popular: an *image map* is an image containing 'hot' areas, which are associated with URLs. Clicking on such an area causes the resource identified by its associated URL to be retrieved. Figure 12.3 shows such an image map: it looks like just a picture, but each of the flower heads is the source of a link. To make an image into an image map, it must be associated with a map element, by giving it a usemap attribute whose value is a fragment identifier. This must match the value of the name attribute of a map. Thus, for example,

```
<img src="flower1.jpeg" usemap="#image-map-1" />
```

associates the image flower1.jpeg with a map whose start tag looks like:

```
<map name="image-map-1">
```

The content of a map is a series of area elements, each having an href attribute whose value is a URL in the usual way, together with two attributes shape and coords, which together describe a region within the image which is to be linked to the specified URL. The options for shape and the corresponding interpretation of coords are listed in Table 12.1. The map element associated with the flower image looks like this:

```
<map name="image-map-1">

<area shape="rect" coords="65,351,166,413"
  href="section1.html" />
<area shape="rect" coords="64,353,167,410"
  href="section1.html" />
<area shape="rect" coords="106,324,124,442"
  href="section1.html" />
<area shape="rect" coords="351,420,452,482"
  href="section2.html" />
```

eleven more area *elements*

```
</map>
```

(As you can see, area is an empty element type.) Each flower head is approximated by three intersecting rectangles.

Almost nobody will want to measure or calculate the coordinates of areas such as these. Fortunately, many tools are available that enable you to construct a map by selecting an area and typing a URL. Most graphics packages are also capable of constructing image maps. The particular example just shown was made in Illustrator, where it suffices to select an object and type a URL in a text field in the attributes palette. If you then export the image as a GIF or JPEG file you are given the option of having an HTML file containing the image map generated at the same time. Note, however, that whatever the shape

Figure 12.3 An image map

Table 12.1 Shapes and coordinates

Shape	Coordinates
rect	*left-x, top-y, right-x, bottom-y*
circle	*centre-x, centre-y, radius*
poly	$x_1, y_1, x_2, y_2, \ldots, x_n, y_n$

of the object you select, only rectangles, circles and polygons can be used as areas in the HTML code.

Exercises

1   Show how you can simulate bidirectional links and multi-links with simple unidirectional links. What advantages are there in using the more general forms of link instead of simulating them in this way?

2   In regional links, the source and destination of a link are arbitrary rectangular areas that may contain some text. Why cannot HTML use this model for anchors?

3   Regional links allow for the possibility of links whose sources overlap. How would you cope with the problems this causes?

4   Can a single resource be identified by more than one URL? Can a single URL identify more than one resource?

5   An area element may have an attribute nohref, which, if true, specifies that the designated area has no URL associated with it. Since no part of the image is associated with a URL unless it is within the shape defined by some area, what possible use could you make of this attribute?

6   The *Encyclopedia Britannica* and several good dictionaries are now available online, so, in principle, every term used in any Web page could be linked to its definition in one of these reference works. Would this be (a) practical and (b) useful?

13

Design Principles

- Structure and Navigation in Hypermedia
  - Complementary Navigation Structures
- Non-linear Time-based Structures
- Design Problems of the WWW
- Accessibility
  - Textual Equivalents
  - Markup
  - Structure, Navigation and Links
  - Colour and Motion
  - Flash and Accessibility
- Web Design Issues
  - Correctness
  - Content
  - Usability
- Conservatism and Progress

In the introduction to *Story*, his influential book on screenwriting, Robert McKee makes the following observation:

> "A rule says 'You *must* do it *this way*.' A principle says, 'This *works*... and has through all remembered time.' [...] Anxious, inexperienced writers obey rules. Rebellious, unschooled writers break rules. Artists master the form."

You might consider the phrase "through all remembered time" a little extravagant, or worry about the cultural sensitivity of any alleged principles, but within a given historical and cultural context, the essential point of McKee's thesis is a valid one, which applies to all media, not only screenwriting: following rules and guidelines does not make great art, nor does deliberately breaking them. It is only a mastery of form and the principles underlying it that will allow you to create great work.

This is no less true in multimedia than it is in traditional media. However, in digital multimedia – and, in particular, Web design – we have only a few years' experience, not the thousands of years that we can draw on in the case of story-telling, drama or visual communication. This puts us all in the position of 'anxious, inexperienced' designers, and has led to a positive explosion of rules and guidelines, design tips and 'how-to' manuals from the pens of self-appointed design gurus and usability consultants. And of course, the existence of such a plethora of rules and guidelines has brought forth 'rebellious, unschooled' designers to break them.

In this chapter we will examine the nature of multimedia productions in general, and Web sites in particular, in an attempt to illuminate some of their underlying principles. We will begin by looking at structure.

Structure and Navigation in Hypermedia

Hypermedia consists of a collection of nodes (in Web terms, pages) connected by links. The generality of this model allows nodes to be combined in completely arbitrary ways: any node can be linked to any other and in consequence there can be any number of ways to reach any particular node. In the absence of any organized structure, as soon as there are more than a few nodes, the resulting network will be hard or impossible to navigate, and users will rapidly become 'lost in hyperspace', as the cliché happily puts it. The combination of nodes into a coherent navigable structure is one of the two main design problems posed by hypermedia. (The other, which we will discuss later in this chapter, is the visual design of individual nodes.) From here on, we will consider this problem in the context of the World Wide Web, which is by far the most important example of hypermedia.

A Web site could be defined as a collection of Web pages, all of which have URLs beginning with the same *domain name*. (For Web pages, the domain name is the part of the URL between http:// and the first /, so in http://www.digitalmultimedia.org/index.html, the domain name is www.digitalmultimedia.org.) Almost always, a site also has a home page, which is accessed by a URL consisting of just the domain name. Visitors to the site will most often (though not always) arrive at the home page first. This definition characterizes a site purely in terms of the way it is addressed; normally we expect a site to have a more or less unified theme (often being a collection of information or services provided by a single organization) and to be arranged in a coherent structure, so a better definition of Web site is *a collection of Web pages with a theme, a coherent structure and a home page.*

Well designed sites will have a clear structure and provide a means of navigation that expresses that structure. We can identify four different possible systematic site structures that people find natural and easy to understand and navigate.

Totally connected

Every page has a link to every other page. As you can see from Figure 13.1, even for a small number of pages, this structure requires a large number of links, and is hard to make sense of. (The difficulty of drawing a structure provides a good indication of how difficult it is to perceive.) For a small site, though, it can be the best form of organization. For example, consider a Web site for a small company

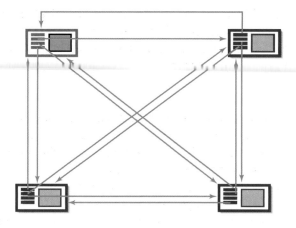

Figure 13.1 Fully connected organization

providing self-catering holiday accommodation in three cottages. This could have a welcome page as its home page, one page for each cottage, a page for contact details, another giving the weekly rates, and perhaps a page with some information about the local area. Visitors might want to look at some or all of these pages in any order, so it is most helpful to link them all together. This can be done by providing a standard navigation bar on each page, containing a set of links to each of the others. Figure 13.2 shows a page from such a site; the navigation bar is laid out horizontally below the design at the top, which also appears on every page to give the site a unified identity. It

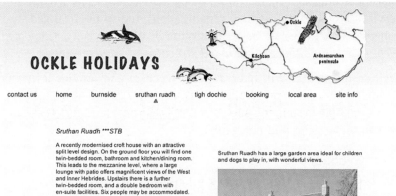

Figure 13.2 Navigation bar for a fully connected site

is useful (some would say essential) to provide an indication within the navigation bar of which page is currently being viewed. In the illustration, note the small triangle underneath one of the navigation bar links, which serves this purpose.

Hierarchical

For larger sites, a hierarchical organization is the most popular. Here, the home page contains pointers to a subset of the other pages in the site. Each of the pages accessible via direct links from the home page can be considered as the home page of a sub-site, and each of these 'sub-home pages' contains links to its own set of pages (as well as a link back to the site's home page). Each of these sub-sites can itself be a hierarchy, containing sub-sub-sites, and so on, to an arbitrary depth, as shown in Figure 13.3. In a pure hierarchy, the pages in any sub-site would not appear in any other sub-site. Each of the sub-sites normally corresponds to a sub-topic within the main topic of the whole site. Thus, for example, it is common for sites belonging to software vendors to have sub-sites devoted to company information, the programs they produce, customer support, and contacts. Within the products sub-site, there will often be a sub-site for each program, and similarly, the customer support sub-site might be divided into support pages for each program.

Although the essential structure of a site may be hierarchical, there can be other links besides those connecting pages with their descendants in the hierarchy. Often, each sub-site is accessible from every sub-home page, and often from every page. A navigation bar

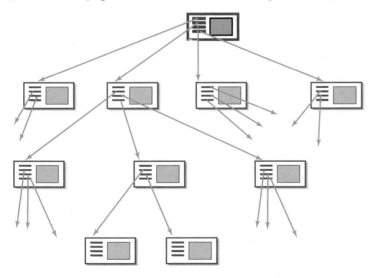

Figure 13.3 Hierarchical organization

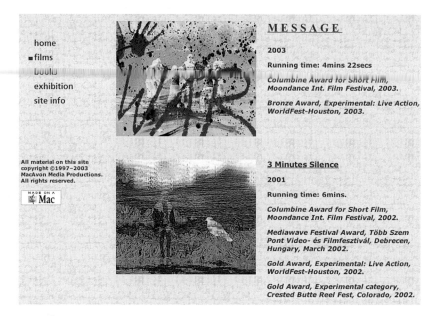

Figure 13.4 Embedded links within a sub-site

on every page can provide these links, while the links within sub-sites can be embedded in the pages themselves, as in Figure 13.4, or in additional navigation bars that appear within the sub-site, as in Figure 13.5. Alternatively, hierarchical drop-down menus can be used to provide access to pages at any level in the hierarchy, as in Figure 13.6. Whichever approach is taken, for hierarchies with more than a couple of levels, it is also helpful to provide some indication to users of where they are in the hierarchy, and a means of moving back upwards. 'Breadcrumbs' – a sequence of links to the sub-home pages of the enclosing sub-sites, as shown in Figure 13.7 – have become a popular way of providing this information.

There is a natural correspondence between the hierarchical logical arrangement of a site, as defined by the links between pages, and the hierarchical structure of the directories and sub-directories holding the pages on the server, but it is not necessary or automatic that the two should be images of each other. A hierarchical site could be stored in a flat directory structure.

Company	Products	Online shop	Dealers	Training	Support	Contact us
	Staff	History	Mission	Locations	Opportunities	

Company	Products	Online shop	Dealers	Training	Support	Contact us
	Gromet plunging	Flume wrangling	Fish walking	Rain preening	Sea strengthening	

Figure 13.5 Navigation bars within a sub-site

Company   Products   Online shop   Dealers   **Training**   Support   Contact us

Gromet plunging
Flume wrangling
Fish walking
Rain preening
Sea strengthening

Figure 13.6 Drop-down menus for navigating sub-sites

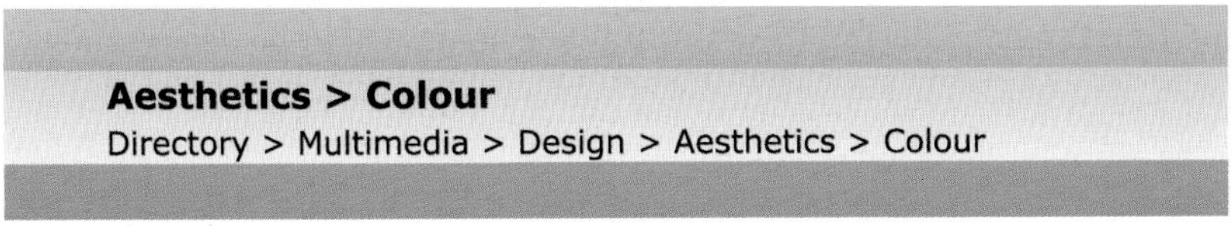

Aesthetics > Colour
Directory > Multimedia > Design > Aesthetics > Colour

Figure 13.7 Breadcrumbs

Sequential

Although we have stressed that hypermedia supports non-linear structures (see Chapter 1), sometimes a simple linear sequence is an appropriate structure for a Web site. (See Figure 13.8.) An artist's or designer's small online gallery is an example. The aim of the site is to display a series of images. Since each image will have to occupy most of a typical user's screen, and since images are relatively large files, it makes sense to restrict each page to one image, thereby avoiding the need for the user to scroll or wait for several images to download. If the image pages are linked together in a sequence, the user can look at each one in turn, as if watching a slide show. In gallery sites, it is common to link the home page to each image page, using a set of thumbnails of the full-sized images as the links.

For a sequence, the only navigation that is strictly required is a button on each page pointing to the next. However, it is advisable to provide a button pointing to the previous page as well and one to the first page. (Visitors to a site do not always arrive at the home page.) Sometimes, as when a sequence is used to display the results of a search, or the

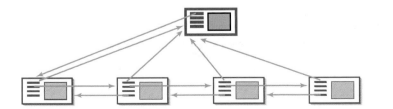

Figure 13.8 Sequential organization

available in a wide range of sizes
to fit children of all ages, and in
the following colours:
navy ■ red ■ grey   black ■

previous<   1 2 3 4 5 6 7 8 9 10 11 12 13 14 15 16 17   >next

Figure 13.9 Navigation links within a sequence

entries in a Weblog, it is also a good idea to provide direct links to every page in the sequence. This actually turns the sequential site into a totally linked site, but if the links identify each page numerically by its position in the sequence, as in Figure 13.9, we would be justified in considering the essential site structure to be sequential.

Hybrid

Many medium- to large-sized Web sites do not fall neatly into any of the three categories just described, but they can be seen as being composed of sub-sites which do. Commonly, a site will have one or two levels of hierarchy, with the bottom levels being either totally linked or a sequence, or both.

Navigation in a hybrid site will make use of the structures appropriate to its sub-sites. If the large-scale structure is hierarchical, then a navigation bar with links to the roots of each of the sub-sites would appear on each page, together with whatever links were appropriate to the sub-site – a subsidiary navigation bar for totally linked sites, next and previous links for a structure.

In our description of site structures, we have implicitly assumed that sites are made up of static pages, that is, pages which are stored in files on a server (see Chapter 2). Increasingly, Web sites are dynamic, with their pages being generated on the fly by programs running on the server, which gather information from a database and format it as a Web page. This doesn't materially alter the structure of the site: the linked pages as they are made available to a browser will still fall into one of the four categories just described, although hybrid structures are more likely to be seen in dynamic sites. Sequentially organized pages within a site are often the result of database queries that return a sequence of records. The most significant difference between dynamic and static Web sites is that the former are potentially infinite, in that, practically speaking, if not mathematically, there is an infinite number of pages that can be generated by a program using different data (think of the number of potential results pages that might ever be generated by Google), whereas a static site is necessarily finite.

Complementary Navigation Structures

In the preceding section we have suggested ways in which navigational information that expresses the underlying structure may be presented for each of the four possible site structures. However, it is also possible to provide navigational structures that do not map directly on to the actual site structure. For example, the support Web site for the first edition of this book had a hierarchical structure. One of the major sub-sites contained information for the book chapters, with a sub-sub-site for each chapter. All of these chapter sub-sites had an identical structure: for each chapter, we provided a list of key points, a set of links, a list of errata, some hints and answers to exercises, a collection of online examples and some extras. Although the site is hierarchical, conceptually these pages form a matrix, where each page corresponds to a combination of chapter and topic. This conceptual structure is expressed in the navigation for the site, shown in Figure 13.10, where the tabs along the top and left edges allow the site visitor to select any combination.

Another, more common, way in which navigation is provided that is complementary to the structure, rather than an expression of it, is the *site map*, which in its pure form is simply a list of the titles of all the pages in the site, with each title being a link to the corresponding page. Site maps are helpful to users who want to reach a particular page directly without following a series of links through a structure. They may also be useful when users get lost in a site, although if the site has a coherent structure which is expressed through its navigation, this should not happen.

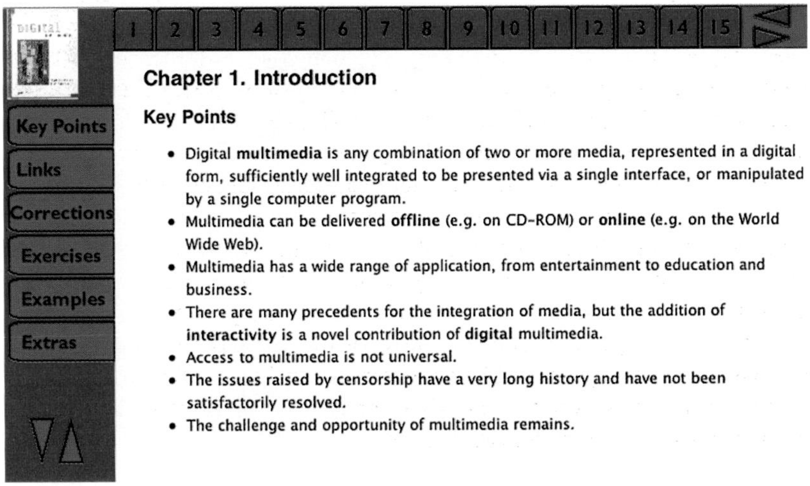

Figure 13.10 A hierarchy presented as a navigational matrix

Finally, complex sites usually provide a *search* facility, which enables users to find pages of interest and go directly to them (or, equivalently, to generate pages dynamically from database records that satisfy certain criteria). It is still important that users have some way of navigating from a page that they have reached via searching. A search may provide a starting point for further browsing, so it must be clear where the retrieved page fits within a site's structure, and which pages can be reached from it. In other words, searching is not a substitute for structure and navigational features.

Non-linear Time-based Structures

The structure of time-based media is determined by the order in which individual elements can be played. All traditional time-based media have a linear structure: the elements are frames of film or video, or notes in a piece of music, and so on, which are displayed or played one after another. In digital media, this linear order can be altered in response to input from the user. The creator of the presentation must provide controls to accept this input, and use the scripting facilities of the particular technology being used to provide a means of jumping to a different point in the presentation. These jumps define a structure for the presentation. In addition, time-based multimedia may exhibit parallelism, with several things going on at once, independently of each other. This parallelism provides additional, more radical, opportunities for non-linear structures. We will consider time-based structures in the context of Flash movies.

Loops

As we saw in Chapter 8, by analogy with film, Flash movies are divided into frames, which, in the absence of any scripts, are played back one after another at a fixed rate – the playback head moves along the movie one frame at a time, displaying the frame it is currently over. A script can be executed to transfer the playback head to any frame. As we will describe in more detail in Chapter 16, scripts may

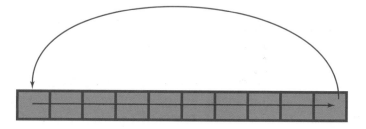

Figure 13.11 A simple looping structure

be attached to a frame, so that they are executed whenever the play-back head reaches that frame. A movie can therefore be made to loop: a script attached to the last frame causes the playback head to go to the first, as shown in Figure 13.11. This is a trivial structure, but more elaborate variations are possible.

For instance, the jump back may not be to the first frame, but instead to an intermediate frame, as shown in Figure 13.12. This gives rise to a structure consisting of an introductory section, which only appears once, followed by a loop. The introductory section might be a credit sequence or a copyright warning.

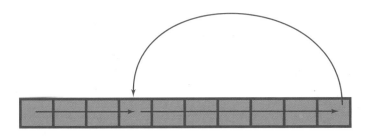

Figure 13.12 Introduction plus loop

More sophisticated looping structures make use of the ability to count within scripts, which makes it possible for a loop to be executed a specified number of times. (We will describe how this is achieved in detail in Chapter 16.) Figure 13.13 shows an example. This might represent a movie being shown in a kiosk at a trade show: the body of the inner loop could be some product presentation. After this had been shown five times, the movie loops all the way back to the beginning to display the company's animated logo. Thus the logo appears fairly often, but not between every presentation.

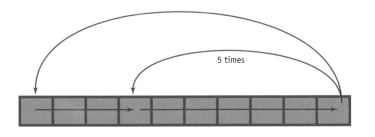

5 times

Figure 13.13 Counted loops

A script can also be used to stop playback, freezing the movie on the current frame. Like jumps, stops can be executed conditionally, so for example, a movie can be made to loop five times and then stop.

Another use of frames in which the movie always stops is error handling. In complicated interactive Flash movies, unexpected conditions can occur: a user may enter invalid data, or a network connection may fail, for instance. In such a case, if it is not possible to recover from the error, one response is for the movie to jump to a frame where a suitable error message is displayed, and then stop.

Branching

Looping structures which depend on scripts that are executed when the playback head reaches a particular frame are deterministic: you can predict exactly what will happen purely from inspecting the scripts and knowing which frames they are attached to. Richer structures require the jumps to be executed in response to user input. In Flash, this can be done by attaching scripts to buttons, which are graphical objects that appear on the screen when the movie is played back, but which respond to events, in particular to mouse clicks which occur when the cursor is over the button. In this sense, they are just like buttons in any graphical user interface, but in Flash movies, an arbitrary action can be made to occur in response to a mouse click, by attaching a suitable script to the button. In particular, the playback head can be made to jump to a different frame. This gives rise to some useful structures.

Perhaps the most common structure is a set of selections on a menu. The movie is divided into independent sections, together with a single menu frame, which contains buttons, each of which has attached to it a script causing a jump to the beginning of one of the sections. The menu frame has a script attached which stops playback there, and each section ends with a frame that causes a jump to the menu frame.

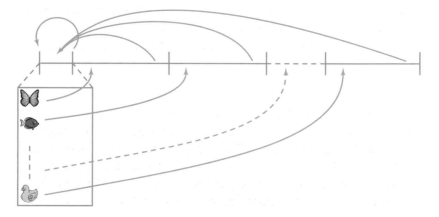

Figure 13.14 Selections

Figure 13.14 shows this structure in schematic form. Each of the icons shown on the menu frame will be a button.

You should be able to see that what we have referred to as the menu frame does indeed behave like a menu in a conventional user interface. However, the technique of providing a set of buttons in a stopped frame does not necessarily have to be used in the conventional way. It is an implementation of a more general *branching structure*, in which the user is able to choose from a set of alternatives the part of the movie to play next by clicking on one of a set of buttons. This general structure is equivalent to the network structure of hypertext, with the links being provided in the form of scripted jumps. Thus, using this method, a time-based presentation can be structured hierarchically or sequentially, or a mixture of both, just as a Web site can. However, whereas the destination of a link in a Web site is a page, which is essentially independent of time, the destination of a jump in a Flash movie is a section of movie, which plays through time, so the jump is like a cut to another scene in a film.

On a Web page, links are usually displayed in one of a few standard forms (underlined text, small image with rollover, etc.), with some ingenuity being required to change their appearance, but Flash buttons can be any shape and may be animated; they can be integrated into a movie in many different ways, so that, although the structure of a movie may be formally equivalent to a hierarchically organized Web site, it may work in a completely different way. By making the buttons appear as part of an animation – for instance, as signposts or characters – interaction more akin to that found in games can be provided. Generally, the time-based, graphical nature of Flash movies allows for a more playful approach to navigation than that which goes naturally with Web pages. At the same time, where conventionality and predictability are important, more advanced scripting techniques can be used to make elements of Flash movies look and behave like conventional interface elements such as checkboxes, radio buttons and drop-down menus.

Parallelism

As we explained in Chapter 8, a Flash movie can contain elements known as *movie clips*, which are self-contained movies-within-a-movie, each with its own timeline. A movie may contain many movie clips, which play back in parallel. In the absence of scripting, this is merely a convenient way of organizing a complicated movie. With some extra work by the animator, any scene built out of instances of

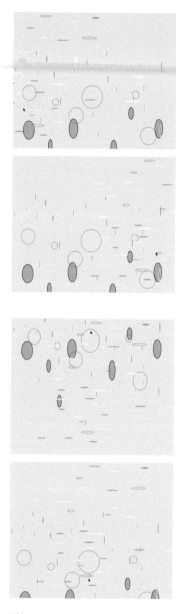

Figure 13.15 An animation responding to mouse movements: top pair, horizontal movement; bottom pair, vertical movement; facing page, random movements

movie clip symbols could be produced by animating each instance individually as a separate object, so the parallelism of the movie clips is not providing anything new by way of structure: the movie still plays back linearly.

However, movie clips can be controlled by scripting, just as movies can. A clip can be started, stopped, sent to a particular frame of its own timeline, or made to disappear, independently of any other clip or the main movie. Since scripts can perform arbitrary computation as well as controlling movie clips, this permits essentially infinite variations of behaviour, particularly as the computation can take account of variables such as the position of the cursor.

A very simple structure illustrates the richness that the combination of parallelism and interactivity permits. A Flash movie can be constructed that consists of a single frame, in which the playback head is stopped by a script. In this frame are placed two movie clips, both of the same size as the frame, positioned with their top left corners at the top left of the frame. For this to work, the foremost clip must have some transparent areas. If it does, when the movie is played, the user will see a composite frame composed of one clip overlaid on the other. Even if the two clips just loop, unless they are the same length, as the movie plays, a sequence of different composite frames much longer than either of the individual clips will be seen. For example, if one clip has 13 frames and the other 11, there will be 143 frames before the movie repeats. To make the movie more interesting, scripting can be used to arrange that the particular frame displayed from each clip at any moment is controlled by the position of the cursor. The clip at the front can be sent to a frame which is a function of the horizontal mouse coordinate, that at the back to a frame which is a function of the vertical coordinate. (For instance, when the cursor is half-way across the window, the front clip would go to its middle frame, when the cursor was at the extreme left, it would go to its first frame, and so on. Similarly, if the cursor was at the top of the window, the rear clip would be in its first frame, and so on.) If this is done, as the user moves the mouse, the two movies will interact in unpredictable (at least to the user) ways. Figure 13.15 shows a simple animation, which has been designed to emphasize the vertical and horizontal components, responding to mouse movements in this way – the pinkish shapes move across the screen in one movie clip, the green elements move down in the other. Note the position of the cursor in each screenshot.

Parallelism combined with interactivity offers a wealth of possibilities for organizing Flash movies, which we will explore in more detail in Chapter 16. Unlike hypermedia structures, structures of this sort do not readily lend themselves to systematization and classification. By the same token, they offer more possibilities for expression and innovation – and for confusion and obscurity.

In our description of structures, we have concentrated on the ways in which hypermedia or interactive time-based media can be put together in a navigable way. There is another layer of structure that is found in conventional media, concerned with the way in which narrative and exposition develop over the course of a film, book, piece of music, and so on. In narrative forms, such as film or the novel, there are well-developed theories that seek to explain how stories work, in terms of character, motivation, conflict and action. Narratives can be non-linear, in the sense that events do not unfold in the order they occur in the fictional time of the story. Discursive forms such as textbooks and lectures have their own theories that lead to familiar forms of exposition ('Say what you're going to say, say it, then say what you've just said', for example) and pedagogical features, such as summaries. As yet, there has been little or no attempt to develop corresponding theories of non-linear structures in hypermedia and interactive time-based media. Such a theory would help us answer questions such as, How can we encourage users to follow links? and, How can we ensure that users leave a site with a feeling of having reached a satisfactory conclusion in some sense? For some sites, there are clear answers to these questions. The sequence of forms you have to fill in in order to purchase items from an online store has an obvious, almost classical, 'narrative' structure – the user, as protagonist, overcomes a sequence of obstacles, such as filling in their address and credit card number, in order to achieve a desired goal, the purchase. Less goal-directed sites have less easily identifiable structures of this sort, which may explain why they are often unsatisfying.

Design Problems of the WWW

At first sight, apart from its horizontal orientation, a Web page is little different from a printed page in a book or magazine, and so you might expect that the principles familiar to graphic designers from print media could be applied directly to Web page design. Although it is true that valuable lessons can be learned from print design, certain technical constraints that the Web imposes make it impossible to transfer print-based designs directly to Web pages.

It must never be forgotten that Web pages are distributed over the Internet (or an intranet). This has three important implications. First,

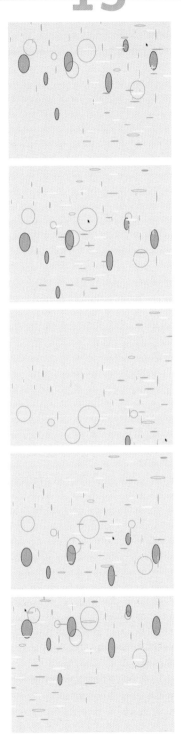

as we showed in more detail in Chapter 2, it takes time for a Web page to be downloaded to a user's machine and displayed there. Second, a page may be viewed on any machine connected to the network. Somehow, you need to make sure that a Web page will look good at any screen resolution, no matter which browser is being used, and how it has been configured, under any operating system. Finally, since the Internet at least is a public network, the designer is largely in the dark about the identity of the visitors to a Web page. They may come from a wide range of cultural and educational backgrounds, with different levels of computing skills, and some of them may possibly suffer from physical or cognitive disabilities.

Until relatively recently, the first of these restrictions had a clear and immediate consequence. As we have seen, still and moving images and sound all occupy large files, which take a long time to download over a slow connection. Therefore, it was prudent to avoid such media elements wherever possible. Of course, for some sites, images are essential, and for many others, the use of visual material can add interest, help with exposition, or simply improve the appearance of a page. There was thus a conflict between designers' ambitions to use images and the network's ability to deliver them. Where the vast majority of network connections are slow (56K modems or slower), the network inevitably wins in this conflict: even if designers use many large images, users don't bother to wait for them to download.

Now, however, matters are less clear-cut. Broadband access is available to consumers in many countries, but the availability is patchy, and the speed of connections that are defined as broadband varies surprisingly widely. The result is that visitors to a Web site may experience download times differing by a factor of up to 40, and there is no easy way of deducing whether a particular target audience will have a slow or fast connection. Blanket advice to eliminate graphics is no longer appropriate, but the designer is left with the dilemma of how to provide users who have a diverse range of connection speeds with a satisfying experience.

This dilemma is just one aspect of the overall Web design dilemma, which results from the heterogeneity of the Internet and its users. In an ideal world, a Web page will look good on a high-resolution monitor with millions of colours, the 14-inch monitor of a bargain-basement PC with limited graphics capabilities, a laptop's small screen, or even in greyscale on the tiny screen of a handheld PDA. It will look good no matter what set of fonts the user has available on their system, and it will look good on any browser the user may choose. In reality, few if any Web pages achieve this ideal.

The inventors of the WWW were aware of these problems from the first, and the original design of HTML and of Web browsers attempted to provide a solution. Text was allowed to reflow, in order to occupy the available window size; elements of a page could not be positioned absolutely, only placed within a single text flow; fonts were not specified explicitly, and type sizes were not absolute, only relative to a base size. The user was allowed control over the base size, as well as being allowed to choose the default fonts, and set the window size. Control was deliberately taken away from the page designer and given to the user.

Over the years, as we saw in Chapter 11, HTML has been extended and augmented with CSS stylesheets, to restore some of this control, and designers have devised various techniques that subvert the restrictions. However, because users still retain control over many aspects of the display of Web pages, and because Web browsers do not all implement the newer features of the Web completely or correctly, it is still quite likely that a particular page may appear very different

Figure 13.16 A Web page based on a printed design...

on different users' machines, and that many traditional design ideas from print media fail to work on the Web.

Figure 13.16 shows a Web page whose design could have been based on a company's printed flyer, as it appears in a browser window on a 1024×768 monitor. The page uses some simple but effective design tricks to help attract the reader's attention and convey its message: the company's name is set in a large distinctive font; less important information ('By appointment to the gentry') is set much smaller so as not to distract from the main message; whitespace is used to separate the elements of the page and to give it a neat and open look; strong vertical alignments connect the discrete blocks of information, with a horizontal rule being used to tie together the two sides of the page; the vertical block of colour leads the eye to the crucial contact details in the bottom right corner. The design is not particularly exciting, but it helps the page do its job of telling the reader what the company does and how to get in touch.

Figure 13.17 shows the same Web page as it would appear in a browser on an old 640×480 monitor, of the sort still found in many homes, schools and corporations. The alignments are now completely ineffective, because you can't see the elements that are aligned at the same time. The whitespace has become a waste of screen area, which has to be scrolled over to find the information on the page. It is just about possible that a user who, following the visual hints in the horizontal rule and the vertical bar of colour, scrolled across the page and then down, might fail to see the company address and telephone number in the bottom left corner. Matters are not much better on a typical 800×600 laptop screen.

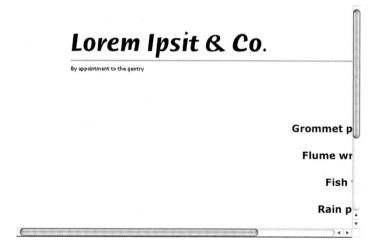

Figure 13.17 ...displayed on a small monitor...

However, small screens are just one of the perils that threaten our page design. A user may not have the fonts used on this page installed on their system. As a result, the default that they had set in their browser would be substituted. This would not cause any information to be lost, but it would undermine the visual design, making the company name less prominent, and possibly suggesting a different character for the company. In Figure 13.18, for instance, the default Times Roman font has been substituted, giving the company a much more formal conservative image than the original design. In this screenshot we have also shown the effect of letting the browser choose the colours of links, instead of having this specified on the page. (This is an option that a user may choose to set in some browsers, including Internet Explorer.) Some usability studies suggest that users prefer to have all links signified by the default blue text, but the effect here is an unpleasant colour clash. You may dismiss this as 'mere aesthetics', but for anyone with an eye for colour, it diminishes the impact of the tastefully restrained colour scheme of the Web page as it was designed, suggesting that the company too might be a bit tacky.

Another way in which users may choose to control the appearance of pages in their Web browsers is by changing the base font size. There are two main reasons for this. One is poor eyesight, something

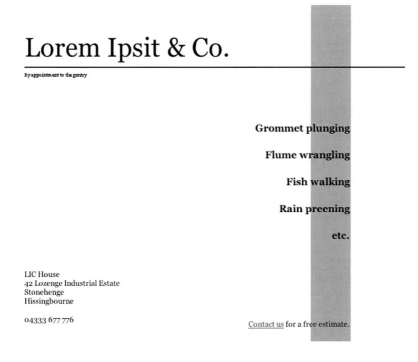

Lorem Ipsit & Co.

By appointment to the gentry

Grommet plunging

Flume wrangling

Fish walking

Rain preening

etc.

LIC House
42 Lozenge Industrial Estate
Stonehenge
Hissingbourne

04333 677 776

Contact us for a free estimate.

Figure 13.18 ...with substituted fonts and altered link colour...

that affects everybody as they get older. The other is high-resolution screens. People whose monitors are capable of displaying at high resolutions often choose to maximize the size and number of windows they can get on the screen by setting the resolution very high, and then, in order to read the text in the windows, increasing the font size. Figure 13.19 shows the sort of disaster that may result.

Figure 13.19 ...with font sizes increased...

Worse things can happen to a carefully designed layout. The page shown in these illustrations was laid out, in accordance with current thinking on best Web design practice, using CSS positioning. Older browsers do not implement CSS positioning, and most modern browsers allow the user to disable CSS. Figure 13.20 shows what happens to the page when this is done. It's little wonder that many Web designers are reluctant to use CSS, and prefer to resort to tricks involving tables and images to give them precise control over layout. As we will discuss shortly, this is, however, undesirable from other points of view.

Finally, although no reliable estimates of their number are available, there are Web users who prefer to use a purely text-based browser. Figure 13.21 shows our example page in such a browser. It is instructive to observe that the result is actually more readable than the

Lorem Ipsit & Co.

By appointment to the gentry

LIC House
42 Lozenge Industrial Estate
Stonehenge
Hissingbourne

04333 677 776

Grommet plunging

Flume wrangling

Fish walking

Rain preening

etc.

Contact us for a free estimate.

Figure 13.20 ...without CSS...

```
                                                    Lorem Ipsit
item5

LIC House
42 Lozenge Industrial Estate
Stonehenge
Hissingbourne

04333 677 776

Contact us for a free estimate.

Grommet plunging

Flume wrangling

Fish walking

Rain preening

etc.

Lorem Ipsit & Co.

-----------------------------------------------------------------------

By appointment to the gentry
```

Figure 13.21 ...in a text-only browser

display in a conventional browser without CSS support shown in the previous screenshot.

This small example should be enough to demonstrate that if you approach Web page design with the idea of creating a layout that everyone will see in the same way, you are doomed to failure. Responding by attempting to force as much of the design as you can into a fixed format will usually just make matters worse. Some designers are so attached to their choice of fonts, for example, that rather than allow browsers to substitute a different font on a system where the chosen one is not installed, they will render their text and incorporate it in the page as a GIF image. This slows down page loading, but more seriously, if a user has disabled image loading or is using a text-only browser, the text will not appear at all, just a missing image icon.

The approach of reducing everything to the level of the most primitive text-based browsers is equally unsatisfactory. Graphic design achieves a purpose in facilitating visual communication. If you reduce your pages to a single text flow in Times Roman, you will not be communicating as effectively as you could. You might justly be accused of abdicating your responsibility in some cases. It is well known to book designers, for example, that text divided into excessively long lines is difficult to read, but since HTML text will reflow to fit into the browser window, users who stretch their windows out to fit a wide screen will inevitably be confronted with long lines if you fall back on default HTML layout. (The lines will be too close together in most browsers, too.) You should not overlook the fact that having something nice to look at pleases most people and is more likely to generate a positive response to the site. This is an important consideration in any commercial site that is trying to persuade visitors to part with money.

Some designers prefer to sidestep the issue by designing for one particular configuration, usually on the grounds that it is the most common among their target audience. This might be acceptable if your pages were going to be distributed over a company intranet, in an organization where every employee had been issued with an identical standard PC which was set up in an approved manner by the corporate IT department. (But what happens when the budget allows everybody to upgrade?) However, on the Internet there is such a diversity of systems that a design that only displays well in Internet Explorer 5.5 under Windows XP on a 17-inch monitor will not appear to its best advantage for many users. Whatever the purpose of your Web site, whether it is to provide information or entertainment, to advertise goods or services, or to provide ecommerce facilities, it should reach as many people as possible, and it is foolish to, in effect, turn people away just because they choose to use an unconventional Web browser or operating system.[†]

† In any case, Internet Explorer allows the user to change so many settings, that you would also be insisting that they use all the defaults.

A much better solution to the dilemma, one which has many additional advantages, is to face the fact that a Web page is not like a printed page, which always looks the same. The same page may appear differently to different users. The important thing is to ensure that the page *transforms gracefully*. That is, although your page may not always display the way you designed it, it should remain readable and navigable – and, whenever possible, attractive – in browsers that are not able to cope with the full range of features you have used. The good news is that this isn't particularly difficult. We will describe specific techniques in the next section.

Flash movies on the Web suffer from some of the same problems as HTML pages: they might be too large to be displayed on a small monitor without scrolling, large SWF files take a long time to download over a slow connection, and complex animations may not play smoothly on an older machine. Flash does, however, allow fonts to be embedded in a movie, so that the problem of font substitution need not arise. Within a Flash movie, the layout of objects is fixed, making Flash attractive to traditional designers who do not wish to compromise their layouts. Also, since Flash movies are always played by the same plug-in, no matter which browser is being used, there are fewer problems with incompatibilities between different systems. (Flash is not entirely free from platform-incompatibility, since the plug-ins for different operating systems are not quite identical, and there are now different versions of the plug-in, corresponding to different releases of Flash.)

Accessibility

The problems of designing Web pages that work effectively on any browser are thrown into sharp focus by considering design for users with disabilities of one sort and another. Among the people who might wish to visit your Web site, there may be some who cannot see or whose vision is impaired to some extent in some way (for example, they may have limited colour perception); there may be people who cannot read, or understand what they read, very easily; there may be people who are unable to use a mouse or keyboard; and there may be people who cannot hear. Any of these disabilities may make it difficult or impossible for them to use a conventional Web browser, and they may therefore rely on *assistive technology* – specialized hardware and software, such as screen readers – to access Web pages. In such a case, it is desirable that a page should transform gracefully into a form that can be rendered using such assistive technology. As a bonus, pages that are *accessible* in this sense will also tend to transform gracefully when they are viewed in browsers that do not support all the features of modern Web pages, or on limited hardware – a page that is accessible to people who are colour-blind will be readable on a PDA with a greyscale screen, for example. Thus, by attending to accessibility concerns, you will overcome some of the problems resulting from the heterogeneous nature of the WWW described in the previous section.

If you are not convinced that accessibility is desirable for helping your Web sites reach the largest possible audience, and do not feel any moral obligation to make them accessible to people with disabilities, you should at least be aware that in many countries legislation places an obligation on those who maintain certain Web sites to ensure that they are accessible. In the United States, for example, Section 508 of the Rehabilitation Act requires that all Federal Web sites, including those maintained under contract by private companies, must conform to accessibility standards based on the Web Accessibility Initiative Guidelines for Accessible Content (which we will describe later in this section). In the United Kingdom, the Disability Discrimination Act 1995 covers (among other things) 'access to and use of information services', and makes it an offence to discriminate against a disabled person by making it unreasonably difficult for them to access the services, and imposes a duty to rectify the situation. Similar legislation in Australia was successfully used to sue the Sydney Organizing Committee for the Olympic Games for failing to make their Web site accessible to blind users. Many other countries have similar legislation.

Most Web designers have little or no first-hand knowledge of the problems disabled users face, or any experience with the specialized hardware that is employed to help them use their computers and browse the Web, so when it comes to accessibility, there is a need for guidance from specialists in the field. The World Wide Web Consortium's *Web Accessibility Initiative (WAI)* has issued a series of documents offering guidelines for accessibility of pages and techniques for achieving it. We will summarize some of the most important guidelines, but strongly urge you to read the relevant documents in full.

Textual Equivalents

One of the easiest and most helpful things you can do is provide textual equivalents for all the non-textual elements of your page, such as images and applets. HTML provides several attributes for this purpose, as well as the **object** element, which can have alternative text as its content, as we described in Chapter 12.

The **img** element has an attribute **alt**, whose value is a string which provides a textual alternative to the image. This should be a brief description. Where the image has an iconic function, the attribute should describe its purpose, not its appearance. For instance, if a picture of a house is used to indicate a link to the site's home page, the **alt** text should be "home page" rather than "little house". Generally, the **alt** text should be precise and concise, but provide as much detail as necessary. For instance, if an image shows a histogram of the number of Web users with certain disabilities, the text should be something like "histogram showing distribution of disabilities among Web users" rather than something vague, like "data graph". On the other hand, the text should not be too long. If a long description is needed, use the **longdesc** attribute, described below. If you really must render some text as an image, you can use the **alt** attribute to provide an alternative version of the textual content. Where images have no semantic content, for example when they are used as spacers, the **alt** text should be an empty string "". User agents will be able to recognize such images as insignificant and skip them.

The **area** element used to create hotspots in image maps also has an **alt** attribute, which can be used to supply textual links as an alternative. In the case of image maps, if you want to be on the safe side, it is also advisable to provide redundant textual links elsewhere on the page. The **alt** text is also displayed in place of the image or hotspot by text-only browsers. In fact, a text-only browser such as Lynx provides a good way of judging the way a Web page will be presented to a blind user, since the text read aloud by a screen reader will often be approximated by such a browser's rendering of the page.

Where an image contains substantive information, as in our example of a histogram being used to display statistical data, the **alt** attribute on its own cannot offer the same information as the image. Instead, a longer textual alternative, such as, in this case, a list of the data values, should be supplied in another document, and the **longdesc** (long description) attribute should be used to point to it: this attribute's value is the URL of the document containing the long description. In cases where **longdesc** is used, the **alt** text should provide an indication of the type of information in the image, so that a user can decide whether it is worth following the **longdesc** link. It is not appropriate to place a complete long description in the page, because some users will not want to read it, so its presence will just interfere with their reading of the page's main text.

Where multimedia elements are embedded using object elements, a textual alternative can be provided in the element's content, as we mentioned in Chapter 12. If embed must be used, it too has an alt attribute. So does the deprecated applet element, but in the case of applets there are additional considerations: an applet provides its own interface, which must be made accessible too. This can only be done by the programmer who creates the applet. Wherever possible, it is better to avoid the use of applets in Web pages where accessibility is important.

Providing a text string as an alternative to an embedded video clip is better than nothing, but it is preferable in such a case to add a *synchronized* textual description to the movie, which describes what is going on as the movie plays. Users should have the option of hiding or displaying the textual description. QuickTime allows you to create text tracks which are synchronized with a movie's audio and video tracks, which serve admirably for this purpose. Where other time-based media are being used, it may be possible to take advantage of SMIL (see Chapter 15) in order to provide a synchronized text track.

We have concentrated on providing text alternatives for the benefit of blind users, because text can be read by software, but text can also be used to provide a transcript of audio tracks, for the benefit of the deaf and hard of hearing, just as closed-captioning and teletext captions are used on television. If a text track includes both a transcription of any dialogue and a summary of what is being shown on the screen, it can serve the needs of both blind and deaf users.

In this section we have advocated the use of text alternatives to other types of content. We should stress that it is not necessary to *replace* images, video, and so on, with text. The important thing is to provide an alternative to allow the page to transform gracefully into a textual form. In fact, it would be a mistake to remove all images in favour of their textual alternatives on the grounds of accessibility. People with dyslexia, and people who never learned to read very well, will find it easier to absorb information when it is presented in the form of an image or an animation instead of as text. Images can often convey information more concisely and effectively than words to any users who are able to to see them – consider a weather map, for instance. Opportunities for communicating effectively using such images should not be discarded, but an alternative should be provided as well. Accessible sites should be accessible to everyone, so the ideal is to provide information in different ways where necessary, rather than catering for any one class of users at the expense of others.

Markup

The second major step that you can take to make pages accessible is to use structural markup. Separating structure and content from appearance, by using CSS to specify layout and typography as we explained in Chapter 11, allows assistive technologies to present the page in whatever way is appropriate to a particular user's needs. If you tag headings as such, by using h1, h2, and so on, software can identify the headings and present them to the user as an outline of the page. A blind user can thus scan the headings rapidly to get some idea of what the page is about before having it read by their screen reader in detail. Similarly, using the various list elements for marking up lists allows them to be presented in a suitable way. Abusing document elements as a way of imposing a particular form of presentation instead of tagging structural elements of the document (for instance, using blockquote as a way of indenting a paragraph that isn't a quotation) can interfere with the efforts of assistive software to extract a document's structure in order to present it in a suitable way. If the markup itself contains just the structural information, then the structure can readily be extracted. If the appearance is controlled by a stylesheet, it can be overridden by a user who needs information displayed in a particular way.

The WAI guidelines tell you not to use deprecated attributes, such as font, since these do not conform to the principles of structural markup. However, the XHTML standard stipulates that user agents should ignore attributes that are not part of XHTML, so their use should not do any harm. In fact, using such attributes can help your pages transform gracefully: they can provide a fall-back for browsers that do not implement CSS. You might argue that they prevent a user turning off all typographic styling by turning off stylesheets. There is something to be said on either side of the argument. However, since the guidelines do not allow the use of deprecated attributes and elements in pages, if you wish to conform to the guidelines, you should not use them.

A special case of the use of structural markup and stylesheets is the use of CSS positioning instead of tables to control the layout of text. (The use of tables to lay out images is less contentious.) Consider the two-column layout shown in Figure 13.22. If the two columns had been laid out as columns of a table, a screen reader, reading the text

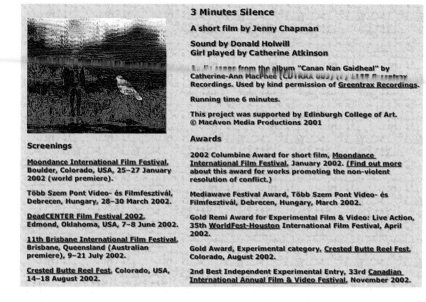

3 Minutes Silence

A short film by Jenny Chapman

Sound by Donald Holwill
Girl played by Catherine Atkinson

from the album "Canan Nan Gaidheal" by Catherine-Ann MacPhee (CDTRAX 003) Recordings. Used by kind permission of Greentrax Recordings.

Running time 6 minutes.

This project was supported by Edinburgh College of Art.
© MacAvon Media Productions 2001

Screenings

Moondance International Film Festival, Boulder, Colorado, USA, 25–27 January 2002 (world premiere).

Több Szem Pont Video- és Filmfesztivál, Debrecen, Hungary, 28–30 March 2002.

DeadCENTER Film Festival 2002, Edmond, Oklahoma, USA, 7–8 June 2002.

11th Brisbane International Film Festival, Brisbane, Queensland (Australian premiere), 9–21 July 2002.

Crested Butte Reel Fest, Colorado, USA, 14–18 August 2002.

Awards

2002 Columbine Award for short film, Moondance International Film Festival, January 2002. (Find out more about this award for works promoting the non-violent resolution of conflict.)

Mediawave Festival Award, Több Szem Pont Video- és Filmfesztivál, Debrecen, Hungary, March 2002.

Gold Remi Award for Experimental Film & Video: Live Action, 35th WorldFest-Houston International Film Festival, April 2002.

Gold Award, Experimental category, Crested Butte Reel Fest, Colorado, August 2002.

2nd Best Independent Experimental Entry, 33rd Canadian International Annual Film & Video Festival, November 2002.

Figure 13.22 A two-column layout

as it appears on the screen, might well read straight across, producing garbled text like "Find out more Boulder, Colorado…" However, if the two columns were div elements, positioned absolutely with CSS, the text would naturally be read correctly, provided only that the two divs appear in the correct order (first column first) in the HTML file. Since they are absolutely positioned, they could appear in either order and still be displayed correctly in a CSS-enabled browser, while a screen reader or any user agent that ignored the stylesheet would present them in the order they appear in the HTML source. If the HTML is generated automatically by a Web authoring application, the divisions may be placed in the file in the order they were created, the reverse of that order, or according to their z-ordering. It is usually possible to reorder items, and this should be done to ensure that they will be in the right order in the generated HTML.

Structure, Navigation and Links

Using markup correctly makes a page's structure evident, but this leaves open the question of how a page ought to be structured. Various techniques, which will probably be familiar to you if you do much technical writing, are advocated for making pages easier to scan, and helping people with cognitive problems more easily appreciate the relationship between elements of the page. These include using headings and sub-headings to identify the main divisions and sub-divisions; using bullets and numbered lists to itemize groups of related points; using one paragraph per idea; and introducing each paragraph with a sentence that summarizes that paragraph's idea. If your intention is to convey simple information in a direct way, these rules will help you do so, whoever is reading your page, but they are too simple-minded to be used as a guide to writing style for all occasions.

At the beginning of this chapter we examined the structure of Web sites and the navigational mechanisms that go with them. Accessibility guidelines stress the importance of providing a navigational overview of the site, preferably in the form of a navigation bar that is separate from each page's main content, to help orient people who easily become confused, and to make it easier for assistive technology to isolate the navigational elements of a page. This simply reinforces current practice.

Because links might be removed from their context, the text that is the content of the a element (or the alt text if the link is attached to an image) should be meaningful in isolation. For instance, a link to a page from which a user can download a demo version of some software should be implemented along the lines of the upper example in Figure 13.23, rather than the lower, since the text Click here in isolation provides no clues about where you might end up if you click on it.

Download a demo version [5MB]

Click here to download demo

Figure 13.23 Good (top) and bad (bottom) link text

Assistive technology may become confused by frames. In Chapter 11, we briefly discussed some of the disadvantages of frames. Accessibility provides you with another reason to avoid them. If you must use frames, consult the WAI Content Accessibility Guidelines for some advice on how to make them more accessible.

Colour and Motion

Roughly 5% of the male population are unable to distinguish between certain colours, usually reds and greens. A much smaller number of people suffer a similar inability to distinguish between blues and yellows, and a few are totally unable to distinguish colours at all, seeing entirely in shades of grey. Many more use PDAs and old computers with black and white monitors, so in total there is a large number of users who cannot always discern colour contrasts. The WAI therefore advise you not to rely on colour alone to convey information. If you wish to be entirely safe, this means that any colour coding of information should be backed up by some other form of discrimination.

Figure 13.24 Distinguishing confusable colours by brightness

For instance, if you use a stylesheet to indicate hypertext links by setting them in a different colour from the main body text, you should also underline them or use some other typographical treatment to make them stand out. Similarly, if you display several sets of data on the same histogram, as well as colouring the columns for each set in a different colour, you could use cross-hatching and other patterns to distinguish them.

This may be going too far, though. When we say that people cannot distinguish colours, in terms of the models described in Chapter 6, what we mean is that they cannot reliably distinguish different hues. This still leaves saturation and brightness. As long as your chosen colours differ sufficiently in those parameters as well as hue, they will be distinguishable: a light red will look different from a dark green, even in greyscale. (See Figure 13.24.) If your page has a coloured background and you use coloured text, it is particularly important that your colours have good tonal contrast, otherwise some people may not be able to read the text at all. Notice, though, that the eye may not be a very good guide: in the pair of images at the right of Figure 13.24, the red and green look as if they are equally bright, but in fact they can be distinguished in greyscale. It is necessary to try reducing your image to greys to determine whether or not colours will become indistinguishable.

The worst of the vogue for using animated GIFs, dynamic HTML and Flash to make elements of a page move and blink on and off seems to have passed, but, in case it makes a comeback, you should bear in mind that rapidly flashing elements can trigger epileptic attacks, so blinking text should be avoided on health grounds if for no other reason.

If you do want to use animated effects on your pages, you should only do so in a way that users can easily turn off, since the movement may be an additional unnecessary distraction for people who already have difficulty understanding information. Most browsers allow the user to disable JavaScript and to display animated GIFs as static images. If Flash animations are used, some controls should be provided to allow the user to stop them or skip to another page. It is also the case that users with cognitive difficulties (as well as technically unsophisticated users) can become confused if windows open spontaneously, so you should avoid using scripts that cause windows to pop up. Many browsers and utilities now block the opening of pop-up windows, since they are most often used for advertisements, so it is prudent to avoid their use anyway.

Flash and Accessibility

Although Flash is increasingly being used to provide forms and other interactive user interfaces to Web applications, it is still basically a time-based visual medium, which by its nature is not readily accessible to those with impaired vision. Even allowing for that, until recently, Flash was widely criticized on the grounds that no content from a Flash movie could be made accessible – the text and structure of the movie's content are embedded in the SWF file in a way that is not readily accessible to screen readers or other assistive technology. With the release of Flash MX in 2003, Macromedia took some steps to remedy this defect. The main innovation is a facility for providing names for all elements of a movie that are used for interaction, so that they can be identified textually. This means that, where Flash has been used as an alternative to HTML for creating a user interface to a Web application, blind users can access the elements of the interface. In addition, the contents of all text fields are automatically made available to screen readers, so that any text that appears in a movie can be read. This means that it is possible to use Flash text to provide a synchronized text track to a movie.

The interface between the Flash movie and screen reading software is provided by Microsoft Active Accessibility (MSAA), a standard technology for interfacing applications to screenreaders. MSAA is only available on Windows systems, so users on other platforms cannot benefit from Flash accessibility. If accessibility is important, it is better to stick with W3C technologies, since these all have accessibility features built into them.

Web Design Issues

Multimedia design is a big subject, which we cannot do full justice to in the space of a single chapter. In this section, we will identify some of the remaining important issues, concentrating on the Web as the most important means of multimedia delivery.

So far as they concern layout, presentation and content, ideas of 'good' design are very much a matter of fashion and cultural sensitivity. It is true that a few classics of design may be widely admired and achieve a relatively long life, but on the whole, what looks wonderful in one decade (or even one year) becomes outmoded, or positively unthinkable, in the next. Fashion in clothing illustrates this most effectively – consider the history of flared trousers, or the bustle. But it applies equally to all aspects of design, from fonts to tableware to billboards and TV advertisements. In the heterogeneous environment of the World Wide Web, it is important to remember that what may be the height of good taste and fashion for one group of people could be grossly offensive to another. Even at a particular moment in time, and in a single place, many different standards of design will obtain among different social, economic and cultural groups. With multimedia productions often intended to reach a worldwide audience, the picture is extremely complex and unclear. It is highly probable that what seems good to you, or in your immediate social and cultural context, will most certainly seem bad to at least some part of a world audience. So, the wider the audience you wish to reach, the greater the challenge – but where you have a specific and restricted target audience, your task will be less difficult.

Besides the subjective and aesthetic aspects of good and bad design, there are some more tangible issues which must be addressed.

Correctness

In the entirely justifiable desire to encourage interface design that is easy to use, HCI and usability consultants have tended to overlook a fundamental requirement: *things have to work*. There is nothing less usable than a site that does not render properly, reacts to a user's input with an error message or causes a browser to crash or freeze. If any of these things happen, it does not matter at all how well designed the placement of the navigation bar is, or how readable the text is by colour-blind users.

Problems with correctness can arise even with the simplest of static HTML pages, as Figure 13.25 demonstrates. Image distortions such as this (which arise from explicitly setting the width and height attributes of an img tag to values that do not match the actual dimensions of the image in the version at the top) can arise if an image is carelessly replaced by another one when a page is being edited, or a template is being instantiated, either manually or automatically. Less extreme distortion than that exhibited here might not be noticed on a cursory examination.

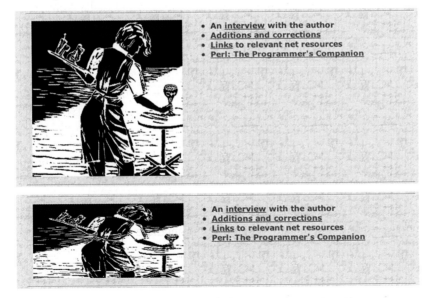

Figure 13.25 An incorrectly scaled image

More commonly, errors are associated with scripting. Scripting is a form of programming, and programming is difficult and error-prone. (Don't let anyone tell you otherwise.) Unlike mainstream programming languages, scripting languages such as JavaScript do not provide much linguistic support for ensuring the correctness of scripts. Declarations are not mandatory, typing is dynamic and thus cannot be checked at compile-time, objects are constructed dynamically and not constrained to a class with a well-defined set of methods. All of these factors mean that most errors in scripts can only be detected when the script is run, with the result that the user, not the scripter, gets to see error messages. Some errors, such as referring to an object that doesn't exist (for instance, by mis-spelling its name), do not even generate messages; the script just doesn't work. If a malfunctioning script prevents parts of a page being displayed or stops a navigation bar working, the page is useless. Scripts that are handwritten must be scrupulously checked and tested. If scripts are generated automatically by a Web-authoring program, they are likely to be more reliable than those you write yourself if you are not an experienced programmer, but they should still be tested. If there is any doubt that a particular page element that relies on a script will work reliably, leave it out.

Errors in HTML syntax can cause a page to render incorrectly, or not at all. Even cursory testing will show up many such errors, but, paradoxically, the fact that Web browsers have traditionally been forgiving of ill-formed HTML means that mistakes of this kind may only show up in certain browsers, while others manage to cope with them. To be sure that your HTML will work on any browser, you should validate it, using one of the available online validation services or the built-in validation tools of any Web authoring package you use. This will ensure that it conforms to the relevant standard, so that it should display on any browser that correctly implements the standard. You may, however, find that validation is too strict, since the use of deprecated elements and attributes is tagged as an error, whereas it may actually assist in the page's graceful transformation, as we described earlier. You should, however, always avoid extensions to HTML which are specific to one browser, such as the **bgproperties** attribute of the **body** element, which only works on Internet Explorer for Windows, and may produce a complete mess on other browsers.

The penultimate sentence of the previous paragraph conceals the flaw in the arguments for correctness that we are putting forward. Browsers can contain bugs, too, and most of them do. You have no control over this; all you can do, and all legions of Web developers have done, is devise work-rounds to avoid the more common browser bugs. This can give rise to a vicious circle, whereby new browsers have to be written to accommodate the work-rounds that have been used to accommodate the bugs in older browsers, otherwise established Web sites fail to work under the new browser. Sadly, many of the worst bugs in the leading browsers are concerned with their support for CSS, otherwise the salvation of Web design. Pragmatically, the best thing to do is to try and avoid using features that are not correctly implemented in commonly-used browsers. If this cannot be done, then stick with the standards and do whatever you can to encourage the browser vendors to implement them correctly. (This is easier for Open Source browsers such as Mozilla, of course.)

Our remarks about the importance of correctness in scripts apply with even greater force to server-side programs that are part of a Web application. When the server-side logic fails, the whole application cannot perform its function. Many such programs are written in Perl or PHP, which suffer from the same shortcomings with respect to correctness as JavaScript. Server-side Java applets and JSP pages are more likely to be reliable. In complex Web applications, which use a mixture of client-side and server-side scripts, together with a database system running on the server, there is considerable scope for errors, not only in the coding but also in the logical design of the system. Here, the full gamut of testing and quality assurance techniques developed by software engineers over the years should be employed. Multimedia professionals who are only amateur programmers should think twice before attempting to implement such systems.

Content

One thing on which usability studies, anecdotal evidence, the example of established media, and common sense all agree is that the most important thing about a Web site is its content. The most beautifully designed and accessible site will fail to attract visitors if the material on the site is of no interest to anybody. In contrast, visitors will keep coming back to a site that offers interesting, informative or entertaining content, even if its design and usability leave something to be desired in conventional terms.

This has become evident in the phenomenon of *Weblogs*, which are no more than pages of chronologically arranged entries (usually a paragraph or two of text) that can easily be updated by a non-technical user. The ease of updating means that Weblogs tend to be updated frequently and provide a rapid form of publication that is available to just about anyone with an Internet connection. The immediacy of Weblogs and the broad range of facts and opinions that are published through them makes them highly attractive to many people, who see them as fulfilling one of the original promises of the Internet, to provide an alternative and independent means of information dissemination, and a platform for views outside the mainstream establishment. As a recent instance, during the US-led invasion of Iraq in 2003, usage statistics show that a huge number of people turned to Weblogs as an alternative to the government propaganda being put out by the mainstream news media and their associated Web sites. At least one of these sites (the BBC's news site) even added their own Weblog page that was updated by their reporters in the region. This often provided a more vivid account of what was going on than the edited reports presented on the site's conventional, more elaborately designed, pages.

Weblogs can be made quite attractive, but usually they are no more than a long page of text divided into short entries. Design skills are rarely in evidence, and the usual length of the pages demands scrolling, but the immediacy and personal nature of the content makes up for these shortcomings. Although the inference that people will put up with indifferent design and certain usability problems in order to get at content that they consider worthwhile should not be taken as an excuse for poor design or inscrutable user interfaces, it should be borne in mind that design is subservient to content and it should not become an aim in itself. (Unless, that is, the design *is* the content: showcase sites for designers' skills are a special case.)

Weblogs are not the only sort of page whose content can be compelling irrespective of its design. Pages containing hard information, such as the support knowledge bases of software vendors, online lecture notes for college courses, and academic research papers, are usually spartan in design at best, and often are barely designed at all, simply consisting of the text and some images laid out using the default HTML layout. People will read these pages because they need to know what they say. However, even in the case of pages where the need to know is compelling, good design has an important role to play, just as it has in the design of a textbook or an academic journal. Fonts can be more or less readable; line length and leading can make the text tiring or easy to read; whitespace, font changes and alignment can be used to separate or group together elements and to make headings and emphasized text stand out. Navigation bars can be easy to find and obvious to use, and colour schemes can be chosen to be easy on the eye and distinguishable by colour-blind users, and so on. All of these traditional design factors should be used not only to make a site on which users will find the information they are looking for, but to make them feel welcome and comfortable using the site, and not feel that they are fighting to extract information from it.

Some content, however, can interfere with a site as badly as poor design can. We refer, of course, to advertisements. For many sites, carrying advertising is the only means of making money. Web users are reluctant to pay directly for access to sites, being accustomed to most things being free on the Internet. However, it costs money to maintain and host a Web site, and many excellent sites are only able to continue in existence because of advertising income. In return for this income, advertisers require that their adverts attract attention. Hence, advertisements often use animation, since movement draws the eye. For a long time, advertisements nearly all took the form of banners at either the top or bottom of a page. This was relatively easy to accommodate in a page design, but it also made it easy for people to ignore advertising banners by not looking at those regions of the page. Increasingly, advertisements are occupying more conspicuous locations, including in the worst case, a box in the middle of the page, forcing text to run round it. Scripts are often used to spawn pop-up windows with advertising messages in.

Many users object to intrusive advertising on the Web and take steps to frustrate it, by turning off GIF animation, blocking pop-up windows and even disabling image loading in their browsers. Browsers cannot reliably distinguish between advertisements and legitimate uses of animated GIFs and pop-up windows by the site itself, so effectively these techniques are no longer available to the Web designer. (It might be argued that this is no bad thing.)

On the other side of this issue, designing banner ads is itself something of a design challenge. The space is limited and an unusual shape, and has to be used to get across a message to an unreceptive audience. It appears to be the case, though, that banner ads are on their way out, to be replaced by larger advertisements, which more closely resemble their printed equivalents, on the one hand, and text-only ads, often returned along with the results from a search engine, on the other. It seems certain, though, that for the foreseeable future, Web designers are going to have to cohabit on commercial sites with advertisements, and modify their designs accordingly. At the least, by using alt attributes and so on, you should ensure that advertisements do not compromise your site's accessibility.

Usability

Graphical user interfaces are a relatively late arrival on the computing scene. For many years, users barely interacted with computers at all. Programs took input data from a file, or a deck of punched cards, did some computation with it, and produced output data, which was often printed out to be perused away from the machine. It was entirely natural under those circumstances that computer scientists and programmers should be primarily concerned with data structures, algorithms and programming techniques. This emphasis continued when interactive terminals and personal computers appeared, but these new sorts of computing system provided opportunities for interacting with programs while they were executing, and this in turn demanded that programmers provide some sort of interface with the user in order for that interaction to take place. However, in many cases, this interface was considered a mere cosmetic embellishment to the serious business of computation, and little thought was given to its design.

The graphical user interface (GUI), designed at Xerox Palo Alto Research Labs, popularized by the Macintosh computer, and developed commercially into the dominant interface paradigm by Microsoft Windows, changed all that. GUIs made computers more accessible to people with little technical knowledge, who tended to perceive the interface as being identical with the computing system. Interface design moved from a marginalized cosmetic function to acquire central importance, and the discipline of human–computer interaction (HCI) began to receive considerable attention. HCI is a multi-disciplinary subject, embracing sociology and cognitive psychology as well as computer science and software engineering.

Interactive multimedia by definition presents a user interface. In the case of Web applications, we might well say that the multimedia element (the Web pages that users see in their browsers) *is* the user interface to the computation that is going on in the server. It should not be surprising, therefore, that in recent years the HCI community has begun to examine multimedia, in particular the WWW. Most of the work has concentrated on the *usability* of Web sites – how easy is it for visitors to a site to find information they are looking for, or use services offered through the site?

Clearly, these are questions of enormous importance. Unfortunately, although a great deal of work has been published on the subject, and guidelines and rules are offered with an air of immense authority, much of the underlying research is poor and the data used to support the conclusions are flimsy. HCI aspires to an empirical, scientific approach to its subject matter, but it has long been plagued by poor experimental methodology. Results are often based on small, unrepresentative samples, analyses of the statistical significance of data are rudimentary, experiments are poorly designed, and experimental controls are weak or non-existent. Web usability studies are often subject to the same faults. For example, Jakob Nielsen, the author of one of the most influential books on Web usability, proudly tells us that his conclusions are based on observations of 400 users – compared with the hundreds of millions of Web users, a sample of homeopathic potency! (To put this in perspective, medical studies of the influence of diet on aspects of health often use samples of around 100,000 subjects, and the results are frequently considered inconclusive.) Not only are the numbers of experimental subjects dwarfed by the size of the total user population; more seriously, no attempt is reported to have been made at ensuring that the sample is representative of the distribution of Web users according to age, sex, culture, intelligence, linguistic competence, educational level, cognitive ability, experience with computers, manual coordination, visual acuity, or any of the other variable factors that might reasonably be expected to influence users' perception of a site's usability. (This would not be easy, in any case, since there is no reliable data on the distribution of these variables among the total population of Web users.) There is a distinct enthnocentric bias to the published research, with most experiments being based on observations of English-speaking subjects in developed Western countries, despite the huge growth in Web use that is occurring in the Far East, in particular, and the rest of the world, in general.

Most seriously, the necessity of having something to measure in order to obtain results tends to lead to goal-oriented experiments: users are asked to do something, such as find a particular piece of information or perform some task, and their success in doing so is used as a measure of a site's usability. This is to simplify the nature of the Web browsing activity, and to underestimate the Web's function as a communication medium. For instance, in one study looking at the influence of writing style on usability, Nielsen and a colleague presented users with several different versions of a travel site about the state of Nebraska in the United States. The original version was written in what the authors of the study call a 'promotional' style ("Mother Nature offers Nebraska a great variety of weather, including

Figure 13.26 Would this site make you want to visit Glenfingal?

sunny skies and cool summer breezes, as well as tornadoes, thunderstorms, and blizzards", and such-like) the second combining various modifications – a more concise objective style ("Nebraska experiences a variety of weather, including sunny skies and cool summer breezes, as well as tornadoes, thunderstorms and blizzards") and the use of bullets and other layout features to make the text easier to scan. Their conclusion was that the latter version was exactly 124% more usable than the first. However, this was based on an assessment of tasks such as answering the questions "Which Nebraska city is the seventh largest, in terms of population?" and "Do you remember any names of tourist attractions mentioned in the website?", neither of which is particularly relevant if the purpose of the site is to persuade visitors to go to Nebraska. To be fair, one of the questionnaires given to participants in the study asked "How much would you like to visit Nebraska?", but it is not clear how the answers to this question were incorporated into the results, if at all. Certainly, this was not taken to be the most important factor, when in fact that, rather than education in geographical trivia, is the primary purpose of a site trying to promote tourism. The truth is that none of the versions of the site was particularly well written or enticing, and to draw general conclusions about how text on Web pages should be written from the participants' ability to answer questions after reading them is unjustified.

Glenfingal

Location: west of Scotland. See <u>map</u>
Population: 450
Bird species: 121
Local **industries**: <u>tourism</u>, agriculture, fish farming

Glenfingal can be reached by a range of <u>transport</u> facilities and offers varied holiday <u>accommodation</u>.

Glenfingal offers:
- a *peaceful*, remote location
- plentiful *wildlife*
- natural *beauty*
- long *summer evenings*
- frequent *sunsets*

Figure 13.27 Would this site make you want to visit Glenfingal?

This is not to say that usability studies are entirely worthless, simply that their implicit claims to provide a rigorous scientific basis for design are severely exaggerated. Observing what people actually do can provide important information about how well designed a Web site is, and help designers resist the temptation to assume that everyone else is just like them, but experiments on a practical scale cannot hope to provide a complete picture.

As we stated at the beginning of this chapter, good design can only come from an understanding of underlying principles. For effective design, you need to understand not only the principles behind the technology, but also the principles of effective communication. In the graphical environment of the Web, you need a 'designer's eye': the ability to organize the elements of a page so that they attract and hold the attention and convey the information it contains – both explicit information, in the form of text and images, and implicit information, in the mood and image that the page is intended to evoke. Usability experts coming from a scientific background tend to denigrate the skills of designers, often implying that designers are only interested in creating something that 'looks cool', irrespective of its usability. This may be true of the horde of self-taught designers who flourished in the first wave of the World Wide Web, but the skills and intuition of properly trained designers, based on insights passed on from the tradition of many years of experience in print design, are more effective in creating usable and effective Web pages than any list of rules derived from goal-oriented small-scale experiments. It is important, though, that designers be aware of the limitations that the Web imposes on design, and that they adapt their expectations and practices accordingly.

There are, however, a few guidelines that it is sensible to follow when designing Web sites, to ensure they are usable, in a broad sense. For the most part, these are little more than common sense and courtesy, but it is sometimes easy to omit to do the things that you know you ought to. The following guidelines are not cast-iron rules, but you should check your design to see whether you have followed them, and if not, identify a good reason for not doing so.

Put the user first

Everything follows from this, really. There is no point creating a Web site – and certainly no point in putting it up on the Internet – if you don't want someone to look at it. Once you accept this, you must also accept that the users who look at the site are the people who should be considered first. This doesn't mean that you should always try to pander to the tastes of a mass audience. You might only be trying to reach a small minority, or your intention might be to startle your visitors, take them to places they didn't know existed, cater to a small clique of cognoscenti or deliberately baffle and bemuse. Even so, you need to think about the visitors to see how you can most effectively accomplish your intention. The results of usability studies and surveys may help in some cases, but you will also have to acquire the skill of putting yourself in somebody else's place, to see how your site will affect them. If you believe that some visitors to your site may suffer from disabilities – in most cases, a realistic assumption – then this principle will naturally lead you to consider accessibility.

Put the user in control

This is one of the basic rules of human–computer interaction, although it is frequently broken, even by some of the biggest software companies. Users should not feel that the computer is forcing them to do things in a certain way, or that it is making decisions on their behalf. Because you cannot know everything about every user, you cannot know what is best for them, so give them choices, don't choose for them. A specific example in the context of Web pages is the use of scripts or **target** attributes to open a new browser window when a user clicks on a link. Users already have a way of opening new windows if they want to, by holding down the appropriate modifier key when clicking on the link, so let them decide whether or not to do so. If they prefer to open the new page in the same window, they can easily go back if they wish to. If they use a browser that supports tabbed browsing, they may very well prefer to open new pages in new tabs, an option you are denying them if you force the link to open in a new window. As in this case, it is usually a simple matter to give the user a choice; what may be less simple is relinquishing control yourself.

Don't provide too much choice

This guideline doesn't really contradict the preceding one. The user should be in control, but not forced to make unnecessary decisions. For instance, when Web pages do spawn new windows, the designer often supplies a button within the pop-up window to close it. The operating system already provides users with a familiar way of closing windows, so don't confuse matters by duplicating this function and forcing people to decide which method to use. In this case, it would be better not to spawn the window in the first place, but the principle applies to any sort of control that duplicates the functions of the browser.

Don't make assumptions about users' behaviour

Don't, for instance, assume that visitors to your Web site always arrive at the home page. Often they will arrive from a search engine's page of results, which may direct them to any page in the site. Therefore, you should provide a link to the home page on every other page, if you want to give all visitors the chance to explore the whole site. It is also important that every page states clearly what it is and where it belongs in the site as a whole – a task made easier if the site is organized in a structured way, as we described earlier in this chapter. Similarly, never assume that visitors will look at every page on a site, or follow links in any particular order.

Use technology judiciously

In other words, don't do things just because you can. During periods when new Web technologies become available, it is tempting to apply new techniques because they are exciting and because you don't want to get left behind. There are, however, practical reasons for treating new developments with caution; in particular, browser support for new features is usually patchy and unreliable for some considerable time after they are first developed. More fundamentally, though,

Figure 13.28 Presentation and interpretation of content is affected by graphic design choices

any technology should only be used if it serves the basic purpose of communication, and is of benefit to the users. One striking example of technology being used injudiciously on the Web is provided by animated welcome pages, which often make impressive use of Flash or dynamic HTML, but, for visitors to the site, simply delay access to the site's actual content. Remember too that regular visitors to a site may not welcome unnecessary change and redesign undertaken simply to keep up with new technology. To take an analogy from everyday life: when supermarkets rearrange all their stock on different shelves, it takes a regular shopper longer to complete a normal task. Similar frustration can result when a familiar Web site is redesigned to use Flash.

Understand your site's context

Any site is just a small part of the complete World Wide Web and needs to fit in to the whole. This is often taken to mean that every site should use conventional navigational elements, link colours, and so on, but that does not follow automatically, as we will discuss at more length in the next section. You might want to use unconventional elements, but you can only do that if you know what the conventional ones are. Just as a symbol is, according to some linguists, defined by its difference from other symbols, so a Web site may be defined by its difference from other sites. Usually, you will want this difference to reside in its content or its appearance, but possibly you may wish to differentiate your site by the way apparently conventional elements behave. In all cases, you must be aware of the context of the site, which is no less than the entire World Wide Web.

The Web is not, however, a homogeneous entity. There are fairly clearly defined categories of Web site, such as ecommerce, news, corporate advertising, technical support, art, personal home pages,

and so on. Each of these categories has its own conventions and set of aesthetic criteria: animal-shaped buttons that might be great fun on a site for small children would look out of place on a support site for the sufferers from a rare fatal disease, to take an extreme example. In Figure 13.28, graphic design and colours which might look attractive in another context undermine the gravity of the content; some design looks poor in any context, and a plain text presentation, which might be appropriate in this case, would be too austere for many other sites. You need to understand how your site fits into the taxonomy of the Web, and thus what conventions apply to it, so that you can follow them, extend them or consciously defy them.

Keep up with change

The Web is constantly changing, socially, culturally and aesthetically, as well as technically, with new conventions developing and old ones being discarded. You need to be aware of changes in all these areas, to ensure that the image and messages your site conveys do not change as their context alters. Or, in more prosaic terms, you have to make sure your site does not become old hat.

Don't neglect aesthetics

As we pointed out earlier, Web browsing is not purely a goal-directed activity. Users are concerned with the complete experience, which includes obvious factors such as whether it is easy to find their way around, but also includes less easily quantified factors that determine whether they find a Web site pleasant to visit. Appearance and aesthetics are thus usability issues. As we have explained at length, you will have to accept that the appearance of your site will not be the same for every visitor, and take steps to ensure that it transforms gracefully. However, the state from which it transforms, which hopefully will be what most users see, should look as good as you can make it. This is not just a cosmetic matter. For example, extensive research has established that different colours provoke different psychological responses, and this has informed serious real-world design issues, such as the treatment of colour schemes in hospitals. In the same way, it is therefore important to realize that while shocking pink may be perfect in some contexts, pale green would be much more appropriate on a support site for cancer patients. However, you also need to be aware that different cultures attach different symbolic significance to colours, icons, and so on. In the West, for example, black is typically associated with death, whereas in Asia, white may play this role.

The mood and feel of a site are heavily dependent on design aesthetics – in this respect, the WWW is no different from any other visual medium.

Know your limitations

It is tempting to have a go at everything, but while we encourage a spirit of adventure, it is as well to recognize that you can't be good at everything. Programmers and others who are familiar with the technical aspects of Web design may feel that layout and other aesthetic aspects are easy in comparison. The feeling that graphic designers don't actually do anything difficult is widespread, and the fact that cutting-edge design often looks bizarre and unattractive to the uninitiated does not help encourage respect for the profession. However, design skills are valuable, and the cutting edge is moving ahead of a body of practice and expertise that has proven its effectiveness over the years. Amateur design looks amateur; if you need graphic design, get a professional, otherwise you will get a mess.

On the other hand, programming is also a highly skilled occupation, with its own body of knowledge and techniques. The ease with which behaviours and preprogrammed scripts can be added to Web pages in an authoring environment, and the deceptive simplicity of scripting languages, may tempt designers into thinking that they can handle any scripting tasks that may be required. The result is likely to be unreliable behaviour and error messages.

Web design and multimedia design in general require a mixture of skills that are rarely combined in a single individual. You should recognize where your skills lie, and turn to other people to fill the gaps in your expertise.

Conservatism and Progress

For most people, the things that are easiest are the things that are familiar. User-oriented design is therefore inherently conservative. The glib implication is that good design is therefore conservative, and that designers should stick to familiar layouts, fonts, and controls; standard colours should be used for visited and unvisited links; navigation bars should be in predictable places; and so on.

There is some justice in this advice. Where designers take advantage of the freedom offered by Flash, for example, to design and implement controls that look and behave in completely different ways from familiar desktop icons and dialogue boxes, the result can easily be a site that visitors cannot understand how to use. If a site's content is utterly compelling but the navigation controls for the site are so obscure that users cannot easily reach the content, they will never discover the fact. Content can only overcome difficulties in using a site if those difficulties are not so severe as to prevent users ever reaching the content; preferably, users should not have to struggle at all – the struggle won't improve the content. Hence, navigation bars need to be clearly identifiable as navigation bars, links need to be followed by clicking, not by some other gesture such as dragging, scroll bars need to be recognizable, and so on.

However, this advice fails to take account of the evolution of both Web technology and users' sophistication and experience. Links provide a good example. Early Web browsers displayed links as underlined blue text, and so users became accustomed to equating blue underlining with a link. There is nothing about the colour and typographic style inherently link-like; it is simply an arbitrary convention. Even after HTML and browsers provided the capability of using different colours for links, it made sense to stick with the defaults, because users could immediately recognize links if and only if everybody used the same convention. Even though it would be pretty obvious that a bold red word appearing in the middle of some text was probably a link if there was no other reason for it to be that colour and weight, there would be some doubt and hesitation, whereas a blue underlined word would be recognized by reflex.

Once browsers supported scripting and CSS pseudo-classes, however, it became possible to use rollovers to denote links. A rollover provides a more positive indication: the text or image is visibly altered, by changing colour or acquiring a drop shadow or whatever, when the cursor moves over it. This change conveys the message that the particular location does things, and hence that it is more than likely that clicking on it will do something more; in the context of a Web page, this is most likely to be jumping to another page, although rollovers are also used to control image swaps and perform other actions on a page. The convention that change on rollover means something will happen on a click therefore provides an improved replacement for coloured links, and makes guidelines that assume links can only be indicated statically by colour and typographic effects obsolete. But if everyone had gone on following those original guidelines and providing users with familiar design elements because that is what they found easiest, rollovers would never have become part of the set of Web conventions.

As this example shows, conventions for Web design need to evolve to take advantage of the evolution of the technology. The methodological inadequacies of usability studies mean that this evolution cannot take place in the manner of conventional research and development, with prototypes being implemented and carefully tested: the huge and heterogeneous population of Web users, and the difficulties of measuring satisfaction without being misled by task-oriented experiments, make testing infeasible. The only feasible sort of testing is live on the Web. This requires some site owners to take risks and use leading-edge design, even though this may cause them to lose visitors if it turns out that their designs are not popular or usable. Obviously, it would be foolhardy to carry out such experiments on ecommerce sites, where lost visitors are lost customers, or on government information sites and product support sites, where the responsibility to pass on information to the public is paramount. However, where sites (or parts of them) are functioning just as online advertising hoardings, for example, one would hope that far-sighted companies would be prepared to host innovative designs, in the same spirit as they might sponsor works of art or commission unconventional advertising posters or films. And just as innovations in fine art have influenced graphic design, and *haute couture* filters down to high street fashion, there is a place for Web sites whose sole purpose is the exploration of the Web as a medium, from which successful radical ideas can be passed on to the wider Web design community.

Exercises

1. What conditions must the structure of a Web site satisfy for a matrix such as the one in Figure 13.10 to be an appropriate navigational mechanism?

2. Explain how you would structure a Flash movie hierarchically.

3. Whereabouts on a Web page should you place important contact information, and why?

4. Since every browser has a back button, why is it necessary for the pages in a Web site to have a link to the site's home page?

5. A *storyboard* is a planning aid used by film makers and animators. It consists of a sequence of still pictures showing the composition of shots at key points in a scene. Storyboards are sometimes advocated as a means of planning multimedia productions.
   (a) Select a music video or a scene from a film that you have access to a copy of, and construct a storyboard that describes it.
   (b) Choose a popular computer game, and carry out a reverse storyboarding process similar to the one described above – this time for a non-linear structure – to convey the essence and possible developments of the game to someone who doesn't know it.
   (c) Based on your experience with these tasks, evaluate the potential usefulness of storyboards as an aid to the design of multimedia productions.

6. Design a Web page advertising your home town, which will work equally well for users with good and with seriously impaired eyesight.

7. Usability studies frequently conclude that users dislike scrolling down long Web pages. For what types of page would scrolling nevertheless be preferable to breaking the page up into a linked sequence? How would you expect users' attitudes to scrolling to be affected by (a) the type of connection someone is using, and (b) any disabilities they may suffer from?

8. Web pages must often provide a means for visitors to contact the site's owner electronically. One way of doing this is by embedding links with URLs beginning mailto: in the page. When a visitor clicks on such a link, their email program is launched with a blank message whose To: field contains the address in the link, so they can fill in the body of the message and send it. Discuss the benefits and disadvantages of embedding mail links in this way for (a) the Web site's visitors, and (b) the Web developer. What other means could be used to provide a means of contact within the site?

9   Look at the six designs in Figure 13.28. Discuss what type of site, if any, each style of design might sensibly be used for; explain why.

10 You are designing a tourist information Web site intended to attract visitors from around the world to a little-known area. Which of the following would it be a good idea to put on the home page of the site, which would be good on a subsidiary page, and which would you omit altogether? Explain the reasons for your choices.

(a) a clickable Flash panorama of a local beauty spot

(b) a timetable for local transport services

(c) a collection of hi-res photographs of the area's best features

(d) a collection of lo-res photographs of the area's best features

(e) a detailed list of places to stay with links to their own sites

(f) a street map of the area's main town

(g) a short written paragraph describing the area

(h) a long written description of the area

(i) a simple large-scale map indicating the area's place in the world

(j) advice on how to reach the area from elsewhere in the world, with links to appropriate travel sites

(k) eye-witness accounts of local festivals and events

(l) a list of local festivals and events

(m) a summary of the area's visitor facilities

(n) a set of links to Web sites of related interest

(o) a large collection of photographs of the area's flora and fauna

(p) photographs of scantily-clad sunbathers

(q) animated advertisements for local businesses

(r) a directory of local businesses with small-scale graphics

(s) a banner across the top of the page with a small animated element (e.g. an eagle flying across a static landscape)

(t) a fully animated graphic banner across the top of the page

11 You are designing a Web site for a cosmetics company which wishes to promote its products worldwide. Which of the following are likely to be good choices for the site, and which bad? Explain why.

(a) Flash movies advertising each product

(b) long descriptions of the products in English

(c) 'standard' icons for links such as a house for the home page, an envelope for contacts, and so on

(d) multi-ethnic models in photographs showing selected products

(e) a list of each product's ingredients

(f) pictures of farm animals in a rural scene to emphasize the company's use of 'natural' ingredients

(g) colour coded pages for product types (e.g. blue for shampoos, yellow for perfumes, etc.)

(h) drop-down menus for site navigation

14

XML and Multimedia

- XML
  - Basic XML Syntax
  - DTDs
- Namespaces
- Stylesheets
  - CSS and XML
  - XSLT and XSL-FO
- Linking
  - XPath
  - XPointer
  - XLink

W e explained in Chapter 11 that the best way of organizing information to cope with the heterogeneous nature of the WWW is by separating content and structure from appearance, and we showed how the use of CSS to specify typographical and layout properties in conjunction with HTML provides a start in approaching this ideal. However, the limited repertoire of tags provided by HTML limits the extent to which this separation can be achieved.

Although they are adequate for marking up the simple, mainly textual, papers for which they were originally intended, HTML's layout tags are by no means sufficient for all the diverse types of material that have found their way onto the World Wide Web, particularly since its commercialization during the middle of the 1990s. Consider, for example, a restaurant wishing to post its menu on a Web page. What tags should be used for each of the dishes on offer? Probably, using a level 2 or 3 header would produce appropriate formatting, but dishes from a menu are not headings, any more than blocks of text laid out on a grid are entries in a table, or mathematical equations are illustrations. If structural markup does not describe the structure of a document, but rather another structure that happens to look like what the designer had in mind as the visual appearance of the document, then much of the point of structural markup is lost. In particular, automatic searching and indexing programs cannot correctly identify the elements of the document. For example, it would be hard to write a program to search for restaurants that served chocolate mousse unless it was possible to distinguish occurrences of the phrase 'chocolate mousse' that announced its presence on a menu from all others, such as headings in online recipe collections or studies on nutrition.

Since HTML's tags are not sufficient for the class of Web pages as it has evolved, new tags are required. Any attempt to add tags to HTML to accommodate absolutely any sort of document that someone might one day want to make into a Web page is doomed to failure, and would leave HTML bloated and unmanageable. A much better solution is to provide Web designers with a facility for defining their own tags. A solution to this problem has existed for some years in the form of the *Standard Generalized Markup Language (SGML)*, which is extensively used in the publishing industry. SGML is not, however, entirely suitable for use over the Internet; certain of its features make parsing it too difficult to be done efficiently enough to provide the required response times. Work on adapting SGML to the Internet led to the definition of a subset, known as *XML (eXtensible Markup Language)*, which provides all the important facilities of SGML without the overhead imposed by the full language. In particular, XML allows Web designers to define their own sets of elements for any type of document. Web pages are thus freed from the limitations of HTML's definition of a document. A formal definition of a set of elements and their attributes, together with constraints on the way they may be combined, can be created in the form of an XML *Document Type Definition (DTD)*. In effect, a DTD defines a specialized markup language.

XML 1.0 was adopted as a World Wide Web Consortium Recommendation early in 1998. It is unlikely that XML will be used directly to mark up individual Web pages by many designers. It is more likely that XML will be used indirectly: experts will produce XML DTDs that define new markup languages for specific tasks. Although this will lead to a proliferation of special-purpose languages, they will all share some syntactic features, such as the form of tags, and will all be based on the underlying technology of XML, so that it will not be necessary to add interpreters for each new language to every browser. So long as it can interpret XML DTDs, a browser can interpret pages marked up in any language defined by one. XML can thus function as an infrastructure supporting a wide variety of mechanisms for organizing text and multimedia content. There is no reason for it to be restricted to the World Wide Web in this role; XML can function equally well with other delivery media.

The process of defining new languages as XML DTDs began before XML 1.0 was even adopted as a Recommendation. Among the DTDs produced are *SMIL (Synchronized Multimedia Integration Language)*, *SVG (Scalable Vector Graphics)*, *MathML (Math Markup Language)* and *XFDL (eXtensible Forms Description Language)*. XHTML is a definition of HTML using an XML DTD.[†] A somewhat different application of XML is as a concrete syntax for *RDF (Resource Description Framework)*,

† HTML 4 and earlier versions of HTML were defined by an *SGML* DTD, not an XML one. They use some of the features of SGML which were dropped in the XML subset.

which is intended to provide a standard for *metadata* – data about a document, such as its language, or labels describing its content for the benefit of filtering services.

XML

Although XML itself has no direct support for multimedia, it underlies the more specialized markup languages SMIL and SVG, which do, and which we will describe in Chapter 15. XML has the potential for providing other multimedia frameworks, so it is important to have a basic understanding of XML's syntax and how new markup languages can be defined using it.

Basic XML Syntax

To begin with, you will get quite a long way if you think of XML as being the same as XHTML except that you can make up your own tags and attribute names. In fact, it would be more accurate to say that XHTML is XML with a fixed repertoire of tags and attributes. Therefore, you already know that tags are written between angle brackets, as in <tag>, and, unless the element is empty, must be matched by a closing tag, which has a / before the element name, as in </tag>; attributes' values are written enclosed in double quotes and assigned to attributes following the element name using an = sign; empty elements can be written like a tag with a / before the closing >; elements must be properly nested; character and entity references beginning with an & can be used for certain characters that are hard to type or, like <, are reserved for a special purpose. Simply following these rules allows you to write what are called *well-formed* documents. Well-formedness simply means that a document obeys the rules of XML syntax that allow it to be parsed correctly. For many purposes, this is adequate: it lets us create documents whose structure is expressed with markup tags, which can be processed by a computer program.

To a programmer, creating a well-formed document is like writing a program with no syntax errors: you might still have type errors, and the program logic may still be faulty, but your program or document does obey the syntax rules of the language.

The following XML document shows you what well-formed XML looks like.

```
<books>
    <book id = "cpp">
        <title>The Late Night Guide to C++</title>
        <author>Nigel Chapman</author>
        <price sterling="29.95" euro="50" />
        <publisher>John Wiley &amp; Sons</publisher>
        <numberinstock current="1" ordered="6" />
    </book>

    <book id = "perl">
        <title>Perl: The Programmer's Companion</title>
        <author>Nigel Chapman</author>
        <price sterling="24.95" euro="44" />
        <publisher>John Wiley &amp;Sons</publisher>
        <numberinstock current="0" ordered="0" />
    </book>

    <book id = "dmm">
        <title>Digital Multimedia</title>
        <author>Nigel Chapman</author>
        <author>Jenny Chapman</author>
        <price sterling="27.95" euro="48" />
        <publisher>John Wiley &amp;Sons</publisher>
        <numberinstock current="12" ordered="20" />
    </book>
</books>
```

The document provides a list of books, with their basic bibliographical details. It might be part of the stock inventory of an online bookshop, so the data also includes the current prices in two major currencies and a record of the stock situation.

We have chosen element names that make it clear to an English-speaking reader what each element is supposed to represent, but the actual names have no formal significance. We could just as easily have used aardvark elements to record the authors' names. The meaning only resides in what is done to the document by software.

A little thought will tell you that there is considerable scope for choice in representing a particular set of data as XML. In particular, there is no clear-cut criterion for deciding whether to use an element with an attribute to record values such as, in this document, the publisher's name, or an element whose content is the value. For example,

```
<publisher>John Wiley and Sons</publisher>
```

or

```
<publisher company="John Wiley and Sons" />
```

Here, we have used a mixture: the price and number in stock are recorded using attributes, this has made it easy for us to combine two different values in both cases: the price in sterling or in euros, the number in stock currently and in a few days time. Using attributes avoids multiplying the number of elements. On the other hand, placing the author in the content of an element has made it possible to have two author elements for the jointly written book. This would help indexing and searching software to identify the book from either author. The decision to use element content to record the values of the remaining fields is somewhat arbitrary.

The structure which XML markup imposes on a document can be represented in the form of a tree, sometimes called a *structure model*. The structure model is essentially an abstract representation of the way in which document elements are ordered and contained within each other. Figure 14.1 is a picture of the structure model for the books document shown earlier. Each document element is represented by a node in the model, as is each section of text. Each node corresponding to an element that is not empty has some child nodes representing its content; as you might expect, such a node is the *parent* of its children, and the terminology is extended to refer to *siblings*, the children of the same parent, and the *root*, the unique element with no parent representing the entire document. The structure model is a tree, with each node having exactly one parent, except for the root, which has none.

Software that processes XML documents often works by parsing the XML input, building a structure model (either as an explicit data structure, or implicitly) and traversing the model, performing computation on the nodes as it goes. There are several APIs in use for performing such traversals. The best known are the W3C's *Document Object Model (DOM)*, which we will meet again in Chapter 16, and the *Simple Application Programming Interface for XML (SAX)*.

DTDs

You can use any elements and attributes you like in a well-formed XML document, providing you obey the simple rules of XML syntax. If, however, you supply a specification of a set of permitted elements, the attributes each may have and which elements they can contain,

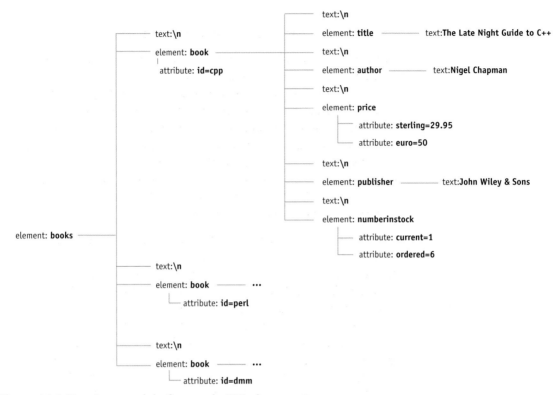

Figure 14.1 Structure model of example XML document

and require that your document conforms to the specification, you can ensure that it belongs to a class of documents with a well-defined structure. (The set of XHTML pages is an example of such a class of documents.) This means that any software that processes documents knows what tags to expect and how they will be related to each other. It can check that documents do indeed conform to the specification, thereby catching a whole class of possible errors, and it can provide specific functionality based on the document class's structure. For example, a browser can provide default formatting for each element, or an editor can show a list of all the permitted attributes when you type an opening tag. If a well-formed document has a specification attached to it and conforms to the rules in that specification, the document is said to be *valid*.

In XML, there are two ways of providing such a specification. The older, better-established method is by means of a *Document Type Definition (DTD)*; a newer method, which is gaining in popularity, is by an XML *Schema*. Schemas[†] are somewhat more powerful than

† Dictionaries and people with a classical education will tell you that the plural of 'schema' is 'schemata', but this is considered pedantic in XML circles, and the XML Schema specification prefers 'schemas'.

DTDs, and provide means akin to the type-definition facilities of modern programming languages for specifying more elaborate constraints on document content. The advantage of schemas is mostly felt where XML documents are used for storing structured data, as if they were databases. For more traditional text-oriented documents, the simpler DTD mechanism is largely adequate, and it is the mechanism used for defining the current versions of XML-based multimedia markup languages like SMIL and SVG, so we will concentrate on DTDs. Some references to descriptions of XML schemas can be found in the bibliography.

Since a DTD defines a set of allowable document elements and their attributes, and the constraints on how you can combine them, we could well say that it is, in fact, a definition of a markup language, and this is often the best way of looking at things. XHTML, for example, is defined by a DTD. Formally, this DTD defines the set of all legitimate XHTML documents, but in practice we take the DTD to be the definition of the XHTML language. In this sense, XML, with its DTD and schema mechanisms, can be thought of as a *metalanguage* – a language for defining other languages.

A DTD may be included within an XML document, but it is more common, especially where the DTD defines a complex language like XHTML, to store the DTD in a separate file, and reference it from within documents that use it. Two pieces of XML boilerplate are required for this to happen. They both use a slightly different syntax from the elements and attributes with which you are familiar. First, there should be an *XML declaration*, which usually takes the form:

```
<?xml version="1.0" encoding="UTF-8" ?>
```

In future, it is to be expected that, when newer versions of XML are defined, higher version numbers will be used in place of 1.0. The value of the encoding attribute specifies the character set used in the document – in this case it is UTF-8-encoded ISO-10646 (see Chapter 10). An XML declaration is, strictly speaking, optional,[†] but it may assist XML parsers to do their job, and should be included. If it appears, the XML declaration must be the very first thing in the document.

† The XML specification states that 'XML documents may, and should, begin with an XML declaration'.

The XML declaration is an example of a *processing instruction (PI)*. PIs are strings of characters enclosed between <? and ?>. They are used to control the processing of an XML document. The first thing in the enclosed string is a *target name*, which is often the name of some program to which the remainder of the PI is sent as an argument.

PIs beginning with xml are used for special purposes in XML processing. We will see an example when we describe how stylesheets are associated with XML documents.

If a DTD in an external file is being used, the XML declaration should be followed by a *DOCTYPE declaration* resembling the following:

```
<!DOCTYPE books PUBLIC "-//DMM//BOOK Bibliographic
information 1.0//EN" "http://www.digitalmultimedia/DTDs/
books.dtd">
```

Note the use of <! and > as delimiters. These are used in those parts of XML concerned with the DTD, in much the same way as < and > are used in markup. The DOCTYPE declaration declares two separate things. First, the name of the *document element*, which will contain the document's entire content, is given after the keyword DOCTYPE. In this case, we have specified the element books, since our entire document is delimited by <books> and </books>, just as an HTML document is delimited by <html> and </html>. After this comes a specification of where the DTD is to be found. The keyword PUBLIC is followed by two different specifications of the DTD's location. The first, "-//DMM//BOOK Bibliographic information 1.0//EN", is the DTD's *public name*. Its peculiar syntax is a relic from XML's SGML ancestor. The public name identifies the organization responsible for the DTD – here a fictional enterprise, DMM – the name, a description and version number of the DTD, and its language (the natural language used for comments, element names, and so on, not the language of the DTD itself, which is always XML, of course). The public name is followed by a conventional URL, at which the DTD is located. This URL is known as the DTD's *system identifier*. XML processors that read DTDs may look for the DTD here, or they may use some implementation-dependent mechanism to find it somewhere else using the public name. If you are using a publicly supported XML-based language, such as XHTML, SMIL or SVG, the language's description will include the appropriate public name and a URL for the DTD. Note that, although you have to specify these, there is no implication that any program that processes your XML document will actually fetch the DTD and use it in its processing. Normal Web browsers, for example, don't fetch the XHTML DTD before processing a Web page; the DTD's rules are built in to the browser's code.

An alternative form of DOCTYPE declaration uses the keyword SYSTEM instead of PUBLIC and omits the public name. This is more convenient for DTDs that are only used locally.

We will not go into the full details of what might be in a DTD, since we do not expect many of our readers will be writing their own DTDs, and the more obscure features involve some wearisome details and specialized jargon. The following brief introduction should convey the essence of how a DTD can specify a markup language. If you are prepared to take on trust the fact that a markup language can be specified by a DTD, you may prefer to skip the rest of this section.

An external DTD (one stored in a separate file from the document) is itself an XML document, so it begins with an XML declaration. After this, though, instead of marked-up text there are special *markup declarations*, which provide the definitions of the set of elements and attributes, and constraints on how they may be combined. A markup declaration begins with <!, followed by a keyword that specifies the kind of markup being defined. After this comes some information that depends on the kind of declaration, and then the declaration is closed with a >. We will only consider elements and their attributes.

An element declaration gives the element's name and specifies what may appear in the element's content. For instance,

```
<!ELEMENT price EMPTY>
```

This is about the simplest element declaration, which says that the element price is an empty element (can have no content). Note the use of upper-case letters for the keywords in the DTD.

EMPTY is an example of what is known in the XML standard as a *content model*. Other content models may appear in the corresponding place in the element declaration. The next most simple is (PCDATA#)* (the brackets are required), which is an obscure way of referring to textual content. The authors' names in our example are of this type, so the declaration of the corresponding element is:

```
<!ELEMENT author (#PCDATA)* >
```

The book and books elements are more complicated, because they can contain other elements, and we need to specify which ones, the order they can occur in, and how many of each there may be. Actually, with a DTD we cannot specify exactly how many times an element may occur within another; we can only state broadly whether it may occur once or several times. In the case of books, for example, the content must consist of one or more book elements. This is expressed in the following element declaration:

```
<!ELEMENT books (book+) >
```

The + following book indicates that the preceding element occurs one or more times. If the + was omitted, there would have to be exactly one book element inside books. You can also follow the element with a * indicating zero or more occurrences, or a ? indicating zero or one (an optional element). These notations may be familiar to you from regular expressions, as used for pattern matching in text editors and programming languages such as Perl.

Where a sequence of elements must occur in order, they are written one after another, separated by commas, as in:

```
<!ELEMENT book (title, author+, price, publisher, numberinstock)
>
```

which you should be able to see correctly specifies the structure of a book element. Note the way that you can use repetition (author+) within a sequence. Note also that this specification fixes the order of the elements within the book element. In a DTD it is not possible to specify that every element of a set must appear without also specifying the order they appear in (but you can do this in a schema). For more complicated constraints, you can use brackets for grouping. (Note that the brackets surrounding all the content models except EMPTY are required, even for trivial cases, such as the declaration of books.)

An additional possibility for content models is the use of the | operator to indicate a choice. Suppose, for example, a book could have some authors or some editors, but not both. Then, assuming an element editor had been declared somewhere, the declaration of book could look like this:

```
<!ELEMENT book (title, (author+ | editor+), price, publisher, num-
berinstock) >
```

(Note the use of brackets to delimit the choice.)

In a DTD, an element's attributes are listed in a separate *attribute-list declaration*. This is introduced by <!ATTLIST, followed by the name of the element whose attributes are being declared. Following this is a sequence of declarations, one for each attribute, declaring the attribute's name and specifying the type of values it may contain, and whether it is compulsory or optional. For example, the attributes for the price element could be declared like this:

```
<!ATTLIST price
          sterling CDATA #REQUIRED
          euro CDATA #IMPLIED >
```

For each attribute, its name is followed by a keyword declaring the type and a specification of the default behaviour. Some new keywords are used in attribute-list declarations: CDATA indicates that the attribute takes values which are character data (strings). Note that, in XML, numerical values are represented as strings, so there are no number data types. As an alternative to CDATA, an attribute's type can be an enumerated list of possible values. This would be used where it only makes sense for an attribute to have certain specific values. For instance, if an element had an attribute day, which could only be assigned the abbreviated name of a day of the week as its value, the corresponding part of the attribute-list declaration would be:

day (mon|tue|wed|thu|fri|sat|sun) #REQUIRED

There are several special types which are also sometimes required. The most common is ID, which is used for attributes that serve as identifiers, like the name attribute of HTML's img element. Although values of type ID look like strings, the XML processor must ensure that IDs are always unique within a document, so that they can be used to address an element uniquely, in a script for example. ID would be the appropriate type for the id attribute of our book element.

```
<!ATTLIST book
          id ID #REQUIRED >
```

The meaning of #REQUIRED following the type in these declarations and that of sterling above should be evident: the attribute must be given an explicit value in the start tag of the element it belongs to, so <book> would be an invalid start tag. #IMPLIED, as used for euro in the attribute-list declaration for price, means that the attribute is optional and that no default value will be assumed, so in this declaration we are saying that it is all right to specify a price just in sterling, without giving the euro equivalent.

For some attributes, it makes sense to specify a default value, meaning that the attribute may have a value assigned to it, but if it does not, the default specified in the DTD will be used. For example, we might assert that, unless we are told otherwise, there are no copies of a book on order, in which case the ordered attribute of the numberinstock element could be left out, and the value "0" would be assumed. That is,

<numberinstock current="1" />

would be equivalent to

<numberinstock current="1" ordered="0" />

This would be declared as follows:

```
<!ATTLIST numberinstock
          current CDATA #REQUIRED
          ordered CDATA "0" >
```

Note that we are still requiring the number currently in stock to be explicitly specified, even if it is zero.

The preceding description should be sufficient to enable you to read the following complete DTD for our books example.

```
<?xml version='1.0'?>
<!ELEMENT title (#PCDATA)* >
<!ELEMENT author (#PCDATA)* >
<!ELEMENT editor (#PCDATA)* >
<!ELEMENT publisher (#PCDATA)* >

<!ELEMENT price EMPTY>
<!ATTLIST price
          sterling CDATA #REQUIRED
          euro CDATA #IMPLIED >

<!ELEMENT numberinstock EMPTY>
<!ATTLIST numberinstock
          current CDATA #REQUIRED
          ordered CDATA "0" >

<!ELEMENT book (title, (author+ | editor+), price, publisher,
  numberinstock) >
<!ATTLIST book
          id ID #REQUIRED >

<!ELEMENT books (book+) >
```

We must emphasize that although we have covered all the basic aspects of DTDs, there are additional features, which are important for the DTDs used to define large-scale languages like XHTML, and which are not entirely straightforward. If you need to write or understand more realistic DTDs you should consult a specialized reference work.

Namespaces

Although a DTD is necessary for checking a document's validity (or, in fact, for the concept of its validity to make sense), it has always been a design aim of XML that well-formed documents can be processed without a DTD, since it is not always practicable to use DTDs on the Internet. Where no DTD is present, a document can use any set of element and attribute names. Since there is no overall control over how names are used, it is more than likely that different document authors will use the same name in different ways. Consider, for example,

```
<lecturer>
      <title>Dr</title>
      <forename>Froederick</forename>
      <surname>Frankenstein</surname>
</lecturer>
```

and

```
<paper>
      <title>On the use of brains</title>
      <author>F. Frankenstein</author>
</paper>
```

Here, both uses of the name title make sense, but they mean something completely different, and software that had to process both of the documents from which these fragments are taken would have no way of distinguishing between the two. Indeed, it might make sense for both fragments to appear in a single document (a university department's annual report, for instance).

If, as is quite likely, both <paper> and <lecturer> elements were used in several different documents, sometimes together, sometimes separately, it would be sensible to construct document-processing software in a modular fashion, with modules for each of the two element types that could be combined as necessary. In that case, it is important that the right module is used to process each element, a task made much simpler if the elements have unique names.

In order to make it easy to generate unique names, *XML namespaces* define a two-level naming system that ensures that different names can be referred to differently, without requiring any administrative mechanism to control the use of names globally (a practical impossibility).

Where namespaces are being used, an element or attribute name may have a *prefix*, which is separated from the name by a colon. Thus, we might use bbl to denote names taken from a bibliographical namespace, so that the titles of papers would be bbl:title elements, while the titles of lecturers might be ppl:title elements, where ppl was the prefix for a personnel namespace.

On its own, the use of prefixes wouldn't help at all – it merely restates the problem as that of ensuring that prefixes are unique and used consistently. However, XML namespaces provide a way of associating a prefix with a URL, allowing the (usually short) prefix to stand in for the (comparatively cumbersome) URL. Since domain names are unique, and there exists an administrative mechanism to ensure that they are so, and each domain is usually under the control of a single organization, it is comparatively easy to make sure that the URLs associated with namespaces are unique. Thus, if URLs were used as prefixes, all would be well. All that the namespace declarations that we will describe shortly really do is allow the author of a document to use an arbitrary prefix that, within the document, does the same job as the namespace's full URL. (You couldn't actually use a URL as a prefix for element names, because URLs can contain characters that aren't allowed in XML names.)

At this point, most people ask what is stored at the URL associated with a namespace, expecting that there is some sort of namespace declaration that can be stored in a file. There isn't (although in principle there could be). A URL is used simply because it is easy to ensure that it is unique. It is not being used as a pointer to a resource, the way it is in a link. There is no need for a namespace URL to point to anything at all.

To declare a namespace in a document, you assign its URL to an attribute whose name consists of the prefix xmlns: followed by the namespace prefix you want to use in the document. So, if you wanted to use names like bbl:title and the bibliographic namespace had been given the URL http://www.digitalmultimedia.org/biblio, you would use the assignment

xmlns:bbl = "http://www.digitalmultimedia.org/biblio"

You can use this attribute with any element, and the namespace will be in scope within that element. (The scope includes the element's start tag, so the element's own name can come from the namespace and use the prefix you are declaring.) Most often, the namespace is declared by assigning to an attribute of the document element, so that the prefix can be used anywhere in the document. For example,

<bbl:books xmlns:bbl = "http://www.digitalmultimedia.org/biblio">

You can also assign a namespace URL to an attribute simply called xmlns, with no colon or suffix. This declares a *default namespace*. Within its scope, names without prefixes are considered to be in the default namespace. In other words, an empty prefix is mapped to the namespace URL. Where all the elements and attributes in a document belong to the same namespace, this will be the most convenient thing to do. For example, all the names in XHTML belong to the namespace with URL http://www.w3.org/TR/xhtml1, and so the start tag for the html element usually declares this as the default namespace:

```
<html xmlns="http://www.w3.org/TR/xhtml1">
```

allowing all the familiar HTML tags to be used without any prefix.

(Strictly speaking, xmlns and attributes with xmlns as a prefix only look like attributes; they aren't really attributes. This has implications if you are writing software to process XML.)

The names of attributes do not have to be unique: different elements can have attributes with the same name. In effect, an element defines its own local namespace for its attributes, so there is usually no need for attribute names to belong to a namespace or be qualified with a prefix. Sometimes, however, it is necessary to introduce attribute names that are supposed to have the same meaning wherever they are used, and for these, the namespace mechanism provides a way of identifying a particular attribute, no matter what context it appears in.

You can't use a namespace declaration inside a DTD, but you can use prefixed names, so that, after the DTD has been processed, documents that use it will be valid. For example, if we wished to use the namespace prefix bbl for bibliographic data, the DTD defining the language for our bibliographic databases could include declarations such as the following:

```
<!ELEMENT bbl:book (bbl:title, (bbl:author+ | bbl:editor+),
  bbl:price, bbl:publisher, bbl:numberinstock) >
<!ATTLIST bbl:book
          id ID #REQUIRED >
```

It would also be necessary to add the following attribute list to the document element books, in order to allow the namespace declaration:

```
<!ATTLIST bbl:books
          xmlns:bbl CDATA #REQUIRED >
```

With these modifications to the DTD, our sample XML document could be rewritten to use a namespace, while being valid with respect to the modified DTD, like this:

```
<?xml version="1.0" encoding="UTF-8"?>
<!DOCTYPE bbl:books PUBLIC '-//Books' 'books-ns.dtd'>

<bbl:books xmlns:bbl = "http://www.digitalmultimedia.org/bbl">
    <bbl:book id="cpp">
        <bbl:title>The Late Night Guide to C++</bbl:title>
        <bbl:author>Nigel Chapman</bbl:author>
        <bbl:price sterling="29.95" euro="50" />
        <bbl:publisher>John Wiley &amp; Sons
                            </bbl:publisher>
        <bbl:numberinstock current="1" ordered="6" />
    </bbl:book>
```

And so on.

There is a possibility that we did not mention earlier for declaring attributes with a constant value. This value is specified in the DTD, and used, like a default value, if the attribute does not appear in an element's start tag. The difference between a fixed attribute and one with a default is that in the former case you may not assign any other value to the attribute. This provides a way of ensuring that the correct namespace declaration is always used in conjunction with a particular DTD. For example, if we changed our DTD as follows:

```
<!ATTLIST bbl:books
xmlns:bbl CDATA #FIXED "http://www.digitalmultimedia.org/bbl" >
```

then the namespace prefix **bbl** could only be used to refer to the namespace identified by the specified URL.

Stylesheets

You will recall from our discussion of structural markup in Chapter 11 that the intention is to separate a document's structure and content from its presentation. XML certainly achieves this, because it has no facilities whatsoever for controlling presentation. Where XML is used as a format for exchanging self-describing structured data between computer programs, this doesn't matter, but often the program that receives an XML document has to display it to a human user. Since XML does not have a fixed repertoire of elements, like HTML has, there is no question of coding a default style of display into the program. The document's layout has to be specified explicitly, and since there is no mechanism within XML for specifying layout, this must be done with an external stylesheet.

Actually, most Web browsers that implement XML *do* provide a default style of layout, simply in order to be able to display XML documents at all, but it isn't much use. For instance, Mozilla browsers just display the content of all the elements with no other formatting; some versions of Internet Explorer produce a pretty-printed listing of the XML source.

You can't use an element to associate the stylesheet with the document in XML the way you use link in HTML, because there is no reason to imagine that any particular DTD will declare a link element. Instead, the same notation is used as we saw in the XML declaration: a processing instruction delimited by <? and ?>. For linking to stylesheets, this begins with the name xml-stylesheet, and has an attribute href, whose value is the URL where the stylesheet can be found. As with link in HTML, you must also specify the type of the stylesheet as the value of the type attribute. Thus, to attach a CSS stylesheet to our books example, we could use the following processing instruction:

```
<?xml-stylesheet href="books.css" type="text/css" ?>
```

As this example suggests, CSS stylesheets can be used with XML, although this is not required. Stylesheets of any type that can be processed by a browser can be used, provided the correct type is specified in the xml-stylesheet instruction.

CSS and XML

Using CSS with XML is a straightforward generalization of using CSS with HTML: you simply define rules for each element type in your XML document. Since you can, in effect, make up your own element types as necessary, defining layout for each type is usually sufficient to define the formatting of the whole document. XML tends to be used in a slightly different way from HTML, so in this section we will introduce some new features of CSS that are more often required with XML than with HTML. Most of these are CSS2 features. (Browsers that can render XML usually implement CSS2, so this is not a problem.)

When you are creating stylesheets for use with XML, it is important to remember that the program processing the document has no knowledge about the element types in the document, beyond the syntactic constraints which may be specified in a DTD, if one is being used. In particular, neither the XML document nor its DTD provides any information about which elements are inline and which are blocks. You must always bear in mind that the names you choose for elements have no meaning to the XML processor. (You should still use names that are meaningful to people, in order to make your documents easier to maintain.) You can call an element paragraph but this won't make a browser insert a new line before it. The CSS property display must be used to set the display type explicitly. In CSS2, it has a lengthy list of possible values, many of them concerned with table elements, but of most interest for the present discussion are block and inline, with the expected meanings; list-item, which formats the element like a list item, with a list marker in front of it; none, which generates nothing for the element (this is not the same as hiding it by setting its visibility off); and compact, which sets the element as an exdented header in the margin, running on the following element if there is room, or starting a new paragraph for the following element if not. (Apart from compact all these values can be used in CSS1.)

When you are laying out an XML document whose elements contain the values of logical components of some structure, like a bibliographic record for a book, the punctuation that is often needed to combine the elements when they are printed out may be omitted, as it has been in our example. CSS provides some elementary features for inserting text before and after elements, which goes some way to allowing you to insert such punctuation automatically. This is done by appending the pseudo-class selectors :before or :after after an element name in a rule, and using the content property to specify text to be inserted before or after the element, respectively. For instance,

```
title:after { content: ", " }
```

would insert a comma after each book's title to separate it from what followed.

Here is a simple stylesheet for laying out the books document; the display of the document in a Mozilla browser is shown in Figure 14.2.

```
book { display: block;
       width: 360px;
       margin: 15px 35px 2px;
       text-indent: -15px;
       font-family: Verdana,Arial,Helvetica,sans-serif;
       font-size: 14px; }

title { font-style: italic; }

title:after { content: ", " }

publisher { text-decoration: underline;}
```

The Late Night Guide to C++, Nigel Chapman <u>John Wiley & Sons</u>

Perl; The Programmer's Companion, Nigel Chapman <u>John Wiley & Sons</u>

Digital Multimedia, Nigel Chapman Jenny Chapman <u>John Wiley & Sons</u>

Figure 14.2 Browser display of document formatted with CSS stylesheet

This display is not entirely satisfactory. Normally, we would expect the names of the authors of *Digital Multimedia* to be separated by the word 'and' or an ampersand. Where there are more than two authors, we would expect that commas would separate all but the last two, which would be separated by 'and'. In order to do this by inserting text before or after an **author** element, it is necessary to identify both the special case of a single author, and, for books with multiple authors, the penultimate name in the list of authors. In CSS, there is no way of doing this: it requires some of the features of a programming language.

One way round this would be to modify the DTD to allow **PCDATA** to appear among the elements inside a **book**, and insert the punctuation in the document between the **author** elements. This is not a very good solution, though, because the punctuation is really part of the appearance of the displayed document, which we have been eager to separate from the structure. A better way would be to use different elements for the first and last authors, a solution we leave to the exercises.

If we wanted to display a price list of our books, we would need to extract the values for the attributes of their **price** elements. Normally, attribute values are not displayed, only element content. In a CSS rule, you can use the notation **attr(X)** as the value of the **content** property in order to insert the value of the attribute named **X** of the element that matched the rule's selector. For instance, to print the sterling price of a book, the following rule could be added to the stylesheet:

price:before { content: "\00A3" attr(sterling); }

to produce the display shown in Figure 14.3. (The mysterious \00A3 appearing in the string is the Unicode escape for the pound symbol.) Note that we have to use the :before pseudo-class, because nothing is actually displayed for the content of the **price** element.

You will recall that the euro price is optional. We would therefore only want to display it for those books that did specify it. To identify

The Late Night Guide to C++, Nigel Chapman
£29.95 <u>John Wiley & Sons</u>

Perl: The Programmer's Companion, Nigel Chapman
£24.95 <u>John Wiley & Sons</u>

Digital Multimedia, Nigel Chapman Jenny Chapman
£27.95 <u>John Wiley & Sons</u>

Figure 14.3 Displaying attribute values

these, a form of selector is used that matches on the attributes of an element. If the element name is followed by an attribute name in square brackets, as in price[euro], the selector only matches elements with that attribute defined in the document. Thus, we might use a rule like:

price[euro]:after { content: "/\20AC" attr(euro); }

to add the euro prices for those books that had them. (\20AC is the Unicode escape for the euro symbol.) The addition of this rule causes the browser to display the XML document as shown in Figure 14.4.

The Late Night Guide to C++, Nigel Chapman
£29.95 <u>John Wiley & Sons</u>

Perl: The Programmer's Companion, Nigel Chapman
£24.95/€44 <u>John Wiley & Sons</u>

Digital Multimedia, Nigel Chapman Jenny Chapman
£27.95/€48 <u>John Wiley & Sons</u>

Figure 14.4 Displaying optional attribute values

It is also possible to select elements whose attributes have a specific value, by putting an = sign and a value after the attribute's name in a selector of the form we just used. For instance, to display the information about *Digital Multimedia* in red, we could add the following rule to the stylesheet:

book[id='dmm'] { color: #C00; }

You cannot use class selectors in CSS stylesheets for XML, since the attribute class has no *a priori* special meaning in an XML document. If you need to simulate matching on class attributes, you can just use a selector of the form elem[class='val']. Even if your document uses a DTD that declares attributes of type ID, you cannot rely on its being processed by a program that uses the DTD, so you cannot use id selectors either. Again, the answer is to use a selector that tests the value of the attribute, as we did in the example above.

XSLT and XSL-FO

CSS can get you a long way with formatting XML documents, but as we saw in the case of multiple authors, some formatting which one naturally wants to perform cannot be carried out in a natural way using CSS rules. In general, CSS cannot perform any formatting that involves displaying elements in a different order from the one in which they appear in the XML document. CSS cannot perform any arithmetic or other non-trivial computation either, so you cannot use values calculated on the fly from the actual content of the document. Nor can a stylesheet be used to derive and format tables of contents, lists of illustrations, and so on, where information derived from one part of a document must be used elsewhere. Finally, although CSS2 has some facilities for controlling page layout, CSS does not really incorporate a layout model suitable for paged media, such as print.

The *Extensible Stylesheet Language (XSL)* was devised to overcome these deficiencies of CSS. It is a much more complex language than CSS, having many of the characteristics of a functional programming language with pattern matching. Its approach to formatting uses a two-stage process. First the structure tree of the original XML document is transformed into a new tree, possibly with the reordering, removal or insertion of nodes. The nodes in this new tree represent elements known as *formatting objects*, which attach layout and typographical information to the original document content. In the second phase of processing, these formatting objects are interpreted, and the document is rendered, to screen, paper or some other medium.

At an early stage of its development, XSL was split into three components, which are the subject of separate W3C Recommendations. The *Extensible Stylesheet Language for Transformations (XSLT)* is concerned with the first stage of the formatting process, transforming the structure tree of the original document into a different tree. It had been realized early on that such a transformation language could have many useful applications beyond laying out documents with formatting objects. In particular, it could be used to transform arbitrary XML documents into XHTML, which could be displayed using a browser's built-in mechanisms. (This approach to displaying XML was used from an early stage by Internet Explorer.) Thus, although XSLT retains the word 'stylesheet' in its name, it is not really a stylesheet language in the same sense as CSS. In fact, it is better thought of as a rather odd programming language.

In order to transform the nodes of a tree, it is necessary to be able to address them using their position in the hierarchy of the tree structure. *XPath* is the second of the three XSL components, and it is used for this purpose. XPath is defined separately from XSLT, because it is useful in other contexts. In particular, as we will see in the following section, it can be used to define links between XML documents.

The remaining component comprises the formatting objects themselves. Formally, this is now known simply as XSL, but because of the possible confusion this may cause, it is more often referred to as *XSL-FO*, where the FO stands for 'formatting objects'.

XSLT and XSL-FO are themselves XML. That is, an XSLT stylesheet (or program, if you prefer) is an XML document that uses a vocabulary of elements suitable for specifying tree transformations. Essentially, an XSLT stylesheet comprises a collection of *templates*, which define how to build part of a new tree out of parts of the old one. Templates are applied to elements of the tree using *selectors*, which, like CSS selectors, match certain elements. However, XSLT selectors may be more complicated than CSS selectors, and are based on properties of tree nodes (including their position and context as defined by XPath expressions) rather than the tags appearing in the document.

All of this adds up to a language more suited for programmers than Web designers. (Even if, as a designer, you are comfortable with JavaScript, the concepts and model of computation used in XSLT are quite different.) For this reason we will not attempt to teach the syntax and use of XSLT here.

XSLT provides a good example of the need for XML namespaces. An XSLT stylesheet must include elements defined in the XSLT Recommendation, and also elements that will correspond to nodes in the transformed tree. No special syntax is available to distinguish between these (since an XSLT stylesheet must be well-formed XML), but a namespace prefix does the job.

Although XSLT is defined in terms of transformations between trees, you can think of it, if you prefer, as transforming one XML document into another. XSL-FO defines an XML-based language that is suitable for marking up a document with tags that describe how it should appear when formatting. The formatting objects incorporate typographical and layout information that resembles and extends that described by CSS properties. You would almost never want to use such a language to mark up your documents – presentation should be separate from content and structure – but such a document is an ideal input format for programs that actually display information. (Here, we consider both the generation of a display-oriented format such as PDF or HTML with CSS, and actual rendering to an output device to be displaying.) Hence, the two-stage approach of transforming a structurally marked-up XML document into an XSL-FO document provides a way of formatting XML documents while preserving the separation of content and structure from appearance. Note that the XSLT stylesheet will specify which formatting objects to generate, so that the stylesheet does specify the formatting to be applied, but in a less direct fashion than a CSS stylesheet does.

You might wonder why we need yet another programming language in the form of XSLT. You can transform XML structure trees using any language which has an API for parsing XML; Java, Python and Perl all fall into this category. An XML document could be transformed into XSL-FO or HTML on the server using a program written in one of these languages before being sent to a client for display. The main advantage of using XSLT is that everything is then within the framework of XML.

Linking

XML goes well beyond HTML in its support for extended links. This support consists of two components: a special language for identifying link destinations within a document, known as *XPointer*, and a set of attributes that can be used to construct elements which serve as links; these are considered to belong to a language called *XLink*. XPointer is built on top of *XPath*, a language, which we mentioned briefly in the context of XSLT, for addressing nodes in a document's structure tree. We will describe linking in XML in a bottom-up fashion, beginning with the relevant parts of XPath, before going on to show how XPath expressions can be used to construct XPointers, which can be used in XLinks.

XPath

Unlike most of the languages described in this chapter, XPath does not use the syntax of XML proper. It uses its own notation, which is more suited for the purpose of describing locations in a document. A location or set of locations is described in XPath by a *location path*. You can think of a location path as being a set of instructions giving you directions to follow in the order specified to reach the intended point in the document. Each instruction is specified by a *location step*, which selects a set of nodes, relative to the *context node*, which is the node you have reached so far by following any preceding location steps. The location path usually begins with the root node of the tree (which corresponds to the document element), which is written as a single /. The subsequent steps (reading from left to right) tell you how to get from there to where you are going, by choosing, for example, the third child or the fourth subsequent paragraph. Location steps are separated within a location expression by / characters.

A location path that begins with a / is an *absolute* path; one that begins with any other location step is a *relative* path. Relative paths are evaluated starting at the current context node. If an Xpath expression occurs within an XML document (as the value of an attribute, for example) the context node is the node corresponding to its position in the document. When XPath expressions are used in XSLT, the context node may be established by other means during the evaluation of the stylesheet. Using the analogy of navigating in a file system on disk, you can think of the context node as the current directory. Just as relative path names are evaluated relative to the current directory, relative XPath location expressions are evaluated relative to the context node. Absolute path names are always evaluated starting from the root of the filesystem, and similarly, absolute location expressions are evaluated from the root node of the tree.

The simplest form of location step consists of the name of an element type, such as book or author in the example XML document given earlier. It refers to the set of nodes of that type among the children of the context node. Referring back to Figure 14.1, if the context node corresponded to the book element for *Perl: The Programmer's Companion*, then the location step price would identify the node for the element <price sterling="24.95" euro="44" />. A location path consisting of steps of this form looks like a list of node types separated by slashes, so it resembles the path part of a URL, but, since each location step may identify a set of nodes, it does not specify a hierarchical path to a particular node in the way a URL path specifies a path to a file or directory. Instead, it builds up a set of nodes by working down the tree, using the set of nodes defined at each step as context nodes for the next step. For instance, / is the root node, /books is all the books nodes it has as children – since books is the document element there is only one – /books/book refers to all the books (all the children of the document element are book nodes) so /books/book/price will identify the set of all price nodes.

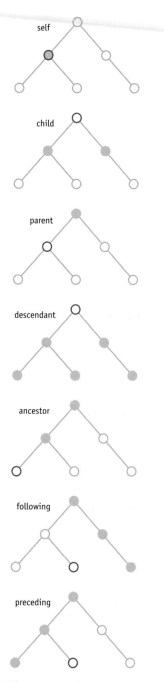

Figure 14.5 Axes

What if you wanted to refer to the price of a specific book, say the second? You can add a number in square brackets after the element name to select a node other than the first one of that type. For instance, book[2] identifies the second book among the children of the context node, so /books/book[2]/price refers to the price of the second book. The nodes are counted started from one (not zero, as programmers might have expected).

Location paths of the form we have described are adequate to specify any node in the document's tree, but they are just a shorthand form of a special case of the more general form of location path provided by XPath. Instead of selecting a node by name from among the context node's children, you can select it from various other sets of nodes, which are structurally related to the context node in various ways. These sets are known as *axes*. Figure 14.5 illustrates most of the available axes. Using the full verbose XPath syntax, a location step may have an axis followed by a double colon :: before the element name, as in descendant::author, which means all the author nodes that are in the descendant axis of the context node.

In addition to the axes shown in Figure 14.5, the attribute and namespace axes are also available. These are necessary for XPath expressions in XSLT, but are not relevant to our discussion of links.

The set of nodes can be restricted by adding a *predicate* in square brackets at the end of a location step. This is an expression which is applied to each node in turn, returning true or false; only nodes for which the predicate is true are included in the set specified by the location step. In general, predicates can be arbitrarily complicated expressions involving arithmetic, comparisons, Boolean operators and a limited repertoire of functions. The most commonly used predicates use the position() function, which returns a number corresponding to the node's position (first, second, etc.) in the set. Thus, the location step child::book[position() = 2] has the same meaning as our earlier example book[2]. (C++ and Java programmers take note that equality is denoted by a single =.) This illustrates the shorthand conventions that led to the notation we used to begin with: child:: can be omitted, and a predicate consisting simply of a number n is taken to mean position() = n. Also useful in predicates is the function last(), which returns the number of the last node, allowing you to count nodes from the end. For example, position() = last()-1 would select the penultimate node from a set.

You may wish to select a node on the basis of the value of one of its attributes. In a predicate, a name prefixed by an @ sign is treated as an attribute name. Its value may be tested using the conventional operators, so to choose all books costing more than €50, you could use the predicate @euro > 50. Hence, a complete location path that matched all the prices exceeding €50 would be /books/book/price[@euro > 50]. (Note that if you are using XPath expressions inside an XML document, you must use < and > for the comparison operators < and >.)

A few other pieces of XPath notation are useful. The expression node() selects all the nodes in a set, so child::node() selects all the context node's children. As in URLs, . denotes the context node, and .. its parent. Formally, . is an abbreviation for self::node() and .. for parent::node(). Hence, if you wanted all the titles of expensive books, you could use the location path /books/book/price[@euro > 50]/../title.

A * stands for all element nodes. This is subtly different from node(), because a document will generally contain text, and possibly processing instructions or comments, which give rise to nodes, but are not elements. The expression child::text() selects only the text nodes. Finally a double slash // is an abbreviation for /descendant-or-self::node(). This can be used wherever a single slash is allowed, so, for example, .//title selects any title nodes in the context node or any of its descendants. As a special case, //title matches any title nodes anywhere in the document. (Note, however, that in a large document, matching within the descendant-or-self axis of the root or a node high in the document tree may be a time-consuming operation.)

Most of the time, the simple abbreviated syntax will be adequate to specify link destinations; the more powerful variations we have described here allow you to specify parts of a document in more flexible ways. For a full description of the remaining features of XPath, consult the references in the bibliography.

XPointer

As we mentioned in Chapter 12, in HTML documents, the value of an a element's href attribute may be a URL with a fragment identifier appended to it. The fragment identifier is a name matching the name or id attribute of some element in the document identified by the URL. This method of addressing within a document only works if the elements you want to address have the necessary attributes defined.

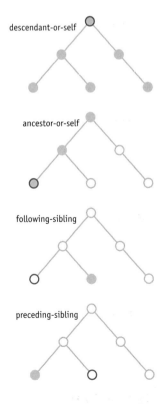

descendant-or-self

ancestor-or-self

following-sibling

preceding-sibling

This may not always be the case, especially if your link points to a document you don't own. For example, in a document dealing with consumer rights in the UK, you might want to include a reference to the relevant legislation, in the form of a link to a section within the online version of the applicable Act of Parliament. Unless the government has attached named anchors to every section, you will not be able to do this, and would have to content yourself with a pointer to the entire Act, which would be less helpful to your readers.

XPath provides a way of describing a location in a document in terms of its structure, which does not require that all the elements be labelled before you can point to them. XPointer is a language for specifying fragment identifiers, which uses XPath and some additional constructs, to provide a flexible means of identifying parts of an XML document. Like HTML fragment identifiers, XPointers (as we shall refer to pointers using XPointer notation) are appended to a URL after a # sign to identify a location within the document identified by the URL.

To begin with, XPointer does provide a way of referring to named locations in a document. The simplest XPointer expression is called a *shorthand pointer* and consists of a name. It refers to the first element within the document that has an attribute whose type is defined in a DTD (or schema) to be ID, and whose value matches the name in the pointer. In other words, a shorthand pointer works like an HTML fragment identifier, except that, since the element and attribute repertoire of an XML document is not fixed, it can refer to any attribute or element of the requisite type. Note, however, that a DTD is necessary to determine the type of the attributes in a document. With our example DTD for books, the shorthand pointer #perl would identify the start of the book element for *Perl: The Programmer's Companion*.

More complex XPointers are identified by the name of a *scheme*, which indicates what syntax is used within the pointer. Schemes[†] allow XPointers to be extensible – new schemes can be added if an improved method of addressing document fragments becomes available. At present, only two schemes are defined: xpointer() and element(). A *scheme-based* pointer consists of a scheme name followed by some data, specific to the scheme, in brackets. In the case of the xpointer() scheme, for example, the data would be an XPath expression (with a couple of extensions which we will not describe here), so a fragment identifier using this scheme would look like #xpointer(/books/book[2]/price). This would point to the price element of the second book; note that this element does not have an ID attribute, so it could not be addressed otherwise.

The element() scheme provides a simpler but less powerful way of addressing the nodes in a tree using a sequence of numbers. A pointer using this scheme begins with either a /, which refers to the root of the tree (the document element) as it does in XPath, or a name, which is interpreted as in a shorthand pointer. Following this is a sequence of numbers, which are interpreted by counting the children of the context node from left to right. Thus element(/1/2) is the second child of the first child of the root, that is, in the books example, the book element for *Perl*. The price element of that book could be identified as element(perl/3) using this scheme.

Different schemes can be combined in the same XPointer. In general, a scheme-based pointer may consist of a number of *pointer parts.* These are evaluated from left to right, and the first one that leads to some location is used as the value of the whole pointer. This allows for the possibility that a browser may not implement all the available schemes. The pointer xpointer(/books/book[2]/price) element(perl/3)element(/1/2/3) provides three different ways of identifying the same element in the example document. A browser that implements XPath and the xpointer() scheme would be able to evaluate the first pointer part to reach the price of the Perl book. One that did not implement the xpointer() scheme would skip over the first pointer part (whose end is unambiguously defined by the closing bracket) and evaluate the second part by counting elements. However, if the browser did not use the DTD, it would not be able to determine which attribute to use to resolve the ID, so it could fall back on the final, purely numerical, pointer part.

It is intended that XPointers should also be able to identify points as offsets within an element, and ranges as pairs of points. This way, it will be possible to point to, for example, a word within a paragraph, or refer to a passage of text that begins in the middle of one paragraph and extends into another. At the time of writing, the notation for this extension has not been fully defined, however.

XLink

Although XPointer provides a flexible method for identifying fragments of documents, we still need a way to use these fragments – and indeed URLs – as links in XML documents. Once again, we must stress that XML allows you to define your own collection of elements, so it is not possible to define a set of linking elements analogous to HTML's a element as part of the XML language. What is needed is a way of allowing elements to be defined which will act as links. XLink provides this by defining a namespace which contains a collection of attributes. Any element which uses attributes from the XLink namespace will be treated as a linking element by software which implements XLink.

It follows that, in order to use XLink, you must include a namespace declaration. Conventionally, the prefix xlink is used for XLink attributes, and the XLink namespace's URL is http://www.w3.org/1999/xlink, so you would add

xmlns:xlink = "http://www.w3.org/1999/xlink"

to the start tag of the document element of your document.

Although XLink does not define a set of elements, it does define a set of types of element, where the type of an element determines how it behaves with respect to linking. The type is determined by the value of the xlink:type attribute. This can take on several different values; for the moment we will only consider one of these: simple, which is used to implement links similar to those with which you are familiar from HTML. In general, if an element's xlink:type attribute has a value *X*, the element is said to be an *X-type* element. For instance, an element with an xlink:type value of simple is a simple-type element.

A simple-type element may have (and usually does have) a *locator attribute*, xlink:href, whose value is a URL (which may have an XPath fragment identifier on the end). It may contain other elements and text, which will provide a visual representation of the link in the XML document, or they may be empty. In addition, it can have two other attributes, xlink:show and xlink:actuate, which determine what happens when a link is followed. The values which can be assigned to xlink:show include replace, which stipulates that the document being pointed to by the link should be displayed in the same window as the document containing the link, replacing its original contents, new, which specifies that it should be displayed in a new window, and embed, which specifies that it should be displayed as part of the original document. By analogy with HTML, replace and new correspond to links with target values of self and blank, respectively, while embed is more like the behaviour of an img: the simple-type element points to an external resource which is incorporated in the display of the document. Unlike imgs, though, the resource pointed to by a simple-type element with xlink:show="embed" is not necessarily displayed when the document containing it is loaded. The behaviour is controlled by the value of the xlink:actuate attribute.

This attribute may have a value of onLoad, which causes the link to be followed as soon as the document is loaded, or onRequest, which means that the link is not followed until an event, such as a mouse click, occurs. Thus, the following element will behave much like an img element in HTML, causing the JPEG image pointed to by its locator attribute to be displayed in-line in the document:

```
<picture xlink:type="simple" xlink:show="embed"
  xlink:actuate="onLoad" xlink:href="../Images/diagram2a.jpg" />
```

whereas the following will behave like an HTML link implemented as an a element:

```
<go xlink:type="simple" xlink:show="replace"
  xlink:actuate="onRequest" xlink:href="books/books.xml#
  xpointer(/books/book[2])> Perl" </go>
```

If you were using a DTD to define your document elements, you would normally use FIXED attribute values for xlink:type, xlink:show and xlink:actuate, so that the behaviour of a simple-type element was determined by the DTD, and document authors didn't have to include those attributes.

XLink as we have described it so far simply provides XML with the same linking functionality as HTML. The XLink Recommendation goes much further, however, by providing for extended-type elements, which connect together more than just two documents. Theoretically, this is an important generalization, allowing linked XML documents to model more complex relationships among information than simple links can support. In practice, extended-type elements present implementation problems, and lack the intuitive appeal of straightforward hyperlinks, so they are not widely implemented and have attracted relatively little attention. For this reason, we will confine ourselves to describing a simple example of how extended links can be used, in order to convey the flavour of extended linking without going into too much technical detail.

Suppose that we wish to expand and reorganize our bibliographic information, so that it includes more information about authors – a brief CV and perhaps a picture, for example – and that we want to allow users to be able to start from an author and find out what books they have written or co-written, or to start from a book and find out about its authors. The obvious way to proceed is by creating an additional XML document containing the authors' details and put links between it and the original document with the books' bibliographic data. A straightforward way of doing this would be to turn the author element into a simple-type link that points to the relevant element in the authors document, and include an author-of element in the latter, which would look roughly as follows:

```
<authors xmlns: xlink="http://www.w3.org/1999/xlink">
     <author id="npc">
         <name>Nigel Chapman</name>
         <picture xlink:type="simple" xlink:show="embed" xlink:
actuate="onLoad" xlink:href="../Images/nchapman.jpg" />
         ...
         <author-of xlink:type="simple" xlink:href=
"books.xml#cpp" ... />
         <author-of xlink:type="simple" xlink:href=
"books.xml#dmm" ... />
     ...
     </author>
     <author id="jsc">
         <name>Jenny Chapman</name>
     ...
         <author-of xlink:type="simple" xlink:href=
"books.xml#dmm" ... />
     ...
     </author>
</authors>
```

This will work, but requires that the links be embedded in the XML documents containing the bibliographical and biographical data; the latter would have to be updated every time a new book was written by one of the authors in the database. More importantly, if the same biographical data was needed for other purposes, such as recording awards and prizes, extra links for that purpose would have to be added. The semantics of the document would become a confusion. A better solution (which has the added benefit of allowing you to create links between documents to which you do not have write-access) is to put the information about links between documents in a separate place. Extended links allow you to do this in an elegant way.

The idea is conceptually simple, and will be familiar if you have ever worked with relational databases, or the entity-set/relationship model of data. A link is considered to be a relationship between a collection of resources (in the usual WWW sense), and following mathematical usage, this relationship is simply the unordered collection of resources that participate in it. So, a possible link consists of the book element for *Perl: The Programmer's Companion*, the author element for Nigel Chapman, and the JPEG image of his picture. In order to put these resources together into a link, we need elements that point to all of them. In XLink, such an element has an xlink:type attribute equal to locator, so following the convention introduced previously, it is called a locator-type element. A locator-type element must have an xlink:href locator attribute that points to the resource in question. It may also have a label attribute, which serves to identify it when it is referred to by other elements. So, for our example, we would have elements such as

```
<authorrsrc xlink:type="locator" xlink:label="npc" xlink:href=
  "authors.xml#npc" />
```

```
<authorpic xlink:type="locator" xlink:label="npc-pic" xlink:href=
  "../Images/nchapman.jpg" />
```

```
<bookrsrc xlink:type="locator" xlink:label="perl" xlink:href=
  "books.xml#perl" />
```

To express the existence of a relationship between the resources identified by these locator-type elements, we enclose them in an extended-type element, for instance:

```
<authorship xlink:type="extended">

        <authorrsrc xlink:type="locator" xlink:label="npc"
                xlink:href= "authors.xml#npc" />

        <authorpic xlink:type="locator" xlink:label="npc-pic"
                xlink:href="../Images/nchapman.jpg" />

        <bookrsrc xlink:type="locator" xlink:label="perl"
                xlink:href="books.xml#perl" />

</authorship>
```

This expresses the existence of the link, which simultaneously models the relationships that we might call *written-by* between books and authors, and *author-of* between writers and books. Note that, in general, both of these relationships may be 'many-to-many', that is, any writer may write several books, and any book may have several authors.

Normally, we want to be able to follow links. A link considered as an unordered relationship is too abstract to follow; it needs to be supplemented by information about how to perform traversals between resources participating in the link. This is done by adding arc-type elements to the extended link. These elements have attributes xlink: from and xlink:to, which take labels of locator-type elements as their values, to indicate that traversal should be possible. Additionally, arc-type elements may have the same xlink:actuate and xlink:show attributes as simple-type elements, to specify how they are traversed. In our example, it would be natural to embed the author's picture in the author information document, and to allow traversals between the author and book resources in both directions, so the arc-type elements could be added like this:

```
<authorship xlink:type="extended">
```

locator elements as above

```
        <pic xlink:type="arc" xlink:from="npc" xlink:to="npc-pic"
            xlink:actuate="onLoad" xlink:show="embed" />

        <author-of xlink:type="arc" xlink:from="npc" xlink:to="perl"
                xlink:actuate="onRequest" xlink:show="replace" />

        <written-by xlink:type="arc" xlink:from="perl" xlink:
                to="npc" xlink:actuate="onRequest" xlink:
                show="replace" />
```

```
</authorship>
```

To complete the example, locator-type elements for all the books, authors and their pictures would be added to the authorship element, together with arc-type elements to allow traversal from each author to their books and vice versa. Since, in general, there would be more than one arc from any author or book, a simple click on underlined text could not be used for following arcs when the document was displayed. A possible implementation would be to have a pop-up menu of arc destinations attached to each resource that had an arc going from it.

With extended links, linking information is no longer usually embedded in a document, as in the model of hypermedia that has become familiar from the WWW, but is separated from it. This arrangement permits a greater degree of flexibility, but raises problems of link management. It is envisaged that links will be stored in resources called *linkbases* which will be accessed in conjunction with ordinary documents to provide the linking information that connects them into a Web.

At the time of writing, not many browsers implement XLink. The most notable exception is Mozilla and the browsers based on it, including Netscape 7, which implement simple links. The behaviour of simple links can be simulated using CSS and scripting, however.

Exercises

1   In HTML, any element may have a class attribute, and the values of these attributes can be used to distinguish different ways of using the same element. Discuss whether this provides an adequate alternative to XML as a way of defining document structures to cope with different sorts of content.

2   Rewrite the example XML books document, (a) using no attributes, and (b) using nothing but empty elements. Discuss the relative merits of these two versions and our original.

3   Every valid XHTML document begins like this:
```
<?xml version="1.0" encoding="utf-8"?>
<!DOCTYPE html PUBLIC "-//W3C//DTD XHTML 1.0 Strict//EN"
        "http://www.w3.org/TR/2000/REC-xhtml1-20000126/DTD/
xhtml1-strict.dtd">
<html xmlns="http://www.w3.org/1999/xhtml">
```
Explain carefully what each part of this rubric means, and why it must be present. What would you expect to find after the closing </html> tag in such a document?

4   Write an XML document for a bibliography which includes books with several authors. Use the elements that we used in our example, but, for authors, use firstauthor, otherauthor and lastauthor to distinguish the first (or only) and last authors. Write CSS rules to format lists of authors with appropriate punctuation.

5   The XPath specification states that 'An axis is either a *forward* axis or a *reverse* axis. An axis that only ever contains the context node or nodes that are after the context node in document order is a forward axis. An axis that only ever contains the context node or nodes that are before the context node in document order is a reverse axis.' Classify the axes in Figure 14.5 in accordance with this definition.

6   Assuming HTML tags and attributes, write down XPointers for the following:
(a) The third level 1 header in a document.
(b) The second paragraph after the anchor with name References.
(c) The third anchor element in the fourth paragraph following the second level 2 header.
(d) The first span element in the same paragraph as the anchor with name References.

15

SMIL and SVG

- SMIL
  - Synchronization Elements
  - Links
  - Animation
- SVG
  - Shapes
  - Stroke and Fill
  - Transformations
  - Other Features

As we explained in the previous chapter, XML is a metalanguage, which can be used to create new markup languages. In this chapter, we will consider two such languages, which have been developed for time-based multimedia and vector graphics. It must be admitted that, at the time of writing, neither of these languages is very widely used. Both time-based multimedia and vector graphics on the Web are almost invariably realized by way of Flash. However, Flash uses a proprietary, binary format, whereas the XML-based alternatives are open W3C standards with a textual representation. This means that, by examining the structure and contents of documents and reading the relevant standards, it is easy to see how concepts such as synchronization and filled and stroked shapes can be represented in a way that can be processed by computer programs. This should provide an indirect insight into their representation in other formats, including Flash.

SMIL

SMIL (Synchronized Multimedia Integration Language) is a tag-based language for specifying the temporal structure of a presentation, in a similar way to that in which the structure of a hypermedia document can be specified in HTML. Like HTML, SMIL, being a purely text-based language, can be written using any text editor; it doesn't require special authoring tools (although, again like HTML, elaborate tools can be used to generate SMIL code from a more comfortable environment – for example, a timeline). For our purposes, SMIL has the additional advantage that its textual representation lays bare some of the details of synchronization that are concealed by the timeline metaphor used in authoring tools, and does so in a way that provides a direct comparison with the page-based hypermedia facilities of HTML.

The SMIL 1.0 specification, which was adopted as a World Wide Web Consortium Recommendation in June 1998, defined a first version of a language for defining time-based multimedia presentations in XML. This recommendation was superseded in August 2001 by SMIL 2.0, which enhanced the language with support for animation and transitions, and modularized its definition, to make it easier to integrate parts of SMIL into other languages which need the same facilities. For example, SMIL animation is incorporated into SVG.

SMIL has been implemented in several programs for playing multimedia over the Internet. The widely used RealPlayer G2, although generally thought of as a program for watching streamed video over the Internet, is actually a SMIL player, and is capable of showing synchronized clips in parallel and sequentially. Similarly, QuickTime 4.1 and higher versions incorporate some support for SMIL.

SMIL is defined by an XML DTD, so the form of its tags is identical to that of XML and XHTML, with angle brackets, attribute assignments, and so on. The DTD's public name is -//W3C//DTD SMIL 2.0//EN and its system identifier is http://www.w3.org/2001/SMIL20/SMIL20.dtd. All the element and attribute names belong to a namespace identified by the URL http://www.w3.org/2001/SMIL20/Language; this should be declared as the default namespace for a SMIL document. At the outermost level, the document structure resembles that of an HTML document: the entire document is a smil element, whose content comprises a head followed by a body. Hence, a valid SMIL document has the following outline structure:

```
<?xml version="1.0" encoding="UTF-8"?>

<!DOCTYPE smil PUBLIC "-//W3C//DTD SMIL 2.0//EN"
    "http://www.w3.org/2001/SMIL20/SMIL20.dtd">

<smil xmlns="http://www.w3.org/2001/SMIL20/Language">
    <head>
    ...
    </head>
    <body>
    ...
    </body>
</smil>
```

The head may contain meta elements, which, as in HTML, provide an open-ended mechanism for including in the document information about the document. The head may also include layout information, describing the spatial disposition of the elements of the presentation on the screen. This takes the form of a layout element, which contains definitions written either in CSS2, using its absolute positioning facilities, or in a simpler notation called the *SMIL Basic Layout Language*.

In either case, it is conventional (in SMIL Basic it is necessary) to define the location and dimensions of a collection of *regions*, each associated with one or more of the elements that occur in the document body. These have a region attribute identifying which of the defined regions should be used to display the element; its type attribute indicates the layout language being used. If you are using CSS to specify the layout, within the layout you provide rules whose selectors match on the value of region. For example,

```
<layout type="text/css">
      [region="topleft"] { top:0px; left:0px; width:100px;
                                height:0px; }
</layout>
```

This layout would place any element whose region was set to topleft in a 100-pixel square region at the top left of the window. SMIL Basic provides similar placement facilities to be used by systems that do not support CSS. We will not describe the syntactical details here – consult the SMIL specification if you need to know about the SMIL Basic Layout Language – and in the examples that follow we have elided references to layout and regions to avoid cluttering the presentation. If they are omitted from a SMIL document, a default layout is applied.

Synchronization Elements

As you would expect, the real substance of a SMIL document is its body. The most interesting elements that may appear in the body's content are the *synchronization elements*, for which temporal properties can be specified.[†] These include two compound elements, par (short for 'parallel', and nothing to do with paragraphs) and seq (sequence). Each may contain *media object elements*, which specify the actual images, video clips, sound, and so on, that are used in the presentation. To accommodate complex synchronization relationships, compound synchronization elements may be nested. Elements that occur within a par element may overlap in time, whereas those within a seq are displayed in sequence. A simple example will illustrate how this works, and serve to introduce the attributes that SMIL uses to specify timing and synchronization.

Suppose we wish to assemble four elements for a presentation: two images, a QuickTime movie, and a sound clip, and that we want to

[†] These synchronization elements and the associated attributes form part of the Timing and Synchronization module in the SMIL 2.0 specification.

present them so that the movie starts to play at the beginning of the presentation, and plays in its entirety. Initially, the first image is displayed together with the movie, but after five seconds it is replaced by the other image, which is displayed for 10 seconds before the first image comes back for another 15 seconds. While this is going on, the sound should start playing after five seconds, and continue until 20 seconds into the presentation. (You can safely assume that the layout defined for this presentation causes the various components to be arranged in a sensible way on the screen.) We have three things going on in parallel here: a movie, images, and sound, with the images themselves being displayed in a sequence, so the structure of the SMIL document's body will be a par element containing media objects for the movie and sound and a seq element containing the sequence of images. The complete body is as follows:[†]

† We have used indentation to emphasize the structure of the document; it has no syntactical significance.

```
<body>
    <par>
        <video src="movies/m1.mov"
                type="video/quicktime"/>
        <seq>
            <img src="images/image1.jpeg"
                type="image/jpeg"
                dur="5s"/>

            <img src="images/image2.jpeg"
                type="image/jpeg"
                dur="10s"/>

            <img src="images/image1.jpeg"
                type="image/jpeg"
                dur="15s"/>

        </seq>
        <audio src="sounds/sound1"
                type="audio/aiff"
                begin="5s" end="20s"/>
    </par>
</body>
```

The media object elements are all empty; they each use a src attribute to provide a URL specifying the whereabouts of the media data. (Here we have used relative URLs.) The media object elements allowed are animation, audio, img, ref, text, textstream, and video. The intention of most of these should be clear. The ref element is a catch-all for media that are not accurately described by any of the other tags. In fact, the other tags are purely descriptive synonyms for ref: the type of data is determined by the type attribute, which specifies a MIME type, or by information provided by the server.

The first element in the par thus specifies the movie. The next is a seq for the sequenced images. We must use three img elements, even though two of them relate to the same image – each element corresponds to an occurrence of the image during a particular period of time. The elements within a seq are displayed in the order they appear textually, as you would probably expect. The duration of each can be specified using the dur attribute, which takes a SMIL *clock value*. Clock values can be specified either as a number of hours, minutes, seconds (as in our example) or milliseconds, using the abbreviations h, m, s, and ms, or in the form *hours:mins:secs.fraction*, which is much like a timecode, except that a fraction is used instead of a number of frames, since, in general, we cannot rely on any particular frame rate. The *hours:* and *.fraction* parts are optional. A special value indefinite can be used for dur to specify that we wish an element to continue playing indefinitely.

Instead of specifying a duration, we can specify a start and end time for the display of a media object, using attributes begin and end, as we have done for the audio element in the example above. Whereas durations are time differences, and therefore need no frame of reference, start and end points must be specified relative to some time origin. What this is depends on the enclosing synchronization element. For elements occurring within a par, times are measured relative to the start of the whole par element; for those occurring within a seq, they are measured relative to the end time of the preceding element. Hence, when we specified the begin attribute of the audio clip in the example above as 5s, this made the sound start playing five seconds after the beginning of the presentation (since the containing par element is the outermost synchronization element of the whole document); specifying its end as 20s truncates the clip's duration to 15 seconds. Figure 15.1 illustrates the synchronization of this presentation on a timeline. The natural duration of the video clip, which is used in the absence of any explicit attributes, is 10 seconds.

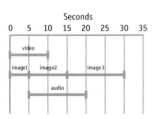

Figure 15.1 Effect of SMIL synchronization elements

The SMIL specification includes rules to ensure that synchronization attributes can only be used sensibly. For example, an element's end value must not precede its begin.

The timing of the sequential elements in this presentation was specified purely by their duration, so they butt together in time. If we use begin and end, we can create pauses between them. For example, if we change the second img element as follows:

```
<img src="images/image2.jpeg"
    type="image/jpeg"
    region="upper"
    begin="5s" end="20s"/>
```

there will be a five-second gap between the display of image1 and image2 – because this is a seq element, the start time is not evaluated relative to the start of the synchronization element, but to the end of the preceding element. Figure 15.2 shows the effect of this change on the presentation's timeline.

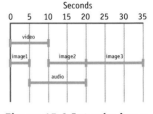
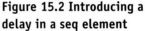

Figure 15.2 Introducing a delay in a seq element

The begin and end attributes can be thought of as specifying the position of SMIL elements on the presentation's timeline. Media elements such as video and audio clips or streamed text have their own internal timeline (cf. movie clips in Flash); the attributes clipBegin and clipEnd can be used to specify offsets within an internal timeline, in order to extract a section from within a clip. For example, if the movie movies/fullmovie.mov was one minute long, the element

```
<video src="movies/fullmovie.mov" clipBegin="20s" clipEnd="40s">
```

would define a 20-second clip from the middle of it. The use of these attributes removes the need to create a separate movie for the extract.

Elements can be synchronized with reference to each other. For this to be possible, each media element must have an id attribute with a unique name as its value, which identifies the element in the same way as id attributes identify HTML document elements. A time value can then be specified as a *syncbase* value of the form *element-id.time-symbol*, where the *time-symbol* is one of begin or end. These denote the start and end times of the element identified by *element-id*, respectively. You can also specify an offset from the beginning or the end, by appending +*clock-value* or −*clock-value*. For example, to delay the onset of the sound track of our example presentation until two seconds after the video had finished playing, we could make the following modifications:

```
<video src="movies/m1.mov"
    id="vid"
    type="video/quicktime"/>
```

```
<audio src="sounds/sound1"
       type="audio/aiff"
       begin="vid.end+2s"/>
```

This way of specifying times, using a syncbase value, is often more convenient than specifying them relative to the start of the enclosing synchronizing element; if the duration of some of the media elements is not known, it is essential.

When a par element contains elements that do not all finish at the same time, the question arises of when the whole par ends. Looking back at Figure 15.1, you will see that there are at least two reasonable candidates for the end time of the combination of video, images, and sound: at 10 seconds – the earliest point at which one of the elements finishes, and at 30 seconds – the latest. Probably, the latter seems the more sensible interpretation, and that is what SMIL takes as the default: the end time of a par element is equal to the latest end time of any of its children (the elements it contains). The endsync attribute may be used to change this behaviour. Its value may be last, which is the same as the default; first, which makes the end time of the par equal to the earliest end time of any of its children; or *element-id*, which makes the end of the par equal to the end of its child with id equal to *element-id*. For example, to make our presentation finish as soon as the video ended, we would change the start tag of the par element to:

```
<par endsync="first">
```

or

```
<par endsync="vid">
```

If we use any endsync value other than first, what should happen to elements that terminate before the end of the par? Looking at Figure 15.1 again, you will see that there is a 20-second gap between the end of the video and the end of the whole presentation. What should happen to the video during this gap? Should it disappear from its allotted region, or should it be held frozen on its final frame? SMIL lets us choose between these two alternatives using the fill attribute, which can take either of the values remove or freeze (the default). To make our video disappear after it has reached its end, we would use the following tag:

```
<video src="movies/m1.mov" fill="remove"
       type="video/quicktime"/>
```

An alternative you might prefer to either of these options is to have the video start playing again from the beginning. Generally, you can arrange for any synchronization element to be repeated a specific number of times using the repeatCount attribute, whose value is a number, indicating the number of times the element is to play.

Since our video is 10 seconds long, we can fill the entire presentation using three iterations of the video.

```
<video src="movies/m1.mov" type="video/quicktime"
       repeatCount="3" />
```

The value of repeatCount can also be indefinite, which, as you would expect, means that the element loops indefinitely – not, though, forever. If an element has an indefinite repeat count, it runs for as long as it needs to in order to 'fill up' an enclosing par or seq. If, in our example, our video element had the following tag:

```
<video src="movies/m1.mov" type="video/quicktime"
       repeatCount="indefinite" />
```

the clip would play until the last image had been displayed for its full duration, no matter how long the video was. The repeatCount attribute can be applied to a par or seq, as well as directly to media elements, so that combinations of media elements can be made to repeat as a unit.

At first sight, although they may be awkward to work with, SMIL's synchronization elements and time-related attributes appear to be sufficient to allow a multimedia author to specify precisely any possible temporal relationship between the individual media elements of a presentation. It doesn't require much imagination to see how SMIL, or its equivalent, could be generated from a timeline, so it would appear that implementing synchronized multimedia presentations is fairly trivial. In reality, things are not quite so rosy. SMIL's synchronization mechanism depends on the assumption that we can unambiguously measure the time taken to play any media element. For time-based media such as audio and video this is not the case. There are two distinct ways of measuring the time that elapses during playback. Consider a video clip that is intended to play at a rate of 15 frames per second. Assuming its id attribute's value is clip1, what time does the value clip1.begin+3s specify? Is it the time at which playback of the clip reaches its 46th frame, or is it three seconds after the clip starts to play, as measured by the clock of the computer system on which it is playing? There is no guarantee that the two will be the same,

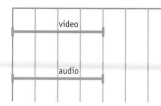

Figure 15.3 Video and audio perfectly synchronized

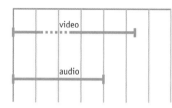

Figure 15.4 Soft synchronization

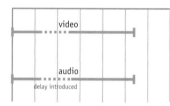

Figure 15.5 Hard synchronization, audio delay introduced

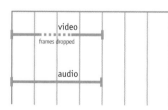

Figure 15.6 Hard synchronization, video frames dropped

because there can be no guarantee that the clip will really play at the correct frame rate: the processor or disk may not be fast enough, or, if the clip is being streamed over a network, transmission delays may occur, causing some frames to be delivered too late. Hence, we must distinguish beween *media time*, the time measured by counting how much of the clip has been played, and *presentation time*, the elapsed time measured with reference to an external clock. SMIL clock values could be interpreted as either, producing different results. If they are interpreted as media time, then media elements wait for each other if a delay occurs; if they are interpreted as presentation time, synchronization may be lost, but the total running time of a presentation will be maintained. In SMIL 2.0, the former interpretation is adopted: the specification states that, 'There is no direct relationship between the local "time" for an element, and the real world concept of time as reflected on a clock.'

The same effect shows up in a different guise when we consider the moment-to-moment synchronization of elements within a par. If, for example, an audio clip and a video clip are playing simultaneously, we would expect them both to play at the same rate; in other words, media time in the two should pass at the same speed. If this is not the case, then the audio and video could slip relative to each other, leading to undesirable effects, such as loss of lip-sync, or the displacement of cuts in the video relative to the tempo of music on an accompanying sound track. On real computers and over real networks, independent delays can occur to either audio or video. Again, there is a choice between two possible responses, and a SMIL player is permitted to use either: it can use *hard synchronization*, with the elements within a par being synchronized to a common clock (thereby effectively matching their presentation times); or *soft synchronization*, with each having its own clock. Soft synchronization is really no synchronization, but it ensures that each element is played in its entirety. Hard synchronization maintains the temporal relationships between the elements (as nearly as is possible in the presence of delays), but distorts playback.

Suppose, for example, that we have one video and one audio clip of identical durations, playing in parallel (see Figure 15.3), and that the video element experiences a delay of some sort during playback. If soft synchronization is used, the audio will carry on playing, and when the video resumes it will be out of sync (see Figure 15.4, where the dotted portion of the video line indicates a delay). To preserve hard synchronization, one of two things must be done. Either the audio must also be stopped until the delayed video data arrives (Figure 15.5), or some video frames must be dropped until the picture catches up with the sound again (Figure 15.6). The latter option is usually less intrusive, but, in the worst case, the picture may never catch up with the sound, so neither is very satisfactory.

SMIL allows the synchronization behaviour of elements to be specified using the syncBehaviour attribute. This may take the value locked, to force hard sync with the synchronization element containing the element (and thus if the synchronization element is a par, with all the other elements it contains), or canSlip, to allow slippage (i.e. soft sync). Where hard sync is specified, delays are introduced – all elements wait for the one that has been delayed.

In contrast, the synchronization of separate tracks in a QuickTime movie, which we sketched in Chapter 9, is equivalent to hard synchronization, with frame dropping. Note that the use of the QuickTime time base is essential to detecting and correcting for loss of synchronization.

The problems just outlined are not a specific shortcoming of SMIL but are inevitable where synchronization is desired, but unpredictable delays can occur. Ideally, one would like to ensure that delays cannot occur, or are kept so short that they do not interfere with playback. This can never be guaranteed, but we can assist by selecting versions of video and audio clips whose data rate is matched to the capabilities of the user's computer and network connection (the latter usually being the limiting factor). SMIL's switch element may be used for this purpose.

A switch may contain any number of other elements, each of which has one or more *test attributes*, which behave in a somewhat different way from other attributes. Their value is tested against some system parameter; if the test succeeds, the element may be selected and rendered. Only one of the elements within a switch is selected; they are considered in the order they appear in the document, and the first one whose test succeeds is chosen. The test attribute that is most relevant to our present discussion is systemBitrate, whose value is a number that is interpreted as a bandwidth in bits per second, and tested against the system bandwidth. This latter value may be simply taken from a user preference, for example specifying a modem connection rate, or it may be calculated from actual measurements of the system's performance. The mode of calculation is implementation-dependent. A test of this attribute succeeds if the available system bandwidth is greater than or equal to its value. Hence, a sequence of media elements can be provided in decreasing order of bandwidth requirements, with corresponding systemBitrate values, within a switch, so that a version can be chosen that is within the capabilities of the system. For example, we could prepare several different versions of a video clip, at different frame sizes and compression quality settings, and choose one of them as follows:

```
<switch>

    <video src="movies/mpeg4-full-size-movie.mov"
           system-bitrate="56000"
           type="video/quicktime" />

    <video src="movies/sorenson-full-size-movie.mov"
           system-bitrate="28800"
           type="video/quicktime"/>

    <video src="movies/cinepak-quarter-size-movie.mov"
           system-bitrate="14400"
           type="video/quicktime"/>

    <img src="images/movie-still.jpeg"
         system-bitrate="1"
         type="image/jpeg"/>

</switch>
```

Note the final element in the switch: this is a default option (presumably the test will always succeed); a still image is selected, which does not place any strain on the capabilities of a low bandwidth system.

Other test attributes include systemLanguage, which is used to select between different languages for text and speech, based on the user's preferences; systemCaptions, which can be set to the value on to display subtitling captions, for example to supply a transcript of an audio soundtrack for the benefit of deaf people; and systemScreenSize and systemScreenDepth, which are used to choose between different versions of images designed for particular screen sizes or colour depths.

Links

We remarked in Chapter 1 that the distinction between page-based and time-based multimedia is not an absolute one: each style may possess characteristics of the other. As a prime example, SMIL provides simple unidirectional links, using linking elements modelled on HTML's anchors; however, the extra dimension of time that is central to SMIL calls for some refinement of the notion of linkage.

There are two linking element types in SMIL, the simpler being a, which behaves as a link source, much as HTML's a element type can. The mandatory href attribute holds the URL of the link's destination; the attributes show and actuate are used in the same way as they are in XLink's simple links, described in Chapter 14. The default value for actuate is onRequest, so normally, clicking on the a element's content causes a jump to the destination, which will usually be another SMIL presentation. Formally, a elements have no synchronization properties and do not affect the temporal behaviour of any elements they contain. Since the content of an a is all that is actually displayed, and since the elements in the content will, in general, have a specified duration, the a element will behave as if it is only there while its content is being displayed. Consider the following simple presentation, for example.

```
<seq>
    <a href="presentation1.smil">
        <img src="images/image1.jpeg"
            type="image/jpeg"
            dur="15s"/>
    </a>
    <a href="presentation2.smil">
        <img src="images/image2.jpeg"
            type="image/jpeg"
            dur="15s"/>
    </a>
    <a href="presentation3.smil">
        <img src="images/image3.jpeg"
            type="image/jpeg"
            dur="15s"/>
    </a>
</seq>
```

Three images are displayed in sequence. Each of the images is contained in an a link, whose href points to a presentation – presumably one which expands on the content of the corresponding image. During the display of an image, clicking on it will activate the enclosing anchor, causing the linked presentation to begin playing. By default, the new presentation replaces the old one; the show attribute has the value replace by default. As well as new, which causes the new presentation to start up in a new window, leaving the old one playing in its original window, show may have the value pause, which causes the new presentation to start up in its own window, but leaves the old presentation paused at its current point, from which it resumes after the new presentation has finished. This attribute value is specific to SMIL, since it only makes sense in the context of a time-based presentation.

Like HTML, SMIL supports the use of fragment identifiers in URLs, so that links can point to individual elements (identified by the value of their id attribute) within a presentation. Again, the temporal dimension complicates matters. Consider a link such as the following:

```
<a href="presentation2.smil#vid1">
    <img src="images/image2.jpeg" type="image/jpeg"
        dur="15s"/>
</a>
```

and suppose that presentation2.smil has the following body:

```
<seq>
    <video src="movies/m1.mov"
        id="vid0"
        type="video/quicktime"/>

    <par>
        <seq>
            <img src="images/image1.jpeg" type="image/jpeg"
                id="img1" region="upper" dur="5s"/>

            <video src="movies/m1.mov" id="vid1"
                type="video/quicktime"/>

            <video src="movies/m1.mov" id="vid2"
                type="video/quicktime"/>
        </seq>

        <audio src="sounds/sound1" type="audio/aiff"
            begin="5s"/>
    </par>
</seq>
```

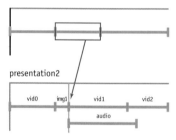

Figure 15.7 Effect of a fragment identifier

(The lower part of Figure 15.7 shows its timeline.) When the link is activated (at any time during the display of the image it contains, as shown in the diagram), a jump is made to the element with id equal to vid1. This element is not displayed until five seconds into the par element that follows the first video clip (vid0), so the effect of the jump must be to start presentation2.smil at that point, skipping the initial video clip and image. In general, when the destination URL of a link has a fragment identifier, the effect of following the link is to start the presentation containing the element it identifies, but as if the user had fast-forwarded to the point at which that element begins. Note that, where the element in question is within a par, all of the elements that are specified to play at the same time will be displayed. Hence, in the example just given, when the link is followed the sound will play as well as the video clip vid1.

SMIL's a elements, in conjunction with fragment identifiers, provide links between entire elements; in other words, they connect identifiable points on the timelines of presentations. SMIL allows a more refined sort of link, based on identifying regions within the individual timelines of media elements. It provides the area element for this purpose. These elements are the only ones that can appear in the content of a media element. (Previously we have always supposed that media elements were empty.)

An area is similar to the element of the same name used in HTML to define hot spots in image maps. It has an href attribute to specify a link destination, and shape and coords attributes, which together define a hot spot within the region in which the media element that contains it is displayed. A media element containg areas behaves in the same way as an image map in HTML, but in SMIL, areas can be associated with other media besides images.

An image map divides up the spatial region occupied by an object, associating links with different sub-regions. Since SMIL elements have a temporal dimension, it is also possible to divide up the time occupied by an object, and associate links with different intervals. The begin, end and dur attributes may be provided for an area for this purpose; here, they have the same meaning as they do for media elements. Suppose, for example, that the file trailers.mov contains a 30-second movie, consisting of three 10-second segments, each of which is a trailer for some other movie (say an original Hollywood blockbuster and its two sequels). The following SMIL code will cause the trailer movie to play indefinitely; during each segment, if a user clicks on it, the corresponding full movie will be streamed from a video server.[†] Notice that, for the first time, the video element has separate start and end tags, because it is not empty.

†See Chapter 17 for an explanation of rtsp://.

```
<video src="trailers.mov" type="video/quicktime"
       repeatCount="indefinite">

    <area href="rtsp://movies.com/blockbuster.mov"
          id="trailer1" begin="0s" end="10s"/>
```

```
<area href="rtsp://movies.com/first_sequel.mov"
    id="trailer2" begin="10s" end="20s"/>

<area href="rtsp://movies.com/second_sequel.mov"
    id="trailer3" begin="20s" end="30s"/>
</video>
```

The id attributes of **area** elements can be used as fragment identifiers in URLs, so that segments of a movie can be used as link destinations. (The SMIL 2.0 specification permits the use of XPointers, too, but does not require it.) For example, if the previous example appears in a file called trailers.smil, a presentation in the same directory could include an image map built out of anchors, such as the following:

```
<img src="poster.jpeg" type="image/jpeg">

    <area href="trailers.smil#trailer1"
        shape="rect" coords="0, 0, 100%, 50%" />
    <area href="trailers.smil#trailer2"
        shape="rect" coords="0, 50%, 50%, 100%" />
    <area href="trailers.smil#trailer3"
        shape="rect" coords="50% 50% 100% 100%" />

</img>
```

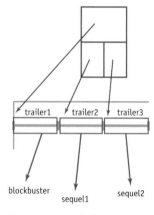

Figure 15.8 Link sources and destinations

Assuming that the top half of the image holds a still from the original blockbuster, while the bottom half is divided into two, showing stills from the two sequels, clicking on a still will cause the trailers video to start playing at the beginning of the trailer for the appropriate movie (see Figure 15.8).

We have used SMIL 2.0 syntax throughout this section, but all the functionality we have described so far is also available in SMIL 1.0, with some minor changes of syntax. In particular, attributes with compound names such as clipBegin used hyphens to separate words, as in clip-begin, and syncbase values of the form *identifier*.begin+*time* would be written id(*identifier*)(*time*). Also, the **area** element's function was provided by **anchor**. These SMIL 1.0 forms can still be used in SMIL 2.0, but they are deprecated, meaning that support for them may be dropped in the future and the newer syntax should be used in preference.

Animation

In SMIL 1.0, the only way to incorporate animation in a presentation was by using an **animation** element to embed an animation, for example a SWF file, held in an external file. SMIL synchronization elements could then be used to determine when the animation played within the timeline of the larger presentation. Since much animation of a certain type is concerned with changing the position and other properties of objects on a timeline (consider motion tweening in Flash, for example), there is scope for animating directly within the framework of SMIL. In SMIL 2.0, support for this sort of animation has been added.

The basis of the animation mechanism is the animate element (which is wholly distinct from the animation element). The attributes of this element specify a property of some other element to be animated and the way its values should change as the animation proceeds. By default, the animation is applied to the parent element of the animate element. For example, to animate an image, an animate could be placed inside an img. Alternatively, the id value of any element may be assigned to the targetElement attribute of an animate element, to identify the element whose property is to be animated. The animated property may be a CSS property that has been applied to the element, or one of its attributes. It is identified using the attributeName attribute, which must always be present. In the case of name clashes, a SMIL processor uses a default algorithm to determine what to animate: CSS properties are given priority over attributes. If necessary, you can explicitly specify the type, using the optional attributeType attribute, which may be set to "CSS" or "XML", for CSS properties or XML attributes, respectively, or to "auto" to specify the default behaviour explicitly.

The time-varying changes to the animated property may be specified in several different ways. The simplest uses two attributes of the animate element: from and to, whose values provide an initial and final value for the property. Having specified what is to change, using attributeName and the changing values, using from and to, it only remains to specify when the change should take place, which is done using the dur, begin and end attributes, which we described in the context of SMIL's synchronization elements.

This animation mechanism can be illustrated using a simple example. Suppose we want to zoom in to an image, by expanding the height and width of an img element. This can be done in the following way:

```
<img src="Images/logo.jpeg" type="image/jpeg" >
    <animate attributeName = "width" from="10" to="100"
                                        dur="9s" />
    <animate attributeName = "height" from="10" to="100"
                                        dur="9s" />
</img>
```

Starting as a small, 10 pixel square, image, the logo will grow uniformly by a factor of 10 over the course of nine seconds. The time at which the animation occurs will be determined by any synchronization element enclosing the imq element. Note that the img is no longer an empty element. The same effect could have been achieved by providing an id attribute for the image and moving the animate elements out of it:

```
<img src="Images/logo.jpeg" type="image/jpeg" id="thelogo" />
<animate targetElement="thelogo" attributeName = "width"
                                 from="10" to="100" dur="9s" />
<animate targetElement="thelogo" attributeName = "height"
                                 from="10" to="100" dur="9s" />
```

The syntax we have described, using from and to attributes, is a special case of a more general way of describing an animation with a set of values, which the changing property takes on over the course of the animation. These values are given as a list, separated by semicolons, which is assigned to the attribute values. For instance,

```
<animate targetElement="thelogo" attributeName = "width"
                                 values="10;20;40;80;160" dur="8s"
/>
```

Clearly, this causes the logo's width to grow from 10 to 160 pixels over the course of eight seconds, but at what rate? By default, linear interpolation is used between the specified values. In this context, this means that the duration of the animation is divided into $n-1$ intervals of equal length, where n is the number of values specified. At the beginning of each interval, the property is set to the corresponding value in the list (i.e. to begin with, it is set to the first value, at the end of the first interval, it is set to the second value, and so on, until at the end of the duration it is set to the final value). During each interval, the value changes steadily, at a uniform rate. In our example, therefore, the width of the logo would expand at an exponentially increasing rate, doubling every two seconds (see Figure 15.9). This form of interpolation can be explicitly specified by setting the calcMode attribute of animate to "linear".

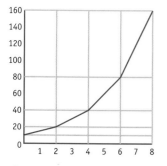

Figure 15.9 Linear interpolation

As you might expect from this, other values may be used for the calcMode. If calcMode="discrete", the duration is divided into equal intervals, as before, but n intervals are used and the property is held steady during each, jumping straight to the next value at the end of the interval (see Figure 15.10). Finally, the value can be "paced", where the lengths of the intervals are adjusted so that the rate of change is constant (see Figure 15.11).

You should now be able to see that an animation as we originally described it, using from and to attributes, is equivalent to an animation with just two values and a calcMode of "linear". For convenience, three other shorthand forms are provided. Instead of using the to attribute to specify an absolute final value for the property, you can instead specify a relative final value, using the by attribute. For example,

```
<img src="Images/logo.jpeg" type="image/jpeg" >
        <animate attributeName="width" from="10" by="90"
                                        dur="9s" />
        <animate attributeName="height" from="10" by="90"
                                         dur="9s" />
</img>
```

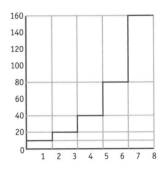

Figure 15.10 Discrete interpolation

has the same effect as our original animation. This may be more convenient on occasion, but is especially useful in an even more shortened form, where from is omitted. In that case, the original value of the animated property is used as the starting value, so by can be used to specify a change. You can also omit from when you include to; in this case, you are specifying a target value for the property to reach over the course of the animation, starting from whatever value it had to begin with.

If you set the value attribute to a list whose first and last members are the same, you will have a looping animation, that ends up where it started. (The loop will only be smooth if the calcMode is "linear" or "paced".) This suggests the possibility of making animations repeat, and indeed you can use the repeatCount and repeatDur attributes on an animate element, with the same meaning as we described for synchronization elements.

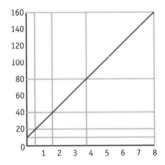

Figure 15.11 Paced interpolation

In general, if an animate element is set to repeat, it will go back to the beginning at the end of each iteration. (If the repetition is specified as a duration, with repeatDur, or if the repeatCount is not a whole number, it may not finish before jumping back to the beginning, or the fill attribute may need to be used, if the duration of the animation does not match the repeat duration.) This will happen whether or not the start and end values match, though the result will only be a smooth loop if they do. You may prefer a different sort of behaviour, though: the animation could loop, and then start again at the point it had reached at the end of the first loop. This would allow you to build up complex movements by accumulating the effect of simpler ones. Consider, for example, the following variant of our logo animation:

```
<img src="Images/logo.jpeg" type="image/jpeg" >
    <animate attributeName="width" values="0;15;10"
                            dur="2s" repeatCount="10" />
    <animate attributeName="height" values="0;15;10"
                            dur="2s" repeatCount="10"/>
</img>
```

The logo will expand from nothing to 15 pixels square, then contract to 10 pixels; it will repeat this ten times. However, if we set the attribute accumulate to "sum", like this:

```
<img src="Images/logo.jpeg" type="image/jpeg" >
    <animate attributeName="width" values="0;15;10"
                dur="2s" repeatCount="10" accumulate="sum"
/>
    <animate attributeName="height" values="0;15;10"
                dur="2s" repeatCount="10" accumulate="sum"
/>
</img>
```

the logo will first expand to 15 pixels and contract to 10, but then it will expand by a further 15 pixels to 25, before contracting to 20, and then expand to 35, and so on. Over the course of the repeated animation, it will expand to 100 pixels in a pulsating motion.

It should be clear that the animation facilities provided by SMIL are extremely primitive, and it would be very tedious indeed to try and create animation by writing these elements by hand. Even though there are some extra facilities, which we have not described, this remains the case. However, if you think about motion tweening in Flash, you should be able to see that it would be possible to express any sort of tweened motion using an animate element, and that ordinary sequencing of frames can be expressed using the synchronization elements. Thus, relatively sophisticated animation can be built up by a suitable combination of SMIL elements. This would only be a feasible way of creating animation, though, if the SMIL was generated automatically from some authoring environment with similar facilities to Flash.

SVG

The *Scalable Vector Graphics (SVG)* language provides a way of describing two-dimensional vector graphics using XML. In the words of the SVG specification:

> "SVG allows for three types of graphic objects: vector graphic shapes (e.g., paths consisting of straight lines and curves), images and text. Graphical objects can be grouped, styled, transformed and composited into previously rendered objects."

This should sound familiar, since these are the types of object that can be manipulated by vector graphics packages such as Illustrator, and which we described in Chapter 4. Indeed, the usual way of producing SVG documents is by exporting them from such a program. Our purpose in describing SVG here is not to enable you to write SVG by hand but to show you how vector graphics objects and transformations can be represented in a format that can be processed by a computer. For this reason, we will make no attempt at completeness in our account.

The simplest way to introduce SVG's manner of representing vector graphics using XML constructs is with a trivial example.

```
<?xml version="1.0" encoding="utf-8"?>

<!DOCTYPE svg PUBLIC "-//W3C//DTD SVG 1.0//EN"
"http://www.w3.org/TR/2001/REC-SVG-20010904/DTD/
svg10.dtd">

<svg xmlns="http://www.w3.org/2000/svg">
    <rect x="120" y="120" width="126" height="126" fill="lime"
          stroke="magenta" stroke-width="4" />
</svg>
```

The first line is the familiar XML declaration, which you should have expected. This is followed by a DOCTYPE declaration, declaring svg as the document element, and showing the public name and system identifier for the SVG DTD. These lines are just the usual XML red tape. After them comes the document proper, which is contained in the svg element. Unlike XHTML and SMIL documents, SVG documents are not divided into a head and body. In this example, the only attribute we have provided for svg is xmlns, which declares the SVG namespace as the default namespace, so within the svg element we can use SVG element and attribute names without a prefix. This is the normal arrangement for SVG documents that are intended to stand alone; it is, however, possible to embed SVG fragments inside other types of XML document, in which case it is necessary to use a namespace prefix, usually svg:. We will not go into this possibility any further.

If you want to examine some SVG code that has been generated by a program, you can export any drawing from Adobe Illustrator by choosing the Save As... command from the File menu, and choosing SVG from the pop-up menu of file types. When the options dialogue appears, make sure that the option Preserve Illustrator Editing Capabilities is off, otherwise a lot of confusing extra data will be generated.

Shapes

Figure 15.12 Display of a simple SVG document

Within the svg element comes the real business of the document: the representation of graphic objects. In this case, there is only one, a coloured square (see Figure 15.12). This shape is described by a single element, of type rect, whose attributes provide all the pieces of information necessary to draw the square in its chosen position. The x and y attribute's values are the coordinates of the upper left corner of the rectangle; the height and width attributes set its size. The remaining attributes specify the presentation (i.e. appearance) of the rectangle; they use the same names and values as corresponding CSS properties. Here, we have set the stroke and fill colours, using the attributes stroke and fill, and the width of the stroke, using stroke-width.

When you draw a rectangle in a program such as Illustrator, you first set the fill and stroke colours and stroke width, then you position the rectangle tool at the place where you want to draw the rectangle, and drag out the shape. That is, the drawing operation actually involves setting the three appearance attributes, the position of the shape and its dimensions, the latter two being set by mouse gesture. Thus, the attributes of the rect element store the same values as we set when we draw a rectangle. You will see that the other SVG elements we will describe exhibit a similar pattern: their attributes (or sometimes the element content) holds the same values as are set, implicitly or explicitly, when drawing the corresponding object in an illustration program.

In particular, the expected repertoire of simple shapes – rectangles, circles, ellipses, lines, polylines and polygons – each have their own element. These elements have attributes controlling their appearance in common; each has its own distinctive attributes for specifying the

Table 15.1 SVG shape elements

Element name	Attributes	Notes
rect	x	coordinates of top
	y	left corner
	width	
	height	
	rx	*x* and *y* radii of
	ry	rounded corners
circle	cx	coordinates of
	cy	centre
	r	radius
ellipse	cx	coordinates of
	cy	centre
	rx	
	ry	*x* and *y* radii
line	x1	
	y1	coordinates of
	x2	end points
	y2	
polyline	points	list of points – see
polygon	points	text

shape and its position. Table 15.1 summarizes these elements and their attributes. Figure 15.13 is a rendering of the following SVG document, which uses some of the shape elements and their attributes.

```
<?xml version="1.0" encoding="utf-8"?>

<!DOCTYPE svg PUBLIC "-//W3C//DTD SVG 1.0//EN"
"http://www.w3.org/TR/2001/REC-SVG-20010904/DTD/
svg10.dtd">

<svg xmlns="http://www.w3.org/2000/svg">
     <circle cx="50" cy="50" r="50" fill="#F67155"
          stroke="none" />
     <polygon points="50,10 66,10 76,27 66,42 50,42 40,25"
          fill="#697FBA" stroke="none" />
     <polyline points="40,25 1,50 50,99 99,50, 76,27"
          stroke="#99A6CF" stroke-linejoin="round"
          stroke-linecap="round" fill="none" />
</svg>
```

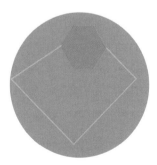

Figure 15.13 Shapes

Note the form of the points attribute values for the polygon and polyline. Strictly speaking, these values may comprise a sequence of coordinate values, separated by whitespace, commas or both. Here, we have adopted a convention whereby two coordinates that should be understood as points are separated by a comma, and each pair is separated from the next by a space. This convention is merely intended to improve readability; whichever separators are used, the coordinates are always examined from left to right, and considered as alternating *x* and *y* values. (This example also illustrates some further presentation attributes, which we will explain shortly.)

In vector graphics, shapes are special cases of a path consisting of a sequence of lines and curves, as we decribed in Chapter 4. SVG provides a path element for the general case. The description of the path is given in a string containing the *path data*, which is the value of the d attribute. This path data consists of a set of instructions for drawing the path, as if with a pen. These instructions are written in a special compact notation. Each instruction is represented by a single letter, which is followed by a series of coordinates; the number and interpretation of these coordinates depends on the instruction they belong to.

Every path begins with an M instruction; M is short for 'move to'. The following two values are taken as the coordinates of the point at which the path begins, and the instruction establishes a *current point*. In other words, they tell you where to move the pen to before you start drawing with it. Straight line segments are drawn by the L instruction. This instruction is also followed by a pair of coordinates, separated by whitespace or a comma; its effect is to draw a straight line from the current point to the point specified by those coordinates, which then becomes the new current point. Sometimes, it may be more convenient to specify the end of the line as an offset from the current point. This is done using the l command. The two coordinates that follow it are treated as offsets in the horizontal and vertical directions from the current point. The polyline in Figure 15.13 could have been drawn using the following path element (see Figure 15.14):

```
<path fill="none" stroke="#99A6CF" stroke-linecap="round"
    stroke-linejoin="round"
    d="M40,25l-39,25l49,49l49,-49l-23,-23"/>
```

Figure 15.14 A polyline

Here we have used an additional notational shorthand: whitespace can be omitted where doing so causes no ambiguity. The reason for this is that, when SVG documents are generated from complicated graphics by a program, it is likely that the path data will be the single largest contributor to the size of the resulting file. Since SVG is a Web format, it is desirable to keep the file size to a minimum, and condensing the path data in this way helps do so.

Since horizontal and vertical lines are more common than lines at any other orientation in most types of graphic illustration, there are special instructions for these: H and h are each followed by a single value, and result in a horizontal line from the current point to a point with the same y coordinate and the specified x coordinate. In the case of H, the value is treated as an absolute coordinate; for h it is an offset from the current point. Similarly, V and v are absolute and relative instructions for drawing vertical lines; the coordinate following them gives the y coordinate or offset of the end point. (In general, as you will no doubt have guessed, an instruction with a lower-case letter is a version of the instruction with the same letter in upper-case, which uses relative coordinates instead of absolute ones.)

In Chapter 4, we described how Bézier curves are used to construct smooth flowing paths and outlines, since they can be combined without discontinuities. SVG supports Bézier curve segments within a path. The C instruction is followed by six coordinate values; call them x_2, y_2, x_3, y_3, x_4 and y_4. These are interpreted as the coordinates of three points, $P_2 = (x_2, y_2)$, $P_3 = (x_3, y_3)$ and $P_4 = (x_4, y_4)$, corresponding to the two control points and the endpoint of a Bézier curve segment that begins at the current point. If you let P_1 be the current point, then the naming of the points corresponds to Figure 4.8 from Chapter 4. The c instruction is used to specify a Bézier curve using relative coordinates.

The typical way of combining curve segments into a smooth path, by using the endpoint of one segment as the start curve of the next, keeping the gradient constant by using control points that are placed symmetrically, is optimized with the S and s commands, which each take just four coordinates. In the notation used in the previous paragraph, these are $P_3 = (x_3, y_3)$ and $P_4 = (x_4, y_4)$. The missing control point P_2 is taken to be the same as the second control point on the preceding curve segment, reflected in the current point. Figure 15.15 illustrates how C and S instructions may be combined to produce smoothly joined curves; the highlighted control point is implicit in the use of S. The path element for this curve is:

```
<path fill="none" stroke="#99A6CF" stroke-width="2"
    d="M0,0C80,50,80,60,0,80S0,150 80,120"/>
```

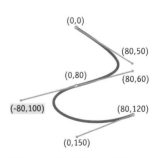

Figure 15.15 Smoothly joined Bézier curves

Stroke and Fill

The examples given so far illustrate the way in which simple stroke and fill properties are represented: the various shape elements and the path element can all have stroke and fill attributes to specify the stroke and fill colours. Their values may be given in any of the forms used in CSS for colour properties; SVG offers an extended range of named colours, but since SVG is almost always automatically generated, colours can just as well be specified as hexadecimal colour codes, which we have used in most of our examples. As you would expect, the width of a stroke can also be specified; this is done using the stroke-width property. Stroke widths are specified by default in pixels. When a path is painted with colour, the colour is applied symmetrically about the zero-width path that the pure geometrical specification of the corresponding document element describes. Hence, the following element specifies a square whose exterior height and width are 130 pixels:

```
<rect x="120" y="120" width="126" height="126" stroke-
    width="4" fill="lime" stroke="magenta" />
```

The width and height attributes specify a 126 pixel square, and the coloured stroke extends two pixels each side of this.

The way in which lines are terminated and joined can be specified using the stroke-linecap and stroke-linejoin attributes. The former may take any of the values "butt", "round" and "square", while the latter has the possibilities "round", "bevel" and "miter" (*sic*). For this last case, there is also a miterlimit attribute to restrict the length of projecting mitred joints. These attributes' values correspond to the properties of line ends and joins described and illustrated on page 106 in Chapter 4.

Both stroke and fill can be made partially transparent. The attributes stroke-opacity and fill-opacity are used for this purpose. A value of zero makes the stroke or fill completely transparent, a value of one makes it completely opaque. Values between these extremes are used to produce partially transparent strokes and fills. We will use these attributes in some later examples.

By default, all fill and stroke attributes are inherited from enclosing document elements, in the same way as the similar properties are inherited in CSS.

The case of gradient fills is more interesting, both in the way gradients are defined and in how they are used. SVG supports linear and radial gradients, with the linearGradient and radialGradient elements. Both of these elements have some attributes that are used in a technical way to map the gradient onto the area it is used to fill, but we can safely ignore these and concentrate on the elements' content, which is where the gradient's colours and spacing are specified. It is important, though, to provide an id attribute value for gradients, since, as we will see, these are used to identify a particular gradient when it is applied.

The content of a gradient element of either sort consists of stop elements. These correspond directly to the gradient stops used in drawing programs to define gradients interactively. Figure 15.16 shows the Gradient palette in Adobe Illustrator, for example. The bar at the bottom of the palette shows the gradient under construction. Each of the little tabs underneath the gradient is a point at which a colour value is set. Between the tabs, the colours blend gradually to form the gradient. Tabs are added just by clicking under the bar, and the colour is set by clicking on a tab and then using the colour selection facilities of the program. Here we have created a linear blend from blue to yellow and then to red, with the yellow being just off the middle of the gradient.

This gradient could be represented in SVG with the following element:

```
<linearGradient id="lgrad_1">
    <stop offset="0" stop-color="#0C419A"/>
    <stop offset="0.4494" stop-color="#F7F632"/>
    <stop offset="1" stop-color="#F5160F"/>
</linearGradient>
```

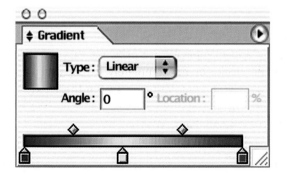

Figure 15.16 Illustrator's Gradient palette

For each stop, the offset specifies the position of the stop as a number in the range 0 to 1, which is interpreted as a proportion of the length

Figure 15.17 Filling with a linear gradient

† See Chapter 12 for an explanation of URI.

of the gradient. The **stop-color** attribute specifies the colour at that point, in the same way as fill and stroke colours are specified.

The **linearGradient** element does not cause anything to be drawn, it merely defines the gradient. To use it, the fill attribute of some shape or path must be set to a value of the form url(#*idref*), where *idref* is the value of a gradient's id attribute, as in url(#lgrad_1). Thus, the following element produces the circle shown in Figure 15.17.

```
<circle cx="50" cy="50" r="50" fill="url(#lgrad_1)"
        stroke="none" />
```

You can probably guess that this example is a special case of a more general way of referring to elements. The value of several SVG attributes, including in particular fill, may be a *URI reference*,† which, despite its name, takes the form url(*URL*), where the URL may have a fragment identifier or an XPointer appended. If, as in this example, the URL proper is omitted, leaving just a fragment identifier, the notation refers to an element, such as our gradient, defined elsewhere in the same document. By specifying a relative or absolute URL it is possible to refer to gradients defined in other documents (although this may not be very efficient).

Radial gradients are defined using stops in the same way as linear gradients are. If the example just given is modified as follows:

```
<radialGradient id="rgrad_1">
    <stop offset="0" stop-color="#0C419A"/>
    <stop offset="0.4494" stop-color="#F7F632"/>
    <stop offset="1" stop-color="#F5160F"/>
</radialGradient>

<circle cx="50" cy="50" r="50" fill="url(#rgrad_1)"
        stroke="none" />
```

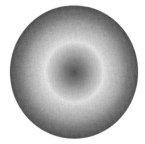

Figure 15.18 Filling with a radial gradient

it produces the result shown in Figure 15.18. Note that the gradient stops run from the inside out in a radial gradient.

In Figure 15.16, the small diamond shapes above the gradient in the palette are mid-point markers. These can be dragged to move the point at which two colours set by gradient tabs are mixed equally, thus altering the rate at which the colours change during the blending. SVG has no facility for specifying mid-point markers, but Adobe's SVGViewer plug-in supports an extension for this purpose.

Transformations

In Chapter 4, we introduced a collection of transformations that can easily be performed on vector graphic objects: translation, scaling, rotation, reflection and shearing. Four of these transformations can easily be expressed in SVG. Reflection is the odd one out, which requires a little more work. The others are all applied using the trans- form attribute, which can be used with any graphic element.

The value of transform is a string consisting of *transformation specifications*, separated by whitespace or commas. Each specification consists of a transformation name, followed by some arguments in brackets. The available transformation names are translate, scale, rotate, skewX and skewY, whose meanings should be apparent. The arguments to each are interpreted according to the transformation.

For a translation, one or two arguments may be supplied. The first is the amount by which the object should be moved in the *x* direction; if the second is present, it is the amount by which it should be moved in the *y* direction; if the second argument is missing, it is taken to be zero. Figure 15.19 shows the display of the following SVG document. (For this and subsequent illustrations, we have drawn a blue rectangle with its top left corner at the origin, to provide a frame of reference for the coordinate system, and a copy of the original rectangle, faded down to 60% opacity. We have also shrunk the pictures to fit the available space, so pixel dimensions will not be consistent with other figures in this section.)

```
<?xml version="1.0" encoding="utf-8"?>

<!DOCTYPE svg PUBLIC "-//W3C//DTD SVG 1.0//EN"
"http://www.w3.org/TR/2001/REC-SVG-20010904/DTD/
svg10.dtd">

<svg xmlns="http://www.w3.org/2000/svg">
    <rect x="0" y="0" width="300" height="350" fill="none"
        stroke="#99A6CF" stroke-width="0.6" />
    <rect x="120" y="120" width="126" height="126" fill="lime"
        stroke="magenta" stroke-width="4" fill-opacity="0.6"
        stroke-opacity="0.6"/>
    <rect x="120" y="120" width="126" height="126" fill="lime"
        stroke="magenta" stroke-width="4"
        transform="translate(-50,64)"/>
</svg>
```

Figure 15.19 Translation

The transform value for scaling is similar: one or two arguments may be supplied. The first or only argument is a horizontal scale factor;

if the second is present, it is a vertical scale factor; if it is omitted, it is taken to be equal to the first argument. That is, if only a single argument is provided, the object is scaled uniformly. Figure 15.20 shows the effect of changing the second rect element in the previous example as follows:

```
<rect x="120" y="120" width="126" height="126" fill="lime"
    stroke="magenta" stroke-width="4"
    transform="scale(1.1,1.4)"/>
```

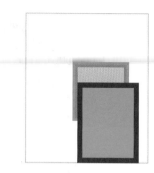

Figure 15.20 Scaling

You can see from this example that scaling is performed by multiplying all the object's coordinates by the specified scale factors, so that the object moves as well as getting bigger. To scale an object in place, the scaling transform would have to be followed by a translation that moved the top left corner of the object back to its original position.

The rotate transform takes either one or three arguments. The first argument is an angle in degrees, by which the object is rotated. If there are no other arguments, the rotation is around the origin. Hence, changing our transformed rect element as follows produces the result shown in Figure 15.21.

```
<rect x="120" y="120" width="126" height="126" fill="lime"
    stroke="magenta" stroke-width="4"
    transform="rotate(45)"/>
```

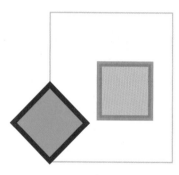

Figure 15.21 Rotation

If you wish to rotate an object about a different point, you specify two additional arguments, which are the coordinates of the centre of rotation. Figure 15.22 shows the effect of the following transform:

```
<rect x="120" y="120" width="126" height="126" fill="lime"
    stroke="magenta" stroke-width="4"
    transform="rotate(45,183,183)"/>
```

Finally, both the skew transform functions take a single argument, the skewing angle in degrees. You must specify skewing along the x and y axes separately. To produce a combined skew, such as the one shown in Figure 15.23, you must combine two transforms. This can be done, for any number of transforms of any type, by including them all in the same transform string, separated by whitespace or commas. Figure 15.23 was produced by the following, for instance:

```
<rect x="120" y="120" width="126" height="126" fill="lime"
    stroke="magenta" stroke-width="4"
    transform="skewX(-30),skewY(-45)"/>
```

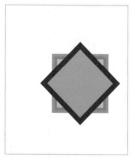

Figure 15.22 Rotation about a specified point

You can see from the illustration that, as with scaling, skewing moves the object as part of the transformation. A translation could be combined with the skewX and skewY transforms to move it back to its original position.

If you transform a shape that is filled with a gradient, the transformation is applied to the gradient too. For instance, if you rotate a shape filled with a linear gradient, the blending will occur along a slanted line, as in Figure 15.24, which was produced by modifying the circle element that produced the circle in Figure 15.17 as follows:

```
<circle cx="50" cy="50" r="50" fill="url(#lgrad_1)" stroke="none"
       transform="rotate(45)" />
```

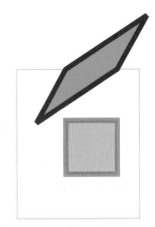

Figure 15.23 Skewing

If you have studied computer graphics, you will be familiar with the idea that any transformation can be expressed as a 3×3 matrix, three of whose coordinates are constant. Hence, six numbers suffice to express a transformation or combination of transformations. SVG supports this notation, allowing you to use matrix(a,b,c,d,e,f) in the value of the transform attribute. Among other things, this allows you to specify the missing reflection transformations. A reflection in the vertical axis is matrix(-1,0,0,1,0,0), a reflection in the horizontal axis is matrix(1,0,0,-1,0,0), a reflection in the line $x = y$ is matrix(-1,0,0,-1,0,0), and so on.

You may want to apply the same transformation to several objects at once. In Illustrator, you would do this by grouping the objects and then applying the transformation to the group. You can do just the same in SVG. The g element forms a group; its content comprises the objects in the group. A g element can have a transform attribute, and the transformation will be applied to all the child elements of the group. For instance, to rotate and enlarge the entire design in Figure 15.13, you could group the elements and transform the group, in the following way:

Figure 15.24 Rotating a gradient fill

```
<g transform="scale(1.5),rotate(-90,50,50)">
    <circle cx="50" cy="50" r="50"
            fill="#F67155" stroke="none" />
    <polygon points="50,10 66,10 76,27 66,42 50,42 40,25"
            fill="#697FBA" stroke="none" />
    <polyline points="40,25 1,50 50,99 99,50, 76,27"
            stroke="#99A6CF" stroke-linejoin="round"
            stroke-linecap="round" fill="none" />

</g>
```

Figure 15.25 shows the result – the pale blue circle indicates the original position of the design; it is drawn by an element that is not part of the group.

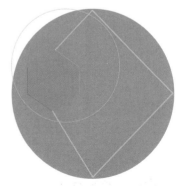

Figure 15.25 Transforming a group

Other Features

Links

SVG documents may incorporate XLink attributes for linking purposes. SVG provides an a element, by analogy with HTML, for creating links to other resources on the WWW. In XLink terms, SVG a elements are simple-type links which are always activated on request. That is, xlink:type is equal to "simple" and xlink:actuate is "onRequest". Usually, an xlink:href attribute whose value is the destination of the link is all that is required. In order to make the names of the XLink attributes available in an SVG document, a namespace declaration for the XLink namespace must be present. To make it possible to use links anywhere in the document, this would be attached to the svg element, which would therefore normally look like this:

```
<svg xmlns="http://www.w3.org/2000/svg"
    xmlns:xlink="http://www.w3.org/1999/xlink" >
```

The first namespace declaration makes the SVG namespace the default, so SVG names can be used without a prefix; the second declaration declares xlink: as the prefix for XLink attribute names, in the conventional manner.

As in HTML, the content of an a element acts as the link source. In SVG, elements typically represent graphical objects, so the usual effect of enclosing an element in an a is to make the graphical object it represents into a hotspot, which can cause a jump to the link destination when it is clicked on, or activated by some equivalent event. For instance, wrapping an a element around the polygon in our example of shapes (Figure 15.13), as shown below, has the effect of making the hexagon into a hotspot. Clicking on the shape will cause the *Digital Multimedia* home page to be retrieved and displayed.

```
<?xml version="1.0" encoding="utf-8"?>

<!DOCTYPE svg PUBLIC "-//W3C//DTD SVG 1.0//EN"
"http://www.w3.org/TR/2001/REC-SVG-20010904/DTD/
svg10.dtd">

<svg xmlns="http://www.w3.org/2000/svg"
    xmlns:xlink="http://www.w3.org/1999/xlink">
    <circle cx="50" cy="50" r="50" fill="#F67155"
        stroke="none" />
    <a xlink:href="http://www.digitalmultimedia.org/">
        <polygon points="50,10 66,10 76,27 66,42 50,42 40,25"
            fill="#697FBA" stroke="none" />
```

```
      </a>
      <polyline points="40,25 1,50 50,99 99,50, 76,27"
               stroke="#99A6CF" stroke-linejoin="round"
               stroke-linecap="round" fill="none" />
</svg>
```

Text

We described in Chapter 11 how text can be readily integrated with vector graphics. Their text manipulation facilities are a major feature of illustration programs. Hence, SVG must provide support for text.

Since SVG is XML, the only sensible way of representing text is as XML characters inside a suitable element. This means that any Unicode characters can be used in text, but that character entities must be used for ampersand and angle brackets. The text element is used to hold text strings that are incorporated in an SVG document. It has several attributes, the most important of which are x and y, which hold the coordinates of the string's anchor point (usually its left end), and a collection of attributes with the same names and semantics as CSS's font properties: font-family, font-weight, and so on. Since SVG is a vector format, fonts will be outline fonts, whose glyphs consist of vector shapes. To set their colour, the fill attribute is used, since vector glyphs usually have no stroke. The following element produces the text shown on the left of Figure 15.26.

```
<text x="0" y="0" font-family="Officina-Sans" font-size="7"
      font-style="italic" font-weight="bold" fill="#F67155">
No more cakes &amp; ale
</text>
```

Within a text element, the tspan element can be used to change the styling of selected spans of text. It, too, takes font and appearance attributes, so it can be used, for example, for setting part of a string in italics or boldface for emphasis, or, as in the following example (shown in the middle of Figure 15.26), for changing the colour of some characters.

```
<text x="0" y="0" font-family="Officina-Sans" font-size="7" font-
      style="italic" font-weight="bold" fill="#F67155">
No more <tspan fill="#697FBA">cakes</tspan> &amp; ale
</text>
```

You can also specify independent x and y attributes for a tspan element, which allows text to be precisely positioned. In a typical application where a block of text is to be laid out as a paragraph of equally spaced lines, for example, tspan elements with y values

Figure 15.26 Text in SVG

No more cakes & ale   *No more cakes & ale*   *Ha   l   l   o   o!*

that increase by the required amount of leading can be used for the separate lines.

In fact, the full range of attributes available for text and tspan elements provides a high degree of typographical control over text in SVG. Kerning and baseline shift can be controlled to arbitrary accuracy, allowing fine typesetting within an SVG illustration. We will not go into the full details, but we will mention the fact that the x and y attributes may take a list of numbers as their values. If a list is supplied, the values are taken to be the coordinates of the successive characters of the text: the first sets the position of the first character, the second that of the second character, and so on. Normally, this would be used to control kerning and inter-word spacing precisely, but it can also be used for special effects. For instance, the geometrically spaced text in Figure 15.26 was produced in the following way:

```
<text x="0,5,15,30,50,75" y="0" font-family="Officina-Sans"
     font-size="7" font-style="italic" font-weight="bold"
     fill="#F67155">
Halloo!
</text>
```

If you count them, you will see that there is one more character in the text than coordinate in the list. In such a case, the remaining text is set using the normal spacing, following from the last character that was positioned explicitly. This is why the exclamation mark is closely spaced next to the second letter 'o'.

Setting type on a path is one of the standard facilities offered by vector graphics packages, and this can be done straightforwardly in SVG (although the full details of how the spacing and positioning of the characters is determined are quite complex). First you need to create a path. Since it will have to be referred to when you set the type on it, the path element must have an id attribute. The type itself is created using a text element, as we have described, and its font characteristics are set using attributes here. You can also use tspan elements within the text to change the styling of parts of it. To associate the text and the path, you use a textPath element within the text. This has an xlink:href attribute (so you need to declare the XLink namespace if you are setting type on paths) which identifies the path. We could set some text along the polyline from our earlier example in the following way:

```
<path id="the_path" fill="none" stroke="#99A6CF"
      stroke-linecap="round" stroke-linejoin="round"
      d="M40,25l-39,25l49,49l49-49l-23-23"/>
<text font-family="Officina-Sans" font-size="7"
      letter-spacing="1.5%" font-style="italic" font-weight="bold"
      fill="#F67155">
      <textPath xlink:href="#the_path" spacing="auto">
More bears and pigs and chickens and whatevers
      </textPath>
</text>
```

The possibility of including text in SVG documents raises the question of fonts. We saw in Chapter 11 that CSS allows you to specify a list of fonts for the **font-family** property, so that a user agent can select whichever is available. This is all right for HTML's model of text display, but SVG's precise typography could get messed up if a different font from the one you intended was substituted. To preserve the appearance of text, it is necessary to make fonts available for downloading, or to embed them in the SVG document.

The preferred mechanism is to use a special sort of CSS rule, called an **@font-face** rule, which declares a location on the Web from which the font can be downloaded. The drawback of this approach is that several different font formats are in use, and there is no guarantee that any particular agent being used to render an SVG document will support any specific font format. It may be necessary to supply fonts in several different formats, or risk text not being rendered correctly in some user agents.

To overcome this problem, SVG allows fonts to be embedded in documents, using the **font** element, which contains data describing the font metrics and the actual glyphs making up the font. As with all font formats, the details are quite complicated, but since font data will almost always be generated automatically, you do not need to know about them, unless you are writing a program that writes SVG. If you are exporting a document from a program such as Illustrator, you will be offered the choice of embedding fonts, in which case **font** elements will be generated and included in the document, or linking to them, in which case, an **@font-face** rule will be used.

Animation

SVG has a simple, but potentially powerful, animation facility, based on SMIL animation, as described earlier in this chapter. In particular, any element may contain an **animate** element, which targets some attribute and specifies how its values should vary over time. For example, the colour of the polygon in our design could be animated in the following way:

```
<polygon points="50,10 66,10 76,27 66,42 50,42 40,25"
        fill="#697FBA" stroke="none">
    <animate attributeName="fill"
            values="#697FBA;#F67155;#697FBA" dur="2s"
            calcMode="discrete" repeatCount="indefinite" />
</polygon>
```

The effect is to change the colour of the polygon from its original blue to the same shade of red as the circle and back again over the course of two seconds. Since the calcMode is set to "discrete", the changes of colour are abrupt, so that the polygon appears to blink on and off – it disappears when its colour matches that of the circle. (We're not claiming it's an inspired piece of animation, but it illustrates the point, we hope.) Almost all attributes in SVG can be animated in this way, so that, by combining animated elements, SVG can serve as an implementation language for Web-based vector animation. Naturally, it would only be sensible for such animations to be generated by a program.

SVG extends SMIL animation in a few ways, but the only major incompatibility is that, if you wish to target an element that is not the parent of the animate element, you must use an xlink:href attribute to identify the target by a URI reference, rather than SMIL's targetElement attribute.

Exercises

1 Write a SMIL document that describes a slide show, during which five images are displayed one after the other for 20 seconds each, while a 30-second soundtrack loops continuously. (Make any convenient assumptions about the locations and file names of the media.)

2 Write SMIL elements to display a video clip and an image together so that, no matter how long the video clip is, (a) the image always appears five seconds after the beginning of the video, and (b) the image always appears five seconds before the end of the video.

3 Add a looped soundtrack to your answer to exercise 2, which always ends at the same time as the video clip.

4   Suppose you have a video clip, an accompanying soundtrack, and a second video clip containing captions for the hard of hearing. Show how you would choose in SMIL between displaying captions or soundtrack, depending on the value of systemCaptions.

5   Write suitable SMIL documents to describe a presentation consisting of a slide show of images in parallel with a video clip, where each image represents the section of the video that plays at the same time. (For example, it may be the first frame of the scene. Assume that a suitable set of images is available.) If a user clicks on an image, the presentation should be replaced by one consisting of the image followed by a video clip.

6   Create two SMIL presentations, the first comprising a sequence of video clips, the second a slide show of the same number of images. When a user clicks on an image, they should go to the point in the video presentation where the corresponding clip is being shown. (Make as few assumptions as you need to about the duration of the video clips.)

7   Write a simple SMIL animation that moves an image along an approximately circular path over the course of a minute.

8   Write SVG code to draw a smiley face, in appropriate colours. If you have it, draw the same face in Illustrator and export it as SVG. Compare the machine-generated code with the code you wrote by hand.

9   Show how you can use a combination of transforms in SVG to scale a 300×400 rectangle in place. Can you write a general transform which will scale any object in place?

Scripting and Interactivity

16

- Scripting Fundamentals
- ECMAScript
  - Expressions and Variables
  - Control Structures
  - Arrays
  - Functions
  - Objects
- World Wide Web Client-Side Scripting
  - Event Handlers
  - Scripts and Stylesheets
- Behaviours
- Scripting in Flash
  - Attaching Scripts
  - Movie Clip Methods and Properties
  - Creating Applications in Flash

T he graphical user interface provided by contemporary operating systems is a paradigm of an *event-driven* system: the user does something (double-clicks an icon, for example), and something happens in response (an application program is launched). Hypermedia navigation, as we described it in Chapter 12, can be seen as a special case of this general model of interaction: clicking on some highlighted text, an image, or a hot spot in an image map, causes the destination of a link to be displayed. While this form of interaction can take you a long way, incorporating more general event-driven interaction into a multimedia production opens up additional possibilities.

The idea is to associate *actions* with *events*. We first need to identify a set of events. Most of these are initiated by the user – mouse clicks and movements, key presses, and so on – but some events are generated internally, for example when a movie finishes playing, or simply after a specific period of time has elapsed. There is even a *null* or *idle* event that is generated when nothing else happens. The set of available events is not fixed, but depends on the particular combination of hardware and software being used.

As well as identifying the set of events, we need to be able to specify actions. Some multimedia environments provide a predefined set of actions (often called *behaviours*) to perform common tasks, such as opening a window, playing a movie or replacing one image with another. More sophisticated environments let you define your own, by providing a *scripting language*: a small programming language with facilities for controlling user interface elements and multimedia objects. You write a script that performs the desired action when it is executed; you then associate that script with an event, using a tag, or some command in an authoring environment, so that it gets executed when the user clicks on a particular image, for example.

One reason for associating actions with events is to provide interactivity: if the system can respond to events generated by the user, then the user can control the system's behaviour. In particular, users can direct the flow of information that they receive – requesting Web pages with a click of the mouse, and so on. Events that occur at specific times provide another reason for using associated actions: they allow time-based behaviour and synchronization to be introduced into systems, such as the World Wide Web, that do not support it directly as part of their model of multimedia. Contrariwise, actions embedded in the timeline of a synchronized multimedia production can be used to provide branching and other forms of non-linearity. It is only a slight over-simplification to say that scripting can add the characteristic features of hypermedia to time-based presentations; it can add a temporal dimension to hypermedia; and it can add interactivity to both, so that multimedia productions that make use of scripts can provide the same experience to every user, no matter which model of media combination they start from.

Scripting Fundamentals

One definition of a *scripting language*, taken from the ECMAScript specification, is

> "...a programming language that is used to manipulate, customize, and automate the facilities of an existing system."

The authors of the specification go on:

> "In such systems, useful functionality is already available through a user interface, and the scripting language is a mechanism for exposing that functionality to program control. In this way, the existing system is said to provide a *host environment* of objects and facilities which completes the capabilities of the scripting language." [Our italics]

Scripting languages can be distinguished from mainstream programming languages such as C++ or Java. These provide some control structures, abstraction mechanisms, and built-in data types, such as numbers and pointers or references; the abstraction mechanisms of a modern programming language allow you to define your own data types, constructed out of the basic types provided by the language. A scripting language provides some control structures and a few basic types too – and may provide some abstraction mechanisms – but it also provides objects and data types that belong to some 'existing system'. For example, a scripting language for use with a relational database system will provide data types corresponding to relations and tuples; one for use as an operating system command language will provide data types corresponding to processes and files. (Note that here we are using the expression 'data types' in the modern sense of *abstract data types*: a set of values together with a set of operations.)

Our concern is with multimedia, so the scripting languages we are interested in must provide objects corresponding to the elements of a multimedia production. It is not adequate to provide a type for each medium – text, sound, video, and so on; the types of objects available need to take account of the way in which media objects are combined within the production. (Recall from the passage just cited that a scripting language provides program control equivalent to the user interface.) Thus, in a scripting language for use with XML or HTML, objects must be provided that correspond to document elements *and* to elements of the user interface, such as windows. In a language whose host environment is a timeline based system such as Flash, we need objects corresponding to frames and the various elements that may appear inside them.

The scripting language will allow us to perform computations on the attributes of these objects, or create new ones, and thereby affect their appearance and behaviour. This computation will be triggered by events. Some of these events will be initiated by the user, so scripted actions provide a means of allowing user input to affect the flow of control, or putting it another way, they allow certain elements of a multimedia production to function as controls providing interactivity. For example, an action may be attached to an image, with the effect that clicking on the image causes a particular movie to start playing in another window.

ECMAScript

The first scripting language for the World Wide Web was a proprietary product called LiveScript, which was embedded in Netscape's Navigator Web browser; LiveScript changed its name to JavaScript shortly after its release, even though its actual relationship to the Java programming language is slight and the resemblance between the names has been a source of some confusion ever since. Microsoft, in its role as the other major browser manufacturer, produced its own version of JavaScript, known as JScript, which was not quite identical to Netscape's. To avoid yet another source of browser incompatibility, the European Computer Manufacturers' Association (ECMA) was called upon to produce a standard based on JavaScript and JScript. This standard gave the name ECMAScript to the language it defined.

It was always the case that JavaScript comprised a core language, providing general-purpose programming facilities and some rudimentary object-oriented features, and a set of built-in objects that allowed JavaScript programs to interact with some other system. In the most familiar case, the other system is a Web browser, and the built-in objects correspond to elements of Web pages and browser windows. By providing a different set of built-in objects, the same language can be used to interact with other systems. Server-side JavaScript, for instance, lets scripts interact with Netscape Web servers and with files and databases.

ECMAScript is a formally defined version of the core language only. The standard explicitly concedes that ECMAScript is not 'computationally self-sufficient': it has to be combined with *host objects* that allow scripts to manipulate a host system, such as a Web browser.

The World Wide Web Consortium has defined a set of interfaces, collectively known as the *Document Object Model (DOM)*, to provide programming access to the structure and content of XML and HTML documents. ECMAScript objects can be defined that implement these interfaces. The combination of ECMAScript and these DOM objects should, therefore, provide a standard framework for World Wide Web client-side scripting, permitting scripts to be written that will perform correctly on all browsers.

In practice, not all browsers conform to the standards as well as one might expect, and browsers that predate the standards are still in use, so Web developers who require their scripts to work on as many browsers as possible must resort to tricks and redundant programming. Hopefully, in time the standards will prevail, so we have made no attempt to describe the idiosyncrasies of any particular browser.

Meanwhile, scripting of a sort was available in early versions of Flash, using an *ad hoc* system of 'actions'. This system was limited, and it was apparent that the full potential of scripting in Flash could only be realized with a full-blown scripting language. Sensibly, Macromedia chose to adopt ECMAScript as the basis of such language when Flash 5 was released in 2000. Unfortunately, for reasons of backward-compatibility, ActionScript, as Flash's scripting language is called, does not conform entirely to the ECMAScript standard, but, to a first approximation, it was created by adding a set of host objects for elements of a Flash movie to the basic ECMAScript syntax. Thus, scripting for the Web and scripting in Flash share a basic syntax. In other words, ActionScript is close enough to ECMAScript and ECMAScript is close enough to JavaScript for the syntax and core semantics of ActionScript to be immediately comprehensible to anyone who already knows JavaScript, and vice versa. We will therefore begin by considering ECMAScript without reference to any particular host environment.

In the interests of simplicity we will only introduce the minimum of syntax, so much of our coding will be less elegant than it could be – ECMAScript allows some sophisticated programming techniques to be employed by those who know how. In the following sections we have attempted to introduce both the language and some of the basic ideas of programming. We realize that some readers from a non-technical background may find this material hard going. If you find you are not comfortable with these ideas, you may still benefit from skimming through the rest of this chapter, just to get a feeling for what can be achieved with scripts. On the other hand, if you have done some programming and know Java, C or C++, the form of ECMAScript programs will contain few surprises. If you are only familiar with Visual Basic, or with the Algol and Pascal family, you may find the detailed concrete syntax slightly odd, but the statement and expression forms available will be roughly as you expect: assignment statements, a variety of loops and conditionals, function definition, call and return, and so on.[†]

† Parts of the remainder of this chapter have been adapted from material that first appeared in *Flash 5 Interactivity and Scripting* by Nigel Chapman (John Wiley & Sons Ltd, 2001).

Expressions and Variables

The best place to start a description of any programming language is by considering the different types of value that are available.

Values and Expressions

ECMAScript recognizes three different types: *number*, *string* and *Boolean*. Numbers are used for arithmetic, and strings for storing and altering text, while Booleans are truth values, which can be used to control the flow of execution of a script.

‡ Internally, all operations are performed on IEEE 754 double-precision floating point quantities.

Generally speaking, the way ECMAScript handles numbers and arithmetic follows the way it is normally done on paper, with no arbitrary additional rules for the benefit of the computer, although some notational compromises are made with the keyboard. No distinction is drawn between integers and floating point numbers.[‡] Numerical constants (or literals) are written using ordinary decimal notation, as, for example, 158 or 14.673, or 'scientific' notation, using e to indicate a decimal exponent, as, for example, 12e35 (for 12×10^{35}) or 1e-4 (for 0.0001). The usual operations of addition, subtraction, multiplication and division are available, using the conventional operators (conventional in programming languages, that is) +, -, * and /. Unary - can be used to negate a value, and unary + can be used to do nothing. The remainder (or modulo) operator is written as %, and differs from that provided in many languages by not being restricted to integers. That is, as well as being able to write 8%3, which gives 2, the remainder on dividing 8 by 3, you can also write 4.5%2.1, which gives 0.3, the remainder on dividing 4.5 by 2.1. Also unlike most languages, ECMAScript defines what happens if the operands of % are negative: the result is negative if and only if the left operand is negative; the magnitude is the same whatever the signs.

ECMAScript also deals with the tricky questions that arise from division by zero and other dubious operations. The number data type includes special values Infinity and NaN. Infinity is the result of operations whose size exceeds the range of numbers that can be represented; for example, 1/0 yields Infinity. NaN stands for 'Not a Number' and is the result of undefined operations. In particular, 0/0 produces NaN.

The precedence of the arithmetical operators holds no surprises: 8*4+3 is equal to 35, for example. Round brackets are used for grouping where it is necessary to override the usual precedence rules: 8*(4+3) is 56.

Strings are sequences of characters. String literals are written enclosed in either double quote marks "like this" or single quote marks 'like this'. Any programming language that uses quote marks to enclose string literals presents the problem of how to include quote marks inside a string. If the delimiters are double quotes, a single quote presents no problem, and vice versa. For the problematical case of the same quote mark being used as the delimiter and within the string, ECMAScript adopts what has become the classic solution to this problem: inside a string literal, special *escape sequences* can be used. An escape sequence consists of a backslash character, \, followed by some other character or sequence of characters; the whole sequence stands for a single character that cannot otherwise be included in the string literal, either because, like the quote mark, it is used for some other purpose, or because it is difficult or impossible to enter using a conventional keyboard. In particular, a double quote mark is represented inside a string literal by the escape sequence \" and a single one by the sequence \'. (Note that the escape sequence is only used to write down the string literal; it is the single character, " or ', that is stored in the string itself.) The escape sequence \\ is used to represent a single backslash in a string literal. Table 16.1 lists all the escape sequences provided by ECMAScript.[†]

† At present the full range of Unicode characters is not supported by all Web browsers. Flash MX ActionScript uses Unicode for strings, but earlier versions of Flash were restricted to ISO Latin1.

Table 16.1 Escape sequences used in string literals

Escape sequence	Character	Unicode code (hex)
\b	backspace	08
\t	tab	09
\n	line feed (newline)	0A
\f	form feed	0C
\r	carriage return	0D
\"	double quote	22
\'	single quote	27
\\	backslash	5C
\o1o2o3	octal byte	o1o2o3 octal
\xx1x2	hexadecimal byte	x1x2
\ux1x2x3x4	Unicode character	x3x4

The only infix operator available for strings performs concatenation – sticking one string on the end of another – and is written as a + symbol. For example, "Digital"+"Multimedia" is equal to "DigitalMultimedia". Since the result of concatenating two strings is a string, you can concatenate another string to the result – in other words, you can build up expressions using strings and +. For instance, "Digital"+" "+"Multimedia" gives "Digital Multimedia". You could have written that string literally, of course. Concatenation, like all other operators, is only interesting if some of the operands are variables, which we will consider shortly.

Comparisons between values are performed using the variations on conventional operators introduced by C and copied by many subsequent programming and scripting languages: > and < have their usual arithmetical meaning; <= and >= are used for ≤ and ≥, while == and != are used for equality and inequality respectively. The result of a comparison is a Boolean value, true or false, depending on whether the comparison succeeds or fails.

The unary operator ! (logical NOT) is used to invert the result of a comparison, or any other expression producing a Boolean value: if E is an expression, !E is true if E is false, and false if E is true. The infix operator && (logical AND) produces true if both its operands are true; || (logical OR) produces true if one or other of its operands, or both, is true. These Boolean operators have a low priority, so that an expression such as 2 > 10 && "2" != 2 has its apparent meaning. It never does any harm to insert brackets if you are in doubt about the binding of operators, and it often makes your meaning clearer. As the example just shown suggests, strings of digits are converted to numbers when they are compared with actual numbers; the same thing happens when they are used with arithmetic operators. If, however, strings of digits are compared with each other, they are not converted and a lexical comparison is used: "2" > "10" is true.

Variables and Assignment

As we remarked earlier, expressions that only consist of constants and operators are of no interest – you always know their value already. It is only when *variables* are introduced that any useful computation can be done.

In programming, variables are containers – or *locations*, in the jargon of programming languages – that have a name (often called an *identifier*) and can hold a value. The value stored in a location can be changed by the operation of *assignment*. It has been argued that assignment is the essence of programming; it is certainly what distinguishes it from mathematics (where variables don't have values that can be changed), and it is central to the way in which computation is organized as a sequence of steps, since assignment allows you to remember values computed in previous steps.

A major difference between ECMAScript and Java, C++, Pascal and most other mainstream programming languages is that ECMAScript is an *untyped* language. To be precise (since the term 'untyped' does not have a unique meaning), a variable is not restricted, either by declaration or any other mechanism or convention, to holding values of just one type. The same variable can hold a string at one time, a number at another, and a Boolean at another – not that we recommend the practice. There can therefore be no type checking. This is regrettable, since it means that many errors that could have been caught earlier will only show up when a script is running. The absence of type checking is usually justified in the name of simplicity, since scripting languages are often used by people who are not experienced programmers.

As is the case with other untyped languages, there is no need to declare variables before you use them – although it is good practice to do so. A variable can be created just by using its name.

Usually, the first thing you do with a variable is assign a value to it – before it has explicitly been given a value a variable holds the special pseudo-value **undefined**. Using an undefined variable is almost always an error, and always unwise. In ECMAScript, = is used as the assignment operator (which is why equality is written ==). A value is assigned to a variable using an assignment of the form *identifier = expression*. For example, to initialize a counter to zero, you would use the assignment

the_count = 0;

where the_count was the name of your counter variable.

ECMAScript is slightly more liberal than most programming languages in the characters that can be used as part of an identifier: upper and lower case letters, digits, underlines and dollar signs are all permitted, subject only to the restriction that the first character cannot be a digit. By convention, identifiers beginning with underlines or dollar signs are used for properties of built-in objects and other predefined values. In theory, an identifier can be as long as you like, though the finite size of computers means that ultimately there will be a limit.

Although you don't have to introduce variables with a declaration before you use them, you can if you like. The reserved word **var** introduces a declaration. It can be followed by a list of identifiers, or, more usefully, by a list of assignments, as in:

var book= "Digital Multimedia", edition= 2;

The individual assignments are separated by commas. Using this form of declaration ensures that you always give a variable an initial value before you use it.

Once a variable has been given a value, the value can be used in expressions just by writing the variable's name. Hence, if the_count had been initialized as above, the expression the_count+1 would have the value 1, and the following statement could be used to add one to the counter:

```
the_count = the_count + 1;
```

Assignments such as the one just shown, that compute a new value for a variable by applying a simple operation to its old value, are common; ECMAScript follows Algol68 and many subsequent languages (most influentially, C) by providing shorthand *compound assignment operators* that combine the operation and assignment. For example, += is an operator that adds its right operand to its left and assigns the result back to the left, so the assignment above could be written as

```
the_count += 1;
```

Such compound assignment operators are available for all the binary operators in ECMAScript.

The case of adding one to a variable is so common that an even more compact notation is provided, in the form of the ++ operator. The precise effect of this operator depends on whether it is written before or after its operand. If written before, as in ++the_count, it increments the value, and the result of the expression is the new value; if written after, as in the_count++, it performs the same increment, but the value of the expression is the original value of the_count. The difference only matters if the increment is used as a part of a more complex expression (for example, new_count = ++the_count), or in a condition (for example ++the_count > 10). The most common way of using ++, though, is in a statement on its own, when, unless you are doing something very obscure, the difference between the prefix and postfix versions is a matter of taste.

Control Structures

Once you have understood the use of variables, it is possible to write scripts using basic *control structures* to perform some simple computation.

The 'structured programming' movement in the late 1970s identified three basic control structures: *sequencing*, *selection* and *iteration*, as being necessary and sufficient for implementing any algorithm. In a sense, therefore, the corresponding ECMAScript statements are enough to allow you to write scripts to perform any computation you want. However, for most non-trivial tasks, higher level features, such as functions and objects, are needed to make scripts comprehensible and easy to maintain. ECMAScript provides these features, too, but in a less fully developed form than that in which they are found in mainstream programming languages, such as Java and C++. Some of the help that objects, in particular, provide for large-scale program construction in these languages is not available in ECMAScript because it lacks static type checking.

Some features to assist with writing more robust scripts, such as class-based objects, have been added to more recent versions of ECMAScript, but have not percolated down to practical use on the Web or in Flash as yet, so we will omit any description of these developments.

The semantics of the three structured control forms is probably familiar, and the syntax used in ECMAScript for each is similar to that used in many other programming languages. The statements in a sequence are written in order, with each one terminated by a semi-colon, as $S_1;S_2;...$, and are executed one after the other. A selection is written if (E) S_1 else S_2. The expression E is evaluated and if it is true the first statement S_1 is executed, otherwise the second, S_2. An iterated statement, written while (E) S, is repeated as long as the expression in brackets after the reserved word while continues to hold true. In all these forms, the names S, S_1 and S_2 denote either a single statement (including conditional and iteration) or a *block*, which is a sequence of statements written between curly brackets, { and }. E denotes an expression, usually some sort of comparison.

Note that loops can be nested inside other loops and a selection can have more than two alternatives – since either or both can themselves be selections. (In fact, one of them can be empty, in which case else is omitted, giving the single-branched conditional if (E) S.) Since a block is really just a sequence, with curly brackets round it to show where it begins and ends, loops can also contain sequences and selections, sequences can include loops and selections, and so on.

Although it is not necessary to put curly brackets round a single statement when you use it as the body of a loop or an alternative in a conditional, it does no harm to put them, and a lot of people prefer to do so. We prefer to omit them unless they are needed, but there is no virtue in this.

The use of sequences is straightforward: you use them when you need to perform several actions one after the other. Non-trivial scripts invariably use selections and iterations, often in sequence or containing sequences. We will introduce the use of these simple control structures with a few examples. These will inevitably have a somewhat artificial air, because ECMAScript on its own cannot communicate with a host system, or even write messages to a window.

As a first example, suppose to begin with that you wish to compute a payment, perhaps a commission. Say the payment is 10% of some total amount, except that amounts less than 10 (euros, dollars, zlotys, or whatever) are not paid. Assume that the total is held in a variable called **amount**, defined elsewhere, and we want to compute the payment and store it in a variable called **payment**, also defined elsewhere. This can be achieved in the following way:

```
var commission = amount * 0.1;     // 10% = 0.1
if (commission < 10)
        payment = 0;
else
        payment = commission;
```

The characters from // to the end of the first line are a *comment* – text that has no effect on the computation, but serves as an annotation for the benefit of people reading the script. You will see few of them in this chapter, because the accompanying text does the job of explanation. However, large or subtle scripts benefit from the use of meaningful comments, and you should develop the habit of adding them, if only to help you remember what you have done when you come back to it after an interruption. Note here (and in earlier examples) that all the single statements are terminated with semicolons. You can, in fact, leave these out when they occur at the end of a line, but most people either find it easier to put them in than to remember the few special cases where they can't be omitted, or are so used to writing in other programming languages that they insert semicolons from habit.

Before leaving this example, consider a possible variation. You may have realized that the variable **commission** is redundant. I could have assigned the commission provisionally to **payment** and then reset it if it was too small. This would use a single-branched conditional, like this:

```
payment = amount * 0.1;
if (payment < 10) payment = 0;
```

You use a conditional statement when you need to make a choice, as in the example just given. Loops are used when you need to repeat an operation. As a simple example, suppose you wished to replicate a string a certain number of times, and that variables s and **repetitions** held the string and the replication count, respectively. So, if the value of s was "ECMA" and that of **repetitions** was 4, you would want to produce "ECMAECMAECMAECMA". The following code will accomplish the task.

```
var ss = "", i = 0;
while (i < repetitions) {
      ss += s;
      ++i;
}
```

The strategy, which will become familiar to you if it is not so already, is to use a variable, in this case i to serve as a *loop counter* that keeps track of the number of times we have gone round a loop. It is initialized to zero before the loop starts. (We haven't gone round any times yet.) Another variable ss, which is going to store the result, must be initialized to the empty string. It will always be the case that ss holds i copies of s; presently it holds none, since i is zero. The number of times that the loop must be executed is equal to the value stored in repetitions, so, provided we add one to i every time round the loop and do not change the value of repetitions, we know we have to go on executing the loop body as long as the value of i is less than that of repetitions, which is what the condition at the head of the loop in this script asserts. Inside the loop we first do the actual work of constructing the result ss by appending a copy of s to the end of it (using an assigning operator), and then increment the loop counter, thus maintaining the truth of the claim that ss holds i copies of s. It follows that when the test at the head of the loop fails, and we exit from the loop, ss holds the required string.

Loops like this one, which are controlled by a counter that is incremented on every iteration, are very common. In many programming languages, some special syntax is provided for them. The *for loop* provided in C is probably the most elaborate example, and it has been adopted with minor modifications in many later languages, including ECMAScript. The for loop has the following syntax:

for (*initialization* ; *condition* ; *increment*) *statement*

and it is equivalent to the following loop:

initialization;
while (*condition*)
{
      statement
      increment
}

That is, the *initialization* is performed before the loop begins; the *condition* is tested to see whether the loop body should be executed;

the *statement* is repeatedly executed, followed by the *increment*. The previous loop could be rewritten as:

```
for (var ss = "", i = 0; i < repetitions; ++i)
    ss += s;
```

As you see, the initialization can include var declarations, though the equivalent while loop tells you that the variables are not confined to the loop.

In a **for** loop, all the book-keeping concerned with iteration is kept together at the top of the loop, separate from the loop body in which the iterated computation is specified. Such special loops are convenient: most programmers have at some time in their career written a while loop and forgotten to add the code to increment the loop counter or whatever it is that is needed to move the loop on for the next iteration. It is strangely easy to do; the result is a loop that goes round forever. It is provably the case, though, that any looping computation can always be written using no more than the while loop and sometimes this will be more suitable than a for loop. In the end, the difference comes down to style and choice.

Arrays

It is often convenient to be able to treat a collection of values as a single entity. For example, suppose you are collecting statistics about the different browsers that visitors to a Web site use in their work. You could keep a count of the number using each program in a different variable, such n_explorer, n_safari, and so on, but this makes it awkward to compute such things as the mean number of users of each browser, or the most popular browser. *Aggregate data structures* allow us to combine a set of values, giving the collection a single name, and to access the individual ones in a simple, uniform way.

The simplest aggregate data structure is the *array*, which is a sequence of values, each of which can be identified by a numerical *index*, which is its position in the sequence. The individual values are the array's *elements*. The process of extracting an individual element using a number is called *indexing*, written by putting the index in square brackets after the array's name: a[0], a[1], a[2], ... are the first, second, third, ... elements of the array a. In general, if a is the name of an array, and *E* is an expression that evaluates to a number greater than or equal to zero, a[*E*] gives the value of the element stored in the array at the corresponding position. Notice that the index values start at zero, not one, even though we invariably refer to the first element, and so on. This is a prolific source of stupid programming errors – but so is using one as the first index.

Arrays must be created explicitly. The expression new Array() can be used for this purpose: it returns a new array, which can be assigned to a variable. Unlike some other languages, ECMAScript does not require you to specify how many elements there are in the array when you create it; it will grow as necessary as soon as you assign a value to an element. Note that if an array a has n elements, the highest element is at a[n-1]. The number of elements in a is given by the expression a.length (this notation will be explained shortly), so a[a.length] is always the first free element beyond those that are occupied.

Numerically indexed arrays are the oldest form of aggregate data structure, and have been used in programming since the earliest days, for a range of purposes. Many of these purposes are concerned with numerical computations and are unlikely to be needed in scripts on the Web or in Flash. One way of using arrays, though, is to provide a mapping from numbers to some other sort of value, often strings, and this can be necessary in such scripts. Months provide a commonly encountered example. If you wish to find out the date six months from now, for instance, it is easiest to represent months by numbers (0 for January, 1 for February, and so on). When displaying the result, it is often better to use the month's name. In particular, because of the different conventions used in the United States and in Europe for writing dates numerically, using the name avoids some ambiguity. An array can be used to turn numbers into names.

Since there is no pattern to the names of the months, the array has to be set up by a sequence of assignments.

```
var month = new Array();
month[0] = "Jan";
month[1] = "Feb";
month[2] = "Mar";
```

and so on. Now, if m holds the number corresponding to a month, (m+6)%12 will be the number corresponding to the month six months later (taking the remainder ensures that values greater than 11 wrap round in the proper way), and month[(m+6)%12] holds its name. For example, if m is equal to 8, denoting September (not August, since our numbering starts at zero), m+6 is 14, so (m+6)%12 is 2, and month[(m+6)%12] is month[2], which is "Mar", i.e. March, which is six months later than September.

It is often the case that you need to access the value of each element of an array in turn. This is best done using a for loop in which the loop variable ranges from 0 to the highest element. In general, it can use the length property of the array as the upper limit of the loop variable, like this:

```
for (var i = 0; i < a.length; ++i)
```

Loops with headers of this form can be used for any task that computes some function of every array element or applies some operation to every element, for example, adding them all up, computing their average, setting them all to zero, adding one to them all, and so on. For example, if browser_users was an array in which browser_users[i] held a count of the number of people using the ith browser in some list of browsers (which could be stored in another array, like our list of months), we could compute the total number of users and the mean number per browser like this:

```
var total_users = 0;
for (var i = 0; i < browser_users.length; ++i)
        total_users += browser_users[i];
var mean_users = total_users/browser_users.length
```

Arrays are potentially large complicated things, so they are manipulated via 'references' – things that point to the whole array. This means that if you assign an array to a variable, only the reference gets copied, not the array elements, so if a is an array (or, strictly speaking, a variable containing a reference to an array), an assignment like b = a creates a synonym for a, not a copy of the array it refers to. This means that writing ++b[7] will increment a[7] too. If you do want to copy an array, you must use a loop to assign a copy of each element explicitly, like this:

```
for (var i = 0; i < a.length; ++i) b[i] = a[i];
```

ECMAScript goes beyond the traditional concept of arrays as numerically indexed sequences, by providing *associative arrays*, which are indexed by strings. Associative arrays are sometimes called *lookup tables*, which conveys an idea of how they work: a string is associated with some other value, and the indexing operation lets you look up the value, given the string. For example, we could reverse the mapping from numbers to the names of months using an associative array. This is still created in the same way as a numerically indexed array:

```
var month_values = new Array();
```

Usage is similar, too, the only difference being that we write strings inside the square brackets:

```
month_values["Jan"] = 0;
month_values["Feb"] = 1;
month_values["Mar"] = 2;
```

and so on. If m_name is a variable whose value is a string, the expression month_values[m_name] gives the corresponding number. With months initialized as it was in our earlier example, it will always be the case that months[month_values[m_name]] is equal to m_name, if the value of m_name is a valid month name abbreviation.

Functions

One important principle – arguably the most important principle – of program construction is *abstraction*. A full account of abstraction would take an entire book, but for our present purposes it is sufficient to recognize it as the process that takes place whenever we take a complex idea or procedure and give it a name so that we can refer to it as if it was an indivisible entity, without worrying about its internal details. For example, Scotland is an abstraction, encompassing the diverse landscapes, history, people and culture of part of the British Isles – itself another abstraction. Abstraction is an absolute necessity of language: we wouldn't get very far if, instead of referring to 'Scotland', we could only point to the tangible individual elements that the abstraction encompasses. Matters are not quite so serious in programming, where it is possible to express any computation using the basic control structures enumerated earlier in this chapter and a set of primitive operations. The result is clumsy, though, and leads to a great deal of repetition. It also makes programs harder to understand, because any logical structure they may possess becomes submerged.

If the preceding discussion strikes you as itself being too abstract, consider the matter from a purely practical point of view. If you can take a computation, express it as a sequence of code in a programming or scripting language, and then give it a name so that, from then on, you can use the name instead of the sequence of code, it means that you can concentrate on that computation once, get it right, then forget about it and simply use it. And if, by some mischance, you get it wrong instead of right, you only have to mend it in one place. As a bonus your programs or scripts will be shorter, occupy less disk space and demand less bandwidth from networks.

The oldest form of abstraction in programming languages is *functional abstraction*, where we consider part of a computation as an abstraction called a *function*, which we give a name to, so that subsequently we can perform the computation just by *calling* the function using its name.

argument₁ argument₂ argument₃

The easiest way to think about a function is as a box, containing some computation, with an input slot on the top and an output slot on the bottom. You feed values, or *arguments*, in at the input slot, computation happens inside the box (but this is an abstraction, so we don't need to worry about how that computation happens) and a result comes out of the output slot. (See Figure 16.1.) Notice that a function may have any number of arguments, but only ever produces one result.

Earlier, we wrote some code to compute the commission on a payment. If you frequently need to perform this computation, you would have to cut and paste this piece of script wherever it was needed. If, however, it could be turned into an abstraction, you could just call it rake_off, say, and then use its name, as rake_off(11450) or rake_off(the_price), for example. A suitable definition of such an abstraction based on the original code would look like this:

result

Figure 16.1 Functional abstraction

```
function rake_off(amount)
{
    var payment;
    var commission = amount * 0.1;
    if (commission < 10)
        payment = 0;
    else
        payment = commission;
    return payment;
}
```

The definition is introduced by the reserved word function, which identifies what follows as a function definition. Next comes the name of the function, in this case rake_off. Following this, in brackets, is an identifier, which is sometimes called a *formal parameter* of the function. When the abstraction is used, the value supplied as its argument is assigned to the formal parameter. Inside the function, it is used just like any other variable.

The code enclosed between curly brackets (which are required here) specifies the computation that the function performs. It is called the function *body*. As you can see, it is quite like the original code fragment. One significant difference is that the value for the formal parameter amount is supplied by the argument when the function is called, whereas before we had to assume that a value had been assigned to it somewhere else. The other difference between the function body and the original script is that we have declared payment, and after the result has been assigned to it, it is used as the value of the return statement at the end of the function body. This value will be the result of the abstraction (the value that comes out of the output slot).

When this function is called, by writing an expression such as rake_off(11450), the code in the function body is executed, with the formal parameter amount set to 11450. At the end of the computation, payment will hold the value 1145, which is returned as the value of the function call. A function call can be used as part of an expression, wherever any other value can be used. For example,

```
var year_total = 12*rake_off(11450);
```

assigns 12 commissions on an amount of 11450 to year_total.

When you write functions you need to think carefully about any assumptions that your code embodies about the arguments, and arrange to cope with any values that do not conform to them – or, if that does not seem possible, at least to document the assumptions clearly. For example, the rake_off function works on the assumption that its argument is a number. What if it isn't? In this case, the value NaN (not a number) will propagate through the arithmetic and be passed back as the result, which is probably the correct thing to do, but the fact ought to be documented. A comment at the head of the function definition is the conventional place for such documentation.

Objects

The use of objects to structure programs is one of the most important developments in the history of programming. The concept has many ramifications which we cannot go into here, but the basic idea is a simple and intuitively appealing one. A program is organized as a collection of *objects*, which together form a model of whatever the program implements. For instance, a Web browser could be made out of objects that model documents, windows, images, and so on. Objects can be understood in anthropomorphic terms as things that possess some knowledge about themselves and understand how to perform certain operations. In the case of a window object, for example, this knowledge would include its size and position on the screen, and whether it is the frontmost window; the operations would include refreshing its contents and closing itself. In more formal terms, we could say that an object consists of a set of data elements together with a set of operations. An important principle here is that an object's operations should only modify the object itself, not other arbitrary objects. (In practice, this principle is often compromised, but it is the ideal, and should be followed if possible, since it makes understanding and modifying programs much easier.)

ECMAScript is usually described as an *object-based* language. This means that it supports the creation and manipulation of objects, but these are not systematically organized into hierarchical classes as they are in an *object-oriented* language, such as Java. An object in ECMAScript is just a collection of named data items, known as *properties*, and functions (i.e. operations), known as *methods*. Any collection will do, and properties and methods can be added to or removed from an object at any time. If a variable called, for example, the_window, holds an object, you can access any property, such as x_position using the notation the_window.x_position, and call a method, close for instance, with the_window.close(). If the method takes any arguments, they are written inside the brackets, separated by commas, as in the_window.move_to(100,10).

Objects are implemented simply as associative arrays, indexed by the method and property names. This works because, in ECMAScript, functions are 'first-class' values, and can be stored in an array like any other value. The apparently anarchic properties of ECMAScript objects follow from this implementation. If you are writing complex scripts that require you to define your own objects and you wish to impose some order on them, in the way you would do with classes in C++ or Java, you can do so by using a *constructor* to build them. Whenever a particular constructor *K* is called to build an object, it will always do the same thing, so, apart from any differences deriving from the arguments to *K*, the objects it initializes will be the same – they will have the same methods and properties, although the initial values of the properties may be different. We could very well say the objects built by *K* are all instances of the same class.

ECMAScript provides syntax for calling constructors when objects are created, and even supports a form of inheritance (based on object *prototypes*). Since we are not going to require these more advanced features in our example scripts, we will not pursue these matters further. If you are interested in these features, or need them, consult the detailed references provided in the bibliography.

You can define your own objects in ECMAScript, but doing so is only necessary when you are writing complicated scripts that you want to reuse. For most scripters, the importance of objects lies in the way they are used to provide scripts with access to the host environment, and we will look at this in detail in later sections. ECMAScript does have some built-in objects of its own, which are often useful in any host environment.

The Math object has properties that hold the value of useful mathematical constants, such as π, $\sqrt{2}$ and e, written Math.PI, Math.SQRT2 and Math.E, respectively. (The use of capital letters for constants is a convention.) These properties can be used in just the same way as any number; for example, the area of a circle whose radius is held in the variable r is Math.PI*r*r. Math's methods provide useful mathematical operations, including exponentiation, trigonometrical functions, logarithms and random number generation. The full list of methods is quite extensive; consult the ECMAScript standard, the ActionScript documentation for Flash or a good book on JavaScript for the complete list. The methods of built-in objects are called in the same way as the methods of any other object, as we described above. For example, to compute the distance between two points, whose coordinates are held in the variables x1, y1, x2 and y2, you could use the expression

Math.sqrt(Math.pow(x2-x1, 2)+Math.pow(y2-y1, 2))

Math.sqrt computes the square root of its argument, and Math.pow raises its first argument to its second (though in the case of squaring the first argument, it might be quicker and more perspicuous just to multiply it by itself).

Every array has some properties and methods (which rightly belong to the built-in Array object). We have already seen the length property. The array methods allow you to sort arrays, reverse them, and turn them into strings by concatenating all the elements. We will not go into the details.

In a similar way, strings have methods and properties. Typical scripting applications often call for the use of the string methods to analyse data that has been entered as a string by the user. Like arrays, strings have a length property, which holds the number of characters; "four".length is a perverse way of writing 4. The property is more often used in conjunction with strings stored in variables, but as this example shows, even literals can be treated as objects.

The string methods include several different ways of taking strings apart: charAt takes a number and returns the character that it finds at the corresponding position in the string: "Video".charAt(2) is "d". Note that character positions start at 0 for the first character, and that the value returned is itself a string, of length one – there is no such thing as a character type in ECMAScript. The substr method allows you to extract parts of a string; it takes a starting position and length as arguments: "Video".substr(1, 3) is "ide" – the substring of length 3 starting with the character at offset 1 within "Video". If a negative starting position is specified, characters are counted from the end of the string, with –1 being the last character, so "Video".substr(-2, 2) produces "eo". If the offset lies outside the string, an empty string is returned.

ECMAScript with its built-in objects allows you to perform computation, but it is host objects which allow that computation to influence a Web browser of a Flash movie. Although our account of ECMAScript is incomplete, we will now go on to consider its use with these host systems, to demonstrate how scripting drastically alters the nature of multimedia.

World Wide Web Client-side Scripting

The World Wide Web offers two potential host environments for a scripting language – servers and browsers (clients) – giving rise to two types of Web scripting: *server-side* and *client-side*. Server-side scripting, which we will discuss in Chapter 17, is used to enable an HTTP server to communicate with other resources, such as databases, and incorporate data obtained from them into its responses. In particular, server-side scripts are used to enable a server to construct Web pages dynamically from time-varying data, and form the basis of Web applications. In this chapter, we will confine ourselves to client-side scripting, which is used to control the display of media elements that have been retrieved from a server. The development of scripting on the client-side was a significant step in the development of the World Wide Web, which transformed the appearance and behaviour of Web pages.

Executing a client-side script means allowing executable code that has been downloaded from the Internet to run on your machine. Since you have no real guarantee that the person whose code you have downloaded is not malicious or deranged (or both – even politicians have access to the Internet), this would be a foolhardy thing to do if scripts were able to perform arbitrary computation. So they aren't.

In particular, scripts running in a Web browser cannot access any local resources, such as files on your hard disks, or make any network connections, and their interaction with the server from which they originated is limited to requesting new resources and posting information from HTML forms.

As a result of these restrictions, client-side scripts are secure, but limited in the useful work they can do. In effect, they cannot do more than modify the browser's display in response to events. Generally, client-side scripts are used to provide feedback to users (for example, by changing the colour of a clickable item when the cursor is over it) or, more often, just to add interest to a site by providing a richer user interface than the simple one consisting of loading a new page when a link is clicked. Where forms are embedded in Web pages, client-side scripts are often used in a more utilitarian way, to validate input to fields, without the need to contact the server and run a CGI script.

In order for ECMAScript to be able to interact with a Web browser, there must be a well-defined interface between the two. As we explained earlier, this can be provided in the form of a set of host objects representing the elements of an HTML or XML document and any styles applied to them, and the components of the browser interface. The W3C's *Document Object Model (DOM)* defines an abstract, language-independent definition of such an interface, and recent versions of most Web browsers provide objects which implement this interface. You should be aware, though, that if you wish to support older browsers, a lot of effort and ingenuity is required to ensure that scripts will work as intended on every browser that supports client-side scripting. We will, however, ignore this complication in our examples, and stick to the standard interfaces.

Among the host objects provided by Web browsers to allow scripts to manipulate HTML documents, the **document** object plays a primary role. As you would expect from its name, it provides an interface to an HTML document. It contains properties holding the document's title and various pieces of information derived from the HTTP request used to access it, such as the URL and referrer; there are also properties which are arrays, containing all the links, images, and embedded objects in the document. The **document** object also has several methods, including **write**, which writes its argument into the current document. Individual elements can be accessed using the method **getElementById**, which takes a string and returns an object corresponding to the element whose **id** attribute matches the argument. For example, if a document contains a paragraph element with id value 'opening', document.getElementById('opening') will return an object describing that paragraph. Using the same device as that which lets strings and arrays share a set of properties and methods, any object returned in this way will have certain properties and methods, including getAttribute, which is a method taking a string and returning the value of the element's attribute whose name matches the string. For instance, if the element returned by the previous example had been assigned to a variable para1, para1.getAttribute('id') would return 'opening'. Elements also have methods which can be used to navigate within the document – retrieving an element's children, and so on – and modify the document by inserting new elements and attributes, and changing the value of attributes.

Which document is the document object related to? It is the document currently being displayed when the script is executed. But how is a script to be executed in conjunction with a document? The HTML script element is used to embed scripts in documents. When a page is loaded, all the scripts embedded in it are executed, with the document object providing its interface to that page. A simple example will make this clear. Consider the following:

```
<html>
<head>
<title>Dynamically generated content</title>
</head>
<body>
<script type="text/javascript">
document.write('<h1>' + document.title + '</h1>');
</script>
</body>
</html>
```

When this page is loaded into a browser, it produces the display shown in Figure 16.2. The interesting part is the script element, enclosed between start and end tags in the usual way. The start tag sets the value of the type attribute to the MIME type text/javascript – other scripting languages may be used, so we must identify the one

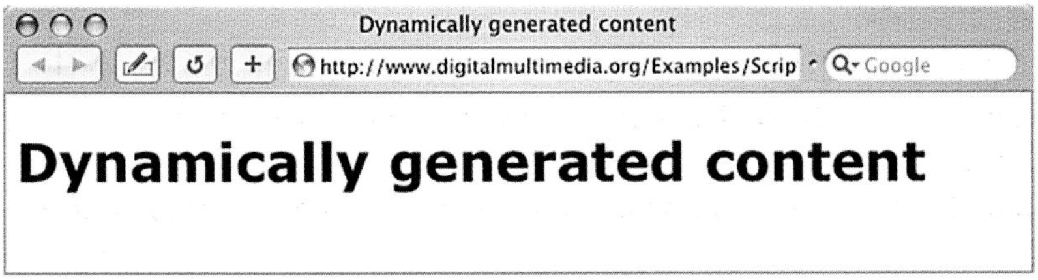

Dynamically generated content

Figure 16.2 Web content generated by a script

being used; despite the anachronism the javascript sub-type is the appropriate one. The script itself is just the single method call:

```
document.write('<h1>' + document.title + '</h1>');
```

The script is executed at the point it is encountered by the Web browser as it parses the HTML document. The write method of the document object takes a string as its argument. Here, we have used the + operator to construct it out of three pieces: the first and last are literal strings containing the start and end tags of an h1 element; in the middle is the value of the title property of the document, and this is a string containing the content of the title element of this page, i.e. 'Dynamically generated content'. The write method does what you probably expect, writes its argument into the document. Since the script is executed when it is encountered during the parsing of the document, the text it writes replaces the script element, so it is as if the document's body were:

```
<h1>Dynamically generated content</h1>
```

and, indeed, the display produced looks exactly as if it was.

It doesn't take a very astute reader to recognize this script as totally pointless – we knew the text of the title and could have more economically embedded it directly in the document, in the form just shown, without executing any script. Now that we know how to combine script and document, via the script element and the document object, though, we can go on to produce genuinely dynamic pages.

A clumsy but effective means of generating dynamic page content is to build it out of text solicited from the user. The function prompt can be used for this purpose.[†] It takes a single string argument, and when called it causes a dialogue box to be displayed, with its argument as a prompt and a text entry field. Any string typed into this field is returned as the result of prompt when the user dismisses the dialogue. For example, the following code will cause the dialogue shown in Figure 16.3 to be displayed; if the OK button is clicked with the text entered as shown, the variable their_name will be set to the string 'Wilfred'.

```
var their_name = prompt('Who are you?');
```

The value of this variable is in scope in all other script fragments embedded in the document after this call, so it can be used to put together some text incorporating the user's name, which can be put into the document with document.write. A good place for the call of

† Technically, prompt is a method belonging to the window object that is attached to the window in which the current document is displayed. All unqualified names (including document) are implicitly methods or properties of this object, so, nearly all the time, you do not need to be aware of it. Note that, since the DOM is only a model of documents, the window object is not part of the standard.

Figure 16.3 Prompting for user input

prompt is in the document's head. The script is executed – so the dialogue is displayed – when it is encountered. The head is completely processed before the content of the body is displayed, so the prompt will appear before the page itself. If prompt is called from within the page body, the dialogue may appear while the page is in the middle of being rendered, which will usually be distracting. Hence, we might use a prompt in the following manner:

```
<html>
<head>
<title>Dynamically generated content</title>
<script type="text/javascript">
var their_name = prompt('Who are you?');
</script>
</head>
<body>
<script type="text/javascript">
document.write('<h2>Why a Duck?</h2>');
document.write('<p>Especially one called ' +
    their_name + '</p>');
</script>
</body>
</html>
```

The dialogue box will appear as we saw previously, and then the page shown in Figure 16.4 will be displayed.

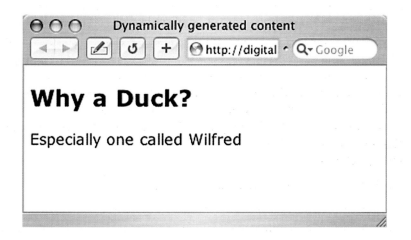

Figure 16.4 Interactively generated content

You probably want to know what happens if the user clicks the cancel button in the dialogue box. An undefined object is returned, and production code should check for this eventuality and do something sensible. If you want to see what happens without any check, try it.

This example is fatuous, but it demonstrates a serious point: information obtained on the client machine at the time the data is downloaded from the server is incorporated dynamically into the page when it is displayed. In other words, interaction with the user has influenced the appearance of the page.

Event Handlers

Much of the interaction required from multimedia presentations and Web pages is concerned with controlling the flow of information. This can be achieved gracefully by using on-screen controls – icons, images, or text – that respond to user events, such as mouse clicks. A simple mechanism for associating a script with an event and a document element is provided by HTML.[†] Almost any document element can have attributes whose name identifies a class of events and whose value is a short piece of code to be executed when the event occurs to that element. Table 16.2 shows the names of the event-related attributes that can be used with most elements, and the events that cause the script that is their value to be executed. Certain elements (for example head) cannot sensibly have these attributes; others, particularly those representing HTML forms, may have extra attributes, but we will not go into the detail of these here, since forms are not often used in conjunction with multimedia pages.[‡]

The code which is the value of an event-related attribute is known as an *event handler*. It is normal for it to be a call to a function. This way, the code that must be included in line with the element tag is compact, and that which performs the actions can be kept separate and easy to read. In this case, we usually refer to the function as the event handler.

One use of event handlers has become a cliché of client-side Web scripting: the 'rollover button'. This is a button – i.e. a small image that serves as a control – whose appearance changes when the cursor is moved over it, to indicate that a mouse click at that point will activate it. This provides some useful feedback to the user, if it is not overdone. The essence of the effect is captured in the following example.

[†] HTML 4 and XHTML, to be precise. Earlier versions of HTML only provided patchy support for events.

[‡] Note, though, that in versions of HTML earlier than 4.0, *only* form elements had any event handlers, so they were often used for purposes other than data entry where event handling was required.

The change of appearance is achieved simply by assigning to the src property of an object corresponding to an image. As we mentioned earlier, the document.images array has an element for each image; it is, in fact, an associative array, indexed by the img elements' id attributes. The following two event handlers update the src of an element with id equal to 'circlesquare', the first setting it to a GIF whose name suggests it is a picture of a circle, the second to a similar image of a square.

```
function in_image() {
        document.images['circlesquare'].src = 'images/circle.gif';
}
function out_of_image() {
        document.images['circlesquare'].src = 'images/square.gif';
}
```

These definitions would be placed in the head of the document. The names of the functions have no semantic significance; they are chosen purely to indicate their function to human readers. They are associated with events in the img tag of the circlesquare element:

```
<img src="images/square.gif" alt="square or circle"
  onmouseover="in_image()" onmouseout="out_of_image()"
  id="circlesquare" />
```

Setting the value of the onmouseover attribute to the string "in_image()" ensures that whenever the cursor is moved over the image, the function in_image will be called, to set the image to a circle. Similarly, the onmouseout attribute has been set to call out_image to make the image revert to the original square. The combination of these handlers ensures that the image displays as a circle whenever the cursor is within its bounds, and as a square the rest of the time. In a practical situation, the images would portray, for example, a push-button in different colours, to indicate readiness when the cursor was over it. Additional onmousedown and onmouseup handlers could be defined to show the button being pressed and released.

The technique of updating the src property of an image object can be used to add animation to a Web page, under the control of a script. This is an improvement on the use of animated GIFs in some ways, since these cannot be controlled: they play once on loading, or for a specific number of times or forever in a loop. Using a script, we can arrange for an animation to be started and stopped by a control or some other means. In the following example, we make a simple

Table 16.2 HTML event handlers

onClick	a mouse button was clicked
onDblClick	a mouse button was double-clicked
onKeyDown	a key was pressed down
onKeyPress	a key was pressed and released
onKeyUp	a key was released
onMouseDown	a mouse button was pressed down
onMouseMove	the cursor was moved
onMouseOut	the cursor was moved away from the element
onMouseOver	the cursor was moved over the element
onMouseUp	a mouse button was released

animation play only as long as the cursor is over it – a moving version of the rollover we just described.

The strategy is easily grasped, but a number of tricks are required to make it work properly. We want to associate a sequence of frames – we will use 10 – with an image element, and cycle through them in turn. The onmouseover event handler for our image will start the cycle going, and the onmouseout will stop it. We can write the image tag straight away:

```
<img src="images/animation/frame1.gif" alt="boing"
  id="the_image" onmouseover="start_animation()"
  onmouseout="stop_animation()" />
```

We are assuming that the images for the animated sequence are in a directory images/animation below the document, as files named frame1.gif, frame2.gif, ... frame10.gif. The first frame is displayed in the image element with id the_image when the page is loaded; the two relevant handlers are set to call functions to start and stop the animation. All we have to do is define those functions, and supply any supporting code they require. The appropriate place to do so is in the document's head.

We know that what we need to do is assign a new value to the src attribute of the object corresponding to the_image at regular intervals – let us say every 80 milliseconds, to give a frame rate of 12.5 fps – and we know what those values should be (the URLs of the frames of the animation). If we assume that we have a function animate that does that as long as a Boolean variable continuing is true, we can define the handlers in terms of it:

```
function start_animation()
{
      continuing = true;
      animate();
}
function stop_animation()
{
      continuing = false;
}
```

We don't need to declare continuing – undeclared or uninitialized variables have an undefined value, which evaluates to false in a Boolean context, when they are first used – but we can if we like (before the functions):

```
var continuing = false;
```

Our problems now seem to be concentrated in the **animate** function. We know from the rollover example how to update images, and it's fairly clear how to use a counter variable to cycle through the frames, but how are we to produce the necessary delay between them? The answer lies in a built-in function[†] that we have not yet described: **setTimeout**. This takes two arguments. The first is a string of code; the second is a number, which will be treated as a time interval in milliseconds. The effect of **setTimeout**(*code, delay*), is to execute *code* after a delay of *delay* milliseconds. In order to repeat an action at regular intervals, all we need to do is make *code* be a call to a function that calls **setTimeout** with a call to itself as the first argument. This is what our **animate** function does. We need some globals first:

[†] Like prompt, actually a property of window.

```
var delay = 80;
var num_frames = 10;
var i = 0;
```

(Two of these are actually constants; in ECMAScript if you want to give memorable names to constants you must use variables.) Now we can write **animate**:

```
function animate() {
    document.images['the_image'].src
                    = images/animation/frame + (++i) + .gif;
    if (i == num_frames)
        i = 0;
    if (continuing)
        setTimeout('animate()', delay);
}
```

The expression on the right of the first assignment builds the name of the next frame using the value of the variable i as the frame number – the prefix ++ operator pre-increments the value, which ensures that it cycles correctly through the frames. The test for equality with num_frames is used to make the value wrap round to zero when it reaches the last frame number, so that we do truly cycle. The last conditional is the key: we test **continuing** to see whether to go on – remember that this variable is set to false when **stop_animation** is called. If we are continuing, we set a timeout, so that **animate** is called again after another delay.

The code just given works after a fashion, but has a major defect: the first time a URL is assigned to the image's src, the image file has to be fetched over the network, which may cause an appreciable delay, so the first cycle of animation may be slower than intended. Subsequently, the file will be cached, and loaded much faster. We would like to be able to preload the images so that every cycle runs at the proper speed. The way this is usually done is by constructing an array of image objects, and populating it with the frames of the animation:

```
var frames = new Array;
for (var j = 0; j num_frames; ++j) {
frames[j] = new Image;
frames[j].src = 'images/animation/frame' + (j + 1) + '.gif';
}
```

Although these images are not displayed, this code is sufficient to cause them to be downloaded and cached. We can now copy the src of one of the images in the array when performing the animation:

```
document.images['the_image'].src = frames[i++].src;
```

which is slightly faster than assigning the URL directly and means that we only have to change the initialization code to get a different animation.

Scripts and Stylesheets

In a well-designed Web page, content is separated from appearance, with the latter being controlled by stylesheets. In order to be able to make changes to the appearance, scripts need to be able to manipulate stylesheets.

There are two ways in which we can change styles: either by changing the style applied to a particular document element, or by altering the stylesheet applied to an entire document. The former is the easier option: each object corresponding to an element of the document has a style property, which is itself an object with properties (in the ECMAScript sense) corresponding to the CSS properties applied to the element. By assigning to these, its appearance can be changed. Suppose, for example, a document has the following stylesheet applied to it:

```
h1 {
     color: lime;
}
```

```
h2 {
      color: blue;
}
```

Then the following HTML element will produce a lime-coloured header:

```
<h1 id="intro">Introduction to Limes</h1>
```

Its colour can be reset to a more sober value by the following assignment, which might be put into an event handler:

```
document.getElementById('intro').style.color = 'black'
```

Altering the stylesheet itself is slightly more complicated. The document object has a property styleSheets, which is an array containing an object for each style element in the document. This in turn includes an array CSSRules containing an object for each rule in the style element. Each rule object has a selectorText property, which allows you to extract the selectors from the corresponding rule, and a style property, which provides access to the values of the CSS properties set by the rule. By assigning to these properties, changes to the styles affecting the entire document can be made. For example, executing

```
document.styleSheets[0].cssRules[1].style.color = 'fuchsia';
```

would change the colour of every level 2 header in the document. Access to style elements and the rules within them is by numerical index, *starting at zero*. Here, styleSheets[0] is the first style; assuming its content is the rules shown above, then styleSheets[0].CSSRules[1] is the object corresponding to

```
h2 {
      color: blue;
}
```

so our assignment has the same effect as transforming this rule into

```
h2 {
      color: fuchsia;
}
```

and applying it, with garish results.

Combining the scriptability of styles with absolute positioning enables you to move document elements about the screen. In conjunction with the use of setTimeout described earlier, this allows you, among other things, to animate text, in a style often favoured for the opening credits of television news bulletins and sports programmes, for example. Generally, the practice should be avoided – it more often irritates users than impresses them. However, occasionally animation of this sort may serve a purpose.

As an example, consider making rollovers where the rolled over element moves while the cursor is over it, instead of just changing its appearance when the cursor first rolls over. In particular, let us make a link that jumps up and down eagerly while the cursor is over it. The relevant part of the HTML document could look like this:

```
<a id="jumper" onmouseover="start_jumping()"
    onmouseout="stop_jumping()"
    href="http://www.digitalmultimedia.org/">
    Jump up and down
</a>
```

The link text has its own id, so that we can apply positioning style to it. Before looking at the rollover script, we need to see the CSS rule applied to the link.

```
#jumper { position:absolute;
      top: 35;
      left: 40;
      font: x-large ;
      color: blue;
}
```

Recall that we use fragment identifiers as selectors to apply a style to a specific element. The rule thus positions the link text at (40, 35), using absolute positioning; an extra large blue font is used to make the word conspicuous.

Now to make things move. We use exactly the same technique as we used to animate a sequence of images: the functions jump_up and jump_down update the top property of the jumper object's style, thereby moving it up and down; each function then sets a timeout, with the other as the code to be executed after the delay, so that the link alternately moves up and down. Auxiliary functions, called by the event handlers, are used to start and stop the movement, as before.

Here is the complete code of the functions, with their associated variables:

```
<script type="text/javascript">
var delay=180;
var continuing = false;
```

```
var the_style;

function jump_up() {
     if (continuing) {
          the_style.top = 32;
     setTimeout('jump_down()', delay);
  }
}

function jump_down() {
     the_style.top = 35;
     if (continuing)
     setTimeout('jump_up()', delay);
}

function start_jumping() {
     the_style = document.getElementById('jumper').style;
     continuing = true;
     jump_up();
}

function stop_jumping() {
     continuing = false;
     jump_down();
}
</script>
```

There are a couple of additional subtleties here. First, to avoid repeatedly writing and evaluating the long complicated expression to access the style object, we have assigned it to the variable the_style in the start_jumping function; the other functions use this variable to change the top property. Second, we want to ensure that the link goes back to its original position after the cursor has moved off it; this is the purpose of the call to jump_down in stop_moving. However, it is possible that a time-out will cause jump_up to be called again after this. The slightly different organization of the test in the two jump functions ensures that, at whatever point in the cycle stop_moving is called, the movement will indeed cease after the link text has moved down to where it belongs.

We should emphasize again that in these examples we have only sought to demonstrate how ECMAScript in conjunction with the DOM can be used to add interactivity and dynamic effects to Web pages. We have not tried to demonstrate good programming style or page design, nor to address the real practical issues concerning compatibility between different browsers and different versions of browsers.

Behaviours

Scripts offer the potential for controlling the user interface to a multimedia production on the basis of elaborate computation, carried out using most of the facilities of a modern programming language. Much of the time, authors only require a limited repertoire of interface enhancements and animation facilities, such as those illustrated in the previous section. If an authoring system can provide a set of parameterized actions that is adequate to satisfy most needs, and a suitable interface for attaching them to elements of a multimedia production, then much of the necessity for scripting is removed. This means that designers can add interactivity and animation to their productions without having to acquire programming skills on top of their design skills. Conversely, it means that programmers can employ their skills in a way that can be exploited by designers, rather than involving themselves in design. Parameterized actions provided by an authoring system to be used in this manner are usually called *behaviours*. Since behaviours are going to be extensively reused, considerable care must be taken in writing them, so that, for example, JavaScript behaviours cope gracefully with the divergent object models and capabilities of different user agents.

What do we mean by describing behaviours as *parameterized* actions? Simply that each behaviour is an abstraction that captures a class of actions – such as displaying a message to a Web browser's status line – from which individual actions, such as writing the specific message Please wait to the status line, can be generated by providing a value for some variable, the behaviour's *parameter*. In this case, the parameter is the message to be displayed; in general, a behaviour may have several parameters. It follows that an authoring system that supports behaviours must provide some means for authors to provide parameter values, and be able to generate code by combining these values with a behaviour. They must also be able to attach the resulting actions to events chosen by the author.

The simplest approach is to build a limited set of behaviours into the browser. You might consider the link-following and history navigating capabilities of all Web browsers as an instance of this approach. Modern Web browsers also include code to interpret a scripting language, so that arbitrary actions can be written in that language. You should be able to see in outline how, instead of being written by hand like the examples in the previous section, ECMAScript actions can be parameterized as behaviours and incorporated into HTML semi-automatically. In order to fill in the details, we will describe

▼ Behaviors

├── <img> Actions
Call JavaScript
Change Property
Check Browser
Check Plugin
Control Shockwave or Flash
Drag Layer
Go To URL
Hide Pop-Up Menu
Jump Menu
Jump Menu Go
Open Browser Window
Play Sound
Popup Message
Preload Images
Set Nav Bar Image
Set Text ▶
Show Pop-Up Menu
Show-Hide Layers
Swap Image
Swap Image Restore
Timeline ▶
Validate Form

Show Events For ▶

Get More Behaviors...

Figure 16.5 The Behaviours panel in Dreamweaver MX

the interfaces to behaviours provided by a representative HTML authoring program, Macromedia Dreamweaver, and sketch their implementation.

Most HTML authoring programs (as against general-purpose text editors with HTML modes, such as BBEdit or Emacs) use a similar interface, comprising a document window providing a view of the document being composed, and several context-sensitive floating palettes (or panels, as they are called by Macromedia), whose contents change according to the element selected in the document window. These palettes allow attributes of the selected element to be changed. Dreamweaver's Behaviours panel (shown in Figure 16.5) is used to attach actions to events associated with the selected element. Clicking the + button causes a pop-up menu to appear, as shown, listing the names of all the available behaviours – Dreamweaver ships with a collection of useful behaviours; others can be added, as described later. Menu entries for behaviours that, for some reason, are not applicable to the currently selected element are disabled. For example, unless an image is selected the Swap Image behaviour will not be available. When a behaviour has been selected, a dialogue box is displayed, with fields for any parameters that are needed to generate the code. Once these have been supplied, the behaviour is shown in the panel, as in Figure 16.6; the event to which the action is to provide a response is shown beside it in the column labelled Events. Each behaviour has a default, but any other event supported by the DOM can be chosen instead, using the pop-up menu next to the event, as shown in the illustration.

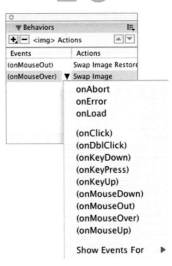

Figure 16.6 Events for behaviours

Since Dreamweaver is an HTML editor, its basic function is to change the contents of HTML documents. It can therefore embody the association of element, event and action by writing suitable ECMAScript code in the document's head to define a handler function, and then inserting an on*Event* attribute into the start tag of the selected element. For example, suppose an img element is selected, and two instances of the Set Text of Status Bar behaviour are attached to it, one for the event onmouseover, the other, with a blank message, for onmouseout, so that the first message will be displayed for as long as the cursor is over the image. Dreamweaver will insert a script equivalent to the following one into the document head:

```
<script type="text/javascript">
function displayStatusMsg(msgStr) {
     status = msgStr;
}
</script>
```

and decorate the <img> tag with attributes similar to the following:[†]

```
onmouseover= "displayStatusMsg('The cursor is inside the image')"
onmouseout= "displayStatusMsg(' ')"
```

The collection of behaviours shipped with Dreamweaver provides an insight into the range of actions that can be readily added to a Web page in this way. (Looked at more cynically, since most of the other powerful HTML tools presently available support roughly the same set of actions, this collection provides an insight into Web page design clichés – at least until the next round of updates to these programs is released.)

Probably the most popular group is concerned with images and motion graphics. **Swap Image** provides the action needed to implement rollover buttons, or to perform image replacements in response to any chosen events. **Preload Images** performs the preloading operation described previously, to ensure that image swaps work smoothly. It is usually included automatically with **Swap Image**.

Image rollovers are such a common requirement for fashionable Web pages that Dreamweaver provides an **Insert Rollover Image** command,[‡] which allows you to create a rollover effect simply by selecting the images for the two states. Inserting one of them and creating the necessary code is all done in one step. Most HTML authoring packages provide this function, as do many graphics packages that have been augmented with Web capabilities or designed for preparing Web graphics.

Other behaviours allow you to animate absolutely positioned elements, control their visibility and even add basic drag and drop functionality. The last of these in particular provides a powerful argument in favour of the use of behaviours, since implementing dragging within the confines of ECMAScript and the DOM requires some non-trivial programming: all mouse movements must be tracked and the position of the dragged object updated in response. Care must be taken to observe the physical constraints of the page. If you also want, for example, to reserve certain areas of an image as 'drag handles', or to provide a target for each dragged object, allowing it to snap to its destination when it is close enough, or to support several draggable layers on the same page, and to work with as many versions of different browsers as possible, you would have to write quite a lot of code. As it is, it may be necessary to add hand-made code to the basic behaviour to monitor the position of the moving element. Be

[†] If you try this and examine the code, you will see that Dreamweaver actually wraps an a element round the img and attaches the attributes to that. This is for compatibility with older browsers that only allow event handlers on a few element types.

[‡] In Dreamweaver MX you can find this command on the Interactive Images sub-menu of the Insert menu.

that as it may, there has been a substantial backlash against the use of such dynamic HTML effects since their first appearance – they are unreliable and users don't like them. It is usually advisable to stick with familiar behaviours, especially rollovers, unless you are designing a Web site as a showcase for scripting.

The behaviours that we have described are not built in to Dreamweaver; new behaviours can be added to extend the repertoire. The mechanism by which this is achieved is an interesting exercise in economy, since all it requires is HTML and ECMAScript – which Dreamweaver has to be able to interpret already.

A behaviour is just an HTML file, whose head contains some ECMAScript definitions, and whose body is a document that will be rendered in a dialogue box when a user selects this behaviour from the pop-up menu in the Behaviours palette. Usually, the document will contain a form element, with fields for accepting the values of the behaviour's parameters.[†] When the form is filled in, these values become available to scripts within the behaviour via objects in the same way as elements' attribute values.

The author of the behaviour must provide two functions: behaviorFunction and applyBehavior, which both return strings to be inserted in the HTML document being edited. The first returns the code for a handler function definition, the second a call to that handler, to be inserted into the selected element's start tag. Typically, the strings returned by both these functions will incorporate values elicited from the user by the form in the behaviour's body. Behaviours may include several other function definitions, notably canAcceptBehavior, which returns a list of events with which the behaviour can be associated, allowing Dreamweaver to correctly set up the pop-up menu by which the event is chosen when a behaviour is added to a document. A displayHelp function can also be defined, which returns a string describing the behaviour when the help button in the behaviour dialogue is pressed.

One can imagine simpler ways of implementing behaviours – using action templates, for example – but this approach permits great flexibility, since all the features of ECMAScript are available for creating the function definitions and calls.

[†] We have not described HTML forms, since they are quite complex and not particularly interesting in the context of multimedia. Consult one of the HTML references for details on forms, the elements that may be used within them, and the special events that are associated with form elements.

Scripting in Flash

Flash's scripting language ActionScript consists of ECMAScript furnished with a set of host objects corresponding to elements of Flash movies, and some additional objects that provide for communication between movies and servers, including XML objects that allow scripts to analyze XML data read from a server. (In fact, as we noted before, there are some minor incompatibilities between ActionScript and ECMAScript, but these have little practical impact.) To complete the interface between the scripting language and movies, Flash must also provide a way of including scripts within movies and arranging for them to respond to events.

Scripts may be written within Flash's authoring environment. The Actions panel shown in Figure 16.7 is used for this purpose. It can be used in two different modes, *normal* and *expert*. In expert mode, you simply type your script into the main pane of the panel. In normal mode, you build up the script by selecting elements from a list and entering parameters into a context-sensitive dialogue in the upper pane. The advantage of this is that it is impossible to introduce syntax errors, and you do not have to remember the details of every ActionScript construct. It is, however, slower, and experienced programmers normally prefer the expert mode. Whichever mode you use, the result will be a script in the ActionScript language. In our examples, we will only concern ourselves with the code. If you need more practical information on entering scripts in Flash, consult the manual or *Digital Media Tools*.

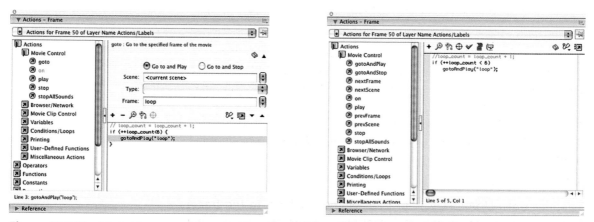

Figure 16.7 Flash's Actions panel in normal mode (left) and expert mode (right)

Attaching Scripts

There are three types of element to which scripts can be attached, each of which determines a set of events which will trigger the attached script. We will consider each of these in turn.

Frame Scripts

A script can be attached to any keyframe, by selecting the frame in the timeline and then entering the code in the **Actions** panel. It is good practice to create a layer for scripts in the timeline; that way you can add keyframes anywhere you want, without upsetting any animation going on on other layers, and alter the animation without disturbing the scripts. A frame script will be executed when the playhead enters the frame to which it is attached. Putting this another way, frame scripts respond to the single event caused by the playhead entering the frame. This is easy to understand, but makes such scripts of limited use. Often, though, scripts attached to dummy frames at the beginning of a movie are a good place to define functions for use elsewhere.

Although we have claimed that the interface between ECMAScript and Flash consists of a set of host objects, the simplest operations are provided as functions. (Purists can finesse this by considering the functions to be methods of an implicit **movie** object, in the same way that functions in JavaScript are methods of the **window** object. The Flash documentation does not do this, though.) Some of these simple functions can be used to implement looping structures in Flash movies.

Normally, when a Flash movie is played in a Web browser or the standalone Flash Player, it will play from beginning to end and then return to the beginning and loop indefinitely. Suppose instead you wanted an introductory section to be played once, and then for the remainder of the movie to loop (see Figure 13.12 in Chapter 13). This can be achieved easily by attaching the following code to the final frame of the movie.

```
gotoAndPlay("loop");
```

The effect of **gotoAndPlay** is to transfer the playhead to the frame identified by its argument, and continue playing the movie from there. Here, we have used a string as the argument. This identifies a frame by its *label*. Frames are given labels by selecting them in the timeline and typing the label into a text entry field in the property inspector panel.

It should be clear that the above script achieves the desired aim. In early versions of Flash, this was about as sophisticated as scripts could be, but in Flash 5 and later versions, arbitrary computation can be carried out by scripts. As a slightly less trivial example, consider modifying the behaviour of this movie with its introduction and loop, so that, after the introduction, the loop only plays a set number of times – let's say six. To achieve this, we need to use a variable to count the number of times we go round the loop, and a conditional statement to make sure that we only loop back if the limit has not been reached.

It is not strictly necessary, but we would always advise declaring the counter variable and explicitly setting it to zero to begin with. This is done by attaching the following single line to the first frame of the movie:

```
var loop_count=0;
```

If you don't do this, the script will still work – variables don't have to be declared and are set to zero automatically – but it will be harder for anyone looking at the movie to understand what is going on.

The script on the last frame can be modified to increment and test the counter. Using the pre-increment operator ++ allows this to be done succinctly:

```
if (++loop_count < 6)
      gotoAndPlay("loop");
```

Button Symbols

It's best to think of button symbols as being a distinct type of symbol in Flash (see Chapter 8), designed to accept user input by responding to events such as mouse clicks and rollovers, but they are built as animations that have exactly four frames. These are given the special labels Up, Over, Down and Hit. The first three correspond to states of the button, relative to the cursor. Up is the normal state, when the cursor is not over the button, while Over, as you might guess, corresponds to the cursor being over the button. Thus, by putting different graphics in the Up and Over frames, a classic rollover effect can be produced: the appearance of the button changes as the cursor passes over it, providing useful feedback to the user. Typically, the two states will be similar, with different shading, for example. The Down frame is displayed when the mouse button is depressed while the cursor is over the button symbol, i.e. the user has pressed the button. Again, the intention is that the display should provide feedback, so typically the Down frame will show an image that indicates the button being operated. For example, if a three-dimensional image of an actual button was being used, the Up frame might show it slightly elevated, while the Down frame showed the same button pressed down. However, these are only conventions. The frames can show any images, or none (for invisible controls), and the same image can be used for all three, if it is felt that conventional feedback is inappropriate.

The final frame, Hit, is different from the other two, because it is not displayed. It is used to indicate the area within which the cursor is considered to be over the button – its *active area*. Often, this will match the bounding box of the image in the Up frame, but it need not do so. For example, Figure 16.8 shows the frames of a button taken from the library distributed with Flash. Here, the active area is extended beyond the button icon, to allow a text label to be placed next to the button icon within the active area, so that it seems to be part of the button although it is not. Clicking on the word Register invokes the same action as clicking on the button icon.

Figure 16.8 Frames of a button symbol and a labelled instance (right)

The frames of a button symbol are composed on the stage like any other frame. Graphics may be imported, and symbol instances can be incorporated in the button. Movie clip instances can be used to create animated buttons. Sounds can also be attached to some of a button's keyframes, by placing them on a layer as event sounds, so that the button clicks when pressed, and so on.

Instances of button symbols, referred to simply as buttons, are created by dragging a symbol from the library onto the stage. As far as animation is concerned, buttons may be treated like any other sort of symbol, although when they are used conventionally to provide controls for interactivity, buttons are usually left in a fixed position on the screen. Normally, one tends to think of buttons as static controls, which sit on the screen waiting to be pressed. This is often the best way of using them; it conforms to users' expectations and provides a simple organization for your movie. Buttons can be placed in a keyframe that is extended over the whole movie, on their own layer.

However, sometimes it may be useful to employ buttons in less conventional ways. One particularly handy technique is to create a button with no content in its Up, Over or Down frames, and a rectangle equal in size to the stage, in the Hit frame, and place an instance of it in the frontmost layer of a movie, extending the image over as many frames as is appropriate. The result is that this invisible button instance will receive events anywhere on the screen. Such a button can be used to create an interface in which all a user has to do to make something happen is click somewhere. You might use this in an introductory section of a movie to allow the user who is familiar with its contents to dismiss the introduction.

Table 16.3 Button events

press	rollOut
release	dragOver
releaseOutside	dragOut
rollOver	keyPress

If a button is selected on the stage, an event handler may be attached to it, using the Actions panel. Unlike frame scripts, button scripts may be triggered by different events. Table 16.3 lists these. The script attached to a button must specify the particular event that triggers it. This is done by enclosing the body of the script in some boilerplate code, of the form:

```
onEvent {
}
```

where *Event* is one of the events listed in Table 16.3. (If you enter scripts in normal mode, this boilerplate is inserted for you when you attach a script to a button.) Conventionally, a mouse click occurs when the mouse is released, so if you wished to provide a control for users to stop the movie, you would place a button on the stage and add the following script to it:

```
on (release) {
        stop();
}
```

When the button was clicked, the movie would stop. To ensure that the button was always available, you could put a keyframe in the first frame of the movie on the button layer, and extend it to the full length of the movie.

With Flash MX (and version 6 of the Flash Player) a more sophisticated event handling model was introduced into ActionScript, whereby handlers could be defined as methods of movie clip objects (see later). Thus, instead of the code shown above, the event handler could be attached to the button by assigning a function to its onRelease method. The advantage of this is that handlers can be assigned dynamically as the movie plays. This technique is somewhat advanced, though, so we will not pursue it further.

Movie Clips

Buttons have been available in Flash since its early days, and many Flash programmers use them as their primary means of recognizing events triggered by user actions, but in more recent versions of Flash, any movie clip can receive events and have scripts attached to it. Table 16.4 lists the clip events. The set is different from that which buttons can accept, and for simple purposes, buttons provide an easier mechanism for adding interactivity. For example, when a user clicks on a button, that button is the only one to receive the release event. In contrast, all movie clips will receive a mouseUp event, and the script attached to each one will have to examine the current mouse coordinates to determine whether it should deal with the click. This is not arduous, in fact, and movie clip events provide a more systematic framework for dealing with user input. For the simple examples that space permits in this book, we will stick with the more established method of using buttons, however, and leave clip events to some of the exercises.

Table 16.4 Clip events

load	mouseUp
unload	keyDown
enterFrame	keyUp
mousemove	data
mouseDown	

Again, things changed slightly with the new event handling model in Flash MX. It is now possible to create a 'button movie clip' by assigning to an event handling method for a button event with a movie clip object. This saves the effort of the previously common technique of embedding buttons inside movie clips, so that the combined object would be able to respond to button events, while having the other properties of a movie clip.

Movie Clip Methods and Properties

In Chapter 8 we introduced *movie clips*, which, in Flash, are instances of symbols that behave as self-contained movies within a movie, with their own independent timelines. Scripts can be used to control movie clips in response to events. This opens up the possibility of *interactive animation*, where the movement of objects on the stage is controlled by user interaction.

In order for a clip to be controlled by scripts, it must be given an *instance name*. This does not happen automatically when the instance is created; you must select the instance and enter a name explicitly in the property inspector (see Figure 16.9). Flash does not check whether any instance name you use actually refers to anything, so if you forget to give an instance a name, but use one anyway believing you had done so, you will not be warned about the error; your action will just do nothing, silently, probably leaving you baffled. As well as

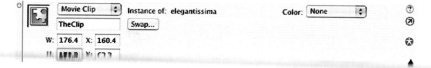

Figure 16.9 Setting a clip's instance name

having an instance name, a clip must also be in existence when it is referred to in a script. A clip comes into existence in the first frame in which it is present, and ceases to exist after the last. If a script refers to it outside its time of existence, nothing happens, and once again there is no error message.

A movie clip's instance name can be used in scripts as if it were a variable containing an object. All such objects that refer to movie clips have a collection of properties corresponding to attributes of the clip, such as its total number of frames, current frame, dimensions, and so on, and methods, which can be used to start and stop the clip, go to a particular frame, and control it in other ways. Several of these methods have the same names and effect as the functions we used to control the playback of a complete movie in earlier sections.

As a simple example of controlling movie clip instances, consider making a movie player, so that the playback of a clip can be controlled using buttons. We will provide buttons to play, stop, rewind and go to the end of a movie clip. The first step will be to create a movie with a single frame and attach **stop()** to it. This frame will just be a container for the movie clip being controlled and the buttons that control it. Next, a clip symbol must be created and an instance of it placed on the stage. Any Flash movie converted to a symbol can be used for this purpose. To emphasize the point once again: the instance must be given a name. Let's suppose it is called **TheClip**. At this point, you will probably realize that we are going to end up with this particular movie clip wired in to the player, rather as if your DVD player came with one disc in it and no means of changing it. Later we will see how to turn this basic movie into something like a Flash movie jukebox that lets you select a movie to play. This will require some additional movie clip methods, so for now, let us concentrate on controlling the playback of a fixed clip.

The next step is to add controls in the form of buttons. You can design your own or use one from the collection of VCR buttons you will find among the libraries distributed with Flash. (To access these, choose **Buttons.fla** from the **Common Libraries** sub-menu of the **Window** menu. A library window will open, from which you can drag instances to the stage.) Figure 16.10 shows a possible design for the

Figure 16.10 A movie player

player, though of course many variations are possible. An instance of a movie clip symbol has been placed within the white area, and given the instance name TheClip. To prevent it playing spontaneously, the statement

TheClip.stop();

is added to the first frame of the main movie. This is our first example of a method being called on a movie clip.

In a similar way, the statement TheClip.play(); calls the play method of our clip – which causes it to play. Hence, the Play button of the movie player needs to have the following script attached to it:

```
on (release) {
      TheClip.play ();
}
```

and then when it is clicked, the clip will start to play, as required. You should be able to see from this what scripts should be attached to the Stop and Rewind buttons.

Going to the end of the clip is marginally more difficult. You can probably see that we need to use the gotoAndStop method, but how are we to know which frame to go to? For a single fixed clip we could just count the frames, but that is inelegant and inflexible, and will go wrong if the clip itself is ever edited in a way that changes its length. A much better way is to use the _totalframes property of the clip, which always holds the total number of frames in the clip. Taking this approach, the script for this button becomes:

```
on (release) {
        TheClip.gotoAndStop(TheClip._totalframes);
}
```

The next step in developing this movie player is to remove the single hard-wired clip, and provide a way of selecting from a range of clips. We won't attempt to provide a way of accessing arbitrary movie clips, but we will use a jukebox as our model, and assume that there is a set of clips from which the user may select one to play. A first require-ment is that there must be additional controls for selecting the clip. We will keep matters simple by assuming that there is only a small number of clips, so we can just add one button for each. Figure 16.11 shows the modified player design.

Figure 16.11 A movie jukebox

The loadMovie method can be used to load a new movie from a SWF file into a movie clip, replacing its original contents. This makes it very simple to implement the jukebox player, since all we need to do is attach scripts to each of the clip buttons, which use this method to load a different movie into TheClip. The argument to the method can be a URL; in the common case that the movie to be loaded is held on the server with the main movie, a relative URL can be used. Hence, if we assume that there is a sub-directory called sub-movies in the

directory housing the jukebox movie itself, we simply need to attach scripts such as the following to each of the movie-selecting buttons:

```
on (release) {
      TheClip.loadMovie("sub-movies/red.swf");
}
```

We could begin by loading one of the clips arbitrarily when the movie starts up, but it might make more sense simply to have no movie until the user loads one explicitly. This is easily accomplished by making TheClip an instance of a dummy symbol, consisting of a single blank frame. It doesn't matter what sort of clip instance you load a movie into, the loaded movie will replace it entirely, so the use of a dummy symbol like this is quite common.

Creating Applications in Flash

Although ECMAScript lacks some of the essential features of a programming language for large-scale programming, it remains powerful enough for fairly serious computation. This means that it is possible to use Flash not as an animation tool with some interactivity, but as a means of developing applications, whose user interface is provided by Flash's graphics and animation capabilities. A relatively simple example will serve to introduce this approach to development.

The application will be a loan repayment calculator, which will allow a user to enter an amount to borrow, using a numeric keypad, and then select a repayment period. The calculator will then work out and display the monthy repayments. Figure 16.12 shows the interface to the calculator. Since this was created in Flash, it is not restricted to standard user interface elements. Here, we created a distinctive calligraphic style for the keypad, and used a complementary font for the display.

There are only two frames in this movie: the one whose stage is shown in Figure 16.12, where data is entered, and one other in which the calculation is performed and the result will be displayed. To enter data, the user clicks on the numbers, as if using a calculator. Each button is, in fact, an instance of a button symbol. (The numeric labels are on a layer on top of the buttons themselves.) The following script is attached to the first frame.

```
var amount = 0, period = 0;
stop();
```

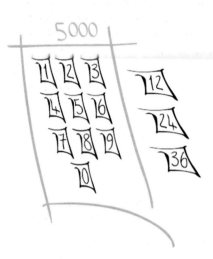

Figure 16.12 A repayment calculator

The variable amount will hold the amount to be borrowed, while period records the term of the proposed loan. Every time one of the buttons on the keypad is pressed, a new value is computed for amount, to correspond to the number formed by appending the new digit to those entered so far. This is achieved with scripts such as the following (for the button labelled 7):

```
on (release) {
    amount = 10*amount + 7;
}
```

The buttons' scripts differ only in the digit added to the end of amount (except for the zero button, which has the obvious optimization). Similarly, the scripts attached to each of the three buttons for selecting the loan period closely resemble each other. For example, the 36 month button has the following:

```
on (release) {
    period = 36;
    gotoAndStop ("Calculate");
}
```

The other selection buttons' scripts just assign a different value to period. The period is thus set to correspond to the button's label, and the playhead is moved to the second frame (labelled "Calculate").

While the user is setting the loan amount by clicking buttons, it is customary to provide feedback by displaying the current value. This is easily done by adding a *dynamic text field* to the calculator. A dynamic text field is created like any other text field using the text tool. When the field is selected, it can be specified as dynamic text using the pop-up menu on the property inspector (see Figure 16.13). When this is done, a field labelled Var appears; a variable name should be typed in here. When the movie is played, the current value of that variable will be converted to a string, if necessary, and displayed in the text field.

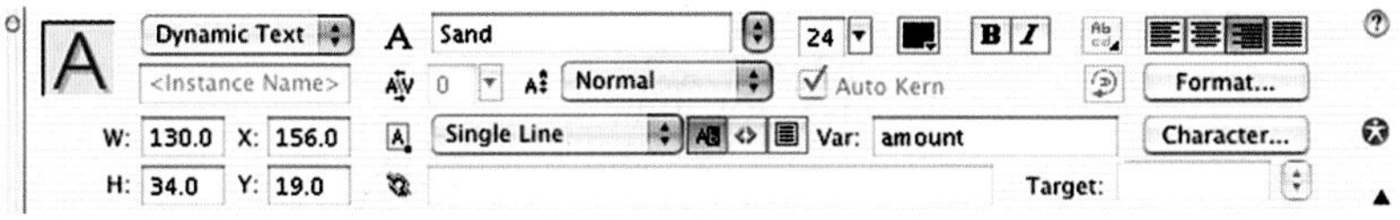

Figure 16.13 Creating a dynamic text field

Thus, simply by making amount the variable associated with the text field above the keypad, the required feedback is provided.

The script attached to the second frame calculates the total amount that must be paid back, using compound interest calculated monthly. That is, we pretend that the loan is being held for the full length of the period, and work out the total that is obtained by adding interest at a fixed monthly rate each month. Then we divide that total by the number of months to arrive at a monthly repayment. (It should be stressed that this example should not be used for making any financial decisions. Interest can be calculated in many different ways, and we do not claim to understand all the subtleties employed by banks and other lending institutions.) There is a simple formula for this calculation, but since we are using a computer, not a slide rule, it is as easy to work out the amount by brute force in a loop that adds the interest accrued each month. We need to know the monthly interest rate. A deceptively modest-sounding value (three-quarters of a percent per month) has been embedded in the code as the value of a variable rate, on the assumption that it will change relatively rarely. (A better approach would be to obtain the current rate dynamically. This can be done easily, but space does not permit us to describe all the necessary ActionScript.)

```
var rate = 0.0075;
```

The main calculation is a for loop. Before it starts, a variable must be initialized to hold the total amount after interest.

```
var total = amount;
```

Paraphrasing this initialization, after no months all that is owed is the original amount borrowed.

The loop is executed for a number of times equal to the period of the loan. Each time, the amount of interest incurred during the month on the total owed is added to produce a new total for the next month.

```
for (var t = 0; t < period; ++t)
    total = total* (1+rate);
```

When the loop exits, the monthly repayment can be discovered by dividing the total by the period over which the loan is taken out.

```
repayment = total/period;
```

It only remains to break the news to the user. A naive way of displaying the result would be to create a dynamic text field, associating it with a variable called **message**, and assigning a suitable string containing the repayment details to it, like this:

```
message = period + " repayments of £" + repayment;
```

Unfortunately, if you try this, you will see output like this:

24 repayments of £249.252818623463

The repayment should be a sum in pounds and pence; that is, the value of **repayment** should be rounded to two decimal places. The following code achieves this – if you can't see how it works, just take it on faith; the details of the arithmetic aren't important.

```
var i = String(Math.floor(repayment));
```

```
var f = Math.round((100*repayment)%100);
```

```
f = f < 10? "0" + f: String(f);
```

```
repayment = i + "." + f;
```

With this modification, the movie now produces acceptable output, such as:

24 repayments of £249.25

As it stands, this little application has some serious shortcomings: there is no way for the user to correct mistakes or start over again, for instance. However, it should serve to demonstrate that creating applications by using Flash as the front-end and ActionScript to perform computation is a viable alternative to conventional software development, at least for some applications. Since Flash can communicate with a server, and parse XML data, it is possible to use the same approach to create the client-side components of serious Web applications.

Exercises

1   An old story relates how a king offered a reward to a wise man who had performed a valuable service for him. The wise man made a seemingly modest request: the king should take a chess board, place one grain of rice on the first square of the first row, two grains on the next square, four on the next, and so on, doubling the number of grains on each successive square. A chess board is eight rows by eight columns. Write a script to compute the number of rice grains on the last square and the total number the wise man was asking for. Either embed the script in a Web page and use document.write to display the answers, or attach it to a frame in a Flash movie and use a dynamic text field.

2   Modify your script from the previous exercise to store the number of grains on each square in an array. Print out the values in the array in a suitable format.

3   [For keen programmers.] You will have discovered that the number of grains of rice is very large indeed, so that it will be displayed by your scripts in scientific notation. Write a function that takes an integer and returns a string of digits that is its decimal representation.

4   Modify the 'Why a duck?' script so that it checks for an undefined return value and takes some appropriate action.

5   Construct an HTML page that behaves like an animation player. That is, there should be buttons to start, stop, and single-step through an animation. Add event handlers to make these buttons play a simple animation, held as a sequence of individual GIF files on the server.

6   How would you make text tumble across the screen in a Web browser?

7   Write the scripts to stop and rewind a movie in the Flash movie clip player example.

8   Fill in the details of the movie jukebox and implement it. Extend the interface so that it more closely resembles a real jukebox of a certain era. Use two columns of selection buttons, labelled with letters and numbers, and use the combination of letter and number to select a movie. (If you have four letter buttons and four number buttons, you will be able to choose one of 16 movies to play.)

Multimedia and Networks

17

- Protocols
  - Network and Transport Protocols
- Multicasting
- Application Protocols for Multimedia
  - HTTP
  - RTSP
- Quality of Service
- Server-side Computation
  - The Common Gateway Interface
  - Beyond CGI

The relationship between computer networks and multimedia is a contradictory one: they are incompatible perfect partners. As the preceding chapters have shown, multimedia places considerable demands on resources: files are often very large, complex processing, such as decompression, may be required, response times must be short, and tight, sometimes complex, synchronization constraints must be respected. Networks are particularly poorly placed to satisfy these demands, because of the inherent limitations of present day technology, and because of the complex and unpredictable effects of the interactions between network components and patterns of network traffic. At the same time, it makes a great deal of sense to maintain multimedia data in a central repository, to be accessed over a network. Wasteful duplication of those same large files is avoided, there is no need for any physical medium, such as a CD-ROM, to be used for distribution, and the approach fits in with the current trend towards distributed systems of desktop machines connected to central servers. Furthermore, the combination of networks and multimedia makes new applications, such as video conferencing and live multimedia presentations, possible.

The considerations in favour of delivering multimedia over networks are generally held to be so compelling as to make it worth living with and trying to overcome the limitations.

In this chapter we will take a closer look at the mechanisms, which we have so far only glanced at, that are provided to make it possible to deliver multimedia over a network. This material is among the most technical in the book, and you probably won't find it of much interest unless you have some knowledge of how computer systems and networks operate. Readers without this technical background may prefer to skim the opening paragraphs of each section to get some idea of what is involved in meeting the demands of distributed multimedia. Computer scientists and engineers will be able to appreciate why the main thrust of academic and industrial research in multimedia is concentrated on the matters covered in this chapter.

We will concentrate exclusively on TCP/IP networks. Bear in mind that this includes not only the Internet – although that was where these protocols were developed – but also 'intranets': local area networks utilizing the same set of protocols. Because of their generally higher speeds and more centralized management, intranets are better able to support some of the distributed multimedia applications, such as video conferencing, that can be implemented using the real-time protocols we will describe. For the Internet, universal deployment of these applications is still in the future, although the growth in broadband means that they are beginning to become more widely feasible.

Protocols

Protocols are the rules governing the exchange of data over networks. They are conceptually organized into *layers*, stacked on top of each other, with the lowest layer protocols dealing with the actual physical signals transmitted over wires and optical fibres. Above these, slightly higher level protocols handle the transfer of packets of raw data, and ensure that they reach their correct destination. The highest layers implement more application-oriented services, such as file transfer or Web browsing. The protocols on each layer are implemented using those on the layer below.

When a Web server and client exchange information using HTTP, for example, it appears as though the client sends HTTP requests to the server, which replies with HTTP responses. To the Web software, no other protocols appear to be involved, but in fact, what actually happens is that the HTTP messages are translated into streams of TCP packets, which are themselves translated into the format of the actual networks over which the data must pass; at the receiving end, these packets are used to reconstruct the incoming HTTP message. Thus, we need a little understanding of the lower level TCP/IP protocols before we can appreciate the characteristics of the application-oriented protocols that are used for multimedia.

TCP/IP networks are *packet-switched* networks, which means that all messages transmitted over the network are split into small pieces, called *packets*, which are sent separately. This enables network bandwidth to be shared efficiently between many messages, since, if the rate at which packets are generated for one message is lower than the available carrying capacity, packets belonging to other messages can be transmitted at the same time; we say messages are *multiplexed*.

Contrast this with the telephone network, where a connection is established between the caller and the person being called, and this connection is held open for the exclusive use of their conversation until the caller hangs up, whether or not anybody is speaking. The advantages of this *circuit-switched* approach, which can be used for data exchange as well as spoken conversations, is that there is no need to distinguish between packets belonging to different messages on the same circuit – there is only ever one message – and that the two parties can rely on the availability of all the bandwidth provided by their circuit. On a packet-switched network, neither of these is the case: packets must carry additional information identifying (at least) their source and destination, and the rate at which packets can be transmitted between two points will depend on what other traffic the network is carrying. For real-time distributed multimedia applications this last factor is particularly problematical.

Network and Transport Protocols

† It's impossible to talk about networks without using sets of initials and acronyms – that's how network people talk. We've tried to keep them to a minimum, and will always tell you what they stand for.

IP† is the *Internet Protocol*, both in the sense that that's what IP stands for, and in the more fundamental sense that it's what makes internets and the Internet possible. IP defines a basic unit of transfer, called a *datagram*, and provides a mechanism for getting datagrams from their source to their destination through a network of networks. The machines that actually exchange messages – the sources and destinations of datagrams – are called *hosts*. Each host will be connected to one of the networks making up the internet. It is identified by its *IP address*, a set of four numbers uniquely identifying the network and host, which is used by IP to send datagrams to the right place.

IP addresses have a hierarchical structure; the assignment of numbers at the top level of the hierarchy is done by IANA. The organizations to which the top-level addresses are assigned take responsibility for assigning sub-addresses at the next level down, and so on. (ISPs frequently assign IP addresses to their dial-up customers dynamically.) In this way, the uniqueness of IP addresses is ensured.

Datagrams belong to the category of data structures comprising a header, containing administrative information about the datagram, followed by the actual data. The header contains the source and destination IP addresses, as well as some additional information concerning routing and optionally security. The detailed layout of an IP datagram depends upon the version of IP being used. IPv4 is the 'classical' IP that has been in use for many years; IPv6 is a newer, more flexible, version. An important difference is that, whereas IPv4 addresses are 32 bits long, IPv6 addresses are 128 bits long, so the new version can accommodate many more hosts and networks. A datagram may be made up out of several packets on the underlying physical network that is carrying it.

As well as hosts, an internet includes machines called *routers*, connected between its component networks, which maintain information about the network topology so that they can work out where to send a datagram to. In general, an IP datagram may have to pass through several routers during its travels over several networks. By inspecting the destination address in a datagram's header, a router can determine whether or not the datagram should be sent to a host connected to the same network as it is. If it should, the router translates the IP address to the native address format of the network, if necessary, and sends the data to its destination. Otherwise, the datagram is passed on to another router. Dynamically updated tables are used to determine which of the accessible routers a datagram should be forwarded to.

IP treats each datagram individually, recognizing no connection between the datagrams that make up a Web page, for example. Furthermore, it cannot identify the application that generated a piece of data, nor the one that should receive it. All that IP does is attempt to deliver individual datagrams from one host to another. It doesn't even guarantee to succeed. In particular, if some datagram has failed to reach its destination after a certain length of time,†it will be discarded. This is more efficient than continuing to try to deliver it – its destination is probably unreachable for some reason – and has the beneficial side-effect of preventing rogue datagrams going round and round forever. It follows, though, that if an application sends a stream of data, it may arrive at its destination with some pieces missing. It is also possible for some pieces to arrive in the wrong order. Since IP treats each datagram individually, and calculates routes dynamically, it is possible for a packet to overtake others sent before it. For example, a router that was down, forcing data to be sent round by a long route, may come back on line, and later packets will take a shorter, faster route to their destination, arriving earlier than packets sent before them.

The majority of applications that communicate over TCP/IP networks require the data they send to arrive intact and in the right order at the receiving end. Consider an email system, for example. If we send you a message, you won't consider it very satisfactory if it arrives in

† In practice, after it has passed through a certain number of routers.

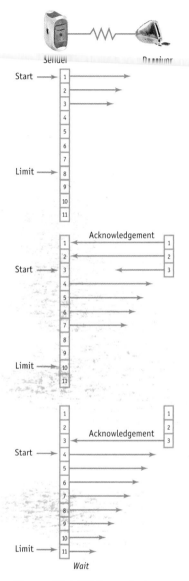

Figure 17.1 Sliding window acknowledgement

your mailbox with key passages missing, and others in the wrong order. If applications had to rely on IP alone, this could happen, so, to provide the required service, the application would have to implement some mechanism for putting packets back in order, and requesting the retransmission of any that are missing. It would be unreasonable to expect every application to implement these functions; instead, a reliable transport protocol, *TCP (Transmission Control Protocol)*, is layered on top of IP.

TCP provides reliable delivery of sequenced packets. It does this using a system of acknowledgement. A simplified version of the protocol would work as follows. When the destination receives a packet, it sends an acknowledgement, and the sender does not transmit another packet until it gets the acknowledgement. If the acknowledgement is not received within a specified period of time (the *time-out*), the packet is sent again. The algorithm as described is prohibitively slow, and TCP actually uses a more sophisticated technique, based on the same principle, using a 'sliding window' of unacknowledged packets. Instead of sending a single packet and waiting for an acknowledgement, it sends several, let's say eight for concreteness. As each packet is received, it is acknowledged; because of the time packets and acknowledgements take to traverse the network, the acknowledgement of the first packet will probably not reach the sender until several others have been sent. That is, there may be several unacknowledged packets in transit at one time. If the acknowledgement of the first packet has not been received by the time the eighth has been sent, the sender waits, and retransmits, as before, if the acknowledgement does not come in time. On the other hand, once the acknowledgement of the first packet is received, the limit on the number of packets to send before waiting is incremented, so the sender will send up to the ninth packet before waiting for the acknowledgement of the second, no matter at which point in the transmission of the first eight the acknowledgement arrives. Once the second acknowledgement is in, the limit is advanced to packet number 10, and so on (see Figure 17.1).

Notice that retransmitted packets may arrive out of sequence, and also that the possibility exists for packets to be sent twice, if an acknowledgement goes astray, for example, or a packet turns up long after it should. TCP thus introduces new opportunities for packets to arrive out of sequence. However, the finite number of packets that is allowed to be transmitted without acknowledgement imposes an upper bound on how far out of sequence a packet can be.

An analogy that is often used to describe the difference between IP and TCP concerns pouring water onto a burning building. IP is like a bucket brigade: water (data) is poured out of a hydrant into buckets (datagrams) that are carried by a disorganized crowd of volunteers (the network). A bucket may be carried some distance, then passed from hand to hand to the next volunteer. Some buckets will get dropped in the process; others will work their way through the crowd at different speeds, so that the order in which they arrive at their destination bears little resemblance to the order in which they are filled up and sent on their way. In contrast, TCP is like a firehose that carries the water straight from the hydrant to the fire; the water just goes in one end and comes out the other, in an orderly stream, without loss.

The analogy is not perfect. A firehose is a much more efficient way of transporting water than a crowd of bucket carriers, but TCP is *less* efficient than IP, because it is actually implemented using IP, but then adds extra overheads with its system of acknowledgements and retransmission.

Besides the overhead incurred by acknowledgement, TCP also incurs a cost in setting up a connection. This is necessary, in order for the acknowledgements to work, and in order to ensure that packets are sent to the appropriate application. Recall that IP addresses only identify hosts, and that IP accordingly only attempts to transport data between hosts. In order to identify a particular application running on a host, the IP address must be extended with a number, called a *port number*. Ports are associated with applications according to the protocol they use. For example, programs communicating via HTTP conventionally use port 80. The combination of an IP address and a port number is called a *transport address*, and enables the protocols running on top of IP to provide communication facilities between programs running on different hosts. TCP uses a pair of transport addresses to set up a connection between two programs, and subsequently these can communicate as if there was a reliable data conduit between them.

For some networked multimedia applications, the possibility of lost packets is more acceptable than the overhead of TCP. Streamed video and audio are the prime examples. Suppose, for example, a speech is being transmitted live over a network. If the video data were sent using TCP, then every frame would arrive complete and in the correct order, but the rate at which they would arrive would be unpredictable.

Jerks and pauses might occur as packets were retransmitted and acknowledgements were awaited. Almost inevitably, the display would fall behind the actual delivery of the speech. The transient glitches caused by the occasional loss of a frame or fragment of audio would be less intrusive, if they permitted an otherwise steady frame rate to be maintained instead. An alternative to TCP is needed to transport data with these characteristics.

The *User Datagram Protocol (UDP)* is built on top of IP, like TCP, but is much simpler, doing little more than ensure that datagrams are passed to the correct application when they arrive at their destination host. Like IP, UDP only tries its best to deliver datagrams, it does not offer the reliable delivery provided by TCP. Nor does it set up connections: port numbers are included in the source and destination fields of every UDP packet to ensure data finds its way to the right place. UDP does perform some elementary error checking that is not provided by IP, to help ensure that datagrams are not corrupted.[†] These features of UDP make it a suitable basis for building protocols for delivering data such as streamed video and audio, for which real-time constraints are more important than totally reliable delivery.

† We might say UDP notices if water sloshes out of the buckets, extending the analogy we used earlier.

The low-cost delivery of UDP is not enough, on its own, for such purposes. The *Real-Time Transport Protocol (RTP)* typically runs on top of UDP, adding extra features that are needed for synchronization, sequencing, and identifying different types of data – or *payloads* as they are called in this context. RTP itself still does not guarantee delivery and it does not prevent packets arriving in the wrong order, but it does enable applications to reconstruct a sequence of packets and detect whether any are missing. It does this by including a sequence number in the header of each packet belonging to a particular stream – RTP sets up connections between applications, so that the stream of data belonging to a particular connection is an identifiable entity. Each time a packet is sent over a connection, the sequence number is incremented; thus, it is clear to the receiver what order packets should be in. Depending on its requirements and the way in which it treats data once it has arrived, a receiving application can reconstruct the correct sequence, discard packets that are received out of sequence, or insert them in their correct places in some data structure being built from them.

An RTP packet's header also identifies the payload type – whether it is video, audio, and so on – which determines, by implication, the format of the data contained in the rest of the packet. This allows different payload types to employ formats that are optimized for their special characteristics; in particular, it allows appropriate forms of compression to be applied to images, video, and sound. Where several different media types are being transmitted – typically video with accompanying sound – they must be sent over separate RTP streams with different payload types. It is therefore necessary to synchronize them when they are received. A timestamp is included in the header for this purpose. It records the instant at which the first byte contained in a packet was sampled. This can be collated with the timestamps in other, related, streams, to ensure that simultaneously sampled data is played back at the same instant.

RTP can be tailored to different applications' requirements and extended to cope with new types of payload – it is a framework for an entire family of protocols, rather than a protocol in the traditional sense. RTP *profiles* define subsets of the protocol's features that are suitable for particular applications. In particular, the audio-visual profile is intended for use with audio and video streams.

A complementary protocol, the *RTP Control Protocol (RTCP)*, can be used in conjunction with RTP to provide feedback on the quality of the data delivery – statistics such as the number of packets lost and the variance of the time between packets' arrival. This data can be used by the application sending the data, to adjust the rate at which it does so, for example.

Multicasting

Previously, when we considered bandwidth limitations and how they affect online delivery of multimedia, we concentrated on the speed of users' connections to the Internet, via modems or cable and so on. These connections are usually the slowest link in the communication chain, but the high-speed networks that provide the skeleton of the Internet are also of finite bandwidth. Here, too, new technologies are leading to increased speeds, but traffic is also growing at a considerable rate, and new types of traffic – especially that associated with bulky time-based media such as video – are adding to the demands placed on the Internet as a whole. Speeding up the network is one way of coping with these demands; reducing the volume of traffic by eliminating duplication is another.

A common situation where data is unnecessarily duplicated arises when a group of Internet users require access to the same resource at the same time. This situation is often associated with multimedia. Suppose, for example, a well-known musician – let's call him Tim

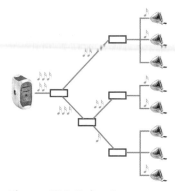

Figure 17.2 Unicast transmission

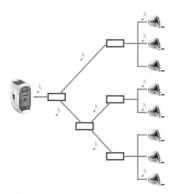

Figure 17.3 Multicast transmission

Linkinwater – has arranged to transmit a live video feed from a concert over the Internet. Every Tim Linkinwater fan with Internet access will want to watch this Webcast. The data being sent to every fan is identical, but conventional (*unicast*) transmission will require that the server from which the video is being streamed send a copy of it to everybody who has set up a connection to watch this concert. If the concert is taking place in New York, but Tim Linkinwater is big in Europe, many copies of the video data will be sent across the Atlantic, putting a strain on both the transatlantic links and the video server. This strain could be reduced by sending a single copy over the Atlantic and not duplicating it until it became necessary to do so in order to distribute the data to all the people who wanted it.

The scenario just outlined is the basis of *multicasting*. Figures 17.2 and 17.3 illustrate the difference between unicasting and multicasting. In unicasting, a separate packet is sent to each user; in multicasting, a single packet is sent, and is duplicated along the way whenever routes to different users diverge. For this to be possible, hosts must be assigned to *host groups*, with certain network addresses identifying groups instead of single hosts. A range of IP addresses is reserved for this purpose. From the sender's point of view a multicast address behaves rather like a mailing list – although mailing lists are implemented quite differently (using unicast). One difference is that the sender does not know who belongs to the host group, if anybody.

A packet that is intended to go to a group is sent to the appropriate multicast address. Routers must be enhanced to cope with multicast addresses, duplicating packets where necessary. They must also be able to perform the routing calculations necessary to determine optimal routes – which may be different from optimal unicast routes. These technical issues, while difficult, are amenable to technical solutions. Other problems that arise when multicasting is attempted on the scale of the Internet are less straightforward.

On a LAN, there are no routers, so multicasting is simpler. Multicast packets will go to the network interface on every host. Each host just has to look at the multicast address and determine whether it belongs to the corresponding host group; if it does, it accepts the packet, in the same way as it accepts a packet sent to its individual address. Multicast applications are therefore more common on LANs than the Internet, at present.

The main problems concern management of host groups. These will typically be spread across different networks, so the information about which hosts belong to a group must be distributed to routers. Group membership has to be dynamic, to accommodate applications such as the Webcast described earlier, so a mechanism is required for a host to join a group, and subsequently to leave it. Routers must then be able to adjust to the new state of group membership. At a still higher level, some mechanism is needed for users to find out about the existence of host groups, what their multicast addresses are, and how to join them. (Again, compare this with discovering mailing lists.) Essentially, when a multicast session is set up, an address must be chosen from the available range, and then advertised – by email, newsgroup, Web site, or a dedicated application that serves the function of a listings magazine.

Many distributed multimedia applications, including live video streaming, and conferencing, have characteristics that make them suitable for multicasting. Protocols such as RTP can run on top of IP multicast.[†] Considerable experience of doing so has been gained using an experimental sub-network of the Internet, known as the *MBone (Multicast Backbone)*, and multicast capabilities are now being provided in routers as a matter of course. ISPs are beginning to offer multicast services, but this emergence of multicast into the world of the commercial Internet raises new questions. Above all, how should multicasting be charged for?

† TCP cannot, however.

There is a third alternative to both unicast and multicast transmission: *broadcast*. A broadcast transmission is sent to every host on the network, and it is up to the host to decide whether or not to ignore it. This is very efficient for the sender, and it may be an efficient way of using network bandwidth, but for most purposes it imposes an unacceptable load on hosts, since it requires them to look at every packet sent to a broadcast address and determine whether it is interesting. Broadcasting is used on the Internet for monitoring the status of the network and for maintaining routing information, amongst other things.

Application Protocols for Multimedia

The network and transport protocols we have described do no more than deliver packets of data, more or less reliably, to their designated destinations. Higher level protocols must run on top of them in order to provide services suitable for distributed multimedia applications. We will describe two such protocols: HTTP, which is the basis of the World Wide Web, and RTSP, a newer protocol designed to control streamed media. Our description is not exhaustive, but is intended to show what is involved in mapping the requirements of some kinds of distributed multimedia applications on to the transport facilities provided by the protocols described in preceding sections.

HTTP

Interaction between a Web client and server over HTTP takes the form of a disciplined conversation, with the client sending requests, which are met by responses from the server. The conversation is begun by the client – it is a basic property of the client/server model that servers do nothing but listen for requests, unless they are asked to. To start things off, the client opens a TCP connection to a server. The identity of the server is usually extracted from a URL. As we saw in Chapter 12, the URL contains a domain name; TCP only works with numeric IP addresses, though, so the name must be translated into an address. This translation is done transparently, as far as HTTP is concerned, by DNS (Domain Naming Services), so HTTP can always work in terms of names (although numeric addresses are occasionally used instead). By default, Web servers listen to port 80, so this will normally be the port number used when the connection is opened.

Originally, prior to version 1.1 of HTTP, a connection was used for each request and its response only: that is, the client opened a TCP connection and sent one request; the server sent a response to that request and closed the connection. This way of using connections is very efficient from the server's point of view: as soon as it has sent the response and closed the connection it can forget about the transaction and get on with something else, without having to keep the connection open and wait for further requests to come over it, or close the connection if it times out. The disadvantage is that accesses to Web servers tend to come in clusters. If a page contains 10 images most browsers will make 11 requests in rapid succession – one for the page itself and one for each image – so 11 connections between the same pair of hosts must be opened and closed. For technical reasons, to help minimize lost packets, a TCP/IP connection starts out at a slow rate and gradually works up to the best speed it can attain with acceptable losses in the existing state of the network. Hence, in our example, the data for the page and its images will not be sent as fast over the 11 connections as it would over a single connection, since each new connection has to start over and work up to speed. HTTP version 1.1 has therefore introduced the possibility of a persistent connection, which must be explicitly closed by the client (although the server will close it after a specified time has elapsed without requests).

Nevertheless, the structure of an HTTP session retains the form of a sequence of requests that evoke responses. No state information is retained in the server, which is therefore unaware of any logical connections between any requests.

HTTP requests and responses are collectively known as *messages*. Both consist of a string of 8-bit characters, so they can be treated as text by programs that read them (and can be read by humans if they have a program that can eavesdrop on HTTP). Messages conform to a simple rigid structure, consisting of an initial line (the *request line* for a request, the *status line* for a response) containing the essential message, followed by one or more *headers*, containing various parameters and modifiers. These may be followed by the message *body*, which contains data, such as the contents of a file being sent by the server, if there is any. Headers are separated from the data by a blank line.[†]

A request line comprises three elements. The *method* is a name identifying the service being requested; the most commonly used method is GET, which is used to request a file or other resource (we will not consider other methods in any detail). The *identifier* comes next, and tells the server which resource is being requested, for example by giving the path name of a file. Finally, the HTTP *version* indicates which protocol version the client is using. For example, if a user clicked on a link with URL http://www.digitalmultimedia.org/DMM2/links/index.html, their Web browser would connect to the host with name www.digitalmultimedia.org, using port 80 so that communication would go to the Web server on that machine. It would then send an HTTP request, whose request line was:

GET /DMM2/links/index.html HTTP/1.1

The headers that may follow a request line all take the form of a header name followed by a colon and some arguments. For example, the following two headers can be found after the request line shown above:

Host: www.digitalmultimedia.org User-Agent: Mozilla/4.0 (compatible; MSIE 4.5; Mac_PowerPC)

The Host header tells the server the host name that the request is directed at;[‡] User-Agent identifies the Web browser (or other user agent) that is making the request. This will allow the server to make allowances for any known problems with this particular browser, if it chooses to.

[†]On the Internet, the combination of a carriage return followed by a line-feed is defined as the line terminator; this is not the same convention as all systems use, so HTTP clients and servers must take care with line termination. Not all do so.

[‡]Sometimes, several host names correspond to a single IP address, and this might make request identifiers ambiguous.

One of the most commonly seen headers in GET requests is Accept. Its arguments indicate, using MIME content types, the range of types of data that the browser can deal with. For example,

Accept: image/gif, image/x-xbitmap, image/jpeg

is sent by a browser to indicate that it is able and willing to display GIF, JPEG and X bitmap images. Browsers may send several Accept headers instead of combining them. Web servers will only send them data that is of an acceptable type. In a MIME type used in this way, a * can be used as a wildcard character, so

Accept: text/*

indicates that the browser will accept any text format.

Two similar headers, Accept-Charset and Accept-Language, are used by browsers to inform servers about the character sets and languages they will accept. The following would be typical of the headers sent by a browser set up in an English-speaking country:

Accept-Charset: iso-8859-1 Accept-Language: en

Since a GET request does not send any data, its body is empty – the message terminates with the blank line.

The first line of an HTTP server's response is the status line, indicating how it coped with the request. This line begins with the protocol version, telling the client which HTTP version the server is using. Next comes a numerical status code, whose meaning is defined by the HTTP standard, followed by a short phrase, explaining to human readers what the code means. If all goes well, the code will be 200, which means OK, as shown:

HTTP/1.1 200 OK

Just as the client told the server who it was, in the User-Agent header, the server introduces itself in the Server header. It also dates and times the response, and, as we saw in Chapter 12, uses the Content-type header to inform the client about the MIME type of the data being returned. For example:

Server: Netscape-Enterprise/3.5.1G Date: Sat, 17 Jul 1999 14:27: 17 GMT Content-type: text/html

We will describe some other noteworthy headers shortly.

Typically, a server's response does contain some data; in the case of a response to a GET request, this will be the contents of the file that was requested, for example.

Where a persistent connection is being used, the client must be able to determine when the end of the data has been reached – when servers closed the connection immediately after sending the response this was not a problem, because data obviously finished when the connection closed. Two mechanisms are now provided. Either a Content-length header can be sent, or the response can be broken into 'chunks', each of which is self-delimiting. For the details, consult the HTTP 1.1 standard.

The status code in a response is not always 200, unfortunately. The HTTP 1.1 standard defines many 3-digit return codes. These are divided into groups, by their first digit. Codes less than 200 are informative; the only such codes presently defined are 100, which means 'continuing', and is only applicable to persistent connections (see the asides earlier in this section), and 101, sent when the server switches to a different protocol, for example to stream some real-time data. Codes in the range 200–299 indicate success of one sort or another. Those in the three hundreds are used when the server must redirect the request to a different URL. For example, a code of 301 ('moved permanently') indicates that the resource identified by the URL in a GET request has been permanently moved to a new location (the server sends a Location header giving the new URL).

Codes that begin with a 4 or a 5 represent errors, by the client and server, respectively. Probably the two most commonly encountered error codes are 400 and 404. 400 means 'bad request' – the request was malformed in some way. This error usually occurs when requests are manufactured by programs other than Web browsers. Error code 404 is 'not found' – the URL in a GET request does not correspond to any resource on the server. This is the code that results from broken links. Other error codes in this range correspond to requests for services that are denied by the server, such as attempts to access protected files. Another interesting code is 406 ('not acceptable'), which is sent if the requested resource's MIME type is not listed in the Accept headers of the request. Server errors include 500 ('internal server error'), which should never happen, and 501 ('not implemented'), which is sent when the server does not know how to implement a requested method.

Caching

The World Wide Web has made information accessible over the Internet in a way that it had never been previously. This has led to an increase in network traffic as people take advantage of this new found accessibility. In order to help alleviate the strain this could cause on the network, HTTP provides support for a system of *caching*, which allows copies of pages that have been received to be kept on a user's machine, and on other intermediate machines between it and the server from which they originate. When a page is requested more than once, it can be retrieved after the first time from a cache instead of from the server. If the cache is on the local machine, this may not require any network access or action by the server at all.

The full extent of HTTP 1.1's support for caching is quite extensive, supplying several alternative mechanisms; we will only describe a subset.

The trouble with caching is that a version of the requested resource that is newer than the version in the cache might have appeared on the server. In that case, the new version should be retrieved, and the old one in the cache should be discarded. The simplest way for the client to find out whether that is the case is to ask. It does so by sending an **If-Modified-Since** header, giving the date and time of its cached copy (which it knows from the **Date** header in the response to its original request). The request is then said to be *conditional*, and the server only sends the requested page if the condition is satisfied, that is, if the page has been modified since the date specified in the header. If it has, the server sends a response containing the modified page, as before. If not, it sends a response with status code 304, which means 'not modified'. On receiving this code, the browser displays the page from its cache.

Conditional requests of this sort eliminate the need for servers to send complete responses in all cases, thus reducing the volume of data transmitted. A further facility potentially eliminates the need for servers to send any response at all, by eliminating the need for clients to send requests. A server can include an **Expires** header in its response to a **GET** request, indicating the date and time after which the data it returns should no longer be considered up-to-date. Until that time, the client is free to use a cached copy of the data to satisfy any subsequent requests for the same resource. Thus no network activity at all is required to obtain the same page until it reaches its expiry date.

While this mechanism is sound, it begs the question of how servers are to assign expiry dates to arbitrary pages. Most of them appear not to try, although one can imagine tightly controlled environments in which it would be known how long a page would remain valid.[†] In the absence of any widespread use of Expires headers, Web clients fall back on their own *ad hoc* devices for avoiding unnecessary network accesses. For example, Internet Explorer offers an offline browsing mode, in which all requests are met from the local cache, if possible. This allows previously visited Web sites to be accessed without the user even being connected to the Internet.

So far, we have assumed that a cache is maintained on a user's machine. There are other places that data can be cached, though, sometimes more effectively. In particular, *Web proxies* usually maintain large caches. A proxy is a machine that handles requests directed to some other server. So when a client that is configured to use a proxy sends a request, the request is sent to the proxy, which then forwards it to its designated destination, receives the response and passes it back to the client. This apparently pointless exercise is often needed when clients are operating behind a 'firewall' – a specially modified router that filters packets to provide additional security. Firewalls prevent users inside them from making HTTP requests, so a proxy is used, which has access to the outside world and the protected machines. Security can be added to the proxy to prevent unauthorized access across the firewall, in either direction. This implies that all responses to requests sent by any machine inside the firewall pass through the proxy, which means that a cache on the proxy will end up holding a pool of data that is of interest to people in the organization maintaining the firewall. This is likely to mean that many requests can be met from the proxy's cache.

Proxies can provide effective caches whenever they are placed somewhere that many requests pass through. ISPs, in particular, can employ proxies with extremely large caches to intercept a high proportion of their customers' requests.

Caches cannot help with pages that are dynamically generated, as an increasing number are, in ways that we will describe briefly in a later section. Nor do they help users who never visit the same page twice unless it has been updated. And caches are finite, so that, sooner or later, cached copies of pages must be discarded, and retrieved again if they are requested subsequently. Nevertheless, they are widely

[†] The HTTP standard suggests the use of heuristics based on, for example, the Last-modified header, but does not specify any detailed algorithms. It recommends that heuristics be applied with caution.

considered to be making a useful contribution to keeping network traffic within bounds.

RTSP

HTTP provides the services necessary for implementing a distributed hypertext system: it should be easy to see how HTTP requests can be constructed in response to mouse-clicks on links, and how a browser displaying the data in their responses can provide the experience of following a link to a new page. HTTP can cope with embedded images, sounds, and video, by downloading a complete data file. Streaming audio and video require a different treatment, though.

In the first place, HTTP runs on top of TCP, and, as we explained earlier, the overheads incurred by the reliable delivery that TCP provides are unacceptable for streamed media, which are better served by a less reliable but more efficient protocol. Its use of TCP also makes HTTP unsuitable for multicasting. RTP, as described earlier, is adequate for carrying streaming media data, and can be used for multicasting, but it does not provide all the necessary functionality required by streams of such data. We usually want to be able to start, stop, and pause them, and possibly (for streams that are not being transmitted live) go to a particular point in the stream, identified by a timecode. For live streams, we might want to schedule a time at which to start the display; for example, if a concert was being transmitted over the Web, we might want to skip the support band and start listening when the headline act was due to go on stage.

The *Real Time Streaming Protocol (RTSP)* is intended to provide these services. It is often described as an 'Internet VCR remote control protocol', which conveys much of the flavour of what it does. Syntactically, it closely resembles HTTP, with request and status lines and headers, many of which are the same as in HTTP, but there are some differences. In particular, RTSP uses ISO 10646 (with UTF-8 encoding) as its character set, unlike HTTP which is restricted to ASCII in its messages.[†] In RTSP requests that include an identifier, an absolute URL must be used, instead of the pathname that may be used in HTTP; RTSP consequently does not need a separate Host header. Most importantly, RTSP responses do not carry the media data, in the way that HTTP responses carry Web page data. Instead, the data is transmitted separately, often using RTP; RTSP merely coordinates the transmission.

† But not its data, of course.

Before an RTSP session can be set up, the client must obtain a *presentation description*, which contains information about the data streams that are to be controlled, which together make up a multimedia presentation. The RTSP specification does not stipulate the format of a presentation description; the *Session Description Protocol (SDP)*'s format is commonly used, but the prevailing applications using RTSP (Streaming QuickTime and RealPlayer G2) take advantage of that format's extensibility to customize it to their own requirements, so, in effect, presentation descriptions largely conform to proprietary formats.

A typical description will include one or more *media announcements*, including the transport address and protocol (e.g. RTP) of one of the session's component streams, and information about the encoding used, including the type of compression, if any. Each stream will have an rtsp:// URL. It is quite possible for different streams to be served from different hosts. The presentation description will also provide a *connection address*, to which subsequent requests are addressed. This is necessary because RTSP does not specify the mechanism whereby presentation descriptions are to be retrieved. There is a DESCRIBE request that is often used for this purpose, but it is permissible for the presentation description to be retrieved using HTTP, or even sent to a user by email.

In practice, both RealPlayer and Streaming QuickTime use DESCRIBE requests, but need a bootstrapping step before they can find out where to send it to. Typically, HTTP is used to obtain the URL of the presentation description; this will begin with rtsp://, to indicate that it can be accessed using RTSP. QuickTime uses a self-contained approach: a small movie containing URLs for different versions of a session corresponding to different connection speeds is presented as the representation of a streamed movie – for example, it might be embedded in a Web page, where a user can click on it, causing it to be retrieved by HTTP. RealPlayer uses a small file with a distinctive extension for the same purpose, although it does not provide for different versions.

Once the necessary URLs have been obtained by the client, it sends a DESCRIBE request, to which the server responds with a message containing the required presentation description. The client's request can include an ACCEPT header, indicating the description formats it understands. Once it has a presentation description, the client can send a SETUP request. The server responds with a message that includes a *session identifier*, an arbitrary string that is used by both client and server to identify messages associated with the same session. (RTSP does not use connections in the way TCP does, partly because the actual streamed data is sent over a separate transport protocol, and partly to enable it to be used for controlling multicast streams.) Everything is then in place for the streaming to begin.

A significant difference between the way QuickTime and RealPlayer G2 use RTSP lies in their approach to presentations comprising several streams, such as a video stream and accompanying audio. QuickTime treats these as separate tracks of a single movie (although they will be transmitted separately), so the presentation description provides details of every stream. RealPlayer G2 is a SMIL player (see Chapter 15), and uses SMIL to coordinate the separate streams. The presentation description it originally retrieves only describes a single SMIL document; this contains rtsp:// URLs for each of the streams in the presentation, and the player sets up separate RTSP sessions for each.

In the simplest mode of operation, an RTSP client sends PLAY requests to cause the server to begin sending data, and PAUSE requests to temporarily halt it. As we mentioned earlier, a PLAY request may include a header specifying a range within the duration of the stream; SMPTE timecodes or clock values in a standard format may be used for this purpose. A session is ended by the client sending a TEARDOWN request, which causes the server to deallocate any resources associated with the session. It is, of course, conceivable that something might go wrong. Status codes are used in responses to indicate any errors that might occur, just as they are in HTTP. Indeed, wherever it makes sense, RTSP uses the same status codes as HTTP.

We emphasise that RTSP messages travel separately from the streamed data they relate to. Usually, RTSP will operate on top of TCP, so that it can rely on delivery of its messages, although it can as easily run on top of UDP, if efficiency is important. For the streamed data, there is no such choice. As we explained previously, TCP is not suitable for carrying the streamed data itself, and this will usually be carried over RTP, which in turn runs on top of UDP. Nevertheless, there is always a logical connection between the streamed data and the RTSP messages. For example, RTSP supports the same headers for controlling caching as HTTP does, but, although the headers are transmitted as part of RTSP messages, it is the streamed data that is cached, not the messages.

RTSP can be used for unicast and multicast streams. Where unicast is used, it provides services such as video on demand: a client requests, say, a movie to be streamed from a server, and the data is sent exclusively to the client who controls its playback with RTSP requests. Multicasting provides services more like conventional television broadcast: a client joins a multicast session that has been set up beforehand, to transmit a concert, for example. Where RTSP is being used with a multicast service, the main difference from the client's point of view is that the server has to tell it the multicast address for the transmission, whereas, in the unicast case, it is the client that has to tell the server where to direct the data stream.

Figure 17.4 summarizes the relationships between the protocols we have described. Video conferencing and similar applications require additional protocols for session management and the equivalent of rules of procedure. We will not describe the protocols presently available for these purposes, since they take us too far away from our main concerns.

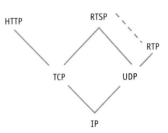

Figure 17.4 Relationships between TCP/IP protocols used for multimedia

Quality of Service

Normally, when data is being transmitted over a packet-switched network, it is subject to the vagaries of network performance, which depends on many factors, most of them unpredictable. This can interfere with the satisfactory streaming of media in several ways. First, *delays* can be introduced. There is always some delay due to the distance signals must travel at a finite speed; the operations that must be performed by routers contribute additional delays. Whereas traditional network applications, such as email and file transfer, can tolerate considerable delays, real-time and streamed multimedia are much less tolerant. You are probably familiar with the slightly disconcerting effect of the transmission delays that occur when live interviews are conducted over transatlantic links for television news bulletins. The effect of similar, or longer, delays on a real-time application, such as a video conference, can seriously interfere with its effectiveness. Streamed applications can tolerate longer delays, although the appeal of live streaming often lies in its immediacy, which is compromised by excessive delays.

Typically, the delay experienced by a particular stream of data will not be constant, but will vary continuously. The variation in delay is called *jitter*; it means that the time between the arrival of successive packets will vary. Jitter causes two kinds of problem for multimedia. First, the variation in the time between packets can result in time

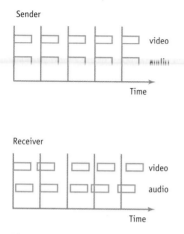

Figure 17.5 Effect of delay jitter on synchronization

base errors; that is, samples will be played back at the wrong time. This is most likely to affect audio streams, where it manifests itself as noise. Second, where a presentation comprises several streams that are transmitted independently, as they will be over RTP, for example, the streams may jitter independently, resulting in a loss of synchronization between them (see Figure 17.5). Unless this can be corrected at the receiving end, disturbing – or unintentionally comical – effects may occur, since people are sensitive to tiny errors in lip-sync. As with delay, different applications can tolerate different amounts of jitter. For example, a video application might buffer incoming data streams, so that it could smooth out jitter and synchronize video and audio streams, provided the jitter was within certain limits.

In addition to delay and jitter, there may be packet loss, since, as we explained earlier, streamed media cannot be sensibly transported using a reliable protocol such as TCP. Once again, different applications can tolerate different amounts of packet loss.

Delay, jitter, and packet loss are measurable quantities. We can, therefore, quantify the amounts of each which a particular application can tolerate. The values of these parameters, together with the bandwidth it needs, define the *quality of service (QoS)* required by an application.

Established types of network service do not require much in the way of quality of service. Mostly, they are based on the transfer of entire files, such as a mail message or the HTML and embedded images of a Web page. They can tolerate as much delay as users' patience allows, and jitter is irrelevant, since nothing will be done with the data until it has all arrived. However, it is generally the case that packet loss is completely unacceptable. These characteristics led to the development of transport protocols like TCP that are reliable but pay no other attention to the requirements of applications. On the contrary, their performance is driven by the availability of bandwidth, and their objective is to make the best use of that bandwidth – which is how delay and jitter are introduced, since the bandwidth available to any one connection is not constant or guaranteed. Integrating support for streamed and real-time applications with their more demanding requirements for quality of service is thus quite a challenge.

New high-speed network technologies are coming into use, which are able to reserve resources for individual connections. The best known of these is *ATM*, which stands for *Asynchronous Transfer Mode*. A pure ATM network can offer guarantees about the quality of service it will provide. Applications can reserve resources to satisfy their requirements, and the network will honour those reservations, so that the application can be assured that delay, jitter and packet loss will be kept within tolerable limits. In order to maintain the quality of service to some applications, the network may have to restrict the resources it allocates to others, perhaps even refusing to accept any new traffic after a certain point. The network is thus behaving much more like a circuit-switched network, such as the telephone system, than an ordinary packet-switched network.

Making an open heterogeneous network of networks, such as the Internet, behave in the same way, while still providing the traditional services that users have come to expect, is problematical. Parts of the Internet are presently ATM networks, but other parts are not, so the quality of service support has to be implemented at a higher level, by way of protocols. A framework known as the *Integrated Services Architecture* has been developed for this purpose. It defines different classes of service, such as 'best effort', which is the traditional IP approach to delivery, and 'guaranteed', where an absolute upper bound is imposed on the delay of packets. Several mechanisms for controlling network traffic to ensure that specified classes of service are actually provided are defined, together with a protocol for reserving resources, *RSVP (Resource Reservation Protocol)*. Some effort has been made to ensure that the facilities of the Integrated Services Architecture work with multicasting, since it is expected that many applications, such as video conferencing and live video streaming, requiring guaranteed quality of service will employ multicasting.

Server-side Computation

In previous sections we described protocols that allow multimedia data to be carried over a network, but we have not considered where that data ultimately comes from. Consider the World Wide Web, in particular. Using client-side scripting, as described in Chapter 16, we can produce Web pages that are responsive to user input in a limited way, but they must be made up from a fixed collection of elements – typically stored in files accessible to a server, although video and audio streams can also be incorporated by a server that understands the appropriate protocols. Using this approach, we cannot even embed the time of day in a Web page.

Server-side scripting is used to enable an HTTP server to communicate with other resources, such as databases, and incorporate data obtained from them into its responses. In particular, server-side scripts are used to enable a server to construct Web pages dynamically from time-varying data. The *Common Gateway Interface (CGI)* provides a standard mechanism for communication between a server and server-side scripts, although, as we mentioned in Chapter 2, other mechanisms and proprietary scripting interfaces tied to a particular server are also widely used. Server-side scripting is not used much for multimedia yet, but as the limitations of client-side scripting become more apparent, and multimedia databases become more widely available, server-side scripting will become more prominent.

The Common Gateway Interface

Earlier in this chapter, we described how a client sends HTTP requests to a server, which sends responses back. The Common Gateway Interface provides a mechanism for the server to pass on data in a client's request to a script[†] – referred to as a *CGI script* – running on the server's machine, and for the script to pass data back, which the server then sends on to the client. An important point to realize is that the communication between the client and server takes place using HTTP, so the output of a CGI script must be something from which the server can construct an HTTP response. Some scripts – technically known as 'non-parsed header' scripts – actually generate complete HTTP responses, but more often a CGI script produces some headers, together with the response body, and leaves the server to add the status line and other headers, such as **Server**, which it is better placed to generate.

CGI is a mechanism for communication in both directions between client and CGI script, via the server. A CGI script is called by the server when the identifier in the request line denotes a script (usually because it refers to an executable file in a designated script directory). How does the client send data to the script? There are three possible places.[‡] First, there are the headers in the HTTP request. Some of these might contain information that is useful to a CGI script. Second, as we mentioned in Chapter 12, a *query string* may be appended to the end of the URL – it is then added to the identifier in the request line. Third, a similar string can be sent as the body of a request whose method is **POST**. We must begin by looking at the format of these query strings, and how they are constructed by browsers.

A query string assigns values to named parameters. In this respect, it is rather like the **<param>** tag in HTML, but its syntax is quite different. A query string consists of a sequence of assignments of the form *name* = *value*, separated by & characters. Within the *value*, spaces

[†] Or program, but most server-side computation is done using scripting languages, especially Perl.

[‡] Actually, there's a fourth, but it is something of a security risk, and therefore is not used much any more, so we won't tell you about it.

are encoded as + signs, and other special characters are replaced by code sequences in the same way as they are in URLs (see Chapter 12). Thus, an HTTP request for a CGI script called register.cgi, with a query string setting the value of a parameter called Name to the string MacBean of Acharacle, and that of Profession to Piper would look like this:

GET /cgi-bin/register.cgi?Name=MacBean+of+Acharacle&Profession =Piper HTTP/1.1

Such a request can be generated by any program that has opened an HTTP connection, but most commonly HTTP requests are constructed and sent by Web browsers. There isn't much point in using URLs with fixed query strings in anchors; to be useful, query strings need to be constructed dynamically from user input. The traditional way of doing this is by using HTML's facilities for constructing and submitting forms, comprising text boxes, radio buttons, pop-up menus, and check boxes. These facilities are quite elaborate, and we will not describe them in any detail. Suffice it to say that each element within the form has a name attribute, whose value is used as a parameter name when the browser constructs a query string. The value of the parameter is taken from the user's input in the form element. Text fields are HTML input elements with a type attribute of text, so a simple form that was used to elicit a user's name and profession for registration purposes might be constructed in the following way:

```
<form method="get" action="cgi-bin/register.cgi">
  <p>Your name:
   <input type="text" name="Name" size="54" />
  </p>
  <p>Your profession:
   <input type="text" name="Profession" size="49" />
  </p>
  <p>
   <input type="submit" name="Submit" value="Submit" />
  </p>
</form>
```

Your name:

Your profession:

Submit

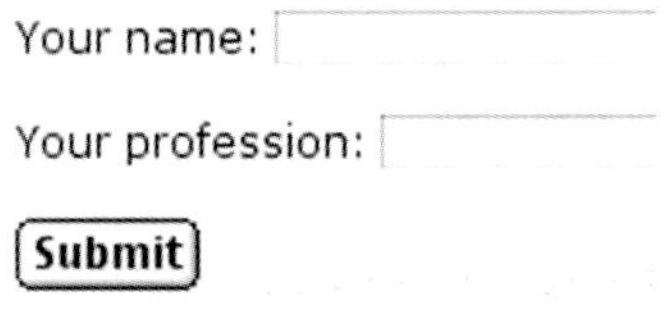

Figure 17.6 A simple HTML form

The displayed page produced by this code is shown (truncated) in Figure 17.6. The method attribute of the form element is used to determine the method in the HTTP request (GET or POST), and its action attribute identifies the CGI script. The input element whose type is submit is a button that can be clicked on to submit the form. This causes the browser to send the HTTP request shown earlier to the server, which in turn passes the parameter values and request headers to the script register.cgi.

As we remarked earlier, a CGI script must pass back to the HTTP server (most of) an HTTP response. Often, CGI scripts construct HTML, by carrying out some computation based on the input they receive, and place it in the body of their response; that is, they provide a means of building Web pages dynamically. They can, however, send data of any type in the response, providing they supply a suitable **Content-type** header specifying the appropriate MIME type. Browsers cannot distinguish between a response generated by a CGI script and one sent directly by an HTTP server,[†] and will display any type of data that is generated by a script, using plug-ins and helper applications where necessary. CGI can therefore form the basis of a distributed multi-media application, with a Web browser providing a front-end to elicit user input with a form and display multimedia elements generated by a script's computation. Often this computation will include accessing a database, possibly containing the multimedia data itself, or possibly just providing information about the data, which is stored separately. In that case, users will be able to construct queries specifying desired properties of the media they wish to retrieve.

HTML forms provide a familiar and effective interface for eliciting user input, and you can use stylesheets to format them in a way that harmonizes with the rest of your page. However, there are other ways of invoking CGI scripts that may be more suitable for some sorts of application.

We mentioned in Chapter 16 that assigning to the href property of a window's location object has the effect of loading a new page. If we assign the URL of a CGI script, and append a query string, the new page will be constructed from the script's output in the usual way. The query string can be constructed by a script running on the client machine, on the basis of whatever logic is written into it, within the restrictions that must be applied to client-side scripts. Conventional form elements may not be required to obtain the necessary user input to construct the query; it may be sufficient to detect events on elements of the page, such as images that can be chosen with a mouse click. In a similar spirit, the additional scripting facilities introduced into Flash with the release of version 4.0 include the capability to send an HTTP GET or POST request, with a query string constructed by a script associated with elements of a Flash animation.

[†] This isn't quite true. In fact, they need to be able to distinguish between them, since it is not sensible to cache the output of CGI scripts.

Beyond CGI

The CGI mechanism has two significant limitations. The first is that it can be slow, which makes it unsuitable for applications that may receive many hits. Various techniques have been and are being developed for improving performance while retaining the essence of the interface. A more fundamental limitation is that the output of a CGI script is returned to the client as an HTTP response. In many respects, this is actually a good thing. It means that any HTTP client can communicate with any CGI script, and that caching and security are handled automatically by HTTP. At the same time, it limits the way in which the client and script can interact to the possibilities supported by HTTP – a protocol explicitly designed for the efficient transport of hypermedia, which is not the only model of multimedia, as we have seen.

A major shortcoming of HTTP for performing complex transactions between clients and servers is the lack of any persistent state in the server. Even though HTTP 1.1 allows connections to be held open, the server still deals with each request in isolation. This extends to requests that invoke CGI scripts: each such request causes a new process to be started to run the script, and terminated once it has done its work. This is the main source of CGI scripts' inefficiency. In order to maintain continuity between a series of requests from the same user, various more or less underhand ruses have to be employed, such as embedding a connection key in a hidden form field in the script's output, using 'cookies' to remember state information on the client's machine (if the client accepts cookies), or using non-standard server features instead of CGI.

An alternative strategy is to bypass CGI and HTTP entirely, by writing a special-purpose server and client to implement a specific distributed application. This can be where Java comes into its own, because the libraries distributed with it provide extensive support for network programming that is (relatively) easy to use – opening a TCP connection and creating an input stream that enables you to read from it as if it were a file only takes a couple of lines of code, for example. UDP connections are also supported. Java also supports remote method invocation, meaning that a program can be truly distributed, with code running on a client calling methods on objects running on a server, in almost the same way as it calls methods on local objects. This provides for seamless cooperation between the client and server.

Java's APIs also offer a range of facilities for multimedia programming on the client side. It should be evident that it is quite possible to construct distributed multimedia applications that combine media types – possibly including new or special-purpose ones that are not supported by mainstream HTTP clients – and protocols – again, possibly including ones that are not otherwise supported. The applet mechanism makes it possible to embed the functionality of such applications in the ubiquitous Web browser, and to allow users to download the client software when they need it. Alternatively, the reusable component technology known as Java Beans makes it possible to construct clients in a form that can be easily incorporated in other applications.

Where the computation in the server is mainly concerned with accessing databases, as it often is, the *Java Database Connectivity (JDBC)* API can be used. This provides platform-independent access to databases that use SQL as their query language. This is the vast majority of serious conventional relational databases. Although commercial database systems do not allow media data to be stored directly in databases, they can be used to store and retrieve data about such data. For example, an index to a collection of video clips, storing their title, length, the codec used to compress them, the date they were made, the director, and a summary of their contents, could be stored as a set of relations. A URL at which it was stored could be used to represent each clip – being a string, a URL can be stored in a database where a QuickTime movie cannot. A client program could provide a user-friendly interface to such a database, and construct SQL queries from a user's input. A server could then execute these queries, via JDBC, and send the URLs of clips satisfying the user's criteria back to the client, which could then retrieve the clips and display them, using the facilities of the Java Media Framework or QuickTime for Java.

Exercises

1   True or false: file transfer applications such as FTP can only run on top of a reliable protocol such as TCP?

2   Why is a sequence number on its own not sufficient to synchronize separate RTP streams?

3   Explain why TCP cannot be used as a multicast protocol.

4   Since the Internet is a network of networks, packets often travel over networks belonging to several different ISPs. Normally, ISPs operate 'peering agreements', whereby they provide their services free to

other ISPs of roughly the same size, in return for reciprocal services. This way, ISPs don't have to keep track of where packets come from and go to, and charge each other for carrying them. Discuss how the commercial provision of multicasting may affect such arrangements.

5   The HEAD method of HTTP is much like GET, except that it causes the server only to return headers, and no body, in its response. What might this method be used for?

6   If RTSP is used to control a multicast stream, what would you expect to happen if a client sent a PAUSE request to the server? Discuss the implications of your answer.

7   Is it true that, as we claimed on page 613, 'There isn't much point in using URLs with fixed query strings in anchors'?

8   RTSP allows the client to randomly access any frame in a video stream (provided it is not live) by specifying its SMPTE timecode. If you were designing an application that allowed users to control streamed video, what controls would you provide to give them this facility? Would your design task be any easier if additional information about the video stream could be transmitted separately? If so, what information would you use?

9   Video streams are often described as 'bursty': that is, the data rate is not constant, but exhibits bursts or intermittent peaks. Explain why this pattern occurs, and describe the problems it presents to networks.

10   The application outlined in the last paragraph of this chapter could largely be implemented using client-side scripting, CGI and HTTP. Describe how this could be done. What desirable features of such an application require you to step outside this technology?

Projects

Projects

This chapter is different from the rest of the book, both in its form and in the nature of its content. It is entirely concerned with putting ideas into practice – with learning through doing – and is presented as a series of multimedia projects, preceded by some general advice and explanation. It is not intended that these projects should represent a general cross-section of real-world briefs – their purpose is to focus learning through solving a range of different problems. Each one has been designed to highlight certain areas of difficulty in practical multimedia, and to stimulate original and well thought out responses. Nevertheless, many of the briefs do draw their inspiration from existing or potentially real multimedia productions, or from actual problems we have been asked to solve in practice. There are no trick questions – the challenge lies only in planning or carrying out the projects themselves. In order to assist you in reaching appropriate and satisfying solutions, each project is discussed in some detail, and the main areas of difficulty are clearly identified.

We know that very different kinds of practical facilities will be available to different readers, and that the amount of time it will be possible for you to allocate to any project will also vary considerably. Some of the projects are small, some could be very ambitious indeed, and one or two could not actually be implemented with currently available technology. However, for each one, a variety of approaches is possible, and you should tailor your response to fit your personal situation. What you cannot execute in practice, you might still be able to plan fully on paper; where only some of the necessary media tools are available to you, you can try to improvise an alternative implementation of the brief with the facilities that you have got. However, some of the briefs have been limited with certain restrictions for a good reason, which will be clearly indicated – to ignore the restrictions in these projects would be to miss the point. Even if you cannot do any practical work at all, much can be achieved simply by reading, thinking, and planning.

You may be working independently, or in a group – this too will determine how much you can achieve. Do not set out to do what is clearly impossible, but try to be realistic. To put ideas into practice successfully, you need to make an accurate assessment of what you, or your group, can actually produce. You will need to distinguish between the more ambitious and imaginative projects, and those briefs which are relatively simple and realizable. It is intended that a few of the projects will function primarily to stimulate thought and problem-solving abilities, and these may be very difficult or impossible to actually carry through in practice. Others – the vast majority – could be realized without too much difficulty or the need for unusual equipment. If you are working in a group, there will be additional questions of project management and the division of labour to address, which will add a further challenge to the realization of each project. Groups need to agree upon an effective and productive organization of work, taking into account the personal strengths, weaknesses, skills and experience of group members. We do not offer guidance on specific management strategies, as each project is open to many possible approaches, both by individuals and by groups of varying sizes and abilities.

Inevitably, when it comes to actually creating a digital multimedia production, you are dealing with design: design of an interface; design of a coherent production; content design and creation. It is most important that you make an honest assessment of your own competence in this respect. Unless you have spent several years on a studio-based course in a design school, or have equivalent work-based experience, you need to recognize that you do not have the advantages and experience which others, properly trained in their field, are expected to have. Chapter 13 offers some advice, but it is no substitute for a full-time course of study in design. Never be afraid to seek whatever help you can get from specialists – whether from fully-trained professionals or from people studying in appropriate areas. This is a fundamental part of good professional practice, and your work can only be the richer for adding other expertise to your own. However, if no such help is available, clear thinking, common sense, and a keen awareness of other people's work and your audience's needs or desires, can take you a long way. By studying both traditional and new media, and using the World Wide Web, you can gain unprecedented access to other people's work and ideas; if you analyze contemporary practice in individual media and multimedia, and examine design precedents carefully, you can build up a sound and informed basis for your own work. Much time and effort – not to mention disappointment – can be saved simply by learning from other people's successes and mistakes. It may sound like a piece of advice too obvious to be voiced, but it is so often overlooked, or scarcely acted upon, that it can hardly be repeated too often.

What is true for technical people who lack training in design, applies even more to multimedia designers lacking technical expertise. Again, you must be aware of the limits of your expertise and be prepared to seek skilled help with technical matters. But for you, if help is not readily available, a study of other people's work will not serve as a substitute. Too often we have seen multimedia presentations where inadequate technical knowledge has resulted in serious flaws in functionality, such as leaving users without a way of stopping a certain part of the presentation, or without any exit option at certain points. Where scripting or other programming skills, or highly technical knowledge, is necessary to make a presentation work, do not try to take a shortcut around this requirement – and be wary of the claims of software that promises to make scripting easy. If it is impossible to obtain skilled assistance, you must either look for a solution to the problem which will fall comfortably within your own – or your group's – sphere of competence, or you must undertake to acquire the missing skills or knowledge at an adequate level.

Underlying principles and theory may be learnt from a book, such as this one – but to put this theory into good practice is another matter. Your multimedia work will be judged not by what you know, but by the practical results. Make yourself aware of the context in which you are working, make good use of specialist skills and your knowledge of precedents, and then *practise*. We all make many mistakes, and where practical work is involved these will quickly become apparent. Test out your designs and ideas at all stages – whether they are still in your head, planned on paper, or actually realized as multimedia projects. Avoid choosing your test audience from the people you believe will respond most favourably, but instead seek out impartial or unlikely test subjects – and then listen to what they say and watch how they behave. You may ultimately dismiss some people's responses as being irrelevant to what you are doing, or you may decide that you are right and they are wrong, but make sure that you have both heard and understood their criticisms, and can give good reasons for dismissing those that you reject.

Any practical challenge offers scope for the imagination and for ingenuity. In some cases the result could be wildly fantastic, and in others a simple but elegant piece of classic design. The key to the successful realization of a project is never to pre-judge or copy, but to think through each task that has been set until you have reached a clear personal vision of your best solution. Then keep that vision in mind throughout all the stages of development, to use as a measure of your progress. Sometimes it will prove necessary to amend your original plan – so be it. The ability to adapt can be a key virtue in a designer – but do not lose sight of your goal, even though you may have to alter the route by which it is reached.

In thinking about and carrying out the projects described in the remainder of this chapter, you should feel free to ignore any of the advice we have given. This is a chance to explore multimedia production in a safe context, free from the pressures of deadlines, clients, and the test of public opinion. Hopefully, the experience you gain will help you avoid some of the worst pitfalls when you are exposed to those pressures on real projects.

The projects have been presented roughly in order of increasing difficulty, but what presents a big challenge to some readers will be an easier task for others, so this ordering only provides a rough indication of the relative complexity of the projects. With one or two clearly indicated exceptions, projects do not build on the results of earlier ones, so there is no reason for you to attempt them in the order they are presented. You can find more projects, organized around the use of specific programs including Flash, Photoshop and Dreamweaver, at the end of *Digital Media Tools*.

One important final note: some of these projects require you to use existing material from the Web, while others will benefit from the use of images and sounds which may be copyright material. Never use such material without obtaining the copyright owner's permission; where you are creating a Web site that is not intended for public access, this should not be difficult to obtain. If you wish the public to be able to see the results of your work, be very careful about obtaining permission to reproduce other people's work. It is safest, and honest, to use only material for which you or your institution holds either the original copyright or explicit permission from third-party copyright owners.

The Projects

1   Choose a personal hero or heroine – living or dead, famous or unrecognized, real or imaginary, human or non-human – and design a *single* Web page (i.e. one without links), using whatever media and software are available to you, to present your chosen figure in the best light to a worldwide audience. Make the design of your Web page 'fit' your hero or heroine in every possible respect, and keep the total size of the content below 250 kbytes. (If you want to make this a bit harder, keep the content down to 100 kbytes.)

This project is about effective communication in a very small space, and about sensitivity in design. You will need to be highly selective about the material you choose, process it sufficiently to reduce its size to meet the target, and design and organize your page in an appropriate way. In asking you to make the design 'fit' the figure you have chosen, we mean that you should choose and integrate all the elements of the page in a way that is sensitive to your subject. For example, if you choose a great political or religious leader, you might wish to encourage viewers in a feeling of respect and admiration for their achievements or philosophy – an irreverent comic strip or a quirky font would be out of place. If you were to choose a film star, on the other hand, a touch of glamour and a showbiz aura for the whole page might not go amiss … unless, perhaps, you wanted to convey their personal strength in some aspect of life unconnected with the film industry. If you were to choose your pet dog, or Bugs Bunny, a completely different solution would be appropriate. So think hard about exactly what it is that you are trying to communicate, and then make sure that every aspect of your design works towards that end. Be aware of the difficulties in addressing a world audience effectively, and think about ways of getting your message across to as many different kinds of people as possible. Do not be discouraged if you have only limited technical resources – results can often be more effective when the means are simple. If you do have substantial resources, exercise discretion in their use, concentrating primarily on effective communication within the limits set. Don't forget that less is quite often more.

2   Repeat the previous project, but this time create a media-rich site to celebrate your hero, consisting of between three and six pages, suitable for viewing over a broadband connection.

Here we are using the term 'broadband' in its contemporary sense (see Chapter 2), so you cannot assume that you have unlimited bandwidth, merely enough for some Flash and/or video and audio, and relatively large images. Since you are now free to incorporate these elements, you will need to think about a design in which these form a natural part of the site. You will also need to consider questions of control over playback, such as whether Flash movies or video clips play automatically or under user control; if the latter, what controls will you provide, and how will you make sure that visitors to the site know how to use them? As in the first version of this project, your design should reflect the personality of its subject and your attitude to it.

3   Create a very simple, low-budget presentation of a set of instructions of your choice – for example, the best way to brush your teeth, or how to give basic first-aid. Assume that this presentation may have to be installed on a very

old computer. The instructions are to be text-based, with links via clear and appropriate icons to a pure graphic exposition of the same instructions.

This apparently simple project is not easy to do well. The challenge is to communicate absolutely clearly, in either text *or* pictures, but not in both at the same time. The design of the presentation should also promote clarity, both in the general layout and ordering and in the design and placing of the icons for the links. Think about the presentation of material one screen at a time. If you do not have graphic design or illustration skills, you could usefully collaborate with someone who does for this project, as the purely graphic exposition of instructional material presents a substantial challenge in itself. However, if this isn't possible, you could use photographs or existing material (providing you observe copyright restrictions).

Remember that the brief specifies that this production must be capable of running on a very old and basic system – don't deny information to people who do not have access to the latest and most powerful technology.

4   In Chapter 1, we invited you to choose a Web site and identify at least five ways in which you thought it could be improved. Return to your chosen site and redesign it, using its existing content, so that it is as good as you can make it.

This ought to be a simple project by now. You should be able to determine which of your original suggestions for improvement are implementable, and implement them. It may be that, having now learned more about multimedia technology, you must accept that some of the site's features which you found inadequate are unavoidable consequences of Web technology. For these, consider ways of changing the site to reduce their impact. In order to make your changes, you should either rewrite the HTML by hand, or import the site into an authoring application and change it there.

5   Traditionally, museums and galleries prevent visitors from approaching valuable objects or works of art too closely. Many items are protected by glass cases or barriers, and very delicate objects may be displayed under low lighting conditions. It is almost never possible to see the objects displayed in any context or arrangement other than the one ordained by the exhibition organizers.

Design a simple Web site which exhibits a number of artefacts of your choice, and allows the user to view and examine the items as they might wish.

This brief may seem straightforward – there is no particular difficulty in setting up a virtual exhibition. The challenge lies in going beyond the confines of the exhibition paradigm. Imagine what visitors might like to do with paintings, if they were allowed to take them off the wall and look at the back, examine them very closely, or from a distance, perhaps judge the effect of looking at them upside down. What about an exhibition of early Renaissance paintings, or aboriginal cave paintings, which are known to cover earlier paintings lying beneath? And different artefacts raise different possibilities. What might you want to do in an exhibition of ancient Egyption artefacts, or a display of stained glass window panels? It is your task to enable the virtual museum visitor to control the way in which they view and interact with the virtual objects to the greatest extent possible. Note that the emphasis here is strictly on the visual – the intention is not so much to inform as to provide a wide, user-defined range of visual interaction with the objects on display.

You will need to design an interface which allows satisfying displays of the objects while providing a simple and effective way of interacting with those displays to change them in a number of different ways. As direct interaction with the artefacts on display is the primary focus of this project, the business of having to interact with the computer as an intermediary will be intrusive, and your interface should minimize this disturbance as far as possible.

More ambitious solutions to this project will require considerable expertise and a wide range of software. So, be aware of your own limitations – and therefore of areas which you should steer clear of.

Clearly, if you have the necessary software and the skill to use it, one fruitful approach to this project could be based on 3-D representations and VR, but this is by no means the only option.

6   An old harbour town has decided to mount an exciting multimedia installation as a tourist attraction – to be sited in a boat moored by the waterfront. Inside the boat, visitors are to be given access to a vast amount of information and material in all media on the subject of 'harbours through the ages'. Devise an effective and realistic implementation of this installation, with an interface suitable for constant use by the general public, and some measure of control which will prevent the visitor from being overwhelmed by excess material or getting disoriented.

The first problem here is obtaining the material. A possible approach is to hook up the boat to the Internet, but a conventional Web browser is too general a tool.

You might write a dedicated Web client that automatically queried the major search engines at intervals and then provided a set of links for users to follow (but how would you prevent them getting lost in hyperspace, or stepping outside the material on harbours?). Alternatively, you could download the material, and convert it to some standalone form of multimedia production. How would you store, organize and retrieve the material – and make sure it stays up to date – in this case? As a third alternative, consider how you would obtain suitable material from conventional sources, and digitize it. Make some estimates of the costs of this approach, and consider the problems of copyright and clearances.

The second challenge lies in designing a suitable interface for use by people of all ages and abilities. This is a classic design problem, without an emphasis on special needs. For this particular project it would be a bonus if the interface could relate to the subject of the installation (harbours) in some way.

7   Create a Web site guide to an art college's annual degree show. This needs to display a wide range of work in such disciplines as glass, ceramics, fashion design, theatre design, graphics, illustration, photography, video, animation, painting and drawing, sculpture, etc. It should convey the scale of work, and the spaces in which it is displayed in the real show, where that is appropriate, and it should allow for each student to include a written statement and short personal profile to accompany their degree display. Your production should provide adequate navigational controls for the user to find their way around both the virtual and the real degree shows.

This might almost be called a classical problem in multimedia, so commonly is it required. Remember that, in this case, the multimedia production is subsidiary to the real show. Although it should be attractive and useful in its own right, its primary function is to advertise the degree show and serve as a guide to it. Thus you should, in some way or other, represent the physical space of the show, whether as a map or using QTVR or some other 3-D representation. You must also respect the students' work. Where it is represented, you should do it justice, and not subsume it to some grand design scheme of your own. Different types of work – painting, sculpture, video, and so on – need different treatment to convey their nature. Do not fall into the trap of trying to produce a solution that will work for any show. Fit your solution to the specific task in hand.

The best results will be produced if you are able to work with an actual art college or faculty on real students' work.

8   A chain of estate agents wishes to provide computers in each of their branch offices which will access a central database holding pictures, video and VR material relating to the properties for sale. Devise such a system – using the Internet and not a local network – which allows for this centrally held material to be pulled down for display to walk-in clients.

This brief is representative of a class of multimedia applications that is being deployed in the real world. It is a large-scale, technical project, and should only really be attempted by a team that includes a high proportion of technically skilled people. Its importance lies in the need for design and computation on both the server and client sides. On the server, it will be necessary to design and implement a database that can hold (or at least point to) multimedia data. On the client side, an interface that can be used by office staff to display property details in a suitably impressive manner to clients is required. The client and server must communicate. HTTP and CGI may be adequate with a conventional Web browser interface, but you may be able to design a better (at least a more efficient) solution.

9   Produce an interesting and enticing presentation of life on your campus which uses just recorded and remixed sound and still images (no video), to play as a looped show on a simple fixed installation without interactivity, in a foyer or waiting room where potential students are waiting to be interviewed.

This is an exercise in production and communication skills using relatively simple means. The result will essentially be a looped slide show. To compensate for this simplicity and to avoid possible boredom on the part of the viewers, make your production as imaginative and interesting as possible. Avoid the obvious: consider using devices such as humorous or ironic juxtapositions of pictures and/or sound, and consider how to achieve emphatic effects. Think about the pace and flow of the production – try to create variety and dynamic relationships between elements of your material. Make the most of the media you are working with – still images could come from many different types of sources and may be treated or combined digitally. Sound alone can be extremely powerful, so make the most of its potential.

10   Thinking about how hypertext, displays, frames, etc. work, design a layout for an on-screen presentation of a substantial and heavily annotated

manuscript such as the Koran, the Buddhist Sutras, the Bible, the Vedas, the complete works of Shakespeare, or whatever.

Footnotes and endnotes, as we know them, are a device entirely dictated by the physical form of books and the process of printing. Digital media free us from those forms, but what are we to do instead? Is putting an HTML anchor node wherever you would place a footnote marker any more convenient than putting numbered notes at the end of the text? The aim of this brief is to utilize the dynamic nature of screen layout to devise a mechanism for associating annotations with a text – a mechanism that is convenient, placing the annotation where it is needed, but unobtrusive. It is a good discipline to try and work within the limits of Web technology (you will probably need to write some scripts), and this may allow you to produce a prototype. You could also think about ways of automatically generating texts in your layout from XML markup.

11 Create an instructional road safety installation specifically for teaching blind or severely visually impaired children how to interpret sounds at the roadside. This should incorporate some very simple interaction with an appropriate interface for these users – to allow, for example, for repetition of elements, starting and stopping the instructions, and so on.

This is not simply an exercise in applying the WAI Content Accessibility Guidelines. Here, sound is a vital part of the system, but must be interpreted. What is required is not a guide, or a collection of information, but a complete learning environment. This offers an opportunity for you to research and think about educational uses of multimedia, as well as designing both for children and for special needs. The interface does not just duplicate the familiar functions of a Web browser, but has to provide special controls suited to the teaching purpose of the installation. Flash may be a suitable tool for implementing at least a prototype.

12 Import a short (say five minutes or so) but already edited piece of video or an animation into a video editing application. Study it carefully and choose 20 or 30 single frames which you feel will best convey the narrative or import of the whole clip on their own. Produce these as (a) a storyboard, and/or (b) a time-based animatic.

A storyboard is a sequence of still images that tells a story, like a comic strip. An animatic is a sort of sketch of a movie composed entirely of still images within a time-based environment; each image is held for the duration of the scene it represents in the final, full-motion, movie. Each still image should capture the essence of a scene. The animatic will show the rhythm of the edits that are proposed (or, in this case, have already been made) and the flow of the whole movie. The difference between the storyboard and the animatic is that a storyboard is static – something you might pin to the wall – whereas an animatic is time-based and plays for the full length of the finished piece.

This is an exercise in reverse storyboarding. Its purpose is to make you think hard about how time-based visual media are constructed and developed, and to enable you to identify and subsequently plan structures and narrative development for such work of your own. The challenge lies in identifying a few key frames out of some 9000 candidates. You should test out your result on someone who has not seen the original piece you started from – your success will be measured by how accurately they are able to understand the story or development of the piece from your storyboard or animatic.

13 Design an interface – and make a mock-up if appropriate tools are available to you – for an international tele-conference for students to exchange thoughts on their experiences of multimedia courses.

Think about what you need to control; what you need to indicate and the best means of doing this; what analogies you should be thinking in terms of (is this to be like using the phone, watching TV, being in a conference centre, or what?); and what assumptions about the underlying technologies you are or should be making.

There are several tele-conferencing applications in use, and you should look at their interfaces as a starting point. Try to think of an interface that is suited to the application, not the desktop context in which it will be used. One possibility is to use a three-dimensional representation of the conference.

14 Create for yourself a showpiece Web site which you could use to exhibit your design skills to a potential employer or client. This should be a no-budget production (except for using such equipment as is available to you) – the content should be entirely comprised of royalty-free material trawled from the Web or elsewhere.

The purpose of this project is to help you to understand and maximize your own particular Web design skills, without being concerned with the production of content. However, you should ensure that you choose and organize your found content in such a way as to create a successful and coherent Web site. Make use of the full range of Web technologies if you wish, but ensure that your page transforms gracefully on older browsers, or when viewed over a slow link. And be careful to test it on as many different platforms as you can – you won't impress many clients if the first thing they see is a scripting error message.

15 Devise a multimedia application to assist in the identification of birds in a specific geographical area. This should use still images, sound and text – and Flash movies or video if possible (but if not, do without moving images). It should include an interface that allows the user to obtain, for example, a view of typical tail twitching behaviour, or a sample of warbling song, as well as stock responses to filling in a form with details of the bird to be identified.

The aim of this project is to make the end product serve a precise requirement in the best possible way. The requirement is for an aid to the *identification* of birds – not a catalogue or other attractive presentation. Birds are usually identified by information such as size, colouring and markings, voice, habitat, behaviour, and so on. You need to decide (or research) what features will aid identification, and then assist the user in both recognizing these features and matching them to the birds of your chosen area. Try to think through the ideal solution to this brief from the ground up – you may learn by looking at similar multimedia applications which already exist, but avoid copying them.

16 An artist wishes to convert a many-layered screen print into a multimedia gallery presentation. The original printed image consists of 24 layers, which will be scanned in separately. Each layer contains one coloured abstract shape or mark; some are opaque and some are semi-transparent. In the presentation – on a computer screen installed in an art gallery – these shapes and marks are to move around in an apparently random manner, independently of one another, giving an almost infinite possible number of permutations of the image. The ultimate purpose of this display is to enable the viewer to halt the movement at any time, and request a printed version of the particular permutation of the image which is displayed at that moment.

This is another brief which appears deceptively simple: several of the technologies described in earlier chapters, including Flash and JavaScript, will enable you to animate layers. However, you must ensure that the technology you choose does justice to the material. Does it handle transparency correctly, for example? There is also an interesting problem in deciding what constitutes random motion of the layers. Presumably, an unpredictable swirling effect is required. How will you achieve this? And if the user's reactions are a little too slow, such that they stop the movement beyond the state which they wished to freeze, how will you ensure that they can retrieve the image they actually wanted?

The real difficulty of the project is concealed in the innocuous final requirement that the user be able to request a printed version of the current display. This is a fine art project, so screen resolution prints will not be acceptable. Accurate colour is important, both on-screen and when printed. How will you arrange that a high resolution image can be printed that is identical to what is displayed on the screen at the instant the print is requested?

17 This project should be done in groups. Each of you should obtain or make one or more pieces of text, audio, video, animation, and one or more still images – you each need a total number of media elements sufficient to send a different one to each of the other members of the group. (So if your group has ten members, for example, you each need to collect and send nine media elements.) Each group member will end up with a collection of elements, with no particular logic to their combination. The task is to create a rich media Web site out of those elements, first by working individually, and subsequently by combining your individual productions into a larger whole.

It is important for group members not to collaborate beforehand; the idea is that each of you is presented with a collection of elements over which you have no prior control. It may be that one member ends up with nothing but pieces of text, or a large collection of sound files, or things may work out so that everybody ends up with a balanced number of elements of each type. The point is to make the best of whatever turns up. This means looking for ways of using the particular mix of media that you have been sent, looking for connections or contrasts between media originating from different people, and so on.

This project can be carried out on a small scale – within your particular class, for example – or on a much larger scale, by collaborating with other groups around the world. You can choose whether or not to focus it around a specific subject, or to leave it wide open (which is more difficult to do well).

18 Weblogs are an increasingly popular form of Web site. Short, mostly textual comments are posted frequently to the site – usually a single page – where they are organized chronologically. Design a layout for such a site, which will provide a suitable framework for presenting the Weblog entries. If you have access to a Weblogging system that allows you to create your own templates, then implement your design in this form.

You will need to design the layout of the whole page and of the individual entries. Remember that the page will grow over time, so it cannot be designed around a fixed height and will almost inevitably require scrolling. You can assume, though, that entries will be periodically archived, so that the page does not have to accommodate an unbounded number of entries. Try to get away from the spartan appearance of a page of short text snippets arranged one after the other. Think about how you can incorporate graphics, or use an interesting page layout, without substantially increasing download time.

19 Find an informative Web site that is slow to load over a dial-up connection because it uses a lot of graphics or Flash movies. Produce a lightweight version that is more suitable for low bandwidth connections but retains the same information.

There are two sub-problems here. First, you need to extract the information from the original site and make it independent of its current presentation. Then you need to find a new way of presenting the same information with lower bandwidth requirements. Don't assume that pure text is the only way to do this: a diagram in a vector format may be quicker to load than a textual description of the same information, for example. The challenge is to maintain the integrity and accessibility of the original information while changing the way and even the medium in which it is presented.

20 Choose an HTML-only Web site that you find dull and create a livelier Flash version. Make sure that your new site still loads quickly.

It's easy enough to animate everything in sight and convince yourself that the result is lively, but it will soon pall. What you need to do is look at the function and content of the original site and use animation, colour, interactivity and so on, to draw visitors in so that their experience of using the site becomes both more enjoyable and more profitable. This is not so easy.

21 Design a Web site with a theme that can naturally be presented in a chronological fashion, such as the history of some domestic appliance, or the career of a celebrity. Use a timeline as the fundamental organizational device for the site, and add navigational controls that fit this organization.

Here we are considering the timeline as a form of presentation, rather than as a means of constructing a time-based presentation. The user should be able to see an overview of the chronological development of the subject of your site, with important events highlighted on the timeline. You should add links to sub-pages corresponding to such events, and these sub-pages should also be linked to reflect the chronology. Each page should provide some indication of where it fits on the main timeline – one possibility is to include a graphic of the whole timeline, with the current location highlighted.

22 Work as a group to produce a Web site consisting of film reviews (not necessarily new films; you could use films you have recently seen on TV or rented on video or DVD). The group should design a standard layout for each review, with standard elements, such as a cast list, synopsis and star rating, and then individuals should create pages based on this layout.

If you are using a Web authoring package that supports the use of templates, you should create the standard layout as a template, or set of templates, that can be filled in to create the individual reviews. Each review need not be restricted to a single page; you may find it better to have a summary page with links to more detailed sub-pages, for instance. Feel free to incorporate multimedia elements, such as images, and links to other sites.

If your group includes people with suitable skills, and you have permission to create programs on a server, extend this idea into a Web application that allows readers to annotate the basic review with their own comments and ratings.

23 Choose a subject that interests you – your favourite band, sports team or video game; current political or environmental issues; local history, stamp collecting, anything you like. You can be sure that there are plenty of sites on the Web related to it. Trawl the Web and collect as many links as you can (at least 100), and then build a Web site that presents those links in an organized way.

Some sort of subject classification will help people find their way around. Classification is, of course, a long-established area of study, and you could usefully investigate the classification schemes used in libraries when you are thinking about how to organize your links. You might want to investigate ways of presenting the same set of links organized in different ways, by providing different routes through your site, or, if you have the knowledge and facilities, using server-side computation to generate lists dynamically. As well as classification, you also need to think about presentation. A long list of URLs is not very helpful to anybody. What text will you put in the links? How will you organize the list on the page so that it is readable. Will you break the list into several pages, or use layout to express the organization?

24 Take a sequence of screenshots showing how some short operation is performed in a computer application with which you are familiar. Use these screenshots and a minimum of explanatory text to create an instructional Web page or pages showing novice users of that application how to perform this particular operation.

The sort of operation we are thinking of here would be something like resizing an image in Photoshop or setting tab stops in MS Word – anything that requires you to bring up a dialogue or use a floating palette to make settings. You will need to decide at which points in the operation to take a screenshot. (There are several utilities available for taking screenshots on both Mac and Windows platforms if the facilities built in to the system are not adequate for you.) You may need to crop or blow up your screenshots to bring out important features, and it may be necessary to apply sharpening and other filters to make sure that text in dialogues is readable. Think about annotating the screenshots – highlighting relevant controls by drawing a ring round them and so on – but make sure that users can tell the difference between your annotations and the image taken from the screen. Finally, make sure that the images are arranged on the Web page in a clearly understandable sequence.

25 Create a simple Web site listing all the entertainments in your local area, designed for maximum accessibility by handicapped people of all kinds. Try to make the site as attractive as possible for all users, disabled or otherwise.

The WAI Guidelines for Accessible Content provide a starting point for this project, which is essentially an exercise in careful implementation within those guidelines. One of the points the WAI make is that accessible design does not have to be dull; you just have to make sure that you provide some way of reaching information and navigating the site for everyone. Additionally, adding alt attributes to all your images is not all that is needed: you must design the site so that it presents the information in a way that makes it easy to find out what is on in the area. Ideally, you should test your design on real users with different sorts of disability, and using different assistive technologies.

The emphasis of the project is on accessibility, so don't spend too much time trying to produce a definitive entertainment listing. If you live in a big city, for example, don't try to cover every venue; just choose a small area, or a few representative places of entertainment. You can usefully do some research and include information on disabled access to venues, though.

26 Take two sets of photographs of a place. First, find a suitable vantage point and take a set of pictures that can make up a 360° panorama of the general area. Second, visit some selected locations inside that area, and take photographs at those specific locations. When you have all the pictures you need, create a Web site consisting of a draggable panorama made by stitching together your first set of photographs, with hotspots within the panorama at each location you visited for your second set of photos; clicking on a hotspot will allow the visitor to see the corresponding detailed photo. You will have to provide clear instructions, so that visitors to the site know what to do, and make sure that there are some visual indications of where the hotspots are.

Taking the first set of pictures and stitching them together may pose a challenge. Specialized tripod heads and software for creating panoramas are available, and you should use these if you can. Otherwise, you will have to improvise: careful use of an ordinary panning head should enable you to take a set of photos covering 360° in the same plane. These photos can be combined in Photoshop, but you will probably have to do some manipulation of the images to make sure that they join up seamlessly, or nearly so.

You have a choice of technologies for making the panorama draggable and adding hotspots. Flash is probably the easiest option, although QuickTime VR is also a possibility; programmers could perhaps create a Java applet.

27 A maker of short animated films wishes to give the audience a new level of interaction with her work. A ten-minute film has been made frame by frame with traditional animation techniques, and captured to computer disk, complete with sound track. The film-maker would like the audience to understand more about how the film was made, and to be able to view individual frames or selected sequences at will. More challengingly, she would like any viewer to be able to re-edit the film, and play back their own edited version. This version would persist until either the computer was instructed to return to playing the original version, or another re-edit took place. Devise an implementation of this brief which would be suitable for installation in a public space, with the display of the film versions maintained on a TV monitor or video projector separate from the computer interface.

it's hard to see how this can be implemented without some custom programming. You might consider using one of the consumer-oriented desktop video editors, such as Apple's iMovie, but before doing so, you should think very carefully about whether an untrained audience could make use of it, without getting into difficulties. If you prefer a custom solution, you will need to devise a minimal interface that lets the user perform enough re-editing to obtain some feeling of control, but is simple enough to be mastered without instruction. (Non-programmers can usefully try to design such an interface without implementing it.)

The technically minded should also consider the problem of how to maintain the display of one version of the movie while somebody is creating a new edit.

28 Imagine a portable tourist's companion of the future. When turned on, this hand-held digital device will tell you where you are in the world (or galaxy), ask you what you would like to know, show you appropriate multimedia material, give you directions on how to get where you want to be from where you are now, make reservations for travel, accommodation, etc. on your behalf, and connect to Web sites for further information where appropriate. It will update itself to remove redundancy, and hold a memory of your personal use for user-sensitive assistance. Specify a design for such a system, and if you feel you have the skills and necessary facilities, implement such parts of it as you can.

Which may be none of it .... This is an ambitious project that goes beyond the capabilities of today's technology (doesn't it?). This should not prevent you from thinking about what is required, from hardware, software and telecommunications. A possible starting point would be to look at how nearly you can approximate this device with the facilities currently available: hand-held PDAs, mobile phones, and the Internet. It may not be too big a technological step from there to the full system. However, you should also think about what is required beyond the technology: who is going to provide the information? How is it going to be paid for?

You may find it possible to implement some of the sub-tasks; if so, try to combine as many as possible into a single system that approximates the intended implementation. Make an honest assessment of how nearly your prototype approaches a genuine realization of the brief. (Try to see this from an ordinary consumer's point of view.)

29 Malcolm McCullough suggests "we might say that postmodern consumers are ceasing to spin their own yarns, figuratively, every bit as much as the artisans of industrializing Britain stopped spinning their own yarns, literally." [Malcolm McCullough, *Abstracting Craft: The Practiced Digital Hand*, MIT Press, 1998, p. 73]

Thinking again of the dark and stormy night in the Introduction to this book, design an exciting and enabling Web site which will allow postmodern consumers to spin their own yarns once again, with the only constraint being that the yarn commences with the expression (not necessarily in words) "It was a dark and stormy night ...".

This is one to dream about and plan; it is not expected that you will attempt it in practice – unless you really feel that you are in a position to do so. This is not about providing a ready-made story with alternative branches – or anything like that. It is about trying to invent a mew multimedia form for the future. What would be required from a multimedia production that enabled each user to spin a yarn, using all possible combinations of media, which was completely of their own making but from a single starting point? Give free scope to your imagination, but temper it with some hard thinking about what is required for this to become possible. Somebody has to lead the way ahead ...

Bibliography

The references that follow have been selected as suitable sources of additional information, or to provide useful background. Since this is an introductory text, we have concentrated on books and tutorial articles, and have made no attempt to provide a guide to the research literature.

Because of the changing and ephemeral nature of the World Wide Web, we have only included a few Web pages among our references. For the most part, these contain standards documents, on the assumption that their location is likely to remain fixed for some time. The Web site that accompanies this book, at www.digitalmultimedia.org, includes a collection of links to relevant Web sites, as well as an expanded classified version of this bibliography.

Adobe Systems Incorporated. *Adobe Type 1 Font Format*. Addison-Wesley, 1990.

> ⇥ This specification provides information on how PostScript Type 1 fonts are stored, and what hints can be provided by the font designer.

Adobe Systems Incorporated. *Portable Document Format Reference Manual*. Addison-Wesley, 1993.

> ⇥ In case you ever wondered what PDF is actually like.

Apple Computer, Inc. *Demystifying Multimedia: A Guide for Multimedia Developers from Apple Computer, Inc*. Apple Computer, Inc, 1993.

> ⇥ While this book, which is directed primarily at managers, has negligible technical content and is dated (it is mostly about CD-ROM production), it is good on the process of multimedia production – especially on the different jobs involved – and remains worth reading. It includes interviews with people working in multimedia, and case studies.

Roland Barthes. *Image – Music – Text*. Fontana, 1977.

> ⇥ Nobody who is at all interested in the cultural aspects of media and

multimedia can afford to neglect this collection of essays. Barthes has written several other books, and if you find his ideas interesting and wish to pursue them further, you should track them down.

Gregory A. Baxes. *Digital Image Processing: Principles and Applications.* John Wiley & Sons, 1994.

> ▸▸ Most books on image processing (apart from introductions to tricks you can get up to with Photoshop) are highly mathematical and mainly concerned with image analysis and recognition, so this book is especially valuable, as it covers a range of image manipulations in an accessible way. Many examples of the effects of the processes on sample images are included.

Tim Berners-Lee, Roy T. Fielding and Larry Masinter. *Uniform Resource Identifiers (URI): Generic syntax.* RFC 2396, IETF, 1998.

> ▸▸ The formal definition of URIs, which includes URLs as a subset.

Lewis Blackwell. *20th Century Type.* Laurence King Publishing, 1992.

> ▸▸ An extremely good history of the important developments in typography in the last century. Anyone who has any interest in fonts and typography should read this book.

Scott O. Bradner. *The Internet standards process – revision 3.* RFC 2026, IETF, 1996.

> ▸▸ How a document becomes an Internet standard: this description of the process provides an insight into what it means to be a standard.

Rob Carter. *Experimental Typography. Working with Computer Type 4.* RotoVision, 1997.

> ▸▸ More of a guide than other books on the subject, which tend to be mere showcases. This book includes a description of the rules traditionally used for layout, and then goes on to offer advice about breaking them. There are plenty of examples.

Cascading Style Sheets, level 1, www.w3.org/TR/CSS1.

Cascading Style Sheets, level 2, www.w3.org/TR/CSS2.

> ▸▸ These two documents define the CSS language, including its absolute positioning facilities.

Jenny Chapman. *www.animation: Animation Design for the World Wide Web*. Cassell & Co, 2002.

▸▸ A concise survey of Web animation techniques, including an extensive showcase of animated sites that were on the Web at the time the book was written.

Nigel Chapman. *Flash 5 Interactivity and Scripting*. John Wiley & Sons, 2001.

▸▸ An account of some of the more advanced techniques of scripting in Flash, suitable for programmers. Slightly out of date now.

Nigel Chapman and Jenny Chapman. *Digital Media Tools*. John Wiley & Sons, 2nd edition, 2003.

▸▸ The practical companion to *Digital Multimedia* contains tutorial introductions to six widely used applications for creating, manipulating and combining digital media: Flash, Dreamweaver, Photoshop, ImageReady, Illustrator and Premiere.

Jeff Conklin. Hypertext: An introduction and survey. *IEEE Computer*, 20(9):17–41, September 1987.

▸▸ An early standard survey reference on hypertext and hypermedia, which has not dated as much as you might expect. Although the WWW has appeared and grown up since the publication of this paper, many of the issues Conklin considers remain relevant, and are only now being addressed with the development of XML.

Jon Crowcroft, Mark Handley and Ian Wakeman. *Internetworking Multimedia*. Taylor & Francis, 1999.

▸▸ A comprehensive account of the issues we described briefly in Chapter 17, including multicasting, protocols and videoconferencing.

Document Object Model (DOM) level 1 specification, www.w3.org/TR/REC-DOM-Level-1.

Document Object Model (DOM) level 2 specification, www.w3.org/TR/WD-DOM-Level-2.

▸▸ These two documents provide an abstract, language-independent definition of the model of XML and HTML documents that is the basis for scripting on Web pages.

ECMA. *ECMAScript: A general purpose, cross-platform programming language.* Standard ECMA-262, 1997.

> ⯈ The reference manual for the ECMAScript language, which is the basis of JavaScript and ActionScript. Does not describe any host systems, so cannot be used as a complete reference for Web scripting.

Elaine England and Andy Finney. *Managing Multimedia: People and Processes.* Addison-Wesley, 3rd edition, 2002.

Elaine England and Andy Finney. *Managing Multimedia: Technical Issues.* Addison-Wesley, 3rd edition, 2002.

> ⯈ The complexity of many multimedia projects implies the need for management – a topic we have barely touched on. These books (two volumes of what was formerly a single work) are devoted to it.

Christine Faulkner. *The Essence of Human-Computer Interaction.* Prentice-Hall, 1998.

> ⯈ A concise survey of mainstream thinking about HCI and usability.

Roy T. Fielding, Jim Gettys, Jeffrey C. Mogul, Henrik Frystyk Nielsen and Tim Berners-Lee. *Hypertext Transfer Protocol – HTTP/1.1.* RFC 2068, IETF, 1997.

> ⯈ Full details of the latest version of HTTP, with all the request and response headers, and status codes.

David Flanagan. *JavaScript: The Definitive Guide.* O'Reilly & Associates, Inc., 4th edition, 2001.

> ⯈ There are many books currently available on JavaScript, JScript, or DHTML, but this is one of the best, providing a clear and thorough account of the JavaScript language and its uses on the WWW. This edition covers the standards as well as actual implementations in common browsers.

James D. Foley, Andries van Dam, Steven K. Feiner and John F. Hughes. *Computer Graphics: Principles and Practice.* Addison-Wesley, 2nd edition, 1996.

> ⯈ This well-established academic text contains a thorough account of the theory of computer graphics. It concentrates largely on vector graphics, and includes an extensive account of all aspects of 3-D graphics. The authors' approach is mainly mathematical, and many readers will find it dry. Available in both Pascal and C editions.

Veruschka Gotz. *Digital Media Design: Color and Type for the Screen*. RotoVision, 1998.

> ⇥ An excellent succinct introduction to the issues raised by the differences between display and print in connection with colour and typography. Instead of laying down rules based on established practice, the author encourages us to look at digital media in their own right, and to take advantage of their special qualities.

Ian S. Graham and Liam Quin. *XML Specification Guide*. John Wiley & Sons, 1999.

> ⇥ The title parses as 'a guide to the XML specification': the book is mostly an annotated version of the specification. For anyone seriously interested in XML, this is essential reading.

Ian S. Graham. *XHTML 1.0 Language and Design Sourcebook*. John Wiley & Sons, 2000.

> ⇥ One of the better books on HTML and CSS. Although there are many others to choose from, this is clear and accurate.

Ian S. Graham. *XHTML 1.0 Web Development Sourcebook*. John Wiley & Sons, 2000.

> ⇥ A companion to the preceding entry, which describes wider aspects of Web design, including HTTP and CGI, as well as design methods.

Jed Hartman and Josie Wernecke. *The VRML 2.0 Handbook: Building Moving Worlds on the Web*. Addison-Wesley, 1996.

> ⇥ A tutorial and reference on VRML, showing how the language is used to construct models, arrange them into scenes and add interactivity.

HTML 4.0 Specification, www.w3.org/TR/REC-html40.

> ⇥ Technically, this specification has been superseded by XHTML 1.0, but the latter is almost entirely specified by reference to HTML 4.0. In addition, HTML 4.0 remains the most widely used version of HTML.

Bob Hughes. *Dust or Magic: Secrets of Successful Multimedia Design*. Addison-Wesley, 2000.

> ⇥ An experienced practitioner's account of many design and management issues in multimedia production.

ICC Profile Format Specification, version 3.4. International Color Consortium, 1997.

➤ The complete definition of the format of the profiles used by colour management software, such as Colorsync. Much of it is concerned with print issues, but multimedia authors must be increasingly aware of colour management. The specification is presently available in PDF from the ICC's Web site at www.color.org/profiles.html.

Introduction to ISO, www.iso.ch/infoe/intro.htm.

➤ ISO's own account of their history and role in the standards process. The page includes a good discussion of the nature of standards.

Johannes Itten, *The Elements of Color*, John Wiley & Sons, 2001.

➤ A treatise on the color system of Johannes Itten, based on his book *The Art of Color*. A classic text on colour with superb illustrations.

Richard Jackson, Lindsay MacDonald and Ken Freeman. *Computer Generated Color: A Practical Guide to Presentation and Display*. John Wiley & Sons, 1994.

➤ A short introduction to the perception, representation and display of colour, covering physics, psychology and physiology, as well as computational topics. The book is arranged as a series of short articles, which gives it a superficial flavour, reminiscent of popular science magazines, but it actually contains much useful information on a topic that is generally somewhat neglected.

Bruce F. Kawin. *How Movies Work*. University of California Press, 1992.

➤ Film shares many qualities with multimedia, but it is a more mature technology, with well-developed conventions and working practices. Understanding film can provide useful insights into multimedia, and possibly show us some ways in which it might develop. This book is a comprehensive introduction to all aspects of film. (The author is a professor of English and film studies, so his account of the importance of critics should perhaps be taken with a pinch of salt.)

Isaac Victor Kerlow. *The Art of 3-D Computer Animation and Imaging*. John Wiley & Sons, 2000.

➤ A guide to 3-D modelling, rendering and animation, illustrated with lots of examples (and some cartoons).

Dave Kosiur. *IP Multicasting: The Complete Guide to Interactive Corporate Networks*. John Wiley & Sons, 1998.

➤ Despite the intimidating sub-title, this is actually one of the most readable books on networking that we know. It clearly describes the motivation behind multicasting as well as the technology itself, including the main protocols used for multimedia.

Kit Laybourne. *The Animation Book*. Three Rivers Press, 'new digital' edition, 1998.

▸▸ An excellent practical introduction to the techniques and equipment used in animation. As the 'new digital' tag indicates, the current edition takes account of the impact of computers on the animator's craft, but it still includes an extensive coverage of traditional media, and the author is at pains to emphasize the common underpinnings of both approaches.

David Lowe and Wendy Hall. *Hypermedia and the Web: An Engineering Approach*. John Wiley & Sons, 1999.

▸▸ The authors of this book believe that the application of software engineering principles to multimedia production will improve quality and reduce costs. This seems to be a somewhat dubious claim from several points of view, but if you share their faith, you may find this book helpful.

Malcolm McCullough. *Abstracting Craft: The Practiced Digital Hand*. MIT Press, 1996.

▸▸ The expression 'thought-provoking' is overworked, but it is hard to describe this book any other way. The author raises many questions about the relationship between traditional craft and digital technology, and, indeed, between people and digital technology. His answers may not always be convincing, but the issues are of considerable importance to anybody working in multimedia. If you only read one book from this list, this should be it.

James D. Murray and William vanRyper. *Encyclopedia of Graphics File Formats*. O'Reilly & Associates, Inc., 2nd edition, 1996.

▸▸ The bulk of this book comprises descriptions of the internal layout of nearly 100 graphics file formats, including those commonly encountered in multimedia (GIF, JFIF, PNG, etc.). As such, it will only be of interest to programmers. The introductory chapters provide a useful review of some aspects of computer graphics and a general description of how the necessary information can be stored in a file. Extensive pointers to defining documents, standards, and so on are included, and the book has a companion Web site, where updated information and descriptions of new formats are available.

Mark Nelson and Jean-Loup Gailly. *The Data Compression Book*. M&T Books, 2nd edition, 1996.

>> A general account of data compression algorithms, aimed clearly at programmers – all the main algorithms are implemented in C in the text. The emphasis is on practicalities – this book will not satisfy mathematicians. Among the algorithms included are Huffman, Lempel–Ziv in all varieties, and JPEG.

Jakob Nielsen. *Designing Web Usability: The Practice of Simplicity*. New Riders. 2000.

>> A very influential polemic on usability. Contains much good advice, and a certain amount of dubious empirical justification. The author's dogmatic approach will not appeal to every taste.

Michael O'Rourke. *Principles of Three-Dimensional Computer Animation*. W.W. Norton & Company, revised edition, 1998.

>> A good accessible survey of 3-D techniques.

Ken C. Pohlmann. *Principles of Digital Audio*. McGraw-Hill, 4th edition, 2000.

>> Since this is the only serious technical book on digital audio, it's fortunate that it is very good.

Charles A. Poynton. *Digital Video and HDTV Algorithms and Interfaces*. Morgan Kaufmann, 2003.

>> A detailed and highly technical account of video technologies, covering digital video and its analogue background. Mostly concerned with broadcast TV, but still relevant to multimedia.

Jennifer Preece, Yvonne Rogers and Helen Sharp. *Interaction Design: Beyond Human–Computer Interaction*. John Wiley & Sons, 2002.

>> A well-regarded text on user-oriented design and usability.

Paul Resnick and James Miller. Pics: Internet access controls without censorship. *Communications of the ACM*, 39(10):87–93, 1996.

>> A tutorial introduction to the mechanics of PICS, and the rationale behind it. Also available online at www.w3.org/PICS/iacwcv2.htm.

Joseph Rothstein. *MIDI: A Comprehensive Introduction*. Oxford University Press, 1992.

▸▸ The description of MIDI software is out of date in the details, but overall, this is a straightforward, accurate and accessible description of the MIDI protocol and how it is used.

Rosemary Sassoon, editor. *Computers and Typography*. Intellect Books, 1993.

▸▸ A nice little collection of essays, which concentrates on the relevance of established typographical practice to digital typesetting.

Scalable Vector Graphics (SVG) 1.1 Specification. www.w3c.org/TR/SVG11.

▸▸ The formal definition of SVG.

Henning Schulzrinne, Stephen L. Casner, Ron Frederick and Van Jacobson. *RTP: A transport protocol for real-time applications*. RFC 1889, IETF, 1996.

▸▸ Full details of RTP and RTCP.

Henning Schulzrinne, Anup Rao and Robert Lanphier. *Real Time Streaming Protocol (RTSP)*. RFC 2326, IETF, 1998.

▸▸ Full details of RTSP, with all the methods, status codes, and so on.

Michael Stokes, Matthew Anderson, Srinivasan Chandrasekar and Ricardo Motta. *A standard default color space for the internet – sRGB*, www.w3.org/Graphics/Color/sRGB.

▸▸ The document that defines the controversial sRGB colour space.

Synchronized Multimedia Integration Language (SMIL 2.0). www.w3.org/TR/smil20.

▸▸ The formal definition of SMIL.

Roy Thompson. *Grammar of the Edit*. Focal Press, 1993.

▸▸ This book is simply an account of different types of shots and transitions used in film and video, how they may be combined, and the effects that result. Useful both as a guide for video editing and as a reference point when considering ways of combining media, especially in time-based multimedia.

John Tollett, Robin Williams and David Rohr. *Robin Williams Web Design Workshop*. Peachpit Press, 2002.

▸ One of many books offering advice on Web design, this one is attractively produced, mostly sensible and based on practical experience.

P. N. Tudor. MPEG-2 video compression. *Electronics and Communication Engineering Journal*, December 1995.

▸ A very clear short description of MPEG-2 (and, by implication, MPEG-1) compression. Also available (at the time of writing) online at www.bbc.co.uk/rd/pubs/papers/paper_14/spaper_14.htm.

John Vince. *3-D Computer Animation*. Addison-Wesley, 1992.

▸ An unpretentious introduction to 3-D modelling, rendering and animation techniques.

Alan Watt and Mark Watt. *Advanced Animation and Rendering Techniques: Theory and Practice*. ACM Press/Addison-Wesley, 1992.

▸ If you want to know how ray tracing, radiosity, and other advanced 3-D algorithms work, this book will tell you, in considerable technical detail.

Web Content Accessibility Guidelines 1.0, www.w3.org/TR/WAI-WEBCONTENT.

▸ Compulsory reading for anybody designing Web pages.

Raymond Williams. *Television: Technology and Cultural Form*. Fontana, 1974.

▸ A classic and influential study of the cultural aspects of television, which provides an important reference point for any attempts to analyze the cultural impact of multimedia.

Adrian Wilson. *The Design of Books*. Chronicle Books, 1993.

▸ A description of the practice and values of traditional book design, from a leading designer. Predates the digital revolution, but contains many things that remain relevant.

Extensible Markup Language (XML) 1.0, www.w3.org/TR/REC-xml.

▸ The official XML specification is dense and quite hard to read; generally, you are better off with Graham and Quinn. Related specifications (XPointer, XLink, XSL, and others) can be traced from www.w3.org/XML.

Glossary

24-bit colour

A **digital** colour representation using 3 **bytes** (24 **bits**) to represent each **pixel**; one **byte** for each of the red, green and blue components.

3-D

Three dimensional. Applied to genuinely three dimensional models, images generated by those models, or applications for the production of such models, but also to two dimensional images giving an impression of depth (using perspective, stereographic projection, shading etc.).

accessibility

In the context of the **World Wide Web**, features of **Web sites** which ensure that the content of the sites can be accessed by people with disabilities of any kind. See also **Web Accessibility Initiative**.

ActionScript

The Macromedia **Flash** scripting language, based on **ECMAScript**, intended for the creation of interactive features in **Flash** movies and **Web sites** and the control of **Flash** movies.

ActiveX

A Microsoft component technology which permits programs (ActiveX Controls) to be transmitted over the **Internet** to interact with the user and applications running on the client machine. ActiveX is platform-specific, being only supported by Windows **operating systems**.

ADPCM

Adaptive Differential Pulse Code Modulation. A **digital** audio **compression** technique, based on storing the differences between consecutive samples.

ADSL

Asymmetric Digital Subscriber Line. A high-speed **data** connection for **Internet** access, using existing copper phone lines. An ADSL connection is many times faster than a dial-up connection in the downstream direction. Upstream data rates are typically significantly slower than downstream rates.

AIFF

Audio Interchange File Format. A **file format** commonly used on Apple platforms for storing **digital** audio data. AIFF supports a variety of **bit resolutions**, sample rates, and channels of audio.

algorithm

A set of rules giving a sequence of operations for solving a particular problem.

aliasing

An **artefact** in signal processing resulting from undersampling, whereby frequency components get transformed into other frequencies. The phenomenon manifests itself differently in different media. In audio, it is heard as distortion of the sound; in images it is seen in the form of jagged edges or Moiré patterns.

alpha channel

A **greyscale mask** used to specify different degrees of transparency in an image.

analogue

An adjective applied to **data** which can have arbitrary real values and can therefore represent continuously varying signals and phenomena such as brightness.

animated GIF

A **GIF** file that contains more than one image. Because **Web browsers** and other programs will display each image in turn, this format is suitable for **animation**. Animated **GIF** is the only **file format** for animated sequences which does not require a browser plug-in for playback on Web pages. See **GIF**.

animatic

A sequence of key still images, presented with assigned durations in a **time-based medium**, which conveys the pacing and narrative development of a project. Each image is held for the length of time which the sequence it represents will take.

animation

Since the beginning of the twentieth century, animation has meant the creation of the illusion of movement by the rapid display of a succession of still images – drawings, paintings or photographs of manipulated objects or materials. The term is derived from animate, meaning to give life to or to bring alive. In the context of the **World Wide Web**, animation may be any technique which brings Web pages to life through movement or change using images which are created or computed one at a time.

antialias; antialiasing

The replacement of **pixel** values at a contrasting edge in an image (especially a diagonal edge) with values between the original extremes. This softens the coarse, step-like appearance (**pixellation**) often seen in low **resolution** images.

API

Application Programming Interface. A set of well-defined interfaces by which an application communicates with an **operating system** or other programs.

applet

A very small program, usually in **Java**, downloaded from a **Web server** to run inside a **Web browser** on a **client** machine.

artefact, artifact

A usually undesirable side-effect of data processing during **compression** etc. which results in a perceivable distortion of the original.

ASCII

American Standard Code for Information Interchange. A **character code** providing a standard for the interpretation of **bit** patterns to signify letters,

dlghs, punctuation and control operations.

assistive technology

Devices for people with disabilities to
allow them to use computers and to
access information. For example, voice
input **software**, Braille writers, large
character displays, etc.

attribute

A named property together with constraints on permissible values of that
property. For example, in **HTML**,
tags of different types have named
attributes such as height, width, etc.

bandwidth

A measure of the maximum possible
data transfer rate available over a communication channel.

Bézier curve

A curve defined by two end points
with a pair of direction lines at each
end to indicate the directions and rates
at which the curve leaves the two end
points. Bézier curves are particularly
useful because they may be connected smoothly.

bit

A binary digit; the smallest unit of
digital information, taking one of the
values 0 and 1.

bit depth

The number of **bits** being used to represent each **pixel** in an image. This can
be as low as two **bits** for a **greyscale**
image comprising only black and white
pixels, but is more frequently a multiple of eight.

bitmap

An array of values in which the colour of every **pixel** in a **digital** image
is specified. The term bitmap is often
used to refer to the image itself, and
is contrasted with **vector graphics**.
Bitmapped images are typically complex and have large file sizes; images
from a scanner, camera or video source
(whether **digital** or not) are all represented by bitmaps in a computer.

broadband

Broad **bandwidth** connectivity, typically 500 **kbps** or greater over, for
example, **ADSL**, cable modem or satellite.

browser

See **Web browser**.

button

See **navigation button**.

byte

A **data** storage unit comprising an
ordered sequence of eight **bits**.

cache

Temporary storage held either in
memory or on **disk** in order to retain
recently accessed **data** so that subsequent requests for the same **data** may
be satisfied quickly. **Web browsers**
typically use a cache for this purpose.

Cartesian coordinate system

A mathematical representation of
points in space. Each point is uniquely
represented by an ordered set of numbers representing the distances from a
fixed point (the origin) to the point in
question measured along axes mutual-
ly at right angles.

Cascading Style Sheets

See **CSS**.

CCIR 601

A standard for **digital** video **sampling** (properly known as ITU-R 601), defining a horizontal **sampling** picture format providing 720 luminance samples and two sets of 360 colour difference samples per scan line. An **NTSC** frame according to CCIR 601 consists of 720×480 **pixels**; a **PAL** frame consists of 720×576.

cel

In traditional **animation**, a sheet of transparent acetate on which images for **animation** are drawn and painted, allowing layering of images to build up a scene. This technique is closely echoed in many **digital animation** applications which use multiple layers and transparency.

CGI

The Common Gateway Interface. A mechanism for a **Web server** to pass **data** contained in a **client's** request (using **HTTP**) to a script running on the **Web server**. The output from a CGI script is a complete or partial **HTTP** response, for example to build a **Web page** dynamically.

channel

In graphics, each of the separate **greyscale** images making up a colour image. For example, the red, green and blue channels of an **RGB** image.

character code

A number representing one of the characters supported in a **character set**, for example in the **ASCII character set**.

character entity

A symbol reference in **XML** or **HTML** used to insert characters which would be hard to type, which are not available in the chosen character encoding, or which form part of an **XML tag**, for example the < symbol.

character set

An association between a set of integers and the characters they are used to represent, defined by an unambiguous set of rules.

CIE

Commission Internationale de l'Éclairage (International Commission on Illumination). An organization which has defined stardards in colour perception, for example the CIE chromaticity diagram.

client (1)

See **client–server**.

client (2)

A term used generally to refer to a computer running a client program.

client–server

The model of interaction in a distributed **system** such as the **Internet** in which a client program running on one computer sends a request which is responded to by a server program running on another computer, often at a different location.

clipping

A form of signal distortion, usually caused by over-amplification, where the output signal is limited or 'clipped' to the maximum amplitude that can be represented.

clipping path

In a **bitmapped** image, a vector path which defines a shape used as a **mask** when importing the image into other applications.

CLUT

Colour lookup table. An indexed table used to map a limited set of index values to **RGB** components, up to a maximum of 256 colours. See also **indexed colour**.

CMS

See **colour management system**.

CMYK

Cyan (C), magenta (M) and yellow (Y) – the three subtractive primary colours – together with black (K): the process colours used in colour printing.

code

Part or all of a computer program, in particular the source or compiled instructions forming user applications. Also used informally to refer to **markup** in **HTML**, etc.

codec

A component performing the **compression** and **decompression** of video signals (a contraction of *co*mpressor/ *de*compressor).

ColorSync

Apple **software** providing colour management at a **system software** level.

colour depth

The number of **bits** used to represent each **pixel** in an image.

colour management system

Software which compensates for variations in device-dependent colour

handling in order to achieve accurate and consistent colour reproduction.

colour profile

A description of the colour characteristics of a device used for mapping between colours and colour values, used by a **colour management system**.

component video

An **analogue** video **system** comprising three separate video signals: one for luminance and two for colour difference values. These signals carry picture information in **YUV** colour.

composite video

An **analogue** video signal which combines Y, U and V on a single carrier with a sync component.

compression

An operation performed on **data** to reduce the space required to represent it, for reasons of economy or efficiency. Used very frequently with **bitmapped** images, and in all but the highest-end video work. See also **lossless compression**, **lossy compression** and **decompression**.

cross-platform

A term applied to **software** and **data** formats which may be employed essentially unmodified on a variety of computer platforms and **operating systems**, for example on Apple, Unix and Windows machines.

CSS

Cascading Style Sheets. A language defined by a **World Wide Web Consortium** Recommendation for specifying the formatting and layout of the elements of structurally marked-up documents such as **HTML** or **XML** documents.

DAT

Digital Audio Tape. A **digital** sound recording format using cassettes of 4 mm tape employing **sampling** rates of up to 48 kHz. DAT is also used to store **data**.

data

The values which are input, stored, manipulated and output by computer **software**, which may represent or be interpreted as text, sounds, images, **software**, etc.

database

A large structured collection of persistent **data** which may be accessed using a query language.

data transfer rate

The speed at which **data** is transmitted across a **network**, usually measured in **bits** per second (bps).

decompression

An operation performed on previously compressed **data** to restore it as far as possible to its original, pre-compressed state. Used frequently in image and video work. See also **compression**, **lossless compression** and **lossy compression**.

de-interlace (ing)

The separating of the two **fields** of a video **frame**.

DHTML

See **Dynamic HTML**.

digital

An adjective applied to **data** which can only have a finite set of discrete values and can therefore only approxi-

mate continuously varying signals and phenomena, but which is in a form amenable to computer processing.

digitize, digitization

The construction of a **digital** representation of an **analogue** signal. See also **quantization** and **sampling**.

disk

A computer storage device which records **data** using patterns of magnetization in a thin layer of magnetic material on a rotating disk.

dither(ed), dithering (1)

In image processing, a method based upon the principle of optical mixing which uses patterns of **pixels** of available colours – for example, the colours in a **CLUT** – to simulate missing colours. Dithered images often have a 'dotty' appearance.

dither(ed), dithering (2)

In **digital** sound processing, the addition of small amounts of noise to mitigate the effects of an inadequate number of **quantization** levels.

Document Object Model

A standard defined by the **World Wide Web Consortium** specifying an interface between the components of a **Web browser** and objects representing the elements of an **HTML** or **XML** document, together with any styles applied to them.

document type definition

See **DTD**.

DOM

See **Document Object Model**.

download

The transfer of **data** from a remote **server** to a local machine.

downsample, downsampling

Changing the **resolution** of a **bitmapped** image to a lower value in order to restrict **data** size or to match the image **resolution** to that of an output device. See also **upsample**.

Dreamweaver

A Macromedia Web authoring application.

DTD

Document Type Definition. A specification method for **XML** which defines the grammar for a class of documents.

DV

A consumer and semi-professional **digital** video standard which uses a fixed (**lossy**) **compression** ratio of 5:1.

DVCAM, DVCPRO

Variations of tape format for **DV** using the same **compression** algorithm and data stream as DV.

DVD

Digital Versatile Disk (originally Digital Video Disk). An optical high capacity removable storage format used to record video and computer **data**. A double-sided DVD can store up to 17 Gb but smaller sizes are more common.

Dynamic HTML

A term used to refer to the combination of **JavaScript**, **CSS** and basic **HTML** which implements dynamic **Web page** features such as **animation** and **rollover** buttons without relying on **browser** plug-ins or **Java**.

ECMAScript

A core **scripting language** which provides computational facilities that can be augmented with objects to control host environments such as **Web browsers** and **Flash** movies.

edit(ing)

In video or sound applications (and in film), the operation of constructing a finished piece from a collection of individual clips, or from a longer piece, by cutting and joining.

effect(s)

Alterations made to the values of **data** in **bitmapped** images (including video) and sound in order to achieve enhancements or special visual or aural effects.

element

In an **XML** document, the basic logical unit used to define its structure.

field

In most video (but not in film) each **frame** is composed of two **interlaced** fields, transmitted one after the other (but see also **progressive scan**).

file

A **data** storage unit, generally on **disk**, which contains an ordered sequence of **bytes**. Each file has associated **attributes** such as name, owner, type, file creation date and time, etc.

file format

A specification of the internal structure of a class of **files**, often forming part of a standard (e.g. **JPEG**, **TIFF**, **AIFF**). File formats are understood by the set of applications which read or write that class of file.

filter

The selective removal or modification of some **data**, for example the removal of high or low audio frequencies in a sound sample, or the removal of certain spatial frequencies in an image.

Final Cut Pro

An Apple application for professional desktop video **editing** and post-production work.

Fireworks

A Macromedia application for the creation of **Web** graphics.

Flash

A Macromedia application for the creation of **animation** and front ends to **Web applications**.

font

A collection of **glyphs** sharing the same basic design so that they are visually related and work well togehter for the display of text.

fps

Frames per second. The units in which **frame-rate** is usually measured.

frame (1)

In **animation**, a single still image which is part of an animated sequence. In film or video, each discrete photograph in the sequence, and therefore the smallest possible unit available in **editing** (but see also **field**).

frame (2)

In **Web** design, an area within a **Web page** which is independently updatable.

frame-rate

A way of specifying the speed of playback of a sequence of video, film or **animation**.

FreeHand

A Macromedia application for vector drawing.

FTP

File Transfer Protocol. One of the **TCP/IP** family of **protocols**, used for transferring **files**.

gamma

A single number used to approximate the relationship between input **RGB** values and the intensity of light emitted by a monitor. In image processing a filter may be used to simulate the effect of change of gamma.

GIF

Graphics Interchange Format. An 8-**bit bitmapped Web** graphics **file format** using **indexed colour**, which can permit one arbitrary colour to be defined as transparent. See also **animated GIF**.

glyph

A visual representation of a character's shape. Glyphs are grouped to form **fonts**.

graphical user interface

See **GUI**.

Graphics Interchange Format

See **GIF**.

greyscale

A range of colours comprising shades of grey from white to black, in graphic applications generally restricted to one **byte** per **pixel**, i.e. 256 greys.

GUI

Graphical user interface. A way of interacting with a computer that uses graphical elements such as windows, menus and icons together with a pointing device such as a mouse, trackball or touchscreen.

hardware

The physical components of computers and peripheral electronic devices, including the media on which **data** is stored.

HCI

Human–computer interaction. The study of the ways in which people interact with and use computers.

hotspot

An area on an **image map** that is 'active', such that a **mouse event** in that area will trigger some action.

HSB

See **HSV**.

HSV

Hue (H), saturation (S) and value (V), or (synonymously) brightness (B). A colour model in which hue is modified by white and black, roughly imitating the way in which artists work with colour in traditional media.

HTML

HyperText Markup Language. A document **markup language** used to create **Web pages**. HTML 4.0 is formally defined by the **World Wide Web Consortium**.

HTTP

HyperText Transfer Protocol. A simple **protocol** for the fast transmission over the **Internet** of **hypertext** information, usually documents marked up in **HTML**.

human–computer interaction

See **HCI**.

hypermedia

A collection of different media elements such as text, graphics, sound and video connected by **links**. The **World Wide Web** is the best known example of hypermedia.

hypertext

Text augmented with **links** which are pointers to other pieces of text, either elsewhere in the same document, or in another document, possibly stored at a different location.

ICC

International Color Consortium. A group set up in 1993 to promote the standardization and evolution of an open, **cross-platform color management system** architecture and components.

Illustrator

An Adobe **vector graphics** application.

image map

An interactive image, unique to **Web applications**, which contains active areas known as **hotspots**.

ImageReady

An Adobe application, usually supplied packaged with **Photoshop**, for the creation of **Web** graphics.

image slicing

The division of a **digital** image into rectangular areas or slices, which can then be optimized or animated independently. A sliced image has attached

HTML code which puts the slices back together on a **Web page**.

in-between

The in-between **frames** in an **animation** are those created by reference to **key frames** at each end of a sequence, in order to complete the movement or action. In digital **animation** this can be done by computation. See also **tween**.

indexed colour

A method of representing colours indirectly. Each **pixel** holds a value which is used as an index into a table (see **CLUT**) holding the colour components to be used.

interface

See **user interface**.

interlace(d), interlacing

A standard for the scanning of a video **frame** such that the two **fields** are displayed alternately, giving a set of odd and even raster lines. See also **deinterlacing**.

Internet

A huge, world-wide **network** of computers, now principally used for access to the **World Wide Web**.

Internet Content Rating Association

An international organization that administers the labelling of Web sites' content.

interpolation

The calculation of additional, approximate values between known values in a set, typically used in the **upsampling** of images, where additional **pixels** are required, and in the calculation of **in-between frames** in **digital animation**.

intranet

A local area **network**, for example within a company, which uses **Internet protocols** and **systems**.

inverse kinematics

A method of computing the **animation** of any structure that takes the form of a chain of elements, by working backwards from effect to cause. This is generally used for **animation** of human and animal bodies – the position of the bones of the leg, for example, is calculated from the position of the final element in the chain, the foot.

ISO

International Organization for Standardization. Responsible for setting international standards in all technical fields except electronic and electrical engineering. In information technology ISO works together with the International Electrotechnical Commission (IEC).

ISO 10646

An **ISO**/IEC international standard that defines a **character set** including characters for all known written languages. **Unicode** is a subset of ISO 10646, currently considered adequate for practical purposes.

ISO Latin-1

Also known as ISO/IEC 8859-1. An 8-**bit** character set of which the first 128 code points are identical to **ASCII** and the remaining 128 are used for additional characters in Western European languages.

ISP

Internet Service Provider. A company providing **Internet** services such as dial-up access, domain name registration and **Web site** hosting.

Java

A computer programming language designed by Sun MicroSystems which is especially suited for **Internet** use because it can run on any platform. Java programs can be turned into **applets**.

JavaScript

An **object-based scripting language**, based on **ECMAScript** and the **DOM**, used to embed functions in **Web pages**.

JPEG

Joint Photographic Experts Group. Usually used to refer to the **bitmapped** graphics files which use JPEG **lossy compression**, especially suited to photographs. JPEG is widely used on **Web pages**.

JSP

JavaServer Pages. A mechanism that allows **Web** developers to dynamically generate **HTML**, **XML** and some other types of **Web page** using **Java**.

kbps

Kilobits per second. A measure of how many thousands of **bits** pass a designated point each second, used to express **data transfer rate** across a **network**. See also **Mbps**.

key frame (1)

In traditional **cel animation**, principal animators drew key images of characters etc. at the start and finish of an action, and the **in-between frames**

were drawn subsequently by other people. In **digital animation** and motion graphics a key frame is thus a **frame** whose contents are fully specified by drawing and/or by the setting of precise parameters, as opposed to those **in-between frames** which are **interpolated**.

key frame (2)

In video **compression**, a **frame** stored in its entirety, possibly compressed, as the basis for inter-frame **compression** of subsequent **frames**.

link

In **hypermedia**, a pointer or reference to a location in a document. Usually, links are embedded in documents – as highlighted text, for example – to connect locations in two documents, and may be followed using some interface gesture such as clicking with a mouse.

link base

A collection of **links** stored externally to any document to allow flexible linkage, including **links** between more than two documents.

lossless compression

A reversible **compression** technique which permits the original values of the **data** (before **compression**) to be recovered exactly.

lossy compression

Data compression which cannot be exactly reversed, so that the **decompression** operation restores only an approximation to the original **data**.

LZW (Lempel–Ziv–Welch)

A **lossless** data **compression** algorithm, patented by Unisys, used in **GIF** files.

markup

Instructions, often in the form of **tags**, inserted into a document to specify its structure or control its formatting.

markup language

A language consisting of a set of **tags** and rules governing their usage, for applying **markup** to documents.

mask, masking

In **bitmapped** image processing, including video, a **greyscale** image which defines an area to be excluded from processing or considered transparent. A mask may be saved as part of another image as an **alpha channel**, or may exist independently. See also **alpha channel** and **clipping path**.

Mbps

Megabits per second. A measure of how many mega**bits (1024×1024 bits)** pass a designated point each second, used to express **data transfer rate** across a **network**. See also **kbps**.

memory

Hardware components of a computer **system** in which **data** may be stored for subsequent retrieval. See also **RAM** and **disk**.

MIDI

Musical Instruments Digital Interface. A standard for communicating between electronic musical instruments and music **software** such as sequencers.

MIME type

A specification used on the Internet to describe the type of data; a MIME type is used to specify the type of data contained in an HTTP response, for example.

mini-DV

A miniature videocassette tape standard used at consumer and semi-professional level to record **DV**.

MJPEG

Motion JPEG. A form of video compression that works by applying **JPEG compression** to each frame.

morph(ing)

In **animation**, the transformation of one shape into another over time. Shape **tweening** in **Flash** is a computed form of morphing; Aardman's famous plasticine character Morph illustrates the original concept.

mouse event

Any mouse input occurring at a distinct point in time, e.g. movement of the mouse over an active area of the screen, clicking the mouse button, etc.

MPEG

Motion Picture Experts Group. Usually used to refer to the set of standards for video and multimedia defined by this group. These include MPEG-2, the **compression** method used for **DVD** video, and MPEG-4, a high quality, low bitrate **codec**, increasingly used on the **Internet**.

navigation bar

A set of **links**, often using **rollovers**, placed on a collection of **Web pages** to provide standard navigational access to each page.

navigation button

A **link** in the form of a small image or **rollover** embedded in a **Web page**, often as part of a **navigation bar**.

network

A collection of computers, bridges and routers, connected together by wires, optical fibres or wireless links, so that they can exchange **data**. Also used to refer to the connections between computers in a network.

non-linear

A term primarily used in multimedia and **time-based media** to describe any sequential production which is not played back or experienced in an order predetermined by the producer(s). This normally implies some measure of user control or interactivity, although we sometimes speak of a non-linear narrative or structure within a linear work such as a book or film.

NTSC

National Television Standards Committee. More usually used to refer to the composite colour video standard which that committee devised for use in the USA, consisting of 29.97 **interlaced frames** per second, each with 480 lines of vertical **resolution** out of a total of 525.

object-based

An adjective applied to programming languages which provide facilities for the creation of objects, comprising values and methods, but lack the systematic class-based organization provided by **object-oriented** languages.

object-oriented

An adjective applied to programming languages which provide facilities for the creation of objects as instances of classes, hierarchically organized using the principle of inheritance.

Open Source

Computer **software** which is made freely available in source form, i.e. with the program source code and compilation and build operations made public.

operating system

The computer **software** which directly manages the machine **hardware** and provides the mechanisms by which applications make use of the computer.

packet

One of the small pieces into which messages are split when transmitted over a **network** such as the **Internet**.

PAL

Phase Alternate Line. A composite colour video standard consisting of 25 **interlaced frames** per second, each with 625 lines of vertical **resolution**. PAL variants are used in most of Europe, Australia, New Zealand, China and some other areas.

PDF

Portable Document Format. A **file format** capable of displaying graphics and text, developed by Adobe for transferring and presenting electronic documents in a way independent of the original **hardware**, **software** or **operating system** used to create them.

Perl

A computer programming language often used for **Web applications**.

Photoshop

An Adobe application for the manipulation of **bitmapped** images, generally considered the industry standard for this task.

PHP

PHP Hypertext Processor (a recursive acronym). An open source language for specifying **server**-side computation and embedding the results in dynamically generated **Web pages**.

PICS

Platform for Internet Content Selection. A system of metadata for describing the content of **Web pages**, used by filtering services to restrict access to pages.

pixel

The smallest element of a **bitmapped** image, capable of displaying a single colour. Pixels are usually square and are assembled into images in rows and columns.

pixellation/pixellization

In **bitmapped** image processing, including video, a visible 'blockiness', usually the result of **artefaction** following **downsampling** or **lossy compression**. So named because it seems as though the individual **pixels** are themselves visible, though usually they are not.

plug-in

A small computer program that can be attached to a larger program in order to execute specific functions, such as the display of a certain type of file. Plug-ins are frequently used with **Web browsers** to display formats not supported directly by the browser itself.

PNG

Portable Network Graphics. A relatively new **bitmapped** graphics **file format** that uses **lossless compression**. Being unpatented, use of PNG on **Web pag-es** avoids any potential licensing issues involved in the use of **GIF**.

Premiere

An Adobe desktop video **editing** application.

progressive scan

In a video **system**, the display of all the raster lines in each **frame** in consecutive order, instead of alternately as **interlaced fields**.

protocol

A set of rules governing the exchange of **data** between programs over a **network**.

quantization

In signal processing, the restriction of any continuously varying signal to a finite set of discrete values.

QuickTime

A multimedia architecture developed by Apple, available on Macintosh and Windows platforms, most widely used as a **cross-platform** video format with synchronized sound.

QuickTimeVR

A **QuickTime** component used for interactive **3-D** scenes and objects, providing a primitive form of virtual reality.

RAM

Random Access Memory. A computer's high speed **memory**, arranged so that each **byte** has an address, permitting direct access to any individual stored value.

rasterize(d)

Conversion of a **vector graphics** image into a **bitmapped** image, a process which may introduce **aliasing**.

ray tracing

A **rendering** technique for **3-D** models that produces photo-realistic results.

Real Time Streaming Protocol

See **RTSP**.

Real-Time Transport Protocol

See **RTP**.

Real Video

A proprietary **Web streaming** video format which requires a **plug-in** in the user's **browser**.

render(ing)

In all kinds of **digital** image processing, including video and **3-D**, the generation of a final 2-D **bitmapped** image or image sequence by computation from a set of parameters input by the user, for example, after applying **effects** or defining the setup of a three-dimensional scene.

resolution (1)

The number of **pixels** per unit length (e.g. **pixels** per inch) displayed by an output device or recorded by a scanner.

resolution (2)

The number of horizontal and vertical **pixels** in a **digital** image or **frame** of video.

RGB

A colour model, based on additive colour mixing, in which each colour is represented by three values denoting the proportions of red, green and blue light it contains.

RLE

See **run length encoding**.

rollover

An image or a piece of text which changes its appearance when the cursor moves over it, usually to indicate that it will respond to a mouse click. Often used in **navigation buttons**.

RTP

Real-Time Transport Protocol. A **protocol** used on the **Internet** for the delivery of **streamed** media. RTP does not guarantee reliable delivery of **packets**.

RTSP

Real Time Streaming Protocol. A **protocol** used on the **Internet** to control **streamed** media, sometimes decribed as an 'Internet VCR remote control protocol'.

run length encoding

A **compression** technique which replaces multiple consecutive copies of a repeating string (a run) with a single copy together with a repeat counter.

sampling

In signal processing, the recording of values at discrete intervals in time. Part of the process of **digitization**. See also **quantization**.

script

A program written in a **scripting language**.

scripting language

A programming language, often with a restricted syntax, used to manipulate the facilities of an existing **system**, as, for example, **JavaScript** is used to manipulate a **Web browser**.

search engine

A program relying on automated **data** collection which is designed to allow the user to enter specific search criteria when looking for material in documents held on a computer or **network**, usually on the **World Wide Web**.

server (1)

See **client–server**.

server (2)

A computer running a server program.

SGML

Standard Generalized Markup Language. A structural **markup languages**, the precursor of **HTML** and **XML**.

SMIL

Synchronized Multimedia Integration Language. A **markup language**, based on **XML**, for describing multimedia presentations with synchronized elements.

software

Computer programs.

sprite

In **animation** controlled by computer programming, a character or object which is animated by the substitution of a different image or **sprite face** for each state (e.g. each position of the body in a walk cycle) and by the adjustment of its position within the **frame**.

sprite face

A still image representing one single state of a **sprite,** for example, one position of the body during a walk cycle.

stop-frame, stop-motion

In traditional **animation**, a technique in which objects or characters are photographed one **frame** at a time, being moved or altered a small amount between each **frame** so that an illusion of motion is created when the frames are subsequently played back in sequence.

storyboard

In any time-based production involving visual material, a series of small drawings representing key moments, actions and development in the production, presented in sequence like a comic-strip. A storyboard may include notes describing action and sound.

stream(ed), streaming

An adjective applied to **time-based** media which is transmitted over a **network** and played back as soon as it arrives.

SVG

Scalable Vector Graphics. A **vector graphics** format for use on the **Web**, defined by a **World Wide Web Consortium** Recommendation.

SWF

Originally Shockwave **Flash**, but no longer considered to stand for anything. The format of movies generated for playback by the **Flash** Player or **plug-in**.

system

An integrated collection of components, functioning together as a composite entity, for example, a computer system composed of processor, **memory**, peripherals and **software**.

tag

An instruction in a **markup language**, usually delimited in some way, for example by being enclosed in angle brackets.

TCP/IP

Transmission Control Protocol/ Internet Protocol. Loosely used to refer to all of the **protocols** used on the **Internet** and **intranets**. TCP and IP are the lowest level **protocols** used to communicate between applications and hosts respectively.

thumbnail

A small, **downsampled** version of a larger image.

TIFF, TIF

Tag Image File Format. A **cross-platform bitmapped** graphics **file format** designed to store raster data, usually **uncompressed**.

time-based

An adjective applied to any medium that inherently has extent in time, for example video or sound.

timecode

A notation for precisely identifying a frame in a video sequence, also used to specify time within an audio track in an editing application. Timecode enables frame-accurate editing and is used to synchronize picture and sound. When written to tape, it permits logging and offline capture of clips.

transition

In video **editing**, the join between one discrete clip or scene and the next. The term is especially applied to joins which involve some **effect**, such as the fade-out/fade-in of a cross dissolve, rather than to simple cuts.

tree

A hierarchical structure in which each node has exactly one ancestor.

tween(ing)

In **animation**, the **interpolation** of additional **frames** between **keyframes** to complete the illusion of motion or action.

UDP

User Datagram Protocol. A simple communications protocol for communicating between hosts using **packets** of **data** called datagrams. UDP does not guarantee delivery of individual datagrams.

Unicode

A 16-bit subset of **ISO 10646** which represents text in most of the written languages of the world.

upload

Transfer of **data** from a local machine to a remote machine.

upsample, upsampling

Changing the **resolution** of a **bitmapped** image to a higher value by means of **interpolation**. This may be in order to match the image **resolution** to that of an output device, or to increase the number of **pixels** for use in further processing. See also **downsample**.

URI

Universal Resource Identifier. A **URL** or **URN**.

URL

Universal Resource Locator. A means of identifying any resource on the **Internet**, comprising a **protocol**, domain name and a path.

URN

Universal Resource Name. A name that identifies a resource on the **Internet** in a location-independent way.

usability

A measure of how easily anything, but particularly computer **software**, can be operated by users for the purpose for which it was intended.

user interface

The set of elements such as commands, icons, menus and dialogue boxes, available to the human user for interaction with the programs running on a computer; for example, the desktop interface to an **operating system**. See also **GUI**.

UTF-8

Unicode Transformation Format-8. An encoding for representing single **Unicode** characters by variable length sequences of **bytes**.

vector graphics

Images entirely composed of mathematically defined shapes and paths, which can nevertheless be very complex visually. Vector graphics are compact, scaleable and **resolution** independent.

VHS

Video Home System. Since the 1980s, the world-wide domestic consumer standard for video recording and playback, using half-inch magnetic tape in cassettes. VHS emerged as the consumer standard for home video after competition with the much better quality Sony Betamax. Now being superseded by **DVD**.

visualization

The presentation of complex information in an easily grasped visual form, which may be anything from a simple graph to an elaborately animated reconstruction of a scene based on a collection of **data**.

VRML

Virtual Reality Modelling Language. A standard **markup language** for describing interactive **3-D vector graphics**, designed particularly for use on the **World Wide Web**.

W3C

See **World Wide Web Consortium**.

WAI

See **Web Accessibility Initiative**.

Web

See **World Wide Web**.

Web Accessibility Initiative

A **World Wide Web Consortium** programme which develops guidelines for enhancing the **accessibility** of **Web sites**.

Web application

A distributed **system** which uses a **Web browser** as an interface with the end user, and **HTTP** to communicate with programs running on a **server**.

Web browser

A program for displaying **Web pages**.

Web page

An **HTML** document, usually held on a remote **server** and accessed with a **Web browser**.

Web-safe colours

A set of 216 colours that are guaranteed to be displayed correctly on any of the major computer platforms.

Web server

A program that responds to **HTTP** requests by returning **Web pages** to be displayed in a **Web browser**.

Web site

A collection of **Web pages** with a common theme, a coherent structure and a home page.

Windows Media

A Microsoft multimedia format widely used for **Web** video.

World Wide Web

The global distributed **hypermedia system** hosted on the **Internet**.

World Wide Web Consortium (W3C)

The organization that creates Web standards and oversees the evolution of the Web.

WWW

See **World Wide Web**.

XHTML

A version of the **HTML markup language**, defined using **XML**.

XLink

A means of specifying **links** in **XML** documents, using a collection of **attributes** defined for the purpose.

XML

Extended Markup Language. A **markup language** with facilities for defining **tags** and specifying restrictions on their usage; hence XML may be considered a metalanguage for defining other **markup languages**.

XPath

A notation for addressing elements within an **XML** document.

XPointer

A language, which uses **XPath**, for specifying fragment identifiers to refer to locations in an **XML** document.

XSL

Extensible Stylesheet Language, often known as XSL-FO, XSL Formatting Objects. A **markup language** defined in **XML** for creating documents that describe formatting and layout.

XSLT

Extensible Stylesheet Language for Transformations. A language defined in **XML** for describing transformations that alter the structure of an **XML** document.

YUV

A notation used to refer loosely to any component video **system** using a luma (Y) and two colour difference (U, V) components.

z-order(ing)

In **Web pages**, **3-D** scenes or image manipulation programs, a stacking order from front to back of the objects or layers.

Index

3–2 pulldown, 202
3-D animation, 266–272
3-D graphics, 103–116
3-D rendering, *see* rendering
3-D software, 106

A

A-law, 297
absolute positioning, 375–377
abstraction, 552
abstract characters, 315, 333
abstract data types, 538
accessibility, 20, 433–441
    Flash and, 441
    see also WAI
access to multimedia, 17–20
    and disabilities, 19
    and PDAs, 44
actions, 536
    in Flash, 539
ActionScript, 254, 539, 573–
    588, 574
    see also Flash
ADPCM, 297
ADSL, 52
advertisements, 447
AfterEffects, 261–266
    interpolation in, 263
AIFF, 302
aliasing, 41, 282
alignment of paragraphs, 349
    in CSS, 373

alphabets, 315
alpha channels, 133–135, 182
alt attribute, 435
analogue representations, 35
    and noise, 36, 195
    reconstruction of, 37, 41
analogue to digital converters,
    36
anchors, 399–400
    images in, 408
anchor points, 96
animated GIFs, 248–249, 563
animation, 190, 242–272
    3-D, 266–272
    cel, 243
    interactive, 579
    in SMIL, 512–516
    sprite, 250
    stop-motion, 244
    SVG, 531–532
    techniques, 243–246
    use of JavaScript for,
    563–566
ANSI, 59
anti-aliasing, 89–91, 133
    of fonts, 341
API, 49
applets, 405
ascenders, 335
ASCII, 317–319, 323
ASP, 56, 397
aspect ratio, 203

assistive technology, 433
ATM networks, 610
attributes, 360
AU, 302
audio, *see* sound
Augmented Human Intellect
    Research Center, 385
authoring systems, 48
    for HTML, 571
    see also Dreamweaver
AVI, 222, 223
axes, 87
    in 3-D, 103

B

B-pictures, 213
backward prediction, 213
bandwidth, 197, 295, 507, 610
baseline, 335
base URL, 398
behaviours, 536, 570–573
    applied to objects in 3-D,
    267
Bézier curves, 91, 92–95, 236
    drawing, 93
    joining, 94–95
bitmapped fonts, 338
    scaling of, 339
bitmapped images, 67, 79,
    118–153
    combining with vector
    graphics, 73–75

compared with vector
    graphics, 68–73
embedding in HTML,
    405–406
text in, 345
transformation of,
    148–151
using in drawing
    programs, 74
bits, 32
block formatting, 347,
    348–351
blue screen, 182, 231
    see also chroma keying
blurring, 143, 144
BMP, 80, 167
bold fonts, 329, 341, 370
bookmarks, 391
breadcrumbs, 416
brightness, 173
brightness and contrast
    adjustments, 136
broadband, 18, 51–53, 197,
    426, 591
browsers, 387
    see also Web browsers
BSI, 59
bump mapping, 115
bytes, 33, 161

C
caching of Web pages,
    604–606
calligraphic fonts, 329
cap height, 336
CCIR 601, 202
CD-ROM, 8–9
censorship, 24–29
    and the World Wide
        Web, 25
CGI, 56, 397, 612–614
    limitations of, 615
    query strings, 612–613

channels, 179–181
character entity references,
    358
character repertoire, 316
character sets, 33, 316–324
    ASCII, 317–319, 323
        in URLs, 396
    encodings, 321–323
        Quoted-Printable,
            322
        UCS-2, 323
        UTF-16, 321
    in HTML, 364
    ISO 10646, 319–324
        Basic Multilingual
            Plane (BMP), 321
    ISO 646, 317–318
    ISO 8859, 319
    platform-specific, 318
character styles, 348
chromaticities, 183
chroma downsampling, 183
chroma keying, 162, 231
chrominance sub-sampling,
    203, 210, 214
    see also sampling
CIE chromaticity diagram,
    160
Cinepak, 216
CJK consolidation, 320
class attribute (HTML), 366,
    367
client-side scripts, 557
clients, 54, 615
    World Wide Web, 55
        see also Web browsers
clipping, 287
closed paths, 96
    closed, 96
CLUTs, 166
    see also palettes
CMS, see colour management
codecs, 196, 206–219, 222

animation, 249
asymmetrical, 208, 216
compared, 217–219
symmetrical, 208
code points, 316
code values, 316
ColorSync, 186
colour
    16 bit, 161
    24 bit, 161
    additive mixing, 160
    and accessibility, 439–
        441
    and CSS, 372–373
    CMYK, 170–173
    device-independent
        specification of, 177
    direct, 163
    indexed, 163–170
    physics of, 157
    RGB, 158–161
    saturated, 174
    specifying in SVG, 522
    sRGB, 187, 372
    subtractive mixing, 160,
        171
colour correction, 180–183
colour depth, 161–163, 236
    and image file size, 163
colour gamut, 159
    CMYK, 173
    RGB, 159
colour management, 184–187
colour pickers, 176
colour profiles, 184
    ICC, 186
colour temperature, 183
colour vision, 158
colour wheel, 174
colour blindness, 439
comments
    in ECMAScript, 547
    in HTML, 359

companding, 298
complementary colours, 171
compositing, 73, 76, 134
    video, 231–232
compression
    dictionary-based, 124
    inter-frame, 207
    intra-frame, 207
    Lempel-Ziv, 125
    lossless, 79, 123, 124–125
    lossy, 79, 124, 296, 298
    LZW, 125
    of images, 79, 122–129
    of sound, 295–301
        perceptually based, 298–301
    of speech, 296–298
    of video, 193, 206–219
    see also codecs
    spatial, 206
    temporal, 206, 211
compression artefacts, 129, 191
condensed fonts, 329
constructive solid geometry, 106
control characters, 317
control points, 92
convolution, 140–145
cookies, 615
coordinates, 87
coordinate geometry, 86–89, 103
    use of equations in, 88
coordinate transformations, 87
corner points, 96, 97
CSS, 326, 360–381, 427, 531
    absolute positioning, 375–377, 430, 437–438
        and scripts, 567–569
    alignment of text in, 373

and fonts, 368–371
and images, 406
and SMIL, 500
and XML, 478–481
colour and, 372–373
declarations, 361
inheritance, 370
properties, 364
    changing with scripts, 566
pseudo-classes, 400, 479
rules, 361
selectors, 361, 368

D

DAT, 281, 286
datagrams, 592
data rate
    of CCIR 601 video, 203
    of CD-quality sound, 287
    of compressed sound, 300
    of DV, 210
    of motion JPEG, 209
    of MPEG-2, 205
    of video, 192
data structures, 34
DCT, 126–127, 140, 209, 210, 211
    inverse, 128
DC component, 39
definition of multimedia, 7
deinterlacing, 201
delays, 609
descenders, 335
design guidelines, 412, 452–456
desktop publishing, 333
device control, 193
difference frames, 207
digital cameras, 47, 64
Digital Versatile Disk, *see* DVD
Digital Video Disk, *see* DVD

digitization, 35–42
    of sound, 281–285
    of video, 191–196
DIN, 59
dingbats, 321, 334
direction lines, 93
direction points, 92
Discrete Cosine Transform, *see* DCT
display fonts, 331–332
dithering
    of colours, 168–169
    of sound signals, 284
DivX, 205–206, 215
DOCTYPE declaration, 469
document element, 469
Document Type Definitions, *see* DTDs
DOM, 466, 539, 558
domain names, 395, 396, 413–418
dominant wavelength, 173
dots per inch, 118
downsampling, 121
drawing programs, 70, 72
    rulers in, 87
Dreamweaver, 571–573
    behaviours palette, 571
DTDs, 363, 463, 466–472
    attribute-list declarations, 471–472
    content models, 470–471
    element declarations, 470–471
    markup declarations, 470–472
    namespaces and, 476
    public name, 469
    SMIL, 499
    SVG, 517
    system identifier, 469
DV, 193–194, 204, 228
    compression, 210–211

shuffling, 211
video segments, 211
DVCAM, 193
DVCPRO, 193
DVD, 9, 195, 205, 209, 214
dynamic HTML, 441
dynamic range, 278

E

easing, 253
ECMA, 538
ECMAScript, 537, 538–556, 558
   arithmetic in, 540–541
   arrays in, 549–552
     indexing of, 549
   assignment in, 544
   associative arrays in, 551–552
   Boolean operators in, 543
   comments in, 547
   comparison operators in, 542
   conditional statements in, 547
   control structures in, 545–549
   data types, 540
   escape sequences in, 541–542
   functions in, 552–554
   loops in, 547–549
   methods, 555
   objects in, 555–562
     built-in, 556–557
   properties, 555
   strings in, 541–542
   variables in, 543–545
     declaration of, 544
elements, 357
   block-level, 365
   classes of, 361

div, 366
inline, 365
parent, 358
span, 367
ellipses, 92
em, 336
em-dashes, 337
empty elements, 359
en, 337
en-dashes, 337
envelope shaping, 294
EPS, 82
ethics, 17, 24
event-driven systems, 536
events, 536
event handlers, 562–566
   and Flash buttons, 578
ex, 336
extended fonts, 329
extended links, 491–494
eXtensible Markup Language, *see* XML
extrusion, 107

F

faders, 294
fantasy fonts, 329
favourites, *see* bookmarks
fields, 200
file formats
   audio, 302–303
   graphics, 78–83
     conversion between, 83
   MIDI, 304
fills, 96, 98
   gradient, 98
   pattern, 99
film, 3, 22
   censorship of, 27
   editing, 225
     conventions, 223
   frame rate, 191

history of, 5–6
filters, 39, 102, 139
   high pass, 291
   low pass, 291
   notch, 292
   sound, 290–292
firewalls, 605
FireWire, 46, 47, 193, 228
Flash, 12, 50, 60, 254–265, 420–424, 498
   actions, 539
   and accessibility, 441
   and HTTP requests, 614
   buttons, 576–579
     and event handlers, 578
   button events, 578
   clip events, 579
   creating applications in, 583–586
   dynamic text fields, 584–585
   easing in, 253
   frame scripts, 575–576
   graphic symbols, 257
   loading movies into clips, 582–583
   motion tweening
     compared to SMIL animation, 516
   movie clips, 257–259, 579–583
     and scripts, 579
     instance names, 579–580
   scripting, 573–587
   stage, 255
   symbols, 256–259
     instances, 256
   timeline, 255
   tweening, 256–257
   using bitmaps in, 255

Flash movies, 433
    structures in
        branching, 422–423
        implementing, 575–576
        loops, 420–421
        parallelism, 423–425
    see also SWF
floating boxes in CSS, 375
fonts, 324–342
    and CSS, 368–371
    and SVG, 531
    and Web pages, 429–430
    bitmapped, 338
    body size, 335
    bold, 329, 341
    calligraphic, 329
    condensed, 329
    dingbat, 334
    display, 331–332
    embedding in files, 326
    extended, 329
    fantasy, 329
    italic, 328
    modern, 337
    monospaced, 327
    old-style, 337
    OpenType, 338, 340
    outline, 338
    pi, 334
    proportional, 327
    Roman, 327
    sans serif, 327
    serifed, 327
    slanted, 328
    small caps, 329
    substitution of, 326, 333
    symbol, 334
    text, 331
    TrueType, 339
        instructions, 341
    Type 1, 339
        hints, 340

    upright, 328
    weight of, 329
font families, 330–331
font metrics, 338
formatting objects, 482
Fourier Transform, 39, 126
fractals, 108–109
    random, 109
fragment identifiers, 399, 409, 487–489
    in SMIL, 510
frames, 367–368, 439
frame grabbing, 245
frame rate, 236
frequency, 38
    negative, 39
    of sound, 276
frequency domain, 39, 90, 126
frequency spectrum, 39, 276
FTP, 55
fusion frequency, 190

G

games, 14
gamma, 184, 237
Gaussian blur, 143, 146
General MIDI, 306
GIF, 79
    and indexed colour, 167
    see also animated GIFs
Gimp, The, 131
glyphs, 324, 333
    bounding boxes of, 337
Gouraud shading, 113
graceful transformation, 433
gradient fills, 98
    in SVG, 522–524
graphics, 64–83
    text as, 344–346
graphics metafiles, 82
graphics tablets, 47
graphic equalization, 293

greyscale, 161
grotesques, 328
Group of Pictures, 213

H

hard synchronization, 506
harmonics, 38
HCI, 448, 452
HDDV, 204
HDTV, 202
helper applications, 404
hidden surface removal, 112
home pages, 413
hosts, 592
href attribute
    HTML, 399, 401
    SMIL, 509
HSV colour model, 173–176
HTML, 4, 49, 54, 60, 326, 356–368, 427, 462
    and hypermedia, 403–410
    class attribute, 361, 366, 367
    correctness of, 443, 444
    deprecated elements, 360, 364
    embedded objects, 405, 407–408
    embedding scripts in, 559
    forms, 613
    frames, 367–368
    headers, 365
    href attribute, 399, 401, 403
    id attribute, 368, 401
    links in, 395–401
    lists, 365
    tables, 365
    text layout algorithm, 374
    validation of, 444

HTTP, 54, 55, 322, 396, 399, 402, 403, 591, 600–606
   caching, 604–606
   requests, 601–602
      conditional, 604
      for CGI scripts, 613
   responses, 602–603
      constructed by CGI scripts, 612
      status codes, 602–603
      use of MIME types in, 56
HTTP streaming, 197–198
hue, 173
Huffman coding, 124
   of sound, 295
   use in JPEG compression, 127
human–computer interaction, *see* HCI
HyperCard, 386
hypermedia, 10, 55, 384, 403–410
   structure in, 413–418
   see also HTML
hypertext, 384, 385–389, 395, 398–401, 403
   browsing in, 390–391
   history of, 385
   nodes, 389
hyphenation, 349

I

I-pictures, 212
IAB, 60
IANA, 57, 60, 322, 592
ICRA, 28
id attribute
   HTML, 368, 401
   SMIL, 503
IEC, 58
IEEE 1394, 193
   see also FireWire

IETF, 60
iLink, 193
   see also FireWire
Illustrator, 70, 91
   autotrace tool, 74
   brush strokes in, 74
   files, 82
   filters in, 102
   gradient mesh tool, 98
   pencil tool, 96
   pen tool, 93, 96
image histograms, 136
image manipulation, 130–148
   applied to video, 230–231
image maps, 408–410, 511
   use of alt attribute, 435
image resolution, 120
in-betweening, 252
indentation, 350
indexed colour, 163–170
information kiosks, 386
inline formatting, 347, 348
Integrated Services Architecture, 611
Intel Indeo, 216
interactive animation, 579
interactivity, 4, 12, 13–16, 48, 537
   see also scripting
interface elements, 16
interlacing, 200
interleaving, 311
Internet, 18, 50, 591
   demands on, 597
   dial-up connections to, 51
   quality of service and, 611
Internet cafés, 18
interpolation, 71, 120, 149–151, 252

bicubic, 151
bilinear, 150
in AfterEffects, 263
nearest neighbour, 150
intranets, 56, 591
Inverse Fourier Transform, 39
inverse kinematics, 268
in points, 226
IP, 592–593, 595
   addresses, 592
      for multicasting, 598
ISO, 57, 58
ISO 10646, 319–324, 369
   see also character sets
ISO 646, 317 318
ISO 8859, 319
ISO Latin1, 319, 320, 323
ISPs, 50, 55
   Web caching by, 605
italic fonts, 328
ITU, 58, 59, 159

J

jaggies, 89
Java, 615
JavaScript, 538
   server-side, 539
   see also ECMAScript, scripts
JFIF, 80
jitter, 197, 282, 609
JPEG, 80, 125–129, 167, 182
   quality setting, 128
   quantization matrix, 127, 128
   zig-zag sequence, 127
JPEG2000, 128
JScript, 538
justification of paragraphs, 349–350
   in CSS, 373

K

kerning, 337
keying, 231
key frames, 231, 251
    and video compression,
      207
    interpolation between,
      252–254
    in Flash, 256
kinematics, 268

L

LANs, 50, 54, 56
    and multicasting, 598
lathing, 108
layers, 75–78
    animating with, 249–250,
      261–266
    combining, 78
    tracing with, 77
leading, 335
left side bearing, 337
letterpress, 324, 331
letter spacing, 338
levels adjustments, 136
ligatures, 338
lighting, 105, 113
Linear Predictive Coding, 298
line joining styles, 98
    in SVG, 522
linkbases, 494
links, 10, 384, 386, 388–389,
    457
    between entire
      documents, 403
    bidirectional, 389
    destination, 389, 401
    display of, 390
    extended, 389
    images and, 408
    in HTML, 395–401
    in SMIL, 509–512

    in SVG, 528
    in XML, 484–496
    regional, 389
    semantics of, 402
    simple unidirectional,
      389
    source, 389, 400
    see also multi-links
link types, 402
lists, 365, 374
LiveScript, 538
localization, 354
longdesc attribute, 435
luma keying, 231
luminance, 160, 177, 203

M

macroblocks, 212
margins, 374
markup, 351
    accessible, 437–438
    structural, 353–355, 462
    visual, 353
markup languages, 344, 498
    see also HTML, XML
masking curve, 299
masking of sounds, 299
masks, 132
    greyscale, 133
    see also alpha channels
MathML, 463
mattes, 231–234
    garbage, 231
    travelling, 233, 264
media time, 506
Memex, 385
metaballs, 110
metadata, 394, 464
meta elements, 364
MIDI, 303–309
    controllers, 305
    editing, 308
    messages, 305–306

MIME types, 56–57, 322,
    403–404, 407, 602
    of scripts, 559
    of stylesheets, 364
mini-DV, *see* DV
modalities, 7
modelling
    3-D, 106–111
    free form, 106
    hierarchical, 105
    physics-based, 110
    procedural, 108–110
    terrain, 109
modems, 51
    cable, 52
modern fonts, 337
Moiré patterns, 41
monitors, 47
    calibration of, 186–188
    effect of resolution on
      Web pages, 428
monospaced fonts, 327
monostyled text, 325
morphing, 257
motion compensation, 210,
    212
    global, 215
    sub-pixel, 216
motion graphics, 261–266,
    572
motion JPEG, 209–210
motion paths, 257, 266
movie clips, 423–425
movie controllers, 221
MP3, 289, 300, 302
MPEG, 211–216
MPEG-1, 211
MPEG-2, 204
    profiles, 204
MPEG-4, 12, 205, 215–216
μ-law, 297
multi-links, 389
multicasting, 597–599, 611

and LANs, 598
host groups, 598–599
multimedia, 2, 7
    definition of, 7
    page-based, 10
        see also hypermedia
    scene-based, 12
    time-based, 11
multimedia applications, 6
    distributed, 614
        see also Web
        applications
multimedia architectures, 49
multimedia PC specification,
    43
multimedia presentations, 11
multimedia productions, 6
multiple media, 7

N

navigation bars, 414, 416
navigation in hypermedia,
    413–419
networks, 50–57
nodes, 389
    in structure models, 466
noise gates, 290
non-linearity, 10–13, 387–
    388, 420–424
non-zero winding number
    rule, 100
NTSC, 199, 202
    CCIR 601 sampled, 203
    frame rate, 191, 200
    resolution, 119
numeric character references,
    359
NURBs, 107
Nyquist rate, 40

O

objects, 554
    in ECMAScript, 555–562

media, 500
offline delivery, 8
old-style fonts, 337
online delivery, 8, 9
online stores, 23
OpenType fonts, 338, 340
open paths, 96
optical character recognition,
    325
outline fonts, 338
    scaling, 339
out points, 226
oversampling, 121
overshoot, 336, 340

P

P-pictures, 212
packet-switched networks,
    591
packets, 591
page-based multimedia,
    see hypermedia
page layout, 405
Painter, 70
painting programs, 65, 72
PAL, 199, 202
    CCIR 601 sampled, 203
    frame rate, 191
    resolution, 119
palettes, 164, 166
    Web-safe, 169, 170
paragraph styles, 350, 353
particle systems, 110
paths, 94–96
    motion, 257
    open, 96
PDF, 68
persistence of vision, 190,
    200, 242
personal digital assistants, 44
Phong shading, 113
Photoshop, 48, 70, 187, 261
    colour correction in,
        180–182

curves dialogue, 138
files, 82
Gaussian blur, 143
interpolation in, 150
lasso tool, 131
layers, 75
    adjustment, 78
magic wand, 132
magnetic lasso, 132
marquee tools, 131
plug-ins, 130, 230
vector-based text in, 346
PHP, 397
pica (pc), 335
PICS, 27–29
pitch alteration, 294
pixels, 66
    CCIR 601, 203
    identifying by
        coordinates, 87
    logical, 68
    physical, 68
pixels per inch, 120
pixel dimensions, 119
pixel group processing,
    139–148
pixel point processing,
    136–139
pi fonts, 334
plug-ins
    parameters for, 408
    Photoshop, 130, 230
    Web browser, 50, 405
PNG, 80, 125, 129, 162, 167
points (pt), 334
polygon meshes, 107
polylines, 91
portals, *see* Web portals
port numbers, 595
Poser, 268
post-production, 223, 230–
    236
posterization, 41, 167
PostScript, 81

and SVG, 62
 fonts, 339
 line caps in, 97
 points, 335
PowerPoint, 12
Premiere, 234
 sound effects plug-ins,
   290
 stop frame capture in,
   245
presentation time, 506
primary colours
 additive, 158
 subtractive, 172
procedural modelling,
   108–110
processing instructions, 468
process colours, 173
programs, 34
progressive scanning, 200
 see also deinterlacing
proportional fonts, 327
protocols, 54, 591–597
 in URLs, 395
 layered, 591

Q

QTVR
 see QuickTime VR
quality of service, 610
quantization, 36, 283–285
 of rhythm, 42, 308
quantization levels, 36, 283
 insufficient, 41
 non-linear, 296
quantization noise, 42, 283
QuickTime, 56, 205, 220–223,
   311
 and file format
   conversion, 83
 and MIDI, 306
 and SMIL, 499
 as a multimedia

architecture, 49
audio CD import, 288
components, 221
file format, 222
for Java, 222
MIME type for, 57
MJPEG-A format, 209
movies, 220
 self-contained, 237
Musical Instruments, 306
plug-in, 222, 271
sprite tracks, 251
streaming
 and RTSP, 607
synchronization in, 507
VR, 271

R

radiosity, 114
RAID arrays, 46–47
rasterizing, 73
ray tracing, 114, 267
RDF, 394, 463
RealAudio, 303
RealMedia, 205
RealPlayer G2, 499
RealVideo, 222
rectangles
 drawing, 92
reflection, 101
reflection mapping, 115
rendering, 66, 89
 3-D, 104, 105, 111–115
Requests for Comments, 60
resolution, 70, 118–122
 image, 120
reverb, 293
RLE, 123, 249
 use in JPEG, 127
robots, 393
rollovers, 457, 562–563, 572
 and Flash buttons, 576
 animated, 568–569

Roman fonts, 327
rotation, 101
 in 3-D, 104
rotoscoping, 247
routers, 593
 and multicasting, 598
RSAC ratings, 28
RTCP, 597
RTP, 221, 596–597, 606
 payloads, 596
 profiles, 597
RTSP, 221, 606–609
 presentation descriptions,
   607
 session identifiers, 608
run length encoding, see RLE

S

samplers, 306
sampling, 36, 89, 118, 149
 4:1:1, 204
 4:2:0, 204
 4:2:2, 203
 of sound, 281
 of video, 202
sampling rate, 36, 281, 287
 inadequate, 37
Sampling Theorem, 40
sans serif fonts, 327
saturation, 173
SAX, 466
scaling, 101
 of bitmapped images,
   71, 149
 of vector graphics, 71
scene-based multimedia, 12
schemas, 467
scripting, 12, 420–424
 errors in, 443–444
scripting languages, 536
 defined, 537
scripts
 and Flash buttons, 578

and Flash movie clips, 579
and stylesheets, 566–569
attaching to Flash movies, 574–578
CGI, 397, 612–614
embedding in HTML, 559
in Flash, 573–587
server-side, 611
use of for animation, 563–566
searching, 420
on the WWW, 391–394
search engines, 23
SECAM, 199, 202
selections, 131–133
feathered, 133
Semantic Web, 394
sequencers, 304
software, 308
serifed fonts, 327
serifs, 327, 337
server-side scripts, 557
servers, 54, 590, 600, 615
HTTP, 611
and MIME types, 403
World Wide Web, 591
SGML, 463
shading algorithms, 113
see also rendering
shapes, 91–92
sharpening, 144
see also unsharp masking
shearing, 101
applied to fonts, 328
signals, 36
site maps, 419
slanted fonts, 328
small caps fonts, 329
SMIL, 436, 463, 498–516, 608

animation, 512–516
interpolation modes, 514–515
looping, 515–516
Basic Layout Language, 500
clock values, 502
deprecated syntax, 512
DTD, 499
linking element types, 509
links in, 509–512
media object elements, 500
regions, 500
syncbase values, 503
synchronization behaviour, 507
synchronization elements, 500–505
test attributes, 507–508
Sorenson video codec, 216
sound, 274–312
digitization of, 281–286
editing, 289–290
effects, 292–295
importing from CD, 288
loops, 289
physics of, 275–277
psychological aspects of, 280–281
recording, 286–288
setting levels, 287
sampling of, 281
streamed, 302–303
Source Input Format, 214
spectral power distributions, 157
specular reflection, 113
spiders, 393
SPIFF, 80
sprites, 250
sRGB colour model, 187, 372

standards, 57–60
for character sets, 317–323
for video
analogue, 199–202
digital, 202–206
Internet, 60
stereophony, 280
strokes, 96
dashed, 97
line cap, 97
structural markup, 353–355, 437, 462, 477
structure model, 466
stylesheets, 356, 360–362, 368–381
and anchors, 400
and XML, 477–483
cascading, 380
see also CSS
links to, 377
scripts and, 566–569
stylesheet languages, 356
see also CSS, XSL
SVG, 60, 68, 69, 82, 86, 91, 97, 463, 517–532
animation, 531–532
Bézier curves, 521
DTD, 517
fonts and, 531
gradient fills, 522–524
groups, 527
links in, 528
paths, 520–521
shapes, 518–519
stroke attribute, 522
text in, 529–531
transformations, 525–527
transformation specifications, 525
SWF, 82, 86, 254, 260
symbol fonts, 334

synchronization
   hard, 506
   loss of, 610
   of RTP streams, 597
   of sound and video,
      309–311
   soft, 506
synthesizers, 306

T
tables, 351, 365
   as layout grids, 373
tags, 352, 357, 358
TCP, 594–596, 606
TCP/IP, 50, 591
   and LANs, 56
textual equivalents, 434–437
texture mapping, 115
text fonts, 331
text formatting
   tag-based, 352
   WYSIWYG, 352
TGA, 81, 167
threshold of hearing, 298
TIFF, 80, 167
time-based multimedia, 11
timecode
   and sound, 310
   drop frame, 227
   SMPTE, 227
timelines, 11
   for sound editing, 289
time bases, 220
time stretching, 294
tracking, 338
tracks, 289
transformations, *see* vector
   graphics
transitions, 223, 226, 229
translation, 101
transparency, 77
   and GIF files, 79–81
transparency mapping, 115

transport addresses, 595
tremolo effect, 294
tristimulus theory of colour,
   158
TrueType fonts, 339
   instructions, 341
tweening, 256–257
typefaces, 330
Type 1 fonts, 339
   hints, 340
typography, 314
   and CSS, 368
   specialized terms in,
      334–338

U
UCS Transformation Formats,
   323
UDP, 596
underlining, 330
undersampling, 38, 41
unicasting, 598
Unicode, 320, 323, 334, 358
   see also character sets
unsharp masking, 145
upright fonts, 328
URIs, 395
URLs, 55, 367, 391, 395–399,
   413, 600
   and XML namespaces,
      475
   base, 398
   escape sequences in, 397
   fragment identifiers, 399
   in RTSP requests, 606
   partial, 398
   path component of, 396
   query strings appended
      to, 612
   use in SMIL, 501
   use in SVG, 524
URNs, 395
usability, 448–456

research, 448–450
   see also design guidelines
user agents, 357
user interfaces, 15–16,
   448–456
   event-driven, 536
   for time-based media, 16
   innovative, 16
   use of icons in , 65

V
valid XML documents, 467
vectorizing, 73
vectors, 88
   3-D, 103
vector graphics, 68, 86–116
   animating, 252
   origin of term, 88
   text in, 345
   transformations, 70,
      101–102
      defined
         mathematically,
         101–102
   see also SVG
vector quantization, 216
video, 190
   capture cards, 194
   capturing, 46
   composite signals, 195
   editing, 223, 226–227
      conventions, 223
      digital, 228–230
      traditional, 226–227
   interactive, 198
   live, 198
   post-production
      see post-production
   progressive download,
      197
   resolution, 119
   streamed, 197–199

video conferencing, 54, 197, 199, 590
virtual reality, 269–272
visualization, 64, 103
voices, 306
voxels, 86
VR, *see* virtual reality
VRAM, 164, 166
VRML, 12, 269–270

W

W3C, *see* World Wide Web Consortium
WAI, 434
    Guidelines for Accessible Content, 434
WAV, 302
waveforms, 276, 289
    use for synchronization, 310
wavelength of light, 157
Weblogs, 445–446
Web Accessibility Initiative, *see* WAI
Web browsers, 384, 606, 613
    and distributed multimedia applications, 614
    downsampling in, 122
    history list, 390
    plug-ins for, 50, 405
    text-based, 430, 432
Web crawlers, 393
Web portals, 23
Web proxies, 605
Web sites, 398
    defined, 413
Web site structures
    hierarchical, 415–416
    hybrid, 418
    sequential, 417–418
    totally connected, 413–414

well-formed XML documents, 464
whitespace, 359–361
white point, 183
Windows Media, 205, 223
wire frame previews, 111
World Wide Web, 4, 8, 10, 49, 54, 386
    and censorship, 25
    and sRGB colour, 187
    as a graphical medium, 65
    as publishing medium, 21, 23
    clients, 55
    colour and, 372
    design problems, 425–432
    graphic bias of, 19
    hypertext links in, 399
    index sites, 392
    popular sites, 23
    QuickTime and, 222
    scripting and, 557–569
    searching, 391
    servers, 55
    standards, 60
    video delivery over, 197
World Wide Web Consortium, 60
    and accesibility, 20
WWW, *see* World Wide Web

X

x-height, 335
Xanadu project, 385
XFDL, 463
XHTML, 357, 360, 364, 463, 464, 467, 482
XLink, 484, 489–495, 528
    locator attributes, 490
XML, 49, 323, 344, 389, 462–495, 498, 517, 573

as metalanguage, 468
attributes, 465
CSS and, 478–481
declaration, 468
default namespace, 475–476
document element, 469
namespaces, 473–476
    for XLink, 490
    URLs and, 475
namespace prefixes, 474–475
PIs, 468
processing instructions, 468, 478–483
stylesheets and, 477–483
valid, 467
well-formed, 464
see also DTDs
XML Schemas, 467
XPath, 484–487, 488
    axes, 486
    location paths, 484
    location steps, 484–485
    predicates, 486
XPointer, 484, 487–489
    pointer parts, 489
    scheme-based pointers, 488–489
    shorthand pointers, 488
XSL, *see* XSLT and XSL: FO
XSL-FO, 483
XSLT, 482–483

Y

Y'$C_B C_R$, 177, 183, 203
YUV colour, 177

Z

z-ordering, 375